Luise Zuspann, Augusta Strupp, Caroline Grebe, Sophie Dietz, Margaretha Grabert, Wilhelmine Burgdorf, Adam Borner, Johann Sophias, Christian Sophias, Adam Sophias and Heinrich Sophias.

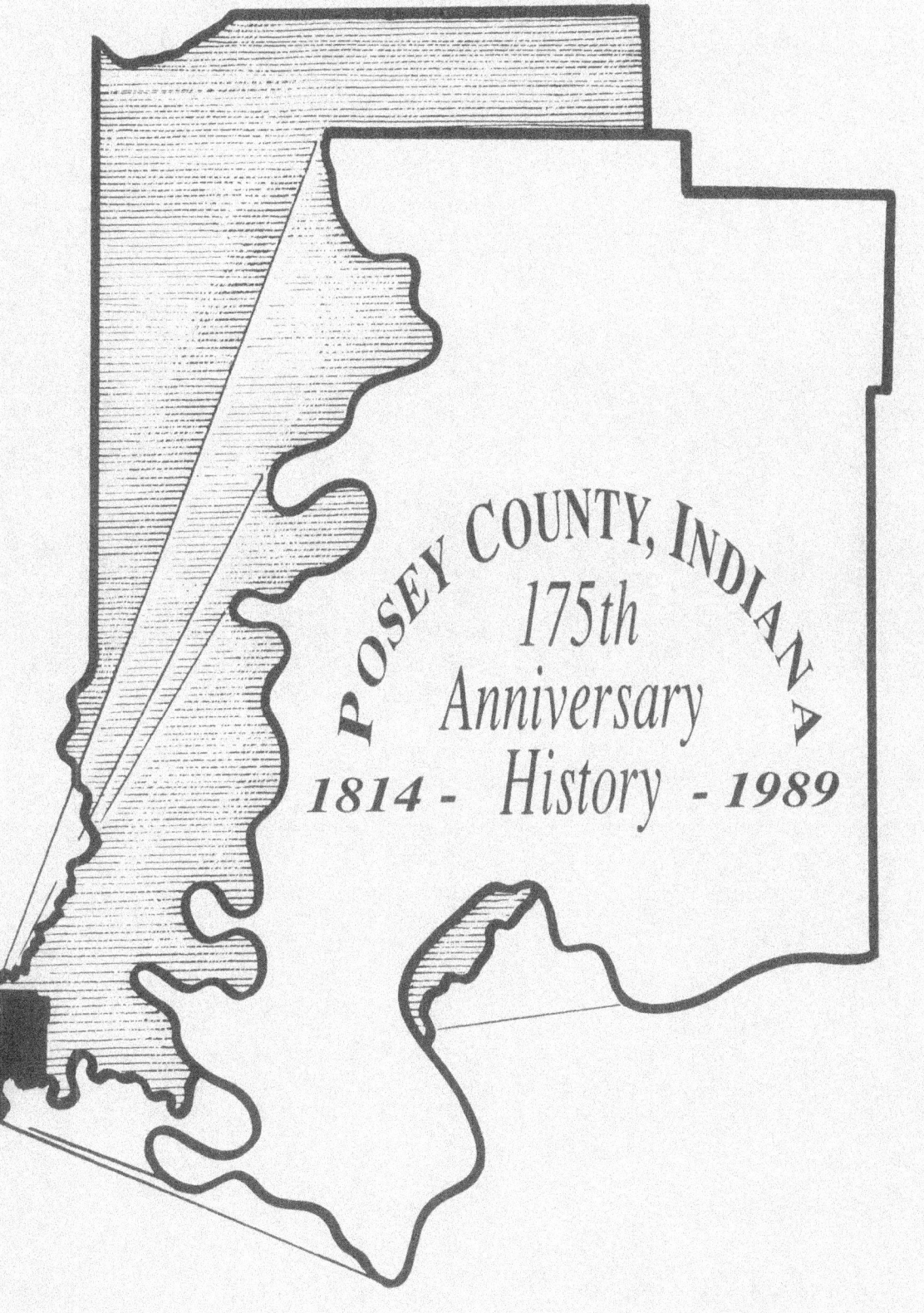

Phil Hagemann's Livery Stable, he is third from right. 120 Main Street

Turner Publishing Company
Publishers of America's History

Copyright © 1989 by Posey County Historical Society

Author: Jennifer St. John

This book or any part thereof may not be reproduced without the written consent of the Author and Publisher

The materials were compiled and produced using available information; Turner Publishing Company and the Posey County Historical Society regrets they cannot assume liability for errors or omissions.

Library of Congress Catalog Card No: 89-051786

ISBN: 978-1-68162-442-6

Created by: Mark A. Thompson, Independent Publishing Consultant for Turner Publishing Company
  Book Design: Elizabeth Dennis

Limited Edition of 750 copies of which this copy is number _____

TABLE OF CONTENTS

Posey County Historical Society 4
Cover Art Seal 5
Introduction 7
Posey County History 1913-1989 9
    Indiana 1913-1920 10
    Posey County 1913-1920 10
    Indiana 1920-1929 23
    Indiana 1930s 30
    Posey County 1930s 32
    Indiana 1940s 37
    Posey County 1940s 39
    Indiana 1950s 45
    Posey County 1950s 45
    Indiana 1960s 51
    Posey County 1960s 51
    Indiana 1970s 56
    Posey County 1970s 57
    Indiana 1980s 60
    Posey County 1980s 60
Church History 65
School History 79
Family History 85
Club-Organization, Business History 179
Index 189

About 1895 neighborhood threshing. Threshing machine owned by Edward Lengelsen. Left to right: Edward Lengelsen, Ida Lengelsen Mime Hengstenberg, Elisabeth Schimmel Lengelsen, 5th person-Luise Becker, 8th person-Wilhelm Becker. Far Right: Emma Winiger second women to her right: "Muttes" Stock (Berge).

POSEY COUNTY HISTORICAL SOCIETY

Book Committee: Left to Right: Anne Doane, Wanda Griess, Glenn Curtis and Ilse Horacek

Early n 1974 the Gamma Psi Chapter of Kappa Kappa Kappa members issued a call to the citizens of Mt. Vernon to form a local Historical Society. The primary purpose of forming such an organization is to collect, restore and preserve the rich heritage of the Posey County area, which unfortunately has been neglected and lost for several years.

On Feb. 24, 1974 an organizational meeting was held in the Mt. Vernon High School cafeteria. Hubert Hawkins, Executive Director of the Indiana Historical Society was present to assist and guide in forming the society. At this meeting a constitution was adopted, a slate of officers was presented and elected and a schedule of membership fees was presented.

At this time it was decided not to limit the society to Mt. Vernon but open it to the whole Posey County. And that the society would not be affiliated with the Tri Kappa club but would be a corporate entity under the management and control of its own officers and members.

The only requirement for a person to become a member of the Society is that he or she has an interest in Posey County. The person doesn't have to live in Posey County to become a member. The first membership classes were $3 for an individual, $5 for a family and $10 for a club, corporation or other group.

The first board of directors were Otis Allyn, Alois Waller, Robert smith, Mrs. Gene Brooks, Mrs. Steve Bach and the officers were: Jerry King, president, Mrs. Charles Lawrence, secretary; Miss Catharine Howard, vice-president and Mrs. John Doane, treasurer. The officers are also members of the board of directors.

The first thing the new society was involved with was the opening of the cornerstone of the Posey Count Infirmary that was torn down in April 1974. A copper container containing several items of interest was placed in the cornerstone when the Infirmary was built in 1889 with appropriate Masonic ceremonies under the auspices of the Beulah Lodge, U.D.f. & A.M.

The first marker placed by the Society was made by the Staples Foundry of Mt. Vernon to be placed in front of Governor Alvin P. Hovey's home on Fourth and Walnut Streets.

The 'Old Timer' columns from the Mt. Vernon Democrat were bound in two volumes in 1976. These were written by Frank "Pop" Fessenden and were a weekly column of reminiscences of Mt. Vernon and Posey County. these articles were divided into chapters with original drawings by Glenn Curtis, a local cartoonist.

The Society has reprinted the 1900 Posey County Atlas, the Goodspeed History of 1886, the Leffel History of 1913 and the Leonard History of 1882 several times.

"The Mount Vernon Wochenblatt" a translation from German into English and "it Was Written" was written by a member, Ilse Horacek. Both volumes were collections of articles published weekly in the Mount Vernon Democrat under the title "One Hundred Years Ago."

Among the many projects of the Society were cooperating with the Indiana Historical Bureau in a survey of historical markers in Posey County, purchasing film for the Alexandrian Library, donating books, time and month to the Alexandrian Library, inventory and publishing a book of historic sites and structures in Posey County and getting the People's Bank & Trust Building (formerly the I.O.O.F. Building) and The Posey County Courthouse entered in the National Register of Historic Places and the 175 anniversary History Book.

In January 1989 the Society began offering their time and knowledge three days a week t the Alexandrian Library in the new Indiana Room for anyone needing help with their genealogy.

The first genealogical seminar was held in April 1989 in conjunction with he Alexandrian Library. A full day with three speakers was enjoyed by the ones attending.

A yearly seminar is planned as long as interest is shown.

The present officers and directors of the Society are Mrs. Simon Griess, president: Mrs. Thomas Horacek, vice-president: Mrs. John Doane, secretary; Mrs. Floyd French, treasurer; Miss Mildred Blake, Glenn Curtis, Merle McFadden, Mrs. Donald Baier and Miss Miskel Wolfinger.

COVER ART SEAL

Inspiration.

That is what it takes to create a unique piece of artwork. Artists may spend days studying their subject, waiting for inspiration to strike.

For artist Glen Curtis, 59 years of inspiration was long enough.

The native and lifetime resident of Posey County spent two or three weeks designing sketches for the seal. He said that he imagined many detailed scenes for Posey County's seal—"my grandfather fighting off Indians"—but finally adhered to the same philosophy on which he has always based his artwork.

"The best idea is the simplest you can come up with," Curtis said.

He explained that people could never quite grasp where his home county was located until he explained that Posey is "settled between the Wabash and Ohio rivers".

For Curtis, the seal was his chance to "show people exactly where it (Posey County) is—its unique location between those rivers. I wanted to give people a quick glance of where this book is coming from."

Since his first professional art job in high school, Curtis has worked as a newspaper cartoonist, a truck driver for a volunteer fire department, a grocery store manager and a city councilman. He currently manages his home farm.

"You know, I think I've forgotten some of my jobs," Curtis stated matter-of-factly. but he never forgot his love for art.

"I don't want to make money at it. It wouldn't be fun."

During his lifetime, the dry-humored artist has held enough jobs to experience all that Posey County has to offer. He has sampled the county's many qualities, leading him to state that Posey is indeed "a complete cross section of all kinds.

"I think it has a cross section of all kinds of people, (different) economic levels, social groups.

"It's got the GE plastic plant—the first in the U.S. It's got the agriculture community, New Harmony community, oil refineries. We've got a lot of churches and a lot of taverns. It's got a little of everything...if you can find it.

"We've even got cypress and pecan trees." Curtis explained that those trees are rarities in that region of the United States. "People drive down to Florida to see those trees.... If you were blindfolded, you'd swear you were in Florida.

"We've got a lot to offer if we'd just tell people about it."

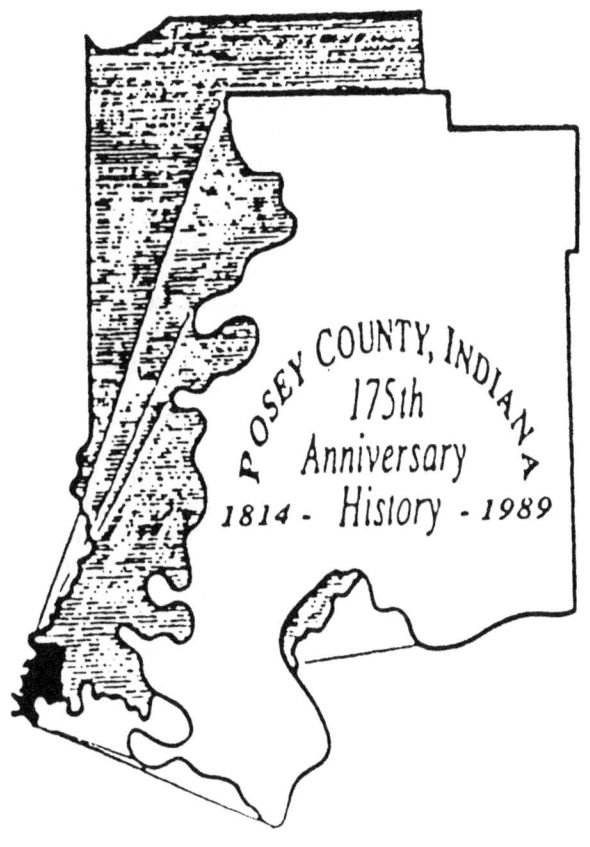

INTRODUCTION

The extreme southwestern corner of Indiana is known as Posey County. Bounded by Kentucky on the south, Illinois on the west, Vanderburgh County on the east and Gibson County on the north, a fruitful valley lies nestled between the Ohio and Wabash Rivers. Small hills and slightly rolling ground cover 402 square miles of fertile land.

It is hard to imagine that less than 200 years ago the native red man still wandered over this land through dense virgin brush and dark forest. Willow trees, poplars, sycamores and cotton woods lined the banks of the rivers. The early pioneers recorded finding wild cherry and peach trees, giant oak, locust, elm, tulip, pine and beech trees in abundance.

History books tell us of a French outpost located at the mouth of the Wabash River in 1763. About 1794, the first white man to venture by foot through this area was believed to have been an Irishman named Thomas Jones who, along with his Indian wife, manned a trading post on the spot known today as Bone Bank.

But the birth of the pioneer settlement came about in 1798 when a lone man came down the Ohio River in a canoe. He turned north and paddled up a small stream with its many twists and turns. Beyond each bend lay the same deep solitude. He saw countless deer tracks in the mud along the water's edge and speckled fish leaped and splashed back into the water all around him. Upon reaching a spot where a storm shattered tree lay spanning the creek, he moved his craft to an overhanging limb and rested in the shade of the natural bridge. There the Scotsman, who had come from the Carolinas and lived in Kentucky, conceived the thought for his future home. He stepped back into his canoe, cast loose and paddled back down the creek and out into the broad waters of the Ohio River. Andrew McFadin had explored the stream that ever since has carried his name — McFadin's Creek.

A few years later in 1806, Andrew McFadin's dream came true. Along with his family and a few friends he returned and established a home on a nearby bluff. Others soon followed, log cabins were built and the new settlement was known for nearly ten years as McFadin's Bluff. Most of these early settlers came from Pennsylvania, North Carolina, Virginia and Tennessee by way of Kentucky and the Ohio River. Their names revealed an English-speaking ancestry. Malinda Weir was the first child born in the new settlement in 1807. It is thought that the Reverend Samuel Jones, as Baptist, was the first minister to preach the gospel in the area.

Land grants were made to the veterans of the Revolutionary War. During the early years, these pioneers pushed further inland and built forts to protect themselves from the Indians; one at Doublehead, southwest of the area now called Stewartsville, the other on the Black River, near Shaw's Fort.

In 1814, the county was formed from sections of formerly belonging to Warrick and Gibson counties. The new county was named for Thomas Posey, the Revolutionary War general who was governor of the Indiana Territory from 1813 until its statehood in 1816.

As an admirer of General George Washington (his father had served under the general), patriotic-minded Samuel Rowe suggested in 1816 that McFadin's Bluff be renamed Mount Vernon after Washington's home on the Potomac. All men present approved the new name. About fifteen families were then living in the settlement. Second Street, north of the water front, was known as "The Row" — named for a row of log cabins built there. Beyond that was a wilderness of mostly unexplored forest. As late as 1824, deer were killed where Second Street today crosses Main Street. A pond provided hunters with fowl — the area not bounded by Fourth, Fifth, College and Main streets. In 1820, a panther killed young James Culbertson under a large locust tree that is now the corner of Fourth and Main streets.

The first county seat was located at Blackford in Marrs Township in 1815. This community was named after Isaac Blackford, the first judge of the judicial district of the southern counties of Indiana. Later it was moved to a more central location at Springfield. In 1825, due to its advantageous location on the Ohio River, Mount Vernon became the permanent county seat. The present courthouse was built in 1875 at a cost of $95,000.

Mount Vernon was incorporated as a town in 1832, and in 1866 it was chartered as a city and received a city seal.

One of the most significant religious settlements in America was founded in 1814 by George Rapp in Posey County. Rapp moved a community of 700 followers from Pennsylvania to land along the Wabash River; it became known as Harmonie. In 1825 the town and almost twenty-thousand acres were sold to a Welsh social reformer, Robert Owen, who renamed the town New Harmony. Owen sought to introduce social reforms and tried to establish a model community He was one of the earliest proponent of women's rights, child labor laws and public education. New Harmony became the home of many early intellectuals, including William Maclure, Thomas Say, Robert Dale Owen, Dr. Edward Murphy and Madame Fretageot. The Owen experiment lasted only a short time. In March of 1827, the dissolution of the community was announced. However, New Harmony remains one of the state's recognized art centers, rich in cultural and aesthetic history.

As New Harmony grew, Mount Vernon also developed into an important town. In 1851, plank road was built to connect the two sites. The road cost $2,000 per mile to build, thus a toll of three cents per mile to each traveler was charged to cover its cost. This toll road provided easier access to both communities: a stage coach delivered mail and travelers, and it is said Mount Vernon's population doubled as a result.

A large influx of German immigrants from 1830 to 1890 became the foundation of for strong agriculture in Posey County. Ninety-three percent of the population of Marrs Township in the 1850 census were Germans and ninety-eight percent resided in Robinson Township. By 1860, the Germans had doubled their number and settled extensively in Mount Vernon. Their frugality and industriousness soon caused the town to flourish. Mount Vernon quickly became an important shipping port for farmers needing to transport their crops.

Many German gravestone can still be found throughout the county, especially in St. Wendel and St. Philip. Bellefontaine, Mount Vernon's largest cemetery, was once known as German Cemetery.

The coming of the railroad in 1871 was the most important catalyst for the county seat's growth. It connected Poseyville and Mount Vernon to

Evansville and other major cities throughout the Midwest. This opened access to new markets and industries.

The editor of a Mount Vernon newspaper described the changing lifestyle of the 1880s in these words: "We live in a modern world."

Posey County was the home of three Civil War generals — Alvin P. Hovey, William Harrow and John Pitcher. General Hovey was elected governor of Indiana in 1888. He died while in office in 1981 and was buried in Bellefontaine Cemetery.

Surely the successful growth of Posey County is in part due to the efforts and sacrifices of its pioneer ancestors. They worked the land and built the communities, ten townships, the city of Mount Vernon, the towns of New Harmony, Poseyville, Cynthiana and Griffin, and many other settlements. All have survived the ravages of hard time in the past.

When storms and floods brought destruction, Posey residents rebuilt. When epidemics took their loved ones — in 1873 almost two hundred people died within two months from cholera — the survivors carried on. Loyal to their country, Posey men and women fought and died in this nation's wars to preserve freedom for all citizens. Posey County's bright future was founded in a strong past. —Written by Ilse Horacek for the Mount Vernon Democrat, July 1987

Solitude Covered Bridge picture taken 1929 source: Alexandrian Library

Evansville & Mt. Vernon Express: Building is on N.E. corner of intersection of 4th & Main Street Mt. Vernon, Indiana.

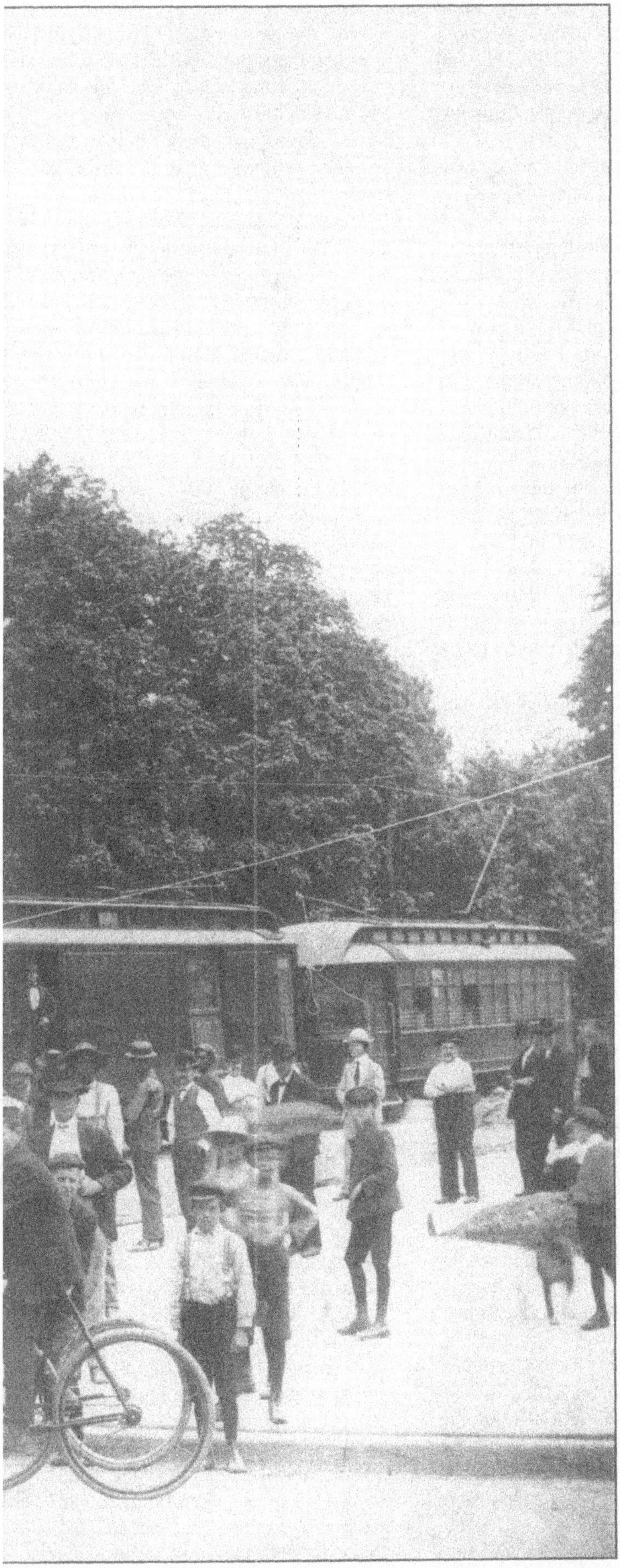

POSEY COUNTY HISTORY
1913-1989

Indiana: 1913-1920

The early years of the 20th century opened with Hoosiers and Posey County residents proud that one of their own would occupy the vice-presidential chair. On March 4, 1913, former Governor Thomas Riley Marshall was sworn in as vice president under Woodrow Wilson. While Marshall never became President, his wit and humor made him a very popular vice president nationwide. He entrenched his place in the history books with his observation that "What this country needs is a good five-cent cigar."

While one Hoosier won the vice presidency that election year, another Hoosier was a candidate for President. In 1912, Eugene V. Debs of Terre Haute, labor leader and organizer of the Pullman strike, headed the Socialist ticket in the 1912 election. Later in the decade, Debs was jailed for speaking out against American participation in World War I. Debs was popular even if his cause was not. In his fifth Presidential race in 1920, Debs received nearly nine million votes while still in a federal prison.

Indiana Democrats had reason to celebrate in 1913. The same 1912 elections that elevated Governor Marshall to Washington, D.C. placed Democrat Samuel M. Ralston in the governor's chair after he defeated former Republican Governor Winfield Durbin and Progressive Albert J. Beveridge. Under Ralston's administration, the state park system was established, a public service commission was created, the state's Workman's Compensation Act was passed, and in 1916 Indiana celebrated her centennial of statehood. But, Beveridge had other honors in the decade -- his 1916 biography of John Marshall won the Pulitzer Prize in 1920.

The second decade of the 1900s saw the first primary elections in Indiana. The general elections that year returned Wilson and Marshall to office, but the governorship went to Republican James P. Goodrich. Goodrich's administration oversaw the planning of the state highway system, the creation of the Department of Conservation and Indiana's contribution to the American effort in World War I.

These teen years were the waning days of Indiana Literature, but many bright lights still shone. Theodore Dreiser published The Titan (1914), The Genius (1915) and A Hoosier Holiday (1916). Booth Tarkington's Penrod and Sam appeared in 1914 and 1916, Seventeen in 1917 and the Pulitzer Prize-winning The Magnificent Ambersons in 1918. David Graham Phillips produced Susan Lenox: Her Fall and Rise in 1917. History was not neglected: Charles Beard wrote An Economic Interpretation of the Constitution in 1913.

Indiana literature lost its most popular representative when James Whitcomb Riley "the beloved Hoosier poet" died in 1916. He was buried at the highest point of Crown Hill Cemetery overlooking the city of Indianapolis.

1911 saw the beginning of two now-entrenched Indiana sports traditions: the Indianapolis 500 Mile Race and the state high school basketball championship. Speeds increased along with the crowds at the "greatest spectacle in racing" throughout the decade. The Indiana High School Athletic Association began sponsoring the state tournament in 1912; by 1916, some 450 member-schools participated. Through 1918, the tourney was held at Indiana University; it moved to Purdue in 1919 and in 1920 came to Indianapolis.

In 1916, an assistant football coach and an aspiring baseball player met in South Bend and in the next five years created a sports legend. Knute Rockne built the Notre Dame football program around George Gipp for the five years he played. (However, 1918 was considered an unofficial season because of World War I.) Gipp's death of pneumonia in December 1920 provided inspiration for future Notre Dame teams (and political candidates) with his last request to "win one for the Gipper."

World War I was the major international event of the decade, and Indiana did her part for the war effort. The state's output of coal, corn and wheat increased during the war years, and some 500,000 war gardens were planted. Indiana sent 146,322 of its citizens to the war; 3,369 of them were killed.

Indiana was the automobile manufacturing capital of the country throughout the decade. Several companies were born -- and some died-- in the teens: The Bush, produced in Elkhart from 1916 to 1924; Interstate, Muncie 1908-1918; Lambert, Anderson 1905-1917; Monroe, Indianapolis, 1911-1924 and Richmond, Richmond, 1902-1916.

While automobiles were being produced throughout the state, the highway system also grew during the teens. After the federal government offered financial support, Indiana began a highway fund and a State Highway Commission to oversee the system's development.

With the developing highway system, however, the annual traffic death toll also rose through the decade. The toll passed 100 in 1915; two years later more than 200 were killed. In 1920, an auto accident claimed the life of former governor Frank Hanley.

Traffic and war deaths were not the only tragedies that impacted Indiana. However bright the prospect of the early teens and had been, the latter years of the decade seemed to bring one disaster after another. Tornados struck in March 1917, killing 46 people in New Albany and 21 in New Castle. A collision and fire on the Hagenbeck-Wallace circus train near Gary in June 1918 destroyed four rail cars and killed 68 circus people.

The number of deaths in the "Great War" paled beside the number of people killed on the home front by influenza, In 1918, flu killed 5,553 Hoosiers; 3,025 died in 1919 and 2,295 in 1920. Flu-associated cases of pneumonia took an even greater toll each of these years.

Worker discord and labor unrest also swelled during the post-war years. A strike in the steel companies nearly paralyzed the Calumet area in October and November 1919.

Other Hoosiers, however, were joining together during the decade. In 1915, the Little Theater Society of Indiana was organized at Indianapolis. Humorist George Ade served as its president. The same year, the Indiana Historical Bureau was founded.

Posey County 1913-1920

Posey County bore the burden of some of the state's many disasters in the teens. While many county residents enjoyed productive days in the year 1913, the first thing it may always remember is the flood. The headlines read, "Posey County Now in Grasp of Worst Flood in History."

For 10 days in March, 1913 the rains did not slaken. Shortly after 15 inches fell, the Wabash river began its rapid rise. Warnings from the weather bureau reached residents when the river marked 17 feet on the gauge in Mount Carmel. A mere 24 hours before, the gauge had measured the river level at seven feet. By March 28 the level reached 29 feet and was expected to reach 25 feet in New Harmony the following day. Panic and fear set in as devastation seemed

Sherburne Park Riverfront off Main Street

inevitable. The livestock seemed to suffer the most with the Western Star newspaper reporting "hundreds of hogs and thousands of chickens and poultry of all kinds were swept away by the rushing waters." Reports poured in from people telling of farm machinery, buggies, wagons and buildings passing by their water-logged homes. Many of these homes were damaged beyond repair or even carried away, leaving thousands of families living as refugees.

In Mount Vernon, the Ohio River water marks reached 52.8 feet -- making it the worst flood in the town's history. The only floods that neared this mark were in 1898 and 1907 when the level had reached 48 feet.

March 30 marked an important date in Posey County history. New Harmony, the highest point in the county and so far practically untouched by previous floods "went under." Three-fourths, or more than 3,00 New Harmony homes were flooded, almost all moved off their foundations by rushing water. At one point, amid the panic, a barge loaded with stone was sent in hope of mending the break in the levee. But, the worst happened instead. The power of the water slammed the barge through the hole making the break all the wider. With practically all of the town flooded, residents took to the hills. May found refuge in the few places the flood did not crush in its journey -- city hall and a few churches. The few places where the water level was low, looked like stockyards as livestock from miles around huddled for safety.

While the newspapers reported many had barely escaped the disaster, no deaths were reported. But the destruction caused by the Flood of 1913 took its toll in property and livestock damage. By April 17, Posey County began the tremendous task of cleaning up what was left. The American Red Cross began efforts to help farmers back on their feet by providing furniture, clothing and food. One prominent worker went so far as to say the Red Cross would "go far enough in each case to make certain that the farmer can make a crop."

A committee in Mount Vernon asked the state for relief writing, "We, the members of the Associated Charities and the Committee of Flood Suffers of Mount Vernon, Indiana respectfully suggest and urge that you send us immediately and all our flood sufferers from all the surrounding country, being cared for by us, one car load of provisions furnished by the state to consist principally of beans, coffee, sugar, molasses, lard, matches, candles, meat, oatmeal, rice, hominy, canned corn, baked beans, flour, meal, baking powder soda, soap, pepper and such other substantial necessaries of life as you may want to send. This being the necessary, not for the citizens of Mount Vernon, but for the flood sufferers of the surrounding country."

Estimated flood damage was not revealed in the newspapers, although one area reported damage figures well above $800,000 -- a devastating sum in 1913.

While the flood of 1913 seemed to shadow the rest of the year's events, Posey County pulled itself together and became caught up in other events.

The county had occasion to put the March flood behind them for a moment to remember those who gave their lives for their country. Memorial Day was celebrated by Posey County in Mount Vernon with a parade of 10 automobiles that slowly made their way to Bellefontaine Cemetery. A bugle was sounded, and those in the parade as well as the onlookers followed by singing "America." Flowers and flags were placed at more than 150 graves. Veterans and youth stood silent as "taps" was played by a solitary bugle. The crowds, moved by the ceremony, dispersed in silence. Later that afternoon, the silence gave way to the shouts of hundreds of people who had gathered for the parade. Veterans led the assembly, followed by a captain and his comrades, displaying light artillery. Following were Mayor John Moeller, the city fathers, the orator of the day and various county officials. More than 400 school children came next, holding American flags and "fanning the air in jubilant extacy of young America," according to Western Star. Dressed in uniform and regalia, the I.O.O.F. followed, then the Woodmen lodges and the city fire department. Numerous automobiles and carriages brought up the rear. The procession ended at the courthouse where they stopped to hear the patriotic tunes of the Imperial Orchestra. The ceremonies ended with prayers and several orations, including one made by Senator George Curtis. He pledged, "that the everlasting remembrances of the custom of commemorating the valor of the Americn soldier will be the endearing thought of the generations to come." Jasmine buds were presented to the veterans attending the ceremony, a benediction was read and the Memorial Day activities ended.

The thoughtful Memorial Day ceremony was followed by a much more joyous -- almost intriguing -- event. A representative of the S & R Film Co. of Evansville, Indiana arrived in Mount Vernon to takes "motion pictures." Residents saw themselves in "action" as the fire department made two calls on Main Street. The city's Chief of Police Smith was filmed as he arrested a chicken thief. Pictures were taken of the Keck-Gonnerman Co. Foundry, the Mount Vernon Strawboard factory and Sherbourne Park. Filming continued with shots of the street-cleaning apparatus, members of the Mount Vernon Commercial Club and the L & N and the C & E I railroad depots. The 1,000-foot-long film was aired to residents the following week.

November is the month for elections, and the vote in the 1913's race narrowly ousted Mount Vernon mayor. The democratic nominee, Alonzo Grant was elected by a plurality of 156 votes over John H. Mueller. The democrats swept the ticket with city clerk, and four of the six councilmen elected. There were no winners on the progressive ticket, although their nominee for mayor, William Ruminer received 91 votes.

The dedication of the new Murphy Auditorium in New Harmony heralded in 1914. The money to build the much-needed auditorium was acquired from the surplus of the lecture fund left by Dr. Edward Murphy -- $28,000. The building held 800 and had "a commodious stage large enough to accommodate the biggest attractions," according to the Western Star.

In June, 1914 came one of the "biggest attractions" in Posey County history. Former President William Howard Taft addressed a large group at the community's Centennial celebration. Taft began his speech saying, "...there is no community the size of New Harmony in America that has contributed so much to industrial and social advancement. Regarding the history of New Harmony, and founder Robert Owen and the Rappites, Taft said the reason the communities failed was directly related to their socialistic principles. He declared that no society can enjoy success

About 1913 boys playing baseball at West Franklin Methodist Church

West Franklin School, Ann Brown, Teacher-Left to right, top row: unknown, Hostettler, Grabert, Albert Grebe, Tom David ?, Albert Boerner, Carl Ernst, George Boerner, 2nd row: Louise Nigg, Leola Nigg, Elnora Noelle, Elnore David, Emma Noelle, unknown Ida Ernst?, Irma Boerner, Bertha Boerner, Alma Wilkens, Carl Hengstenberg. First row: Erwin Wolf, Heinrich Stock, unknown, Rudolph Boerner, unknown Hostettler?, Edward Arnold Becker.

without competition in business. In his own words Taft remarked, "the plan was based on the assumption that man was different being from what he is...Until men are perfect beings of this kind, socialism must either constitute a tyranny so rigid as to destroy not only the right of the liberty and to interfere with the pursuit of happiness, or it must be a failure."

County election day in November saw the entire Democratic ticket elected with the exception of one Republican county councilman, even though The Western Star reported that 538 of 4,955 registrered to vote did not turn up at the poles.

Indiana is often the center of major storm activity, and Posey County is not excluded. During the early hours of one June morning in 1915, 1.6 inches of rain fell, and while no homes were damaged, many feared the worst and fled to high ground. Several trees fell, causing much of the electricity and most telephones to go out in Mount Vernon. The Western Star reported the old grandstand at the Fairgrounds was destroyed. But, by far the farmers of Posey County suffered the most. The paper reported thousands of dollars of damage to much of the wheat and corn crop.

Later, in September, Walter Jackson, a leading member of the Posey County Bar Association died. Jackson was a prominent lawyer for 36 years and known throughout Indiana. Born and raised in Posey County, Jackson was buried in Bellfontaine Cemetery.

That same month, residents read about and witnessed a curious event. Walking on a wager from New York to San Fransico and back, a man passed through Mount Vernon and stopped at the Western Star offices on September 18, 1915. That man was Captain Hicks, an Indian scout and champion long distance walker. Hicks left New York on March 1, 1915 and was on the home stretch when he stopped at Mount Vernon, "as fresh as a daisy," reported the Western Star. With baggage weighing about 100 pounds and a dog as his companion, Hicks supported himself with the sale of postcards on the way west and lecturing on the return trip. Hicks was declared Champion Walker of the World in 1910 when as a missionary, he walked 25,000 miles in two years. Hicks was 72 years old when he made the walk in 1915 and reportedly averaged around seven miles per hour. The wager was set at $10,000 and would be given to Hicks when he returned to his starting point in New York.

By 1915, many Posey County cities were eligible to celebrate their cenntenial. New Harmony honored its centennial in 1914, and in September of 1915, Poseyville marked its cenntenial with a reunion of the descendants of Hugh Frazier.

Brought against his will from Paisly, Scotland in 1700, Frazer was "bound out" to a family in Virginia when he was seven

Mollie Hanes Tobacco Crop

until he turned 21. He later married into the family he had served for 14 years and had a son, George. He later married and had four sons and three daughters of his own. The Frazer daughters moved with their husbands to Harrison County, Kentucky and later to Posey County where they purchased a large tract of land in what is now Robb Township. From all over the country, including California, more than 500 Frazer descendants gathered to celebrate their heritage. The day's events included speeches, the reading of a poem that was also read at the semi-cenntenial 50 years earlier and a presentation of a complete geneological record of the Frazer family.

A year later, out of Bloomington, Indiana came the report of two "beauties" from Posey County. The October, 1916 paper reported that the county's "fame as the home of canteloupes extraordinary and grains of wheat that run five of six to the bushel is in the danger of being eclipsed." It seemed that two Posey County men attending their first year at Indiana Universtiy won honors for their physical qualities. Carl Schnabel of Mount Vernon was declared the most perfect man of the freshman class and French Clements, also of

Mount Vernon placed third. Schnabel weighed 156 pounds and was five feet and seven inches. The head of Deptartment of Physical Training said Schnabel was one of the most perfectly built men that ever entered Indiana University and would most likely have a great athletic career.

Also in that same month, Mount Vernon came face-to-face with a $5,000 law suit. Ernest Alldredge was run over by a horse May 24 during the city's Horse Show Day and was permanently injured. His mother sued Mount Vernon for $5,000 claiming the city for giving the Horse Show Committee exclusive use of Main Street and various other streets. Alldredge's mother alleged that this was a violation of the law of Indiana. No verdict was found in the Western Star. Later the $5,000 law suit that attracted the attention of much of Mount Vernon in October, 1915, was brought to trial in June of 1916. The plantiff still held that the city was responsible for injuries incuured by Alldrege May 24 when he was run over by a horse during Horse Show Day, held on the streets of Mount Vernon. The city claimed no responsibility. After three days, the jury voted seven to five in favor of the defendant.

Poseyville again made the news later in the year...but, this time it was not for its cenntenial celebration. Residents mourned the death of William Walling, a Civil War veteran, and were preparing to hold memorial services in the Old Union Church when a protest formed. The protest was not agianst the funeral or Walling, but agianst the minister who was to conduct the services. It seemed a member of the congregation had accused Reverend Pursinger of a statutory charge brought by a young women at Owensville. The minister, who appeared in court more than a year earlier, said he would fight the charge. The Walling family made a decision to leave the church and conduct the services at graveside in Saulman Cemetery.

"Terrific Hail Storm Hits City," read the headlines of the Western Star on June 8 1916. Hail the size of "moth balls" and later the size of "goose eggs" pelted Mount Vernon and broke quite a few windows. While Mount Vernon escaped the brunt of the storm, Black and Point townships suffered. Many farmers lost their entire wheat and corn crop to the pounding hail. Chicken and turkeys were killed in the storm that left some farmland six inches deep in hail the size of hen eggs.

By July, the effects of the recent hail storm were felt among the farmers of Posey County. The wheat crop, severely damaged by the hail, was barely more than one-third the prior year's yield.

But, an even greater tragedy struck.

Another storm hit the following month with winds that reached 100 mph. Throughout the storm, hail and rain along with the strong winds scattered tree limbs, flooded sewers, and quickly put the entire city of Mount Vernon and surrounding areas in total darkness.

The Western Star reported that "sparrows were blown from their nests, roosts in the trees and drowned by the heavy downpour of rain, thousands of dead bird bodies being found upon all the streets in the city on the following morning and scarcely a live one was to be seen in this section." Only one building was damaged, although the the "light" plant and both of the telephone companies suffered extensive loss, as most wires were down in the city. Again, the farmers felt the power of the storm which resulted in a loss of at least 25 percent of the corn crop.

The effects of the storm were quickly cleaned up and progress continued in Posey County as councilmen formed a committee to survey the need for traffic "posts" in Mount Vernon. The committee was formed in response to the growing automobile traffic over the decade. The intersections of Second, Third, Fourth and Fifth streets on Main and Second Street at Walnut would have the new traffic posts. The Western Star added to its report a suggestion that the committee designate one of the city policeman as a traffic officer and do away with parking on Main Street.

While the new traffic lights were quite a topic of conversation -- they were soon overshadowed by Posey County participation in the State Cenntenial Celebration. Indiana was 100 years old and the citizens of Posey County could be proud that they contributed a great deal to its rich heritage. The entire September 7 front page of the Western Star was filled with news of the preparations. This grand celebration would take place September 12 and 13 and would include a free concert by the Indianapolis Military Band and a "novel and very instructive Water Pageant." All of the business district and much of the residential district in Mount Vernon would be decorated in grand fashion to host the following activities. These activities were listed in the Western Star.

On September 14, 1916, following the Centannial celebration that "surpassed anything in county's history," the Western Star again filled the front page -- this time with a detailed account of the two-day affair. "The beautiful rising of the sun Tuesday morning gave evidence that the

---

STATE CENNTENIAL CELEBRATION ACTIVITIES

TUESDAY, SEPTEMBER 12, 1916
8-10 a.m.-Get together, shake hands, have refreshments.

10-11:30 a.m.-Band concert, Posey County bands.

11:30 a.m.-1 p.m.-Lunch

1-1:45 p.m.-Band concert, Indianapolis Military Band

2 p.m.-Opening address.

2:30 p.m.-Parade. 1. Historical parade. 2. 400 county school children 3. Industrial parade.

5 p.m.-Human flag (400 people make up the flag. This flag will be in position during the parade and will sing some songs immediately after the close of the parade.)

7:30 p.m.-Grand concert, Indianapolis Military band and chorus consisting of 150 Posey County voices. Mrs. Chilton Pleasants will sing "Indiana," which was composed by Mrs. Albert Wade, a former resident of Mount Vernon.)

WEDNESDAY, SEPTEMBER 13, 1916

9:30 to 10:30 a.m.-Concert, Indianapolis Military Band.

10:45 a.m.-"HomeComing" address.

1:30 to 2:30 p.m.-Concert, Indianapolis Military Band.

2:45 p.m.-Address.

4:30 p.m.-Human flag.

4:30 p.m.-Pole dance and other drills

7:30 p.m.-Historic river pageant on river front

The following are the episodes and scenes of the historic water pageant.

INTRODUCTION

1. The Ohio-dance of the water nymphs.
2. The forest primeval. Dance of the Dryds and Fire Flies.
3 Prologue.

EPISODE I

(One hundred years ago or more ago.)

1. Coming of the Indiana.
2. Fur-traders, French missionaries, etc.
3. Early Pioneers

EPISODE II

(Civilization)
1. Coming of the Rappites.
2. The Owen Community.
3. Mount Vernon made the capital of Posey County.

EPSIODE III

(Political unrest.)
1. The Civil war period.
2. The Hovey Campaign.
3. In Memory.

EPISODE IV

(Progress unfolded.)

FINALE

1. Fathers Time & his Winged Fairies.
2. Posey County's contribution to the state.

Creator bestowed his blessings on the people of Posey County, so they could fittingly celebrate Indiana's centennial."

The most notable part of the celebration was the mile-and-a-half long parade that entertained thousands. The Indianapolis Military Band led the troupe, followed by many historical floats including the early settlers and Indian float, the pioneers and their descendents float, and ox team hitched to an old-fashioned prairie schooner, a flatboat float and a "good representation" of the old court house at Springfield, the first capital of Posey County, Dan Rice and his famous market house and talking horse, the Hovey Glee Club, the Posey County product float and finally the ship of stat float representing Indiana.

The Sherbourne Park Band led the second section, followed by the Knights of St. John in full dress. Directly behind these two groups was a float titled "Father Durbin," and one called "Christianity Civilizing the World." Following were the "Boys in Blue," the Loyal Order of Moose and a drum corps from Evansville. The school children of Posey county and the children of the city schools filled much of the parade, escorted by their teachers. The fire department, in full uniform, the Royal Neighbors, the Women's Christian Temperence Union and the Order of the Eastern Star followed the children in floats.

Advertisements galore bombarded the onlookers as the Industrial section of the parade moved along the streets. Twenty-three floats advertising everything from flour and hominy and the Hot Blast Stove to Red Band cigars and the John Deere elevator to the models wearing the latest New York fashions and a float from the Western Star entertained the crowds.

Several automobiles followed representing Ford models from 1909 to 1916. There were also truck and tractors and comparisons of the new and old methods of plowing. "Last but not least," writes the Western Star, "came the horseless carriage of Ed Hanner's which was propelled by a burro."

The two-day grand Centennial Celebration progressed without any problems and ended at the river where and estimated 20,000 from southern Indiana, Illinois and Kentucky watched the Water Pageant.

Posey County's own history was celebrated later that year when Dr. Barton W. Everman, director of the California Academy of Science museum, reviewed zoology in Indiana during the past 100 years in a two-day session of the Indiana Academy of Science. Noted naturalists included were John James Audubon, Alexander Wilson, Constaine Samuel Rafinesque and George Rapp, founder of a society of Rappites or Harmonists. This society came from Butler County Pennsylvania in 1815 to establish its community in New Harmony. Everman was quoted in his review saying, "New Harmony remained for many years the literary, scientific and art center west of the Alleghenies; and to this day it holds its place among the most enlightened and cultured communities in a state distinguished for its scientific and literary prestige."

Early in 1917, before the United States entered World War I, American troops were being sent to patrol and protect the Mexican border. Earlier, California, Utah, Nevada and parts of Arizona, New Mexico and Colorado were acquired by the United States after the Mexican War (1846 to 1848). Twenty-eight years later Proferio Diaz overthrew the elected goverment and appointed himself dictator. Although under his rule the economy improved, only big landowners, businessmen and foreign investors benefited -- the majority of Mexican citizens lived in poverty. By 1911, political unrest came to a climax, and Fransisco Madera, a popular and liberal landowner forced Diaz out of office. Unfortunately, Madero was a weak president and within three years Gen. Victorio Huerta seized power and established a dictatorship. But, the fighting did not stop here. Madero's supporters continued to fight for an elected government. President Woodrow Wilson helped by not officially recognizing Heurta's government. In 1914, United States involvement became imminent. Several American soldiers were arrested in Tampica. In retaliation, United States forces took Vera Cruz to prevent arms shipments to the port from reaching Huerta's armies. Later on that year, revolts forced Huerta to leave the country. But, once again, the new president, Carranza was not completly supported. Two groups in particular, one headed by Fransisco "Pancho" Villa and the other by Emiliano Zapata, wanted stricter reforms. President Woodrow Willson cut off the supply of arms to the two groups in 1915. Seeking revenge, "Pancho" Villa raided Columbus, New Mexico in 1916, killing 16 Americans. In an immediate response, President Wilson sent Gen. John J. Pershing to Mexico to bring "Pancho" Villa to justice. Meanwhile, United States troops were sent to protect the border in the case of another attack.

As soon as transportation was found, 25,000 National Guardsmen including Company L of Mount Vernon were to return from the Mexican border, reported the January 25 Western Star. The organizations mustering by order of Maj. Gen. Funston, the Indiana 2nd Infantry, the ambulance company no. 2 and brigade patrol, leaving 45,000 to 50,000 men on border patrol. Company L of Mount Vernon was one of three battalions composing the 2nd Infantry. Remaining Indiana troops included four Indianapolis companies of the 1st Infantry, field hospital M.2 of Frankfort and D battery of Ft. Wayne.

It wasn't until February 8, 1917 that Capt. Merle Weisinger of Co. L telegraphed his father in Mount Vernon, that the city knew the troops were almost home. The telegraph arrived from Ft. Benjamin Harrion, and Capt. Weisinger couldn't say when they would finally be home. Posey County didn't waste a moment's time preparing "big doings" (as reported by the Western Star) for their return.

Finally, 14 days later, the 52 men of

Company L returned. Capt. Weinsinger and some of Company L remained at Ft. Benjamin Harrison and would arrive a few days later. Since the entire company didn't return, a banquet and celebration planned for Weinsinger were postoned.

Almost as soon as Company L had returned, orders were issued March 29, calling the company to mobilize. None of the 60 members knew where they were going as they awaited further orders from headquarters. "The War Department disclosed for publication only the fact that the state troops now being mobilized will be used to guard government property, munition plant, railroad terminal and bridges and other properties vulnerable to attack by

Factory girls out for a Sunday row. Second from left-Ida Mathilde Becker, right with second oar-Elizabeth Becker

hostile organizations and disloyal persons within the United States," said the <u>Western Star</u>. The call for new recruits was great. During times of peace, a company of peace strength was composed of 80 members -- at war strength, 150. The goal of the officers of the Mount Vernon Company was to reach peace strength by the time they were ordered to leave. "It is your duty as patriots to respond, and you should do so at once and thus show to the world that the some patriotism exists in Mount Vernon today as it did in the early 1860s when your fathers shouldered their guns at the first call." (<u>Western Star</u>)

One week later, the call came. Company L under the command of Capt. Merle Weisinger and First Lt. Ivan Curtis left on a train for Jeffersonville. Here, they were ordered to guard the United States Commissary Department -- the largest in the country. The company supassed their goal of 80 new recruits and reached the required peace strength number. Recruiting continued in Posey County in order to reach wartime strength.

Just one day later, the United States declared war on Germany.

The events leading to the United States intervention in the war are key to Posey County's involvement. Although some county papers made little mention of the war, it began June 28, 1914 when Archduke Francis Ferdinand of Austria-Hungary was assasinated. Exactly one month later, Austria-Hungary declared war on Serbia. Following this, Germany declared war on Russia and then on France. By 1915, Italy had declared war on Germany. Then on February 1, 1917, Germany began unrestricted submarine warfare. Then the British intercepted a message from Germany to Mexico. The message asked the Mexican government to join with them in declaring war on the United States. The offer included the promise to return the lands taken by the United States in the Mexican War. The Mexican government declined the offer. On April 6, 1917, the United States declared war on Germany. At this time the Allies included Belgium,

Brazil, the British Empire, China, Costa Rica, Cuba, France, Greece, Guatemala, Haiti, Honduras, Italy, Japan, Liberia, Montenegro, Nicaragua, Panama, Portugal, Romania, Russia, San Marino, Serbia and Siam. The Central Powers were made up of Austria-Hungary, Bulgaria, Germany and the Ottoman Empire.

A Posey County mass meeting was held on April 7 in the Mount Vernon courthouse. More than 100 farmers, bankers, teachers and other citizens discussed how to increase and conserve the food supply during the crisis. The speakers addresseed in depth the method that could be used to produce larger crops, the benefits of using a commercial fertilizer and using all waste ground that was possible for the farmers to cultivate.

Patriotism was strong with coming of the World War I. Those who "talked too much" or appeared to be disloyal in any way were outcasts in the community. On one occassion in late April, James P. Timoney, a special agent for the Department of Justice (headquartered in Indianapolis) arrived in Posey County unannounced. His mission was to investigate some remarks which fingered those who were "very indiscrete as well as unwise toward the government since its entrance into the World War," reported the Western Star. The paper went on to say that Timoney made it clear that, " we have several here who have been doing too much talking and that unless they cease their talking and change their attitude they will be properly taken care of."

However consuming the war was, there was still time for normal life. One activity was the Calf Club which began in mid-June, 1917. "Just a few words in explanation of our Calf Club, which we have launched, and which we are now ready to turn over to you with sails set for the village of 'Success,' which being reached, means profit to you in dollars as well as experience in caring for a very interesting animal," said club founder William Holton. The Calf Club was apparently welcome among the farmers. One wrote saying: "I am certainly glad I got the calf which is number 498. Although one of the pure-breds might sell for the most money this one is good enough to raise calves and sell milk and cream from...they say I am all smiles and I know it is the truth."

Animals made the news again that June, but this time the breed produced was the first of its kind. Charles Nolan of Point Township showed off his Zebroid, a cross between a zebra and a mare.

In late September, the citizens of Posey County honored the conscripted men leaving for training at Camp Taylor. These 34 men of the National Army were honored by a patriotic parade. Everyone taking part in the parade was asked to carry the flag, and all homes and businesses were asked to display the stars and stripes. A band began the parade, followed by the conscripted men, the Harrow Post, G.A.R., the Women Relief Corps, the Boy Scouts, another band, Secret Orders, citizens, school children and teachers, all labor organizations and finally the fire department. Money was collected in a flag to benefit the conscripted men. This was the only money exchanged that morning, as all business were requested to close their doors from 9 until 10:25 a.m. for the parade.

The third quota of drafted men from Posey County left for Camp Zachary Taylor in Louisville, Kentucky amid cheers. After the band played several patriotic selections, the Honorable Janes Blackburn delivered the farewell address. The speech emphasized that the United States had been "smote on one cheek" and then turned the other. Our flag, he stated, had been fired upon and it is you young men as well as every American's duty to defend it until there is not a thread left."

The response to this farewell address, given by one of the drafted soldiers, William Maurer, had the crowds doubled over

Dr. Hastings Zebroid Hybrids, some were sold to circuses.

in laughter. "Why if you think I am going to stand up here and picture the horrors of war you are badly mistaken. We are not going to war. We are a bunch of big boys going out on a great big picnic, that's where we are going. I feel that we are the whole show and that you people standing out here are trying to get in and just having a peep. In fact, you are not even a side show, we are both and when I express myself in this manner I do so knowing that it is the American boy today who is holding the honors and I am certainly pleased to be one of them."

Thirteen inches of snow covered much of Posey County that December, making it one of the worst blizzards in the county's history. Railroad traffic was delayed and rural mailmen returned without finishing their routes due to the nine-and 10-foot drifts. The Western Star reported that several Kentucky men had walked over the solidly frozen Ohio River. This was the first time since 1907, said the paper, that the river had frozen solid enough to close. Some livestock was reported lost due to the freezing temperatures and many cars were incapacitated. One bright note in the storm was reported by grain experts who predicted that the heavy snowfall would benefit the farmer -- the blanket of snow adding both warmth and moisture to wheat fields, perhaps adding thousands of bushels of wheat to the next year's crop.

While the men of Posey County did their part during World War I, the home front certainly did theirs. Notes from the Red Cross stressed the "grave necessity of every woman devoting her time and energy to the Red Cross...who will win the war by their war work in the front trenches at home." Responsibilities included working four to six hours a day providing for the needs of the army medical corps.

Another way to serve on the home front during the war was to donate a variety of clothes and necessary items to a collection center. These would then be sent overseas to the Belgium and French refugees. Some items were no accepted - men's stiff hats, (derby, straw or dress), women's stiff hats, fancy slippers, goods containing rubber of any kind, such as fancy suspenders and garters, and leather goods not in the best of condidtion. The following items were approved: shirts, light colored flannels, underwear, trousers, garments, overalls and other working garments, three-piece suits, shoes, overcoats, jerseys and socks (sizes 10 1/2 and 11). The women could contribute by sending shirts, underwear, petticoats, blouses, skirts, overcoats, two-piece suits, pinafores, shoes (sizes 7 and 8), shawls, night dresses, girl's stockings and infant clothes.

Stewartsville Depot of Illinois Central Railroad

One Posey County shipment contained 70 hospital shirts from New Harmony, 28 pajamas and 30 hospital shirts from Mount Vernon.

The papers were filled with news of of the war, and the responsibilities of the American citizens at home. In August, a liberty guard was organized in Posey County. White men between the ages of 18 and 45 were asked to join in support of the country. The following letter published in the Weekly Democrat described the organization and its duties. "The Liberty Guard organization is purely a patriotic one, organized at the call of the Governor and is subject only to his orders, or those whom he places over us. It is not subject for riot or guard duty, except under imperative need at home. There are now more than one hundred and fifty companies in the state one in every community, so there would never be a call to go elsewhere than in its own community....By our presence we have made the state safe from outside or unpatriotic interference; and our present duty is to give the conscripted men as much military training as possible before he is inducted into the service; and we would be glad to hear that you had gathered together all these conscripts and made them fit." Membership in the Liberty Guard was dissolved when a man enlisted in any branch of the United States service.

Some townships formed their own liberty guards, as was the case in Black Township. The only other guards in the county at this time were in Poseyville and Cynthiana.

The Patriotic League of Posey County was formed with many of the same objectives. Without using mob force, the members made it their goal to find those disloyal to America. The ultimate goal of the organization was to make Posey County free of disloyalty without exception. To make steps toward this goal, a resolution was adopted asking county schools to stop teaching the German language at the end of the present school term. A second resolution, requesting all ministers in the county to deliver a sermon titled, "Was the United States of America justified in entering upon the war with Germany?" The Western Star added its own views to the article saying, "We are at war with the most savage nation on earth; our boys are on the fining line and are being slain by the most barbarous methods known to man or beast, and citizens native or foreign born, can not lend their sympathy to such a people as the Germans have proven themselves to be."

While men attended patriotic meetings, women also were great supporters of the war. Liberty bonds were big business during war years and they were heavily promoted in the newspapers. Money the government received from bond sales went directly toward the war effort. At the end of the war, the bonds could be redeemed at a higher value. A group of Posey County women representing each of the 10 townships -- Bethel, Black, Center, Harmony, Lynn, Marrs, Point, Robb, Robinson and Smith, conducted a drive to meet a bond sales goal. The message from the committee to other women in Posey County was strong and clear. "This is not a time, when so many are already in mourning, and the ache and fear of all that is most terrible is universally felt, to indulge in the baubles and frivolities that are supposed to be pecularly feminine. Such funds as they have, or can raise, must be turned over to our country to be used for a more serious purpose. In this way the women can and must do their full part."

When the second Liberty Loan drive was established in Posey County, the minimum goal was $329,000 and the target goal was set at $548,000. Posey County well surpassed the minimum, reaching a total of $465,000. The goal of the Third Liberty Loan was set at $398,850, and the chairman of the Liberty Loan Committee was confident that it would be oversubscribed. The committee carefully organized the entire county and sent representatives to doors to help surpass the stated goal.

An organization calling themselves the War Mothers of Posey County served as link between servicemen and their homes, to offer sympathy and encouragement and to build morale. By becoming a War Mother, these women would automatically become a charter member of the National War Mothers Organization. These groups often sent food, letters and small necessities to the soldiers fighting overseas. Garden Parties and raffles helped War Mothers provide services to the soldiers.

A part of the World War I came home to Posey County as a reminder of the battles overseas. A train carrying war relics arrived in Posey County at Mount Vernon. The large display of thought-provoking war items was supplied by the U.S. War Department and the French government. To come in contact with the war, to witness its harsh realities, all the onlookers had to do was touch the German guns, shells, helmets, airplanes, gas bombs, shrapnel shells, mortars, and minatures of the u-boats and models of the submarines used by the American Navy and the navies of the Allies.

Despite the intense patriotism and willingness to fight for America, there were those who appealed to the District Board to be exempt from overseas duties. Only a few were allowed to remain. Most claims were disallowed. One pleaded that he had to support his widowed mother, another that he had only been married one month, another loss of vision in one eye...all these claims were disallowed and the young men were sent to war.

Those who did remain and many women took up a different sort of fight -- one to provide more food for the men overseas. These efforts were called War Gardens, and they would ultimately assist the request of the government in planting and raising more food. Any city lots and unused private lots were immediatley used to create a War Garden. A committee met to discuss how to find unused lots, what to plant and what, if any, ferterlizers should be used.

In October 1918, another killer hit Posey County -- not the Germans -- but the Spanish Fluenza. The State Board of Health closed all public places including schools, churches, theaters and public amusement places. No public meetings could be held.

But then...

PEACE IS DECLARED - About noon today William P. Egli, agent of the L. & N. railroad, caught a message over the wires stating that the German Government had signed the armistice terms as presented by the Allies and that peace had now been declared. The signing of the armistice took place at 2:00 o'clock yesterday afternoon, German time, or 1:00 o'clock this morning, United States time.

The Posey County newspaper carried this joyous message to all on November 11, 1918. At this time, election returns in Posey County showed an almost complete Democratic ticket. Although the early returns had the Republicans smiling, final votes, especially from Black Township turned their smiles to frowns with the Democrats winning. Precincts that normally voted Republican, voted Democrat, and vise versa. In addition to the surprising results, the turnout was low, in part due to the missing soldier vote.

Even with the loss, the Republican Party had reason to celebrate. Everyone had reason to celebrate -- the war was over. The Allies had won. The men were coming home.

"...sleep for the remainder of the night was out of the question." published the Western Star, November 14. Posey County along with the rest of the country and nations once at war celebrated. Streets filled with people... runnings, walking, dancing, driving in decorated cars, all making as much noise as they could. Tin horns, cow bells, dish pans, even wash tubs were used to celebrate the happiness of the county. Factory whistles blew and screeched and music played favorite and patriotic tunes. Amid the chaos, plans were being drawn up to celebrate in a somewhat organized fashion. A parade made up of school children, the Women Relief Corps, the War Mothers, the Red Cross Workers, Boy Scouts, Liberty Guards and at least 100 automobiles filled the streets. A sum of $110 was spent on fireworks to be set off at the river that evening. And although several men were injured by premturely exploding fireworks, nothing could squelch the excitment of the news.

Troops were sent home, inductions were ceased and those organizations supporting the war on the home front were disbanded. But the celebrating that occured from the moment it was heard, could never cover up the grim statistics of the World War that began for some countries in 1914 and for the United States in 1917. In the United States alone, 116,516 men were killed, 204,002 wounded and 4,500 captured or missing. These numbers were relatively small compared to the 4,968,000 killed, wounded or missing in France. And, although the numbers were not official, the Russians were said to have more than 9,150,000 men dead and wounded.

Residents mourned the death of 34 Posey County soldiers:

Arthur Anderson, William Crow, Robert K. Curtis, Owen E. Divine, Charles Dixon, Owen Dunn, Marion Gerton, Frank Goebel, Homer Gordon, Charles H. Hobbs, Sidney Hohimer, Herbert Huck, William A. Kleinschmidt, John Lurker, Lalus McCracken, Oliver Marquis, Lemuel H. Martin, John M. Mitz, Earl B. Neek, Joseph M. Oxford, Marvin E. Pierle, George F. Rabler, Otis M. Redman, Angus P. Reynolds, Albert Roemr, Jesse Russell, Daniel F. Seifert, James W. Showers, Loyd S. Sugg, Frederick S. Wade. George A. Walls, Carl Williams and James Williams.

A month after the war had ended, an end also could be seen to the rampant influenza epidemic. The ban on public meetings was lifted, theaters were allowed to open (although a few remained closed, unable to acquire films on such short notice), the Billard room opened up, the public schools

Lawrence School 1918 Top Row: unknown, Wade, Louis Dornbusch, Edward Becker, unknown Wade, Emily Duncan (teacher), Hilda Hausmann, Edna Schaber, Annette Stephan, Kathryn Keller, Erna Hausmann, Second Row: Hade, Clarence Marx, John Oscar Hast, Lillian Dietz, Wade, Esther Hahn, Thomas Dornbusch. First Row: Cora Stephan, Dora Schisler, Luise Becker, Helen Schaber, Lorena Hahn.

Around 1918 Mt. Vernon to Grandview Traction Car person standing in front of car George Hawey Martin who was a motorman. Herbert Jacobs also of Mt. Vernon standing on car steps was conductor.

were opened and churches could again hold their services. The Western Star in an effort to completely defeat the flu, advised readers to keep up the good work and carefully follow certain rules.

- Don't sneeze or cough in anybody's face.

- Don't neglect or laugh at a "common cold." It may be the first symptom of flu.

- Don't worry. Worry is weakening.

- Don't visit flu victims, unless you really must do so. Then, wear a flu mask.

- Don't use a common drinking cup anywhere.

- Don't use a common towel anywhere.

- Don't put pencils or pencil holders in your mouth. There may be flu germs on them.

- Don't pet dogs or cats. They carry germs in their hair.

The last of the teens passed quietly in Posey County. Former President William Howard Taft and distinguished guests passed through Mount Vernon on his way across country. The group, which also included the President of Harvard University, a professor of international law at Harvard, the president of the National Council of Women and a few others were advocating the League to Enforce Peace.

In other areas, an unusual effort to attract more Saturday shoppers began when the merchants of Mount Vernon combined and invited the whole of Posey County to witness a "marvelous fete." For absolutely no charge, anyone could come and watch Daredevil Smith make an attempt to scale the courthouse without climbing gear. This drawing card, Daredevil Smith, was nationally known for this strange act and was reputed to have climbed buildings in 42 states. Smith told reporters he was confident he could climb the courthouse without the use of rope and would go from bottom to top within 20 minutes. On that Saturday the "human fly" climbed the courthouse, to the delight of the crowds, in eleven mintues.

But, effects of the war were still felt by the citizens of Posey County. Almost daily during May soldiers returned from active duty. Tragically, the paper also reported the suicide of a Marrs township man who had served duing the war and had only been home for two weeks when he hanged himself.

"Hubdeep to a buggy", and "deep enough to swim a horse" were just of few of the descriptions of a storm that hit Posey County in June 1919. Not since the flood

Largest confirmation class ever at Salem Evangelical Protestant Church, Hensler, Indiana 1919. Little boy in window is Melvin Stephan

of 1913 were the waters so high. Transportation was at a standstill until the following day. It was impossible to get from Mount Vernon to New Harmony or Evansville, and the storm was devastating to farmers. Newly cut wheat in Caborn was destroyed by the floods and entire crops of wheat in West Franklin were lost. As in floods past, relatively few buildings were damaged. It was the farmer who bore the brunt of the storm's destruction.

Later that year in September, it was the merchants who suffered loss, not the farmers. At midnight, a fire destroyed seven buildings and killed 70 head of livestock in Mount Vernon. The blaze, repotedly the worst in 25 to 30 years, drew crowds from all over the county. It took until 3 p.m. the following day for fireman to feel confident that the destruction had ended. Although the cause of the fire was unknown, it was beleived to have started in a stable owned by Phil Hagemann. Estimated loss from his big sales stables, horse and mule barn totaled more than $55,000. The danger from the fire -- falling power lines and collapsing walls -- hampered the firemen's work. Due to those fallen lines and a telephone pole, the Mount Vernon Electric Light and Power Company lost $600, and the Southern telephone Company lost $300. One home was destroyed with losses of more than $1,000. Losses reported by the rest of the businesses claimed by fire, The W.H. Fogas Building, the Cartwright Heir Building, the J. H. Perry Shoe Shop, P.W. Wenzel Tailoring and Pressing Shop, the Masonic Lodge (colored) and the Swift & Company Cream Station totaled $11,200.

Indiana: 1920-1929

After the turmoil of World War I and the flu epidemic, Indiana and the nation in 1920 looked ahead to better times. The Republican Party ran on a platform of peace, prosperity, and "normalcy." This appeal won Warren Harding the Presidency, and made Warren T. McCray governor of Indiana. McCray's personal finances, however, deteriorated during his term; state funds found their way into his accounts, and in 1924 he was convicted of mail fraud. Lt. Gov. Emmett Forrest Branch completed the last few months of McCray's gubernatorial term, while McCray served a term of three years in a federal penitentiary. He was pardoned by President Hoover in 1930.

Branch offered no surprises, but his successor certainly did. Ed Jackson was elected governor in 1924 with the enthusiastic support of the Ku Klux Klan. The Klan also saw a majority of its "approved" candidates for the General Assembly elected in that year. Klan-related scandals and corruption spread throughout the state government. In 1928, Jackson was tried for bribing former governor McCray with Klan money. He was acquitted only because the statute of limitations on his crimes had expired.

In the early 1920s, the Klan reached its height of influence in Indiana politics through appeals to patriotism, intimidation, and bribery. In 1923 the Klan sought to buy Valparaiso University. (This plan, fortunately failed; Valparaiso was sold two years later to the Lutheran Church.) Most of the legislative candidates endorsed by the Klan won in 1924. There were a few incidents of opposition -- Klansmen were driven from the streets of South Bend in May 1924--but the Klan held considerable influence in the state government.

All this changed with the fall of David C. Stephenson, former Grand Dragon of the Indiana Klu Klux Klan. In 1925, Stephenson abducted and raped Madge Oberholtzer, a state employee. Distraught, Oberholtzer attempted suicide, but lived long enough to testify against Stephenson. He was convicted of second-degree murder and sentenced to life in prison. With Stephenson's downfall, public opinion shifted quickly against the Klan. The Indianapolis Times' crusade against the Klan was rewarded by a Pulitzer Prize in 1928. Stephenson also helped break the organization by revealing details of its political corruption, including its ties to Gov. Jackson. By 1929, the political influence of the Klan in Indiana was ended.

Corruption seemed a political watchword of the 1920s, from the national Teapot Dome scandal to local issues. In 1925, John L. Duvall was elected mayor of Indianapolis and two years later he was removed and jailed for corrupt practices. During the decade, six Indianapolis city councilmen also were convicted of corruption and one Hoosier congressman was convicted of peddling postmasterships.

Still in other areas, honest Indiana politicans were playing large roles. In 1921, Will H. Hays became postmaster general; he was succeeded in 1923 by another Hoosier, Harry S. New. Former Governor Samuel M. Ralston was elected Senator in 1922, defeating (as he had for the governorship) Albert J. Beveridge. Democrat Reginal H. Sullivan became mayor of Indianapolis in 1929. Indian's only five-time Presidential candidate, Eugene V. Debs, was released from prison in Decmeber 1921 (he died in Terre Haute in 1926). In 1928, two sterling Republicans succeeded to chairs so uneasily held by Harding, McCray and Jackson. Herbert Hoover was elected President and Harry G. Leslie chosen as Governor of Indiana.

The 1920s were hard times for Indiana governors. Aside from McCray's and Jackson's troubles (J. Frank Hanley died in 1920) former Vice-President Thomas R. Marshall and Senator Samuel M. Ralston in 1925 and Winfield T. Durbin in 1928.

Indiana literature continued to flourish in the 1920s, particularly int he field of history. Robert S. and Helen M. Lynd's 1924 work Middleton took Muncie as its "representative American city." Charles and Mary R. Beard wrote The Rise of the

American Civilization in 1927. The next year Albert J. Beveridge's Life of Abraham Lincoln was published posthumously. Claude Bowers produced three major works: The Party Battles of the Jackson Period (1922), Jefferson and Hamilton (1925), and The Tragic Era (1929). Other literature was not neglected. Mary Q. Burnett's Art and Artists of Indiana appeared in 1921, as did Booth Tarkington's Alice Adams. Louise Ludlow's In the Heart of Hoosierland appeared in 1925. And, 1929 saw the last completion of Kin Hubbard's work in book form, Abe Martin's Town Pump. But the book of the decade may also be the greatest book written by a Hoosier, Theodore Dreiser's 1925 masterpiece An American Tragedy,

But, Indiana art lost three of it major painters in the decade, Theodore C. Steele and Otto Stark died in 1926 and James Ottis Adams died in 1927.

And other tragedies struck. A February 1921 train crash at Porter killed 37 people. A mine blast at the City Mine in Sullivan in February 1925 killed 51; 37 died in and explosion at the Francisco Mine No. 2 at Princeton in December 1926. The worst storm ever to hit the midwest struck March 18, 1925. Seventy died in Posey, Gibson and Pike counties (the total midwestern death toll was 689). Traffic and revenues decreased on the interurban lines as more people took to the roads. In 1928 the state's annual traffic death toll topped 1000.

The Indiana auto industry continued to lose ground in the 1920s. Although, two companies that began in the decade survived -- Duesenberg, produced in Indianapolis from 1920 to 1937, and Cord, manufactured at Auburn and Connersville from 1929 to 1937 -- other lines were not so fortunate. Four companies ceased production in 1924 -- Bush in Elkhart, Maxwell in New Castle, Monroe in Indianapolis and Premier in Indianapolis. Indianapolis Cole stopped production in 1925, Connersville Lexington in 1927 and Durant in Muncie and McFarlan in Connersville in 1928. The industry at Kokomo also was hit hard. The Haynes Automobile Company declared bankruptcy in 1924 and the next year the Apperson Company failed, started by Haynes' former partners.

A national coal strike and railway shipman's strike in 1922 also affected Indiana companies, but after these were settled industrial peace was the norm for the rest of the decade. Indiana banks during the 1920s had their own difficulties. Twenty-eight Hoosier banks failed in 1927, 24 in 1928 and 21 in 1921.

The 1920s were the glory years for Notre Dame football and its coach Knute Rockne. His "Four Horsemen" were the stars of the decade, and Notre Dame won the national football championship in 1924 and 1929.

The 1920s was a decade of odds and ends, firsts and lasts, in Indiana. WSBT in South Bend became the first commercial radio station licensed in Indiana in 1921. The 1923 Legislature made the flower of the tulip tree the official state flower. A neighborhood store in Moorseville was robbed in 1924, beginning the career of a man better known for bigger deeds -- John Dillinger. The first scientific archeological excavation in Indiana was made in 1926 by J. Arthur McLean at a mound in Sullivan County. The National Road became U.S. Highway 40 in 1925 when the federal highway numbering system began. The French Lick Springs Hotel introduced a new health beverage, tomato juice, in 1925. Before the end of the year, the Henry P. Williams Company of Paoli had begun the commercial canning of the juice.

The stock market crash of October 1929 brought the "Roaring Twenties" to a sudden halt. Indiana and the rest of the nation waited and watched for what the next decade would bring.

Politically, the big news events of 1920 were the state and national elections. But, up until November, Posey County found itself going about normal business -- almost.

The newspapers in February reported that a certain man's "ponies took a joy ride in a six-cylinder touring car! This sounds a little out of reason, but one can expect most anything in these days of fast living." It seemed that two ponies got out of their stables and headed north "as fast as their little hoofs would permit," reported the Western Star. When the owner heard news of the escape, he used the services of a six cylinder touring car to begin the chase. After the six-mile ride, the ponies were stopped and a decision was needed. Without objection from the owner of the car, the ponies were loaded into the rear seat and driven home.

The Mount Vernon Board of Education assured the families of those children who attended the Western Building school, that a new $17,000 West Side school would take its place and be better able to serve the students. The new school would be one-story high with a basement and would be constructed so that additions could be built when needed. Building began in 1920 on the James Whitcomb Riley Grade School.

Plans were also discussed to erect a new Senior High School with an adjoining athletic field. By April 1, the site for the new Senior High School was selected. Although construction would not begin for a few years, the site immediately purchased was located just southeast of the Central and Junior High School building and also included several lots on the corner of Sixth and Canal streets. The property was bought for $2,250.

At this same meeting, the board decided to increase higher paid teacher's salaries by almost 25 percent and the lower paid salaries by 50 percent.

An "up-to-date" course was added to the curriculum in the Mount Vernon High School and was taken under advisement for schools in New Harmony and Poseyville. The new Vocational Agricultural and Domestic Science course would drop some of the present required classes such as Latin and the students would spend half the day studying agricultural and domestic science. Graduates would still receive a diploma and would be free to go on to college. The program had been tried in other parts of the state with success.

The weather again took its toll in the Mount Vernon portion of Posey County. A wind storm tore off many roofs and toppled a number of barns. The Light Plant was shut down for a time due to the danger of falling wires. Many boats and barges along the stormy waters of the Ohio were washed down river or sunk. A few farmers in Point Township lost livestock and reported downed buildings. Tin roofing on those building that had survived the great fire the year before were blown off, however, the buildings had not yet been repaired and the damage was not great.

The primary elections in April of 1920 were no surprise, as they foretold the winning of the Democratic ticket in the November elections. Posey had been, for a majority of its history, a Democratic county. The only heated contest during the primaries was for sheriff. And, the biggest surprise of the April returns gave Republican presidential candidate Hiram W. Johnson of California the majority of Posey County votes. The other Republican candidates, Frank O. Lowden received 365 votes, Leonard Woods, 283 votes and Warren G. Harding, 85 votes.

The Coliseum board met in May and chose a site for the "big memorial building" to be erected in Mount Vernon. Of the many lots offered, those belonging to Jacob Cronbach and Dr. D. C. Ramsey were selected. The property sold for a total of $11,000 and covered an area of 140 by 140 feet.

The unexpected results of the April primaries were nothing compared the election results in the November race. Headlines of the Western Star paper read, "Republican Tidal Wave Almost Engulfs Posey"..."For Years the Gibraltar of Democracy, Posey County Gives Majority of 204 to Senator Harding for President." The man who had received the least of votes on the Republican ticket from Posey County, was preparing to lead the country. The reports from the newspaper sounded grim, "Posey has always been looked upon by other counties in the state a being as rockribbed solid democratic count. However, the results of Tuesday were surprising but are no indication that the county will remain in the hands of the opposition."..."Apparently the Democrats joined the wave which had struck this country. They wanted a change and made no exception in Posey."

Besides Harding, Republican candidate James Watson carried Posey in his campaign U.S. Senator. Republican Candidate McCray became Indiana's governor by one vote. Republican Edward Jackson was elected secretary of the state.

The county ticket was not caught "in the state and national landslide," and elected all Democrats with the exception of two offices, Circuit Clerk and Surveyor. However well the Democrats seemed to do in the county elections, the vote always seemed to be close. The Democrats were big losers in Robinson Township. Robb, Harmony and Center townships showed that the Democrats didn't fair as well as expected. The women took an active part in the election and the paper reported that "it is safe to say that nine out of every ten voted as their husbands did."

The news of elections quieted and Posey County newpaper began to report other happenings. To bring more culture to Posey County residents, especially school children, the educational committee for Mount Vernon brought the Elson Art Exhibit to the senior high school. The extensive exhibit contained 200 reproductions of the world's most famous paintings. The committee hoped to establish a fund to buy various pictures to decorate the school rooms. Fund-raising enabled the committee to purchase $700 worth of paintings from the Elson Company.

In other news, famous phonograph star Ada Jones arrived in Mount Vernon with a well-known American violinist and a entertainer, magician and trick violin player, and a pianist.

News of the plans to build a coliseum made the papers, this time in an effort to stop its construction. The Cynthiana Argus argued the "Coliseum which is causing so much talk in Posey County will be built under protest, if it is built. Outside of Mount Vernon there seems to be no one in favor of it. The taxpayers of the whole county would be taxed for its erection and maintenance and Mount Vernon would reap the benefit. There are not very many towns in the county and it does not seem just that a town on the very edge of the county should be favored."

Center Township made the Evansville paper in April of 1921, with an article highlighting the only surviving veteran of the Civil War in that area. But not only was John S. Ramsey known for that fact, he was also one of the many in the theater the night James Wilkes Booth shot Abraham Lincoln. Sitting in a box just opposite the President, Ramsey and a companion saw Wilkes enter the booth, heard the shot and saw the assassin jump over the rail and run from the stage.

The battle of the Soldier's and Sailor's Memorial Coliseum continued, and was finally brought to court. A Public Service group that recently organized sought to restrain the Posey County officials from further proceedings in the erection of the coliseum. The judge made a date for a future hearing and stated that, " the case was purely one of law; that he would decide it as such," reported the newspaper. The case had split the county, the north fighting the south.

A Studebaker Light was given the mileage test in July, 21 on the Evansville-Mount Vernon route. The tests were administered by running the automobile several hundred miles, then detaching the carburetor and letting the engine run until it ran out of gas. The car, driven at a steady 23 mph, got 28.4 miles per gallon.

One of Posey County's associations was organized in November 1922 when 53 charter members attended the first meeting of the Posey County Historical Association. The association was a branch of the Southwestern Historical Society, a branch of the Indiana Historical Society, founded in the 19th century. The first Posey County Historical Association was led by Attorney James Blackburn, secretary and curator and Lola Nolte, both of Mount Vernon; Treasurer, Mrs. George Ford of New Harmony; Mrs. B. O. Hanby of Black Township, Mrs. Nora Fretageot of Harmony Township, Mrs. James Gudgel of Smith Township, J. P. Cox of Center Township, Patrick J. Lynn of Marrs Township, James Morlock of Point Township, Mrs Charles Miller of Bethel Township, Rev. Beach of Robb Township, Charles Raben of Robinson Township, Mrs. R. E. Wilson of Lynn Township, vice-presidents and genealogist, Caroline Crease Pelham of New Harmony.

A parade, barbecue, band concert and military ball highlighted the dedication of the new armory building in Mount Vernon in September 1923. Quite a few important military personnel attended from the tri-state area including the Battery E of the Indiana National Guard.

A few weeks later, the city that had just celebrated was -- for a short time -- in a panic.

Not since 1919 had a fire done as much damage as the one that raged in 1923. The American Hominy plant in Mount Vernon was destroyed. The Southern Hotel, Brinkman Building and one residence on Water Street also were damaged. Two box cars of the

C & E I Railroad were destroyed. The entire city was in danger of burning as wind carried sparks over the west side of town and as far out as a mile into the country. Mayor L. T. Osborn even called the Evansville Fire Department to assist, but cancelled the call when the fire chief deemed it unnecessary. The fire was brought under control in two hours, and was completely doused in less than 24 hours. The damage estimate for the Hominy Company alone was $250,000. The company just spent $10,000 on repairs which were to be completed before the company entered its busy season in October 1. The company's products included grits, hominy, flake and meal.

Southern Posey County was hit with 2.42 inches of rain in a little over an hour, flooding sewers, creating electrical problems and flooding many residential homes. The rain posed no serious threat to the county wheat crop, no buildings were damaged and no one was injured.

The post election news to hit the papers included stories of arson. The Hotel Posey, between Third and College avenues in Mount Vernon, was owned by Randall

Mr. and Mrs. Ben McFadden 1922. Fieldon's peddling wagon for store North of Savah

Spence. The hotel sustained little serious fire damage, but was reputedly filled with smoke. But firemen, noting the strong odor of coal oil and after an investigation, decided the fire was cased by "incendiaries." Next, investigators discovered that Spence had a $7,400 insurance policy on the hotel and was experiencing some financial difficulties. Another man seen loitering around the hotel just previous to the fire was promptly identified and arrested. James W. Moore, the father of 10 children living in Gallatin County, Illinois was to have been paid $750 to start the fire. Both men, owner and arsonist, confessed and were imprisoned.

The last half of the decade began rather quietly. The Unafraid Republican, a Mount Vernon newspaper published the following resolution made by the Indiana Historical Society: "Whereas, On the eleventh day of December 1816, President Madison signed the Act of Congress by which Indiana was admitted into the Union as a State and...The year 1816 is inscribed on the seal of the State of Indiana as the most significant date in her history, and...Though there are many national anniversaries officially recognized, there has as yet been no anniversary designated in Indiana which commemorates the State and it achievements or its history, and...The observance of December 11th has of late years become general in the schools, historical societies, pioneer societies, and public gatherings under various names and ...The official designation of December 11th as Indiana Day and the issuance of an annual proclamation by the Governor will still further on these occasions focus the attention of the people of Indiana upon her history and upon the significant place she occupies in the American Union, thus promoting patriotism and good citizenship. The Executive Committee of the Indiana Historical Society on behalf of the Society and of the sixty-five local historical societies of the State, respectfully urges the passing by the General Assembly of the bill now before it which provides 'that the Governor shall issue a proclamation annually designating the eleventh day of December as Indiana Day and in pursuance thereof suitable exercises, having reference to historical event to be commemorated thereby, may be held in the public schools and by citizens generally throughout the state, inappropriate and patriotic observance of the anniversary of the admission of the State of Indiana into the Union.' It will be noticed that this does not in any way create another holiday but merely calls attention to December 11th as the birthday of the State and a day commemorative of an event which symbolizes the whole of Indian History."

A February edition of the Unafraid Republican spent several pages extolling the rich history of New Harmony, Indiana. In the spotlight was the Workingman's Institute founded in 1838. In 1925, the Institute contained 25,000 books and an interesting museum of relics from New Harmony past.

After the legislature adopted statewide prohibition in 1917, amendments where added in 1921 and 1923 adding the "illicit still law," and the "illegal transportation law." A new bill also passed in 1925 (CHECK) that made it unlawful for any person to purchase, receive, manufacture, transport, shop, possess, sell, barter, exchange, give away, supply or otherwise handle or dispose of any intoxicating liquor except for pure grain or ethyl alcohol and alcohol for medical purposes and wine for sacramental purpose only.

A day later, a 100-gallon still of moonshine was seized by a federal agent at a farm just south of St. Wendel. The arrest also turned up four burners, a "hot-shot," 78 glass jugs and 28 barrels of mash.

But this small event did not hold the attention of the county as did an event on March 18, 1925.

By 4 p.m. that day, the town of Griffin in Bethel Township was devasted by a tornado. Every structure in the town of 750 residents was destroyed by the deadly funnel cloud. Driving near Griffin, Graham Endicott of Poseyville saw the terrific storm, immediately left his car and ran to safety in the ditch. As soon as the storm passed, Endicott went to the nearest farm house and telephoned to Poseyville and Stewardsville for aid.

Hundreds of rescue workers were sent to the scene. Every doctor in Mount Vernon traveled to New Harmony to attend to the injured. Firemen from every city sent men to search the debris for the dead and injured. The Posey County Red Cross sent clothing, medicine and food.

The scene, reported by many who answered the calls of aid, was one of total destruction, fear and anger. The Western Star reported that "a great number of persons went to the assistance of the unfortunate, were compelled to turn their heads and leave the scene." Battery E 139th F.A. of Mount Vernon sent truckloads of soldiers to assist the devastated community. Entrance to Griffin required a pass, as the town was put under martial law, to prevent looters. The town attempted to clean up and organize. In the next 24 hours, lines of communication had been set up, basic sanitary measures were in place and the electric light plant began to operate agian. Tragic stories of orphans, residents helpless as they heard the screams of their friends trapped in buildings and reports of more bodies, filled the papers. The death toll reached 48 and hardly anyone escaped injury.

But, the clean up of the storm's aftermath was slow. Griffin school children moved to Poseyville, Stewartsville and New Harmony and were enrolled in those city's schools. The Mount Vernon Chamber of Commerce established a relief fund raising effort for Griffin. More than 250 men of the Modern Woodmen lodge poured into the town to clean roads, alleys and a number of homes in the residential district.

The early April papers reported that martial law had been lifted, Battery E had left, and the town of Griffin was under the direction of the American Red Cross. Fifty-three carpenters, electricians, plumbers and other necessary skilled tradesmen, took on the considerable task of rebuilding Griffin.

By May 5, 27 buildings had been completed and seven others were under construction. The Red Cross had spent $8,983. More than $15,000 had been raised in Posey County to support the rebuilding project -- a great deal more was to be done. One June 9, the paper reported the Red Cross had awarded Griffin $24,814.52 in "awards" to finish the task of building and repairs, household furnishings, clothing,

1925 Griffin Tornado site, Merle & William Allen (Prof), observers

livestock, maintenance, trust funds, cash awards, medical aid, burial expenses, farm implements, farm labor, tools and business rehabilitation. The estimated damage in Griffin totaled more the $250,000.

While Griffin was rebuilding after the immense tragedy, other cities in the county were going about their normal business. Much of the county was still discussing the building of the Coliseum, a new community service center. Contracts were announced for the erection of the building including general construction, heating and ventilating, plumbing and wiring were awarded to J. A. Behrick & Son, L. M. Strack and Oscar D. Keck. But, the planning was not over. In June, Posey County residents began a heated discussion of the advantages and disadvantages of the building. A number of World War I soldiers were present, to whom the coliseum would be dedicated. A reverend who attended claimed that Posey had no YMCA nearby that could hold civic and religious meetings and therefore was in favor of the coliseum. And yet, another Posey County building made the news -- the dedication of the Fauntleroy home in New Harmony. It was considered one of the most interesting and valuable possessions of the Federated Clubs. The Unafraid Republican reported that "Miss Fauntleroy then gave an outline of those who had lived in the home, and with a voice that showed the emotion she felt in the last act of giving up the home of her family, she presented the key of the homestead to the president of the Indiana Federation of Clubs." In response, the president dedicated the home "in the name of God and State to all that is good and great."

But, news of the coliseum again consumed the newspaper, this time in an article titled "The Coliseum, By the People, of the People and For the People of Posey County." It was finally decided that coliseum would be built. This five-year argument was decided by the tax board after a conference in Indianapolis. The lawyers who fought for the building advised "against any demonstration of celebration of the state board decision. It will be a mistake to rub in our victory. Now that the battle is won, the result and achievement belongs to us all."

For the first time, plans for the inside of the coliseum appeared in the paper. The main floor of the building would be entered by a wide flight of steps, with ornamentation on either side. Three entrance doors would signify three branches of the armed service -- Army, Navy and Marines. The first floor would consist of entrance lobby, which inlcuded a hall of fame, restrooms, cloak rooms, and a auditorium capable of seating 1,100. The second floor would include an assembly hall with a 100-seat capacity, a large balcony with accommodations for 40. The basement would boast a swimming pool, lockers, a gymnasium with balcony for spectators and a modern kitchen.

Later articles requested that a room be set aside for the Posey County Historical Society where it could display its historic collections. The Historical Society also requested to aid in deciding to choose an artist to depict Posey County's past. The society then recommended George Hoenig, an Evansville artist.

Driving laws became clearer and were being more strictly enforced as more people took to the roads in the 20s. Posey County drivers were told they must dim their lights when passing another motorist, have two license plates (one on the front and one on the back), and must keep a record of ownership in the car. Also, drivers were told they could not allow children under 17 to drive without a permit or an adult "This applies to girls as well as boys," stated the Western Star.

In an effort to keep the streets safe with the large amount of automobile traffic, stop signs were installed in the county seat, Mount Vernon. On one side was painted, STOP and directly underneath it the words "Arterial Highway." The other side read, "WATCH YOUR STEP." The signs were shaped like a shield and were white with black lettering.

In early 1926, Posey County residents completed a time capsule for the cornerstone of the Coliseum. Quietly, without ceremony, items were carefully laid in a copper box and placed in the northeast corner of the new building. Untouched for perhaps centuries, would remain a list of all sailors, soldiers and Marines of Posey County in the World War, together with the Gold Star roster; a list of officers, membership and brief history of Owen Dunn Post No. 5 American Legion of the city; a list of officers and membership of Harrow Post No. 491, Grand Army of the Republic; a list of officers and membership of Harrow Relief Corps; a list of officers Harrow Relief Corps; a list of officers and membership of Posey County Chapter of Daughters of American Revolution; a list of officers and membership of Daughters of Civil War veterans; a list of officers and membership of Posey County War Mothers of World War; a list of officers Posey county conscription board; a list of officers and membership of Battery E. 139th Field Artillery; a list of officers and membership of Company B local Spanish American War company; a list of officers and membership of Posey County Historical Society, a list of board trustees of Posey County war memorial; names of architects and engineers, names of contracts of building workmen employed at time of laying of corner stone, a transcript of legal history of the coliseum building, a list of officers, membership and history of Mount Vernon Chamber of Commerce, a last statement of the Mount Vernon banks, an issue of the Mount Vernon Democrat of September 13, 1923 known as the Armory Edition which gave a military record of county's issue of the Mount Vernon Democrat of May 25, 1921 coliseum edition.

In May, 1926, it was finally decided that a clock atop the St. Matthews Church did belong to the church. It seemed that one resident thought of installing a town clock next to the town's fire bell. When the clock would reach the top of the hour, it would somehow tap the bell. However, once installed, it did not work. Members of St. Matthew's church said they would make room for the bell in their tower, provided the clock was secured. Funds were raised to buy the clock for the church and $50 were donated every year to maintain it.

A sentimental donation was made to the Posey County Historical Society in August of 1926. The April 15, 1865 New York Herald was given to the society by John Ramsey of Wadesville. Ramsey was present at Ford's Theater the evening President Lincoln was shot.

Progress continued to move into Posey County when one of the largest foundry and machine companies in Southern Indiana started operation from total electricity instead of steam. The plant made the switch slowly and ended up in operation under a 100-horse-power-motor.

"The Garden Spot of World," Posey County, had another claim to fame in July of 1926. "Wheat, Golden Wheat!" applauded the Western Star. Machine measurements recorded that Ed Donaldson who owned and operated a farm just east of New Harmony had set the country's record largest average wheat crop. A total of 60 acres netted 2,753 bushels or an average of just fewer than 46 bushels an acre. The crop promised to garner $1.28 per bushel.

Hay hauling near West Franklin, Indiana around the 1920's. Andrew Ernst, Joseph Bender, Herman Hengstenberg, Carl Ernst, William Ernst, Ed Harris, Wilhelm E. Becker

But, the "Garden Spot" suffered later that month as the county felt the effects of a heat wave and drought. No substantial rain had fallen for three months. Farmers were forced to haul water for their families and livestock. Crops all over the county were burning. Point and Western Black townships suffered the most, while Griffin reported it had not seen rain for two or three weeks.

The Klu Klux Klan suffered defeat throughout the country in the November election of 1926 as Posey County voters nixed Klan-endorsed candidates. Republicans were also big vote-losers, with Paul L. Short was the only GOP winner, elected to serve as the county's coroner.

Eight months after the cornerstone was laid and six years after plans had begun, the Posey County Coliseum in Mount Vernon was dedicated. The $200,000 building was finally ready. It held more than twice as many citizens than the courthouse. A special dedication service, conducted on the eighth annual Armistice Day, honored the heroes of World War I. The guns of 11 soldiers of the Battery E sounded at 11 a.m. and doors of the Coliseum opened. An invocation was read followed by the singing of "Abide With Me." After the reading of the list of gold star men, a speech was delivered on the same subject. This part of the ceremony was held on the steps of the Coliseum, and only after lunch was the crowd permitted inside the 1,100-seat auditorium to hear the afternoon services. They proved to be patriotic, with the singing of "America" and "The Star Spangled Banner." Sunset brought the final event of the dedication when the Owen Dunn Post hosted the Armistice Day Ball.

The Daughters of the American Revolution staged a dedication ceremony of different sorts -- not to a newly erected building, but to a building long since gone. The group, along with state officers and county residents, dedicated two markers designating the original location of the toll-gates on "Old Plank Road." The road, built in 1851, served as a valuable link between Mount Vernon and New Harmony. Lumber was cut into planks 10 feet long and three inches thick. Toll-gates, which charged the traveler three cents a mile were built at the first and fourteenth mile. The road served its duty for several years, but, expenditures for upkeep soon outweighed the collection from the tolls, and the road was abandoned. The only evidence remaining were the two monuments built by the D.A.R.

More than a year after the tornado struck that leveled the small town of Griffin came the final loss report. Griffin was not the only town destroyed by the funnel cloud...14 areas in the midwest received Red Cross support. More than $3,000,000 was spent rebuilding these areas with an average of $494 spent per individual. Griffin residents received an average of $609 per individual case, or a total of $100,000 for the entire community.

Plans were already in the works when the <u>Western Star</u> announced that the J. G. White and Company of New York proposed to both Posey County and White County, Ill a franchise to erect a toll bridge over the Wabash River. While the first of the proposals had placed the bridge at or near New Harmony, Mount Vernon civic clubs began a movement to have the bridge start at Mount Vernon, saying that if erected at New Harmony, it would be too close to the assured state bridge across the Wabash at Mt. Carmel, Ill. In the minds of Posey County citizens, the bridge would be essential in the progress and growth of southern Indiana. The bridge would route much of the county's east and west automobile traffic through the community. The franchise would assure Posey and White counties that the building would begin immediately after legal action had been settled and completion would follow with two years after construction had

Maurice Abel-Abel's Shoe Shop c. 1920 on West Second Street

begun. Tolls were set at 50 cents for pleasure auto and driver (each additional passenger would cost 5 cents), Bus and driver $1.50 (each additional passenger would cost 5 cents); a half-ton truck at $1 (25 cents per additional ton).

A severe cold streak ushered in 1928, sending a blizzard and strong winds countywide. Griffin was without electricity for two days, and all ferries on the Ohio and Wabash suspended operations.

A fire destroyed a shop and residence in Blairsville in Robinson Township mid-March. Flying sparks threatened almost the entire town, but the efforts of town citizens and volunteer firemen from around the county saved any other buildings from being damaged.

Ground breaking ceremonies for the new Mount Vernon High School were held in 1928. Announcements set the completion date for the middle of January the following year. Although the school was open to students at the set date, it wasn't until February 22 when minor details were completed, that the building was officially dedicated.

A well-attended tradition began in 1929 -- the county's annual Fall Festival. The <u>Western Star</u> heralded the event as "the first ever of its kind held in the city will include amusements for all with bargains of unsurpassed values offered by merchants." The Fall Festival, planned in September, went smoothly on October 31. Other festivities included a children's parade, street dancing, concerts by two bands and two drum corps and a gift distribution. More than 5,000 showed up for the celebration, despite inclement weather.

The year ended in celebration and Posey residents looked forward to another enriching decade.

Indiana: 1930s

Paul V. McNutt dominated Indiana politics in the 1930s as completely as Franklin D. Roosevelt dominated the national scene. Both came to power at the height of the Depression; both advocated massive government assistance to overcome the effects of the Depression, both were charismatic patricians with strong appeal to the common people, and both made lasting changes in the governments they directed.

The century's fourth decade began with the Great Depression sweeping across the country. Sixty-four Indiana banks failed in 1930; the next year, another 82 failed. Before the end of the Depression, six Indiana auto companies had ceased production: Elkhart's Elcar in 1932, Marmon, in Indianapolis in 1933, Stutz in 1936, and

Auburn, Cord, and Duesenberg in 1937. In 1933, Studebaker went into receivership. Its president, Albert Erskine, committed suicide. Still, Studebaker managed to weather the Depression, surviving until 1963. Also in 1933, the Monon Railroad filed for bankruptcy. Hoosier farmers continued to produce, but the prices they received for their goods fell; in 1937 and 1938, these declines were especially rapid.

Governor Harry Leslie, like President Hoover, tried several efforts to ease the effects of the Depression. Leslie called a special session of the Legislature in 1932 to reduce taxes and government expenses.

The elections of 1932 firmly entrenched the Democrats in Washington and in Indianapolis. Franklin D. Roosevelt and a solidly Democratic Congress took the reins of the federal government. Paul V. McNutt, dean of the Indiana University Law School, was elected governor, and M. Clifford Townsend, lieutenant governor. All 12 U.S. representatives from Indiana were Democrats; Democrat Frederick Van Nuys was elected senator. Ninety-one of 100 seats in the Indiana House went to Democrats, as did 43 of 50 Senate seats.

McNutt moved quickly to use this majority. His projects, sometimes called the "Little New Deal," meshed well with Roosevelt's New Deal programs to help alleviate the worst effects of the Depression. In 1933, a state gross income tax (combining a sales tax and an income tax) was adopted. The state used the proceeds toward education, increasing its share of school funding to 30 percent. The state Department of Public Welfare and the Division of Unemployment Compensation were formed in 1936. Together they created the Bureau of Personnel. This bureau oversaw state hiring, and allowed a limited merit system in some state operations. The Department of Public Welfare administered Social Security and pension payments.

McNutt also acted to strengthen Democratic control and the powers of governor. The 1933 Reorganization Act consolidated 169 state departments into eight main departments. The act also required all executive branch and many departmental employees to resign for reappointment or replacement by the governor; McNutt saw that slots were filled with loyal Democrats. The Hoosier Democratic Club also was organized in 1933; patronage office holders were expected to contribute two percent of their state income to the "club," supporting the Democratic Party that had given them jobs. This "two percent club", as it became known, shifted to Republican hands later, but payments to the party in power continued into the 1980s.

The stresses of the Depression brought on a wave of labor troubles affecting Indiana. Workers at Real Silk Hosiery Mills in Indianapolis struck in 1934; the next year a strike was called against Wayne Knitting Mills in Fort Wayne. A 1936-1937 strike at General Motors' plant at Flint, Michigan, spread to the Guide Lamp Division at Anderson. The worst strike of the decade, however, began at the Columbia Enameling and Stamping Company in Terre Haute on May 23, 1935. By July, 26,000 workers were on strike. Gov. McNutt declared martial law in Terre Haute and although the strike was called off in July, martial law remained in effect until February 1936.

Despite the strikes and the bank and business failures, new companies were formed in the 1930s. The Indiana Farm Bureau Cooperative began production of crude oil. In 1939, the cooperative built a refinery at Mount Vernon with a capacity of 3500 barrels per day. A Tennessee company, Stokely(CHECK SP) Brothers merged with the Van Camp Company of Indianapolis in 1933 to form Stokely Van Camp. The Stark, Wetzel & Co. meat packing firm was organized in Indianapolis in 1936 by several former employees of Armour Packing Company. The state's largest coal company, Ayrshire Patoka Collieries, was formed in 1939 with the merger of Patoka Coal Company with the Electric Shovel Coal Company. Five years after Prohibition was lifted, Indiana ranked 11th among the states in beer production.

Hybrid seed corn was introduced in Indiana in 1937. One year later, hybrid seed was used in a third of Indiana fields. By 1939, more than half of Indiana's corn acreage was in hybrid corn.

One of Indiana's more famous citizens, John Dillinger was paroled from the State Prison in Michigan City in May 1933. He was re-arrested in Ohio and imprisoned at Lima. Five men broke Dillinger out of the Lima jail in October and in January 1934 he was caught in Tucson, AZ, and brought back to Indiana. Using a wooden gun, Dillinger escaped from the jail at Crown Point on March 3. His freedom lasted only until July 22, when federal agents ambushed and killed him outside the Biograph Theater in Chicago.

Notre Dame was again the national collegiate football champion in 1930. It was the last championship for Coach Knute Rockne, who was killed in a plane crash the following year.

The 1934 elections continued the Democratic stronghold: 1 of 12 Hoosier representatives were Democrats, and Sherman Minton was elected to the Senate. His colleague, Frederick Van Nuys, a more moderate Democrat was becoming disenchanted with both the New Deal and the McNutt administration.

Cliff Townsend was elected governor in 1936, and he set about continuing the policies of McNutt. Sen. Van Nuys became increasingly critical of Roosevelt, McNutt, Townsend and other liberal Democrats. In the 1938 election, Townsend and McNutt attempted to purge Van Nuys, but he narrowly won re-election.

Despite the Democratic successes of the early 1930s, Republicans were still a factor in the state. The Hoosier press was overwhelmingly Republican-oriented and opposed to the New Deal. In 1938, Homer Capehart invited 20,000 Republican precinct committeemen to his Daviess County farm. This "Cornfield Conference" planned a strategy for a Republican resurgence that began with the 1938 elections. The party took 7 of 12 congressional seats and won a majority in the Indiana House.

Three former governors of Indiana died in the 1930s: Emmett F. Branch, Harry G. Leslie and Warren T. McCray. Artists John Elwood Bundy and William Forsyth, Humorist Frank McKinney "Kin" Hubbard also died during the decade.

One of Indiana's major philanthropic institutions, the Lilly Endowment, Inc., was founded by J.K. Lilly Sr. in 1937. Eli Lilly's involvement with Hoosier history began with a visit to Angel Mounds in 1931. With Lilly's support, the Indiana Historical Society purchased the site in 1938, and a WPA-sponsored archeological dig began in 1939. Eli Lilly purchased and restored the home of William Conner, the first settler in Hamilton County, in 1934. In 1937, the Indiana Historical Society published his <u>Prehistoric Antiquities of Indiana</u>.

Some of the worst floods of the century hit Indiana in 1937. In January, floodwaters from the Ohio River covered 46 percent of Evansville, and more than half of New Albany was under water.

The Legislature declared the tulip tree the official state tree, and the zinnia the state flower in 1931. (The peony would replace the zinnia in 1957.) Two years later, the cardinal was named the state bird. The Indianapolis News won a 1931 Pulitzer Prize for its reporting on tax reform. The Indiana State Symphony Society was also organized in 1931. In 1936, Fabien Sevitzky became conductor of the Indianapolis Symphony. The Indiana Pavilion at the 1933 Century of Progress Exposition was decorated with murals by Missouri artist Thomas Hart Benton, who would later paint similar murals in the Indiana Statehouse. William Lowe Bryan retired in 1937 after serving as president of Indiana University for 35 years; Herman B Wells succeeded Bryan. Indiana University organized a building campaign in the late 1930s, erecting the Medical Building in 1936, the School of Business, Physical Sciences Building, and the Auditorium, all in 1939. In 1937, 1938, and 1939, students from the Herron School of Art in Indianapolis won the prestigious Prix de Rome, a two-year fellowship to study art at the American Academy in Rome. Former governor Paul McNutt served as U.S. High Commissioner to the Philippines from 1937 to 1939, then became head of the Federal Security Administration.

After a decade of Republican government, and that government's apparent inability to alleviate the Depression, the Democrats returned in strength in the 1930s. Their efforts did make headway against the Depression, although it would take the mobilization for World War II to bring full recovery. In Indiana, Paul McNutt reshaped the governorship to his taste, and watched as his policies continued after his term. But toward the end of the decade, the first sounds of a Republican resurgence were heard. Some Indiana firms vanished, others were born, and overall Indiana weathered the Depression. The next decade would provide both challenges and opportunities for the Hoosier State.

Posey County

The affects of the Depression were not immediatley felt in Posey County. The Western Star reported that agricultural, school and church interests actually made progress and several conventions held in Mount Vernon enabled business to survive. While crop prices were down, they were not critically low. Only one business, the Mount Vernon Straw Board Company, suspended operations. Others stayed in operation, even if only on a part time basis. The appointment of a county agent, the work of 4-H clubs and three successful farmer's institutes supported agricultural efforts. Adding to the agricultural success of the area, three Posey County farmers qualified in the five-acre state corn contest.

The business and industrial sections of the county showed sign of success despite inclement weather, with the second annual Fall Festival and Trade Day in Mount Vernon. The mile-long line of floats and people paraded through the streets hampered only by occasional rain and snow. Only the dance was cancelled because of the weather. Late that afternoon, school children paraded from all over the county in addition to Battery E, the Boy Scouts and Girl Scouts, high school drum corps, Junior Red Cross members, American Legion, Caborn Band, Mount Vernon High School Band, Mount Vernon Fire Department and a host of colorful floats representing the businesses and industries of the city. This 1930 parade drew crowds of 5,000 spectators, surpassing the attendance of the year before. The Western Star reported that "the prize offered the rural school having the largest percentage of enrollment in the line of march was won by Dunn school...This school has 18 pupils, all of them being in the parade."

A political earthquake hit the county in the elections of the 1930s, destroying the Republican ticket. Posey County proved to be a Democratic stronghold, electing only one Republican to office, John A. Hartman, who became councilman in the Second District.

A drought disaster hit Posey County early in 1931, creating problems for farmers. Wells dried up, and many farmers resorted to hauling water from long distances to save their livestock. The wheat crop was well on its way to failing. A few more weeks without rain would mean certain disaster. The rest of the county also suffered. With increased hardships, the Red Cross came to the aid of the farmer by setting up fund drives. Each county suffering from the drought was given a quota to reach. For each dollar raised, the Red Cross added $4. Posey County's quota was set at $2,000 making it a small part of the $10 million needed to ease the burden of the rest of the country. An estimated 250 Posey County farmers were suffering from the drought and the community was called to action with the following message from the chairman of the National Executive Offices of the Red Cross. "...Minimum ten million dollars needed to prevent untold suffering and actual starvation by thousands of families. Pollution (of) water supply caused by dying cattle has added to winter hardship in some sections. Hoover in proclamation tomorrow will urge immediate and generous response. Confident your people will not fail to meet their share in this humanitarian need... Your chapter quota 2,000 dollars. Report action taken."

What had started in 1911 finally made headway in 1931. The government purchased Mount Vernon property in 1911 with plans to erect a Post Office. Twenty-years later, with the distinguished honor of being the oldest federal building site in Indiana, orders were issued to raise the two-story Rosenbaum building to make way for the postal building. A month later, a $75,000 building was assured when President Hoover signed the second defiency bill. Construction was set to begin in the fall of 1931 and plans were mapped out for a one-story building with a large lobby, work windows, workrooms, delivery areas, private offices, money order, a registered mail department and store rooms.

With attention turned toward a new Post Office, Mount Vernon residents were pleased to host the convention of the Indiana Federation of Rural Letter Carries and the district convention of the Joint Association of Postal Employees. Several hundred guests joined in the July conference held in the Coliseum. The committee in charge of the event posted a notice in the newspaper asking all Mount Vernon residents to display flags and decorate businesses knowing that the "visitors will be more impressed." A special invitation was extended to farmers in the county who benefited directly from the service of the rural carriers. All of Posey County was welcome at the final event of the convention -- a dinner and dance at $1 a ticket. Convention participants were treated to special musical programs and a trip to historic New Harmony. The entire convention, heralded as a huge success, was highlighted when a Mount Vernon man was chosen as the next president of the Indiana Federation of Rural Mail Carriers and a Mount Vernon woman was named head of the new Ladies Auxiliary. The Western Star reported "the convention of both organizations in this city resulted in the Mount Vernon Post Office becoming 100 percent organized in the Indiana State Federation of Rural Letter Carriers and the Joint Association of Postal Employees."

The Mount Vernon Straw Board Plant which had suspended operations a year earlier, readied to begin operations again by June of 1931. The transfer of the property and equipment to form the new Mount Vernon Straw & Paper Board Company, resulted in more than 200 applications for the 110 jobs the new company had available. Following a sale, the old Straw Board company was leased to Alton Paper & Box Company of Alton, Ill.

The business community saw more progress that year with what the Western Star reported as "one of the most important financial transactions in history of Posey County." The result of the merger of Old First National Bank and People's Bank and Trust made the new People's Bank and Trust the only bank in the city with resources in excess of $3 million. In regard to the merger the bank secretary said, "the depression of the past two years has demonstrated that a savings account has been one of the safest if not the best investment of the American public. Some people think large city banks away from home are safer. They may be safe, but you never know. You do know your local people. You know their standards of honor. You know of their financial success...They know a strong bank is essential to the prosperity of the community.

The agricultural community was delighted with the largest peach crop in years. By August, more than 20,000 bushels had been picked in the county and well over 40,000 were still on the trees. Stories in the papers urged county residents to buy up the peach crop and can the fruit because a small crop was expected the following year.

As the Depression continued into 1931, Posey County again avoided many of its effects. Agricultural and industrial activities advanced despite the severe drought. Membership of the Posey County Farm Bureau increased 73 percent and the peach crop broke all records. In the industrial and financial community, the reorganization of the Straw Board Company and merger of the two banks dominated the news. Beside the successful Rural Letter Carriers and Postal Employees Conference, Posey County also hosted the district convention of the Grand Army of the Republic and the meeting of the Pocket Publishers' League. The untiring efforts of civic workers made the Uniontown-Mount Vernon Road and extension of State Rroad 69. Unfortunately, the law enforcement office were kept busy as burglaries were up all over the county.

While 1931 brought the disaster of drought, a severe storm caused most of the county's weather problems in 1932. Point and Marrs townships suffered the greatest damage, and just across the river in Uniontown, Kentucky, two persons were killed when a hotel collapsed. Rain, hail the size of hen eggs and high winds that twisted trees off at the roots, destroyed much property, damaged the electric and telephone companies and moved many buildings from their foundations. Although property damage was high, crops suffered little.

Farmers were pleased when they heard that the Van Camp Packing company, which earlier had announced that it was not operating the following season, was to be leased by the Mount Vernon Canning Company. The objective of the new company was to purchase 325 acres of land to plant tomatoes. Because of the lateness of the growing season, the first crop to enter the canning factory would be purchased. The venture was made possible by the Mount Vernon Chamber of Commerce. Just four days later, after the announcement 382 acres were purchased, and Posey County farmers became very interested in the operation of the plant.

In May, 1932, the newest "talkie" house opened in Posey County. The New Empress Theater operated by the former owner of the Vernon Theater was completely remodeled and on opening night displayed a state-of-the-art "talkie" machine. The Empress reopened under new management showing "Employee Entrance," a First National picture. Prices for all night showings except Tuesday were 10 and 15 cents. Tuesday night was billed as "family night," and all tickets were 10 cents. Matinees on Saturdays and Sunday included a 5 and 10 cent admission.

The greatest increase in countywide school population in recent years also occurred in 1932 -- 109 new students. Only Marrs and Black township school corporations reported a decrease.

As predicted, the 1932 peach crop showed a decline. One orchard picked 500 bushels compared to 20,000 picked in 1931. The apple crop also suffered, producing only one-tenth of last season's yield.

The struggle to erect a Post Office in Mount Vernon stretched into another year, and the federal building was finally dedicated with great celebration in September 1932. A street parade, dedication ceremony, aerial stunts, building inspection, band contest, Terrapin Derby and street dance highlighted the opening of the all-Indiana limestone edifice. More than 6,000 people attended the event that turned the 21-year project into a reality.

But, Mount Vernon lost another building the following month to fire. Blackened brick walls were all that remained of the Milling Company. Fire Fighters from as far away as Evansville fought the blaze, thought to have been started by mechanical friction. A related disaster occurred when a tank containing 7,000 gallons of corn oil exploded, knocking firemen to the ground and shattering windows in the surrounding area. Although there were no serious injuries, the company suffered an estimated loss of $300,000. The mill site was purchased from the American Hominy Company in 1924, just two years after it was destroyed by fire in 1922. By April of 1933, plans were under way to rebuild the needed mill. Bigger and better than before, the new mill would be five stories and the new warehouse would stand two stories. The most up-to-date equipment was ordered and the mill, which would continue to manufacture hominy, meal, grit, hominy feed, flakes, corn oil and brewer's meal, was expected to be complete by June.

The entire nation -- including Posey County -- was swept by the political fire of the Democrats in the 1932 elections. Franklin D. Roosevelt carried the majority of the county with 2,765 more vote than Herbert Hoover.

An outbreak of Hydrophobia, or rabies caused a quarantine in Posey County for 40 days beginning in January 1933. A dog in Point Township was infected as were a number of cows and hogs in Lynn Township and Mount Vernon. A week after the quarantine was issued, a state quarantine of 120 days came into effect. Under the quarantine, dogs and cats, were at all times to be supervised by the owner. Otherwise they were to be killed by police officers. By the end of the month twenty persons in Posey County were being treated for rabies with the Pasteur treatment.

Mount Vernon continued to attract outside conventions to its city and coliseum. In March 1933, it hosted the 8th District Convention of the American Legion and Auxiliary. The two-day convention brought in hundreds of visitors. Hundreds more in Posey County witnessed a grand street parade, a competitive drill, a banquet, religious services and a dance. More than 5,000 enjoyed the parade followed by the competitive drill. The drum and bugle corps of Funkhouser Post, Evansville, won first place and the corps of Tell City and Jasper, Indiana placed second and third. Two-hundred and fifty attended the banquet where Mrs. Gillie Munsey Dunn, mother of the first Posey County boy to die in World War I, was honored as the first Gold Star mother. State Commander William O. Nelson followed this presentation saying, "We have successfully met the challenges that have been hurled at the American Legion and the Auxiliary, with our interest in child welfare and in our service to disabled comrades, widow and orphans, and defy the forces of communism...We are proud of our national legislation committee in what they have done in establishing a fair allowance and benefit and we hope that the USA will continue on the basis of an adequate national defense. We have established this organization on noble ideals, and we hope you will stand behind these great principles on which these great organizations are founded and continue to carry on."

In March, 1932 heavy rains caused flooding in the lowlands of Point Township, forcing many farmers to lead their livestock to higher grounds. The Wabash and Ohio rivers registered high on the gauge, the Ohio at 45 feet and the Wabash at 23 feet. Then in May, the rains returned and flood levels almost matched those of the previous storm. Creeks and ditches in the southern half of the county overflowed, making many roads impassable. At Solitude, Big Creek overflowed and flooded parts of State Righway 69. Although flooded, State Highway 62 still carried traffic. Rains damaged property, and the Western Star reported that a cottage at Dawson's Old Dam Resort, 14 miles north of Mount Vernon, was moved 12 feet off its foundation. Crops in some sections of the county were severely damaged.

Terrible flooding occurred in March of 1935. Mount Vernon recorded 5.28 inches of rain, the heaviest precipitation since the great flood of 1913. Traffic was halted on state roads 62, 66 and 69. Crews worked nights to make the roads passable. The community of Solitude broke the 1913 record, when approximately 500 acres of land was covered with waters from Big Creek. Also in Solitude, a section of the C E & I Railroad was flooded.

Heavy wind storms damaged western Point Township and the southwest tip of Black Township in August of 1936. Fortunately no persons were injured, although homes, barns and livestock received damage. Rainfall and winds were light in the rest of the county and the paper reported that "Poseyville only had enough rain to lay the dust."

Headlines in the April edition of the Western Star announced the arrival of 3.2 beer in Posey County. In rolled the first truck to bring the legal beer into the county from the Falls City Brewing Company in Louisville, Kentucky. The beer, purchased through the Southern Indiana Beverages Corporation, Inc., was sold for $2.75 per case of 24, including an additional dollar deposit for the case. The appointed Wholesaler for Posey announced that due to the small margin of profit on the imported beer, it would be sold for cash only. Posey County residents were allowed to purchased no more than one case each day.

While Posey County, Indiana and the country still abided by the rules of the 18th amendment, a commission was under way to repeal it. While only 15 percent of Posey County residents voted, clearly the "wet" vote won, and Albert Heckman and John Moeller became the delegates to the Indiana Convention for the repeal of the eighteenth amendment. A June newspaper reported that the "wet" vote received 3,037 ballots, with the "dry" vote garnering 1,037. The "wets" carried 56 of the 92 counties in Indiana, making it the 10th state to favor the repeal of the 18th amendment. United States Senator, Frederick Van Nuys, a Democrat from Indiana said, "I thoroughly believe that repeal of the Eighteenth amendment is one of the material steps necessary to proper rehabilitation of social and economic life."

In other news, the state highway commission, ordered ex-servicemen with dependents be given first choice in jobs that would start road improvement on State Highway 62. Unskilled labor was paid the minimum wage of 50 cents per hour and skilled laborers received 60 cents per hour.

The Posey County Circuit Court kept busy in 1934 with a change of venue case from Vanderburgh County. After six hours of deliberation the Posey County court found former deputy Herbert Walker guilty of involuntary manslaughter. Walker was charged with the shooting death of undertaker and cab line operator in Evansville. In his testimony, Walker said he was trying to arrest the man and the gun went off accidentally. The jury was made up of residents from Mount Vernon, Lynn Township, Center Township, Robinson Township, Point Township, New Harmony, Poseyville, Bethel Township and Griffin.

In 1934, the New Harmony Fairgrounds attracted 38,000 spectators to the Tri-State Rodeo. The glamour of the old west thrilled those attending the big event. A mounted march of all the contestants, performers, Indians and officials decked out in western costume, kicked off the rodeo. Events included bareback riding, trick and fancy roping, professional bronco riding, a Roman standing race, a Sioux Indian ceremonial dance, a high jumping horse and trick and fancy riding contest. A Professional Steer Bulldogging event was covered by the Western Star, "Most of us know how difficult it is to gain a close personal acquaintance with a bull in a pasture, but just imagine what its like to take the horns of wild steer that has probably never known what a fence is and endeavor to bring it to the ground ... in record time." Other events included wild Brahma steer riding, bullfighting and a wild horse race.

"We gave the people of the middle west their first taste of a genuine Western Rodeo last year. We know they liked it by the large number of people who came back for more day after day. This year we've put up larger cash prizes to attract a still greater field of champion contestants and you can count on even more excitement than last year," said Fred Gentry, president of the Tri-State Rodeo about the second annual rodeo in 1935. And, the rodeo again attracted large crowds, four top-ranking cowboys and a host of new events. A street parade with a 95-year-old four horse stage coach that once belonged to the Wells Fargo Company highlighted the opening ceremonies. Music was furnished by a 22-piece cowboy band and 200 Indians of the Rosebud Division of the Sioux tribe pitched teepees on the New Harmony fairgrounds. Contestants vied for prizes totaling more than $4,000 during the four-day event.

Mount Vernon hosted the county's next event, the annual Fall Festival, October 15-19. Large crowds enjoyed a number of exhibits including a Purdue agricultural display, the Indiana State Conservation Department Zoo and a cream and Guernsey dairy cow show. Other events included a novelty goat race, ladies bingo, a clowning policeman, a woman contortionist, a cowboy rope spinning act and acrobat. An industrial parade took to the streets followed by a pet parade.

The year 1935 was important for the Catholic Church in Posey County. The Rev. Albert Schmitt, a member of the St. Wendel parish was elevated to priesthood in March. This event was special because he was the first member of that church to take the vows and the first priest ever ordained in Posey County. Bishop Ritter requested that the ordination take place in the Rev. Schmitt's home parish and not in St. Meinrad, where it was usually held. Although a native of Indiana and of the Indianapolis diocese, Schmitt later moved to the diocese of Corpus Christi, Texas.

A discovery of prehistoric bones in a creek near Stewartsville in November 1935 attracted county attention to an early Posey County. Portions of a letter from the Department of Pathology of Washington University in St. Louis, published in the paper read, "Acting upon your suggestion we did drive up to Stewartsville on Thursday morning to see the Schutz find, It is, I believe, destined to be a most remarkable find for Posey County, if not for the state of Indiana. The bones are remarkably well preserved. Of what we saw it could be said that they are those of a mastodon. I think that it is of the Proboscidea. That means the elephant family... I think to learn by way of this find that elephants one time, thousands of years ago, wandered over the terrain of Posey County. The tusks were the most remarkable pieces which I saw, they are very large, larger than any of the elephants which we see this day...The elephant family is as you know a native of Asia and Africa...how and when did they come to Posey County. They are of the tropical area of the world and Posey County is not tropical. There is raised a most interesting subject for thought... I hope care will be taken to get out everything that is in the hole."

A straw-vote, or a Small Town and Rural America sentiment, was taken in Posey County in August 1936 before the presidential election that November. The Western Star was selected as one of the many weekly newspapers across the county to conduct the poll. Residents were asked to clip out a form in the paper, complete it and return it to the Western Star office. Voters were not required to sign their name, but were asked to inform pollsters of the town and state in which they would be voting. The results were first tabulated in Mount Vernon and then sent to New York. A majority of voters cast "ballots" for Franklin D. Roosevelt over Alfred M. Landon, and in the November election, Roosevelt won the presidency.

The memory of storms and flooding in the early 1930s, took a back seat the flood of 1937.

In early January the rains came, and the gauge registered 59.25 feet, six feet higher than the high recorded in 1913. At 46.5 feet the town of Griffin was in serious danger. All communication had been cut and there was no electricity. The rest of the county learned of 37 persons living in one house. The Red Cross was immediately on hand with the objective of evacuating families and supplying them with the needed provisions.

The Coast Guard was busy sending flood victims and refugees to the high and dry city of Mount Vernon. Although no food shortages resulted, residents in the county were asked to cut down on portions. Hoarding was forbidden. All of Point Township, western Black Township and southern Marrs Township were completely evacuated. During the height of the flood, reports told of 2,500 persons driven from their homes. Livestock and building losses were expected to be staggering.

Mount Vernon, still dry when the gauge marked 57.5, became the relief center for the tri-state area. The coliseum was quickly converted into a hospital for many refugees.

The Mount Vernon health officer announced that the overflow had contaminated the water supply. All residents were instructed to boil the water before drinking or using it to cook. Easing the situation in the city was the Consumer's Ice Company, who offered 5,000 gallons of pure water from their wells to help the

Jessie Heckman Reynolds in her Ford. She and her husband Samuel O. Reynolds buried in Stewartsville Cemetery with son Eldon (WW II) Vet., a former teacher

community. The donated water supply was carefully rationed.

Then, for the first time in its history, Mount Vernon along with 25 other Indiana counties was placed under martial law. Lieutenant Beauford Alldredge, Commander of Battery E was placed in charge of Posey County under the order of Governor M. Clifford Townsend. Under martial law, residents and refugees were to obey orders from the lieutenant. Some of the orders included a provision that no refugees were to return to their homes; criminal courts, city police, sheriff and relief agencies were to remain in operation, businesses in unrestricted areas could remain open, the sale of liquors was prohibited, although the sale of beer could continue and no one other than police officers or guardsmen were to carry firearms. Regulations required all refugees to receive typhoid inoculation before returning to their homes.

Under martial law, the Red Cross worked steadily to provide clothing, food and other necessary items to refugees and stranded families. More and more refugees poured into Mount Vernon each day. Almost 50 percent of Evansville was under water and 100 of their flood victims arrived in the city January 28. The Coast Guard did its part and reported that almost 600 people had been rescued through its efforts.

By February 4, the gauge showed that the water was slowly receding. Martial law was still in power by mid-Febraury. More than 2,700 refugees still called Mount Vernon their temporary home and were not allowed to return to their own homes without a military permit.

Only as the threat of flooding lessened, Posey County farmers begin to estimate their losses. The state director of re-settlement revealed a loss of several million dollars to Indiana Farmers -- Posey County accounting for more than a half a million. Livestock suffered a $38,600 loss, corn, fodder, hay seed, oats, soybeans, straw and wheat loss was placed at $209,100, and buildings and other property suffered a loss of $252,30.

February 18, 1937 marked the turn-around in the great flood. Martial law was lifted and the coliseum discontinued its hospital operations. Lieutenant Allderdge lifted martial law saying, "We could not have asked for more co-operation, cheerfully and readily given by the populace of the flood area and civil authorities, than was accorded us. Because of that fine spirit of cooperation we were able to avoid any unnecessary harshness in enforcing regulations. The spirit manifest by Posey Countyites will always be a treasured memory of the officers and men of Battery E."

Mount Vernon Crest Stages

Date	Stage	Date	Stage
Aug. 10 1875	44.5	Jan. 26, 1907	48.5
Feb. 24, 1882	44.9	Jan. 21, 1913	48.1
Feb. 19, 1883	51.0	April 6, 1913	52.9
Feb. 21, 1884	53.0	Jan. 19, 1916	44.5
Feb. 10, 1887	46.4	Feb. 1, 1927	45.4
April 13, 1889	45.8	Jan. 1930	42.0
March 31, 1890	46.3	March 1933	46.1
March 4, 1897	44.7	April 2, 1936	44.3
April 3, 1898	48.4	Feb. 2, 1937	59.2

The Red Cross continued well after the water had subsided in giving relief to flood victims. Rehabilitation programs began offering those qualified families the status of life they had enjoyed before the flood. Records revealed that 65 Posey County homes were leveled, 250 homes home were severely damaged and 176 homes received minor damage. Heavy loss of livestock, feed and farm implemented was reported by 250 families.

A controversy begun in 1936 resulted in law suits 1938 over the proposed construction of a school. The Black Township trustee and board members took all the steps in getting a grant to build a consolidated school for the township. The board also took bids for construction and appropriated $48,000. Five companies made bids and were accepted by the board. But, when the board failed to concur in the sale of bonds because of a disagreement regarding the location of the property, they attempted to cancel all bids. Five different firms filed five distinct law suits involving, architectural and engineering work, heating and ventilation, plumbing and sewage, electrical and profit damage, amounting to $27,000 in damages.

There were no major floods during the final two years of the 1930s, but the county did experience the heaviest snowfall in 21 years in February. The southern portion of Indiana, not used to snow, was blanketed with 11 inches. Traffic was delayed and school children sent home early. With the immediate arrival of warmer weather, the snow vanished in two days.

New Harmony received word early in March that the Indiana Senate unanimously passed a new act which formed a Memorial Commission and provided, through a tax levy, $140,000 for the purchase and restoration of select historic buildings. The four-year tax beginning in 1940, would pay for the restorations of eight buildings. When these buildings where completed, they would be turned over to the State Conservation Department, who would then operate and grounds as a state museum and park. The commission to oversee the project was headed by Professor Ross Lockridge of Indiana University. The eight buildings chosen to be purchased and restored where the Old Fauntleroy home, the Owen laboratory, the MacLure home, the residence of Joseph Neef, the Old Opera House, the Rappite Building No. 2, the Old Fort Tavern, and the monument of Thomas Say. Only the Opera House needed extensive restoration work. The project also relied on private donations. By the next month, the commission had decided to include in its restorations the old Rappite Labyrinth and a replica of The Philanthropist, which transported the "Boatload of Knowledge" to New Harmony. Plans also were being made to make the tourist park on the river front into a small, modern state park.

By 1938, the rabies scare that had begun in 1933 had ended, and attention was turned to a more widespread problem -- tuberculosis. The disease had claimed the lives of five people in the county in 1937, and it was estimated that there were 108 cases being treated in 1938. Because the disease was not diagnosed early enough, it was thought that many would die. The Posey County Tuberculosis Association arranged to furnish a free tuberculosis clinic one day in the gymnasium at New Harmony.

The Posey County Methodists shared news coverage in 1938 when Bishop Edgar Blake, the presiding officer of the Methodist Episcopal church in the Detroit area came to the county for the first time in 25 years. All Methodist churches in Posey closed that Sunday so the congregations could hear his speech. The theme of the talk was the solution to present-day problems through religion and not through political forces.

The ceremonies at the Christian Church in Griffin started out joyously early in February of 1939, but ended in tragedy. After the tornado ripped through the town of Griffin in 1925, the church had to be rebuilt. In 1939 the church was completely finished, and the last note was paid. During a special service in the afternoon, the note was to be burned in celebration of the event. But, during the morning service, a fire swept through the building and destroyed 14 years of work. No injuries occurred and loss was estimated at $4,000. It was believed that the note which was never found, was burned in the fire. Griffin had no fire fighting equipment to battle the blaze.

Street cars, once a popular form of transportaiton and by 1939, replaced by buses, made an appearance in Posey County. But, this time they were not a mode of transportation, but permanent homes. The sale of many of the electric car bodies measuring 42 feet long, eight feet wide and weighing 12 tons, prompted people to buy the cars and turn them into residences.

Indiana: 1940s

Indiana politics shifted back to their more traditional conservative Republican leanings in the 1940s following the progressivism of the McNutt and Townsend administrations. Indiana supported a favorite son for president in 1940, Wendell Willkie. The Republican nominee was born in Elwood, Indiana. Representing the more liberal wing of the Republican party, Willkie drew votes from both his own party and from Democrats disgruntled by the New Deal and Roosevelt's try for a third term. His support was not, however, enough to topple Roosevelt. Willkie became a respected writer and commentator on international affairs, wrote the book One World and died in 1944.

On the state level, the 1940 election also turned sour for the Democrats. Republicans took 8 of the 12 House seats; Raymond E. Wills, an Angola newspaper publisher, captured the Senate seat from Sherman Minton; and the Republicans took control of both houses of the Legislature. Henry F. Schricker, elected governor, was the only Democrat elected to a major state office in 1940; neither McNutt or Townsend supported the more moderate Schricker in the election.

The new Republican Legislature took steps to keep Schricker on a tight rein. The 1941 State Administration Act attempted to deprive the governor of much of his authority. The bill was primarily an attempt to roll back what were seen as the excesses of the McNutt governorship, and to place more of the administration of the state in the hands of the (now-Republican Legislature. The act was ruled unconstitutional by the state Supreme Court in June 1941, but with the Legislature against him, Schricker was never able to wield the power that McNutt and Townsend had in the state.

World War II affected the U.S. early in Schricker's term, and Indiana contributed greatly to the war effort. In January 1941, the Indiana National Guard was mobilized as the 38th Infantry Division of the U.S. Army. While they did not see battle action until late 1944, this division had an important role in such battles at Leyte Gulf and Luzon.

The home front offered other chances for Hoosiers to contribute to the war effort, and opened opportunities which had been denied before the war. In 1942, the Indiana Plan of Bi-Racial Cooperation was put forward, proposing manpower cooperation between blacks and whites for the war effort. African-American Hoosiers fought with whites on the battlefields of Europe and the Far East, and worked with whites on production lines in homefront factories. Women also were integrated into the labor force; by the end of 1943, one-third of Indiana factory workers were women.

The Indiana Ordinance Works, a joint project of the War Department and the DuPont Chemical Company, opened in April 1941. Indiana plants -- Studebaker, General Motors, Bendix, and others -- retooled their assembly lines to produce aircraft parts. Camp Atterbury, Jefferson Proving Ground, and Crane Naval Ammunition Depot were three of many sites created for the war effort which outlasted the war.

Former Gov. Paul McNutt was appointed to head the Federal War Manpower Commission in 1942. That same year, actress Carole Lombard, born in Fort Wayne, was killed in a plane crash on her way from a war bond rally in Indianapolis.

The 1944 elections brought the Statehouse back to Republican control; Ralph Gates was elected governor. Due to the death of Senator Frederick Van Nuys, Indiana had two Senatorial elections in 1944: Homer Capehart was elected to a six-year term, and William Jenner was chosen to fill out the last few months of Van Nuys' term. Jenner was elected to a full term in his own right in 1946.

Labor, in Indiana as elsewhere, was troubled by the controls of the war production. Sixty-seven strikes affected Indiana firms in 1940, 161 in 1941, and 92 in 1942. Except for a coal strike in 1943, most unions held to a pledge not to strike during the war. The United Auto Workers finally succeeded in organizing General Motors' Allison Division in Indianapolis in 1943.

Once the war was won, Indiana and the country set about returning to their pre-war conditions. In the years after the war, Indiana farmers far exceeded their prewar production. Companies returned to their normal production: the first post-war radio produced by RCA at Bloomington came off the line in September 1945; Servel's first post-war refrigerator came out of the Evansville factory in October of that year; and the first Studebaker rolled out of South Bend in January 1946. The reorganization of the Monon Railroad also was completed in 1946. Much of the planning for postwar conditions was instituted in the Indiana Committee for Economic Development and the Indiana Economic Council, both created in 1943.

The Indianapolis 500, suspended during the war, resumed in 1946 under the new ownership of Anton G. "Tony" Hulman, Jr. Former governor Paul McNutt served as the first United States Ambassador to the Philippines in 1946 and 1947.

The wartime cooperation between blacks and whites was just the start of a burgeoning movement for civil rights. A fair employment practices bill passed the Indiana House unanimously in 1941, but was killed in the Senate. The same year, the Indiana High School Athletic Association allowed all-black and Catholic high schools to join the association and participate in the state tournament. A weak fair employment act finally passed the legislature in 1945. The Gary School Board adopted a nondiscrimination plan in 1946; three years later the Legislature passed a law abolishing segregation in public schools.

Indiana lost several of its greatest writers in the 1940s. Humorist George Ade died in 1944 and novelist Theodore Dreiser died in 1945. Ernie Pyle, whose articles brought home the conditions of America's G.I.'s, was killed in the Pacific in 1945. Novelist Booth Tarkington died in 1946, and Meredith Nicholson died in 1947.

Other Hoosier writers, however, created their own lasting works in the 1940s. Most notable were Jessamyn West's 1945 book The Friendly Persuasion and Ross F. Lockridge's 1948 Raintree County.

A series of 1933 Indiana murals painted by Thomas Hart Benton were presented to Indiana University in 1940. The First Christian Church, built in 1942 on Eliel Saarinen's design, became the first contribution toward Columbus' eventual reputation as an architectural center. Major Protestant denominations formed the Indiana Council of Churches in 1943. Indiana's first "theme park," Santa Claus Land, opened at Santa Claus in 1946. Besides Raintree County, another notable work was published in 1948: the first Kinsey report from the Institute for Sex Research at Indiana University. Television came to Indiana on May 30, 1949, when station WFBM (now WRTV) broadcast the Indianapolis 500. Station WTTV began broadcasting from Bloomington and Indianapolis in November 1949.

Indiana began a swing back to conservatism in the 1940s. In 1947, (Ind.) House Concurrent Resolution Number 2 rejected any future "subsidies, doles, and paternalism" from Washington. The resolution had no real effect, but it was an expression

Strawboard Factory, looking North from atop of Strawbale near Ohio River, West End Mt. Vernon, IN

of the mood of the state. This conservatism would continue into the next decade.

Posey County

The new decade greeted Posey County and the tri-state area with temperatures that dipped to three below zero. Reported as the coldest weather in 10 years, the storm also brought along snowfall that impeded country road and highway travel.

Weather caused concern again in March, this time sending hail and rain throughout the county. Pelting hail caused much damage to farm buildings and residences, tore holes in automobile roofs, shattered windows and did major damage to farmland and highways. Wadesville and Oliver, Upper Point, Lynn and Black townships bore the brunt of the property damage by hail. Residents in Wadesville and Oliver reported hail the size of large hen eggs. Cythiana received severe rain and hail storms and Stewartsville and Griffin reported heavy rain.

Then in August, the county received another blow -- a severe heat wave that damaged much of the Posey corn crop.

In April of 1940, the old Mount Vernon Strawboard factory was destroyed -- not by rain or hail, but of fire. The buildings were in the process of being razed to make way for the occupation by a pipe line terminal of the Texas Company. Although the fire meant the building could be razed more quickly, most of the salvage operations were deemed unprofitable by the blaze. Four of the men working on the project narrowly escaped death when walls began to collapse. The blaze raged from 1:15 on a Wednesday afternoon until 9:30 that evening. Other properties near the factory were damaged when a strong west wind carried sparks.

The new Gas Pipe Line Terminal would transport, upon completion, 3,500,000 gallons of gasoline from a 57 mile pipeline annually from the Indian Refinery at Lawrenceville, Illinois to the plant in Mount Vernon where it would then distribute the product by railroad, truck and barge. The tanks in Mount Vernon provided 193,00 barrels of storage. Evansville was one of the other cities considered for the project. But, records showing that the devastating flood of 1937 left the county seat "high and dry," it became the number one choice.

The effects of the flood of 1937, were still being felt years later as Mount Vernon prepared its residents for "Rat Banquet Week," with "Red Quill" as the finishing touch. The flood apparently had driven rats from lower ground to the "high and dry" Mount Vernon. The Chamber of Commerce, who sponsored the event, asked residents to support "Rat Banquet Week" by removal of rubbish and trash, using trash cans with lids and by also using a rat poison known as Red Quill. During the week, the Chamber sponsored "bait night." Here, residents would put out the Red Quill bait in their homes and business to rid the city of the health menace. Residents were carefully advised to "feed their pets well..so that they would not find the bait attractive because of hunger."

Three-hundred and seventy-eight pages were dedicated to the purpose of composing the records of Posey County. Prepared by the Indiana Historical Records Survey of the Work Project Administration, the publication listed and located all county records including an historical sketch of Posey County, an essay on county government, and an article on the housing records, floor plans and a picture of the present courthouse and a county map. The director of the Indiana Historical Bureau stated, "The Posey County inventory of public records is designated to assist officials in locating records and to inform the public concerning the history and government of the county." The state supervisor of the project added, "Part of a nationwide plan to make Americans more conscious of their historical records, the Posey County book should be a quick and ready reference to anyone..." Posey was the 12th county in Indiana to receive this inventory.

For a bond issue of $1,050,000, the Indiana Toll Commission gave two Chicago bond houses the right to finance the purchase of the New Harmony toll bridge across the Wabash River. The sale included the purchase of a ferry operation. Officials stated that the purchase of the ferry would augment the net earnings of the bridge by approximately $12,000. In 1939 the span made a gross income of $120,000. At this rate, further stated officials, the bridge would become toll-free in 11 years. The newspapers also reported that the owners wanted to sell the bridge because it had a greater interest in construction than in management. The company added that under state ownership the span would operate more economically being tax-exempt. However, the sale of the New harmony bridge would indefinitely delay the construction of a similar bridge west of Mount Vernon.

In an attack against the sale the bridge commissioner told Posey residents that the Indiana Toll Bridge Commission offered $300,000 more than necessary for the purchase. Briggs said, "The price of $945,000 at which the commission purchased the bridge is too much in excess of the first cost which is $637,000 or the replacement cost which is $486,000 Why pay more?

"A petition is before the commission to construct a bridge across the Wabash River west of Mount Vernon. The building of such a bridge would substantially reduce the income of the New Harmony Bridge,

thus decreasing the ability to make settlement on the principal and interest on the bonds," he added.

Shortly after these arguments, a suit was filed in Marion County to prevent the Indiana Toll Commission from buying the bridge. The suit was jointly sponsored by the Indianapolis Chamber of Commerce, the Indiana Farm Bureau and the Hoosier Motor Club. The suit was filed under the name of James C. Calvert, a Cythiana farmer and a bridge user. Defendants in the suit included the Harmony Way Bridge Company, present owner of the structure, and the two firms which bought the bonds to finance the transaction. The plaintiffs held that the present reasonable value of the bridge was not more than $500,000. The legislative director of the Indiana Farm Bureau added, "You can't give a half million dollars to somebody without someone paying the bill. This time it is the traveling public."

In June 1941, the New Harmony bridge was purchased by the White County, Illinois Bridge Commission for $895,000. Finances for the purchase were provided by an issue of revenue bonds. It was still believed that the 10-year-old bridge would become toll free within 10 to 12 years. The suit against the purchase of the bridge by the Indiana Toll Bridge Commission was effectively blocked by the Indianapolis Chamber of Commerce, the Indiana Farm Bureau and the Hoosier Motor Club.

Posey County along with the eastern half of the nation, witnessed the spectacular display of the aurora borealis -- or the Northern Lights on September 19, (check). From this mass of light came shimmering swaths of colors including pink and light green. While pleasant to watch, those operating wireless radio and telegraphs found it interfered with communication. The Mount Vernon Democrat reported, "A transient who left his boat on the Ohio river and walked to Greathouse Chapel on the Uniontown road was an example of fear. He endeavored in vain to gain entrance to the church which was locked. Summoning Douglas Dixon, a nearby resident, the transient appealed to Dixon to let him in the church so 'I can lie on the altar and await the end of the world.' Dixon said today that the man evidently spent the night under the church as he saw him crawling out and returning to his boat early this morning."

War

Blitzkrieg, Adolf Hitler, Pearl Harbor and the Atomic Bomb all bring to mind graphic pictures, memories and stories of the World War that, during its time, killed more persons, cost more money, damaged more property, affected more people than any other war in history. In addition to costing $1,150,000,000,000, 10 million Allied servicemen were killed, 6 million Axis military men were killed and more than 50 countries played some part in the conflict.

The first of the lightening war or blitzkrieg from Germany hit Poland on September 1, 1939. Soon after, six more countries, Denmark, Norway, Belgium, Luxembourg, the Netherlands and France all became victims of the new German warfare. Failing to conquer Britain in 1941, The Germans went on to take Yugoslavia and Greece and then moved on to Russia. Also seeking expansion, Japan attacked Pearl Harbor on December 7, 1941, forcing the United States to become a part of World War II. Hanging on after quite a few disasters, the Allies began to take the offensive. They halted the enemy's advance in North Africa, the Pacific and Russia. Italy, France and Germany all felt the growing power of the Allies. Italy surrendered on September 3, 1943, Germany on May 7, 1945 and Japan on Sept. 2, 1945 after the Allies dropped atomic bombs on Hiroshima and Nagasaki. The United States total casualties reached a solemn 1.2 million. Of those, 545,108 were either killed or missing.

"Scrap" was the key word throughout the war on the homefront and by mid-August 1942, the drive to salvage scrap metal was well under way. The Posey County Salvage Committee of the Civilian Defense Council reminded residents that the donation of scrap metal should not diminish after each individual drive. Rags, rubber, metal and kitchen fats were the items most needed by the salvage drives and were required if production of war machinery was to continue. The county agent had organized 216 neighborhood committees to collect the trash. In Posey County and throughout the nation, the American Legion took charge of the collection of all junk autos October, 1942. The chairman of the Posey County Committee said, "We must have scrap and we must have it at once." School reports at the meeting reported that Black School in Point had collected 6,030 lbs; Lawrence school in Point, 9,420; Cronbach school in Point, 8,810; Grafton school in Black, 7,120; Farmersville school in Black, 4,860; Savah school in Lynn, 4,430; and St. Philips parochial school in Marrs, 4,415 lbs. The consolidated school at New Harmony, Poseyville, Stewartsville, Cythiana, Griffin ad Wadesville reported success but could not give total due to the fact that all the scrap had not yet been sold. No reports were received from Caborn, Hartman, Stucky, Lawrence and West Franklin School in Marrs; Jeffries, Upton and Thomspon in Black; Smith and Springfield in Lynn; Schroeder, Huber, Parker, Wateman, Blairsville and St. Wendell in Robinson.

The Posey County Chapter of the American Red Cross never seemed to rest. At the end of the first eight months of 1942, the chapter reported that adult membership had reached 1,062 persons and the junior membership was up to 3,735. Each committee of the Red Cross increased efforts to take part in national defense projects. The production committee made a total of 235 garments and were working on many others. Garment production slowed with a material shortage. Other committees included were the home service committee and the first aid and water safety committees. The chapter set its 1943 War Fund Drive at $8,000, double the 1942 goal. Volunteers were expected to make a house to house sweep of the entire county to fulfill the new goal. The Western Star reported that, "Each contributor to the Red Cross/War Fund will receive the customary Red Cross service flag for display in the windows of their homes and business establishments - but, wartime emergencies have relegated the customary Red Cross metal lapel button into oblivion for the duration."

Meanwhile, the Civilian Defense Board dealt with demolished buildings, fires, scores of war victims and panicked citizens -- all in theory. Each Friday evening in 1942, the board conducted air-raid practices to rehearse their duties. Air raid wardens called in reports of "incidents" which took place in their sectors and the control board handled all crises immediately. Posey County residents were invited to witness the board in its practice activities. The session was to prepare for the first nationwide practice black-out before the arrival of the 1942 winter season.

For the first time since the nation entered the global conflict of World War II, Posey County held county elections. The Western Star reported "...Posey County citizens must go the polls Tuesday and vote for this privilege of the American people which has been a heritage fought for and handed down through the years and which now, in the light and scope of the present brutal war, is a privilege to be preserved for the years of peace ahead. To eliminate confusion and give moral support and encouragement to our leaders who are charting a course of victory through these perilous days, ...Posey County citizens should go to the polls and vote the straight Democratic ticket and thus give these leaders the vote of confidence which they need and deserve."

Apparently, voters paid no heed to this suggestion as the official election results showed the Republican Party to capture five major Posey County offices. This followed a Republican trend throughout the nation.

To further prepare for the blackout, the Mount Vernon Civilian Defense Council asked for 100 percent cooperation in a "dim-out." The difference between a dim-out and a black-out is that street lights are left on during the dim-out and industry operates as usual. For residences, mercantile businesses, public buildings, churches, fraternal homes, taverns, restaurants, and theaters --the dim-out and the black-out were the same. With the sounding of the alarm signal, all lights went out (with the exception of a dimmed night light). The OCD gave specific expections during the dim-out: "1. If you are at home, stay there. 2. If you are not at home, stay where you are and don't try to go home. 3. If you are on the street, get off and take cover. 4. If you are at home when it starts and haven't made advance preparations to cover your windows and doors, turn your lights out. 5. If you are in an automobile, pull over and turn off you lights, or get out and take cover. 6. If you are running a business which is open at the time of the warning turn out all outside lights and window lights. 7. And last, but not least, if your warden knocks on your door and asks you to put out you lights please do as he asks you to, and do it with a smile. Also remember that he is backed up with law and an ordinance, and can cause you some trouble and unpleasant publicity if you decide to have your own way. All places not cooperating in the dim-out will be a matter of record."

Traffic on the highways near Mount Vernon were stopped, slowed or detoured around the city. OCD authorities asked Indiana Bell to block telephone calls for the hour during the practice. The late November paper called the dim-out a success, with almost 100 percent cooperation. Three "incidents" occurred during the dim-out which were immediately handled by the OCD -- an explosive bomb damaged power cables and water mains, an incendiary bomb started a fire damaging power cables, and a man suffered a broken leg in a traffic accident. Except for minor problems, the operation was considered successful, and OCD officials believed that when the War Department ordered a blackout, the community would be prepared. By February of 1943,(check) the civilian defense director for the county seat announced that the first blackout would be during the week of February 21 through 27.

From 8:30 to 9:30 p.m. February 25, the residents participated in their first blackout. Representatives were present from Boonville and Poseyville to observe the staged event. Businesses, homes, clubs, churches all turned off their lights, traffic was stopped and people cleared all outside areas. The OCD immediately went to work coordinating efforts that prompted Lt. Col. M. G. Henley, assistant liaison officer of the Fifth Service Command, U.S. Army to say, "Mount Vernon and its Civilian Defense Organization is fully and well-prepared to meet any emergency." Five "incidents" followed the screaming warning whistles of the Mount Vernon Milling Company, Fuhrer-Ford mill, Home Mill & Grain Company, Mount Vernon Water Works System and the Indiana Farm Bureau Refinery. The first was a poison gas alarm, the second a incendiary bomb in a residence, the third, fourth and fifth involved high explosive bombs that demolished buildings and killed 15 people. All OCD officials responded to the calls as if they had actually happened.

Again, the residents of Mount Vernon were tested, when two months later, they participated in a mock air-raid. The first alert, sounded by factory whistles, warned of the possibility of an air-raid. All OCD personnel were to report to their posts, lights were to be extinguished and traffic was to continue with caution. The second stage, or actual blackout called for all traffic to stop, the streets to be cleared except for authorized OCD personnel. "Bombs" dropped during this period were colored with streamers noting the kind of bomb. The third and final stage, also known as the second alert, was a precautionary period, reminding citizens to maintain blackout procedures with the thought the raiders may return again.

On December 7, 1942, the first anniversary of the bombing of Pearl Harbor was observed under the sponsorship of Owen Dunn Post, No. 5, American Legion and the Mount Vernon Post, No. 3258, and Veterans of Foreign Wars in assistance with the Posey County War Savings Staff. The observance highlighted the challenge to the homefront to continue the purchase of war bonds in the Victory Loan Campaign and continued collection of tin cans, kitchen fats and heavy scrap metal. When all the speeches had been made and the band had played, the audience left the coliseum and burned effigies of Hirohito and Hitler on the court square.

While the war raged on elsewhere, storms raged on in Posey County in early 1943. The Ohio River passed the flood stage of 35 feet on the Mount Vernon gauge and was forecast to reach 45 feet. Although always a serious matter, this year's flood posed an even greater danger... food was as vital as bullets in winning World War II. And, a Posey County record-breaking 2,000,000 bushel corn crop was in danger of being destroyed. A shortage of labor and several weeks of poor weather had left much of the crop unharvested. Posey County focused on beating the waters to the crop...and so did the soldiers of the U.S. Army from Camp Beckinridge, Kentucky. Under orders from the War Department, more than 195 men rushed into the lowland to harvest the corn before the water raged in. The Posey County Red Cross and OCD units transformed the Mount Vernon gymnasium and auditorium into a dining room and sleeping area. Many men and women worked late preparing food for the incoming soldiers. Newspapers reported that one day's harvesting goal was 10,000 bushels. The evening before, 50,000 bushels had been gathered. Workers labored feverishly to build up roads to enable them to reach the corn in the lowlands. Then in March, the rains returned, this time dumping six inches in 20 hours, adding to the two inches from previous night. Farmers in the lowlands were asked to immediately evacuate livestock, transportation in many areas was paralyzed, basements were flooded, electricity was out, power lines blocked roads that were not flooded. Scores of incapacitated autos dotted the roads and Big Creek and McFadin Creek raged across fields. It would be weeks before residents could clean up the county.

Posey residents beheld the first "souvenirs" of World War II in January of 1943. One of Mount Vernon's own, serving as a cook in the Merchant Marine, sent some souvenirs from an interesting experience. A Japanese plane had crashed in his flour bin, leaving behind a portion of the aluminum fuselage and two of the 50 mm shills fired by the American plane which brought down the enemy craft. The boy's father, a local barber displayed these items that had been sent by his son.

In order to ensure that the home front was involved productively in the war, the women's division of the OCD carefully organized a "block plan," to evenly distribute wartime responsibilities. Mount Vernon used the block plan, utilizing a zone leader and a colonel for each half of the city who would direct sector majors. A "block" was not a city block, but an area that was easily handled by a captain and her six lieutenants. Each block was responsible for overseeing salvage, Bonds and Stamps, nutrition, labor, victory gardens, rationing, consumer interest and educational activities. An article in the Western Star concluded a feature on this subject stating, " Inasmuch as personal excuses and refusals are not accepted when a man is called to military service, the same plan will be followed on the home front. Women delegated to service in the block system will be expected to accept their responsibility with the same willingness and desire to service their country as their sons, brothers and husbands on the battle front."

In an effort to acquire money to build a new USS Vincennes (the first cruiser had been destroyed in what the newspaper called "an unequal battle in the vicinity of the Solomon Islands,") the government hoped to sell War Bonds through a Navalcade traveling exhibit. Residents throughout the county were invited to Mount Vernon to hear Naval hero and pharmacist Frederick Moody speak. Moody arrived aboard a motorized replica of the battle cruiser Vincennes, gave an evening address describing the battle in which the first cruise ship was destroyed. Much of the Navy equipment manufactured by Indiana industries was on displayed, including 650-pound and 325-pound depth bombs used in anti-submarine warfare, rubber life rafts, life vests, shells, bombs, a knot board, gunners' protective helmets, and ammunition boxes. Another part of the exhibit featured official Navy Department photographs of battle action and a large mural of the christening of the first Vincennes. The goal of the traveling exhibit was to rebuild the Vincennes at a cost of $22,000,000.

The home front in Posey County suffered damages, not due to the war, but to Mother Nature. Heavy rains submerged approximately 40,000 acres of the county, destroying, without hope of being replaced, the wheat crop. The corn and soybean crops were re-planted. Road damage was estimated at $15,000 due to the rains. The newspaper, reported that the bridge at "Dead Man's Corner" in Point Township near the mouth of the Wabash, was the only span to have been washed out.

While some Posey residents were affected by the rains, all residents were affected by this report from the Mount Vernon Republican. "Your auto should have but one license plate today - the rear 1942 plate to which the 1943 tab is attached." The order was to help provide scrap metal for the ongoing drive.

A project dealing with the installation of automatic warning signals at railroad grade crossing on the state highway system was brought to a virtual standstill by World War II. Only routes having a high military defense rating would receive the new signals.

Salvage articles were given prime space in wartime newspapers and a major drive for tin cans was pursued in fall, 1944. The county salvage chairman urged Posey residents to turn in more tin saying, "Tin is fast becoming one of our chief worries. Japan still holds possession of the largest tin producing mines in the world, and no doubt, they will destroy these mines when the South Pacific Islands are retaken. We need more and more tin for the manufacture of war materials machinery for producing war materials and civilian uses."

The drive for War Fund contributions showed Posey County close to failing as it had the previous year in 1943. Every community, rural and urban was over the top or assured of reaching goal except Mount Vernon -- which was $1,500 short. Black, Center, Harmony, Point and Robinson Townships exceeded or reached their goals, Bethel was only $23 short, Lynn $9 short, Marrs $12 short, Robb $6 short and Smith $65 short.

Other war programs affecting the county included rationing. Although 85 percent of the all meat was ration-free in late 1944, the New Year promised to add more meat to the list as well as vegetables such as asparagus, green and waxed beans, corn, spinach and peas.

The Central Grade School building had little chance of surviving the fire that swept through it in February of 1945 with its wood interior and stairways. Approximately $140,000 of damage in building and school equipment was estimated in the school with an enrollment of 520 students and 15 teachers.

Events of the War dominated the attention of the county for five years. Countless stories of Posey support, crises, tragedies and "miracles" filled the papers. Although nearly impossible to relay all the efforts and events of the county during the war years, the following headlines tell some of the stories. "Posey County Does its Part To Keep 'Em Flying --- With Oil", "Posey County Aluminum Collection is 500 Pounds Above per Capita Quota," Posey Farmers to Mobilize for '43 Production," Posey Farmers Ask Machinery and Manpower," "Coffee Rationing is Next in Order," "Gas Ration Registration on 2nd Day: Supplemental Forms to Be Mailed In," "Volunteers Needed by Fuel Oil Panel," "War Christmas to Be Observed in City, County," "Posey County and State Far Behind Quota in August Sale of War Bonds," "Coliseum Guns Will Go to War as Scrap," "2,910 Pound of Tin Cans Collected Locally in Initial Monthly Pick-Up," "Kitchen Fat Salvage Lagging and Vital Need: 793 Tons of Scrap Goal in Posey," "Battery Leaves Mt. Vernon for Active Service," "Posey Selective Service quota is 57 up to July 1, State Board Announces," "Effect of War is Felt in Posey Co.," "Trainloads of Hoosiers to see U.S.S. Indiana III Launched," "Added OCD Units Prepare to Serve," "Mount Vernon OCD Control Board Plans Graphic Test of Air Raid Facilities," "Tuesday Night Dim-Out Plans in Final Form," "39 New Posey County Soldiers Report for Duty Monday; Leave at 3:00 p.m.," "22 New Posey Co. Soldiers to Camp," "16 Posey Soldiers to Fort Harrison."

Posey County read the following account when they opened their morning newspapers on August 16, 1945.

"Business ...returned to normalcy this morning after coming to virtually a complete halt at 5:00 o'clock Tuesday night when President Truman officially announced that the greatest war in history had come to an end with Japan's acceptance of the peace terms laid down by the United Nations at the Potsdam Conference -- terms which amounted to unconditional surrender. ...citizens greeted President Truman's announcement with typically American enthusiasm that resembled a pow-wow and snake dance preceding an athletic contest. In response to the plea of

Keck Gonnerman Company Southwest corner of Pearl & West 4th Street Mt. Vernon, Indiana. Picture taken in 1940.

M.C. Collins   H.W. Renschler   R.A. Keck   F.L. Keck   J. Dausman
E.V. Green   W.T. Booth   Pete Logan   Al Reich   A. Miles

Employees of Keck Gonnerman Company taken in front of Bean & Pea Huller picture taken in 1946 or 1947.

Mayor Frank Fessenden for a safe, sane celebration, the public co-operated in an excellent manner with unusually good order being preserved and no acts of vandalism reported. The mayor had previously stated "it would be appropriate that citizens pause and give thanks to God for victory, not a victory of mere military might, but a victory of a righteous cause, before any other celebration."

Churches held special well-attended services Tuesday and Wednesday evenings to give thanks for the end of the war and the newspaper reported that taverns closed promptly in compliance with the suggestion of the Alcoholic Beverage Commission and remained closed until the next morning.

Posey County relished the end of the war, because one-tenth of its population had fought for the victory. Much of the rationing halted and local service stations reported a 400 percent increase in gasoline sales. The War Manpower Commission abolished all controls, giving the nation a fee labor market for the first time in more than two years. Of the Posey County men who served during World War II, fifty-six lost their lives. Thirty-four were killed in action, two died of wounds, one died of injuries in the line of duty, 16 died during training or maneuvers, two were missing and one, reported the Western Star "was determined to be dead under Public Law No. 490 which is designated as a 'finding of death'."

Celebrations of the end of the war were dampened by a September rainfall that accumulated 7.26 inches in just 12 hours. Roofs caved in under the weight of the rain, sections of the L & N and C & E I railroads were washed out, traffic was slowed or stopped and one bridge was washed out near the Black-Lynn Township line. Farmers in Black and Marrs townships reported losses of hundreds of acres of soybeans and corn. The years following were no kinder to Posey County farmers. Rain and generally bad weather resulted in a loss of the 1947 hay crop which stood rotting in the fields. The alfalfa crop also suffered along with a damaged 30 percent of the corn and soybean crop. Only the wheat seemed to withstand the inclement weather. Heavy rains came again in April 1947, inundating the lowlands in Posey and isolating Griffin. The Wabash rose to 42 feet, the highest since 1945, when it crested at 51.2 feet. Despite the flooding in farmlands, crops were not severely damaged.

As 1946 arrived, the newspapers turned from wartime events to everyday events. The new Mount Vernon Locker & Packing Plant was established, the Kiwanis conducted a clothing drive, an inspector urged remodeling of the Posey County Jail and the Ohio River was on the rise again.

The first Peacetime Fourth of July in five years was well attended by Posey citizens. The days events were centered around the dedication of the Mount Vernon Municipal Airport. Native Posey resident Gene Dawson was one of the guest speakers. His long list of impressive credentials included aviation editor of the Indianapolis News, secretary of the Indiana Aeronautics Commission, president of the Indianapolis Aero Club, vice-president of the Aviation Writers Association of America and master of ceremonies of a weekly aviation program on WIBC Radio in Indianapolis. After the opening ceremonies, commercial flyers conducting sight-seeing trips for anyone who was interested, and for those who were a little more daring --- stunt riders also were taking passengers. If Posey residents didn't want to fly, there was still plenty to watch. A flight of Army planes passed by and the US Army held an exhibition.

The Mount Vernon Airport services included flight training, aviation ground school, aerial pipeline inspection, insect control and defoliation for farmers and food service on weekends. Model airplane builders had a spot of their own on the east-west runway.

At a cost of $1,375, the town clock that sat in the steeple of St. Matthews Church was removed, repaired and "electrified" in August 1946.

A wrench was thrown in the plans to construct the Wabash River bridge in 1947 by the Volgelgesang-Polk Report given to Governor Ralph F. Gates. The report found it uneconomical to build the bridge. The Mount Vernon Chamber of Commerce immediately protested, saying "Whereas, funds have been made available and necessary legal steps have been taken to make possible the construction of a bridge across the Wabash River west of Mount Vernon, Indiana and Whereas, we believe this proposed bridge to be the most important single fact affecting the prosperity and welfare of the citizens of our community in our generation, and Whereas, the proposed span would provide an avenue of relief to the populations of Southern Indiana and Southern Illinois in time of flood and facilitate the saving of the crops of these naturally rich farming areas, and Whereas, the Volgelgesang-Polk report just filed reveals that in excess of eight hundred vehicles will use the proposed span each day and does not take into consideration the thousands of bushels of corn, wheat, soy beans or the many loads of hogs, cattle, and other livestock that would go to nearby markets in Indiana which now go to the distant market in St. Louis because they cannot cross the Wabash with resultant loss of money and time, and Whereas, the said report while indicating a diversion of traffic from the New Harmony span, shows that the remaining traffic would be sufficient to make it a free bridge eventually, and they have had several years to place the financing of the bridge on a sound financial basis and Whereas, the said report is in error and misleading in that it indicates that the proposed bridge is only nine miles south of the new Harmony span when in fact it will be approximately thirty-five miles south of New Harmony by water and at least twenty five miles south of New Harmony by highway and in fact the distance from Mount Vernon, Indiana to New Haven, Illinois would be decreased from forty-five miles to fourteen miles by virtue of the construction of the proposed bridge, Now Therefore, be it resolved by the directors of the Mount Vernon Chamber of Commerce that the aforesaid Volgelgesang report be corrected to correspond with the facts and the proposed bridge be constructed in the immediate future." Just one week later, the Chamber of Commerce received an encouraging report from Governor Gates saying that he had not yet accepted the Volgelgesang report as final. He further remarked, "I have not as yet had the opportunity to find out how the report affected Governor Green of Illinois...and if Governor Green should take the engineers' recommendation as final, it does not appear our chances are too good."

The Western Star which had long reported the news of Posey County, changed ownership for the first time since it began in 1876. Jack Nix, a World War II veteran and journalist, became the publisher along with co-editors Monica Senecal and Ruth Holmwood in July, 1947. For the past 71 years, the Western Star was published by the Leffel family. John Leffel published the first and only German Newspaper in the county and soon took on the responsibilities of his newly formed Western Star eventually discontinuing the German paper due to lack of time. Leffel was the first publisher in the county to install power presses and the first to purchase a lintotype machine.

Another first for Posey was in 1948 when United States President Harry S. Truman gave a speech from the railway platform at the L&N Station in Mount Vernon. It was the first time in the history of the county that a President had visited Posey citizens. Two other presidents, William Howard Taft and Franklin D. Roosevelt had visited and spoke in Posey, but Taft was an ex-president at the time and Roosevelt was a candidate for Vice-President. Many Posey County schools, businesses and industries closed to hear Truman speak.

Polio cases increased in Indiana and Posey County during the summer of 1949. A vaccine program was started immediately and as an additional precaution against polio, public subscription for funds to spray mosquitoes with DDT was started by the Kiwanis Club of Mount Vernon. Residents responded quickly by donating $1,754.15 for aerial and ground spraying. New Harmony and "across the Wabash" towns also sprayed with DDT.

Indiana: 1950s

The tone of Indiana politics in the 1950s was set more by its U.S. Senators than its governors. Senators William Jenner and Homer Capehart were first elected in 1944 and both rose quickly in the far-right wing of the Republican party. Jenner was a particularly strong supporter of the anti-Communist "crusade" of Joseph McCarthy, and emulated McCarthy's tactics in a vitriolic attack on Secretary of State George C. Marshall in 1950.

The conservatism of Indiana's Senators also was seen in the General Assembly. In 1951, (Ind.) Senate Bill 86 moved through the Legislature. It required that the names of Hoosiers receiving welfare be available for public inspection. The federal welfare system objected to this invasion of privacy, and threatened to withhold $20 million in welfare payments; the General Assembly ignored the threat and passed Senate Bill 86. A showdown was averted by the Jenner Amendment. Sponsored by Jenner in the Senate and Charles Halleck (another Hoosier) in the House, the amendment allowed individual states to decide the confidentiality of welfare records.

The tide of conservatism carried through much of the decade. In 1957, the General Assembly created an Un-American Activities Committee. The same year the Chamber of Commerce and conservative Republicans pushed a right-to-work law through the General Assembly. In 1958, the ultraconservative, anticommunist John Birch Society was organized in Indianapolis.

Indiana governors of the 1950s were far more moderate than its Senators. Henry Schricker enjoyed his last political hurrah in 1952 when he nominated Adlai Stevenson for President at the Democratic National Convention. George N. Craig, a moderate Republican, was elected governor in 1952, and saw many of his progressive proposals rejected by the conservative Legislature. Craig's political star dimmed again in 1958 when several of his close advisors were convicted of bribery in acquiring contracts for state highway construction. Republican Harold Handley, elected governor in 1956, pushed a modest increase in the gross income tax, and lost a race for the Senate in 1958 (tagged "High Tax Harold").

This 1958 election was the beginning of a progressive, Democratic revival. William Jenner decided not to run for re-election, and Evansville Democrat Vance Hartke won his Senate seat. More progressive legislation also began to emerge from the General Assembly; the 1959 School Reorganization Act consolidated many township schools under countywide systems.

Two Democratic former Governors did not live to see the progressive resurgence: Cliff Townsend died in 1954, Paul V. McNutt in 1955. Former Republican governor Ed Jackson, bedfast since a 1948 stroke, died in 1954.

Perhaps the greatest game in Indiana high school basketball was the final of the 1954 state tournament, when Milan (student body 162) defeated Muncie Central with Bobby Plump's last-seconds jump shot. (This game would later be dramatized in the movie Hoosiers.) The championship team of 1955 and 1956, Crispus Attucks, was the first all-black team to win, and included among its players Oscar Robertson. On October 8, 1956, Michigan City-born Don Larson of the New York Yankees pitched the first perfect game in World Series history.

Other native Hoosiers began literary careers in the 1950s: Kurt Vonnegut with Player Piano (1951) and Dan Wakefield with Island in the City (1959). Another career began and tragically ended in the decade: Hoosier-born actor James Dean created a lasting fame with his work in Giant, East of Eden, and Rebel Without a Cause, before his death in a 1955 auto crash.Columbus, in Bartholomew County, continued to build its reputation as an architectural center in the 1950s with buildings designed by Eliel Saarinen and other noted architects.

Indiana passed through the 1950s much as the country as a whole did: a conservative and popular leadership, no major crises, and, by decade's end, a feeling that change was in the air.

Posey County

One of the smallest towns in the state now had something that just a few other towns of its size had -- a medical clinic. Poseyville was caught in a dilemma with many towns of its size. The 1,000 residents had a hard time keeping up with its citizens' medical needs. Residents had to travel to much bigger towns in order to receive adequate care. But, Poseyville solved its own problem when two young doctors showed an interest in setting up a practice in Poseyville. Seeing an answer to its needs, a citizens committee was formed and raised $23,000 to pay for the equipment and the remodeling of a building. One doctor had graduated from Poseyville High School in 1939, and the other was a friend he had met while interning in Salt Lake City. The clinic started with 11 examining rooms, including one equipped for emergency and overnight patients. Both the doctors would one day own the clinic -- a small reward for the heavy debt and responsibilities of the first few years.

Poseyville again made the news in 1953 when it hosted the Posey County 4-H Fair. The high school gymnasium and football field provided enough space to house the home economics exhibit, commercial exhibit, farm animals, machinery displays and refreshment stands. Crowds were large and the 4-H Fair continued to be a most popular event in the county.

One of the oldest telephone companies in southern Indiana, the Marrs Township Telephone Company, sold out to the Indiana Bell Telephone Company. in August 1953. The new telephone company would provide residents with improved telephone services. However, Marrs Township would not receive the new services until a hearing before the Indiana Public Service Commission.

Posey County property value improved in 1953. For the first time in its history, the county's property, real estate and personal totaled more than $30,000,000. By 1956, the assessed valuation of Posey real estate and personal property was $31,821,020 and in 1957 the amount reached $33,872,270. But 1958 saw the tax valuation lower by $1,731,095.

With the end of hostilities in the Korean War, the Posey County homefront slowed its drive for blood always needed on the war front. From three collections, Posey county had given 443 pints of blood. While the quota was established at 546, the American Red Cross was pleased, considering the first drive had begun half-way into the year.

Another excellent record was reported to the papers, lauding Mount Vernon Battery B National Guard. The battery functioned with the 38th Division in a two-week period of intensive field training at the Michigan military center at Camp Grayling, Michigan. The records showed no casualties and Battery B's came home with excellent records on the range and in the camp. In the years following, Battery B received two more "superior ratings," this time from training exercises at Camp McCoy in Wisconsin. Again, Battery B suffered no injuries, accident or illness during the two-week intensive training. After returning from training in 1958, Battery B received an "excellent" rating, just one point from "Superior."

Stretching 230 miles from Mount Vernon to Peru, Indiana -- the Indiana Pipeline was finally completed under the authority of the Indiana Farm Bureau Co-Operative Association Inc. From the Mount Vernon refinery to its destination in Peru, the first products were sent in late August of 1953. The new line, which took three years of planning and one year of construction, meant progress for Mount Vernon and Posey County. It meant that products could be distributed direct to farms in southern, south central, central and north central Indiana.

A Purdue agricultural economist made 1954 farming predictions at the Posey County Outlook meeting in New Harmony. The total message wrapped around a 5 percent decline of the total picture. The predicted decrease was not expected to last long or result in serious damage, and might even lead to a year of increased business activity. The agricultural economist predicted a slightly more than 5 percent decrease in the farmer's cash receipts, but no major decline in farm real estate. Farm produced items, such as feeds, seeds and purchased livestock were predicted to decline. Total grain supplies were estimated to be about 4 percent higher, but the soybean crop might lose in 1954. Returns from beef breeders would show a decrease, but the demand for sheep meat and wool would show an increase. Dairy products would average at a lower level than in 1953 and egg prices would see an increase. The final prediction showed family living cost to stay about the same.

Hoosier hysteria reached all the way down to Posey County. The 33rd annual basketball tourney in 1954 broke attendance records with each successive year. The New Harmony Rappites took the title in 1954 winning their 5th title. Mount Vernon had been a winner nine times, Poseyville eight times, Griffin five times, Cynthiana four times, Wadesville in 1940 and before Stewartsville High School closed, it took one title.

After lengthy negotiations, the date of the purchase of the Marrs Telephone Company had been set on February 9, 1954. The hearing was moved to February 18 when Indiana Bell announced its plans to purchase Caborn Telephone Company also in Marrs township. Indiana Bell Telephone Company was progressing in other parts of the county. An existing telephone building in Mount Vernon was added on to and dial service was begun for New Harmony, Mount Vernon, Oliver and Savah.

The Locker-Packing Plant in Mount Vernon, however, was hit hard when more than $80,000 worth of building and equipment was destroyed in a fire in early February. The plant employed six persons and included 580 individual lockers, 450 which contained large quantities of food. A modern refrigeration system valued at $6,000 was totally destroyed by fire. The destruction in this one building alone was more than the $60,000 damage a fire on the Lower Main Street Business district had caused fewer than six weeks before. The three-story building was erected in 1918 and had been occupied by the packing plant for seven years.

In May 1954 the Indiana Public Service Commission had yet to give approval for the new dial system in parts of Posey County. Before the hearing, Indiana Bell conducted interviews with all but six telephone users and found that 98 percent of the residents in New Harmony were in favor of the service improvement. Indiana Bell had conducted the survey in New Harmony because it was the only town that would see a rate increase due to the new system. The project, once approved, would cost half a million dollars. By October, the Marrs Township telephone companies were finally purchased, and Bell was now asking the Indiana Public Service Commission to approve its proposal to purchase the St. Philip Telephone Company. The town of St. Philip served 225 residents and would also receive the new dial system.

October 30 marked the installation of the long-awaited dial phone system in the Mount Vernon, New Harmony and Solitude exchanges. At 2:30 p.m., the manual switchboards were cut and within seconds the new subscribers were using the direct dialing system. Prefixes were assigned to each town. Mount Vernon was "Poplar," New Harmony, "Overbrook" and Oliver and Savah received "Sunset." The new two-five number system required the caller to dial the first two letters of the prefix followed by five numbers. Days before the dial system was installed, residents were able to practice on phones provided by Indiana Bell. With the new service came a directory.

Mount Vernon's first radio broadcasting station began operation in December. The 1.590-kilocycle, 500-watt power station would operate in the daytime only and would network with the Linton and Booneville stations, airing some of the same programs. The rest of the time, however would be devoted to special interest topics of the Posey County and Mount Vernon area. The battle to build the station was a long and costly one. For more than a year, the application had been before the Federal Communication Commission in Washington along with two other applications, one from Newburgh, Indiana and the other from Indianapolis, both requesting the same frequency. The Commission finally granted the license to Mount Vernon and would award "call letters" at a later date.

Mount Vernon ranked sixth among the seven leading Ohio river ports in freight volume during 1953. The other leaders were, in order: Huntington, West Virginia, Pittsburgh, Aliquippa and Rochester, Pennsylvania, and Louisville. Seventh position was held by Evansville. Mount Vernon moved 1,736,622 tons of gasoline and oil shipments. The total tonnage moved among the seven ports reached 46,304,210.

Water was a key topic of conversation in 1954, but not for the amount of freight that could be shipped on it. Plans were submitted to the Utility Board and the Public Steering Committee to modernize current Mount Vernon facilities and use the Ohio River as a water source. Modernization of existing water works and upgrading the distribution and storage system were estimated to cost $660,000.

The year 1954 marked new attention towards Marrs Township. The July 2 Mount Vernon newspaper announced an addition to the Posey County map -- Marrs Center. With 70 homes, three businesses, one church and 226 people, Marrs Center would be unincorporated. But, the Brotherhood of Immanuel Evangelical and Reformed Church, who headed the committee and the movement, placed road sign along the highway to call the new town to the attention of passing motorists.

Farmers in the new Marrs Center and all Posey County farmers who were interested, could participate in the new agricultural extension program from Congress. The program provided funding to assistant county agents who would then enroll a group of families interested in making a study to improve farming and family living. Posey County was one of 25 counties in the state to take part in this more personal type of government program.

Also under way in 1954 were plans to link a $2,500,000 bridge between southern Indiana and Illinois. The proposed Wabash Memorial Bridge would include 16 piers to support the span. Completion of the bridge was set for September 1, 1955. By November, it looked as though no steel would be installed, although the piers were almost completed. Plans to name the highway routes to the bridge would soon be announced by the Indiana and Illinois highway departments.

Mount Vernon also was experiencing a "first" in 1954. Mayor Paul Hironimus drove up and dropped off his mail into the city's first "drive-in" mailbox. The Chamber of Commerce and the Kiwanis Club requested the "courtesy box," and the post office set the hours of pick up at 1 a.m., 11:15 a.m., 1:15 p.m. and 6:30 p.m., Mondays through Saturdays and 8 a.m.,

1 p.m. and 5 p.m. on Sundays and holidays.

The Alexandrian Public Library was celebrating its 50th anniversary with a newly renovated building. The Library was first opened to the public in 1905 under the direction of Edward E. Highman, the library's first president. Mrs. Matilda Greathouse Alexander was the library's founder, and Mrs. Olive MacGregor served as its first librarian.

More than 14,800 books and 68 weekly and monthly publications were available to the 1,400 registered patrons and many more Posey County residents.

Representatives from New Harmony, Mount Vernon, Griffin, Poseyville, Stewartsville, Cynthiana, St. Wendell, Wadesville and Blairsville formed a committee to lead the 1955 March of Dimes in Posey County from January until February 15. Projects to raise funds included a "Mother's March," a March of Dimes basketball game, a county-wide mailing and coin collections in business establishments.

Still in the planning stages, Mount Vernon's project to improve the water system was finally ready for bidding. They were accepted in May and the committee began work adopting a bond ordinance for the proposed expansion.

Planning stages were long over for the Wabash Memorial Bridge as the State Highway Commission of Indiana began the purchase of the right-of-way for the state road leading to the bridge. The road, which would extend from Black Chapel to Mount Vernon would involve purchasing parts of 13 properties.

A rain and hail storm that hit Mount Vernon and surrounding area, early in March caused $100,000 in damages to businesses and homes. A wall of a burned building toppled into the Plymouth-Chrysler sales service agency, caving in the roof and shattering glass. Two employees were taken to the hospital for injuries. Almost an inch of rain fell within 20 minutes, flodding sewers and basements. Roofs were damaged and some destroyed. No rain fell at Hovey, Solitude and Savah, while the area northeast of Mount Vernon suffered the most. Marrs Township also experienced flooding, but central and north Posey County missed the storm. Almost a week later, first damage estimats were discovered to be conservative. The final losses were set at $250,000.

Health was the issue later in the year, when a service was set up by the County School Board of Education for school children. Nine of Posey County's townships, Smith, Bethel Black, Lynn, Marrs, Point, Robb, Smith, and the Center-Robinson Consolidated schools would benefit from the service which would cost the cooperating schools about $2.16 per student. Responsibilities of the school nurse would include promoting, establishing and supervising a school health program, controlling and preventing communicable diseases, giving vision, hearing and dental tests, advising parents with handicapped children, reporting and recording health data, advising teachers and students on health and safety practices and coordinating efforts for sanitary school conditions.

Already 80 other Indiana counties in Indiana had prepared for Appreciation Days for the Korean War veterans, and October 1955 was the time for Posey County to honor its 550 veterans. The celebration included a parade, with military units and the Mount Vernon High School marching band. Certificates were awarded to veterans and Gold Star men. The celebration didn't mask the reality of the war... there was a prayer, a memorial service and the lingering notes of taps.

In April, Battery B was busy with a preparation of yet another kind. The National Guard field artillery unit had recently received orders that on an unannounced date, it would be participants in Operation Minutemen -- a military exercise that had never before been staged in America. The operation was designed to test the speed and efficiency of the National Guard in an emergency situation. The nationwide drill would include 22 infantry divisions, five armored divisions and more than 100 special units. Operation Minuteman would also extend beyond continental borders into the District of Columbia, Alaska, Hawaii and Puerto Rico. As the test could come at any time during the weekday, businesses were asked to cooperate by letting the men participate without penalty.

Just west of Mount Vernon ground was broken for the new radio station in May. The Federal Communication Commission gave to the station the call letters, WPCO (for Posey County). WPCO, which would broadcast daily from 6 a.m. until 7 p.m. and was expected to go on the air by early September. Employees would then broadcast from a large reception lounge, an air-conditioned studio and office and control room. Twenty-six telephone lines from Mount Vernon were wired into the new station. Ahead of schedule, WPCO went on the air in late August as 500 people stood in the station to watch. The first program aired at 2 p.m. and featured interviews with civic leaders.

While the station was under construction in June, so was work on the Wabash Memorial Bridge. Steelwork began as the pier work finished, with construction crews working 18 hours a day.

Just a year before, Mount Vernon enjoyed its first drive up mailbox. And, now in 1955, the post office added another service to Mount Vernon and Posey County -- certified mail. A mailing and delivery safeguard, it was needed for mail with no intrinsic value but for those who needed a record of delivery. An additional charge of 15 cents gave those who bought the service a certificate showing the mailing date, and later a receipt of the delivery. Certified mail gave mailing and delivery proof without the more costly registered mail fee.

Indiana Bell Telephone Company remained in the news of the 1950s as it was finally approved by the Public Service Commissions of Indiana and the Federal Communications Commission to acquire the property of the St. Philips Telephone Company. Plans were immediately made to change from calling by number instead of by name, with future plans calling for the switch to the dial system.

Probably the biggest news of 1956 was the completion and dedication of the Wabash Memorial Bridge. While the events leading up to the dedication took the attention of most Posey County residents, there were many other happenings that deserved mentioning.

To accommodate the heavy traffic of voters in Posey County, the Posey County Board of Commissioner and the state election committees added Black 13 as the 33rd voting precinct. The new precinct helped relieve the fifth and sixth precincts and was in operation by the May primary.

In order to accommodate the parents of Posey County, the office of the county superintendent of school issued the first publication of The School Reporter.

"For a long time we have felt the need for communicating to parents information of a general education nature which affects our schools and children," wrote Superintendent Eldon R. Crawford. The first issue off the press in January 1956 included articles on school surveys, school health and immunization slips, employment of minors and news about the speech clinic.

With the support of the Posey 4-H Club Council, 4-H Adult Leaders, Home Demonstration Clubs and the County Extension Committee, the Posey County Agricultural Improvement Center purchased 53 acres of land to be fully cultivated into an agricultural youth and community center. Future plans would include the long term objective of the Center to establish a 4-H Club fairgrounds and a center for rural, urban, civic, school and church use. A total of 597 boys and girls were enrolled in 4-H club work when the Posey County Agricultural Improvement Center held the first 4-H Fair on its new grounds in 1957.

Another purchase to aid the county was under way later in the year, this time under the direction of the Mount Vernon Board of Park Commissioners. Plans including the purchase of almost 143 acres, bounded on the south and west by State Highway 62 just northeast of Mount Vernon, to serve as a city park. The Mount Vernon Kiwanis Club detailed the planning of the park. Future purchase and improvement would be funded by special bond issue.

In October, a referendum consolidated Mount Vernon, Black, Lynn and Marrs townships into the Metropolitan School District of Mount Vernon. Point Township, although not at the meeting, later joined the district. At the same time, Robb and Smith townships and Center-Robinson School District merged, with the addition of Bethel at a later date. Due to a protest by Bethel county taxpayers against the addition of Bethel to the district, the commissioners did not include Bethel or Point (because it did not join until later) in the districting. Commissioner established District 1 of the Metropolitan School District of Mount Vernon to include Marrs Township, East Black Township, and Lynn Township. District 2 was composed of Northwest Black Township and Mount Vernon City precincts. Southwest black Township and the other Mount Vernon city precincts comprised District 3. The North Posey County Metropolitan School District included Smith Township and Poseyville precinct 2 in Robb Township. District 2 was made up of precinct 1 in Poseyville and precinct 3 in Stewartsville and North Center Township. District 3 included Robinson Township and South Center precinct.

In addition, all eyes were on the development of the Wabash Memorial Bridge and the plans that would honor its dedication.

As early as December 1955, committees discussed the dedication ceremony. Early in 1956, most of the newspaper article highlighted the completion of final stages. January announced the final "pour" of the bridge floor, completion of the curbing and the installation of handrails. Foreseeing business trends, the Mount Vernon Planning Committee sought to adopt and amendment to re-zone the new state highway leading to the bridge. The amendment would establish an extended 500-foot business zone along each side of the highway.

Meanwhile, the Mount Vernon Chamber of Commerce took the lead in organizing opening events. Letters were sent to 10 cities in Southeastern Illinois inviting them to participate in the festivities. For all the committees that helped to plan the events, a banquet would be held in their honor at an Evansville hotel. The rest of the crowds were ready to enjoy a colorful parade.

As the bridge neared completion, bridge manager Don Blair, tentatively set the toll charges. All tolls would be one-way. Class "A" passenger cars could purchase books of 10 at a cost of $3 or books of 100 at $25. Class "B" trucks would pay $4 for a book of 10 and $30 for one of 100. Class "C" tickets were sold without discount and were used by trucks with more than two axles. There was to be no charge to those who crossed the bridge on the day of dedication.

By May, engineers informed Posey County residents that the bridge would open on July 7, 1956. The governors of Indiana and Illinois as well as the entire staff of the Indiana Toll Bridge Commission were expected to attend the ceremonies. Beside the dignitaries, more than 20,000 people were expected to attend. Speeches, a parade, a small air show, and a banquet would highlight the day's activities. A thousand helium filled balloons were to be released. Attached to the balloons would be postcards which entitled the finder to prizes when returned to the dedication committee.

Then, on July 7, Posey County and thousands of others witnessed one of the biggest events in the county's history. The dedication plaque read," WABASH RIVER MEMORIAL BRIDGE, 1955, This structure is an enduring memorial to those of Indiana and Illinois who gave their lives in defense of their beloved country, constructed by Indiana State Toll Bridge Commission." The new bridge spanned 5,029 feet. Indiana's poet laureate, E. A Richardson (Big Rich) wrote the poem to dedicate the bridge:

"Across the waving Wabash, high in the air,
  appears a piece of art, designed by skill,
  On massive pillars, placed beneath at will,
  It is a safe and solid thoroughfare.
  Upon the long approach, in foul or fair,
  The toll house sits, with ever open till,
  Awaiting willingly or fares to fill,
  Contributed by those who travel there.

So stand the stately, high majestic spa,

Well rated with the beautiful and the best,
A perfect emblem of the gift of man,
Where everyone can travel east or west,
Regardless of his color, creed and clan,
May glory on the bridge and builders rest!"

More than 15,000 people attended the festivities. A-mile-and-a-half long parade boasted 125 spectacular entries. Channel 50 covered the days events.

As the new was ushered in, the old was ushered out. The century-old Mackey ferry made its last crossing. The traffic across the bridge made the ferry operation obsolete. More than 100 trips a day had been made by the operators. Just a week later, the Dogtown Ferry ended its 30-year operation. The road leading to both ferry operations were "abandoned" by the State Highway Department of Indiana and reverted to county highway status. All the signs were left on old Road 762 and Road 62, but stop signs were removed. The new Road 762 leading to the bridge carried both numbers 762 and 62.

Early in 1957, Indiana Bell began the switch to the dial system in the St. Philips exchange area, which included Parkers Settlement, Marrs and parts of Evansville and Caborn exchanges. The switch from name to number gave St. Philip subscribers the exchange "Yukon." The new system was expected to be operating by May and would permit calling between St. Philips, Mount Vernon, Evansville, Solitude, New Harmony and St. Joseph without a long distance charge. In 1956, Indiana Bell reported spending of $25 million in the state of Indiana to install modern systems. This was the second year in a row, that Bell had spent more than $20 million for materials and supplies. The newspaper reported that, "Indiana already is the telephone instrument manufacturing capital of the world, as all Bell system telephones are made in Indiana.

Duck and goose hunters, landowners and the Indiana Department of Conservation were pleased with the Posey County Circuit Court's decision to grant a petition to raise the water level of Hovey Lake. A dam already constructed would flood Dry Lake, just adjacent to Hovey. This plan would provide year around sanctuary for migratory waterfowl. Although illegal to hunt at Dry Lake, hunters were pleased with the decision, knowing that the new lake would attract other fowl to areas where hunted was allowed.

D. Mead Johnson, president of Mead Johnson & Company, announced in May of 1957 that it had purchased approximately 500 acres of farmland just two miles east of Mount Vernon. The manufacturer of nutritional and pharmaceutical products made no plans for immediate for the land.

While Mount Vernon looked forward to the possibility of getting a new industry, New Harmony was ready for the opening of their town's latest industry, Micro-Lab Company out of Anderson, Indiana. The new firm, expected to open in 60 days, would employee 100 New Harmony residents when in full production. The New Harmony Business Men's Association saw the need for a new industry in its community to help ease the unemployment rate. Ground was broken in late July for the new Micro-Lab plant which was in the business of manufacturing radio transmitters and receivers for marine service.

While the business community seemed to grow in 1957, farmers suffered. The Agricultural Secretary declared Posey County a disaster area after an unprecedented growing season weather along with 50 other counties in the state. Although 15 counties were removed from the list, more than half the counties in Indiana remained in the disaster category. Relief was given in the form of low interest loans to farmers.

When the reports came in, it seemed the Wabash Memorial Bridge was a success. The first year's profit totaled $52,177.75 from a total of $96,624.91 in tolls and $44,447.16 in expenditures. The bridge was constructed at a cost of $2,500,000 not including the road construction leading to the span. Average daily tolls were $269.90 with an average of 724.7 vehicles crossing per day. During the first year, more than 264,525 vehicles crossed between the two states. The following year showed a profit of $63,000.

While the traffic over the river increased, the traffic on the river remained about the same, and Mount Vernon held it sixth position among all Ohio river ports in volume of freight tonnage. Statistics in 1953 showed 1,736,622 as the total volume of tonnage with an increase to 2,961,454 tons in 1957.

In the spirit of giving at Christmas time a youth center was dedicated through the generosity of one New Harmony resident. The open house on Christmas night showed off the remodeled First Missionary Baptist Church which would not only serve as a youth center, but also as a center for art exhibits.

Sixteen school corporations in Posey County, including Evansville were invited to participate in an endeavor to bring education through television. The Southwestern Indiana Television Council and the Ford Foundation were interested in using southwestern Indiana as an experimental field for educational television. The experiment would conclude if large groups could be taught as effectively as small groups in a regular classroom. The program would cost the participating schools $75,000 and was subject to the approval of school boards and the Indiana Department of Public Instruction.

DDD, or Direct Distance Dialing, was a common phrase in 1958 among Posey County residents. Indiana Bell added the service allowing Mount Vernon telephone users to call 2,000 communities in 32 states. Resident were able to dial direct cities like San Francisco, Philadelphia, Miami, Detroit, Chicago, Salt Lake City, Dallas, Indianapolis, St. Louis, Phoenix and Denver. With this service, almost one-third of the nation's 60 million telephones would be at Posey County's fingertips. With all the new services and replacing and expanding facilities, Indiana Bell expected to invest $31,000,000 in 1959. Announcements indicated that $9,000,000 would be allocated to local and long distance equipment, $11,000,000 for outside lines, $9,000,000 for equipment installations and $2,000,000 for land purchase and building.

For 71 years, the four-classroom St. Wendell school had served its community well. In 1957, the school, which had stood since 1884, was razed. On its foundation was erected the new eight-room school. And, in 1958, the 118-by-58 foot two-story building with offices, and music rooms, opened to serve the community's students.

While one building went up, another went down. Poseyville's landmark, the Co-Op corn elevator, burned to the ground. With the efforts of the Cynthiana, Evansville, New Harmony and Mount Vernon fire departments, the blaze was confined to the elevator. While the office and scales did not burn, the total damage was estimated at $60,000, with a loss of between 12,000 and 15,000 bushels of corn.

More than 100 calls where placed November 7 to the Mount Vernon Police Station, and the mayor in Herrin, Illinois said he was "knocked out of bed" when the biggest earthquake in 60 years rocked southern Indiana, Kentucky, Illinois, and Missouri. The first tremors, started around

Salem E.&R. Church (Evangelical & Reformed) built 1888, late 1950's

8:41 p.m. and followed by 14 minutes of vibrations, registered between 4 and 6 on the seismograph. Surprisingly, no injuries or damages were reported.

In 1815, the Jesse Nash family had traveled via flatboat from Pennsylvania to Posey County. He purchased property from George Rapp, leader of the New Harmony Rappites and built a log cabin for his family. Two acres of this historic land was purchased by the Indiana Highway Department for the purpose of building a roadside park on Indian 66 west of Wadesville. The dedication of the park, held in late May heralded the park as the finest in the Indiana highway system, boasting six brick ovens with firewood available, tables, modern restroom facilities and parking area.

Cynthiana made the news in 1959 upon the dedication of their new post office. But this was only one of quite a few events that residents of Cynthiana had recently experienced. The new bridge on Highway 65 south of Cynthiana, a new nursing home, new junior and senior high school facilities and the new dial telephone all meant progress for the town.

The school system was an important issue to Posey County, and progress took the form of new facilities. Ground was staked out for the erection of the new Metropolitan High School building in the Mount Vernon area. Financed by the Mount Vernon Metropolitan School Building Corporation, the building was expected to open for the 1960-61 school year. Later in the year, the North Posey Junior and Senior High School, located midway between Poseyville and Wadesville, was ready to serve its first students. The one-story modern structure replaced the high schools at Griffin, Poseyville, Wadesville and Cynthiana. The building handled 600 students comfortably and included a 600-seat auditorium, office, bookstore, lounge, guidance area, library, classrooms, vocational areas, gymnasium, dressing rooms and a health room. Athletic fields and outdoor physical education and recreation facilities were included in future expansion plans.

The Chairman of Educational Administration and Coordinator of Special School Services at Purdue University announced that year that, "it is no exaggeration to say that Posey County ranks at the top in educational improvement in Indiana in recent years... I am sure the people of Posey County have been so close to the development of their new school systems, and have had so many struggles which an outsider would be unaware of, that it is difficult for them to assess the remarkable achievements that have been brought about."

The Posey County School System not only enjoyed changes, so did the industrial community in the last half of the 1950s. The Mount Vernon Industrial Fund not only reached its goal of $100,000 to attract new industries, but surpassed the mark. That campaign, challenged by a contribution of $5,000 by the Mead Johnson Company if it reached $95,000, was then met. The Mount Vernon Industrial Association had seen the effect of attracting new business just one month before when a 16-acre site was selected two miles to the south of the city for a commercial plastics plant operated by General Electric. The Chamber of Commerce interpreted the new local industry as "a rich reward for its years of effort to expand Mount Vernon industrially." Groundbreaking ceremonies for General Electric's Lexan(r) Polycarbonate Resin plant were held in July 1959. When the plant was scheduled to open in early 1960 it would employee 75 persons with the goal of employing 165 when the plant reached full operation.

Construction of the Wabash Memorial Bridge in 1956 proved profitable each successive year, and 1959 was certainly no exception. Toll collections increased $4,420.90, due to the opening of the Evansville expressway and the closing of Indiana 66 between New Harmony and Evansville for bridge widening. Bridge Superintendent Robert J. Hancock reported that during November, 36,442 vehicles crossed between the two states.

Indiana: 1960s

The Democratic revival that began with Vance Hartke's election in 1958 continued in 1960 with the election of Matthew Welsh as governor. While facing a Republican Legislature, Welsh was able to get some progressive legislation passed. In 1961, the Department of Administration was created to organize the purchasing, personnel and administrative procedures of state government. A state Civil Rights Act also was passed in 1961, three years before a similar federal law; in 1963, the law was strengthened and the Indiana Civil Rights Commission created. Legislation also authorized the creation of Indiana Vocational Technical College (Ivy Tech) in 1963.

In 1963, Gov. Welsh called a special session of the Legislature to raise taxes. The compromise worked out provided for two percent individual and corporate taxes, and -- for the first time in the state's history -- a sales tax of two percent. Republican Lt.-Gov. Richard Ristine cast the tie-breaking vote in the Senate to pass the legislation.

In the 1962 Senatorial election, Homer Capehart was ousted in favor of Birch Bayh. Only four years before, Indiana had a moderate Republican governor and two very conservative Republican Senators; now they were replaced by a progressive Democratic governor and two liberal Democratic Senators.

Perhaps the sweetest victory for Hoosier Democrats, however, came in 1964. In the Democratic primary, Gov. Welsh defeated conservative George C. Wallace by 200,000 votes. The Republicans nominated Barry Goldwater, a conservative of the cut of Jenner and Capehart. But in November, Indiana's electoral votes went to Lyndon Johnson. Goldwater's defeat marked the first time Indiana's presidential vote had gone Democratic since 1936. (As of this writing in 1989, it was also the last Hoosier Democratic vote.)

The progressive trend continued with the election of Roger D. Branigin as governor in 1964. During Branigin's term, the poll tax and property tax on household goods were abolished, the 1957 right-to-work law was repealed, and the first statewide reapportionment since 1921 was made.

In 1965, former governor Matt Welsh was appointed part-time chairman of the International Joint Commission on Waterways with Canada. The next year, Henry F. Schricker died; he had been the last Democratic governor before Welsh.

Virgil "Gus" Grissom of Mitchell, Indiana, was selected one of the seven original U.S. astronauts. On July 21, 1961, he became the third man to travel in space, aboard the Mercury capsule Liberty Bell 7. Six years later, Grissom and two other astronauts were killed in a fire on the Apollo 1 capsule. Indiana boasted another early astronaut, Frank Borman, of the Gemini 7 mission, was from Gary.

Gary also attracted national attention in 1967 when Richard Hatcher was elected mayor, the first black man elected mayor of a northern industrial city.

When Studebaker ceased production in 1963, Indiana lost the last car that had been totally Hoosier born and made. Another era in the Indiana transportation industry ended four years later, in 1967, when the Monon Railroad cancelled its passenger service.

Architecture, both old and modern, drew Hoosier attention in the 1960s. The Historic Landmarks Foundation of Indiana was organized in 1960. The former Indianapolis City Hall was renovated, and in 1967 became the home of the Indiana State Museum. New buildings were constructed across the state, most notably in Columbus. Probably the best known of Columbus' landmarks, the Eero Saarinen-designed North Christian Church, was built in 1964.

Composer and songwriter Cole Porter, born in Peru, Indian, died in October 1964. Among his best-known works were "Night and Day," "Begin the Beguine," and "I've Got You Under My Skin."

A devastating snowstorm in January 1965 left 32 people dead in Indiana. And, on Palm Sunday, April 11 of that year, three bands of tornadoes moved across the central and northern parts of the state, killing 140 and damaging more than $100 million in property.

Despite its heavily Democratic representation in Congress, Indiana returned the Statehouse to Republican control in 1968. Edgar D. Whitcomb of Seymour, Secretary of State since 1966, was elected governor. (Escape from Corregidor, Whitcomb's book on his war experiences, was published in paperback in 1967, and helped promote Whitcomb's candidacy.) Whitcomb's election was the first of five straight the Republicans would win and continued a 20 run of control of the governorship.

Posey County

Mount Vernon added a new business to its economy in 1960 when building began on a fertilizer blending plant. Custom Farm Services, Inc. would manufacture and sell a complete line of dry and liquid fertilizers in bag, bulk and tank and offered to blend any materials to suit the customer. By June of the same year, Custom Farm was operating with three full-time employees. The company made plans to double the number of employees by the following year. Veatch, Inc. of Chicago also chose to locate its new plant in Mount Vernon early in 1961. The manufacturer of fibreglass boats, tanks and burial vaults would employ 10 when it first opened and had plans for expansion. The Vernon Coach Company started in Mount Vernon in 1963, manufacturing two 35-by-8 foot trailers each week at a cost of $3,000. Dollar General Stores of Scottville, Kentucky opened its first Indiana store in Mount Vernon. Dollar General, a retailer of dry goods, family apparel, shoes and housewares, followed a policy of even dollar prices (no cents), selling items with prices of less than a dollar value in multiple numbers to reach dollar levels.

The county seat also added a new school to its new buildings. In 1960, constuction began on St. Matthew's Parochial School. Eight classrooms, an auditorium, a gymnasium and kitchen facilities, a lounge and a first aid room were included in the $173,015 project. Opened in September of 1961 and dedicated in October, the building actually cost $238,000. Mount Vernon dedicated its new high school in February 1961 at a cost of $2.5 million.

Expansion also hit Posey County in the 1960s. General Electric's administrative and materials office outgrew locations in 1963 and were moved to a converted residence on Indiana 69 South. B&W's plant had only been in Mount Vernon five years by 1967, but was celebrating its 100th anniversary of world-wide operations. In its five years at the county seat, B&W had become the world's largest, and most modern equipped heavy pressure vessel shop. Beside manufacturing these vessels for nuclear power stations, the plant also produced wall assemblies used in conventional boilers by the electric utility industry. Due to the increased demand for nuclear power plants in the late '60s, B&W was backloged by more than 36 orders. The Mount Vernon plant's payroll was approximately $5 million, employing some 1,000 persons.

51

Posey County found fame when the County Commissioner, a magazine publication of the County Commissioners Association of Indiana sent a representative to Posey County for two-weeks to gather historical information and photographs depicting county history.

New Harmony received its own recognition in 1961 when the American Institute of Architects announced in Washington, D.C. that it selected a newly completed edifice for one of its annual "honor awards." The Shrine in New Harmony was honored as one of the seven in the world for the award. New York Architect, Philip Johnson who designed The Shrine, also won another honor award for his design of the Nuclear Reactor in Rehovot, Israel. Johnson was the only architect on the list to receive two awards.

The Metropolitan School District of Mount Vernon won honors in 1963 when, for the first time, the district was granted First Class Commissions by the federal commission of the Indiana State Board of Education. To receive this recognition, all facets of education were reviewed including inspections of facilities, condition of facilities, equipment and condition of equipment, faculty experience and training, curriculum, extra-class activities and all other factors entering into the education of students.

"Snow... Snow...And More Snow...," read the March newspapers in 1960. Southern Indiana was under a blanket of snow that closed schools and brought most scheduled activities to a halt. The weather bureau in Evansville reported that it was the biggest accumulation of snow since the 20 inches that fell in 1918. With temperatures just above the freezing mark, strong wind and thirteen inches of snow, travel was impossible in many areas of the county. On a lighter note, the newspaper reported, "Of course, we know what caused it as we have heard of some of the Florida vacationers that have returned and it always turns cold when the arrive back." The bitter cold hit southern Indiana again 1963. Not used to such harsh winter conditions, schools were closed and transportation was halted when Posey County measured three inches of snow, temperatures of 15 degrees below zero and hazardous drifting.

Ice was the biggest culprit in a March 1965 storm. All of Posey County was without electricity for at least an entire evening. Cynthiana's power was restored first and Poseyville and Mount Vernon's electricity were not restored until the following afternoon. Many of the rural areas did not receive power until the evening. Besides slowed traffic, the biggest news reported by the newspapers was the postponement of the sectional basketball tourney. Each year, winter storms seemed to be worse than in years past. In 1966, the papers reported the "biggest snow in six years." Schools remained closed for three days and mail delivery was delayed. The weather bureau at Dress Memorial Airport in Evansville measured nine inches, "but local unofficial measurements in this area indicated that it was more like 12 to 13 inches." A savage squall ripped across Indiana in October of 1967, causing considerable damage to many Indiana towns and cities. Posey County suffered power failures and road blockage due to fallen trees.

Despite the decades storms, Posey fared relatively well in other areas. In 1960,(check) Indiana Bell offered an alternative to the big, heavy black and certainly easy to pick out phones that sat in the parlors, kitchens, family rooms and bedrooms of many Posey County homes. A new lightweight telephone, "The Princess," was introduced as a compact, oval-shaped instrument that reduced by more than a third the space needed for current desk-type telephones. The phone weighed 42 ounces and came equipped with a dial which lighted up when the receiver was lifted and glowed during the night with the flick of a switch. Sure to please every customer, "The Princess" came in white, beige, pink, blue and turquoise. The phone carried a $5 charge and extra 75 cents a month to own.

Later in the decade, Posey residents were introduced to another convenient invention. In July of 1963, the ZIP Code was introduced to the nation. The five-digit ZIP Code given to Mount Vernon was 47620. The Postmaster urged residents to use the "revolutionary new system," saying, "The Zip Code is literally the last word in mail addressing...The address on mail most often gets read as many as eight or ten times by postal employees, to get it to the proper destination. With ZIP Code, a clerk needs only to glance at the code to know immediately to what state and post office the letter is destined, and to speed it on its way, cuting up to 24 hours off the time between deposit and delivery." Examples on how to include the Zip Code in correspondence were published in the paper.

The county was concerned about government allocation of state and federal funds in 1960, and public salary schedules. A tentative Federal Census showed a decline in Posey County population. Although unofficial, the census showed Mount Vernon, Cynthiana, Marrs and Robinson Township, the only areas to gain in population in the past decade. Mount Vernon increased by 749, Cynthiana, 64, Marrs 495 and Robinson 186. New Harmony suffered the greatest loss from 1,360 to 1,114. When the results were finally official, only Cynthiana, Marrs and Robinson Township showed a population increase. Mount Vernon, thought to have had an increase of 749, actually decreased in population by 179. The overall Posey County population figure dropped from 19,818 in 1950 to 19,214. The census also showed that Indiana gained 728,264 inhabitants, an 18.5 percent increase over 1950.

Of the 18 batteries that participated in tests at Camp Grayling in Michigan, Battery B of the Mount Vernon National Guard achieved a "high excellent" rating and won second place honors. The Silver Certificate was awarded to Battery B in October, 1960 by the 38th Division Commander for the local unit's high standard performance during the past year. The battery outdid itself the following year, placing first during the two-weeks of intensive training at Camp McCoy in Wisconsin. Battery B received a "Superior" rating after the two-week intensive training. This was the first time any battery of the 1st Howitzer Battalion had received such a high ranking. Late in the spring of 1965, Battery B became a part of a 1,500 man task force that trained in Puerto Rico. The composition of the task force included an Artillery battalion, two Infantry battalions, Medical company, Maintenance company, Engineer company, Military Police platoon, Signal platoon and Headquarters, 3rd Brigade. Just one month later, Battery B received their fifth straight Federal inspection "superior" rating.

Bringing talent and cooperation together to plan and promote projects of countywide interest was the goal of the newly formed United Organizations of Posey County in 1962. Representatives from the Greater Mount Vernon Association, the county council, county commissioners, Cynthiana Town Board, Poseyville Town Board, Farmers Bank of Wadesville, Wadesville Athletic Club and the Mount Vernon Chamber of Commerce met for the first time in June and extended invitations to the New Harmony Town Board, the New Harmony Business Men's Association, the Griffin Town Board the St. Wendell Athletic Club and both the Republican and Democrat county chairmen. The group first tried to hasten construction of the proposed highway Wadesville to Mount Vernon, an entry onto Interstate Highway 64 across the north end of Posey County.

Also formed to aid Posey County was the Gold Ladies, who donated their time as volunteer workers for the State Hospital. Volunteers worked in the clothing shops, mending, pressing and sizing donated clothes, making then ready for the patient to use.

By 1963 another organization was formed, this time dealing with the economic development of the county. A group of farm, business and civic leaders met to facilitate a planned economic development program for Posey County and to help coordinate development programs that were important to the future of the area. Discussions centered on Posey County and southern Indiana lagging behind the industrial northern sections. The group pointed out that areas needing attention included industrial development, recreation and tourism, and up-to-date public and community facilities.

The Rural-Urban League, dedicated to promoting better understanding the problems of both rural and urban people, held its first meeting in January of 1964. Speaking to a group of 200 Posey residents, Director of the Co-Operative Extension Service at Purdue University Howard Dresslin, told listeners about agriculture's tremendous advancement as well as disappointments during the past two decades. Dresslin added that American agriculture's problems stem from over-production and not under-production in contrast to most of the world. He also said that Indiana, which in 1964 had the highest per acre corn yield of any corn-producing state and ranked at the top or near the top in production of virtually every other crop associated with the central states, had the problem of over-production to a marked degree.

The Christian Rural Overseas Program (CROP) was established to help worldwide interests. Every residence and farm in Posey County was given the chance to donate either commodities or cash of the international relief work of the churches. CROP began after World War II as an expression of America's friendship for people in war-torn countries. It was reported in a CROP bulletin in 1947, that 500 million pounds of food were donated.

Posey County set their goal at 3,000 bushels of corn or equivalent cash gifts.

Posey County needed help itself in 1961 as officials investigated the possibility of federal aid for repairing damage to highways and bridges because of recent flooding. Posey was one of 29 counties designated by President Kennedy as disaster area making the county eligible for assistance. Three-fourths of the all the counties damage was to highways and the estimated repair cost reached $8 million. Damage to bridges, culverts and roads reported by Posey County totaled $337,500. Ten bridges in the county were destroyed, eight bridges were damages, five road culverts were destroyed and 55 were damaged.

Through license fees and other funds, Posey County received $466,451 for road construction and improvement in 1963. Statewide showed that $66,875,050 was distributed among the 92 Indiana counties and 539 incorporated cities and towns for road improvements. The county again needed support to rebuild after flooding in March 1964. Evansville recorded 12,23 inches of rain and Mount Vernon 10.69. Highway 68 between Poseyville and New Harmony, Highway 65 between Cynthiana and Evansville, Highway 69 between New Harmony Mount Vernon, U.S. 460 between Wadesville and Evansville were all closed along many county roads.

The worst flooding had occurred in 1937, when the high mark stood at 59 plus feet. The mark was expected to read 47.5 by the time the 1964 rains quit. Although Posey County applied for $82,268,52 of federal aid for damaged highways and bridges, it was allocated only $73,676.52. In 1961, Posey County received $102,718 in two federal grants after major flooding of creeks and rivers.

During 1963, the newspapers reported the Hovey Lake would rise seven feet and double in size when the new locks and dam on the Ohio River southwest of Mount Vernon were completed. The director of the Indiana Department of Recreation announced state plans to develop a 4,000-acre hunting area and wildlife refuge within 10 years. The state also announced plans to bring more activity to New Harmony State Memorial and promised to work on a public access sites to the Ohio River in Mount Vernon. In the last year of the decade, the director of the Indiana Department of National Resources visited Posey County to review the project. The director was accompanied by area leaders including State Senator Robert Orr. The proposed project expanded the 300-acre lake to 1,700 acres when the Uniontown dam was completed and included the purchase of other acreage to expand camping and ground recreational facilities including a new headquarters building would cost around $2 million.

"I envision Hovey as a tremendous facility for Southern Indiana and Posey County...it has great potential," remarked the director. One month later in July, Posey and Vanderburgh County joint state senator announced that contracts for the projects were hoped to be awarded by the end of the year.

Ohio River freight traffic totalled 85,306,058 tons in 1962, ranking Mount Vernon as the sixth largest post on the river and qualified it as the largest shipping port on the Lower Ohio River. Petroleum products, grain, bituminous coal and chemicals comprised most of the local shipping, accounting for most of the 2,746,846 tons. Huntington, Virginia ranked first, followed by Louisville, Pittsburgh, Cincinnati, Alliquippa-Rochester, Pennsylvania and then Mount Vernon.

Sixteen counties in southwestern Indiana pulled together resources to accomplish major breakthroughs in economic development. One project completed by the Hoosier Lincoln Land Travel Association was the printing and distribution of 30,000 Lincoln Land maps showing a trail through the 16 counties and pointing out 59 points of interest including two in Posey County. The map also informed readers of camping, lodging, and dining facilities in each area.

In the heat of the summer in 1964, New Harmony celebrated its sesquicentennial -- 150 years of rich and productive history. The three-day festivities where highlighted by a keynote address from Dr. Herman B. Wells, chancellor of Indiana University. He praised New Harmony as "the greatest cultural and scientific center of its day," and as a "living symbol today of the courage and industry which have made Indiana great." Other events included a large parade, with a number of bands, floats and hundreds of people. More than 6,000 folks celebrated New Harmony's past. The Mount Vernon paper reported: "There is perhaps more of Indiana's birth to be founded in this town of 1,000 people, than in any other point in the state. Indiana's cultural heritage, its scientific development and contributions emanated from her. Bringing history alive is a difficult task, but the Sesquicentennial Committee did a wonderful job in showing that New Harmony is alive and its history lives permanently with its people."

Making New Harmony's rich history better known to all Indiana residents came in June 1965 when it was selected by the United States Department of the Interior as one of two sites eligible for registration as national historic landmarks. Fountain City, Indiana was home to the other possible landmark, the Levi Coffin House. Late in August of the same year, New Harmony was designated by Secretary of the Department of Interior Stewart Udall as a registered national landmark. The state's Governor, the Secretary of the Department of Interior, and Congressman Winfield K. Denton joined in the ceremonies that declared New Harmony as "possessing exceptional value in commemorating and illustrating the history of the Unite States of America." The Mount Vernon paper reported: "The varied history of New Harmony includes the original settlement by George Rapp and the Harmonist Society who built the community in 1814 in the hope that the Lord would begin his 1,000 year earthly reign there. In 1825, the British industrialist and reformer Robert Owen and his partner William Maclure began a second era. Outstanding Chapters in American natural science, education, community development, and social reform were written there. And by the time of the Civil War a brilliant theatrical tradition to last almost 100 years had begun."

Uniontown locks and Dam construction was under way by the summer of 1965, launching the first stage in the $65 million project. The first stage included miles of concrete highway that started at Indiana 69 at Hovey Lake. When the entire project was completed, the Uniontown locks and dam would provide recreational facilities and pleasure boat launching.

Early in 1965, the Posey County Council made emergency appropriations to implement the Federal Food Stamp Program through the County Welfare Department. A caseworker received $5,925 of the $6,925 for salary. An estimated $12,000 in stamps was available for food purchase each month. Posey County hoped to eliminate the monthly distribution of federal surplus food by township trustees.

Daughters of the late Elmer E. Elliot donated 700 acres along the Wabash River just three miles south of New Harmony to the Department of Natural Resources. The heavily wooded area had been in the Elliot family since 1920 and was home to a small 40-cabin resort area. As a state park, to be completed in 1967, it would play an important part in developing historic New Harmony as a recreational, educational and as the paper reported, an "inspirational" site.

Then in 1967, Mount Vernon would have its own park. The late Julius Brittlebank, formerly of Mount Vernon and the manager of the old Hudnut Hominy Mill, willed $89,000 for a city park. Brittlebank first specified that his estate would go to his son Frank's children or child. When Frank died childless, $268,000 was left to Mount Vernon, Terre Haute and Charleston, South Carolina.

Authorized by the United States Department of Agriculture (USDA), a Technical Action Panel was organized in Posey County in September 1967. The panel consisted of top- ranking officials from the Farmers Home Administration, Agricultural Stabilization and Conservation Service and Cooperative Extension Service. The basic objectives were outlined in the Mount Vernon Democrat: The panel would "1. Serve as a channel for carrying out the secretary's directives for assisting people in rural areas. 2. Provide assistance to individuals and groups in rural areas for community-wide projects that benefit low-income farm families and other residents. 3. Identify major problems in rural areas and determine sources of assistance. 4. Assure the availability and use of needed federal and state agency services by individuals and groups in rural areas. 5. Advise agencies outside of USDA on needs for their services in rural areas. 6. Assist individuals and groups in rural communities to plan economic development and community projects and keep plans current by updating needs, inventories and goals. 7. Assist leaders in forming rural development organizations. 8. Assist local leaders and groups to identify problems and develop projects."

A 12-year-old Mount Vernon boy discovered the 20,000 year-old bones of a mastodon near Farmersville in January 1966. A New Harmony archaeologist formerly on the staff of the University of Kentucky examined the bones and confirmed they were of a prehistoric beast. Only parts of the Mastodon were found, including an upper foreleg, several vertebrae, broken rib fragments, a piece of the pelvis two teeth and one tusk. The bones of two other Mastodons had previously been found in Posey County.

Of all the events occurring in 1966, the biggest by far was the celebration of Posey County's Sesquicentennial. Mount Vernon also celebrated it Sesquicentennial, and in April the paper curiously reported the following proclamation: "WHEREAS: The year 1966 had been dedicated to celebrating The One Hundred and Fiftieth year of Mount Vernon's founding, and WHEREAS: The great City of Mount Vernon has set aside the dates of June 27 through July 4 of the year to celebrate this important milestone with Parades, Praise and Pageantry, and WHEREAS: The male citizens of the City are desirous of entering the spirit of the historic event by wearing hair on the face where heretofore it has not appeared to remind us of the customs of our male citizens in the early days. BE IT HEREBY RESOLVED: That I, Harold Gentil, Mayor of Mount Vernon, hereby proclaim that theses public spirited citizens shall become members of the great fraternity known henceforth as "Brothers of the Brush". The proclamation went on to say, "Members in good standing will agree to raise facial adornments in the form of mustaches, sideburns, goatees, full beards, of any combination thereof form March 21 until July 4, 1966...The Proclamation issued the Sesquicentennial spirit of good fun, and in recognition of the importance of visual support by all male citizens of our coming glorious Sesquicentennial Celebration."

Founded in 1906 and operated by Floyd Oursler and his sons since 1928, The Mount Vernon Republican ran its last issue in September 1966.

The Mount Vernon Democrat, published without a break since 1867, printed a special sesquicentennial story in October, 1966. In a four column story, writer Don Blair outlined the history of Posey County.

As a part of the Northwest Territory the area that is Posey County was under various governments: The first organized government being the Indiana Confederacy, then France until 1763; then Great Britain until 1774; then Province of Quebec; then ceded to the United States by the treaty of Paris in 1783. The great state of Virginia claimed the area until it was ceded to the federal government shortly after the Revolutionary War, 1784.

"This Northwestern Territory included all of the lands west of the Ohio River, east of the Mississippi River, south of the Great Lakes and west of Pennsylvania, It was in the area that a great many skirmishes between the American and the allies of Great

Britain took place. This territory included an area of 265,878 square miles.

"Since waterways were the only practical paths of the penetration of primeval forests, the junction of two major streams the Ohio River and the Wabash was an important intersection. Cultures from different parts of the country would meet at this confluence, at times such meets would result in open war fare, at others there would be considerable commerce. The fact that artifacts from widely separated regions are to be found together in Indian mounds in Posey County attest to the mingling of cultures in the area.

"Migration to the Northwest Territory was great from the date of its being made a part of the United States as a result of the Treaty of Paris which had ended the Revolutionary War. In 1800 the population had grown until it was desirable to divide the area into smaller territories, so the Indiana Territory was established with William H. Harrison as the governor.

"The development and the population increased at a rapid rate and in 1815 Jonathan Jennings presented to the congress a "Memorial" requesting statehood for the area. As a result for he the first race for the governorship, Jennings was elected over Thomas Posey who had been the last of the governors of the territory. The formal admission of the state was December 11, 1816, at the time of the admission there were thirteen counties and Posey was one of the smaller ones.

"The name Posey was familiar to the times as he had been an outstanding member of the army during the Revolution, and closely associated with the leaders in the days prior to the Treaty of Paris as well as active in Indiana affairs. The relationship between the Indians and the Whites was of extreme importance as they were making a concentrated effort to repel the Invader from their lands.

"After the defeat in the election for the governorship Posey was appointed in charge of Indian affairs in the state of Illinois and moved to that state, His sons established their home in Shawneetown an took part in the development of that community. Their home was located on the hills above the town where it was free from the flooding Ohio River.

"While on a visit to his sons Thomas Posey died and was buried in the Rose Garden, this later became the Westwood Cemetery located between Old and New Shawnetowns. The cemetery still serves both of these communities.

"The first session of a court in Posey Coney was held in Absalom Duckworth's Jan. 6, 1815. It was at this court that it was decided that the county seat would be located at a spot about one mile south of the present site of (unreadable) and that the town would be called Blackford, the (unreadable) of the town was laid out and the lots sold to secure money for the construction of the court house and jail. The first court session at Blackford was May 1815 in the house of William Hutchison which he had offer for use rent free.

"At the court session Hutchison was allowed a bill of $6 for whiskey to make the potential buyers happy and liberal. At the price of whiskey this would have satisfied a large crowd.

"Travel at this time was most difficult and it was soon seen that Blackford was too far from the center of the county to make a good seat of government and so in May of 1817 a commission appointed for the purpose (unreadable) that they had chosen a site of 100 acres donated by Frederick, more nearly in the center of the county.

"In May 1817, the board ordered the county seat moved to Springfield and a sale was advertised for July of the same year, and again there was to a be the barrel to help encourage the bidders, In November of this year the board met in Springfield in temporary quarters.

"Springfield had neither a railroad nor was on a stream, it was soon seen that this was not the desirable place for conducting county business and so in May 1825 the county officers were instructed to move their offices to Mount Vernon. The first session of the county board held in Mount Vernon was the 4th of July 1825.

"In 1873, as the county had prospered and as the county business had grown to the point of requiring better accommodations, a commission was appointed to investigate the possibility of building a new court house and secure plans for such a building. This group was Thomas Loudon, John Pfeffer, James Sampson, Thomas Jaquess and George Thomas.

"Plans submitted by Vrydale & Clarke were selected by the group and recommended to the board. On the 4th of February 1874 the board received bids for the construction of the building of which one by John McMannomy was the low. The contract price $74,400 plus extras of $1,011 and other costs brought the total for the building ready for occupancy to $88,275 when it was first used in 1876.

"An act of the territorial Legislature dated Sept. 7, 1814 outlined the new county of Posey, this area was taken from both Warrick and Gibson Counties. In 1815 the boundaries were altered so as to include all of New Harmony in Posey County, as by the first description this town was partly in Posey County and partly in Gibson County. Again in 1817 the boundaries were enlarged, to be more consistent with the enlarging population. In 1818 a part of the east side of the county was added to Vanderburg land in 1823 another row of sections was taken from Gibson and added to Posey.

"There has been a great deal of progress and development in the county since its creation in 1814 and some of this progress will be seen in the future articles about the individual communities which make up the total county." The article ended here.

"...concerning public health, providing for state and local health official and personnel, prescribing their powers and duties, establishing a public health code and providing for the administration of public health laws, prescribing penalties, repealing certain laws, and declaring an emergency," was part of an act of the Indiana General Assembly in requiring cities and counties in the state to establish a Board of Health.

In November 1966, Posey County formed their Board of Health which immediately dissolved all part-time health departments and health boards. The records, transferred to the new department, included information from the Vital Statistics Department and the Public Health Nursing Service. The governing board consisted of a public health officer, seven appointed board members, and a sanitation officer who would conduct educational programs, be aware of the cleanliness of milk, food and water, and guide communities and private citizens in the installation of sewage disposal systems, establishing a clean community.

With nearly a century of duty in Posey County, National Guard Battery B was rumored to be moved from Mount Vernon to an Evansville base. In an appeal to keep the battery, a history was relayed in the pages of the Mount Vernon Democrat. Excepts from this history include: "Posey County had five active companies during the Civil War. They were Companies A and F of the 25th Regiment and Companies C, D and H of 1st Calvary Regiment of Indiana Volunteers. Company H was made up of men mostly from Mount Vernon, and was organized June 10, 1861...seven companies at home maintain(ed) the home defense. They were of the 1st Regiment, 1st Brigade of the Indiana Legion.

Company H, 1st Regiment, Indian Legion, Mount Vernon, was organized in 1888 and was the first Guard unit of its kind to be organized locally. Due to no funding the company dissolved. August 1890, a monthly report showed 42 officers and enlisted men, but membership was larger prior to that time...Company B, 161st, Indiana volunteer Regiment was organized during the Spanish-American War. The company was mustered out April 30, 1898. After the turn-of-the-century, Company L, 1st Battalion, 1st Infantry, was formed in Mount Vernon. President Woodrow Wilson ordered the Indiana National Guard and Company L to stop Francisco "Pancho" Villa at the Mexican Border. Company L left Mount Vernon for Ft. Harrison on June 24, 1916. Company L was ordered to mobilize and recruit on March 27, 1917. By January of 1918, 135 men were members of Company L and the unit left for Hattiesbburg, Mississippi. The liberty Guard was formed in Mount Vernon in 1918 after Company L left. Artillery came to Mount Vernon in June 1922, when Battery E, 139th Field Artillery was organized. Battery E's weapons were four French 75's -- horsedrawn. On March 18, 1925, Battery E was called upon in the worst calamity that ever happened in Posey County. The little town of Griffin was completely wiped off the map when a tornado struck, razing every structure to the ground. In 1925, Battery E encamped at Ft. Knox, Kentucky, won signal honors and was selected from the entire Division to fire the salute to Major General Howze, commanding the Fifth Army area. Mount Vernon's present armory was built in 1927 and the battery became truck-drawn on January 1, 1934. For the first time in the city's history, Mount Vernon was place under martial law when the Flood of 1937 hit the county. August 30, 1940, Battery E trained three weeks with the Second Army at Camp Wyeville, Wisconsin. Sixty-five thousand men participated in "war games," Battery B was on the invading "Blue" Army. Battery E was mobilized on January 17, preparatory to beginning a year's active duty. Members and officers of Battery E were to be no longer "watchdogs" of the State of Indiana, but "regulars" in the US Army. Over 3,000 atched them leave on January 29. Early in May, 1941 Battery E was quarantined for measles at Camp Shelby, Mississippi, but later that month battery men ran and jumped to win the 2nd Battalion Track & Field Meet with 42 points. When units of the Indiana National Guard were mustered into federal service, the state was left without a military force for service in the event of civil disturbance or disaster. Out of this imperative need for replacements came the Indiana State Guard and Company F of Mount Vernon. The Mount Vernon company maintained one of the best ratings in the regiment and participated in all regimental maneuvers. Company F was an infantry unit including a rifle platoon, machine gun quad and hand grenade squad.

At the conclusion of Maneuvers in 1942, the local Guard unit did not return to Camp Shelby, but continued its training in amphibious warfare at Camp Carrabelle, Florida. On March 1, 1942 the unit was renamed Battery B, 163rd Field Artillery. After this training Battery B established itself at Camp Livingston, Louisiana and remained there until it left for service with the 38th Division in the Pacific. Battery B sailed from the Port of New Orleans, December 1943 for the Hawaiian Islands, arriving there January 21, 1944. It left for New Guinea and the Philippines July 11, 1944. Battery B men distinguished themselves in the Battle of Zig-Zag Pass and the Island off Coregidor to open the mouth of Manila Bay and also in the defense of the water supply of Wah Wah Dam. The 38th Division killed 26,697 Japanese to lead all Allied divisions in number of enemy killed in any Pacific campaign. The Division was in action for 198 consecutive days. The Battalion was deactivated on November 7, 1945. Battery B, 163rd Field Artillery, was re-organized September 9, 1947." Throughout the following years Battery B was recognized with a number of "Superior" and " High Excellent" ratings during training and federal inspection.

The <u>Mount Vernon Democrat</u> concluded the article writing, "The men and their deeds in days gone by who built the splendid tradition for the Indiana National guard are by now perhaps only vaguely remembered with places and battles. But, this achievement of success in hazardous and dangerous military duties has blended into an immortal fame and respect for the Hoosiers as military men. Then too, maybe the old memories are important enough to instill a fighting spirit into county residents and they will "go to battle" also to keep the Guard in Mount Vernon."

But all the efforts to keep the guard failed. Battery "B" moved to Evansville.

Indiana: 1970s

Indiana government experienced numerous changes in the early 1970s. In 1970, voters approved a constitutional amendment mandating annual sessions of the General Assembly. Prior to this, the legislature had met only every other year. Under the new system, the Assembly would meet for 61 days in odd-numbered years, 30 days in even-numbered years. The first "long" session was held in 1971. Legislation passed in 1972 allowed the governor to serve two consecutive terms. Nominations for governor, lieutenant-governor, and U.S. Senator were made in statewide primaries rather than in party conventions, under legislation passed in 1975.

The state capital experienced major governmental changes of its own. Approved by the Legislature in 1969, UNIGOV began in 1970 to merge the local Indianapolis government with that of Marion County into one city-county government. Indianapolis hosted the U.S. Conference of Cities in 1971, and under the leadership of mayors Richard Lugar and William Hudnut, began a campaign for recognition as an amateur sports capital.

Indiana politics in the 1970s continued a Republicans trend that had begun with Edgar Whitcomb's election as governor in 1968. Speaker of the House Otis R. Bowen was elected governor in 1972 and reelected in 1976, the first Indiana governor since Henry Schricker elected to two terms, and the first since 1852 to serve two consecutive terms. In 1876, Indianapolis Mayor Richard G. Lugar defeated Vance Hartke for his seat in the U.S. Senate. The state went for Richard Nixon by a landslide in 1972, and for Gerald Ford in 1976.

Through Republican leadership, Indiana adopted a number of fairly progressive programs in the 1970s. In 1971, the state set limits on the amount of phosphorus in detergents, becoming one of the first states to act on this environmental concern. Aso in 1971, the Indiana Committee for Higher Education was established. In 1973, state teachers were granted the right to collective bargaining. The state also saw a major property-tax relief bill in 1973. Personal property taxes were frozen or rolled back, while corporate income taxes were raised. The bill also raised the state sales tax from

2 to 4 percent. State aid to schools was increased; following the 1973 bill, the state paid about two-thirds of the cost of public schooling while local communities paid about one-third, reversing the pre-1973 ratio. A step away from the patronage system was taken in 1977, when fee profits from personalized license plates were divided between the Republican and Democratic parties.

Two new facilities opened to take advantage of Indiana's waterway connections. The port of Burns Harbor, on Lake Michigan, opened in 1970. At the other end of the state (at the other end of the decade), the Southwind Maritime Center opened at Mount Vernon in 1979.

The worst tornadoes since 1965 hit southern Indiana in April 1974; the southeast corner of the state was particularly hard-hit by the series of tornadoes moving from Kentucky through Indiana toward Xenia, Ohio.

In 1970, the Indianapolis Museum of Art -- formerly the Herron Museum -- moved to its new building overlooking the White River. The next year, the last all-Indiana railway line, the Monon, consolidated with the Louisville and Nashville system. Former Governor Harold Handley died in 1972, former Governor Roger Branigin in 1975. The first girl's state basketball tournament was held in 1976.

As the decade closed, Indiana and the nation were hit with a severe economic recession; before it ended, more than 250,000 Hoosiers had lost their jobs. The 1970s closed with Indiana looking toward better times ahead in the 1980s.

Posey County

Five-thousand, five-hundred and eighteen trees were to be cleared for Hovey Lake expansion project in Point Township. More than 600 pecan trees and maple varieties were included. Only the cypress trees were excluded from the contract. Jasper Corporation, which was awarded this part of the project, was given three years to clear the area. Swampy conditions in the proposed lake area made it impossible to move heavy equipment around more than a few months out of the year. The Hovey Lake project neared completion in 1976 and the benefits were already evident. Almost 12,000 visitors came to Hovey in 1975, and by April 24, 1976 a total of 13,000 had already been making use of the new facilities. By the end of July, the new checking station and 50-acre campground was completed along with a ramp, dock, picnic area and rest rooms. The Uniontown Ferry Road would be relocated west of the site to avoid intervening with the new activities. Although there were concerns over another type of intervention -- the Harmonie State Recreation Area worries were met with the argument that most visitors to the site near New Harmony were swimmers and campers, while the Hovey area attracted fishermen. The new Hovey Checking Station was designed to attract wildlife enthusiasts and had available a checking counter, offices, kitchen facilities, a bunk room (the later two primarily built for use by biologists). While active in hunting, Hovey Lake's primary purpose remained the conservation and protection of wildlife.

While Hovey was nearing completion, the Harmonie State Recreation Area opened for its new season in May 1976. The Park opened with two new miles of road under construction, 200 modern and 60 primitive camping sites, a new concession stand at the pool, a firewood concession for campers and a campground general store.

Mount Vernon became the subject of a "filler" program for a production company in 1976, when a freelance photographer from Los Angeles began to work on a documentary called "Now and Then." The seven-minute film took an old photograph and recreated the same setting on film. Then when the film was developed, the negatives were spliced forming a serial showing the same scene in different years.

More than 200,000 barrels of crude oil were shipped to the Farm Bureau Refinery in 1976, but the newspaper reported that the plant's refinery capacity had "far outstripped the supplies of domestic oil." The paper went on to say that "...the company is able to refine 22,000 barrels of crude oil each day, domestic supplies of oil only yield an average of 10,000 barrels each day."

"A centuries-old custom will be broken at St. Wendell Church in Posey County..." read the <u>Mount Vernon Democrat</u> in August, 1970. The break in the custom gave three laymen of the parish authority to distribute Holy Communion. Previously, only ordained priests and deacons were allowed this privilege. An Evansville Bishop announced that he had been granted authority from Rome to break the custom, "where a need exists." The need did definitely exist in the Posey County church where only one priest had the responsibility of distributing Communion to more than 300 people.

The 1970s brought a new problem to the county farmers. This time, it wasn't flooding, but a corn blight. Bold headlines appeared in county newspapers in 1970 urging farmers to wear masks in order to stay out of the way of the toxic gases given off by the fungus. The reports also urged farmers to harvest corn early to avoid further spread of the damaging blight. Tests showed that the fungus did not affect cattle. Although the entire state as well as the southern portion of the United States and the northern Corn Belt was affected by the blight, the southern half and Posey County seemed to be the hardest hit. Losses were estimated at almost 50 percent. Again in 1971, the blight hit. This time a prepared Posey County faced the problem. The expected loss of 50 percent turned into only 15 or 20 percent, but caution was still high. Farmers were offered a preventative, a fungicide to spray on corn that showed signs of the blight. It was not a cure. Corn was again harvested early and was dried artificially to prevent the spread of the killer fungus. Former County Extension Agent said "yield will be much better than last year. Last year wasn't anything to remember if you wanted to think of something pleasant to remember." The only good news given to farmers was that the corn blight would probably not be a problem the following year.

An area just east of the county seat drew attention in September 1970, when plans were announced for the construction of a "giant, sophisticated river port facility and industrial court." The 13 million project included the use of 1,110 acres of flood free and flood plain land. Specuatlion included land at the municipal airport site and high-production agricultural land. A thousand acres of land just east of McFadden Creek was included in the plans for future development.

"A daydream might find the train arriving and many people with large trunks and animals unloading at the depot," read the <u>Mount Vernon Democrat</u> in March, 1972. It brought back memories to many residents who remembered the old opera house (in 1972, the Alles Brothers Furniture Store). The three-story building, celebrating its 125th birthday, was erected in 1817 by the Masonic Lodge, which used the third floor. The opera was housed on the second floor and various businesses took up the space on the ground floor. In 1922,

57

the entire building was sold to the Alles family.

While the General Electric Company plant in Mount Vernon brought employment and growth to the county -- it also brought about a tragic incident in August, 1972. Two 26-year-old men who were readying the plant after a weekend shutdown were asphyxiated by nitrogen as they entered a piece of equipment to check it. One man was a Poseyville resident, the other from New Harmony. Both men had wives and small children.

Another mishap of a different kind almost hit Posey County over Labor Day weekend in 1972. Alexander and Duncan Productions were scouting for a rock concert location, and Posey County was among the sites being considered for the "Rockfest." At the end of August, Posey Judge Steve Bach issued a temporary restraining order against the possible staging of a rock festival. The judge ruled that the production company had not made sufficient plans for the expected crowd of 300,000. Sufficient plans included water supply, sanitation facilities, trash disposal and improved roads. He further stated that the event would "constitute a nuisance and deprive Posey County, Mount Vernon, Griffin, Poseyville, Cynthiana and New Harmony of police protection." The final site chosen for the three-day Rockfest was Bull Island, a part of Illinois on the Wabash River. A news editor from the Mount Vernon Paper attended the concert and confirmed what the Judge had feared. He reported, "It was a whole different world...The values, laws and mores which we accept in this world did not apply there." ...Nudity, I later discovered was accepted in this 'other society.'... There was a shortage of everything except drugs, it seemed... At night, some of the girls sold themselves -- to support their drug habit and buy food for the next day."

Two to 10 years and a more than $100 in fines was the penalty in 1973 for cattle rustling, and Posey County was a victim to this crime. Late August, a farmer near Griffin reported six head of cattle stolen and another farmer who left his gate open was missing cattle and was having no luck locating them. More than 85 concerned farmers from Lynn, Harmony and Robb attended a meeting in New Harmony to take a closer look into the situation. The shortage and high price of beef and the opening of Interstate 64 across the Wabash River might have prompted the incident. Farmers were concerned that the toll free bridge invited rustlers because no one was there to notice anything suspicious, especially in the early hours of the morning. Suggestions to combat the problem ranged from making sure cattle were branded or tagged, to a radio link between farmers and the sheriff's office and 24-hour patrols

Beginning in late December and continuing into January 1974 , three winter storms hit Posey County. Each storm dumped layer-upon-layer of snow and sleet, causing hazardous driving, school closings and tired employees from the State Highway Department. Crews worked around-the-clock to plow and salt roads. One county engineer remarked that they were fighting a losing battle, although the severity of the final storm was not as great as the previous two.

Poor weather continued throughtout the year. In August, the county experienced a drought that caused considerable crop damage. But, the story didn't end there. The dryness caused the fire department to respond to grass fires once or twice daily. The Farmer's Almanac showed normal July rainfall in the Ohio River Valley was about 3.6 inches, yet Posey had only recorded .58 inch of rain that month.

One New Harmony resident was so concerned about the water system in the city that he conducted his own tests and show them to the town board in mid-August. The resident claimed that the water was at times unfit to drink, containing impurities such as bug carcasses and wings, sand, lime, rust, calcium chloride and petroleum. He even went as far as to hold a sample of water from his house and a sample of the Wabash River... showing that the River sample appeared clearer than the city water. The waterworks supperintendent countered the claim, saying that there was no way bug carcasses could enter the system due to the high pressure inside the lines. He also explained that several hydrants had been tested recently, causing surges in the water pressure. The town board did not ignore the issue, seeking immediate action from the Posey County Health Department and the Indiana State Board of Health. More than 20 samples were taken from various homes in the community, and chemical samples also were extracted. By the end of August, reports showed that New Harmony's water system was safe, although there were high amounts of iron, manganese and calcium. While the levels were high, they did not pose a threat to residents. The chief of the water section of the state agency recommended a "flushing" of the system, adding that it should be flushed once a year. This process involved opening city hydrants.

The county found itself dealing with another potential health problem in 1976 when the Indianapolis office of the United States Department of Agriculture confirmed that three herds of county beef cattle were infected with tuberculosis. The disease was discovered during a routine check of a slaughtered cow. The USDA was not sure of the source or extent of the problem. There was a sigh of relief among citizens when a newspaper article reported that there was no danger to humans unless they were to drink unpasteurized milk from infected cows, however, none of the diseased animals were dairy cows. After the extent of the problem was discovered, the USDA set about "depopulating" the infected herds.

The Bicentennial year brought out many a flag, patriotic decoration and county-wide festivities. From Los Angels and Washington to Valley Forge, Pennsylvania, the Santa Fe and Oregon Trail wagons headed across America. Posey County, Indiana was the first wagon stop in Indiana after the Ohio River barge trip. The Pennsylvania group sponsoring the pilgrimage also presented a 45-minute Bicentennial show in Mount Vernon. Sixty wagons were crafted for the journey. One representing each state, five Conestogas and five chuck wagons.

There weren't any barges traveling on the Ohio in January 1977. In fact no vehicles could move on the Ohio after a severe cold snap left the river frozen. A minus 21 degree temperature was recorded, making it the second coldest temperature ever recorded in the area. The entire state was suffering the cold weather blast, which closed schools (a total of eight days in Posey county), creating a fuel crisis in some areas and snapping power lines. Another Arctic blast hit the Posey area again in late January averaging minus 38 degrees (including windchill). Cold accompanied with 40-mile-per-hour winds again closed schools as well as businesses and industries. On January 28, the Indiana State Police reported that they were closing all roads north of Terre Haute due to heavy snowfall. Indiana Governor Otis Bowen declared a state of emergency in the state due to a shortage in energy supplies.

February brought its problems when city and county officials were informed of a 70-ton chemical slug of carbon tetrachloride moving toward Mount Vernon. Because traces of the dangerous chemical were already detected in the water, city officials began a combative effort by adding carbon to filtered water removing much of the chemical. Reports showed 42 parts per billion in Evansville. The US Environmental Agency calls anything over 50 parts per billion "unsafe." Residents were at first urged to boil water, then the suggestion was dropped. Carbon tetrachloride commonly used as a cleaning fluid and known to cause cancer in laboratory animals, damages the liver and kidneys.

But, the chemical spill was only one problem the water company faced. The severe cold snap broke many city lines. Water department crews were busy in Mount Vernon with more than 50 reported breaks. It was estimated the frozen pipes left 100 homes in the city without water.

Meanwhile, March brought good news to New Harmony. The Antheneum project in 1975 was well under way in 1977, and was scheduled for completion in 1978. The Antheneum (meaning literary or scientific association) was constructed to begin a major economic boost for the area by providing an interpretive center, a 200-seat theater, a restaurant, amphitheater and surrounding parks and gardens. The interpretive center, only one part of the $1.5 million project funded by the Lilly Endowment, would become home to exhibits and other historic memorabilia of the town. This center for visitor orientation and community cultural event was to be architecturally designed to reflect community life and ecological soundness.

April found Mount Vernon still in the middle of a water crisis that nearly shut down the water works. Samples sent to the U.S. Environmental Protection Agency came back indicating the chemical traces in the water were well above the "concern point" due to a second chemical spill that reached the city in 1977 as a result of a sewage plant accident in Louisville. Hexachlorocyclopentadiene and octachlorocyclopentene were found in the water supply, causing the EPA to contact the Indiana State Board of Health to recommend shutting down the system. However, the city did not hear from the State Board of Health, but finally received word that the city could shut it down if it wanted to play it extremely safe. The shut-down was not imposed, due to the large number of industries dependent on the local water supply. At the same time, residents were urged only to use as much water as necessary until the slugs passed. It was estimated that the two chemicals, which were traveling eight hours apart, would take 30 hours to pass the city. Also, it was estimated that is would cost $3,000 to $4,000 to flush the city lines. The February spill cost $1,200 in chemicals and manpower to combat the slugs.

The last year the statewide War Souvenir Campaign made its rounds was in 1959. Eighteen years later in 1977, a similar campaign began, formed by a special bomb squad from Ft. Benjamin Harrison, They came trained and equipped to handle anything from fire crackers to tactical nuclear weapons. Although the word "souvenir" usually has a positive connotation, the campaign has a far more serious view. The purpose of the statewide sweep was to uncover items taken by residents such as hand grenades, rifle grenades, mortar and small artillery shells, blasting cans and "dud" ammunition. The seriousness of the situation was evident in 1959 when a hand grenade, deemed safe by a war souvenir collector, exploded in Beech Grove, Indiana killing two children and injuring fire others. The 1977 campaign stressed that all items would be picked up with no question asked.

The Federal Housing and Community Development Act, which had funded projects in the Mount Vernon area for the past two year, rejected its 1977 application. The money went to Boonville, which had in the works a $319,000 massive rehabilitation project. Mount Vernon received 66 point on the application, and Boonville got a score of 73. Poseyville sought funding through the HCDA for construction of a multi-purpose park and for tiling a drainage ditch. Reports indicated the Poseyville's application was completely rejected.

July, 1977 weather brought with it storms that raged through the county with 60-mile-per-hour winds. Although no injuries were reported, trees were uprooted, power was lost and several unconfirmed tornados were reported.

Accident victims from the January 1979 storm crowded area hospitals. For a few days in mid-January freezing rain had made transportation nearly impossible, school and businesses closed and weather reports issuing "winter-storm warnings" frequented television and radio broadcasts.

For more than 20 years, two capped bottles sat unnoticed on a shelf at Mount Vernon High School. The contents of the bottle -- picric acid -- had made officials take a second look. The acid, a poisonous chemical, was used by the Japanese and Chinese during World War II to make hand grenades. An Indiana University professor expressed concern that the crystallized acid could explode from the friction created when the cap was removed. Several other Indiana high schools reported bottles of the same acid. These were removed and no injuries were reported. An explosives expert from the Indiana State Police arrived to advise officials on the safest procedure.

The office of County Prosecutor attracted attention from the Federal Bureau of Investigation in 1979 on the 1978 Posey elections. Allegations pointed toward vote buying. The incumbent, Republican Bill Gooden, said, "I'm aware of no vote buying that went on, however, I am not naive that this sort of thing happens." Local attorney James Redwine, who ran against Gooden in the 1978 election stated that he was not the source of the allegations, but had heard the information and had passed it along. The Republican Party chairman felt that even if it had occurred, it was at such a small level it would ultimately prove insignificant in the outcome of the vote. The Federal Bureau found nothing that indicated vote buying.

The complaints had been building since 1904. Actually the complaints were about the building -- the Alexandria Free Public Library. For 75 years the library maintained the same address and the same building. Problems began when the library outgrew its space. A variety of complaints finally spurred efforts to raise the monies needed to erect a new library -- not enough book space, added and makeshift shelving, an increase of 2,100 books since the library opening in 1904, and not enough seating. When anyone wanted to view microfilm, the lights had to be turned out. Not only was the building hard to heat, it was inaccessible to handicapped persons. Only adding to problems was no display area. Two years earlier an organization formed to promote the library called Friends of the Library had donated funds and the project was under way.

1970 Plans for a "giant, sophisticated river port facility and industrial court" were realized in 1979, when the Southwind Maritime Centre was officially dedicated. THe years of planning that preceded the opening actually began in 1969 when the General Assembly of Indiana appropriated $50,000 for study that would ultimately develop a public port on the Ohio river.

Plans turned into steady progress in 1970 when Mount Vernon was chosen as the site for the port. One year later, a contest produced the winning name: South W(estern) IND(iana) Maritime Centre.

A construction permit was issued in 1972 and a contract was awarded the following year. During the ground-breaking ceremonies, Governor Otisa R. Bowen spoke of the port as being an "unparalleled asset" to the state. Although it was not yet completed by 1975, the port handled cargo.

By 1977, 157,324 tons of cargo moved through the Southwind Maritime Centre and in 1978 it handled 385,000 tons of corn beans, wheat, fertilizer and miscellaneous cargo.

Indiana: 1980s

The 1980s opened with Indiana, as well as the rest of the country, in the grip of an economic recession. Manufacturing centers were particularly hard-hit. Muncie and Anderson ranked among the top ten state cities in unemployment, each with a jobless rate of more than 18 percent. More than a quarter of a million Hoosiers lost their jobs before the recession ended in 1982.

Indiana in 1980 approved a $32 million state loan to Chrysler Corporation. Part of the federally-arranged bailout package, the state loan was intended to benefit Chrysler's plants in Kokomo, New Castle, and Indianapolis. In 1984, after an offer of $25 million in state incentives, General Motors agreed to build a truck assembly plant near Fort Wayne. Similar incentive offers brought other businesses to the state, including several cooperative ventures with foreign firms. The new jobs helped revive Indiana's manufacturing sector, still recovering from the 1979-1982 recession.

Indiana politics of the early 1980s mirrored the nation's conservative trend. Republican Lieutenant-Governor Robert Orr was elected to succeed Otis Bowen in 1980; the same year Indiana gave its support overwhelmingly to Ronald Reagan for President. With considerable help from the Moral Majority, Congressman J. Danforth Quayle of Huntington was elected Senator, turning back Birch Bayh's bid for a fourth term. In less than 20 years, Indiana's choice of governor and senators had swung from moderate-liberal Democrats to moderate-conservative Republicans.

In 1981, the selection of candidates for lieutenant-governor was returned to the party conventions. The choice had been made by primary since 1975. The Orr administration increased both sales and income taxes in 1982, shortly after the November elections. Despite the unpopularity of this maneuver, Orr was handily re-elected in 1984.

Environmental concerns captured the attention of many Hoosiers in the 1980s. Several reports raised concern over acid rain, the result (in large part) of the coal-fired power plants Indiana and many other states depend on. Whatever Indiana's concern about coal, the major alternative -- nuclear energy -- proved even less popular. In 1983, bowing to the pressure of environmental, civic, antinuclear and consumer groups, Public Service Indiana canceled further work on its Marble Hill nuclear reactor near Madison.

Songwriter Hoagy Carmicheal died in 1981. Composer of "Stardust" and a number of other classic songs, he had attended Indiana University and lived in Bloomington several years.

The General Assembly offered some sweeping changes in the 1980s. A 1985 law allowed cross-county banking and multi-bank holding companies. Many small banks consolidated with large banks, becoming local branches of the larger systems. In 1989, following a favorable referendum vote in 1988, legislation was passed providing for a state lottery and parimutuel betting. The last major stronghold of patronage, the license branch system, was also overhauled in the 1980s, removing license branches from political control.

Indianapolis, under the leadership of Mayor William Hudnut III, continued to refine and define its image as a city. The 1888 Union Station, something of an eyesore for years, was renovated into an elegant mall of upscale shops and trendy restaurants. The state capitol building was also restored to its 1880s glory. Office space rose in downtown towers and suburban office plazas. New hotels opened to house the expected crowds. Plans moved ahead for the Circle Center Mall, a complex taking a good part of the heart of downtown Indianapolis.

Perhaps the one facet Indianapolis has stressed is its status as "amateur sports capital" of the nation. Various sporting events and championships were lured to Indianapolis. In 1987, the city played host to the Tenth Pan-American Games, the first games held in the U.S. since 1959. While most of the games took place in Indianapolis, some yachting events were held in Michigan City, and equestrian events at the Hoosier Horse Park near Columbus.

Indianapolis' major commitment to its sports-center image was the Hoosier Dome, built in the early 1980s. It was a stadium without a team until 1984, when the Baltimore Colts packed Mayflower moving vans one night and drove from Baltimore to become the Indianapolis Colts. The Colts, like the basketball Indiana Pacers, have had their good and bad seasons through the 1980s. While Indianapolis doesn't yet have a pro baseball team, its AAA Indianapolis Indians had garnered its three consecutive AAA championships in the latter 1980s.

Hoosier politics took several turns in the late 1980s. In 1988 a Hoosier was once again on a national ticket, when Senator Dan Quayle was named Republican George Bush's vice-presidential running mate. Despite questions about his inexperience, scholastic and war records, Quayle proved an effective campaigner. Bush and Quayle were elected in November 1988.

The same election, however, brought another twist to Indiana's political picture. Evan Bayh, son of the man Quayle had defeated for the Senate seat, was elected Governor of Indiana. Democrats came within a few seats of taking the state Senate, and the State House was split between the parties, 50 seats apiece. Since no party could gain a majority to elect a speaker, two speakers -- one Democrat, one Republican -- were elected, to head the House on alternating days.

Congressman Dan Coats, who had been elected to Dan Quayle's House seat, was appointed to take Quayle's Senate seat when Quayle became vice-president. In a special election to fill the congressional seat, Democrat Jill Long, whom Quayle had defeated for the Senate in 1986, was elected.

Posey County

"I wouldn't exactly call them bumper crops," said a Purdue University agronomist, "But they were very good." Posey County did well in overall crops yields for 1978 and 1979, but 1980 proved to be a difficult year. The dry, hot weather that hit the area when the corn was in the reproductive stage made for short ears with few kernels. Crop yields showed a decrease of 35 percent from 1979. The only bright spot was the drier whether meant less mold on the corn crop.

County council candidate Jo Anne Schmitt, with $10 out of her own pocket and $23 in donations, captured her office. The only Democrat elected to the council, and one of the few women to ever hold the position, Schmitt was recognized for her soapbox that she carried around -- everywhere she went. "People laughed about the soapbox, but they asked real questions about what I could do," Schmitt said.

It wasn't razed, it was renovated. The Posey County jail received a $500 donation from the local Moose Lodge to be used for improvemnts. Once renovated, the jail would function as a group house providing shelter and care for up to eight troubled children.

New Harmony wasn't looking for renovation, but a new school. And, that's what a Ball State University team of educators suggested. A study on the district's educational program, facilities and financial capacity found the existing 1913 school building inadequate to handle 1980s New Harmony students. The head of the study team further said "the building is not suitable for elementary or secondary education and has more then outlived its educational life expectancy." The cost of remodeling or sending students to another district did not prove cost effective. Building a 35,000-square-foot kindergarten through 12th grade school using the current gymnasium, would cost $2.1 million. A new building and gym would total $3 million, a K-8 building would cost $2.4 million and a K-6, about $1.8 million.

The sending of most critically ill patients to Evansville and a $50,000 to $60,000 deficit were among the reasons for the closing of Welborn Hospital's Posey County emergency room in mid-July 1982. Only 900 patients used the emergency room in 1982 -- almost one-third the number of patients that checked in the previous year. Other reasons giving for the closing involved a reduction in hours and an incorrect phone listing in the Evansville directory. "Life Flight," a new air ambulance service, took the place of the emergency room. The service was available to people within a 90-mile radius of Evansville, which includes all of Posey County.

Fear of dropping in class rank and grade point average as well as a fear of failing to meet college entrance criteria made many students shy away from taking difficult or honor courses in high school. A faculty committee at the Mount Vernon high school worked on three policies to encourage higher attendance in the more difficult classes. The proposals included a requirement for students to receive at least one "A" to be on the honor roll; to divide honors graduates into groups to recognize the highest ranking students; and to develop a weighted grade point average whereby students taking honor or difficult classes would receive additional credit.

The coliseum that caused so much controversy earlier became property of the county in 1982 when commissioners and the coliseum board signed a 99-year lease on the war memorial. With the lease signed, the county could begin the renovation work needed to house additional county offices. The renovation had been the topic of many discussions in the past year. Even with more than $1 million in courthouse funds and the location of the courthouse in the coliseum could not spur renovation. The county had no legal authority over the building until the lease was signed. A seven-year-old study estimated that the renovations would cost around $500,000.

Controversy played a big part when Busler Enterprises began plans to move to Posey County near Ind. 62. When Bulser Enterprises filed an application for three-way liquor license in July 1983, tempers rose. According to state law, an application with the Alcoholic Beverage Commission that is denied cannot be submitted a second time until a year has passed. However, an application that is withdrawn can be submitted 30 days later. Busler resubmitted its application and was granted permission to serve alcohol in October. Executives from Busler maintained that the application was withdrawn. Demonstrators claimed that it had been denied. No one knew who was right. No minutes were taken at the July meeting. Then in May, eighteen Marrs Township residents living from 400 feet to five miles from the proposed complex filed a petition for a judicial review of the liquor license granted to Busler Enterprises. Although the state commission found that the local board acted properly in granting the permit, that Busler would be located in a non-residential area, that the area had adequate police protection, and that the company's food sales meet the $100,000 per year minimum, residents argued that the officials were "arbitrary, capricious, and abuse of discretion and otherwise not in accordance with law," among other complaints. Marrs residents lost their battle, and Buslers got their license.

Alcohol was the subject of another discussion -- this time in Mount Vernon. City officials considered adopting an ordinance that would prohibit opening alcoholic beverages in public. Resident's complaints began to get louder with recent alcohol-related fighting incidents. Other residents said they would not take their children to the community skating rink because of the groups gathered nearby drinking alcohol. City officials also realized the ordinance would be difficult to enforce and wondered how to take in account festivals and special events that sold alcohol beverages. The following month the same ordinance was one-step closer to becoming reality when the first reading was passed by the city council. Although the first step was out of the way, the proposed ordinance had to go through two more readings before it could be enforced. The punishment for possessing an open alcoholic beverage container in public could result in a fine of no less than $1 and no more than $100. The ordinance passed both readings and the "Broken Seal Ordinance" became law.

Late in 1983, city councilmen showed their support for a proposal which would give Indiana State University at Evansville independence from the controls of Indiana State officials in Terre Haute. USI, if independent, would have total control over all programming and administrative responsibilities. A trustee board, independent of the one at Terre Haute, would maintain, direct and oversee all functions of the campus. USI gained independence July 1, 1985.

A statement by a local attorney promising swift and vigorous legal action brought a crowd of more than 900 to its feet in March 1984 meeting held at the Mount Vernon High School auditorium. The heated statement centered on an application by Elk River Resource to building a coking plant 3.5 miles southwest of the county seat just neighboring the county's largest employer in 1984 -- General Electric. Residents clearly opposed the plant. Controversies between citizens and company spokespersons ranged from traffic problems, and construction procedures to environmental cost and levels of sulfur dioxide emissions. A representative of the Posey County Farm Bureau added that the emissions would have a negative effect on crops. Signatures of 5,000 persons against the building of a coking plant added to the oppositions. The New Harmony town board joined with opposers in mid-March proposing to write a letter to the State Air Pollution Control Board.

It appeared the Elk River had lost in June 1984 when the State Board of Health returned its application. The State Board of Health justified its actions saying it heard the company was seeking a possible site for its plant in Kentucky. Residents were thrilled after also hearing that local officials who studied the application determined the method that would be used to curb the dangerous emissions were not very effective. But, the matter was far from being over. In a response to the returned application, Elk River official stated, "The project in Mount Vernon is still very much alive, and as soon as Inland Steel finalizes its economic studies currently under way, and should the studies be favorable, we will return the application for further processing." Despite the response, Elk River did not locate in Mount Vernon.

When the Alexandrian Public Library turned 75 years old in 1979, it needed a new building. Five years later in 1984, the situation had not changed. During those years a feasibility study conducted by James Associates, and Indianapolis based firm, was under way. Although the figures were not official, James Associates suggested building a new two-story, 21,500 square-foot building which, completely furnished and landscaped could cost $2.75 million. Property eyed by the library board was in the city block just opposite the existing facility. When the final presentation was made, it was unanimously accepted by the library board. The study called for a design that was able to handle 60,000 volumes, twice the existing collection. The block bordered by Main, Fifth, Sixth streets and College Avenue proved to be the best location because of building visibility, public access, traffic patterns and parking and building approach. Some of the land was owned by residents, while the remaining property was owned by the Metropolitan School District of Mount Vernon but operated by the city council. This particular piece of land, College Park, would have to be transferred back to the school system before the library could use it. An agreement was made between the library and the city council. The latter agreeed to transfer powers if the library board agreed to let the land operate as a park unless it was actually used for construction of a new building and the old library would be turned over to the city when the new facility was completed. The board agreed. In June 1984 the city council returned College Park to the school district. Meanwhile, the library board continued to work with those resident who owned the other land needed to build a new facility. By October, a March 1985 grounding breaking was scheduled. The board at the Alexandria Free Public Library began the first steps necessary to sell $2.85 million in bonds to pay for the facility.

With plans well under way to begin a new building, another Mount Vernon operation shut down. In a quick decision, the 37-year-old J.R. Short Milling Company announced it would close it doors. The Chicago-based company said it owed it shutdown to competitive conditions. No further explanations were offered. The closing displaced 70 employees. Late in November 1988, the Milling Company made the news again. An early November morning, many residents awoke to black billowing clouds of smoke over the old J.R. Short building. Four wood floors collapsed, bringing one wall with it. Firefighters from Mount Vernon, Marrs Township and Evansville stayed on the scene until evening to supervise what was left of the smoldering building. A St. Louis resident, who had purchased the building, had planned to open it early the following year as an oats processing company.

Early in January 1985, reports indicated that the operation of Historic New Harmony would by taken over by Indiana State University-Evansville hinging on approval by the Indiana State University board of trustees. When the Lilly Endowment awarded a $25,000 grant to restore and develop the historic aspect of the town, Historic New Harmony, Inc. began. In the past 10 years Lilly Endowment had awarded $12.5 million in additional funds to its development. Lilly officials considered phasing out its involvement when the expected return on the investment was not met. The final $300,000 installment was due in 1985 and Lilly's involvement would end, unless USI took charge. All parties favored the change, and USI became the new manager. 1989 figures show that 50,000 people visit Historic New Harmony each year.

With one part fluoride mixed per billion parts water, New Harmony again made the news January 1985. With the state paying for the fluoride equipment, installation and the initial fluoride supply, the town board unanimously passed a resolution to have fluoride added to the water supply.

"We're asking all people to be patient. We'll get their mail to them sometime." This simple statement reflected only one of many problems caused by a February 1985 storm. Unmatched since the blizzard of 1978, the storm that hit Posey County closed all schools, 740 miles of roads, and delivered seven inches of snow, temperatures of 15 degrees below zero and gusts of 35 miles an hour. Although it did not quite fall under the definition of a blizzard, Sen. Joseph O'Day asked the governor's office to declare Posey County in a stat of emergency and send the National Guard to help clear the roadways.

Another problem affecting Posey County was not seasonal or dependent on the weather -- it was drunk driving. Grim statistics reported in 1985 showed that drinking and driving was the most often committed violent crime and significant cause of death among the young. It was the number one cause of death for all Americans to age 30. In response to the statistics and recent drinking and driving related incidents, 14 Mount Vernon students begin a Students Against Drunk Driving (SADD) chapter. The four goals of the SADD organization were to help eliminate the drunk driver and save lives; to conduct community alcohol awareness programs; to alert and inform students of the dangers of alcohol and driving and to organize a peer counseling program to help students who may have concerns about alcohol.

Early in January 1986 the Advisory Liaison Emergency Readiness Team (ALERT) began a fund-raising project that would bring an emergency warning and communication system to service the county seat. When the $125,902 goal was reached, the city would have sirens installed, the ability to use the 911 emergency number and use of and emergency control center.

If the new emergency system had been installed by May 1986, it would have been used. Two tornados ripped across the county at 4 p.m. on May 16. Several implement buildings were flattened, a Mount Vernon school bus with no one on board was toppled and mobile homes were demolished or severely damaged. Several area in Point Township, St. Philip and Blairsville were hit the hardest. With all the extensive damages, only four injuries were reported. The only fatality was a family dog.

After years of dreaming, planning and petitioning the Alexandria Free Public Library was completed and dedicated. A cornerstone, yet to be finished, would appropriately contain a copy of the invitation to the dedication ceremonies, editions of two county newspaper's containing coverage on the event, and a copy of the board resolution authorizing construction of the facility. A list of all the petitioners, a list of federal, state, city and county official, photographs of the library board and staff and their signatures and a copy of those who attended the dedication and open house were also added to the cornerstone. The final touch included a 1986 50-cent piece, quarter, dime, nickel and penny were among the contents. A finished building didn't mean plans for the new library were complete. Programs including space for literary classes, a tax form service for the elderly and GED classes were ideas already under way. The original structure, dedicated in October 1905, was given to the city, which planned to use the space for fire department sleeping quarters and storage areas. A year later, the newspapers reported that visitation to the new library had topped all records. The increase forced the library to open its doors on Sunday afternoons. Reports indicated that 11,418 persons were registered library-borrowers -- 62.38 percent of the population within the library district.

Posey County first animal cruelty case was tried by the circuit court early in 1987. Two years earlier, 56 dogs were found living on a residential property in very poor conditions. A shed, located in a field contained decomposing animals. Many of the animals were found exposed to the elements and without food or water. In 1987 the owner was given a choice: find homes for the dogs that were suited for adoption, pay for rabies vaccinations and give names and addresses of persons adopting the dogs, or serve six-month in the county jail. Five days later, the defendant chose to euthanize the remaining 24 dogs.

A group of Soviet dancers, usually known to tour the bigger cities, visited New Harmony. During their stay and performance, the Soviets had its first taste of rural America -- a Sunday afternoon barbecue and tours of historic New Harmony and Evansville. Jane Owen, a key figure in bringing the dance group to New Harmony said, "I think they might confuse some of the cities in their memories, but there is no way they will confuse their visit here with their visits to New York and Philadelphia."

And, the Russian dancers did not. After arriving via fire truck, flashing lights and a siren escort, the official tour director Mikhail Musikhim expressed his approval saying, "We have been in the United States six days and have been welcomed everywhere, but this welcome tops them all."

News on a new home arrest system hit the papers in February 1987. The system allowed those serving time and participating on a work release program to live at home while they worked. Previously, when work was completed, persons spent their time in jail. A leg bracelet sent information to a computer at Security Research Inc. in Evansville. Officials there are able to monitor the location of the person and send someone immediately if that person were found leaving the home or tampering with the device. Those desiring to participate in the program were required to pay a $50 starting fee and $49 per week afterward.

"It's kind of a no-win situation," one farmer said. Most of the crops had been planted when the rains came in May -- five inches in all. Thousands of acres of Psoey cropland were covered. Even when the waters receded and farmers could replant, one early frost could wipe out a great deal of crops. Big Creek had flowed over its banks throughout the county and at Solitude, SR 69 N was closed. School opened late due to impassable roads and flash floods occurred near Poseyville. Hearing from the National Weather Service the Wabash would hold steady until early June, didn't ease some farmer's fears near Griffin. Just as this news came, so did the news that the levee north of the town broke. Farmers in that area began the tiring process of ensuring that the southern portion of the levee, in danger of breaking, would be kept from doing just that.

Travelers through Posey County might not recognize the sign that says POSEYVILLE -- but, they might recognize the one that says, "Watermelon Capital of the World." Although there weren't as many melons growers in 1987 as in previous years -- those famous Posey County melons still had a fine reputation. While most of the melons are grown in Gibson County in a four mile wide by 15 mile long sandy stretch. The area just north called Poseyville served as the main marketing center for the melon for years, and therefore gained the fame. The decrease in melons-growers is due to the tremendous amount of work that goes into its production. More than a thousand acres of melons are estimated to be growing in the Poseyville-Johnson area. One melon farmer told this story. "A guy from Illinois who buys from me said he bought some Missouri melons, and they were tough and had no taste at all. From now on, he said if he can't find 'em here he just won't buy 'em." According to newspaper archives, Psoey County has been famous for its melons for more than 100 years.

Posey County Commission gave its okay to a proposal that bring a regional morgue and pathologist to serve an eight county area. Cases had previously been sent to the Pathology Department at Deaconess Hospital. Officials there announced that the practice will stop due to and overload. Without the hospital's service, all cases would have to be sent to the Indiana University School of Medicine in Indianapolis.

The summer of 1988 is remembered for heat, lack of rain and damaged crops. Posey County was no exception. By July of 1988 the county was eight inches below normal in rainfall and the corn and soybean crop were on the verge of destruction. Melon-growers in the county were warned that half the corp would be lost if rain didn't come in the next seven days. Posey farmers and farmers from all 92 counties were able to call the Drought Hotline for advise on everything from insects in the field to where to purchase hay for their livestock. More than 100 calls per day reached the Purdue Ag Center.

The rains finally came, but not in time for many farmers. Those who didn't farm enjoyed the break in dry 100-degree weather. Those who did tried to total up loses. The soybean crop in most areas was saved by the rain, but the corn crop suffered. In some Indiana counties, 50 to 75 percent of the crop was lost. Posey farmers showed a 45 to 50 percent loss. An $11 million debt, resulted from Texaco failed efforts on a takeover bid for the Pennzoil Corporation in 1985, forced the company to sell of many of its assets including quite a few service stations and several refineries. The closed refineries resulted in a loss of 400 in the southern Illinois Community and 40 jobs at the Mount Vernon barging facility on the Ohio River. Three years later, the Oil Producers Association Refining and Marketing Division made plans to put the two facilities back into production. Although no numbers were release by company spokesmen on how many new jobs the refinery would create, they announced that hopes to have the refinery operating by August 1989.

From Historic New Harmony to its most up-to-date industry, Posey County offers to residents and visitors a variety of educational and entertaining experiences.

Zion UCC Posey County, Indiana

CHURCH HISTORY

POSEY COUNTY, INDIANA
175th
Anniversary
1814 - History - 1989

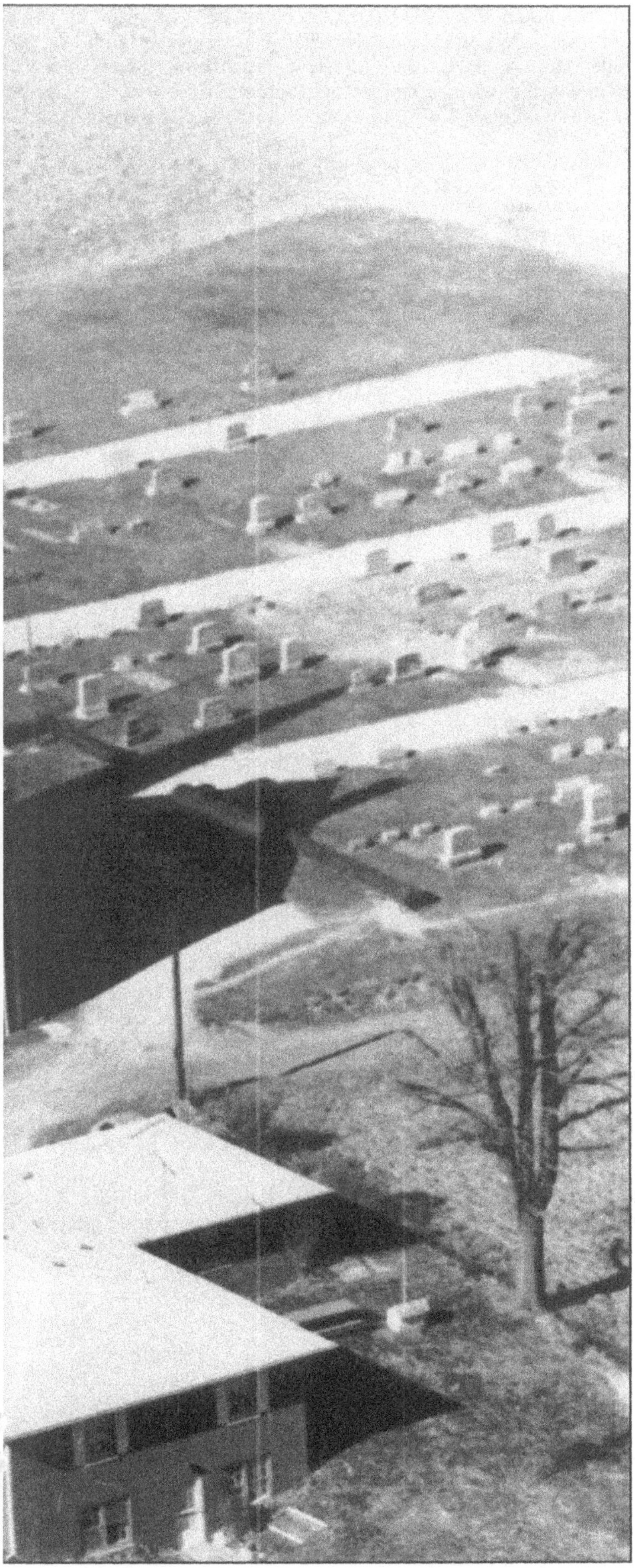

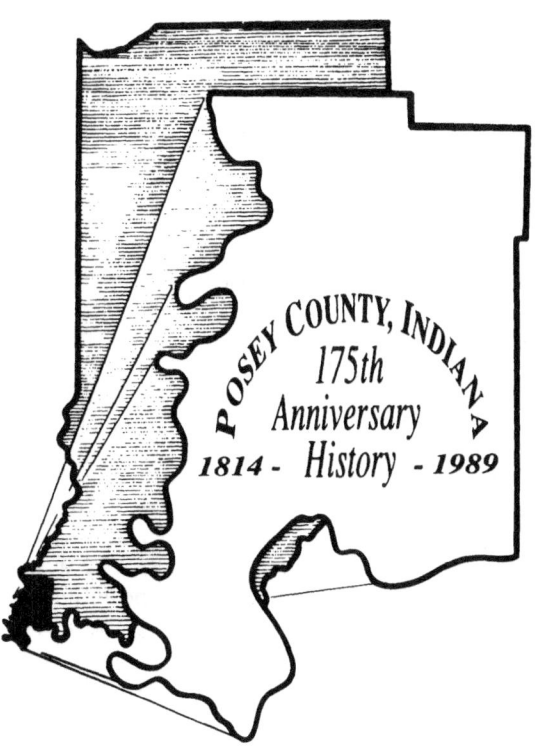

FIRST UNITED METHODIST CHURCH

While Peter Cartwright is credited by some as having launched the Methodist movement in Indiana in 1804. He was preceded by Nathan Robertson in 1799. Robertson moved from Kentucky to Charlestown and three years later organized a class at Gassaway near Charlestown. By 1807 there was one circuit in Indiana, one Methodist preacher, and 67 Methodists scattered throughout the sparsely populated Indiana Territory.

The life of the circuit rider was harsh, demanding, and exhausting: and it claimed its share of martyrs. Many an itinerant preacher was compelled to locate in some community. Such, we believe, was the case of Moses Ashworth, who came to the southwestern corner of the Indiana Territory and began to plant the seeds of Methodism in what is now called Posey County. He lived, worked and died here. From these humble beginnings, the church grew.

Moses Ashworth was buried near the Old Prairie Church in Black Township. The story is told that during the fifties when J. Kenneth Forbes was pastor, he went looking for the grave of Moses Ashworth. While unable to find the grave, he did locate the grave marker in a hog lot. The marker was transported to the campus of DePauw University where it now serves as a monument to our early Methodist circuit riders and itinerant pastors who laid the cornerstone of the church in this new frontier.

By 1810 there were three circuits in the Indiana Territory, four preachers, and 760 members. During this time the itinerants, men by the name of Wheeler, Garnett, Thomas King, Thomas David, and John Shrader, were making an impact upon this part of the territory. It is written of John Shrader, "he was a wonderful preacher and traveled extensively in this state and also in adjoining states."

On June 7, 1815, a preacher by the name of Thomas Templeton came to this area to live. He built a two room log cabin near what is called Templeton Grave Yard and held services there for many years.

The first mention of the Methodist Church in Mt. Vernon occured in 1828. At that time the church was a part of the Princeton Circuit, and services were held in the home of Jesse Y. Welborn whenever the circuit rider came to town. During this year a small brick schoolhouse was built on the northeast corner of Main and Sixth Streets. This community building served as a place of worship for all denominations.

By 1835 the southwestern corner of the state was growing and changing so rapidly that a change in method was imperative and the area became a part of the Evansville Circuit. The following year a Mt. Vernon Circuit was established under the leadership of Isaac McElroy.

In 1840 a church and parsonage were built on a lot on the north side of Fourth Street between Walnut and Mulberry Streets. This lot was donated and deeded to the Church by Jesse Y. Welborn.

In 1851 there were 11 pastoral appointments in the Mt. Vernon Circuit. After much deliberation it was determined that Mt. Vernon should become a station (one church, one pastor). Nathan Shumate was appointed as the first pastor. The church grew and under Rev. Shumate's leadership it was decided that a new building would be erected. A new church was built in 1852 on the west side of Walnut Street between Fourth and Fifth Streets. This lot was donated by Richard Barter. The new adjustment of the charge and the new church proved beneficial and consequently great prosperity was enjoyed.

In the fall of 1888, the Indiana Annual Conference was held in Mt. Vernon with Bishop John H. Vincent presiding.

In 1905 during the ministry of S.S. Penrod, the church decided to build once again when they outgrew its facilities. The new site was on the Corner of Sixth and Main Streets directly across from the first place of worship, the old Brick Schoolhouse. At the head of all of the building committees involved in this project was Milton Black who happened to be in his 96th year at the time. He attended the laying of the cornerstone in his wheelchair but was taken to his reward a few weeks before the completion of the church.

In October, 1915, during the pastorate of Rev. J.A. Breeden, the Centennial of Methodism in and around Mt. Vernon was celebrated.

On October 15, 1933, under the pastoral leadership of Edwin F. Shake, a merger agreement was reached between the First Methodist Church and the St. Paul's Methodist Episcopal Church which was connected to the Central German Conference. The St. Paul's Church was located on the southeast corner of Fourth and Locust Streets and was used as a parish house after the merger.

On February 25, 1939, Grover C. and Lena H. Keck and Franck and Louise K. Keck gave the former home of John and Addie K. Keck, parents of Grover and Franck, to the church for use as a parsonage as an expression of love and affection and tendered in memory of John and Addie K. Keck.

After years of Negotiation, a Plan of Union was agreed upon and on May 10, 1939, the Methodist Episcopal Church; the Methodist Episcopal Church, South; and the Methodist Protestant Church united to form the Methodist Church.

Again, in 1957 the Church outgrew its facilities and the Old Akron Style Church was torn down to be replaced by the present Georgian Colonial Style Church. This building was dedicated to the glory of God on August 31, 1958.

At the General Conference held in Dallas, Texas, on April 23, 1968, the Methodist Church and the Evangelical United Brethren Church merged and formed the United Methodist Church. We became the First United Methodist Church.

On Sunday, June 15, 1980, the Church celebrated a service of Consecration for the newly finished Education Building and the renovated church during the pastorate of Robert W. Koenig.

The people called Methodists have had a long and glorious history in Posey County. The faith and dedication of today's Methodists are not greater and no less than that of those who preceded them. Hearing the call and understanding the need, they respond, without fear of involvement, in the work of ministry to Church and Community. Let us continue to write the faith-history of tomorrow.

Rev. Harold R. Walker, Pastor

Mt. Vernon General Baptist Church

Rev. Samuel Jones is believed to be the first Baptist minister to preach in Posey County. The first services were held in private homes, or in groves with people sitting on the ground. Camp meetings, important for social aspects as well as religious, began in these early days.

In 1814, a small log house was built near the site of Templeton's Graveyard and present Hedges School, to be used by all denominations. In 1828, a small brick building was built near the corner of Sixth and Main Streets and all denominations worshipped either there or in the Court House until 1840. It is said the Hardshell Baptists and Methodists were the most active denominations to use these buildings.

In 1825 the General and Regular Baptists united and built Mt. Pleasant Church about five miles from Mt. Vernon, near Bufkin. Members of this church organized the Mt. Vernon General Baptist Church, April 27, 1873, in the Presbyterian Church. These members were Rev. Jacob Speer, Rev. T.M. Strain and Rev. Wilson Blackburn. Rev. Blackburn was chosen pastor, Daniel Miller, deacon and Robert Dowdy, clerk. The thirteen organizing members met in the homes for services.

In September 1873, the Church joined the Liberty Association of the General Baptists Denomination. There were the usual struggles and adjustments of a new church but by the year 1892, the membership was 137.

In 1887, a small church was built in the 800 block on Walnut Street. For some obscure reason the church became known as "Little Daisy". Church services were held twice a month, with Sunday School every Sunday afternoon. In 1890, with a membership of 150, the building was enlarged to double the space.

November 1891, the church was host to the General Association of General Baptists, the twenty second annual meeting. One important decision made at this meeting was the authorization of the writing of a Doctrine and Usages Book for the denomination.

In October, 1911, a parsonage was rented for the pastor, for $8.00 per month. In the next few years, much discussion was given to the location, building plans and solicitation of funds for a new church. August 1920 a lot on College and Seventh Street was purchased for $1,400.

In 1921, a full time pastor and a church advisory board were chosen, and a first church budget was adopted. The budget of $970.00 was divided in Pastor's salary, $750.00; lights $25.00; coal and kindling $20.00; janitor $75; and incidentals $100.00.

In 1923, the new church was dedicated and services began with the congregation assembling at the Walnut Street Church and marching to the new church at College and Seventh streets. Four long time members in the group were Mrs. Paris Adams, Mrs. Elmer Bergstrom, Mrs. Merle Phelps and Mrs. Vaughn Underwood.

In 1941, property to be used as a parsonage was purchased. In 1953, the church building was renovated and enlarged.

August 21, 1955, the radio ministry was begun at the same time WPCO was established in Mt. Vernon and broadcasts from the church have continued each Sunday morning at 11:00 o'clock since that time.

In 1965, the church purchased six acres of land at 1717 North Main Street for $18,000. The parsonage was built in 1968.

Ground breaking for the church building took place in October 1970 and construction began under the direction of Marvin Deig, the building chairman. More than 100 volunteers, some not members of the church, donated time to save an estimated $35,000 of the total cost of $210,000 for the project.

April 1, 1973, members of the congregation met at the College Street Church for the last time. From there a group of 100, followed by three church buses filled with people, musicians in a pickup truck, police and sheriff escort, marched to their new church home.

Present activities, important to the membership and community since they began, include Vacation Bible School in June each year, 1930; Camp program for all ages at General Baptist Camp Brosend near Newburgh, 1950; Bus ministry for a variety of services, 1959; Children's Church, 1968; Ladies Aid Society, two Missionary Societies, an active Youth Group, and the Men's Brotherhood.

Rev. Wilson Blackburn, the first pastor, was dedicated to this church and brought it through those trying, developing years. Since that time, more than twenty nine other dedicated pastors have served the church faithfully and well. From the membership, a number of young men have entered the ministry or other religious work.

The church membership in 1989 is 468. Services are held each Sunday morning and evening and Wednesday evening. Sunday School has an enrollment of 267. The church gives great support to the Home Mission Work in several states, to missionaries in foreign mission work in the Philippines, Jamaica and India, to Oakland City College, Oakland City, Indiana, a General Baptist College and other outreach projects of the church and denomination.

St. Francis Xavier Church

This historical sketch, written in 1989, spans a century. *The Poseyville News* of September 5, 1885, carried the announcement: "Arrangements are being made to build a Catholic church ... in the near future." The priest who guided the beginnings of the parish was Father Francis B. Luebermann. An acre of ground at the east end of Main Street was purchased from Miss Amelia Endicott in April, 1886, for $500. The foundation of the church was begun in the summer of 1886, and the laying of the cornerstone took place a few months later - Sunday, October 31. It was not until late summer of 1887 that the brick church, 34 x 76 feet, was completed. The cost, including some furniture, was $4,100.

In August of 1895 Father Andrew Schaaf became St. Francis' spiritual leader, and as time passed, he presided over a great deal of expansion. He purchased a second acre of ground from Miss Amelia Endicott for $500. The construction of a rectory, 32 x 42 feet with two stories and nine rooms, was finished in the fall of 1897 at a cost of $1,500. At the same time, one room of the school had been completed, and the school opened on September 13 with an enrollment of 25. In 1901 three acres a mile west of Poseyville were purchased for a cemetery. In 1903 ground adjoining the church property on the south was purchased, and the property included a residence which served as the home of the Sisters of St. Benedict for the next five years. In 1906 the school was enlarged, and in 1907 a tracker action pipe organ was purchased for the church. The present convent was completed in the spring of 1908.

Father Francis W. Wolf was pastor from 1910 to 1920, followed by Father Henry T. Verst. Under Father Verst an addition was added to the church and its dedication was celebrated on September 18, 1921. Father Henry C. Hunger became pastor in 1927. The man who became pastor four years later, Father John Schenk, served the parish for a quarter of a century - 1931 to 1956. He was followed by Father Alfred Niehaus, and during his pastorate - 1956 to 1968 - a new school was built in 1963. During the years that Father Roman Heerdink was pastor - 1968 to 1972 - the difficult decision was made to close the school. The next pastor was Father Alban Berling, O.S.B., and during his pastorate - 1972 to 1975 - the church was renovated. The pastor for the next twelve years was Father Albert J. Scheller. The new rectory was built during his pastorate. Father William Schwenk became pastor in July, 1987.

As of this writing, the number of families in St. Francis Xavier Parish is 284, and the total number of parishioners is 883. They are grateful to God for the first century of their parish and they trust in God's guidance during the months and years to come.

St. John's Episcopal Church
1855-1987

Founding and Early Beginnings

On June 4, 1855, a group of Mt. Vernon residents met at the office of Dr. M.S. Blunt to adopt a resolution organizing "a Protestant Episcopal Church to be known by the name and designation of St. John's Church, Mt. Vernon." The group elected S.S. Dryden, M.S. Blunt, James Cason, J. Conyngton and J. Pitcher as vestrymen. Also attending the meeting were The Rev. W.C. Armstrong, Thomas F. Prosser, John Hancock, W.P. Edson, J.P. Edson and H. Capelburg.

Until 1858, St. John's, a missionary station, was served alternately with New Harmony by The Rev. W.C. Armstrong. From 1858-1861, The Rev. Colley A. Foster, principal of a female seminary in Mt. Vernon, served as missionary-in charge. Services were held in a school room on alternate Sundays. Then, until 1892 when the present church was built, services were held in homes and later in the Lutheran Church of Christ.) (Now Trinity United Church of Christ.)

St. John's affiliated with the Diocese of Indiana in 1857. Bishop George Uphold preached in Mt. Vernon on two occasions, in 1859 and 1861. The Rev. W.S. Rowe is listed as Deacon Minister of St. John's in 1861. The 1862 parochial record reported one infant baptism, one communicant removed, seven present communicants, one funeral, thirty-four services held with thirty-one times preached, contributions and domestic missions collection totaling $1.20.

St. John's history from 1862-1891 has been lost. Other than a listing of clergy who performed baptisms and marriages, those twenty-nine years of worship and service remain hidden. The listing did, however, indicate that clergy did not remain long at the Mt. Vernon church, and often served other area Anglican churches as well.

In 1891, St. John's Women's Guild was organized by Mrs. Emily Uphold, daughter of Bishop Knickerbocker, first Bishop of Indiana.

One year later, in 1892, the present St. John's church was constructed. Bishop Knickerbocker was present on April 18, 1893 to bless the church and conduct the first service held there. Some names listed in the 1893 registry were Fitton, Nolte, Dixon, Fretageot, Hovey, Spencer and Brittlebank.

MINISTRY OF THE WOMEN'S GUILD

Following the building of the church, the Women's Guild assumed the responsibility of handling the church's day-to-day operation and authorized payment of all bills, including the Diocesan Assessment.

Although there were times during the following years that St. John's functioned without the benefit of clergy, it never operated without the benefit of the Women's Guild, once the Guild had been organized.

Throughout the history of the church, the Guild involved itself in outreach projects such as lending the church organ to a local Christian Church for a revival, helping needy churches in Arizona and New Hampshire; and working with the Red Cross during World War I, making surgical dressings and purchasing surgical instruments.

The Guild paid for building the church basement and putting in a furnace in 1916.

St. John's was closed for ten months in 1925 due to a shortage of clergy. The years which followed were years of financial struggle. In 1933, when the fate of St. John's hung precariously in the balance, the church school (organized in 1930) held its classes in homes to save on the coal bill. The future of the small church seemed dim. But the Guild remained active, refusing to give in to discouragement, holding onto faith with an energy and will to continue.

BISHOP'S COMMITTEE

The church survived and in 1937, the Bishop's Committee reorganized with Henry Kling serving as Vice-Chairman. The Committee's stated purpose was to reorganize the church and relieve the women from some of their many responsibilities.

1935 TO THE PRESENT

Again we come to a period of St. John's history, 1935-1944, which is lost. The year 1951 is next mentioned in Guild records as being the year that St. John's hosted the district meeting of the House of Churchwomen which included six parishes. Two years later, records indicate that St. John's elected two delegates to the convention in Terre Haute.

On October 14, 1955, St. John's celebrated its centennial anniversary. The Rt. Rev. Richard A. Kirchhoffer, Bishop of Indianapolis, celebrated Eucharist, assisted by The Rev. Wm. E. Stark, Vicar of St. John's.

Ground was broken on April 3, 1960 for the construction of a parish hall which was blessed on September 18, 1960.

On April 23, 1964, the present rectory was purchased.

The parish hall was remodeled in 1979. Then, Bishop Edward Jones blessed a second-story addition on October 3, 1982. At the time of the addition, a prayer garden was landscaped on the north side of the church.

A LOOK TO THE FUTURE

In October, 1986, St. John's acquired parish status at the Diocesan Convention held at Evansville, Indiana. The church has reached a point in its history where it is financially secure, allowing it to expand its outreach program and deepen its emphasis on a Christian education program for all ages.

The Rev. Joseph J. Dunne has remained with St. John's for thirteen years at the time of this writing and has provided the church with continuity, development of lay ministry, and strong spiritual leadership.

St. John's moves forward to pursue the Lord's work, giving thanks for the perseverance, endurance and great faith of those who have gone before.

LIST OF CLERGY

W.C. Armstrong 1855-1858, Colley A. Foster 1858-1861, W.S. Rowe 1861-?, L.F. Cole 1885-1891, A.A. Abbott 1891-1894, Austen F. Morgan 1894-1896, Fredrick I. Collins 1896-1897, Otway Colvin or Colona 1897-1901, William Duhanel 1901-1914, E.H. Birahby 1914-1915, W.R. Plummer 1915-1920, H.L. Lymon Wheaton 1920, R.P. Eubanks 1920-1924, Charles H. McKnight 1924-1932, Moor 1932-1934, R.S. Ottensmeyer 1934-?, Smith 1939-1949, Rufus L. Simons 1951-1953, Captain Hemphill 1953, W.E. Stark 1954-1957, E.O. Waldron 1958-1962, Earl Conner 1963, M.A. McClure 1963-1966, Kenneth T. Innes 1966-1968, Wm. R. Hall 1968-1970, Peter Van Zanten 1970-1972, W. Robert Webb 1972-1973, Joseph J. Dunne 1973-.

Saint Matthew's Church

Early records reveal that from 1840 to 1844 Rev. E.J. Durbin from Kentucky, Rev. A. Deydler and Rev. C. Schmiederjans attended the parish.

Rev. Roman Weinzapfel was the first to pay Mt. Vernon regular visits, celebrating the sacred liturgy in the house of the brothers Schenk who settled in Mt. Vernon from St. Philip in 1851.

The need for a Catholic Church in Mt. Vernon was felt and in 1856, Hiram P. and Mary Castleberry sold to Rev. DeSt. Palais, Bishop of Vincennes, lots 136 and 139 in the Williams addition. All of lot 139 and the south part of lot 136 were used for construction of the first church. A two-story brick building, 40 x 22 feet, intended ultimately for a schoolhouse or parsonage, but the flooring of the second story being omitted, it was used for church purposes. The citizens subscribed liberally and the total outlay was $2,000. The church was placed under the patronage of Saint Matthew and, in October, 1857, was blessed by Rev. E.J. Durbin.

In July, 1858, Father Weinzapfel visited the church for the last time. For several years different priests from other parishes served Mt. Vernon, Rev. Patrick McDermott from Evansville, Rev. Paul Wagner from St. Wendel, Rev. John Contin and Rev. Gustave Ginsz from Vincennes and Rev. H.J. Destel from St. Philip. In 1867 Rev. Destel erected a spacious one-story frame house, which was to serve as a schoolhouse and parsonage.

Rev. John Sondermann was appointed the first resident pastor on Nov. 11, 1868. He found a small congregation and $2,000. in debts. He paid the debt in a few years and beside, bought ground for a cemetery and added a second story to his residence.

From 1874 to 1976, Rev. Mattias A. Gillig was pastor.

Rev. J.J. Schoentrup took charge in July 1877. At that time the congregation consisted of 73 families. The school had an enrollment of 126 children.

A new church was begun in the summer of 1879 and completed in July 1880. The building was Roman style, 112 by 50 feet, with a steeple 146 feet high. Bishop Chatard blessed the church October 10, 1880. The cost of the building was $10,000, the interior furnishings $1,700.

In 1882, Rev. J.J. Schoentrup purchased lot 137 of the Williams addition for $1,250.

From 1883 to 1917 Rev. A. Koesters and Rev. Francis B. Luebbermann was in charge of the parish.

In 1900, St. Matthew parish acquired 80 acres of land in Point Township, about 12 miles southwest of Mt. Vernon. Forty acres were donated by G.B. Menzies and General Alvin P. Hovey, the other 40 acres being purchased by the parish for the sum of $550. Under the direction of Fr. Luebbermann, a frame church 72 by 35 feet was built there. It was dedicated in October, 1902, under the title of Poor Souls Chapel. This mission was attended from St. Matthew until 1907. The church was destroyed by fire in 1937.

During Father Luebbermann's pastorate of 32 years the present brick convent and rectory were erected with a large two-story brick school building at the corner of 5th and Mulberry Streets.

The Rev. Joseph T. Bauer served from 1917 to 1927. In 1920 Father Bauer purchased from the Spencer heirs, lots 150 and 151 in the Williams addition for $7,600. The present school is on these lots. It was under Father Bauer the Church's beautiful stained glass windows were donated and installed. The stained glass panels on the entrance doors are dedicated to the members of the parish who served in the Armed Forces during World War I.

Rev. Joseph E. Lannert, Rev. Edward A. Cobb, Rev. John J. Rapp, Rev. James Rogers and Rev. Leo Conti served from 1927 to 1951.

Rev. Raymond Smith assumed charge in 1951 and it was at this time that the present elementary school was built and a new organ was donated to the church in memory of Josephine and Catherine Gempler.

Rev. Walden Schiffer and Rev. Eugene Heerdink served from 1968 to 1979.

In July 1979 Rev. Robert Bultman became the pastor. He was active in civic and church affairs, serving as president of the Mt. Vernon Ministerial Association.

August 11, 1981 was the day Rev. Hilary F. Vieck became pastor. Since 1981 two pieces of property were acquired. In 1983 the Fogas property on Fourth and Walnut was purchased and in 1988 the Challman office building was removed to make room for a 35 car parking lot across the street from the west entrance to the church. The associate pastor is Rev. Joseph Swartz. Saint Matthews consist of a membership of 1,676 souls and the school has an enrollment of 151 in grades K thru eight.

At present, plans have been completed to remodel the church by installing heating and air-condition units, painting, plastering, and installing new carpet.

St. Paul's United Methodist Church

The first Methodist congregation met in the home of Jonathan and Rebekah Jaquess. It was organized in 1816, the year they came by flat boat down the Ohio River and settled in Robb Township, Posey County.

Circuit riders stopped in the home from time to time to conduct services. One of these circuit riders was a young German, John Schrader, from Baltimore, Maryland. He married Rebekah, the daughter of Rebekah and Jonathan Jaquess. At that time, he was traveling a circuit of 400 miles; sleeping in the woods with no covering but the sky, no pillow but his saddle bags, no company but his faithful horse, and the howling of the wolves. One day, tired and hungry, he rode up to a cabin by the wayside and stopped for dinner. Coffee was an unknown luxury, but he carried with him a small package of tea, which he gave the woman of the house. When dinner was served, he found she had boiled the tea in the dinner pot with the meat!

John Schrader possessed a beautiful voice. When he sang old hymns, such as "Jesus, Lover Of My Soul" and "Oh For A Thousand Tongues To Sing," his voice filled the whole house with melody. He was considered one of the most powerful ministers of the day. His eloquence and sincerity, his personal appearance, combined with a lovable and happy disposition, helped him win many for the Master. He is buried in the Poseyville cemetery.

The first church was built on the west end of Main Street on land given by Talbot Sharp in 1836. This building was used until 1859. Then it was decided to build a new church and Thomas Jaquess gave the lot, the same lot where the present building now stands. The church was completed and dedicated November, 1860. A bell was purchased for this building which is still in use today.

In 1904 the second building was sold and the present church building was completed by August 15 at a cost of $7,193. It was dedicated December 11, 1904, by Rev. Levi Gilbert, D.D., Rev. J.M. Turner, D.D., Presiding Elder, and Rev. P.C. Lisman, the Pastor. An annex was built in February, 1953. It cost $15,000. Six classrooms and a fellowship hall with kitchen was completed in May 1980, at a cost of $169,500.

Wadesville Christian Church

In 1948 a group of people of different denominations decided to organize a church where all could worship in harmony. It was agreed to meet on January 2, 1949 at 2:00 P.M. in the school building. The group found the building locked so they met at the home of Mr. and Mrs. William Zenthoefer next door. Rev. George Stuckey preached the first sermon. Several meetings were held in homes. A business meeting was held at the home of Mr. and Mrs. Klye Rigg. There a committee was appointed to go to see Rev. Lonnie Haas, Evansville, to get advice as to how to proceed to organize a Christian Church, Disciples of Christ. The group was confronted with several problems, and they were discouraged. But they had faith. They went to Mt. Vernon and talked with Mr. Fred Wilburn, a long time pillar of the First Christian Church of that city. Mr. Wilburn gave them encouragement as well as a donation.

Many meetings and prayers followed that trip. Finally the group rented an empty restaurant building that was located on Highway 66. In April, 1949, Mr. William Seibert decided to sell the building to the group for $5,000.00. This took lots more prayers, unity, and hard work. The Church Board of Extension in Indianapolis gave them a grant of $1,000.00 and loaned them $4,000.00 more. Rev. Henry Taylor of the Poseyville Christian Church helped the Wadesville group organize. The twelve charter members were the following Mr. and Mrs. Henry Clark, Mr. and Mrs. Jess Clark, Mr. and Mrs. Ivan Walker, Mollie Mae Hanes, Faye Williams, Ruth Ann Williams, Mrs. Elizabeth Cox, and Mr. and Mrs. Klye Rigg.

Laymen and ministers from Evansville churches assisted greatly in promoting this new church. Each member assumed his responsibility by teaching and calling. The Wadesville community responded well. Rev. Lester Ringham was the first appointed minister, and he served for 1-1/2 years. The building was paid for in full by March 24, 1954, and on May 9, 1954, the mortgage was burned at a special service. At this time Rev. Henry Kello was the pastor.

Almost immediately the ground was broken for a new addition. The corner stone was laid on June 6, 1954. On October 3, 1954 the dedication of the new addition which cost $8,500.00 was held. The membership at this time was 59. Rev. Kello and his son, Rice, named the group The First Christian Church - Wadesville, Indiana. Rev. Henry Kello died in June, 1959.

It was decided by the congregation that a pastoral unity be established between the Poseyville Christian Church and the Wadesville Christian Church, and July 1, 1959, the pastoral was formed with Rev. Ellis Cowling as pastor of both churches. In June, 1959, the need was obvious for more parking space for the church. The property of Mr. and Mrs. Paul Woolston that adjoined the church to the northeast was purchased for the sum of $6,500.00. Membership at this time was 65.

In October, 1965, the church mortgage was paid in full and the mortgage burned. In December, 1965, Rev. Cowling RESIGNED as pastoral unity minister, and the membership stood at 109.

From 1965 until June, 1967, Rev. L.B. Scarborough served as interim minister and the membership rose to 119. Rev. Herbert Gillen was accepted as minister in June, 1967. Rev. Gillen stayed with the church until September, 1970. By this time the membership was 136.

In the following months, until February, 1971, Rev. Harris B. Erickson served as interim minister. Until December of the same year, Rev. Carl Ham served as pastor.

On August 15, 1972, Rev. Rice Kello was hired by the Pastoral Unity Committee to serve at Wadesville and Poseyville. In April of 1973, the church was again remodeled. The pulpit was moved back, and new pews were added. In 1975 the basement was remodeled to make more room. Cabinets and a sink were added.

In March, 1976, Rev. Rice Kello passed away after four years of faithful service to both churches.

It had been apparent for some time that the steady growth of the church was going to soon warrant the hiring of a full time pastor for the Wadesville Church. The church then took the necessary steps to secure a minister. On August 1, 1976, Rev. Alfred Webb and his wife, Cleta J., became members of the Wadesville Christian Church, and Rev. Webb accepted the position as full time minister here.

Several meetings and discussions about the need of a new sanctuary and a full basement. In 1977 ground breaking ceremony was held on a Sunday morning in June. In December of the same year the basement of the new structure was finished and used for the Christmas party for our congregation.

In January, 1978 the builders completed his contract on the structure and a celebration breakfast was held to signify the completion of phase one of our building program. Phase II of our building was completed by Christmas. On December 17, 1978 services was held in the New Sanctuary. (The mortgage at the Farmers Bank & Trust was $110,000.00. The total cost, with the help of volunteers remodeling Sunday school rooms and many other jobs was estimated at a total of $150,000.00.)

June, 1979, Rev. Webb resigned as pastor. Rev. Keith Hueftle accepted the position of interim minister. On October 19, 1980 the dedication service was held in the new sanctuary.

Rev. Carl Ham and wife Jean, became members of the church on August 1, 1982 and Rev. Ham accepted the position as full time minister. In November, 1984 a Day Care service was established in the church basement. Many things have improved over these years.

On June 1st, 1988 a ceremony was held for the burning of the mortgage. This was a joyous occasion. It was decided that much more was needed and we borrowed $13,500.00. New doors was installed, new windows in the vestibule, the drive and parking area was blacktopped.

On May 15, 1988 a dedication service was held outside of the church for the "Partico" paid for by Dorothy Weber and children in memory of her deceased husband Ernest Weber.

On February 6, 1989, membership of the church was 187, participating members of 108. Church attendance averages about 90 with Sunday school at 55.

We celebrated our 40th birthday of the church with a basket dinner on February 12, 1989. *Submitted by Mollie M. Hanes*

Zion Lippe United Church of Christ

As early as 1836, German immigrants began arriving in this area of Posey County. Those first settlers stayed with no church affiliations. This community was named Tersteegen after the Reformed Pastor and hymnwriter Gerhard Tersteegen. The community name was later changed to Lippe due to the large number of immigrants who came from the state of Lippe in Germany.

In 1842 Pastor Krassauer of St. John's Church on Harmony Way invited families who lived in this area called Lippe to come to church services that he held in a school house about one and a half miles West of the present church.

A group of sixteen members organized in 1844. They built the first church to be known as Zion Church in 1845. It was a simple small church built of logs covered with clap boards and had a few tiny windows. The benches were cut from tree trunks. The church benches and altar were made by the members. This church served the congregation until 1856, when a new structure was built to better house the expanding church community. The ground purchased for the new structure was 90x45 feet.

The congregation continued in its service and growth providing a church operated parochial school for all age groups.

In 1895 the current church was built. In 1959 a new educational building was attached to the church allowing for a more comprehensive religious education program.

This year, 1989 the church will begin a building program, an addition between the educational building and the church. This will allow handicap accessible rest rooms, pastor's office, multi-purpose room, handicap entrance, and Communion preparation area.

The congregation has a strong German Reformation heritage and in its formative years became associated with the Evangelical Church (Synod of the West). The church later shared in the merger of the Evangelical with the Reformed Church. More recently it joined with the Congregational Christian Church to form the United Church of Christ.

In 1949 it gave up German services and conducted all services in English.

Currently the church offers a variety of programs. A Women's Guild helps the church through programs of education, service and worship and it also has an active group of quilters.

Youth programs include Junior and Senior activities throughout the year.

Sponsored by the church, the Sunbeams is a group that visits nursing homes, the sick and shut-ins within the Fellowship. It also sponsors meals and programs for the local Senior Citizens.

The educational facilities enable the congregation to meet the instructional needs from nursery-age children to adults. A nursery center school, one of the oldest in the community, is professionally-staffed and provides services for the community.

The congregation also maintains an outdoor recreation program which includes a modern softball diamond, tennis courts, a basketball court and play equipment for children.

Pastoring the church is the Rev. Conrad Heisner. Rev. Heisner came to Zion in September of 1988.

Rev. Craig Reed is Pastor Emeritus. Rev. Reed retired from the ministry and Zion in April of 1988. He served Zion for eleven years.

The church now has a membership of 300 with a Sunday School enrollment of 140.

Services at the church are at 10 a.m. Sunday. Preceding the worship service is the Sunday School at 9 a.m.

Zion Church, with its tower stretching towards the heavens, is a constant reminder to those who see it from any direction of its witness. We look upon the history of Zion Church not only with a sense of pride and accomplishment, but as a challenge to the future to continue that witness which our forefathers began long ago.

Bethel Primitive Baptist Church

Black's Chapel United Methodist Church

In 1849 friends and neighbors of Ezekiel and Mary Ann Black met in their home in Western Black Township every Sunday morning for church services and always remained for Sunday dinner.

On September 17, 1849 Ezekiel Black and Thomas Harrison gave ground for a new church building, each giving equal parts. Later when the ground was surveyed it was solely on Ezekiel Black and was recorded in the court house at Mt. Vernon, Indiana on August 21, 1860.

The first trustees were Thomas Harrison, Thomas Todd, Samuel Templeton, Joseph Fisher and Ezekiel Black.

Approximately in the year 1881, a new building was erected which served the community for 74 years.

In discouraging years, the church doors were kept open due to the personal perseverance of Mr. Francis Curtis, known affectionately to the community as "Uncle Frank".

In 1937 a flood destroyed the Prairie Church leaving the members without a church home. Prairie members then merged with Black's Chapel.

An informal meeting of friends and members of Black's Chapel was held July 1, 1955 to discuss the pending relocation of the church caused by a new highway being built by the state past the church. The sum of $12,000 was presented by the State of Indiana and accepted by the trustees of Black's Chapel - Everett Topper, Wilford Curtis and Paul McFadin. The church building was sold to Frank Werking for $250 and the church pews were sold for $200. The last service held in the building was August 28, 1955.

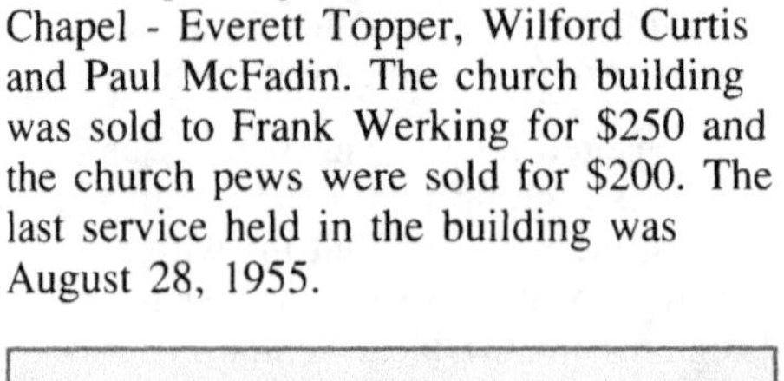

Of the several sites presented by the trustees, an acre from the parsonage grounds was selected as most suitable and the sum of $75 was paid to the parsonage trustees. A committee consisting of Herbert Rowe, Eugene Schutz, Herbert Smith and Harry Stevens was chosen to work with the trustees. Mr. Alton Miranda was selected by District Superintendent Dr. Browning as the architect and Melvin Noelle was the contractor.

Church services were held in the Pentecostal Tabernacle on Bald Knob Road south of where the church was being built until cold weather. Then services were held in the homes of the community, and the church continued to grow. The first service was held in the basement of the new church April 15, 1956.

The first service held in the sanctuary was May 13, 1956. The church was dedicated on October 7, 1956.

The present trustees of the church are Everett Topper, Ronald Smith, Paul E. McFadin, Dennis Angel, Rosa Rowe, Wayne Topper and Geraldine McFadin. *This history was written by Mrs. Otto Rowe, Mrs. Paul M. McFadin and Mrs. Herman Curtis.*

Faith United Methodist Church

The Faith United Methodist Church, corner of Wolflin and Third, had its beginning when a small group of neighbors began to meet together for worship at 1114 W. Third Street. In 1916 the meeting place was moved to 1000 W. Third Street and dedicated as **"The Little Mission"**.

In 1921 the Rev. A.W. Arford organized the church as **"The First United Brethren in Christ Church"** with twenty-five charter members and today only three of these are living: Mrs. Edna Allen, Mrs. Effie Hendricks, and Mrs. Frances Smith.

On April 13th, the cornerstone was laid for the present building and on October 19th, 1924 the building was dedicated to God's service. This building cost $10,000.

In 1946 the merger between the United Brethren in Christ denomination and the Evangelical Church denomination changed our church's denomination and name of our church to **"The Evangelical United Brethren Church"**.

In 1948 a new parsonage was built; previously the church rented homes for their ministers at 830 W. Fourth St., 823 W. Fourth St., and 824 W. Fourth St. A house was then purchased from Arnold Burris at 930 W. Third and was the parsonage until the current parsonage was built beside the church.

In 1959 an addition to the church was built including a pastor's study, nursery, art glass windows, carpet, electric organ, church hymnals, choir robes, and many other improvements followed through the years.

Due to the merger of the Evangelical United Brethren and the Methodist denominations on April 1st, 1968, we became the **"Faith United Methodist Church"**.

Through the years four men have answered the call to the ministry: William Medcalf, John Medcalf, James Bradford, and Andy Kinsey. It is our prayer that we move forward under the leadership of the current pastor, Marvin L. Roeder.

First Baptist Church (SBC)

On Tuesday evening December 19, 1951, the New Harmony Missionary Baptist Mission, which was supported by the Northside Baptist Church, Grayville, Illinois, was organized into the FIRST BAPTIST CHURCH.

Charter members numbered 16 and were as follows: Mrs. Eliza Axton, Lloyd and Ruby Delancy, Earl N. and Ann Frazier, James Frazier, Earlene Frazier, Julia Kirk, James W. and Jewell Powers, Robert and Roberta Powers, Winnie Rambo, Jack Thompson, Louise Turner and Pauline Wilson. Mrs. Ruby Delancy is the only charter member still on the church roll.

Rev. Earl Frazier was called as the first minister. He remained in that position until 1957.

Preaching was first held in private homes, then in a building on Main Street where the TIMES OFFICE is now, a construction company office, and also in the "OLD ROCK HOUSE", which was located on highway 460 east of town. Finally on May 21, 1951, the church body bought the "Jack Beeson House" on North Street for 3,700.00. This is now known as the "Jane Owen Community House". Trustees for this purchase were Earl Frazier, James Powers and Jack Thompson. Many happy times are remembered in this building.

In 1956, the Church bought the "Old Loren Cox Place" on Tavern and First Streets. Construction was begun on the first phase of a new church building that same year. It was a two-story block building and was used for church services and Sunday School classes. It is still in use today.

In 1968 a new building program was begun. The new sanctuary was put under roof by Barton and Spencer. The interior work was completely finished by the people of the church. During the summer of that same year a watermelon crop was planted and harvested on the Hollard McGrew Farm. The proceeds were used to purchase an organ and piano. The exact amount needed to purchase the instruments was received from the sell of the melons.

On May 4, 1969, the present sanctuary was dedicated.

At present the church has a resident membership of ____. There is also a Preschool operated by the church, Harmony Christian Preschool. The enrollment in 1988 was 20 preschool children.

The present membership is very mission minded and has very active mission groups of all ages. These groups are always looking for ways to serve their fellow man who are in need.

Past ministers are: Earl Frazier, 1951 to 1957; Leo Simmons, 1957 to 1960; C.L. Farrell, 1960 to 1962; Ronald Smith, 1962 to 1963; Albert Kemp, 1963 to 1965; James Lawless, 1965 to 1967; John Deason, 1967 to 1969; Paul Davis, 1969 to 1970; David Simpson, 1970 to 1972; Paul Davis (interim) 1972 to 1973; Gary Parker, 1973 to 1974; James Carroll, 1974 to 1983; and the present pastor, Stan Wall, 1983 to present.

Past deacons of the church are: Ray Smith, Jack Thompson, James Powers, Claude Harris, Jesse Franklin, Windell Taylor, Holland McGrew, Albert Travelstead. All of the above have passed on. Present deacons are William Conyers, Loren Spencer, Allen Spencer, Eddie Rueger, George Hatch, Allen Hatch, Larry Conyers, Walter Burks, Clint Stewart, Steve Cooper, and John Carroll.

Salem Church (Heusler)

June 9, 1848, a missionary from Germany, Heinrich Toelke, wrote the American Home Missionary Society he was preaching every Sunday afternoon to a gathering of 12 families in a hilly region near the Ohio River eight miles from the city (Evansville) and not far from the Black Hawk Mill. These families soon organized as a congregation and chose the name of Salem (Peace) as suggested by its location. When Ludwig Austmann arrived in Posey County in March, 1849, he also served the congregation. Later this community came to be known as HEUSLER because of the post office situated for some years in Dr. Heusler's house next to the cemetery.

Many of the early families came to escape poverty, authoritarianism, and military conscription of their sons in the Old Country. Though Salem has never been a large congregation, it was the first of its denomination in the area. Trinity, Mt. Vernon, was founded by a pastor serving Salem in 1853, and Immanuel on Ford Road became an offshoot about 1871.

Land was acquired for a church from John and Lena Hahn. The confirmation class of 1852 was reported to be the first confirmed in a new log church. At some point a parsonage was built, probably also log, and a log schoolhouse. By the time the latter was torn down in the early 1950's, a frame schoolhouse (which existed until the 1960's) had been built in 1901 closer to the Old State Road. The original parsonage was sold to a member and a new frame one built in 1883. This parsonage was in turn replaced by a brick one in 1953. The old parsonage garage roof became a shelter on the picnic grounds, property acquired in the 1950's where an outdoor amphi-theater was developed and served for the commissioning in 1959 of a missionary from Salem to Japan, John Rasche. The stone education building was completed in 1963. The oldest existing picture of the congregation was taken in 1892, with the frame church of 1888 in the background. A bell manufactured in 1891 was hung. In 1972 the congregation approved plans drawn up by the education building's architect, and a stone church was dedicated in 1974. The old church was sold to a member for preservation and use as a retreat center and moved onto the homesite of one of Salem's earliest families.

In the early church, men only were considered members, except in the case of a widow or woman whose husband did not belong; the men sat on one side of the sanctuary, women and children on the other. The bell was run Saturday evenings. Music was important, usually taught by the pastor's wife, who traditionally could play the pump organ and direct the choir, or teach music to the confirmation pupils.

In 1880 a constitution was drawn up with 43 signers. (It used to be the custom that one signed the constitution upon becoming a member.) The beautiful script states that, if attendance at the school should fall below 20, it might be discontinued for the summer. Also, the name was to be the **Evangelische Protestantische Salems Kirche** (Evangelical Protestant Church of Salem), "never ever" to be changed.

The German congregation and pastors had a hard time during the World Wars, when inhabitants were sometimes afraid to speak their own language or carry on their customs. This led to the demise of the culture in a foreign land. 1931 saw some worship conducted in English. The earliest existing tombstone dates from 1857; the earliest record-book dates from 1858, listing information on each member by families, and exactly where prior church records are to be found in Germany.

Although contributions were made to the German Evangelical Synod of North America and pastors were obtained from it, Salem remained completely independent until about 1941. In 1934 the Evangelical and Reformed Churches merged, and in 1957 joined with two English-background churches, Congregational and Christian, to form the United Church of Christ.

April 10, 1892 Oldest picture in existence of Salem Church & congregation built 1888

Zoar United Methodist Church

About 1870 interested persons, living SW of Mt. Vernon, Ind. felt the need of a church. In 1875 a log building was erected on 1/2 acre of donated ground.

It was to serve people of all denominations.

By 1900 the need existed for a larger church. Under the sponsorship of the St. Pauls Methodist Church a new frame structure was erected and given the name, Zoar Methodist Church.

In 1950 more rooms were added. This church has always shared pastors of neighboring Methodist churches.

Zoar United Methodist Church after the Steeple was fixed in October 1983.

JOHNSON UNITED METHODIST CHURCH NEW HARMONY, INDIANA

1840s First recorded Methodist meetings held in the home of a Mrs. Anderson. Early members were Mrs. Anderson, her son and daughter, Mr. and Mrs. Hops, John R. Hugo, Josiah Whitlock, John Beal and H. Dalrymple. In a short time services were held in the ferry house at the foot of the levee north of town.

1846 The first Methodist Episcopal Church was constructed on a lot given by John R. Hugo. This was located on the north side of Granary Street between Main and West Streets. Francis Asbury Hester became the first regularly appointed pastor. A Sunday School was organized.

1905 James N. Johnson donated two lots and $7,000 for the construction of a new brick church and parsonage. Those attending the ground-breaking service were James N. Johnson, John Wilson, John Boyer, E.W. Nash, Lawrence Lichtgenberger, Clinton Sanders, Rose Sanders, Roy Sanders, L. Wade Wilson, T.J. Truscott, Milton Johnson, Charles Sibley, Tom Wells, Frank Sanders, Tom Conner, Joe Brown, Gordon Wilson, Kenneth Nash and the Reverend Benoni A. May.

1906 The Building Committee (James N. Johnson, Dr. S.O. Rawlings, Thomas Truscott, John Wilson, W.O. Tretheway, and John Heuring) reported that Andrew Carnegie gave one half the cost of the pipe organ. Stained glass windows were given in memory of Thomas R. Inwood, Maru Husband Newkirk, Benoni Abner May, Celia C. Chaffin, Martha D. Soper, May Elliott, John and Amanda E. Wilson, James N. Johnson, Thomas J. and Catharine Wilson Truscott, C.U. and N.D. Rawlings, Anna E. Huebner, Mary Langer, Amy Endicott Cox, and organizations of the church. Dedication services for Johnson Methodist Episcopal Church were held July 1, 1906.

1939 The name was changed again due to a merger of three Methodist bodies to the Johnson Memorial Methodist Church. The Reverend Loren N. Campbell was the minister.

1954 The Reverend William R. Kell and family moved to the third and present parsonage located at 918 Main Street. The brick parsonage was renovated for educational rooms and became known as the Church Annex. Helen Elliott wrote a short history of the church listing all the ministers.

1965 An extensive remodeling program was completed. Officers of this project were: Louis H. Stallings, Charles Kemmerling, Charles K. Mann, Allen Cook, Myron Cox Jacob Effinger, Cecil Gooden, Jay Moore, Foster Tolliver, Leslie Wardelman and John Whitmore. E.C. Ford gave a new organ in memory of his wife and mother. The Reverend Paul T. Jump, Pastor, wrote "Historical Notes on the Occasion of the 125th Anniversary of the Methodist Church in New Harmony and the Reopening of the Church for Public Worship: October 31, 1965."

1968 The merger of the Methodists and the Evangelical United Brethren denominations resulted in another name change—the present Johnson United Methodist Church. The Reverend Warren F. Montgomery was the pastor.

1977 A booklet of church history, programs, choirs, and church organizations was compiled by the Reverend Marvin L. Roeder.

1989 Kristy Hein ordered the new Methodist hymnals. The Music Committee is: Carolyn Stone, Helen Stallings, Doris Whitmore, Rita Reynolds, Terry Hon, and Janey Frayser. Trustees of the church are: Joyce Robb, Philip Werry, David VanLaningham Juanita Hyatt, Jack Sweeney, Velma Hein, Harry Bennitt, Fred Frayser and Richard Stone. The Reverend Leslie McKown was the pastor until June when the Reverend Joy Kraft-Lawler was appointed.

Northern Posey County School

SCHOOL HISTORY

POSEY COUNTY, INDIANA
175th
Anniversary
1814 - History - 1989

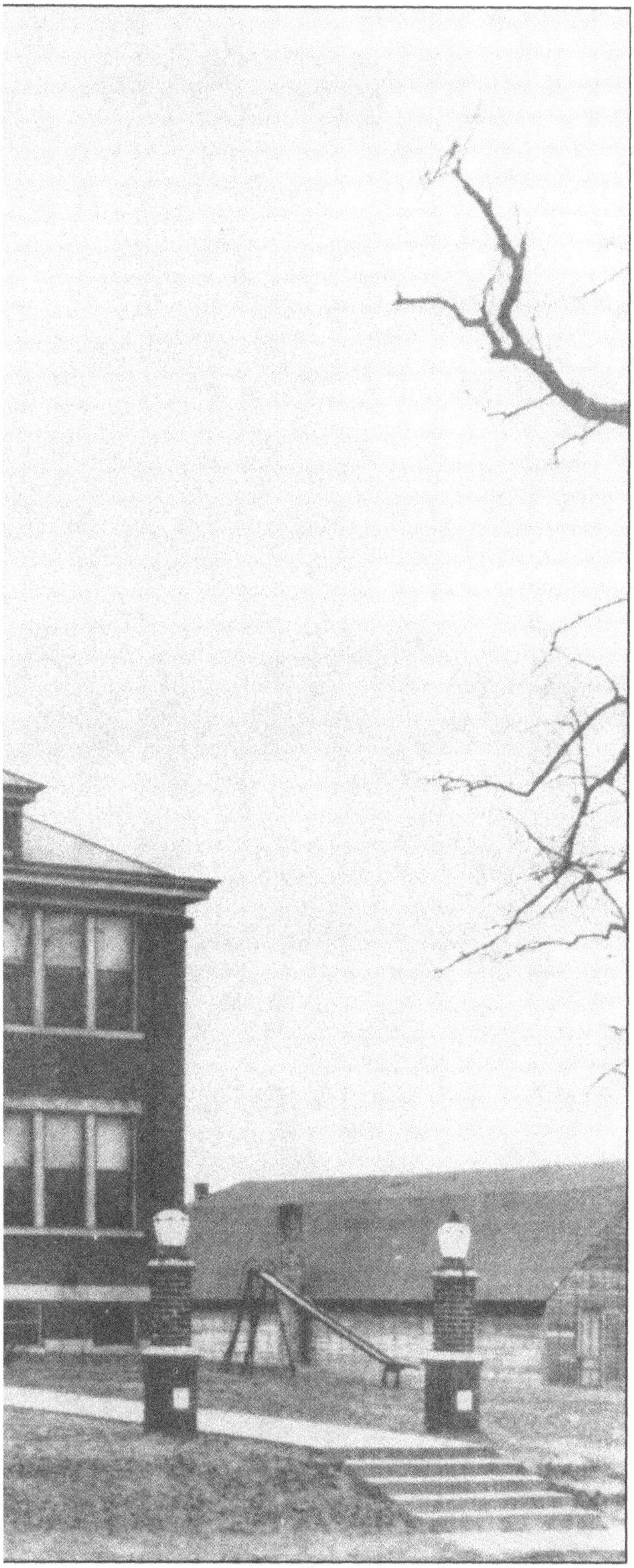

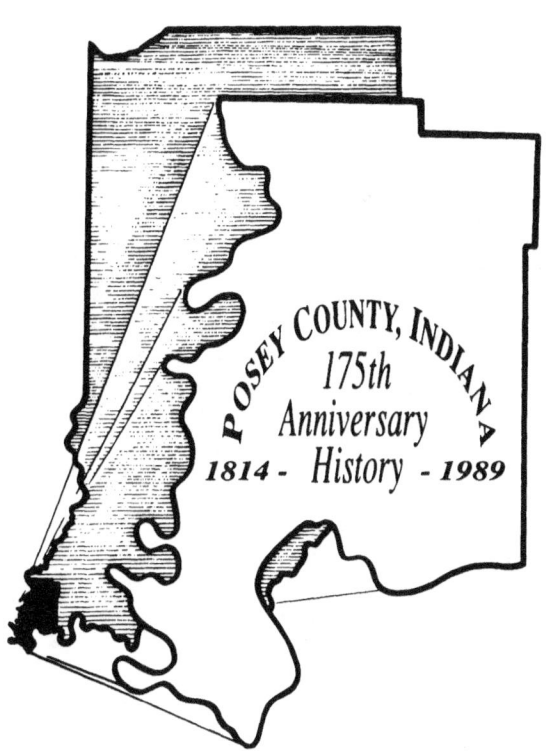

Metropolitan School District of North Posey County

The Metropolitan School District of North Posey County, Indiana came into existence in November, 1956 as a result of a county wide school reorganization election. This election merged Center-Robinson, Bethel, Robb and Smith townships under the provisions of Chapter 226, Acts of 1949 of the Indiana General Assembly. Total land area of the school district is approximately 150 miles. The new school corporation joined together administratively in January, 1957 and assumed all school property, rights, privileges, debts, and liabilities of the previous township school or joint corporations. This included any bonded indebtedness, accumulation of building fund receipts, contracts and tenure obligations which were held by or with the then school townships.

Following the recommendations of a Purdue University survey the South Terrace Elementary School designed for kindergarten through grade six was completed in 1958 to serve the area formerly known as Center-Robinson. The Purdue survey team also recommended that a new Jr-Sr High School be constructed to accommodate students in Cynthiana, Griffin, Poseyville and Wadesville. Construction began in 1958 and the new school was occupied in the fall of 1959. The schools in Cynthiana, Griffin, and Poseyville were converted to elementary schools and continued to operate until the fall of 1964 when the Griffin School was closed and those students were included in the Poseyville Elementary enrollment. Because of crowded conditions at the Jr-Sr High School and lack of proper facilities in the remaining elementary buildings another construction program began in 1969 and resulted in two new buildings, which were occupied in the fall of 1971. The new Jr. High School building serves children in the 7th and 8th grades district wide while the new North Elementary School serves children K-6 in the northern part of the district.

In September of 1984 an educational facility team from Indiana University recommended that six new classrooms be constructed at South Terrace Elementary to accommodate increased student enrollment and Special Education needs. Construction of South Terrace class-

South Terrace Elementary

rooms was completed in 1986. The Board of Education proceeded at that time to accept Indiana University's recommendation to remodel and add six classrooms to North Posey High School. Total work at North Posey was completed in March of 1988. The new additions contain many up-to-date techniques in construction and educational planning.

There are 100 teachers on the instructional staff including the special areas of Library, Guidance, Speech Therapy, Special Reading, Music, Art and Special Education.

A five member Board of School Trustees governs the school corporation; administrative functions are carried out by the Superintendent of schools, appointed by the Board and by staff members.

The Metropolitan School District of North Posey County administration is composed of a central office staff consisting of the Superintendent of Schools and an Administrative Assistant, full time principals for each building and an assistant at the high school.

The school corporation, since 1959, has owned and operated its own transportation system and the buses are so routed that in most cases it is possible for children to ride no longer than one hour going to and from school.

All schools within the Metropolitan School District of North Posey County are dedicated to the youth and citizens of the entire school district.

Note of Interest: There was a school located in Stewartsville, 1st through 12th grades, that burned in the winter of 1944.

POSEYVILLE SCHOOLS

The Poseyville Log School House is, to the younger generation, a myth; to the older, a dream of memories only. It stood about one-half mile north of the village on the road leading to Black River. The ground on which it stood was donated by the Rev. John Shrader in 1820.

It contained but one room, possibly 18 x 20 feet, and the roof was made of clapboards. There was but one door which faced the east. At the left side of the door was a raised platform with a desk and chair for the teacher. To the right was a box, on which stood a watersoaked, wooden bucket with a rusty tin cup from which all the school drank. Germs and microbes were unknown then. On the north side, when the house was first built, there was a huge fireplace which was later torn down and the opening walled up. The

North Posey High School addition 1988

west and south sides each had a small window with panes of glass 6 x 8 inches. Under these windows were placed long split slabs of black walnut which were used for writing desks. The desks were flanked by backless benches in which holes had been bored and sticks driven for legs.

Steel pens were unknown so all writing was done with quill pens, which were made and mended by the teacher.

Massachusetts, the first state noted for its learning, furnished the first teachers of the school. The principal studies were the R's, "Reading, 'Riting, 'Rithmetic, and Spelling." Much stress was laid on spelling. If a boy or girl could spell well, even though ranking low in other studies, he was considered a good student.

The boys' games were town-ball and bull-pen. The girls skipped rope and dropped the handkerchief. Anti-over was a game played by both boys and girls.

Near the school was a forest, untouched by an axe except where a road had been cut through. This forest was filled with grand old trees for which Southern Indiana was noted, the dogwoods and red-buds.

In referring to her little log school of learning, Sarah Bozeman wrote: "within its four walls were certainly instilled those most notable principles of love and loyalty to country. For when the Civil War cloud darkened the land, a call was made which was answered by more than half of the boys whose early training was received within the rude walls of the Old Log School house."

At the beginning of the last half of the nineteenth century, the accumulation of the school funds of Indiana served to arouse an increasing interest in the public schools among the people of our state. The Old Log School was torn down and replaced with a larger and more commodious frame structure. A better class of teachers was in demand. A new series of books known as *McGuffey's Readers and Speller* were introduced.

The spirit of progress reached the patrons of the Poseyville School District in 1851. This new structure was a one-story building of one room about 20 x 40 feet. Bells not being used, no belfry was required. It was lighted with four windows on each side and three on the west end. The room was furnished with a single row of seats with the desks attached, placed along each side wall, and two double rows placed in the center of the room, thus making three aisles. The door, teacher's desk, and a blackboard occupied the east end. The flue was built from "the ceiling up" near the front of the building; to this was attached a stove with a capacity sufficient to hold a stick of wood two feet long.

The house was ready for occupancy in 1852; the school director was then ordered by the township trustee to call a meeting of the patrons and select a teacher.

During this period, 1851 to 1873, the Public School system gradually improved and with it the schools. At first the qualification of the teacher was limited; he had to be able to keep good order, have some knowledge of reading, writing, and arithmetic, be able to superintend the boys, while getting wood for the stove and attend to sweeping the floor. Later, however, the law provided for the appointment of a County School Examiner whose duty it was to examine all applicants to teach.

To supply a growing demand for a higher education, algebra and physiology were in the early sixties added to the course of study.

In 1871 the school house was destroyed by fire and the construction of a new one became necessary. The ground for the new one was donated by Mr. T.C. Jaquess, a progressive citizen. Plans were decided on for a two-story brick building containing three rooms equipped with the latest and best furniture. The building was completed in 1872. It was built on what is now known as Cale Street.

Arrangements were made for employing two teachers. For a period of twelve years school was conducted in this building. This period may justly be termed the transition period from the district school to the high school.

The attendance of the pupils increased until the three rooms were filled and each room supplied with a teacher.

The District School was rapidly becoming an Academy of Learning, when in 1884, for the second time in our history, the building was destroyed by fire. Notwithstanding this calamity a larger and more modern structure was immediately built and in it School District No. 3 at once became The Poseyville High School.

The organization of a high school in the year 1885 was a difficult task for the superintendent. The state furnished very little assistance in outlining a course of study and limited means curtailed the teaching force and shortened the school year. However, a curriculum was arranged giving the pupil the advantage of the first year course of a commissioned high school.

After this the School Town of Poseyville was incorporated, September 8, 1886. In addition to this course a "Normal School" was conducted for a term of three months, after the close of the regular school year. This was continued for three or four years. The number of pupils rapidly increased by transfer from other schools. The school fund also increased and the trustee was able to hire more teachers.

In 1896 it became necessary to build an addition of two rooms to the building. In 1900 the State Board of Education placed us on the Certified High School list. It continued in this capacity until 1908 when it became a Commissioned High School. It was about this time the increased attendance and growing demands of our school called for a larger and more modern building. This demand was complied with by our citizens in 1910 by the erection of the last built known as "Old Poseyville High".

This building was of red brick and was situated on a hill in the north part of town. It was about 80 x 90 feet in structure. There were four entrances, one on each side. Above the main entrance on the south side was the belfry where the old bell rang. On each side were windows.

On entering the building you found yourself in a large hall which had entrances into five rooms. These rooms were used for the grade students. On the west and east side were two flights of stairs leading to the second floor and to the basement. Those on the east side were used by the girls and the west side by the boys.

Going up to the second floor one found the five rooms occupied by the high school. The halls were used as coat rooms. On the north side was the assembly room with windows across the north wall and an exit by a fire escape stairs. In the east part of the assembly was a stage on which class plays and commencements were held. All rooms were equipped with necessary articles for conducting the classes.

The building had its own complete water system with all modern conveniences. Drinking fountains were placed in the hall and basement.

In the basement you would find the Domestic Science and Manual Training rooms, supply rooms, rest rooms, and a large gym. It was used for banquets and entertainment. The first alumni meeting was held here in 1914.

The school ground extended over four acres of land. Playground and a ball diamond were at the back of the building. Baseball was the only sport played by the schools at first.

The Home Makers Club of Poseyville, organized in 1910, played a big part in promoting Domestic Science and Manual Training.

In 1918-1919 basketball became a popular sport and a new gym was built and because of its appearance it became known as "The Barn". At first there were no dressing rooms in the gym, and the boys dressed in the school basement and ran over to the gym, even in the coldest of weather. Later dressing rooms were added on the back side of the gym. This building remained until 1927 when it was torn down and a new and more modern building was erected, which was used for plays, banquets, basketball, and commencements.

The Stewartsville School burned in 1944 so those students were transferred over to our school and the school became Rob Township School.

The attendance kept increasing each year. More and better equipment was added each year to improve the school. Shrubs, trees, and playground equipment made their appearance.

In 1957 and 1958 they were beginning to talk about consolidation and plans were made after much deliberation to build a new high school located about 2-1/2 miles south of Poseyville. This was ready for occupancy in 1960 and is known as "The North Posey High School".

The old school was then used by the Stewartsville and Poseyville grade children. In the fall of 1964 the Griffin grade students were transferred to the Poseyville School. When the new elementary school was built in 1969, the Cynthiana grades and St. Francis grade students were entered with the others at the opening in 1970-1971.

During the years from 1912 to 1959, we saw many of our boys leave for wars and some of these never returned.

Our old Poseyville High holds many happy memories to the forty eight classes who graduated there. Two and three generations of families claim it as their Alma Mater.

Many of us were fortunate in getting one of the bricks from the old school when it was torn down in 1969 with a picture of the school on the brick. This will be nice to hand down to our children and grandchildren.

Sarah Bozeman wrote that no one need be ashamed of "The Old Log School", as one of our greatest presidents, Abraham Lincoln, attended one of these.

From our Alma Mater came some doctors, lawyers, bankers, merchants, teachers, nurses, ministers, farmers, and many others; so we can be real boastful when we say, "We graduated from Old Poseyville High".

Although the old school is gone, the cherished memories we hold will never be forgotten.

Compiled by Ella Fern Williams Class of 1924

West Franklin School March 29, 1893 Top Row right: Wilhelm E. Becker, second row from bottom: Ida Lengelsen.

James T. and Malinda Yeager Hanes family. Martha Frances, James Thomas Hanes, Florence Effie, Welzie Thomas, Emory Eldon, Ora Madison, Ephriam M., Grace, Malinda Yeager Hanes holding Arcie, Nealy William. Taken at old home place at St. Wendel, Robinson Township. Sec. 2R12 Posey County.

James T.d Malinda Yeager Hanes family. Martha Frances, James Thomas Hanes, Florence Effie, Welzie Thomas, Emory Eldon, Ora Madison, Ephriam M., Grace, Malinda Yeager Hanes holding Arcie, Nealy William taken at old home place. St. Wendel. Robinson Township. Sec. 2 R 12 Posey County.

Hengstenberg Homeplace 1886 or so; Edward Lengelsen, Mine and Elizabeth Schimmel Hengstenberg, Wilhelm Hengstenberg (Sr.) Mr. and Mrs. Brandan with child on lap. Ida Lengelsen standing.

FAMILY HISTORY

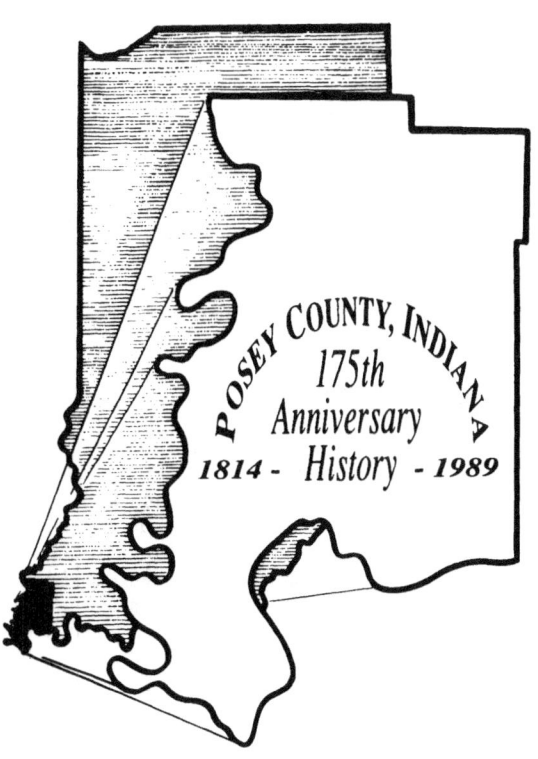

POSEY COUNTY, INDIANA
175th Anniversary
1814 - History - 1989

PAMELIA (THOMPSON) AGOSTINELLI FAUSTO AGOSTINELLI

Fausto Agostinelli and Pamelia (Thompson) Agostinelli presently reside in North Charleston, SC. Pam graduated with the class of 1963 from Mount Vernon High School. Fausto and Pam married Sept. 28, 1968. They have two children Ryan Patrick born Apr. 26, 1970 and Mimi Elisa born Jan. 30, 1974. The Agostinellis lived for a brief time in Mount Vernon and Evansville before moving to South Carolina in August 1969.

Pamelia was the only child of William Clinton Thompson and Anna Marjorie (Head) Thompson. Pam was born July 15, 1945. She has taught school since her graduation from Indiana State University in 1967. She later earned a Masters degree from the College of Charleston in 1976. She currently is active with Beta Sigma Phi: an international cultural, service, and social sorority.

Bill and Ann Thompson, Pamelia J. and Fausto Agostinelli

Pam's father, William C. Thompson, was born July 14, 1923 in Mount Vernon to William Thompson and Minnie (Watkins) Thompson. William, better known as "Bill", served in World War II in the Mediterranean and Pacific. Because his parents died by the time Bill was five, he was raised by his mother's sister and her husband Edith and Charles Hutson. Bill worked for brief time on the Ohio River, and as a dispatcher for the L&N Railroad. He spent most of his life as a watch repairman for Acme Jewelers.

William Clinton Thompson married Anna Marjorie Head July 12, 1942. Anna Marjorie Head was born July 8, 1923 to Richard Harvey Head and Flora (Tongate) Head formerly of Lewisport, KY. The Head family resided in Posey County from 1922 to 1943. Mr. Head worked for a meat packing company and Mrs. Head was employed by the garment factory on Main Street. Anna spent her whole life in Mt. Vernon except during the war when she traveled with her husband in the service.

Anna's paternal grandparents were Handley Head and Alice Kincaid of Kentucky and her maternal grandparents were Francis Marion Tongate and Laura (Adkins) Tongate.

Anna still resides in Mount Vernon. She was educated as a cosmetologist and electrolysis and is self employed in Evansville. She also holds an associates and bachelors degree in health sciences.

Pam's husband came from Italy to Mt. Vernon in 1967. He worked at the Babcock Wilcox plant for his company Innocenti located in Milan, Italy. Mr. Agostinelli was an electrician and traveled worldwide for his company. He is presently employed as a supervisor at Robert Rosch in Charleston, SC.

Fausto is the son of Lorenzo Antonio Agostinelli and Lisetta Chiara (Freddi) Agostinelli. Lorenzo was the electrician for the town of Vaprio D'Adda during World War II, Lorenzo was born Apr. 18, 1908 in Far Gera D'Adda and married June 17, 1933. Lorenzo died repairing a severed line while the town celebrated the end of the war in Italy May 7, 1945. Lorenzo's father was Luigi Agostinelli born Nov. 27, 1863 and married Maria (Signorelli) Agostinelli. Luigi's father was Antonio and his mother was Antonia (Locatelli) Agostinelli.

Fausto's mother still resides in Vaprio D'Adda. She was born June 8, 1911 to Giovanni Freddi and Techla (Urgnetti) Freddi. Techla was an orphan. Giovanni was the son of Pietro Freddi born Apr. 3, 1859 and Virginia (Frigerio) Freddi born Dec. 16, 1856. Pietro was the son of Giovanni Freddi and Marguerita (Preme) Freddi, Virginia was born in Cassano D'Adda to Giovanni Frigerio and Maria (Taola) Frigerio.

THE WILLIAM A. ALEXANDER FAMILY

Between the dates 1800-1810 a fairly large number of good solid families moved into Posey County and became good and outstanding citizens. One such family was that of William A. Alexander, who came via Kentucky from North Carolina. He came to Indiana with his parents when he was about six years old. He was married to Eleanor Allison, and to them was born eight children. He became a very successful farmer and cattle man, acquiring over 1000 acres of the finest farmland in Lynn Township.

Ausburn and Mary A. Stephens

One of his eight children was William David Alexander, who was born in 1837 and married in 1857 to Phoebe Ann Wilson of Virginia. He started in life with a small amount of capital, but through frugal living and hard work he prospered and acquired nearly 500 acres of excellent farm land. Besides farming he, as his father had done, also bred and raised live stock. He had an elegant home situated in a beautiful location high on a hill in western Lynn Township. From this residence one could see Mt. Vernon ten miles distant, and the smoke from steamboats on the Ohio River could be traced from Evansville to the mouth of the Wabash River.

There are few remaining descendants of William A; Alexander living in Posey County today. One of William D. Alexander's ten children was Julius, born in 1875 and married to Idella McFadden. They had four children, one of whom is living today in Mt. Vernon. Lena Alexander Addison, a former school teacher, first in Posey County, then later in northern Indiana, was married to Paul F. Addison, also an educator. Her family lived for many years in western Lynn Township in the same location as her grandfather William David. Her father too was a very successful farmer.

Another member of this family today in Mt. Vernon, is Lillian Lichtenberger Root. Her father, Aaron Lichtenberger, was the son of Harriet Alexander and Lafayette Lichtenberger. Harriet was a daughter of William A. Alexander. Lillian was married to Chester Root, and has lived in Posey County all her life, and is a retired teacher in the Mt. Vernon school system.

Another son of Wm. A. Alexander was Lafayette who was married to Sally French. This family had two sons, Frederick and Alfred. The father died at an early age. Alfred J. Alexander was married to Clyde Conlinand they are the parents of Mary Alexander Stephens, who lives in Mt. Vernon with her husband Ausburn T. Stephens. She too taught in the Mt. Vernon school system for several years. Their daughter, Jane E. Norris, her husband, R. Scott Norris D.D.S., and their two children, Julie and Amy Lynn also live in Mt. Vernon, and represent the fifth and sixth generation descendants of Wm. A. Alexander.

Another son of Wm. A. Alexander was Andrew, whose wife was Matilda Greathouse Alexander. None of this family are living, but due to Matilda Alexander's efforts to give to Mt. Vernon its first library, and to continue for her life time to further the cause for a public library for the city, she deserves recognition and mention in this biographical sketch. Today we have one of the finest public libraries in the state of Indiana, which is named after its early founder.

BRUCE R. AND CHRISTI ALLDREDGE

Bruce R. Alldredge and Christi Quinn were married Nov. 30, 1974 at Welborn Methodist Church, Black Township.

Bruce is the son of Myron Lee and Eileen Alldredge. He attended Upton Elementary School, West Elementary School, Mount Vernon Junior High, and graduated from M.V.H.S. in 1969. He studed at Vincennes University for one year and transferred to Purdue University for his second year. At the end of that year he returned home to associate with his father in farming.

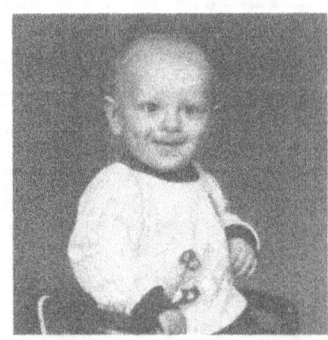
John Robert Alldredge nine months

Christi's father Glenn Quinn, son of Robert and Elizabeth Lee Quinn, was born 1924 at Mount Vernon, IL. He graduated from high school there, then spent 1943-1946 as a mess sergeant with the U.S. Army. He came to Indiana as a young man to be close to his brother and sister-in-law, Lloyd and Reva Nell Quinn, of Mount Vernon. After his marriage to Betty, they settled on a farm north of Upton in Black Township. He engaged in farming and also was employed at the Handle Factory. He was one of the first employees of Babcock-Wilcox when the company came to Mount Vernon. Four children were born to Glenn and Betty: Christy in

1955, Barbara in 1959, Michael in 1960 and Lester in 1961. Glenn cared for them from their infancy. For several years Ben Mayville lived with the family. When the children became older, Rose Schwindel Wainman was their housekeeper.

Glenn's hobbies are rock hunting and collecting Indian relics.

Bruce and Christi made their first home with Bruce's maternal grandmother, Ida Butler. Their first child, Carla Lynn, was born Sept. 2, 1975, while living in a mobile home at the Alldredge farm in Upton. In 1977 they purchased the farm home of Bruce's paternal grandparents, Herman and Grace Alldredge. It is located across the road from his parent's home. The second daughter, Sara Elizabeth, was born Nov. 13, 1979, and a son, John Robert, on Jan. 29, 1988.

Bruce is a beekeeper. He likes to hunt and trap during the winter months. He grows watermelons, cantaloupes, sweet corn, tomatoes and pumpkins for market.

The family is active in the worship services and church school at Welborn Methodist Church.

MYRON LEE AND EILEEN D. ALLDREDGE

Myron Lee Alldredge and Eileen D. Butler were married Sept. 12, 1935, in a ceremony at the Alldredge homestead on Upton Road in Black Township.

Myron Lee, born in 1911, was one of seven children born to Herman and Grace Whipple Alldredge. He attended Upton Elementary School and then started farming. In 1935 he purchased the farm of his grandfather John Sam Alldredge. He and Eileen farmed, raised livestock and for several years operated a dairy.

Myron Lee and Eileen Alldredge

Their children are Rhonda, born in 1940; Treva, born in 1946; and Bruce, born in 1951.

The family worships at Welborn Methodist Church where Lee and Eileen teach in the church school. Lee has been a Boy Scout leader. Eileen was a 4H leader for 12 years and a charter member of Jolly Housewives Homemakers Extension Club. She is educational director for the Posey County Woman's Christian Temperance Union. She graduated from Mount Vernon High School in 1933. She likes to sew, cook, and garden.

Lee's great-grandfather, Samuel Spike Alldredge (1825-1911), farmed in the Upton community. He was the father of seven children and gave them each a farm. He built two log houses and one frame house. Lee's grandfather built the two-story, seven room frame house where Lee and Eileen started housekeeping. The grandfather had a grocery store in Upton and later another one in Mount Vernon. His first wife was Sallie Welborn, mother of Herman, William, and Della. His second wife was Mary Lou Redman, mother of Ethel and Elsie.

Lee's maternal grandparents were Marion and Mary Hall Whipple.

Eileen was born in 1916 to S. Arthur and Ida French Butler. She has a brother, Naurice, and a sister, Lois Blackburn. The Butler family lived on the Butler homestead at Farmersville. The grandfather, Clark Butler (1827-1893), came as an orphan from the east. He worked for the Trafford family, purchased a farm and married Alzina Black (1837-1879). They were the parents of five children. Clark took a trip to California during the Gold Rush of 1849.

Eileen's maternal grandparents were John and Laura Durlin French, of Lynn Township. He was a descendant of the pioneer French family who came to Posey County in 1906. Their five children were Elanor, Ida, Zulah and Zedok (twins), and Lena.

In 1888 the family traveled to Colorado in a covered wagon. They claimed two plots of land and built a sod house. Later they returned to Indiana. John gradually lost his eye sight as the result of an accident.

Ida French was a school teacher. In 1909 she won a trip to Europe by securing subscriptions to the Evansville Courier. In 1910 she married S. Arthur Butler. They resided on the family homestead and farmed. Arthur died in 1932. Ida stayed on the farm, paid off their debts and raised the children. The family were members of the Olive Chapel Methodist Church.

In her memory book Ida wrote: "God will not look us over for our medals, but for our scars."

OTIS BARTON ALLYN

Otis Barton Allyn (deceased) was born in Posey County on Sept. 28, 1912, a son of Abijah Allyn (b. Jan. 5, 1881 - d. May 8, 1957) and Emma Wolfinger Allyn (b. Jan. 22, 1881 - d. Oct. 21, 1960). Otis attended Indiana University and taught school in Posey County for six years before starting an abstract business in Mt. Vernon, which was still in operation in 1989. He served as First Sergeant in the 82nd Airborne Division during World War II. Following a tour of duty in North Africa, Sicily, Italy, Ireland and England, he participated in the Normandy invasion. He later attended Officer Candidates School at Ft. Benning, GA, and served as a Lieutenant at Ft. Hood, TX. After the war he returned to Indiana University and received his law degree in 1950. He was a member of the Indiana Chapter of the Order of the Coif. Otis helped organize the Greater Mt. Vernon Association, was a past president of the Mt. Vernon Kiwanis Club and a lieutenant governor of the district Kiwanis. He was past exalted ruler of the local Elks Lodge. He was a past president of the Posey-Vanderburgh Sons of the American Revolution. He was also a past president of the Posey County Historical Society, the Mt. Vernon Alexandrian Library Board and the Posey County Bar Association. He was a member of Trinity United Church of Christ and was a past president of the Trinity Church Council. He was a member of Owen Dunn Post #5, Western Hills Country Club, Petroleum Club, and Germania Maennerchor. Otis was the senior partner of the Allyn, Givens, and Bender law firm. He died Aug. 30, 1985.

Abijah Allyn and Emma Wolfinger Allyn were also the parents of Louis E. Allyn (b. Dec. 11, 1908), Ruth Allyn (b. Sept. 10, 1906) and Wilma Simpson (b. Mar. 26, 1905 - d. Dec. 17, 1988).

Otis B. Allyn married Helen L. Felker on Dec. 16, 1944, at St. John's United Church of Christ, Evansville, IN. Helen was born Dec. 20, 1913 in Evansville, a daughter of Rosa Reichert Felker and John C. Felker. Both of Helen's parents were born in Wuerttemberg in Germany on the same day, Oct. 6, 1877 - Rosa in Unterturkhim and John in Frauenzimmern. Their families immigrated to the United States in the 1880s when Rosa and John were children. The Felker family settled in Evansville, IN; the Reichert family settled in Lee County, AL.

After graduating from Evansville College (now the University of Evansville) in 1934, Helen taught in the Evansville Public School system for 14 years. She is a member of Trinity United Church of Christ, Trinity Auxiliary and the Tuesday Literary Club.

Otis and Helen Allyn's children are: Emily, born Apr. 3, 1950, and Mary, born Nov. 10, 1956. Emily married Robert Yount. They have one son, Joseph, born Dec. 10, 1981. Mary married Kenneth Juncker. They have three daughters, Rebecca and Anna, (twins) born May 21, 1980 and Dana, born Nov. 15, 1985.

Rosa R. Felker and John C. Felker were also the parents of Gustav F. Felker (b. Jan. 2, 1903 - d. May 30, 1982), Albert J. Felker (b. Jan. 5, 1905 - d. June 30, 1966) and Emma F. Oehlman (b. Dec. 3, 1906).

DONN AND SANDRA ALMON

Donn L. and Sandra R. Almon are residents of Black Township where he is employed by Indiana Farm Bureau as refinery assistant superintendent and she is a homemaker. Sons, Stuart Brent and Derek S., and daughter, Jetta Lynn, are residents of Posey County as are grandchildren Luke and Alex Almon, Chasidy and Joshua Kilgore, and Brandin and Amanda Almon. The grandchildren are of the eighth consecutive generation of Almons to live in Robb Township and Posey County beginning with Thomas Almon Sr. who with his wife, Mary Swanson, and some of their children came from Christian Co., KY sometime between 1792 and 1811. The Almons are believed to have located in Virginia after having migrated from England.

Mr. Almon, a Revolutionary War Veteran, and his wife accompanied their son John, his wife, Holland Murphy, and her mother, Ada Rice Murphy, to Pike County to reside in the early 1830s. John was a farmer and minister. Thomas Almon Jr. accompanied his parents from Kentucky and at the age of 21 fought and was wounded in the Battle of Tippecanoe. He died at age 87 and was buried beside his wife, Ruth Martin, in Black River Cemetery near Pumpkin Run in Robb Township.

One of their sons, Bennett Almon, a farmer, married Maranda Armstrong on Feb. 12, 1846; the previous year she had woven for her hopechest a coverlet which is on display today in Workingmen's Institute Museum, New Harmony, IN. As an adult, Bailey Martin, eighth of their 12 children, lived with his wife, Etta E. Baldwin, on an adjoining farm. In addition to farming, he operated a threshing machine as well as a cider press into which apples were dumped by the wagonload (worms and all). His horses competed in county-fair harness races which were sometimes started by Frank James who had paid his debt to society. It was reported by Larkin, a son, that nobody argued about the fairness of the start.

Due to his father's failed health, Larkin B. Almon and his wife Mary U. Crawford, with their infant son, Donn, joined Bailey and Etta Almon in their home where Donn continued to live until after his marriage in Black River Church on May 24, 1952 to Sandra Saxe, a resident of Robb Homestead and native of Edwards Co., IL.

While serving in the U.S. Army, Donn was stationed in Germany after which residence was taken up in Mt. Vernon. Donn and Sandra are members of First United Methodist Church and are actively involved in the restoration and care of Black River Cemetery.

THE JACK E. AND WANDA D. ANGEL FAMILY

Jack is the second son of William Mathias and Lillie Greathouse Angel. His brother, William R., died in 1978. The family moved from Newburgh, IN to Mt. Vernon in 1934.

Jack and Wanda graduated from Mt. Vernon High School, he in 1946 and she in 1947. They married on June 3, 1947. Jack went to work for Bennett's Harley Davidson Shop in Evansville and Wanda for Peoples Bank & Trust in Mt. Vernon.

Three sons were born to them, Dennis Edward in 1950 in Evansville, IN, Stephan Eugene in 1952 and Jeff Robert in 1953 in Lewiston, ID.

Jack was born in 1929 in Warrick Co., IN. His great grandparents owned the land where Angel Mounds is now located. His mother's family, the Greathouses, migrated from Heidelberg, Germany to Pennsylvania then west to settle in Posey County.

Jack E. and Wanda D. Angel

Wanda's father, Winfred Myron Dunn, the son of Robert Buchanan and Ethel Culley Dunn, ran a Phillips 66 Station on College Avenue. He and Zola Rowe married in 1928. Wanda was born in 1929. They divorced in January 1939 and in December of that year she married Everett "Pete" Ashworth a prominent Black Twp. farmer.

Jack and Wanda with Dennis moved to Lapwai, ID in 1951 where Jack began an auto repair shop located on the Nez Perce Indian Reservation. Their home, west of Lapwai, was once a waystation for stagecoaches.

In 1959 they returned to Posey County to farm with Wanda's parents. Traveling back in a 1935 International 1-1/2 ton truck holding all their possessions, it took them a full week as they very seldom exceeded 35 MPH. They felt like their ancestors had years before, enduring snow blizzards, ice storms and very slow going. In 1959 they bought five acres on Bald Knob Road where they still live. In 1969 they bought a farm bordering the Wabash River known as the Zimmerman Farm.

Along with farming, in 1964 Jack started working for Renschler Farm Equipment in Mt. Vernon, where he still works. Wanda worked for the former Gerber's Supermarket as cashier and bookkeeper.

Their three sons married and so far ten grandchildren have arrived. Dennis married Constance J. Horacek in 1971. Twins, Christopher Scott and Bryan Neal born in 1973 followed by Brock Edward in 1974. Dennis farms in Posey Co., IN and White Co., IL. Stephan married Gail A. Saalwechter in 1973. Twins, Jacob Daniel and David William born in 1983 followed by Benjamin Edward in 1986. Living in Chicago, IL, he is co-owner of a printing and mailing co. Jeff married Patricia L. Richey in 1980. They have one son, Shaun Jeffery born in 1981, two daughters, Rebecca Diane born 1985 and Amanda Lynn born in 1988. Jeff has a son, Clay Robert born in 1975 by a previous marriage. Jeff owns and operates Angel's General Contractors in Posey County.

Jack and Wanda are members of Black's Chapel United Methodist Church where he is lay leader and they both have held various positions through the years.

VIRGIL G. AND MARGIE JEAN (ESPENLAUB) ANGERMEIER

Virgil G. and Margie Jean (Espenlaub) Angermeier reside in Black Township Virgil, born July 17, 1920 in Gibson County, parents, Leo and Olivia (Bender) Angermeier. Attended eight grades of school in Gibson and Posey County. Came to Posey County in 1927. Was active in 4-H projects, sheep and grain. Was a farmer in partnership with his brothers, Cletus and Dale, later he owned and operated Mt. Vernon Feed and Supply (Wayne Feeds) for 28 years. Is now retired.

Leo, born Apr. 23, 1892 in Vanderburgh County, parents, Nicholas and Bertha (Baumgart) Angermeier. Olivia, born June 5, 1985 in Posey County. Olivia's parents were Valentine Bender and Theresa (Will) Bender. Valentine, born Nov. 6, 1863 in Hessen-Darmstadt, Germany, parents, August and Catherine (Berg) Bender, school teacher and farmer, natives of Germany, came to Vanderburgh County in 1865, moved to Posey County, Smith Township in 1888.

Virgil G. Angermeier Margie Jean (Espenlaub) Angerrmeier

Virgil and Margie Jean married Sept. 6, 1950. To this union have been born Glenda Sue, Paul L. and Glenn V. Paul L., born Jan. 24, 1954, attended eight years of school at St. Matthews, graduated from Mt. Vernon High in 1972, graduated from Purdue University and University of Illinois with a Doctor's degree in ecology, now working for Federal Government in Blacksburg, VA. He was an active 4-H member for ten years. Glenn V., born Apr. 16, 1957, attended six years of school at St. Matthews and two years at Mt. Vernon Junior High, graduated from Mt. Vernon High in 1975, graduated from Purdue University and the University of Chicago, with a Master's degree in Business, now working at Chemical Bank, New York, NY. Married to Margaret Brooks, Oct. 8, 1988, residing in Brooklyn, NY. He was an active 4-H member for ten years.

Margie Jean, born Sept. 23, 1922, Marrs Township, parents, Henry C. Espenlaub, Jr. and Emma O. (Miller) Espenlaub. Attended eight years at Stucky school, graduated from Mt. Vernon High in 1941. Worked at the Garment Corp. in Mt. Vernon for 3-1/2 years and presently working at Allyn Abstract Co, Inc. for 29 years. A member of Home Ec. Club for 42 years.

Emma, born in Caborn, Marrs Township, May 6, 1895, parents, Lorenz C. and Margaret (Wimpelberg) Miller. Lorenz, born July 9, 1851, a farmer and road supervisor. Margaret, born Dec. 14, 1858, parents, John and Margaret (Lindeman) Wimpelberg, natives of Germany, came to U.S. about 1840.

Emma, attended eight years of school at Caborn. Married Henry C. Espenlaub, Jr. Aug. 30, 1921. She played piano and organ, loved to play her harmonica and sing german songs.

Henry, born in Marrs Township, Mar. 29, 1893, parents Henry C. Espenlaub, Sr. and Margaret (Jourdan) Espenlaub. Henry, Sr., born May 24, 1861, parents, John C. and Barbara (Muller) Espenlaub. John, born Sept. 26, 1826, migrated at the age of 26 years. Margaret, born Mar. 10, 1861 to Jacob and Margaret Jourdan, both of German parents. Henry attended Carson School, was a life long farmer. Played a violin for dances. Killed under a tractor Aug. 12, 1958.

ASHWORTH

Louise (born Feb. 20, 1900), Mae (born Aug. 25, 1904), and George (born Feb. 20, 1912) were the children of G.A. and Mae (Hurley) Ashworth. G.A. was the son of Andrew Jackson and Sally (Green) Ashworth of Mt. Vernon and Mae was the daughter of James Madison and Elizabeth (Henson) Hurley of Dixon, KY.

G.A. was in the grocery business in Mt. Vernon for many years and was active in local affairs, serving as Posey County Democratic chairman in the early 1920's, as Posey County treasurer, and as a member of the Mt. Vernon School Board from 1935-1948.

Louise, following high school graduation, worked as a secretary in Washington, DC, during the late part of World War I. She married Lawrence Baldwin of Henderson, KY, and has two daughters: Virginia Kraemer (Mrs. Herbert F.) and Ann Heck (Mrs. Alfred D.). She worked in Washington for the federal government until her retirement, was active in Penwomen's Club, is a member of the Daughters of the American Revolution, and lives in Reston, VA.

She has five grandchildren: Dr. Carol Kraemer, Thomas F. Kraemer, Major Karen Heck, USMC, Laura Heck, and Leigh Ann Heck La Rosa (Mrs. J.J.). There are four great-grandchildren: Joey and Anna Louise Chenoweth and Dwayne and Gillian Barton.

Mae graduated from Mt. Vernon High School and received training for an elementary teachers license at Indiana University. After several years of teaching in Mt. Vernon, she accepted a position as editor of "Mothers' Magazine" with David C. Cook Publishing Company of Elgin, IL. She later moved to New York City as a book editor for Friendship Press and to concentrate on free-lance writing of several hundred published stories, articles, plays, and books.

She was honored for her literary accomplishments at the 1989 Mt. Vernon High School Commencement Exercises with the "Outstanding Alumnus of the Year Award."

She is a charter member of the General Thomas Posey Chapter of the Daughters of the American Revolution, is retired, and lives in Reston, VA.

George graduated from MVHS, attended Centre College, and earned BS and MS degrees from Indiana State Teachers College, where he was football captain and received the Hines Medal for scholarship.

On Apr. 12, 1936, he married Helen Louise Lackey of Terre Haute, and they are the parents of two sons: James Michael, born July 25, 1946, and Robert Andrew, born Jan. 25, 1949.

George was a teacher, coach, and school administrator from 1936-1978. Helen, a graduate of Terre Haute Garfield High School, completed work for her college degree at the University of Evansville and taught in the Mt. Vernon schools from 1964-1974. Both were, and remain, active in community affairs; Helen gives book reviews and slide presentations to local and Southern Indiana groups, serves on various church committees, and has served twice as president of Beta Associate chapter of Tri Kappa. George has been active as a director of the Mt. Vernon Chamber of Commerce, United Way of Posey County, Western Hills Country Club, and Posey County Council on Aging. He also served as president of Western Hills Country Club and as the first president of General Thomas Posey Chapter, Sons of the American Revolution.

He has been recognized for his background in athletics by the Champaign News-Gazette, which named him Illinois High School Football Coach of the Year, by induction to the Indiana Football Hall of Fame, and by induction to the Mt. Vernon High School Athletic Hall of Fame. His civic work was recognized by awards from Civitan Club, Posey County Council on Aging, and Mt. Vernon Chamber of Commerce.

Upon his retirement as Mt. Vernon Superintendent of Schools, the University of Southern Indiana conferred an honorary Doctor of Laws Degree.

Mike graduated from Mt. Vernon High School in 1964, where he was class president in both his Junior and Senior years, played varsity football and basketball, and received the American Legion Citizenship Award. He attended Indiana University and Franklin College.

In 1968 he married Dawn Maree Backus, daughter of Denver and Nancy (Jeffries) Backus. They have three children: Jason Todd, born Feb. 22, 1969, Mark Andrew, born June 15, 1975, and Anne Maree-Helen, born Oct. 15, 1980.

Mike is an officer of Posey County Bank, works with United Way, and is a director of Western Hills Country. Dawn is employed by the Metropolitan School District.

Bob graduated in 1966 from Mt. Vernon High School, where he was president of the Junior Class and won all-conference recognition in football and basketball. In 1970 he graduated from Northwestern University, which he attended on a football scholarship, and later earned his MS degree at the University of Evansville.

In 1978 he married Elizabeth Murray of Evansville. They have two sons; Nathan Todd, born Sept. 19, 1985, and John Andrew, born Aug. 9, 1988.

Bob is a teacher and coach at Lawrence Central High School in Indianapolis, where he has twice been named Marion County Football Coach of the Year, and Beth is a surgeon practicing in Kokomo, IN.

ZOLA ASHWORTH

The youngest child of John Lincoln and Clara Hunsinger Rowe, Zola born in 1907 has lived, except for a brief period, in Black Twp., Posey County her entire life. After 81 years, she has returned to live on the property where she was born, on Bald Knob Road.

Her father, John L. was the son of George W. and his 2nd wife, America Baker Rowe. George W. better known as "Hogue" was a large farmer in both Posey Co., IN and White Co., IL. He owned his own ferry boat to cross the Wabash River to his farm in Illinois.

George W. was a staunch Republican, a tradition that has lasted to the present generation. America Baker Rowe owned with her first husband, Jesse, the property now owned by Zola's son-in-law and daughter, Jack E. and Wanda D. Angel.

Zola Ashworth

On June 23, 1902 he along with son Thomas and grandson, Homer, was killed when a steam engine exploded on their farm. They were getting ready to thresh wheat.

John "Linc" and Clara were married in 1891. Linc died when Zola was four months old, leaving Clara with nine children to raise on her own. Claude, Mabel, Ethel, Herbert, Joseph, twins, George and Thomas, Laura and Zola.

Zola's mother, Clara, was born and raised in Burnt Prairie, IL vicinity where her family farmed. Her father, Joseph Hunsinger married Emily Kuykendall in 1857. Besides farming, Joseph served in several political positions and also an elder in the Baptist Church of the community. Joseph died the day after Emily of a broken heart.

Zola married Winfred Myron Dunn in 1928 and a daughter Wanda Dee was born in 1929. Winfred ran a gas station and tire shop. In 1938 he went to St. Louis, MO. Zola worked at the Garment Factory where Posey Warehousing is now located on North Main St., where she sewed pockets in overalls. This was one of the first factories in Mt. Vernon to hire women.

In 1939 she met and married Everett "Pete" Ashworth a prominent Black Twp. farmer. Everett's parents, William and Hannah Fellemande Ashworth, lived in the Prairie community enduring droughts and floods. The 1937 flood destroyed their house. Rebuilding with the help of friends, neighbors and the Red Cross, they continued on. Everett and Zola bought the farm from his mother when William died in 1943.

When Everett died in 1988, Zola sold the farm to their grandson, Dennis E. Angel and his wife Constance, thus another generation carries on.

EUGENE JR. & MARGIE AUSTIN

Eugene (Gene), Jr. and Margarea (Margie) Austin and their daughter Donnagene (Donna) moved to Posey County on June 9, 1969 from Grand Chain, IL. Gene became Lockmaster of the Uniontown Locks and Dam in Point Township and came to observe the last stages of construction in 1968.

Gene was born in Uniontown, KY on July 16, 1919 the eldest son of Eugene and Daisy Austin. He also has a brother James. Gene attended school at the Uniontown Public School and graduated in the Class of 1937. He went to work for the Corps of Engineers on the dredge boat after graduation. During World War II Gene spent three years in the Army Air Force serving in the Pacific. After being discharged Gene returned to the Civil Service Corps of Engineers. Gene worked at Lock and Dam #49 in Uniontown, KY as did his father for many years. He then transferred to Lock and Dam #45 at Addison, KY in Breckinridge County.

Margie was born in Breckinridge Co., KY on Sept. 17, 1929. Her parents were Herman and Dorris Dutschke. She has two brothers Walter and Herman E. and a sister Catherine. The Herman Dutschke family farmed in Breckinridge County at Holt, KY. Margie attended the two room country school at Holt and graduated from Breckinridge County High School in the Class of 1948.

Gene and Margie married on July 1, 1948 in Morganfield, KY. They made their first home at Lock and Dam #44 at Leavenworth, IN. They lived in Leavenworth until May 1951.

Donna was born on June 15, 1951 at the Breckinridge County Memorial Hospital in Hardinsburg, KY. They now lived at Lock and Dam #45 at Addison, KY. The Austin family also lived at Lock and Dam #43 at New Boston, IN, Lock and Dam #48 in Union Township in Vanderburgh County and Lock and Dam #53 in Grand Chain, IL.

Donna attended the Union Township grade school in Vanderburgh County and the Grand Chain Elementary school in Grand Chain, IL. She graduated from Century High School in Ullin, IL in the Class of 1969. She attended Indiana State University of Evansville which is now University of Southern Indiana. Donna married Anthony Wayne (Tony) Gross on Aug. 7, 1971 at the First United Methodist Church in Mt. Vernon.

Tony was born Dec. 3, 1949. His parents are Edwin and Ellie Gross who lived in Posey County. Tony attended West Elementary School in Mt. Vernon and graduated from Mt. Vernon High School in the Class of 1968. Tony attended Indiana State University of Terra Haute and graduated from Indiana State University of Evansville which is now University of Southern Indiana.

Donna and Tony live in rural Mt. Vernon and have two children, Kyle Anthony born Aug. 15, 1979 who is in 4th grade at West Elementary in Mt. Vernon and Brittany Nicole born July 12, 1985 and attends the Susanna Wesley Nursery School at the First United Methodist Church in Mt. Vernon.

On Dec. 30, 1988 Gene retired from the Corps of Engineers after having served as Lockmaster of Uniontown Locks and Dam for 20 years. He had 50 years service with the United States Government. The Austin family do not intend to move from Posey County.

Gene's dad, Gene Austin, Sr. died in March of 1949 and his mother still lives in Uniontown, KY.

Margie's dad died in August 1985 and her mother lives in Maceo, KY.

Tony's dad died in January 1986 and his mother lives in Evansville, IN.

AXTON-HANCOCK

Jeanette Wilson Reynolds of Napa, CA has been

researching her Posey County families for the past 15 years. She was born 1933 in St. Louis, MO the daughter of Marcus Brown and Alice Harriett Dittmar Wilson, moved to Alameda, CA in 1943, attended schools there and married Robert Carl Reynolds in the Oakland, CA Army Base chapel 1953. They are the parents of four sons: Mark Lee; Robert Scott; Jeffrey Wade; and David John.

Jeanette's paternal grandparents were James William Wilson born 1863 Morganfield, Union Co., KY and Idella "Dell" Axton born 1872 Harmony Township, Posey County, to Isham S. (he being a son of Enoch W.) and Sarah Jane Hancock Axton, both having been born Posey County in 1848 and 1850 respectively. The grandfather was a sawyer and owned a sawmill in Brookland, AR, where they resided after their marriage in Posey County in 1901. Dell, who had been a school teacher in Posey County, returned there for the birth of their first three children: Sadie Latitia 1902 and twins James Evelyn and Anna Bridgewater 1904. Another set of twins Marcus Brown and Bessie May born 1905 and daughter Eunice Kathleen born 1909 were born in Brooklyn, AR.

Enoch W. Axton born 1809 Mercer Co., KY died 1885 Posey County married 1835 Margaret Owens born 1813 died 1884 Posey County daughter of Thomas Owens and Elizabeth Rogers, and had siblings Charlotte, Elizabeth, Sarah, Thomas J., Penelope, Levi P., Robert and Leroy.

In 1830 Isham James Axton born 1784-90 North Carolina, father of Enoch W. brought his family to Posey County from Ohio Co., KY, along with his brother William and family. Isham and William had married Murphy sisters in 1808 Mercer Co., KY. Elizabeth "Betsey" Murphy born 1794 Virginia and Isham parented 13 children, with many descendants still in Posey County. Children and spouses are: Enoch W. - Margaret Owens, America-James Odell; William R.-Lucy Ann Hungate; Levi-Elizabeth Moore; John Slaughter- Elizabeth Ann Howery; Isham-Mary Ann Simpson; Margaret-Zachariah Wade; Mary-Armstead Hungate; Prestley-Polly A. Sutton; Ora Jane-Joshua E. Wade; Elizabeth Ann-George Cleveland; Addison-Pamela Acuff; and James M.-America Endicott. The Axton homestead was in Harmony Township.

Sarah Jane Hancock Axton was the daughter of John Hancock Jr. born 1829 Grainger Co., TN died 1857 Posey County married 1849 Catherine Taunt born 1828 Craven Co., NC died Evansville, IN 1904, and had as siblings Samuel Scott, Nancy Jane, Ira Jett Williams and William Asa Williams, the latter two being from the second marriage of Catherine to George I. Williams. John Hancock Jr.'s parents were Benjamin Hancock born 1801 Virginia died 1875 Posey County and Mary Butler born 1803 North Carolina died 1876 Posey County. His grandfather was John Sr. born 1767 Virginia died 1851 Posey County. Catherine was born to Thomas Taunt and Penelope Butler born North Carolina died Posey County. The Benjamin Hancock farm was also in Harmony Township.

JUDGE AND MRS. STEVE BACH

Judge and Mrs. Steve Bach met at I.U., married Sept. 6, 1947 Winchester, IN. Steve; son of Evelyn and Grannis Bach, Jackson, KY - descendant of Revolutionary War Soldier Nathaniel Britton. Rosemary is daughter of Louis and Greta Husted, Winchester, IN. D.A.R. descendant William Ensign.

They have two children: 1951 John C. Bach, 1954 Christine Bockstanz. John, attorney Atlanta, GA, married Patti Calabria, R.N. - 1973. They have two sons: Adam, 1979 and Alex, 1981. Christine, attorney, Allantown, PA, married David Bockstanz, Nuclear Engineer, 1980. They have two children: Katy, 1981 and John, 1985.

Rosemary (Posey) Bach, English Major, I.U. - former president of Tri Kappa, Posey County Mental Health, Regent D.A.R., member of original group re-starting Posey County History Club, was active presenting, programs, book reviews in the community. Wrote articles for Mt. Vernon Democrat, series of the Ohio Riverboats were in archives of I.S.U. She and Judge Bach members of Methodist Church, Posey County Democrats, Western Hills Country Club.

Steve served in World War II in the Intelligence Division of U.S. Signal Corp. He was 1st President of Greater Mt. Vernon Association, serving two terms during its funding. Advanced financing to Waterworks for the water line to General Electric. Was city attorney two administrations, was President of Kiwanis, served as 8th District Judge Advocate for American Legion. He is currently on Community Advisory Council of the Indiana University School of Medicine.

Judge Bach was elected the Posey County Circuit Bench in 1965-1982. Instrumental in restoring Posey County Court Room, using original design. Stressing history of Court House. Served on the Regional Board of Mental Health, also Criminal Justice. He has served on the Governors Juvenile Justice Delinquency Prevention Advisory Board and on the Legislative study commission that formulated the Juvenile Code in Indiana. Served as a faculty advisor of The National Trial Judges College and the Board of Trustees of the National Council of Juvenile and Family Court Judges. Served two terms as President of the Indiana Council of Juvenile Court Judges. He is currently serving as President of the International Institute for Youth and is listed in Who's Who in American Law, Who's Who in America and Who's Who in the World.

BRUCE BAKER

Bruce Baker (1952) is the son of Andrew Charles Baker (1917-1965) of Ullyses, KS. He was of Mormon descent. Andrew came to work in the Griffin oilfields in 1939.

Bruce's mother is Dora Marie Smith of Southern Gibson County. After the death of Andrew Baker, Dora Marie attended Evansville School of Practical Nursing. She married James O. Newman in 1969.

Bruce has two brothers: William Ray and Charles Steven, and two sisters: Suzanne and Andrea Marie.

As a child, Bruce lived in a home built around a log cabin south of Griffin. He moved to Poseyville in 1965. Bruce graduated from North Posey High School in 1970. He served in the Air Force from 1971 to 1975.

Bruce attended the Indiana Law Enforcement Academy at Plainfield in 1976. He served as Poseyville Marshall from 1975-1980, and as a Deputy Sheriff of Posey County from 1980-1984. He joined Farmers Bank and Trust Company in 1984.

Bruce was appointed to the Poseyville Town Board in 1987. He ran unopposed in the election of 1988. He has served as Town Board President since that time.

Bruce married to Lynda Diana Curtis, Evansville

Our Family, April 1986

(1957). Lynda's earliest ties to the southern Indiana area were Carolina Cherokee Indians, who were relocated to this region of the United States. Lynda's father is Charles Eugene Curtis (1935), of Mt. Vernon. Charles is a veteran of Korea and Vietnam. Charles is the son of David Curtis, and the grandson of Raymond Curtis (a former Posey County Commissioner). The Curtis family originated in North Carolina, and settled mainly in the Black Township area as farmers. Lynda's mother is Norma Jean Parson (1935), also of Mt. Vernon. She is the daughter of William Wilford Parson (1909-1976). William was an oilfield worker of Pennsylvania Dutch ancestry. He served in the Navy during WWII in the Atlantic. Norma Parson's mother is Wilma Lee Jackson (1917). She came to Posey County from Springfield, IL in the early 1900s.

Lynda Curtis Baker graduated from Mt. Vernon High School (1976). Bruce and Lynda Baker have two sons. Nathaniel William (Cater) Baker and Andrew Charles (Curtis) Baker. Bruce was instrumental in developing the additions to Poseyville north of Boren Avenue. He was also a leader in the reconstruction of Poseyville streets and sidewalks. The streets were stripped to the soil (1989) and completely reconstructed. A 22 ft. well, and a 16' x 18' cistern used by the old fire "Bucket Brigades" were uncovered during the reconstruction. Lynda Baker has been an emergency medical technician with Posey County Emergency Medical Services since 1980. *Submitted by Lynda Diana Baker*

CALVIN AND LELA COX BARRETT

Calvin and Lela Cox Barrett are residents of Mount Vernon, IN. Calvin, son of Solomon and Maude Ethel St. Clair Barrett, was born in Evansville. He adopted Posey as his home in 1946, when he purchased a farm that is now part of Harmonie State Park. Lela graduated from Springfield Elementary and Mt. Vernon High Schools; is a member of Bethel Church, Posey Historical Society and Nat'l Republican Women Federation.

Aunt Lela, Uncle Calvin

My father, (Joe) Joel Napoleon Cox, born Sept. 1, 1889-Oct. 31, 1971, came to Posey County for employment. In the 1910 Point Census he was a laborer in the home of Robert Wheat. In 1913/14, while a member of the crew on three dredge-boats on Big Creek, south of Solitude, he met Anna, daughter of Charles and Victoria Carroll Phillips. She descends from Nicholas Phillips, who immigrated from England in 1636, and was born July 22, 1897 where he great-grandfather, Elisha Phillips homesteaded. She graduated from Farmersville Elementary School and was a member of Bethel Church, and Royal Neighbor and Lodge. Joel was a member of Bethel Church, which he served as Deacon, Modern Woodman Lodge and a Republican Lynn Twp. Trustee. Their other children are Lorene, married Leonard, son of George Stevens, Charles Joseph, married Marjorie, daughter of Wendalenous Kester, Walter Elbert, married Elizabeth, daughter of Homer Lloyd Tomlinson, Anna Mae, married John Martin, widowed, remarried and divorced Earl Griswold, Harold Lee, married Elizabeth, daughter of Percy McCoy, and Francis Ray, married Phyllis, daughter of Frank Mier. The sons were soldiers; in WWII; Charles in India, Walter in Japan Ray in Germany and Harold in the Korean War.

My grandfather, Joseph Sereneus Cox, born Aug. 28, 1861, Posey, married Sophronia, daughter of Isaac Jesse and Polly Cravens Daniel, in White Co., IL Aug. 26, 1888. Their four sons, Joel Napoleon, James Elzie, William Edward and Charles Henry were born in Illinois. Sereneus died Jan. 20, 1901 and was buried in Mount Pleasant Cemetery, White County. Sophronia died the following year; leaving orphans aged 11 to three. They were reared by her sisters, Lou Carroll and Lizzie Hargrove. Sophronia was born Jan. 22, 1867 and died Feb. 26, 1902.

My great-grandfather, Jackson Cox, born May 8, 1825, Posey, married Cynthia Jane, daughter of James and Edith Fletcher Ramsey, born Sept. 22, 1836 and died May 8, 1898. Their children were James Franklin, Joseph Sereneus, Ananias, Laura Belle, William Edward and Virgil. They sold their Posey farm and purchased one in Wayne Co., IL. They are buried in Mount Pleasant Cemetery.

My great-great grandfather, Joseph Cox, 1794-1865, was a soldier in the War of 1812.

My great-great-great grandfather, John Cox, Sr., 1754-1826/8, migrated from Muhlenberg Co., KY to Posey. He and members of his family were on the roll of Hazel Creek Church there and Bethel, Black River, and Bethlehem in Posey. John and wife, Martha are buried in Cox Cemetery on their farm in Robb Township. *Submitted by Lela Cox Barrett*

BECKER FAMILY HISTORY

The Becker Family while actually living in present-day Vanderburgh County, resided in a log house on 40 acres on the county line, entered from the "hill" road in Posey County, now known as Welborn since Dr. J.Y. purchased so much property along it. The first house on the lane was that of Wilhelm Hengstenberg (II), whose widow later married Ed Lengelsen, and the third was Schimmels', that widow's family. Much of the West side of Evansville, and the hill region of West Franklin in particular, has remaining ties with East Posey County, probably partly because Vanerburgh was carved out of parts of Posey Warrick, and Gibson Counties in 1818.

Jaohannes Becker was mentioned in the inch-

Arnold Becker born 1840 died 1900

thick book about his village, Neumorschen (new marsh), Hessen, as one who failed to pay his school tax, perhaps because of the failure of the potato crop; it was probably financial and perhaps political opportunity that brought them here. The Beckers never seemed to have much money, but they were very particular, always loved books and consideration of intellectual or political matters, such as socialism. Wife Anna Katharina Heinzerling was the daughter of the mayor of the neighboring village of Wichte where the Heinzerlings to this day often serve as mayors, often with the name **Arnold.** Johannes' mother was a Wenderoth, related to those at Wadesville; the Schmucks were also related from the home town in Germany.

An article in **Farm Journal** about a Heinzerling Family Reunion caused this writer to connect with the author, Pat Leimbach, whose husband, Paul, and aunt, Anna Catherine Hartman, were descended from her brother, who had migrated to the area of Elyria, OH. A.G. Hartman had visited the same home areas in Germany as did the great- and great-great-granddaughters of A.K. Heinzerling Becker. Apparently the Beckers came by "sailship" in 1846 to Bridgeport, CT, perhaps as indentured servants to pay their passage, where they remained several years—and left Johannes' brother Wilhelm—before purchasing the Indiana property in 1859. (Six year old Arnold was cautioned not to play on the rigging.)

Arnold, who cut wood and cleared land for a living, married Anna Luise Surbeck of Unterhallau, Kanton Schaffhausen, Switzerland, and had the following children: one son, Ernst Friedrich Wilhelm (who married Ida Lengelsen); daughters Anna Katharina (married Adam Hufnagel), Luise (married George Wilson from England, Emma (married Herman Hengstenberg), Elisabeth Rosa (married Louis Hugo Otto Karn), Ida Marie, Charlotte M., and Ida Mathilda. (latter three died young)

Arthritis remains an inherited affliction of the Becker women, and both sexes were susceptible to lung infections. Arnold's music instrument was the zither, son Wilhelm played bass fiddle.

Arnold's siblings were Wilhelm, who married Elizabeth McCray, and Christine, who married John Hendricks and lived at the corner of Smith-Diamond and Welborn Roads, where he was eventually buried in the corner of the garden after a fight on a boat at W. Franklin.

Johannes was a member of Salem Evangelical Church during the first ten years; son Wilhem was in the first class confirmed in the log church (1852); Arnold helped hang the bell in the new frame church (1888); his son, Wilhelm was general superintendent over 25 years, (a township trustee for eight, then agent for State Farm Insurance 30 years). This writer cherishes a prayer book purchased in the royal bookstore in Kassel, Germany, by John Becker in January, 1839, just off the press, for **Ein Thaler** (one dollar). The Becker homesite though sold after his death in 1900, was redeemed by his son in 1917 and remains in the possession of the fifth and sixth generations.

ALLYN A. BECKER FAMILY

Allyn and Geraldine (Kincheloe) Becker reside in Center Township. They were born, reared and married and have lived all their lives in Posey County. They reside in a house in which three generations of Becker's have called home. They live within site of the old homestead where his great grandfather settled after arriving from Germany in 1852 with his father and four brothers.

They came up the Mississippi River arriving in Evansville, their mother died on their way and after her burial, they resumed their journey to Evansville.

Allyn A. Becker Family

The great grandfather John was employed in Evansville until buying a farm in Robison Township. He later sold that farm and bought one in Center Township. This is where he raised his family. The great Uncle John then built the house where Allyn and Geraldine now live.

His brother, Jacob Allyn's grandfather, bought the house and farm where Allyn's father A .Adriel Becker was born and raised. He married Ruby Rose Allyn in 1918. They had five children, Allyn A., Margaret Rose, Marjorie R., Bettye Pear and Herman.

Allyn and Geraldine were married in December 1939 and raised their family in the same home. Jerry Allyn, the oldest son, was born in 1940, Ronald Roy in 1943, a son, Larry Lee died shortly after birth in 1945. The last and youngest son, Bobby Glen was born in 1953. Jerry Allyn works for Bristol-Myers, Ronald works for Whirlpool and Bob at General Electric.

Both Allyn and Geraldine graduated from Wadesville High School; Allyn in 1937, Geraldine in 1939. They have farmed the Becker Farms (Fairland Farms) until their retirement in 1984.

Geraldine's family (Kincheloe) arrived in Posey County about the same time as the Becker family. Her grandfather, Ora Kincheloe, was a farmer and one of the early deacons of the Mt. Zion General Baptist Church in south Center Township, where Allyn is now serving in the capacity.

There are several Kincheloe families (descendants) still living in Posey County.

Allyn and Geraldine have six grandchildren and one great grandson, Jacob Allen Martin. The eldest of the grandchildren, Scott Becker, is now managing the family farm. *Submitted by Allyn and Geraldine Becker*

JAMES M. BENNETT

James M. Bennett is a resident of Mt. Vernon. He was born Aug. 13, 1899 in Point Township. Son of

John Kelly and Laura Ann (Jameson). He moved to Mt. Vernon with his parents in 1916. Worked at many different jobs as a young man. On the old Straw Board, at the Mt. Vernon Creamery, sold insurance and real estate, was an auctioneer, coal miner and painter before pursuing a career in politics.

He and his brother, Stanley, promoted boxing matches at the Mt. Vernon Coliseum during the 30's, donating all proceeds to charity.

He married Sofhronia M. (Alley) on Sept. 21, 1926. She was born Mar. 23, 1910 in Uniontown, KY to Thelis Alley and Eliza (Cussic). Her father was killed in a logging accident when she was ten days old. She died Jan. 5, 1976. Of this union was born the following children. John Thelis, Ronald Ray, Wanda Lou and Larry Stanton Bennett.

James M. Bennett

James, active in Democrat politics most of his life was elected to office for the first time in 1934 as City Clerk-Treasurer. He went on to be elected Mayor, 1948 to 1952, was elected and served (seven) terms as Clerk-Treasurer 1935 to 1948 and 1956 to 1972. He has worked for County and State government 1952 to 1956 and was bookkeeper at the city garage from 1972 till his retirement in 1985, for a total of 50 years of Public service. He also served as Treasurer from 1971 to 1982, and Board member from 1971 to 1987 of the Alexandrian Library. He is a member of the Odd Fellows Lodge and First United Methodist Church.

He has been honored by his peers in 1980 and 1983 with banquets and commemorative plaques. Receiving letters of recognition from many dignitaries of State and Federal levels, including one from the oval office of, then President of the United States, Jimmy Carter. Also in his honor, in 1972 a newly purchased Fire and Ladder truck (still in use) had his name painted on the sides, at it's dedication at City Hall.

His son, John Thelis, born Sept. 3, 1930. Graduated from Mt. Vernon High class of 1948. Served with the U.S. Army in Germany. Graduated with a BA degree from University of Evansville in 1957. Earned a MA degree in special education from Michigan State in 1969. He has been teaching at the Indiana School for the Blind in Indianapolis since 1964.

Son, Ronald Ray, born Jan. 25, 1933. Graduated from Mt. Vernon High School class of 1951. Served in the U.S. Army in France. Married Pamela (Willis) July 26, 1969. She works as manager of the local cable T.V. station and also as part-time clerical worker for First United Methodist Church. He has worked at J.R. Short Milling Co. and General Electric. Is currently employed as deputy county auditor. Active in sports and community affairs he is secretary of Bellefontaine cemetery board, Treasurer of First United Methodist Church, Park Board and M-Club member. He has been scorekeeper for the Mt. Vernon High School varsity basketball team for over 30 years.

Daughter, Wanda Lou, born Aug. 8, 1934. Attended local schools, finishing high school equivalency at home due to a long illness. Also trained in Commercial Art, she has sold some of her work in Children's storybook and Animal illustrations, advertisements and safety posters. She worked seven years as deputy city Clerk-Treasurer and is currently employed as bookkeeper at the Mt. Vernon Water and Sewage Works.

Son, Larry Stanton, born Aug. 2, 1938. Graduated from Mt. Vernon High School class of 1956. Served with the Mt. Vernon National Guard for seven years. Graduated from Lockyears Business College in 1959. Married Linda (Cook) Feb. 12, 1972. They live in Shoals, IN where he is employed at Buehler's and the Shoals News and she is a teacher at Shoals Jr. High.

Father of James, John Kelly Bennett, born Apr. 3, 1868. Died Mar. 27, 1949. A native of Crittenden Co., KY. Son of James Madison and Mary (Humphrey) Bennett, natives of Tennessee. He came to Posey County as a child. Farmed in Point Township before moving to Mt. Vernon in 1916. He became a familiar figure to the towns people of Mt. Vernon and for many years was affectionately referred to as the "Pop Corn Man", having operated an old coal-oil fueled, push cart, popcorn vendor on Main Street and at ball games. He married Laura Ann (Jameson) Mar. 14, 1897. She was born Nov. 24, 1879 to William C. Jameson, from Fairfield Co., OH and Clarrisa (Parks) from White Co., IL.

To this union was born the following children. James Madison, Pearley Mae, Stanley Marion and Valeria Rose.

Paternal grandparents of James served with Morgans force in the Civil War and was captured by Union forces and remained a prisoner for 22 months. His maternal grandparent served with the Union forces, was captured but survived the notorious Eddyville camp.

The Bennett family are of English ancestry. Worked as blacksmiths and farmers. Prior to the War of the Revolution three brothers, Nicholas L., Walker Marion and Emory Hughs Bennett immigrated to the Virginia Colony. All three served in the Continental Line in the struggle which resulted in the formation of the Union. The brothers were the founders of the family in America.

THE GERALD ELMER BERGSTROM FAMILY

Gerald Elmer and his wife, Bonnie Jean (Willis) Bergstrom are both lifelong residents of Mt. Vernon. Both graduated from Mt. Vernon High School: Gerald in 1948 and Bonnie in 1950. Soon after graduating from high school, Gerald began working for the Chicago and Eastern Illinois Railroad (C&EI) as a fireman and later as an engineer. The C&EI later became a part of the Louisville and Nashville Railroad (L&N). Gerald is presently employed with the CSX Transportation System as an engineer. Bonnie began working as a telephone operator in 1950 at the Mt. Vernon branch of Indiana Bell. She remained there until 1959 when the Mt. Vernon office closed. On Dec. 4, 1955, Gerald and Bonnie were married. They have two children: Tamara Sue (born Sept. 15, 1962) and Brian Elmer (born June 9, 1967). Another child, Roger, died at birth.

Gerald was born on Dec. 24, 1929 in Mt. Vernon,

Gerald Bergstrom Family; Back Row: Jerry, Brian Bottom Row: Bonnie and Tamara

IN, the oldest son of Carl Elmer (born Aug. 19, 1899 in Quincy, MA) and Mary Gladys (Culley) Bergstrom (born Sept. 9, 1908 in Denton, TX). Elmer's parents were both of Scandinavian descent. His mother, Johnna Charlotta Soderblom (born Sept. 15, 1874 in Stromsbro, Sweden) came to America at the age of 19.

Carl Elmer (or more affectionately known as "Turp") was a well known city resident of Mt. Vernon. He met and married Mary Gladys Culley, the youngest daughter of Lemuel and Emma (Gill) Culley, on Oct. 16, 1928. Together they raised two sons: Gerald and Donald Carl. Turp worked at the Mt. Vernon Creamery Company, delivering dairy products to families throughout the community. On Sept. 28, 1965, Turp died after a brief illness. He is buried in Bellefontaine Cemetery in Mt. Vernon.

Bonnie Jean (Willis) Bergstrom was born June 5, 1932 in Mt. Vernon, IN, the oldest of four children — Bonnie, Bobby Dale, John Herbert, and Pamela Sue — born to Homer Dale (born Nov. 21, 1910) and Mary Louise (Bray) Willis (born Jan. 1, 1912). Mary Louise was the oldest daughter of Raymond M. and Elsie Bernice (Alldredge) Bray. Both Homer and Louise have roots planted deep in Posey County. They met in Mt. Vernon and later were married on Nov. 21, 1931. Homer worked as a butcher at several area grocery stores including Mann's Grocery, Sweat's Grocery, and later Lutterman's Market and IGA before retiring in 1972. He died on Feb. 7, 1975 and is buried in Bellefontaine Cemetery in Mt. Vernon.

Gerald and Bonnie's two children, like their parents, have lived in Mt. Vernon all their lives. Tamara Sue graduated from Mt. Vernon High School in 1980. She attended the University of Southern Indiana where she received her Bachelor of Science degree in elementary education in 1984. She currently teaches first grade at St. Matthews Catholic School in Mt. Vernon and working on her Masters degree in elementary education from Indiana State University in Terre Haute, IN.

Brian Elmer graduated from Mt. Vernon High School in 1985. He is presently a Junior at the University of Southern Indiana, majoring in elementary education.

REV. AUGUST E. AND AMANDA D. BINDER

The respective grandparents came with the German immigration movement during the 19th Century and settled in the mid-west.

AUGUST EDWARD:

Parents: Edward and Augusta C. (Kuhnt) Binder

Birth: Apr. 12, 1898, Sedalia, MO.

Early years: Emporia, KS, 1904-1906; Kansas City, MO 1906-1920.

Graduated from Eden Theological Seminary, St. Louis, MO, May, 1920.

Ordained: June 6, 1920, St. Peter's United Church of Christ, Kansas City, MO.

AMANDA DOROTHY:

Parent: Rev. Julius H. and Lyda (Haas) Hortsmann

Birth: Aug. 24, 1897, White Oak, TX, an early suburb of Houston.

Early years: Buckskin, IN, 1898 - 1904; Cannelton, IN, 1904-1906 St. Louis, MO, 1906 - 1920

Marriage: June 22, 1921, St. Louis, MO.

Mr. and Mrs. August E. Binder

Children:

August Edward, Jr. Apr. 1, 1926, married to Louis Savage. An electrical engineer engaged in Nuclear Power Research for 30 years, Albuquerque, NM, retired, living in Parkdale, OR.

Paul Julius, Dec. 3, 1928, electrical engineer for 14 years, then a minister presently serving St. Andrew United Church of Christ, Sarasota, FL. Married Margaret Harding.

Ruth Amanda, Apr. 19, 1932, married to L. Don Duckworth of Mt. Vernon operating his own business of plumbing, heating, air conditioning and electrical wiring.

There are 12 grandchildren and nine great-grandchildren.

CHURCHES SERVED:

Union Evangelical Church, Douglas, MN, temporary assignment for nine months, September 1920-June, 1921, Caroline Mission, St. Louis, 1921-1927, St. Paul's United Church of Christ, Seattle, WA, July 1, 1927-Nov. 1, 1944, Trinity United Church of Christ, Mt. Veron, IN, Jan. 15, 1945 - June 30, 1963.

RETIREMENT

Both served as volunteer missionaries in Honduras for one year. Made five other trips for shorter duration.

Served as interim pastor for many churches in the Evansville-Tri State area.

ASSOCIATED MINISTRIES

President of the Pacific Northwest Synod of the former Evangelical and Reformed Church.

Three times delegate to the national conferences of the denomination. Active in Christian Educational programs and youth work. Member of the Mt. Vernon Ministers' Association. Initiated the efforts to obtain the Cloverleaf apartments for the elderly, serving on the original housing authority.

Developed the Posey County Thrift Shop.

AWARDS

Civitan Club, Senior Citizen, 1969. "The Humanitarium Award For The Preservation of Human Dignity" by the Posey County Thrift Shop, Jan. 17, 1989.

Pastor Emeritus, Trinity United Church of Christ, June 3, 1984.

AUTHOR

"A History of the South Indiana Synod of The Evangelical and Reformed Church, 1963.

"Thots and Words", A volume of Poetry," 1986.

"A History and Analytical Study of Posey County, Indiana, Churches," 1988. Devotional articles published in various magazines.

LAST RESIDENCES

333 W. 6th St., Mt. Vernon from August, 1964 - November, 1988, Good Samaratin Home, Evansville, IN, since November 1988.

BENTON OLA AND BEATRICE (KREUTZINGER) BLAKE FAMILY

Benton Ola Blake was born on Feb. 23, 1884, oldest son of James Isaac and Delia Ann (Wade) Blake. He was born and spent his childhood in a log house on part of the David Caleb Wade farm about two miles from Wadesville on St. Wendel Road which is now known as Blake Road. He attended grade school at Cavett School. He walked to Wadesville to high school and was one of the earliest graduates of Wadesville's three-year high school.

Upon high school graduation, he passed a county exam which was all that was necessary at that time to become eligible to be a teacher. About this time, he lost the vision in his right eye to glaucoma. His first school was Cavett School where he had been a student only three years earlier. The next year, he taught at Oliver School.

Mr. Blake spent some of his summers in school at Indiana University. He was a member of the Wadesville Band that spent the summer on an Ohio River showboat. He played the trombone.

Mr. Blake also taught at a number of county schools. Among them were Fillingim in Center Township and Donner School in Robinson Township. One summer at Bloomington, he met a girl whose sister he had courted earlier in Mt. Vernon. Beatrice Kreutzinger taught for two years in Robinson Township before she married Mr. Blake in 1910. The first piece of furniture they owned was an Everett piano (still in the family) because Mr. Blake was selling pianos that summer. Mrs. Blake played the piano and Mr. Blake learned to play enough to demonstrate his product. One summer, he worked on the construction of the brick Wadesville School Building (1913).

During the years, Mr. Blake had continued to take the county exams until he had a life license to teach 13 high school subjects.

Beatrice Kreutzinger Blake born in Point Township, Dec. 5, 1888, passed away Nov. 17,1973, thus ending a marriage which lasted 63-1/2 years. Mr. Blake died June 26, 1976, at the age of 92 years, four months. They had lived in Wadesville continuously

Beatrice K. Blake, Benton Ola Blake

since July 1945, in the old Cross home which Mr. Blake bought at the time. The couple had eight children. Their children were as follows:

Mildred Beatrice, a retired public school music teacher who is now living in Wadesville, in Posey County. She was a music teacher and band director of the New Harmony Schools during the last 25 years of her 37-1/2 year teaching career.

Anna Dorothy Lewis (deceased), the mother of two sons, Thomas Benton and Kenneth Jay, had been a bookkeeper at the old Home Mill & Grain Company and the Couch Mill in New Harmony and later a piano teacher.

James Kreutzinger (deceased) married Arleta Carroll of Solitude. They had a daughter, Norma Lee Harden. James had been in the automotive industry in Indianapolis.

Ralph Waldo married Louise Vandiver of Madisonville, KY. Their son is Ted Louis. Ralph retired from Whirlpool Corp., Evansville.

Dr. Albert Lea married Doris Hornbostel of Evansville and their sons are Albert Lea, Jr., Randall Charles and Jeffrey William. Albert is a doctor of internal medicine in Indianapolis.

Charles Arthur married Marilyn Thornburgh of Muncie. Their children are Terry Ilenne, Charles Andrew, David Brian (deceased) and Steven Alec. Charles is general manager of radio station WIKY of Evansville.

Two sons preceded them in death: Benton Losey died in infancy and Edmund Thomas drowned in the Ohio River in 1938. *Submitted by Mildred B. Blake*

JAMES ISAAC AND DELIA ANN (WADE) BLAKE

James Isaac Blake was born Feb. 16, 1855, in Perry Co., IN. His father, James Merritt Blake, was, as far as can be traced a circuit rider preacher in that area. His mother was Mary Catharine Cline. James Merritt Blake married three times and had 17 children. As happens so many times, when a new stepmother moved in, the older children left home. James Isaac left home at age 14 when his father married the third time.

James Isaac roamed the country a number of years just drifting from one place to another. Sometime before 1880, he turned up in Posey County, where he met and married Delia Ann Wade,

daughter of Caleb David and Nancy Fleaharty Wade. Caleb David Wade was the son of Caleb Wade and the grandson of Joshua and Polly Conner Wade. Joshua was the common ancestor of most of the Wades in this area.

Upon marriage to Delia Ann, James Isaac Blake farmed acreage east of Wadesville belonging to his father-in-law. Jim Blake did a lot of logging which was an important part of clearing this land to make it tillable. Later, he worked on the township roads and was instrumental in getting the gravel road through to. St. Wendel. He always had time to help out anyone in need. He rode horseback far and wide.

Both Jim and Delia Ann were great story-tellers. His granddaughter, Mildred Blake, recalls: "My first recollection of the song "Old Dan Tucker" was of Grandpa singing it. From him we learned of the wildlife that used to roam this area, of the "beezer" dam on Caney Creek, of the site of an old Indian village, and of the old buffalo wallow."

The Blake's children were as follows: Roberta Pearl (Birdie) who married Elmer Julian and raised eight children. Both are now deceased. A son, Jesse Julian, now owns the old Blake place. Benton Ola (Todd), a teacher, who married Beatrice Kreutzinger, also a teacher, of Mt. Vernon, are also deceased. Of their seven children, a daughter, Mildred, still lives in Posey County. Nola Thomas (Hoop) married Mame Drury of Evansville (both are deceased). Four children issued from their marriage. Hoop spent many years in the employ of the L&N (Railroad) Howell Shops. James D. married Anna Hamilton of Evansville and raised three children in Detroit, MI, where he worked in the automobile industry. James and Anna are deceased.

James Isaac and Delia Ann Wade Blake are both buried in Mt. Pleasant Cemetery near Poseyville, as are David Caleb and Nancy Wade, her parents.

GARLAND HOYT AND GERALDINE SUE BLACKFORD

Garland Hoyt and Geraldine Sue Blackford are residents of New Harmony. They were married on Oct. 17, 1966. Their children are: Robert, born, Dec. 5, 1968 and Angela, born Aug. 9, 1971.

Garland was born June 26, 1939 in New Harmony, IN and was the ninth and last child of Paul Edgar Blackford Sr. and Anna Leora (Martin) Blackford. He attended school in New Harmony for 11 years and graduated from San Lorenzo High, in San Lorenzo, CA. After high school he joined the Navy, where he spent the next 20 years. He is now employed by the University of Southern Indiana.

Geraldine was born July 30, 1936 in Dugger, IN to Carl and Hester (Lutz) Shaw. She worked for the Federal Government until retirement in 1988. She is now employed by the New Harmony Inn.

Garlands parents Paul and Anna Blackford moved to New Harmony in 1920. They were married on July 15, 1916 in Carmi, IL. Their children are: Mildred 29, 1917; Helen, born Aug. 11, 1919; Bill, born Mar. 29, 1921; Paul Jr., born June 8, 1923; Ruth, born Mar. 18, 1925; Tom, born Feb. 4, 1927; Winnifred, born Jan. 23, 1929; Jack, born Apr. 2, 1936; Garland, born June 26, 1939.

Paul Sr. was born Feb. 17, 1893 in White Co., IL. The fourth child of Byron Elliot Blackford and Elisabeth Jane (Hall) Blackford. The family moved from Epworth, IL to New Harmony, IN 1920 while Paul Sr. worked for Elmer Elliot as a farmhand. In 1922 they moved to the Cutoff Island and farmed there for George Griffith until the Depression of 1936. They moved back to New Harmony and Paul St. worked on the W.P.A. until World War II broke out when he went to work at the Shipyard in Evansville. After the War he worked in Southbend for Studebaker and then for Whirlpool in Evansville until he retired in 1958. He died in 1983.

Anna Leora (Martin) Blackford was born Feb. 17, 1896 in White Co., IL. The fifth child of Marshall Martin and Francis Serepta (McGhee) Martin.

F. WILLIAM BRANDT FAMILY

William and Caroline (Boeke) Brandt migrated from Prussia, Germany and into the Evansville area around 1853. William and Caroline were borned in Germany about 1830. They were active in the Zion Evangelical Church in Evansville and their three children were baptized there.

William worked for the Joseph Reitz Lumber Milling Co., in the West Side of Evansville, located along Pigon Creek near the Ohio River. He was a weakly type person and could not hold up with his work so he moved his family to the vicinity of St. Joseph, IN and later from there to Robinson township near Blairsville, where he purchased 40 acres of land in Sect. 28 Twp. 5 R12 and farmed until his death. He was buried at Zion Church Cemetary where the family attended church.

After William's death Caroline married Andrew Sevin. It appeared that they continued to live on the farm and had four other children, attended Zion Church at Lippe and the children were married there. Caroline died in 1917 in Evansville and is buried at Oak Hill Cemetary. Caroline was the daughter of Andrew Drevis Krock.

The William Brandt Jr. Family William, Laura, Elizabeth, Louise, Stella, Henry, William Jr.., August Fred, Lawrence, Ida, Louise Donner

William and Caroline had three children, William, August Jr. and Emma. William married Elizabeth Quander. She was borned in Blairsville and after her father's death (Frank Quander), a civil war veteran, she was taken in and raised by the William Huff family. Elizabeth had three sisters. Her mother was Rachel Huey. August Jr. married Maria Huff and they lived on a farm near Wadesville, they had seven children. Emma married Henry Sparrenberger and moved to the Evansville area.

William and Elizabeth purchased 100 acres of land from Thomas Downen in 1884, it was in Sect. 29 of Robinson township, this is considered the Brandt homeplace and a son Andrew lived on the farm until his death, the land is still in the Brandt family, although the house is no longer there.

Ida Julia Brandt married George Schelhorn in 1910, they lived in the Robinson township area and had five children, Harvey, Elmer, Dale, Walter who is still living in the Mt. Vernon area and a daughter Ruth who married Willie Nowling and lives in Lynn township.

Ida and George moved from Robinson township to West Franklin, then to Point and in their late years lived in Mt. Vernon.

The Brandt homeplace is long gone but the 100 acres of land that was purchased from Thomas Downen in 1884 is still owned by Brandt kin. As you travel through Posey County you will see a Brandt name here and there and when you talk with some of the older ones you can still hear a German accent but long gone is the household filled with only words spoken in their native language.

GLEN & JOYCE BRIESACHER

Glen Arnold Briesacher son of Oscar Briesacher and Buelah Whitsett Briesacher was born May 19, 1925, Hissville, IN. He is the fourth of six children, George, Ida, Frieda, Edward and Geraldine.

Joyce Maunda Loer Briesacher daughter of Barnett Loehr and Carolyn Bell Loehr was born Oct. 18, 1932, Mt. Vernon, IN. She is the fourth of five children; Lois Lowanda, Barnett Edmund, Herbert Earl, Marion Samuel.

Glen and Joyce were married July 13, 1949 at Morganfield, KY. This year they will celebrate 40 years of marriage. They have five children:

Glen Arnold Briesacher, Jr., born Feb. 22, 1951, Gary, IN. Glen attended Mt. Vernon Elementary School for a short period. He graduated from Wirt High School, Indiana University, Iron Workers Apprentice Program and Ivy Technical Vocational School in Evansville. Glen travels a lot and is employed as an Ironworker.

Timothy Bruce Briesacher born Aug. 22, 1953, Evansville, IN. Attended Mt. Vernon Elementary West for a short time. He is a graduate from Wirt High School. Also the Ironworkers Apprentice School. He is married to Gloria Danford. They have two daughters: Heather Melissa born Aug. 3, 1979, Valapraiso, IN. She is a 4th grader at West Elementary School. Tiffany Deseree born Jan. 15, 1982 at Crown Point, IN is also a student in 1st grade at West Elementary School.

Glen and Joyce Brisacher

Daniel Brian Briesacher born Dec. 5, 1955, Gary, IN. Attended West Elementary for a short time. He attended Wirt School in Gary, The Ironworkers Apprentice School. He also attended Indiana State College where he studied management. He is married to Brenda Brueler and the father of Daniel Oscar Briesacher born Aug. 30, 1986, Pheonix, AZ.

David Allan Briesacher born Aug. 22, 1958, Gary, IN attended Wirt School Ironworkers Apprentice School. He is the father of Carrie Lyn Briesacher born Dec. 15, 1987. He is engaged to marry Pearl Bryan. She had two other children Vickie Rios and Chrystal Bryan. They live in Florida.

Gigi Joyce Briesacher was born July 29, 1962,

Gary, IN. She graduated from Calumet Baptist High School, Central Bible College and one year at Evangel College in Springfield, MO. She is a graduate from Deaconess School of Nursing. She is married to Mark Kozinski and they have a daughter, Emily Jane born May 1, 1989. She is a nurse at Deaconess Hospital in Evansville.

Glen and Joyce have moved back to Point Township, where they now live on Graddy Road by Hovey Lake.

Joyce is the native of Point Township, she attended Black School from 1st through 4th grade, her teacher was Miss Goldie, from 5th through 8th it was Mr. B.S. Pindell. She went to Mt. Vernon High School, but dropped out when she was a sophomore. She later received a GED diploma and then went to Indiana University for two years. She has worked with the Lake County Association for the Retarded for 16 years.

Her husband Glen just recently retired from the Lake County Zoning Board. He was also a Ironworker for 25 years. He was in the United States Marines and enjoyed being in politics. He had been a precinct committee man for 20 years.

Glen and Joyce are looking forward to retirement to spend time fishing in Hovey Lake and Stem Pond, and enjoy their grandchildren.

BROADHEAD

Kenneth, Beverly, Jim, and Allison Broadhead live in a two story red brick home atop "Broadhead" hill located four miles north-west of Mt. Vernon on Upton Rd.

Kenneth, a native to Posey County, was born to Walter Broadhead and Lillian Lupton Broadhead in 1940. Both Walter and Lillian have lived in Posey County for all of their lives. Walter's parents Charles Broadhead and Minnie Finn Broadhead have lived in Posey County since the late 19th century.

Lillian's parents, Walter Lupton and Anna Kaffenberger Lupton have lived in rural Posey County for all of their married life. Walter Lupton's parents were William Lupton and Jane Ratcliff Lupton. Jane Ratcliff came over to America from England in 1841. William Lupton served in the Union Army and participated in Sherman's march to the sea during the Civil War. William and Jane Lupton have lived here since the mid-1860s.

Left to right - James W. Broadhead, Allison S. Broadhead, Beverly S. Broadhead, Kenneth L. Broadhead

Kenneth graduated from Mt. Vernon Sr. High School in 1958. Kenneth then began his career as a General Electric employee in 1962. He is currently Operation Lead in Lexan Color Formulation.

Kenneth has a brother and sister who both have been life long Posey County residents. Walter Broadhead, with his wife Sharon, live in rural Poseyville. His sister, Margaret Ann Broadhead Moye, with her husband Don live in the Bufkin area.

Kenneth married Elizabeth Ann Wallis on June 28, 1964 at First Baptist Church in Mt. Vernon. Elizabeth was the daughter of Ralph Wallis and Alice Vaupel Wallis, also of Posey County. She was born on Mar. 2, 1941. She graduated from Mt. Vernon Sr. High in 1960. She has one brother who currently resides in Posey County, Wilbur Wallis and his wife Betty.

Kenneth and Elizabeth moved to rural Mt. Vernon in 1965, and have lived there since. On Jan. 18, 1969, their first child James Walter Broadhead was born. On Jan. 13, 1971, their second child Allison Sue Broadhead was born. Elizabeth died suddenly on Mar. 27, 1983.

Kenneth and Beverly Wilder were married on May 12, 1984. Beverly had previously lived in Warrick County. Both Kenneth and Beverly enjoy gardening and taking walks together.

WALTER BROADHEAD JR. FAMILY

Walter was born Oct. 11, 1928, son of Walter Sr., and Lillian Lupton Broadhead. The Broadheads arrived in Mt. Vernon in 1816 from Manchester, Lancashire, England via Liverpool, Baltimore and Pittsburgh. William Broadhead came first to find a place and work so that he could send for his family. He had a wife, four children, and his Father, Richard. He entered 80 acres of land from the government that was near Black church and worked as a weaver. His family took passage from Liverpool on a sailing vessel. Storms apparently buffeted their ship causing many bruises and broken bones. They lived daily with dread of robbers while traveling in a covered wagon to Pittsburgh. They landed in Point Township on a flatboat from Pittsburgh William, concerned that they had not arrived sooner, went East to meet them. He missed them and consequently it was almost two years before they met again. In the meantime the neighbors had organized a log rolling and built a home for the wife, children and father before William arrived back in the Mt. Vernon area.

From old records it seems apparent that William had brothers who also followed him from England to this area. Their names were James and John Broadhead. Together the Broadheads had extensive land holdings northwest of Mt. Vernon in the Upton area. The generations that followed have been engaged in agriculture since that time.

Walter and Sharon Broadhead

Lillian Broadhead's parents were William Walter Ratcliff Lupton and Anna Marie Kaffenberger Lupton. Abe and Hannah Ratcliff immigrated to this country from England in about 1841. They made a home near the Upton community with their family, consisting of three children, Jane, Sarah, and Uriah. Jane married Mr. William Lupton, a Civil War veteran, in about 1865. Jane and William were Lillian Broadhead's grandparents.

Walter graduated from Mt. Vernon High School in 1946. He immediately followed his father in farming. He served in the U.S. Army during the Korean Conflict. In 1955 he married Sharon R. Hooe from Evansville. They made their home in Mt. Vernon for five months and then moved to a farm just west of Poseyville, IN where Walter continued to farm for a living.

Sharon's parents were Vernon and Alberta Ludwig Hooe, from Evansville. Sharon graduated from Central High School and from the University of Evansville with a degree in Nursing. She also ran a real estate business in Poseyville.

Walter and Sharon are the parents of a son John P., born in 1956 and a daughter, Sherrie L., born in 1957. John is a practicing attorney in Poseyville and is married to Laura Ashley Broadhead from Boonville, IN. Sherrie is a supervisor in Data Processing and is married to Richard A. Maile, from Texas. They each have a daughter, Jessica Broadhead and Katherine Maile.

PAUL HOWARD AND DOROTHEA I. BUNDY

Paul and Dorothea Bundy met in 1944 in San Diego, CA where both were stationed, as Radio Operators, at the U.S. Coast Guard Air Station. They have made their home in Venture, CA since their marriage in 1946.

Paul was born in Mt. Vernon in 1922 and spent a big share of his early and junior high school years in Mt. Vernon and Evansville. His high school and college education were acquired in California. His occupation for 30 years was Wholesale Bread Distributor, retiring in 1978.

Paul and Dorothea Bundy

The Bundy's came to Posey County in 1845 from North Carolina by way of Kentucky, where Paul's great grandfather, Curtis Christopher "Kirk" was born. Kirks parents were William F. and Margaret (Whaley) Bundy. He married Elizabeth Edmonds (Alexander) who was the daughter of Samuel and Tabitha (Goad) Edmonds. Kirk acquired many acres of farm land in the Wabash Bottomland below New Harmony. This land was eventually taken over by the State and became a part of Harmony State Park. Kirk's brother, Thomas, was an itinerant preacher and gained quite a reputation as an Indian fighter when, according to record, he rode into an Indian encampment and single-handedly rescued a white woman. For this act of heroism he received Presidential recognition. Kirk's son, John, married Martha Bray. Their son, (Christopher) Curtis, Kirk's namesake, was Paul's father. In 1916 Curtis took as his bride, Myrtle Mae Strickland, the eldest daughter of John and Sarah "Sally" (York) Strickland.

Dorothea "Dottie" was born in Iowa in 1923. Her parental ancestors, Pike and Sessions, came from England; Samuel Sessions, a former body-guard to the King of England, arrived in Massachusetts in 1630. Her maternal ancestors, Marquardt and Lohmann, came from Germany, settling in Illinois in 1874 and Iowa in 1864 respectively. Her grandfather, Edward G. Marquardt was Mayor of Burlington, IA from 1928 to 1932 and again from 1934 to 1936, serving his fourth term at the time of his death. Her great-grandfather, Carl Lohmann, was Headmaster of his German-American school, served as Police Commissioner, and until World War I, published the "Volksfreund" German Newspaper. His musical accomplishments were also well-known in the area.

Paul and Dottie were married in California in 1946 and have three sons. Jerald married Carolyn Hagans - they have two daughters, Summer and Heather. Michael Peter "Pete" married Marsha Finfrock - they have one son, Micah, and two daughters, Jennifer and Kimberly. Their third son, David, is unmarried. All reside in California.

GEORGE CASSIUS BURKS, SR.
1885-1956

The third son and fifth child of nine children born to Charles William Burks and Martha Ann Hayes. George was born Nov. 13, 1885 in Henderson County, Smith Mills, KY. His parents and family owned property and had business and family ties in both Henderson Co., KY and Posey Co., Mt. Vernon, IN. Which brought him to eventually settle permanently in Mt. Vernon.

At the age of 35, married Ina May (Mayme) Cox, daughter of Charles Lloyd Cox and Charlotte Graul, residents of Wadesville. They were married May 18, 1920 in White Co., Carmi, IL. The couple had 11 children, five daughters and six sons. Mrs. Naomi (Moe) Reinitz, Mrs. Marietts (Sissy) Roberts, Mrs. Charlotte Weatherford, George Cassius, Jr., Charles Millard, Shirley Allen, Mrs. Patricia Brown, Richard Wilson, Walter Lee, Floyd (Pete) Gilbert, Mrs. Sharon Hughes.

George was a commercial fisherman and licensed riverboat pilot on the Ohio River by trade. At one time ran the ferry in Mt. Vernon. During the 1937 Flood, he was one of the engineers who kept a constant vigilant at manning the pumps at the Mt. Vernon Water Works, during that critical time.

He was also in Captain Winston Menzie, Company B, 161st Volunteer Regiment during the Spanish-American War, 2nd Company to represent Posey County during the Mexican border trouble. Although the fighting had halted upon their arrival.

George died in 1956 and Mayme died in 1972.

BURKS-WHITMAN FAMILY

Clayborne Charles Burks and Ethel (Whitman) Burks had two children, a daughter Mildred and one son, Clayborne Charles "Bus". Mildred was born Apr. 11, 1903 and Clayborne Charles "Bus" was born May 18, 1904 after his father died on Feb. 15, 1904. About a year later Ethel married Fred Hutchison and they had a daughter Agnes born Nov. 13, 1906. In 1909 the family moved to Mt. Vernon, IN.

"Bus" was an outstanding high school football player for Mt. Vernon High School. Following is a quote from the year book 1924: "Clayborne Charles Burks "Bus" - Fullback standing out alone in a class by himself is "Bus", the hardest hitting line plunger and fastest field runner in Southern Indiana. Mt. Vernon's opponents met their waterloo many times due to the work of Burks. He is one of the greatest backfield men that Mt. Vernon High has ever produced. He was the only Mt. Vernon football man to receive a position on Heze Clark's mythical all-state eleven."

Charles "Bus" and Vera Burks

"Bus" married Vera Lohmeyer in Edwardsville, IL Nov. 22, 1930. They moved to Evansville, IN where he was employed with Whirlpool Corp. He retired 1969 after 35 years service. Later he went to work for the Machine Equipment Division in Chandler, IN for 13 years. "Bus" and Vera had two children, Donald L. Burks (CPA) and Doris (Burks) Sermersheim of Jasper, IN, Donald L. lives in Evansville, IN. They also had five grandchildren and four great-grandchildren. "Bus" and Vera were longtime members of Parke Memorial Presbyterian Church of Evansville, IN. He being a Deacon and after his death they appointed Vera to fill his place. "Bus" died June 20, 1986 and Vera died Dec. 30, 1988. Clayborne Charles Burks was called "Bus" all of his life.

Fred and Ethel Hutchison moved to Evansville, IN (date unknown). Fred died December 1949. Ethel lived to be 102 years old and died November 1984.

Mildred Burks married John E. "Slats" Martin Jan. 15, 1927, they celebrated their 60th wedding anniversary in 1987. She formerly worked during World War II, she has been a housewife for the biggest part of her married life. John E. "Slats" started out as a successful salesman. In 1942 he went onto the police department of Evansville, IN, worked his way up to Captain, retiring in 1962. He continued as a salesman for number of years and now permanently retired.

Agnes Hutchison married Edwin "Doc" Dausman formerly of Mt. Vernon, IN. She worked for Whirlpool Corp. Evansville, IN and retired from there. "Doc" was employed at Servel till they closed (Evansville, IN), later going to work for M&S Fire and Safety Company of Evansville, IN. "Doc" died in August of 1976. "Doc" and Agnes had one son named Jim who resides in Louisville, KY. They have three grandchildren and three great-grandchildren.

BYRD-BAYER

Lula Catherine Byrd and late Paul Charles Bayer were married Sept. 3, 1943 at Trinity Evangelical and Reformed Church (presently known as Trinity United Church of Christ). Miss Byrd's parents deceased were Lula C. Pfister Byrd daughter of Lina Gerwig Pfister and Louis Pfister both deceased and James Byrd, son of Emma Mills Byrd and Johnathan Byrd both deceased. Mr. Bayer's parents deceased were Elizabeth Schreiber Bayer daughter of Bertha Dietz Schreiber and Henry Schreiber both deceased and Arthur W. Bayer Sr., son of Mary M. Meier Bayer and Adam Bayer both deceased.

Born to Mr. and Mrs. Paul C. Bayer were two sons, Gary and Steven.

The late Paul Bayer was known in the Community as a cabinet craftsman and for his vocal talent. A baritone soloist, he sang for many occasions.

THOMAS J. AND RHONDA L CANALE

Thomas John Canale and Rhonda Lee Alldredge were married Aug. 29, 1964, at Welborn Methodist Church, five miles northwest of Mount Vernon, IN.

Tom is the youngest of eight children. He was born in 1938 to Italian immigrants, Sam Canale (1889-1977) and Kate Porcello Canale (1900-1974). The family lived on a small farm at Albion, NY. The father worked on the railroad. Tom graduated B.S.E.E. from Missouri University, Rolla, MO.

Rhonda is the daughter of Myron Lee and Eileen Butler Alldredge of Posey County. She attended Upton Elementary School, graduated from Mount Vernon High School, and from Evansville College with a B.S.M.T. She worked in the medical laboratory of Deaconess Hospital in Evansville until 1963 when she and three R.N.s from Deaconess drove in two cars to California. All three found employment at the same hospital in Long Beach.

Terry -14, Todd-11, Tom, Tim -16, Rhonda - The Canale Family

At that time Tom was working at Vandenberg Air Force Base for General Electric. He and Rhonda met and spent their courtship in California. After marriage they lived at Long Beach. Tom was transferred to Pennsylvania for a short time and then to Santa Maria, CA, where they bought a home. Their first child, Timothy Scott, was born in 1967. Soon after, they moved back to Norristown, PA, where Tom worked in the Manned Orbiting Laboratory program.

Terence Mark was born in 1969. The family moved again to San Jose, CA. Their third son, Todd Alan, was born in 1972. Tom left General Electric and now is a field sales engineer, working from their home in San Jose.

Rhonda is a Christian Education representative for the Camlorian Park Methodist Church where the family worships. She also works in the office of the San Jose Family Shelter.

Tim and Terry are attending college, Todd attends high school.

CHARLES ALLEN & VEATRICE JO CARL

Charles Allen and Veatrice Jo Carl (known Chod and Jody) were married Oct. 25, 1952 Black River Baptist Church. They are the parents four children. Steven Allen was born Aug. 31, 1955 in Bad Krueznach, Germany. David Wayne (Dane), an engineer, born Aug. 14, 1956, married Pamela Price, a nurse, children Misty and Damon. Gayla Jo, born Oct. 5, 1957, and husband, Bobby G. Becker of the Oliver community, hold degrees in business from ISUE. Damon Thomas, born Feb. 4, 1964, graduated from NSU, Thibadoux, LA where he played Div. I baseball. Steve, Dane, Pam, Gayla, Bob and Tom are graduates of North Posey High School.

Charles and Jody Carl

Charles, born July 22, 1927 in Poseyville, graduated from Griffin High School in 1945. He served with the 264th Field Artillery Battalion 1952-56, during which time he and Jody lived in Oklahoma and Bad Krueznach, Germany. He farmed in the Griffin bottoms and Robb Township until 1984.

Charles' father, Roy, born Mar. 4, 1908 near Patoka, IN, came to the Griffin area with his mother, Rosetta Parsetta (Jordan), and four sisters following the death of his father George on Oct. 28, 1912. George died of blood poisoning after being kicked in the head by a mule. One of the four sisters was killed by the Griffin tornado. Ancestors of this family included "Purty Old Tom" Montgomery. Born in Roanoke Co., VA, 1745, Montgomery married Martha Crockett in 1767 and, as Lieutenant, served under the command of George Rogers Clark, 1781-82.

Charles' mother, Cora Frances, born Aug. 11, 1908 in Cuba, MO, returned to the Griffin area from Arkansas by covered wagon in 1917. The daughter of Charles Albert and Mary Elizabeth (Boyer) McIntire, the granddaughter of James and Lucinda McIntire, Cora married Roy Carl Apr. 23, 1926 in Albion, IL. In addition to Charles they were the parents of Betty (Scott), Delores (Polley), Loretta (Dunlap), Marjilee (Anderson) and Janice (Yancey). Roy, a retired farmer and pumper in the Griffith oil fields, died Apr. 24, 1982.

Jody, born Feb. 16, 1931 near Albion, IL, is a former Wide-A-Wake 4-H Club member, 1949 graduate of Poseyville High School and an employee of the Posey County Co-op.

Jody's parents, Joe and Norma June (Millar) Saxe, married May 17, 1930 in Grayville, IL, became Posey County residents Mar. 11, 1942. Other children of this family are Sandra Rose (Almon), Eugene Wayne, Carroll David and Harriett Ann (Winkleman). Joe was a farmer, and Norma was recognized as an accomplished soprano. Norma was born June 15, 1909. Joe, born Oct. 26, 1902, died Oct. 31, 1980.

Jody's maternal grandparents, Thomas Kent and Rose (Robinson) Millar, came to the Pun'kin Run community in Robb Twp. the day of their marriage, owning land there 1889-93. Ancestors of their's came from Leeds and Sedgeboro, England.

Jody's paternal great-grandparents came to America in September 1856 from Surrey, England; her father's maternal antecedent Claes Martenszen Van Rose came to New Amsterdam with Peter Styvesant around 1636.

Charles and Jody reside in Poseyville and are members of the Old Union Christian Church.

CULLEN W. AND SARAH E. CARR

Cullen W. Carr and Sarah Elizabeth Schneider were married Apr. 17, 1953 at Trinity Evanglical and Reformed Church in Mt. Vernon. Her cousin the Rev. Eugene A. Schneider returned to perform the ceremony. Their great grandfather, John Schneider 1831-1872, was one of the founders of the church in 1853. In 1934 the Evangelical Church merged with the Reformed Church and in 1957 the E and R congregation merged with Congregational Christian Churches. The familiar church with the lighted cross on the tall steeple became known as Trinity United Church of Christ.

Cullen and Sarah Carr

Cullen, the only child of Charles W. Carr 1896-1988 and Gladys Nicholson Carr 1895-1983, was born Nov. 14, 1922, in Mt. Vernon. His father Charles was the son of Sam and Nancy Bray Carr, both natives of Posey County, they operated hotels and dining rooms in various locations in Mt. Vernon. Charles compiled the Carr Genealogy "Ancestors and Descendants of Amasa Carr", which is in the local Alexandrian Public Library as well as the Library of Congress in Washington, D.C. His mother Gladys was a native of Boonville, Warrick Co., IN, however lived most of her life in Posey County. Cullen attended grade school in Mt. Rainer, MD, while his father was Disaster Relief Director with the American Red Cross in Washington, D.C. Returning to Mt. Vernon he finished grade school and graduated from Mt. Vernon High School in 1942. During WWII he served in the Army from January 1943 to March 1946 and was in the U.S. Naval Reserve from September 1948 to May 1956. After his discharge he returned to Evansville College, graduating with a degree in Accounting, in 1950. This school later became the University of Evansville. After graduation he worked as a salesman for Swift and Co., for awhile. He then went to work as an accountant for Continental Oil Co. in Griffin, IN and then Carmi, IL. Starting in March 1974 he became an Audit Examiner for the Indiana Employment Security Division. Because of emphysema he had to take an early retirement in 1982.

Sarah, the only child of Edward G. 1887-1958 and Charlotte N. Schneider 1887-1971, was born Nov. 24, 1926 in Posey County. Edward, the oldest son of Conrad and Katherine Peters Schneider, was a farmer and during the 1920's and 1930's operated his own fruit orchard. For many years he was a

substitute rural mail carrier, starting back in the days when a requirement was to have a "sturdy buggy and a strong horse". His father's ancestors came from Hanover, Germany. Charlotte was the second daughter of Charles and Elizabeth Dietz Nebe, both natives of Germany. Charles was from Dusseldorf, arriving in the U.S. by way of New York City. The Dietz family arrived in New Orleans from Gaugrehweiler. Charlotte was a sales clerk at Rosenbaum's Dry Good Store before she married. Sarah finished Jeffries grade school and graduated from Mt. Vernon High School in 1944. She graduated from DeVry's School of Beauty Culture in Evansville. After working two years for the owner of the Marinello Beauty she bought the shop in January 1947 and continued operating it until the end of 1979. In the summer of 1988 she designed and embroidered a shape of Posey County which was chosen to represent the county in the Heritage Quilt Project. The ten foot long quilt belongs to the Indiana State Museum in Indianapolis.

Cullen and Sarah have enjoyed traveling, photography and theater. It was the little theater, Hoop Pole Players that brought them together. The Hoop Pole Players Inc. was organized in 1949 and produced plays through 1955. For several Christmas seasons they had short plays available for local organization programs. One year presenting the program 11 times in seven evenings. Cullen and Sarah were cast as husband and wife in several plays and decided to make it permanent. They have lived at 402 W. 4th St. since their marriage.

DENNIS J. AND IMA JEAN CARR

Dennis J. and Ima Jean Carr are both Posey County natives and reside in Mt. Vernon. They were married Apr. 25 1964 in Mt. Vernon and have two children, Laura Jean born Sept. 24, 1966 and J. Kevin born Dec. 17, 1970.

Dennis was born Oct. 1, 1943 in Mt. Vernon, the oldest son of Lester J. and Helen L. (Breeze) Carr, Jr. and has one brother, Bruce S. born Feb. 14, 1950. Dennis is an Analytical Chemist working in Technology Research at General Electric where he has been employed since November 1963.

Dennis J. and Ima Jean Carr

Jean, though she still considers herself a Posey County native, was born Oct. 24, 1943 in Norman, OK in a military hospital where her father was stationed with the Marines. She is the daughter of Eugene E. and Ima Lee (Nelson) Morlock and has two brothers, David E. born Sept. 9, 1948 and Jeffrey L. born Dec. 22, 1954. Jean is an X-Ray and Medical Lab Technologist employed by MEC in Evansville.

The genealogy of the Carr family has been traced to Sir Lord Andrew Kerr of Scotland in 1450 whose descendants first arrived in America in Boston in June of 1635 aboard the frigate 'Elizabeth and

Ann'. Eventually descendants Amasa and his wife Lovisa (Foote) Carr settled in Posey County in 1837 in the Bufkin area. The published genealogy of the Carr family "**Ancestors and Descendants of Amasa Carr**" by Charles W. Carr can be found in the Alexandrian Library in Mt. Vernon.

The Morlocks are descendants of Christian II and Christina (Willman) Morlock. Christian I and Louisa Morlock immigrated to America from Baden, Germany. Christina Willman immigrated to America with her parents Johan and Anna (Zimmerman) Willman from Altheim, Germany in 1854. The Morlocks migrated to Posey County from Ohio sometime in the 1830's as reflected in the 1840 census, settling in Marrs Township. Christian I was a farmer and operated the brick yard at Morlock Pond on Tile Factory Road. Christian II married Christina Willman Jan. 27, 1868 in Posey County. Of their children, George Morlock married Elizabeth Bayer July 31, 1892 in Posey County. Of their children Fred Edward married Macil Green Jan. 7, 1920 in Posey County. They had three children, the eldest of which is Mrs. Carr's father Eugene E. Morlock.

Mrs. Carr is continuing to research the Morlock genealogy.

WILLIAM BOWER CHALLMAN M.D. AND DOROTHY BRUBAKER CHALLMAN

The choice of Mount Vernon as a desirable place to live and to set up an office for the practice of medicine brought two newcomers, William B. Challman and his wife Dorothy, to Mount Vernon in October, 1932.

Dr. Challman, born in 1908, the son of Samuel K. and Katharine Bower Challman, was reared in neighboring Vanderburgh County on a farm near Inglefield. This farm had been homesteaded about 1835 by his great-grandfather, Thomas Bower, a native of York, England, and the farm still remains in the family, presently owned by a cousin of Dr. Challman.

He attended grade school in Scott Township, graduated from Central High School in Evansville in 1925 and from Indiana University School of Medicine in 1932.

His wife, Dorothy B. Challman, a native of Warsaw, IN, was born in 1906, the daughter of Walter and Mary Barron Brubaker. Walter Brubaker was an attorney and later Circuit Court Judge of Kosciusko County, and was a veteran of the Spanish American War. Mrs. Challman graduated from Warsaw High School and later met her husband to be while a student at Indiana University from which she was graduated in 1929 with a Bachelor of Arts degree in English and journalism.

Dr. Challman opened his medical practice in an upstairs office on Main Street in a building which was next to the People's Bank and Trust Company. Later he bought a building at 131 West Third Street where he practiced until 1953 when he purchased the George Black residence at 431 Walnut Street. The home was of historical significance and regrettably it was torn down in 1988. It had been built by William P. Edson, an early Mount Vernon attorney and judge. Benjamin Harrison, then a noted Indiana lawyer and later 23rd President of the United States, visited the Edson home several times during business trips to Mount Vernon.

In 1937, Dr. Challman took special training in ear, nose and throat treatment at the University of Vienna Medical School in Austria. This offered an unusual opportunity to see Europe just prior to the outbreak of World War II. He visited relatives of his stepfather in Germany and saw evidence of the military build-up which was later to bring so much havoc to the world.

In 1936, he learned to fly, and flying was a hobby which he and his wife enjoyed for most of the rest of his life. In the late 1930s, during the time that airmail service was being expanded in the United States, Dr. Challman and Dave Alldredge, a longtime Mount Vernon automobile dealer and pioneer aviator flew the first air-mail into Mount Vernon in a bi-plane which they owned together.

Besides the love of flying, Dr. Challman was devoted to the study of astronomy and was a member of the National Astronomical Society and owned several telescopes—one of which he donated to the Mount Vernon High School. He was also a student of Civil War history and an ardent gun collector.

When World War II broke out, Dr. Challman volunteered for service in May of 1942 in the U.S. Army Air Corps as a flight surgeon. He served overseas in the China-Burma-India Theater with one of the first B-29 groups to be deployed. He was discharged in November of 1945 as a Major. He resumed his medical practice in Mount Vernon and was active in many civic and fraternal organizations. For many years he was head of the Posey County Civil Defense. He also served as City and County Health Officer and was President of the Medical Staff of Deaconess Hospital in Evansville in 1959.

Dorothy Challman was also active in civic and cultural affairs in the community and was a teacher in the Mount Vernon schools during World War II and again in the 1960s. For ten years she wrote a popular column for the Mount Vernon Democrat called "Domestic Daze" and also wrote poetry and some drama.

During World War II, Dr. Challman became acquainted with a Chinese diplomat by the name of Dr. George K.C. Yeh. Dr. Yeh was educated in the United States and was a trusted aide to Chiang Kai-Shek, the President of China. Dr. Yeh later became Foreign Minister of Nationalist China in Formosa and then Ambassador to the United States. In 1960, Dr. Challman renewed his friendship with Ambassador Yeh and invited him to address the First District Medical Society, of which Dr. Challman was president at the time. The meeting was held in Mount Vernon at the Farm Bureau Shelter House and was attended by about 200 physicians from southern Indiana and was followed by a reception at the Challman residence at 502 Walnut Street. Dr. Yeh spoke on foreign policy matters and was well covered by the local and national news media.

Dr. and Mrs. Challman reared five children; Stephen C., born 1933; John B., born 1934; Mary Katharine, born 1938; James W., born 1940, deceased 1986; and Martha Challman Debacher, born 1950. All were educated in the Mount Vernon school system. There are three grandchildren, sons of Dr. John B. Challman of Indianapolis — James Cooper, Thomas William and John Curtis, born in 1960, 1961 and 1962.

The Challman sons and daughters carry within their veins a mixture of English and Swedish blood from their father's side of the family and Scottish, German and Swiss through their mother. While their father's ancestors came directly to Minnesota and Indiana, their mother's forebears migrated from their European countries — first to Pennsylvania, then on to Ohio and Indiana. On their mother's side, through her maternal great-great-grandmother, Lydia Peters, is a Revolutionary War soldier, Jacob Peters, and a monument was dedicated to him in Meadville, PA — a ceremony which Mrs. Challman and her sister Margaret attended when they were high school girls.

History became very personal to four of the Challman children in 1942 when their grandmother, Mary Barron Brubaker, and their great grandmother, Mary Eleanor Barron — then 93 years old, visited them in Mount Vernon and related their experiences of journeying West by covered wagon from Pennsylvania in 1878 to a claim in Nebraska and of life in a sod house on the prairie. Homesickness for family, some of whom had moved to northern Indiana by that time, brought Francis Henry Barron, their great-grandfather, and his wife and five children to "civilization" in 1885.

Dr. Challman's mother, Katharine Bower of Inglefield, also enjoyed an early adventure. About 1900, before her marriage, Katharine and her sister Martha traveled by train to Arizona and visited the Grand Canyon. They made the trip to the bottom of the canyon by burro, a classic experience for that time. They told of their adventure for many years, illustrated with stereopticon pictures. This trip was quite unusual because in those days, young ladies just did not do that sort of thing.

Picture taken in June 1960, during the visit to Mount Vernon of Dr. George K.C. Yeh, Nationalist China Ambassador to the United States. Picture from left to right are Ambassador Yeh, holding James Cooper Challman, born just a few days before; Nadra Cooper Challman and John B. Challman, parents of the baby; Frank Tao, press secretary to Ambassador Yeh, Mary Katharine Challman, Stephen C. Challman, Dr. William B. Challman, Dorothy B. Challman, James W. Challman and Martha B. Challman.

In 1965, Dr. Challman had a serious illness, and in 1967, he decided to move his office and home to Evansville in order to be closer to the hospitals and to eliminate the driving to and from Mount Vernon. He continued to practice until 1979 when he died after a short illness. At this writing, Mrs. Challman is still living in her home in Evansville.

JAMES CHAMBERLIN

James Chamberlin was born Jan. 5, 1825 in Posey County. He was the son of Israel and Hester (Russell) Chamberlin, who married in 1820 in Posey County. Israel was born about 1795 in New York or Vermont and died around 1844. Hester was born Mar. 6, 1801 in North Carolina, and died in 1858 on their farm near Mt. Vernon. She was the daughter of William Russell.

James first married Mary Ann Nesler July 20, 1846. One son, Jonathan Chamberlin was born. Mary Ann died Sept. 26, 1848.

James married second, Angelitha Jones Nov. 4, 1849 in Posey County, the daughter of Wilson and Elizabeth (Downey) Jones and the granddaughter of Samuel and Elizabeth Jones.

James Chamberlin farmed and served as a Captain in First Regiment of the First Brigade of the Indiana Legion in the Civil War. Family tradition says they moved to Oregon in 1865 via the Mississippi River, the Isthmus of Panama, landing at San Francisco, then on to Portland, OR were they bought wagons and traveled down the Willamette Valley. They settled near Myrtle Creek, in Douglas Co., OR. There they bought and sold land with the Ridenours, another Posey County family. James and family moved to Idaho Co., ID in 1871. Angelitha died there in 1889. James died in 1892 in Montgomery Co., IL, while he was visiting his brother, Samuel.

James Chamberlin

James' brothers and sisters were Clarissa married David Harris, 2nd married David Utley; John; William married Charity Cully; Lavina married Mac Bell; Lydia married David Anderson, 2nd married Francis Taney; Solomon married Evaline Jones; Samuel married Orilla Utley; Alonzo married Louisa Wilson; Esther married John Mills, 2nd married Clark Rose, 3rd married George English; David married Virginia Robinson; Alvin.

James' maternal grandfather, William Russell was born in 1755 in North Carolina and died May 1850, near Mt. Vernon. He farmed in the Mt. Vernon area and had the following children, all who farmed in Black Twp.: John married Margaret Butler; Lucretia married John Ridenour; William; James W. married Margaret Thomas; Samuel married Lucinda Breeze; Thomas married Celia Cook; Elizabeth married Covington Breeze.

Angelitha (Jones) Chamberlin's paternal grandfather, Samuel Jones was born in 1764 in Rowan Co., NC. He and family moved to Kentucky where his son Wilson, was born in 1793. Two of Samuel's children were married in Lincoln County in 1805. Michael married Nancy Clark and Rachel married Thomas Givens. They moved with Samuel and his family to Posey County. Samuel farmed, served as the first County Treasurer, and was a minister of the Bethel Baptist Church until his death Sept. 11, 1833.

Angelitha's father, Wilson Jones married Elizabeth Downey in 1815 in Posey County and farmed in Marrs Twp. Their adult children: Louisa J. married John Moore; William D. married Rachel West; Samuel R. married Mary Barton; Mary Jane married William B. Barton; Elizabeth married Job Oliver; Margaret married John S. Curtis; Angeline married Aaron McFadden; 2nd married Jacob West; Evaline married Solomon Chamberlin; Emaline married Samuel Dixon; Elva married David Cully; Levitus B. married Anna Knowles; Leroy married Catherine Knowles. He owned a photography studio in Mt. Vernon for many years.

GUY E. AND AMELIA CLEVELAND

Guy E. and Amelia Cleveland are residents of Mt. Vernon, IN. Guy was born in Cynthiana, IN, as were his parents and grandparents. Amelia was born on a farm near Caborn. Her parents were Henry and Matilda (Willman) Pfeiffer. At this writing, Henry is still living and nearing his 108th birthday.

Guy is a graduate of Mt. Vernon High School (1930) and of Indiana State University (1934). During World War II, he served four years in the Navy with the carrier fleet in the Pacific. After the war, he worked for the Post Office Department for 35 years. He retired in 1975.

Guy and Amelia have two sons, Keith and Greg. Keith is married to Susan (Barnett), and they have one daughter, Amanda. They both received Bachelor's degrees from Indiana State, where Susan also earned her Master's. Keith has a Master's from Butler. They are both teachers. Greg graduated from Indiana University and had several years additional study at the University of Missouri and the University of Texas. He is a biologist.

Guy's parents were Guy and Mary (Smith) Cleveland. They had one son and two daughters (one daughter died at birth). The other daughter is Marijohn, who married Clarence Blackburn Jr. (deceased). They have one daughter, Janis. She is married to Randall Brady and they have two children, Erin and Nathan. Janis and Randy are also teachers.

Great-great-grandfather, Micajah and his wife, Sarah (Whaley) came from Fairfax Co., VA, to Harrison Co., KY, before 1800. Great-grandfather, Charles, was born there in May of that year, and was married in Gibson County in 1822 to Phoebe Lunceford. Grandfather Lewis was born in 1842. In 1862, he married Elizabeth Meadows. They had eight children, the youngest being Guy Sr. Lewis was for several years the justice of the peace of Smith Township.

On the maternal side, Mary was the daughter of John Bailey and Viola (Showers) Smith. Viola's parents were Russell and Elizabeth (Duckworth) Showers. Russell was a captain in the Union Army and he and John Bailey served with Sherman's troops in the 80th Indiana regiment. The captain was killed May 13, 1864, at Resaca, GA, the first major encounter of the campaign. The Showers were millers and had a prominent part in the early history of Cynthiana.

John was the son of William Smith (born in Kentucky in 1811). William's father was George R. Smith, born in North Carolina, in 1772. He moved with his family and wife Sarah (Armstrong) to Posey County in 1812. Smith Township was named for him.

CHAMPLAIN ZELLER

Ruth Ann Zeller, the youngest daughter in a family of four children of Clarence and Mary M. (Paul) Zeller grew up on the family farm near St. Wendel, IN. She was born Oct. 25, 1958 in Evansville, IN. She attended St. Wendel Grade School and graduated in 1972.

Ruth Ann, Kevin M., Joseph Earl, Stephanie Renee

Then attended North Posey High School and graduated in May, 1976. Ruth Ann has a sister, Rita Janet and two brothers, Lawrence and Dennis. Larry was killed in the Vietnam War in 1969. Kevin was born in Lincoln, NE on May 23, 1959. He attened Farmersville Elementary School. Kevin graduated from Mt. Vernon High School in 1977. He has a sister Denise and two brothers Keith and Kelly. She started working at McDonald Corporation in July after graduation and is still employed with them as Area Supervisor. On Mar. 28, 1981 Ruth Ann Zeller and Kevin M. Champlain were married. Kevin is employed at General Electric Company in Mt. Vernon. They have two children, Stephanie Renee, born Dec. 13, 1982 and Joseph Earl, born July 1, 1985. They live in Mt. Vernon.

COLLIER

Duane and Marilyn Cullman Collier reside on Bonebank Road, Point Township, S.W. of Mt. Vernon, in the house built in 1885 by John Henry Hinnenkamp, Marilyn's great grandfather

Duane's family is from Lebanon (Boone County) and Sheridan (Hamilton County) Indiana.

Marilyn was born Jan. 22, 1932 to William F. Jr. (1905-1976) and Gladys M. (Hinnenkamp) (1909-1950) Cullman. "Bill" as he was known to family and friends farmed until he retired in 1970.

Gladys was born to John William (1864-1949) and Carrie (Schieber, Weiss) Hinnenkamp (1895-1961).

John William was born to John Henry (1836-1889) and Christina (Zwickel) Hinnenkamp (1842-1927). Both came from Germany as small children with their families.

Carrie was born to John Frederick (1835-1896) and Barbara (Nezer) Schieber (1839-1932).

John H. and John W. Hinnenkamp were both carpenters and helped to build many buildings in Point Township and surrounding areas.

William F. Jr. was born to William Frederick Sr. (1875-1934) and Emma (Morlock) Cullman (1879-1973).

Marilyn and Duane Collier

Duane was born Aug. 18, 1936 to G. Darrell and A. Margaret (Goff) Collier in Boone Co., IN.

Duane and Marilyn were married at Zoar Methodist Church Nov. 20, 1961. They have two children, Mrs. Peter (Carla) Nelson, Indianapolis, IN and Kevin, Mt. Vernon, IN and one grandson, Zachary Nelson.

Duane has been associated with United Farm Bureau Insurance Claims Division since 1956. Duane, Kevin and Marilyn also farm in Point and Black Townships.

CHARLES CONLIN

Charles Conlin was an early landowner and farmer in Point Township, Posey Co., IN. He married Sarah (Sally) Black. Charles was born in Pittsburg, PA on Feb. 13, 1799. His wife was born Dec. 3, 1808 in Vincennes, IN. They lived and farmed in the Wabash bottoms and raised five children. These children were: Samuel, Thomas, Wilkinson, Sarah, and Eleanor. Charles Conlin died Nov. 19, 1845. His wife, Sarah, died Feb. 19, 1880. Both are buried in the Conlin-Rowe Cemetery in Point Township located below the Black Schoolhouse. This cemetery where many of our ancestors are buried has been very well kept thru the years. The tombstones of Charles and Anne are located near many other family members. The Conlins and Black families. Thomas Conlin son of Charles and Sarah (Black) Conlin was born in 1831. He married Mary Ann Rowe. She was born in 1834. They were farmers and owned land in Point Township also. They had ten children:

1. Sarah Abigal - born Dec. 27, 1854. Married Henry D. Goss. Parents of three children: Cora, Frederick, and Thomas.

2. Charles - Born Oct. 17, 1856. Married Viola. Parents of four children: Thomas, Stanley, Martha, Mary.

3. William - Born Apr. 19, 1859. Married Catherine Albright. Parents of three children: Carl, Edgar, Vernie.

4. John - Born 1860. Married Jessie Rosencrantz. Parents of two daughters: Sarah and Jessie.

5. Ellen L. - Born Oct. 6 1864.

6. Mattie - Born 1867. Married Lemuel Osborn. No children.

7. Walter - Born Oct. 13, 1868. Married Minnie Sullivan. One child - Walter Gray.

8. Nellie - Born 1871. Married Frank Pumphrey. No children.

9. Clyde - Born Nov. 2, 1875. Married Alfred J. Alexander. Parents of two children: Thomas Conlin, Mary

10. Parthenia - Married Alexander Hutchinson. Two children: Thomas and John. Thomas Conlin died in 1914 Mary Ann, his wife died in 1924. Buried in Bellfontaine Cemetery near Mt. Vernon, IN.

CONLIN FAMILY
JAMES CONLIN

The Conlin family were among the earliest settlers to come to Posey Co., IN. James Conlin acquired land in Point Township around the year 1818. James, a cabinetmaker in Dublin, Ireland, lost his wife-leaving him with a small baby boy named Thomas. The grandmother took the baby and cared for him. Life became very dreary for James, so he came to America in the late 1700's. He settled in Pittsburg, PA and married a second time to Anne Conklin. Two children were born to them: Charles and Sarah. Not being satisfied with the degree of success he enjoyed in Pittsburg, and hearing of the wonderful opportunities in New Orleans, he (James Conlin) put all his fortune in the purchase of a boat, loaded it with handsome furniture which he made, and started for the city of his dreams to sell his furniture. When he was within a few hundred miles of his destination, the boat sank in a storm, taking with it the work of several years and his hopes for a future in New Orleans. He then made his way back on foot, following the rivers and encountering many hardships. Finally, he came to McFaddins Bluff. He thought the land showed much promise of a good place to live. There was an abundance of game. He entered 400 acres of land which is now the upper Wabash bottoms. During the first year many people and cattle died of milk fever. Thinking it an undesirable place to bring his family he sold this land and moved farther down the river and bought land near Bone Bank in Point Township. Here he built a log cabin. (This land and home was later owned by Will Conlin). He found the people here of good Christian faith. The land was good and there was much wild game. He sent for his family. Charles, being about 19, came with his mother and sister, Sarah. Charles Conlin was born Feb. 13, 1799. He married Sarah (Sally) Black. She was born Dec. 3, 1808. Her parents were James and Eleanore (McMillen) Black. Sarah Conlin dau. of James and Anne (Conklin) Conlin married Jacob Rowe. James Conlin was listed as having voted in the election of Point Township on May 30, 1835. It was held in the home of Samuel Love.

Many wonderful stories of "early" days were told to Clyde Conlin Alexander by her father Thomas Conlin. Thomas was the grandson of James Conlin. He told her he remembered hearing the wolves howl and prowl around the house and his mother (Sarah Black Conlin) could tell of how the Indians would come and take their stores of provisions. The best stories were the hunting of wild turkey and deer. He would rise before sun-up and climb a tree and wait for the turkey to fly from the roost. In the late evening he would wait for the deer to go out to their night lodging. He said of all the deer he killed, and that was many, it was not uncommon to have as many as six hanging in the smokehouse at one time. The early Conlins had a great sense of humor and a quick temper! It is believed that James Conlin, the Irish immigrant, and his wife, Anne are both buried in Point Township, Posey Co., IN. Most likely on the farm where they lived or nearby in a small cemetery. Graves are unmarked. Date of their birth and death are unknown. *Submitted by Wanda Tichenor*

FRENCH COPELAND

French Copeland, Black Township, resides on the farm across the road from where he was born in 1904. He moved to this farm where his grandparents had lived when he married Vivian Noon in 1926.

French's ancestors originated in North Carolina. William Copeland was born July 12, 1783. He married Margery Larmach (June 13, 1786) on Apr. 10, 1805. Of their 13 children only Jacob, born in 1822 in Tennessee, is known.

Jacob married Sally Taylor Barry Apr. 5, 1840. Their six children were: William Marion (Jan. 9, 1847); William Hazel (Sept. 9, 1849); Margery Ann (Dec. 27, 1853); Jessie Milton (Sept. 18, 1858); Amos Lawrence (Dec. 2, 1857); and Joseph Albert (Apr. 4, 1860). Sally Taylor Copeland died Oct. 30, 1862 in Missouri.

Jacob then married Lucinda Sprawle (Nov. 20, 1821) in Wayne Co., MO. Rev. Henry Taylor officiated at the Feb. 26, 1863 ceremony.

Jacob was in the army during the Civil War. He came home on a weekend leave and found that the army had come by his home, cut the clothesline with the washing hanging on it, rode their horses over the clothes, took what they wanted from the garden and trampled the rest. The men killed the milk cow, took what they wanted and left the rest to rot. Two good horses were taken and two lame ones left. Jacob loaded his family and a few belongings into a wagon and left for Indiana during the night. When they arrived in Mt. Vernon, they settled in a log cabin near the present Hedges School.

Amos Lawrence was the only child who remained in Indiana. He was apprenticed to a blacksmith and buggy shop in New Harmony at a very early age. He stayed there until he was 16. He then ran away to Illinois where he worked in a shop for a year. From there he went to Colorado where three of his brothers were living. After a year he returned to Poseyville, IN, and worked in a blacksmith buggy shop. At the age of 22 he married Mary Rebecca Endicott (Feb. 10, 1853) in 1879. Of their six children, two died in infancy. The other four were Samuel, Marion, Clyde, and Robert.

Samuel remained in Posey County and married Ethel French on Aug. 7, 1901. Their three children were Mary Elizabeth (May 4, 1901), French Lawrence (May 20, 1904), and Durward Graydon (1906).

French L. Copeland married Vivian Noon. To them were born Amos Lawrence (Nov. 29, 1927), Richard Bruce (Mar. 18, 1932), Virginia Ann (Sept. 24, 1934) and Charles (April, 1936). Vivian died May 4, 1936. French then married Iona Alldredge Miller Apr. 1, 1944. She died in October, 1983.

French began teaching in the fall of 1922 after a summer session at the teacher's college in Terre Haute. His first job was at Goad Schoolhouse, a one room school in Lynn Township. He taught at many schools in Posey County and farmed for 28 years. Following his retirement from teaching, he continued farming until he retired in 1959. Today he continues to be active in various activities in Posey County.

CORTUS-PHILLIPS

Deena Jean Phillips was born in Evansville, IN on Apr. 1, 1958 to LaRue and Doris J. (McFadin) Phillips. She graduated from Mt. Vernon Senior High in 1976. Until this date she resided with her parents in Posey County.

She attended Western Kentucky University at Bowling Green then graduated cum laude from the University of Houston, TX with a degree in Sociology and Psychology in 1981. She was a member of the Golden Key National Honor Society. In 1984

Deena and Bill Cortus

Deena earned her Master's degree in Sociology. She became the Senior Academic Advisor at the University of Houston. She is currently teaching at Hillcrest Cardin School in Temecula, CA.

On Jan. 19, 1986 in Houston, TX, Deena married William James Cortus. "Bill" was born on Apr. 27, 1956 in Sidney Australia to John and Betty (Feref) Cortus. Bill became a United States citizen in 1977. He graduated from Western Kentucky University with a degree in Public Relations in 1979. He is currently working as a research manager with the firm, Rancon Financial Corporation in Temecula, CA.

Deena and Bill attend San Diego Baptist Church. Deena is a member of the National Council of Teachers of Mathematics. They enjoy many activities such as biking, camping, and aerobicizing.

COX FAMILY

The picture was taken in 1907 at the home of William James and Malinda Zergeibel Cox pictured with their three children - Clara Wilhelmina, Arvin Stinson, and Lester Zachariah. William was the oldest son of Stinson and Sarah Ramsey Cox whose other children were Joseph, Elizabeth, and Leroy. Stinson served as County Commissioner when the present Court House was built and was one of 11 children of Joseph and Elizabeth Hunsinger Cox.

Following the Revolutionary War, Joseph accompanied his father John, - a Revolutionary War veteran - three brothers, and his step-mother through the Carolinas to Indiana. While in Kentucky one brother disappeared and Joseph stayed in Muhlenberg County to continue the search. He married Elizabeth, who was a descendent of a Pennsylvania Dutch family that had lived in the Valley Forge area during the war. He served in the Kentucky Militia and was enroute with them to aid General Harrison in his battles against Tescumseh when the Battle of Tippecanoe was fought. After the War of 1812, they moved to Posey County to be near his family and they were among the founders of Bethleham Primitive Baptist Church.

William James and Melinda Zergeibel Cox. Children: Clara Wilhelmina, Arvin Stinson, and Lester Zachariah.

Malinda was the daughter of Zachariah and Kathariena Zimmerman Zergeibel, whose other children were George, Karl, Amelia, Sophia, and Anna. She and William were married on Nov. 9, 1887, after living in the Wadesville area they moved to the present Cox Farm in 1889. Zacariah Zergeibel was the only member of his family to emigrate from Heidelburgh, Germany. His farm is now the site of Contentinal Grain, Ohio Oil, and Babcock & Wilcox.

Clara lived on the Cox Farm until her death, as did Arvin and his wife, Esther Lillian Roos. Lester married Lela Catherine Ludlow in 1915 and they had three daughters - Wilma Lucille Cox Lengelsen, Mary Catherine Cox Hall McMurry, and Laura Malinda Cox Bullard.

Lela was the daughter of Abe and Laura Rhodes Ludlow whose farm adjoins the Cox Farm and is the present home of Mary Ludlow Rose. Lela had seven brothers and sisters, three died in early childhood or infancy, others living to adulthood were Mary Ina, Aletha Jane, and Elijah Abraham. Abe was the son of George and Sara Ratcliff Ludlow and George was a descendant of a former British sailor who had jumped ship in New England and then served in the American forces. This family settled in Connecticut. Sarah's family emigrated from England. Laura was the daughter of Levi and Malinda Watson Rhodes, who left Harrison County, settled in Mount Vernon and for a short time in the 1880s operated The Green Tree Hotel, which was located on the northeast corner of what is now Water and College.

Wilma Cox married Edgar Lengelsen, son of Gustav and Elizabeth Richter Lengelsen. Mary Cox was married to Thomas Hall and they had three children - Stephen Thomas, Jacquelyn Hall Carney, and Timothy - Tom died in 1960 and she is now married to Jim McMurry. Laura Cox married Robert Louis Bullard, son of Clifford Oval and Lena Cater Bullard. Robert died in 1963 and he and Laura had the following children:

Diane Louise was formerly married to Ret. Major Gerald Campbell and they have two daughters, Carol and Andrea.

Patricia Lynn was formerly married to David Duthie and their children are Heather, Jennifer and Shawn.

Jane Ellen is married to Frederick Lyndon Johnson and they have three sons, Kyle Frederick, Brock Arvin, Zachary Robert. Robert Louis is married to the former Sally Davis and she has a son, Jerry.

Randolph Lee is married to Catherine Giannini and they have a son Robert Louis.

Amy Clair is married to Lt. Colonel Francis McDermott and their children are Leslie, Laura, Frank and Mary.

Sandra Kay, Brock, Tracy, and Megan are the remaining four of Laura and Bob's family and to date are unmarried.

Laura is the present Clerk-Treasurer of the City of Mount Vernon and has been since 1972.

HAROLD L. COX

Though Mr. Cox is a native of Vanderburgh County and a resident of Indianapolis, his paternal line stretches back into Posey County history. In 1815 John Cox, a North Carolinian, and wife, Martha came to Posey County via South Carolina and Muhlenberg Co., KY. They settled near the Robb and Harmony township line and were members of the Bethlehem Primitive Baptist Church. Mr. Cox is a descendant of John Cox's son, Joseph,

Harold L. Cox

who was referred to as "General" Joseph Cox by Posey County pioneers, and his wife, Elizabeth Hunsaker Cox.

"General" Joe had ten sons and one daughter Mr. Cox's great-great grandparents were Joseph's youngest son, Isaac Cox, and Melissa Cater, daughter of Joseph and Jemima Williams Cater of Cynthiana. His great grandparents, Samuel Asbury Cox and Mary Smiley, and grandparents, Cyril Allen Cox and Eulalia Stinchfield were all Posey County natives. Eulalia Stinchfield's parents, John Stinchfield and Louisa Reichert, were the aunt and uncle of Manson Reichert, former mayor of Evansville.

Mr. Cox is a telecommunications computer operator for the state and speaks occasionally with the ladies in the Posey County Welfare Office (Food Stamp Division) from Network Control in the State Office Building.

Mr. Cox has an older brother, Lawrence W. Cox and a younger sister, Karen Cox Book, both of whom also live in Indianapolis. His mother is a native of Ridgway, Gallatin Co., IL.

Mr. Cox is a member of the Sons of the American Revolution and the Society of Indiana Pioneers. He enjoys returning to Posey County for genealogical field trips, collaborating with his cousins, Lela Barrett and Anna Griswold of Mt. Vernon. He has been a guest in the home of Calvin and Lela Barrett on these expeditions.

DARRELL AND DONNA CREEK

Darrell and Donna Creek reside in rural New Harmony. They were married Feb. 13, 1955 in the United Methodist Church in Stewartsville. Darrell serves as a Trustee and Assistant Treasurer and Donna as Superintendant of the Sunday School. They are the parents of two sons, Daniel Wayne, born Feb. 9, 1956 and Douglas Duane, born Nov. 26, 1963. Daniel is married to the former Tamara Blaylock and have one daughter, Lindsay Rae, born Jan. 23, 1982 and a son, Trent Daniel, born Apr. 8, 1986. Douglas is married to the former Valerie Price.

Darrell and Donna Creek 1955 Wedding Picture

Darrell is a native of Posey County and served as Councilman at large for ten years, representing the Democrat Party. Darrell is one of the four chilren born to Charles and Lela Johnson Creek, farmers in Harmony Township. The Creek family moved from Kentucky in 1815, locating in Posey County and engaged in farming. His great grandfather, William Riley Creek, served in the Civil War, Co. E 15th Regiment Indiana Volunteers. This unit organized at Lafayette with many volunteers from Posey County, for which the county never received credit. During this enlistment June 1861, Richard Owen was commissioned Lieutenant-Colonel of the 15th Regiment. William Riley was killed at the Battle of Mission Ridge in Chattanooga, TN, Nov. 25, 1863 and is buried in the National Civil War Cemetery in the city. Darrell's grandfather James Buchanan Creek married Clarrissa Hancock, Dec. 23, 1879, daughter of landowner and wagon maker, Enoch and Mary Stallings Hancock. Enoch's grandparents John and Mary Hancock were from Virginia and had only one child, a son Benjamin. He married Mary "Polly" Butler from North Carolina, Dec. 26, 1826, in Grainger Co., TN. Enoch was born in Grainger County Oct. 15, 1828, as well as his brother John, born Apr. 13, 1829. The rest of his five brothers and sisters were born in Posey County.

Mary was the daughter of Shadrack and Nancy Willis Stallings. The Stallings family entered Posey County from North Carolina in 1818. Enoch and Benjamin Hancock, and Shadrack Stallings jointly owned over 5000 acres in Harmony Township.

Donna was born in Oklahoma and is one of the three daughters born to Don H. Eva M. Probus Strickland, businessman and avid horseman. Donna's maternal great grandfather, John R. Miller staked a claim during the Cherokee Strip Run, Sept. 16, 1893 and homesteaded near Eddy, OK. He married Sarah Elizabeth Jones in 1893 and was ordained in the Baptist Church June 11, 1899.

A. LLOYD CULLEY AND MARTHA M. CULLEY

(Archie) A. Lloyd Culley was born on July 13, 1908, the son of Herman and Katherine (Katie) Shaw Culley in the Caborn area. He and his brother, Edward C. Culley (1912) were raised on the family farm in Eastern Black Township and attended Thompson School. While Lloyd attended high school he resided with his grandparents, Lafayette and Mary Elizabeth Shaw, in town on East Fourth St. and was employed at Rothrock Pharmacy. He was a member of the Mt. Vernon High School Class of 1927.

During school days he met Martha Moore, the daughter of Bertha Hagemann and John Henry Moore. Martha was born Dec. 8, 1908. Because John developed Tuberculosis and died on Feb. 26, 1910, mother and daughter moved to the Hagemann Homestead with Mr. and Mrs. Frederick H. Hagemann. Under similar circumstances, Bertha's sister Elizabeth Blosfeld moved home with her daughter, Augusta. The girls were raised almost as sisters. Martha Moore was a graduate of the Mt. Vernon High School Class of 1928, and was employed in the office of Southland Coal Company in Mt. Vernon following graduation.

Lloyd graduated from the Indianapolis College of Pharmacy in 1930, and was a member of Kappa Psi, national Pharmaceutical fraternity. Lloyd and Martha were married July 28, 1934 at St. John's in Evansville. As a young man, Lloyd was employed by the H.A. Woods and Neighborhood Drug Com-

Lloyd and Martha Culley

panies there. He later had his own store on Kentucky and Wagoner Avenues and worked at Petersheim's Apothecary. During these 27 years the Culley's resided in Evansville with their children, Wayne Lloyd, born Sept. 20, 1937, now of Mt. Vernon, and Jane Gayle (Bonaldi), born Mar. 4, 1942, now of Belleville, IL. Both children graduated from Bosse High School.

In 1961, Lloyd and Martha purchased the Rothrock Pharmacy, where Lloyd had worked as an apprentice during high school. The drugstore at 231 Main Street was completely remodeled and became a popular attraction with its modern soda fountain, large selection of cosmetics, greeting cards, and gift items along with the necessary medications. When Mr. and Mrs. Culley returned to Mt. Vernon to make their home, they resided in the Hagemann home with Martha's mother, Mrs. Moore.

Wayne, a pharmacy graduate of Purdue University (1959) worked closely with his father. Wayne was married to Patricia Kroeger of Yankeetown (1961). Jane holds both a Bachelors and a Masters Degree in Art from the University of Illinois. She married Alfred R. Bonaldi of Oak Park, IL (1969).

The Culley's belonged to Trinity U.C. of C. in Mt. Vernon. A. Lloyd Culley died unexpectedly on Oct. 11, 1973, following a fall from a ladder. Mrs. Culley continued to live alone at the Hagemann home West of town, until her sudden death on Dec. 9, 1986. Both are buried in Bellefontaine Cemetery.

The couple had six grandchildren: John Wayne Culley (1964), Mark Alan Culley (1966), James Scott Culley (1969), and Patricia Lynn Culley (1971), all of Mt. Vernon; and A. Ronald Bonaldi Jr. (1973) and Donna Jane Bonaldi (1981) of Belleville, IL. *By Jane Bonaldi*

THOMAS CULLEY, JR.

Thomas Culley Jr., was born in North Carolina circa 1785. He is first found in the will his father, Thomas "Tupper" Culley where he inherited 200 acres of land on the "old plantation" a feather bed, a cow, calf, and one gun. He married Betsy Canaday in 1804. Around 1811, he moved with his older brother Joseph, younger brother Samuel, sister Lucretia, and her husband, James Breece to Sumner Co., TN. In 1815, they moved from Tennessee to Posey Co., IN.

The Culley brothers and their families remained in Posey County for 30-40 years. Their related families, the Moore's and Duckworth's are found among the first settlers in Black Township. They were members of the Primitive Baptist Church.

The Culleys left many friends and relatives behind in North Carolina. Excerpts from a letter from Easther Garner of Posey County to her sister Sarah Garner of North Carolina shed some light on this period of time:

April 20, 1845

Richard Culley; Mary (Moore) Culley

"Dear Sister,

I received your letter the 19th of this month and was very glad to hear from you one more time and to hear that you and your family are all alive and well and to hear that my family are all alive there, but not all well. I am yet afflicted with the rheumatism at times. My family are all living about me...I received your letter with Indigo seeds in it and wanted to send you an answer but could not get one wrote. I hope you will excuse me, times is dull, money scarce and hard to get but produce is cheap....I will inform you of the death of some of our N. Carolina friends which is Edward H. Bell's wife and son Edward Jacob Benthall and his wife and daughter Rebecca and old Joseph Culley and his Brother Thomas and four of his children. James Breeces wife and three of his children and two of William Russell's children. These have all died since we have been to this country and a great many of our friends besides them have died and you wish to know how we was making out I will inform you that I have a chance of getting along in account of sickness but thank God we have yet made out tolerable well and so I will close as some of the children wants to write a few words. I remain your affectionate sister till death."

After the deaths of Joseph (1841) and Thomas (1844), their children spread out, some remaining in Indiana, others going on to Illinois and some out west to Oregon and Idaho.

Richard Culley (b. 1822), son of Thomas Culley Jr., moved with his wife Mary Moore to Taylorville, IL around 1856. Richard died in 1872 and his son Samuel moved to Pendleton, OR in the late 1880s where members of the Culley family still farm in Weston, OR. Some of Joseph Culley's descendants reside in Ontario, OR. *Submitted by Kathleen Culley Howard*

LOUIS AND DOROTHY CULLMAN

Louis Joseph Cullman and Dorothy Ethel Thompson were united in marriage Oct. 6, 1934. They have been residents of Evansville, IN for more than 50 years.

Dorothy was born in Posey County on Oct. 6, 1914. She was the third daughter of LeRoy and Mattie V. Thompson. Dorothy attended Mt. Vernon, IN high school and for ten years was an employee of I.G.A. Supermarket. Louis and Dorothy had one son, Dennis Raye, who was a graduate of Indiana State University of Terre Haute, IN. Dennis now lives in Lisle, IL. Dorothy also had three sisters....Vera Powell, Beatrice Cobb, and Kathryn Thompson.

Parents of Dorothy are LeRoy Thompson who was born Apr. 20, 1887. He was an employee of

Left to right: Dennis Raye, Dorothy, Louis

Bucyrus Erie of Evansville, IN for many years, he was also a farmer. LeRoy's father was Joseph Thompson and his mother was Susan Cullpepper Thompson. They were also born in Posey County.

LeRoy was a twin to Bessie Thompson Laurence and another sister, Stella Thompson Mann.

Mattie V. Culley Thompson was born Feb. 25, 1888 in Posey County, her parents were Samuel D. Culley and Martha V. Crunk. Mattie had two brothers, Laurence D. and John, and four sisters, Nancy, Ethel, Ella, Grace, all were born Posey County. Mattie and LeRoy were united in marriage on June 7, 1906.

Louis Joseph Cullman was born Mar. 18, 1911 in Posey Co., IN. He is the second son of William and Emma Morlock Cullman. He attended schools in Black Township and schools in Evansville, IN. He was employed at Shane Uniform Company as a Production Superintendent for 41 years, then employed at Fountain Company for ten years. Both companies are in Evansville, IN.

Louis's parents were William Peter Cullman and Emma Christine Morlock Cullman, who were married Aug. 30, 1899 and were farmers. Louis has three sisters....Emma, Anna and Florence, and two brothers...William and Paul, all were born in Posey County.

Louis's father, William Peter Cullman was born in Perry Co., IN, year of 1875, and his father Fred Cullman and mother Erinstine Undgerecht also were born in Perry Co., IN. Fred Cullman's father, Peter Cullman, was born in Germany.

Louis's mother, Emma Christine Morlock Cullman, was born in Posey Co., IN Oct. 1, 1879, and her father Christain Morlock was born in Posey Co., IN and her mother Christine Willman was born in Germany, Jan. 27, 1845.

EMMA AND WILLIAM CULLMAN

Christina Willman was born in Altheim, Germany Jan. 27, 1845. In 1865 at the age of 20, she and her parents Anna and Johann Willman and five sisters and a brother came to America settling in Cincinnati; then later about 1870 they came to Posey County where she met and married Christian Morlock, whose wife Catherine Lang Morlock had recently died leaving him with one son.

Catherine Lang Morlock was the first person buried in the Black Township Cemetery, now Bellefontaine. Christina and Christian Morlock lived east of Mt. Vernon. They were the parents of four sons, Fred, George, John and Edward and two daughters, Mary and Emma. After the death of Christian Morlock in March 1880, his widow Christina with her six children moved into a house on a farm southwest of Mt. Vernon on the Black-Point Twp. Line Road. Her youngest child, Emma, married William Cullman, a native of German

My father and mother William P. Cullman, Emma C. (Morlock) Cullman Aug. 30, 1899

Ridge, Perry Co., IN, Aug. 30, 1899. To this union was born six children: Anna, Emily (who died in infancy) William, Florence, Louis, and Paul. Anna married Carl Weiss in 1920. They were parents of two daughters, Wilma and Wanda. William married Gladys Hinnenkamp in 1930; they had one daughter, Marilyn; Florence married George Upshaw in 1934; they had three children, Glen, Norman and Carolyn. Louis married Dorothy Thompson in 1934, and they have one son, Dennis; Paul married Peggy Rowe in 1948, and they have two sons: Jeffery of Cleveland, OH, and Gary of Mt. Vernon, IN. Every year in July the descendants of Christina Willman Morlock meet for a reunion at Zoar Methodist Church on the Black-Point Twp. Line Road. *Submitted by Anna C. Zuspann*

JAMES CLINTON CUMMINS

I came to Posey County in 1950 from Fairfield, IL where I had been working for the Ashland Oil and Refining Co. They were drilling for oil in the vicinity of The Old Mount Vernon Road and Ford Roads. I went to work for them after my job for the Texas Co. terminated. I asked for a transfer to this part of the country with my wife and daughter. We originated from around Bridgeport, IL, where we both got our schooling. There we married and went to Indianapolis, IN for a couple of years. Then we went to the oilfield of Salem, IL, where I worked for the Texas Pipe line. From there I went to the service for two years. I saw service with the 70, Infantry Division in France and Germany. Was wounded at Philipsburg France, Jan. 8, 1944. When I returned to the U.S., I returned to my old job which didn't last very long. In the mean time we had a little girl which made us very happy. With my wife and daughter I made the move to Mount Vernon, where I remained for 15 years. My company transferred me to Pool, KY. In 1965 when that job played out they sent me back to Mount Vernon again. I worked at Mink Island on the Wabash River for a while then went to Farmersville for yet another job for the same Co. Between Farmersville and Wabash River bottoms for the last six years that I was with them. In the mean time, in the year of 1961, we helped to start a church in a friend's home. They later moved away and we went to the home of Mr. Thomas Horack. We outgrew that and moved to the old store building which was at 300 West Second St. in Mount Vernon, IN. We stayed at this location until we were able to purchase the old church buiding that belonged to the Christian Science people. Where we remained until the present time. We were able to pastor that Church for 28 years. At this writing, at the age of 70 years, I am still pastoring the little church. I hope that I have been able to contribute a little to the spiritual life of Mount Vernon, IN. Here I have made my home less the five years that I was in Kentucky, since 1950.

My daughter, Myrna Faye Cummins, married a boy from Olney, IL. They moved to Mount Vernon where he now works for the Indiana Farm Bureau. Myrna and her husband, Dennis Levitt, live on the old Mackey Farrie Road just west of town with their two daughters, Trisha and Lisa.

GLENN AND DOLORES A. CURTIS

Due to the flood of January 1930, Glenn was born at 925 W. 4th St. in Mt. Vernon at the home of family friends (Bottomly) instead of at the Curtis home in Point Township. His roots in Posey County go back to some of the original settlers including the Curtis, Todd, Conner, Harp, Hill, and Johnson families.

Glenn's parents were Amos W. and Inez Todd Curtis. His father died Aug. 10, 1943 and his mother lived until Jan. 12, 1988.

Dolores was born in Vincennes, moving to Owensville at an early age where she attended elementary and high school.

Her parents were Carl Barry (deceased) and Thelma Byrd Barry. Mrs. Barry presently resides near Owensville.

Dolores received her B.S. degree at Oakland City College and M.S. at Indiana University. She has been teaching elementary school in Gibson County for 30 years.

She is a member of Delta Kappa Gamma, ISTA, NEA, and Eastern Star.

Glenn and Dolores were married on Christmas Day in 1971 at the General Baptist Church in Owensville. This marriage brought together a family of ten children, eight by Glenn's first marriage and two by Dolores' first marriage.

(1986 Picture) Glenn and Dolores A. Curtis

Glenn's children are Linda J. Oliver of Princeton, KY, James K. Curtis and Brenda J. Jones of Evansville, Glenda J. Norvell, J. Todd Curtis, Cinda J. Reinitz and Kenda J. Hartmann of Mt. Vernon. Son, Joseph died at age 30 in 1985.

Dolores' children are Lisa Leslie of Boonville and Cynda Osborne of Terre Haute.

To date, these ten children have produced 17 grand children.

For 15 years Glenn was Editorial Cartoonist for first, the Mt. Vernon Democrat and later, the New Harmony Times.

Currently, Glenn is devoting his time to gardening, farming interests in Point Township, oil painting and pen & ink illustrations including the cover logo of this book. In 1986, he was appointed Posey County Historian by the Indiana Historical Bureau and Indiana Historical Society and is still serving in that capacity.

Away from school, Dolores keeps busy with her crafts and ceramic painting.

Together, Glenn and Dolores enjoy auto travelling and have visited most of the continental U.S., their favorite stops—historical sites and Flea Markets!

After being residents of Mt. Vernon, they are now enjoying their rural home in Marrs Township.

DAVID

William C. and Clara Nurrenbern David reside in Black Township. They married July 23, 1955 in Vanderburgh County, where Clara was born in 1936. William, born in 1933, is the son of Clinton H. and Ida Mae Vaupel David who married, May 21, 1932. William graduated from Stuckey School (two-room) and Mt. Vernon High. He served in the Korean War in Mannheim, Germany. William has worked at Indiana Farm Bureau Refinery since 1956. William's one brother, Jerry W. resides with his wife Betty Fehrenbacher David and children, Jay C. and Kristen at Bloomington, IN. Clinton, a school bus driver and farmer, born in 1911 was the only son of Elmer and Carrie Orth David who married in 1904. They had one daughter, Elnora. For many years Elmer was Marrs Township Democrat trustee. Elmer's parents were George H. and Laura Fisher David and married in 1884. Thomas R. and Mary Moor David (from Virginia), George's parents were extensive land owners in Marrs, West Franklin area. One of the earliest settlers of Marrs Township was Gabriel David, father of Thomas R. Farming was their occupation. Born in Indiana, Gabriel and Polly Carson David married in 1829 and are the great, great, great, grandparents of William

Front Row - Jillian, Cody A., David - children of Rick and Mary; Seated - William - Clois David; Standing - Left to right Jon W. Robert E. - Mary J. - Rick A. Mrs. Rick A., Mark W.

Ida Mae, daughter of William and Rachel Layer Vaupel, was born Dec. 8, 1913, and died July 19, 1985. She had five sisters and one brother. William Vaupel had a short life, 1881 to 1923. His parents were George and Herminia Saalman Vaupel. The Vaupels came from Hessen, Germany in 1866 and were farmers and carpenters. Rachel died July 16, 1959 and her parents were John G. and Lodemia Harrison Layer. John G., a prominent Marrs Township farmer served in the Tenth Indiana Cavalry in the Civil War. His parents, natives of Germany came in 1843.

A 150 year Nurrenbern-Steinkamp reunion was celebrated on the University grounds in 1988. John H. and Elizabeth Steinkamp Nurrenbern came from Hanover, Germany in 1834. He worked in a Cincinatti foundry for two years. In 1836 they received a land grant from the government to purchase 80 acres of farmland at $1.62 an acre near Evansville, IN. John H.'s son John married Barbara Urich and lived on the homestead. This land remained in the Nurrenbern name until 1966 when it sold for the establishment of a college now known as the University of Southern Indiana. In 1937, Robert A. Nurrenbern, Clara's father, expanded his property into the bottomland of Black Township, Posey County. Robert served in World War I.

Robert married Julia Rollett, May 20, 1919. Robert died in 1960 and Julia in 1970. Julia's parents were John and Mary Spieker Rollett. John's parents were Joseph and Sophia Spitzer Rollett, Jr. Joseph Rollett Sr. came from Alsace Lorraine (German-France border), in 1854. The home at 5119 Broadway, Evansville is the original house built in 1855 from oak and poplar trees from his 40 acres. It is still in the Rollett family. They were well known for their carpentry skills.

William C. and Clara M. have four sons who graduated from Saint Matthew Catholic Elementary and Mt. Vernon High. Mark W. born in 1956, Rick A. in 1959, Robert C. in 1961 and Jon Wayne in 1966, still reside in Posey County. Rick married Mary J. Fischer in 1982. They have two children, Cody Alan born in 1985 and Jillian Ann in 1987.

DEIG

Roger Glenn Deig was born May 26, 1967 to Marvin Glenn Deig and Elaine Sue (Adams) Deig of Mt. Vernon, IN. Roger graduated from Mt. Vernon Senior High School in 1985, where he had been active in Football, Baseball and Chorus. Roger attended the University of Southern Indiana. He is currently employed at General Electric in Mt. Vernon as a Chemical Operator.

Roger and Kristine Deig

Kristine Marie (Ritzert) Deig was born Aug. 10, 1967 to David Anthony Ritzert and Ruth Jane (Gries) Ritzgert of Mt. Vernon. Kristine also graduated from Mt. Vernon Senior High School in 1985 where she had been active in the German Club and Chorus, as well as a member of the National Honor Society. Kristine attends the University of Southern Indiana, majoring in Elementary Education. She will graduate in December, 1989. Kristine is currently a substitute teacher for the School District in Mt. Vernon.

Roger and Kristine were married in a 7:00 p.m. ceremony on Mar. 17, 1989 at St. Matthew Church in Mt. Vernon. They reside at 5497 Ford Road in Mt. Vernon with their dog, Lance.

DeKEMPER

Stanley Weyman and Edna L.S. (Schick) DeKemper are residents of Mt. Vernon, IN. They married Nov. 21, 1940 in Henderson, KY. They are parents of two sons: Stanley Weyman II, born Feb. 24, 1948. He is a graduate of Mt. Vernon High School and Purdue University. He married Patricia Young of Indianapolis Sept. 7, 1973 and they had a son Raphael Nafees DeKemper. Stanley works as an intervention trainer and drug counselor in Indianapolis, IN. Kurt Douglas was born Sept. 19, 1958. He is a graduate of Mt. Vernon High School and Purdue University. He married Penny Rene' Mace of Scottsburg, IN Mar. 20, 1982 and they have two sons, Galen Patrick DeKemper and Tyler Douglas DeKemper. Kurt is a research chemist and pharmacist in Indianapolis, IN and lives in Franklin, IN.

Weyman and Edna DeKemper

Stanley Weyman was born Aug. 11, 1915 in Alzey, Henderson Co, KY. He attended schools in Henderson Co., KY and Mt. Vernon, IN. His parents were William E. and Elizabeth (Watkins) DeKemper of Mt. Vernon. They were farmers in Kentucky before moving to Mt. Vernon in 1983. Stanley has three brothers, Jack R. and Rudy E., both of Mt. Vernon and William E. Jr. deceased. Stanley worked for the Consumers Ice & Cold Storage Co. when he married. He worked for the Farm Bureau Refinery for 39 yrs., retiring in 1981 as an electrician. He served in the National Guard and was an electrician's mate 3rd class in the Navy during WWII and was stationed in England. He is a member of Trinity United Church of Christ.

Stanley's paternal grandparents were Benjamin and Emma (Deusner) DeKemper of Henderson, KY where they were farmers. His maternal grandparents were George Lafayette and Janie Gee (Hazelwood) Watkins of Henderson, KY. He worked in the textile mills.

Edna was born Oct. 9, 1921 to George and Louisa (Knopfmeier) Schick of Mt. Vernon. She has a sister, Mildred (Schick) Lee of Ozark, AL; a brother, George E. Schick of Mt. Vernon, a brother, Herman William, deceased and a half-sister, Alma Schick deceased. Her father was a contract thresherman and raised chickens.

Edna graduated from Mt. Vernon High School in 1940 and was working at the Palace Soda Shop. During WWII she worked in the laboratory at the Farm Bureau Refinery. She is a life long member of Trinity United Church of Christ. Her maternal grandparents were Henry and Wilhelmina (Boberg) Knopfmeier of Posey County who were farmers and parents of 11 children. They originally came from Germany. Her paternal grandparents were Peter and Anna Marie (Weirth) Schick of the Caborn area of Posey County. They were farmers and parents of 11 children. They were both natives of Germany.

HENRY J. DENNING FAMILY

In August, 1910 the Henry Denning family moved to Posey County from St. Meinrad, IN. Henry's father, Joseph (1842-1904) and grandfather, Heinrich (1790-1874), a German emigrant, had farmed there since the 1840's. The move was prompted by a growing family and an insufficient amount of tillable land to meet the family needs. Since a brother-in-law, George E. Fischer, already lived in Posey County, it was natural for Henry to seek farm land there. He missed the opportunity to buy land next to George, east of Mt. Vernon, by two days. Instead, he bought 198 acres for $12,000 in Point Township, contiguous to the Lawrence school ground.

Henry, born Oct. 27, 1864 near St. Meinrad, was the first of Joseph's seven children. His mother was Theresia Theile (1843-1865) Denning. He married Theresia Fischer (1871-1950), daughter of John (1845-1915) and Agatha Werne (1850-1892) Fischer in 1891 at Ferdinand, IN. Children followed like clockwork. Leo was born in 1892, Joe in 1894, Wilhelmina in 1896, Aloys in 1899, and Henrietta in 1902. Albert was born in 1910 after the move to Point, as was Mary in 1912.

1941 Photo at Henry and Theresia Dennings 50th Wedding Anniversary Celebration. Front: Albert, Henry, Theresia, and Mary. Back: Aloys, Joe, Minnie, and Henrietta.

The move itself was interesting, taking three days and three nights. Henry and Joe rode wagons, while Aloys got stuck herding the horses and cows on foot. The furniture was sent by rail from Ferdinand. Theresia, who was seven months pregnant, Leo, Minnie, and Henrietta, also rode by train to Evansville, and by Interurban to Mt. Vernon. Aloys remembered difficulties with the Evansville police when the Denning caravan paraded through town leaving souvenir cattle droppings as they went.

Life in Point was good, but not without tragedy. Leo, while helping his uncle Joe Schwindel cut corn fodder, came down with what turned out to be typhoid fever. He became very ill and died in October 1911. Leo's funeral was the first at Short's Funeral Home. Minnie and Henrietta also caught the fever but survived.

Henry farmed until 1924 when Aloys took over the farm. A house was purchased on East Third in Mt. Vernon, where Henry and Theresia lived out their remaining days. Henry helped out on the farm until 1926, when he took the job of janitor at St. Matthew's. That job became available when the pastor decided that the parish could not afford to pay $3.00 a day to the existing janitor. Henry, 62 at the time, accepted the job for $1.00 a day. His duties started at 6:00 A.M. by ringing the Angeles bells at the church. During the depression days that $1.00 a day helped considerably.

All the children but Leo and Albert married. Minnie married Ben Kercher in 1919, Aloys married Anna Fromm in 1925, Joe married Elizabeth Seibert in 1928, Henrietta married Amand Gempler in 1931, and Mary married John Kueber in 1956. Henry and Theresia had 18 grandchildren. (Two died young.)

Theresia's heart failed during a bout with viral pneumonia in July, 1950 at age 78. Henry died the following February at age 86.

WILLIAM F. AND DOROTHY F. DIETERLE

The William F. Dieterle Family have been residents of the Bufkin Community since November 1947. William was the sixth child of seven born (Sept. 5, 1920) to William F. Dieterle Sr. and Katie (Orman) Dieterle. The other six were George O. Dieterle (1904-1974), Mary Wilma Kohler (1906-1967), Irma Cecelia Walker (1910-1983), Kathryn Louise Roos (1913-1969), Elvalena Weber (1918-), Ralph Edward Dieterle (1922-1977) William F. (Sr.) born Oct. 9, 1880, died July 4, 1943. Katie was born Mar. 8, 1880, died May 29, 1951.

William F. attended Mt. Vernon grade and high schools. He worked as a Welder at Servel Inc. until the 38th Div. of Indiana National Guard was called into Federal Service. He served from Jan. 11, 1941 until the end of World War II Oct. 4, 1945.

On Apr. 27, 1943 William F. married Dorothy F. McGhee (born Sept. 7, 1923) the daughter of Alva B. and Elma R. (Gott) McGhee. They were joined in marriage at 338 W. 9th St. by Rev. Walter C. Rasche. While William F. was in service, their first born Sharon Lee (Mrs. Ralph W. Juncker) arrived (Sept. 10, 1944) while William was in New Guinea. Sharon was born at Harrisburg, IL on July 1, 1946 their son Max was born in Deaconess Hospital in Evansville, IN.

Left to Right - Patti, Becky, Max and Sharon, Seated - William and Dorothy Dieterele

In 1947 the family moved from East 10th St. in Mt. Vernon to Bufkin on the Elza Utley Farm. Their second daughter was born on June 22, 1949 and was named Rebecca. These three Dieterle children attended the old Farmersville School until the schools were consolidated. Max and Rebecca graduated from the New Farmersville School. The fourth child Patti Jean was born May 17, 1956 and she attended Hedges Central Grade School. All four Dieterle children graduated from Mt. Vernon High School as had William in 1939 and Dorothy in 1942. Sharon was in the first class to graduate from the New M.V.H.S. in 1961. Then Max in 1964. Rebecca in 1967 and Patti in 1974. William F. and Max both received the Kiwanis Award. The only father and son of this writing.

In 1958 the Dieterles bought the Alanson Allyn farm that joined them on the south and east. In 1967 they built a home on this ground that faces Blackford Road. Dorothy and William are still on this home site and three of their four children are in the Mt. Vernon and Bufkin area. Patti Jean resides in Evansville. Their nine grandchildren are Debra and Alan Juncker, Tami (Dieterle) Straub, Kelli and Max Wm. Dieterle, Jodi and Jeni Merrick, Katie Weintraut and Cari Edge.

William retired in 1982 from Indiana Farm Bureau after 36 and 1/2 years. Besides being a homemaker Dorothy worked as a cook and pie baker for the Posey Bowling Lanes, Pioneer Seed Corn as a scales operator. She cooked at the American Legion home for the Kiwanis dinners and catered meals.

Dorothy has two brothers, Robert W. McGhee of Phoenix, AZ and Donald E. McGhee of Dallas, TX. Their parents and grandparents were residents of White Co., IL and they are buried there.

The Dieterele name is listed in the translation of Mount Vernon Wochenblatt by Ilse Dorsch Horacek and in 1850 Posey County History Book.

DOANE HISTORY

The picture shows Black School in Point Township, one of a group of historic schools in the South Metropolitan School District in Posey County. Anne Doane sketched 31 schools in the late 50s and they now hang in the Mount Vernon High School library.

Mount Vernon has been home to the Doane family since 1946 when they arrived from Long Beach, CA in response to a call from the town Aviation Commissioners. The town had a new airport and needed a manager-instructor to operate it. John Waring Doane, having served as a flight instructor in the Army Air Force during WWII, was qualified for the job. The airport grounds now belong to the Indiana Port Commission, site of Southwind Maritime Centre which, incidentally, was named by John in an area naming contest.

John was born Feb. 15, 1915 to Reverend Clarence E. and Kathryn (Cleary) Doane of Strongsville, OH. He died Apr. 7, 1972. He was named after the first John Doane who left England to come to this country. A notice in a Boston Publication states; "Mr. John Doane came to New England about 1629. Thirty of the Leyden Company, with their families, arrived at Plymouth, Mass." In 1636, the first John dabbled in real estate, was also an innkeeper and court auditor. While living in Eastham, he was town selectman and a Deacon of the first church. He died in 1685, leaving five offspring. In his will, dated May 18, 1678, he declared his age as 88 or thereabouts.

Black School - Point Twp. Posey County

This tenth generation John Doane also dabbled in real estate, was Posey County Coroner, an auctioneer and a photographer of note. On Sept. 12, 1937, he married Anne Marie, born Aug. 3, 1914 to Mihal and Elizabeth (Baloga) Knapik of Thompson, PA. Mihal was born in Austria-Hungary Apr. 12, 1889 and died Mar. 25, 1949 in Thompson. Elizabeth, whose parents John and Anna (Tomko) Baloga came from Slovakia, was born Oct. 11, 1896 and died May 2, 1983.

John Waring Doane Jr. was born to John and Anne Mar. 30, 1940 in Rome, NY. He was schooled in Mount Vernon and attended three years at (then)

Evansville College, and later graduated from McKendree College, Lebanon, IL with a Bachelor of Arts Degree and honors in Psychology. His 22 year military service record included the Aviation Cadet Program at James Connolly AFB in Texas, Strategic Air Command, pilot training at Moody AFB and overseas service where he was decorated with the Third Oak Cluster to the air medal (1971) and the Distinguished Flying Cross (1972). He retired from service in 1984 and is presently employed at Flight Safety International, St. Louis, MO., as a DC-9 instructor.

He is married to Bonnie Lee, daughter of Sylvester (deceased) and Helen (Stephan) Huck of Mount Vernon. Bonnie was born Aug. 17, 1942 and their marriage date is Apr. 27, 1963. They have two sons, Eric John, born June 22, 1965, Caribou, ME, and Mark Waring, born Sept. 14, 1973 at Scott Medical Center, Belleville, IL.

ARVIN AND ANNA DROEGE

Arvin and Anna Droege are very proud of their German heritage.

Arvin was born Apr. 20, 1931 in Robinson Township. He has lived in the same house most of his life. His parents were Edward b. 1896 and Lydia (Papenmeier) Droege b. 1894. They spoke the German language quite commonly in their home. Edward had several work traits; farming, Blacksmith Shop, threshing machine, saw mill and his hobby, broom making. The Blacksmith Shop and broom making machine were passed down to son Arvin.

Arvin's paternal grandparents were; Henry Droege b. 1869 and Katherine (Schelhorn) Droege b. 1873.

Arvin's great-grandparents; Heinrich b. 1829 and Louisa (Schröder) Dröge b. 1833 arrived in Posey County in 1853 from Retzen and Exter, Germany.

Arvin's maternal grandparents, Frederich b. 1856 and Katherine (Dickhaut) Papenmeier b. 1858 were both of German descent. Frederich left Hummerson, Germany with his parents, arriving in Posey County in 1865.

Arvin and Anna Droege

Anna born May 17, 1933 in Vanderburgh County to Arthur and Alvina (Huff) Plassmeyer. The Plassmeyer ancestors lived in Warrick County and came from Niederbeckson, Germany. Arthur b. 1905 was raised in Robinson Township by Philip and Henrietta (Elsfelder) Peters. Alvina b. 1905 in Robinson Township to Philip b. 1877 and Lena (Elsfelder) Huff b. 1877. Anna's great-grandfather Johann Huff b. 1836 left Horrweiler, Germany with parents, arriving in Posey County in 1840. Her great-grandmother Sophie (Roesner) Huff b. 1840, left Germany with parents. Her father died while coming across and was buried at sea. Sophie arrived in Posey County in 1848.

Anna's great-grandfather Lenhardt Elsfelder b. 1834 left his homeland of Neustadt, France, arriving in Vanderburgh County in 1854. Lenhardt's wife Barbara (Reffert) Elsfelder b. 1846 left her native home in Baden, Germany arriving in Vanderburgh County in 1852.

Arvin and Anna married Sept. 9, 1951. Both were employed at Servel until Arvin was called to serve in the Korean Conflict. He served his tour in Germany. Anna joined him in Germany and they lived with a German family.

In 1956 they moved to their present home in Robinson Township.

Arvin has been employed with Farm Bureau Refinery for 33 years.

They have four grown children. Terri (Souders) b. 1954, Larry b. 1956, Gary b. 1958 and Jeri (Sauve) b. 1961. Terri is a school teacher and lives in Dubois County. Larry, Gary and Jeri are employed with General Electric and reside in Posey County.

Arvin and Anna have five grandchildren.

In 1972 they purchased the family farm. They were presented the "Hoosier Homestead Award" in 1983. Their farm has been in the same family since 1853.

The family enjoys working in their Blacksmith and Woodworking Shops. They have created cabinets, furniture and craft items the past 33 years and continue to do so.

Arvin and Anna are active members in Zion United Church of Christ.

Anna has researched family history and completed a book; "Die Schröder Staumbaum" 1985.

Both are members of the Indiana German Historical Society, Tri-State Genealogical Society and New Harmony Twin Cities.

Researching has brought much interest in travels to Germany. They have enjoyed five visits to Germany to visit relatives, cities, churches and farms, where their ancestors lived. They have visited German friends connected with New Harmony Twin Cities and friends in Osnabruck, Germany.

Arvin and Anna enjoy hosting German relatives and friends when they visit in America.

JOSIAH DOWNEN

Josiah Downen, of English and Irish ancestry, was born between the years of 1740 and 1745 and lived in South Carolina. The name is spelled many ways such as Downen, Downend, Downing and Donnan, a South Carolina name. Downing is connected with Downing Street in London, England. Downen is the most common name. All of these names are found on wills, deeds and tax receipts. There were Downens in America as early as 1729 according to Connecticut records of those who fought in the French and Indian Wars.

Josiah Downen served in the South Carolina Militia, 1780-82, in the Revolutionary War, under the command of General Pickens, who lived in this area. Josiah had received a grant of land of 150 acres from George III of Great Britain Feb. 13, 1768 in Granville Co., SC. There were few settlers there this early, most of them coming from the Virginia border in North Carolina. In 1792 South Carolina granted to Josiah Downen 31 acres in recognition of his war service.

Josiah was the father of five sons - Job, William, Timothy, Josiah Jr., and David, and three daughters Elizabeth, Polly and Patsy.

Some of the family migrated to Muhlenberg Co, KY where Josiah was taxed for 120 acres. Here he died between the years of 1801 and 1803. Mary, his wife, died in 1835, aged 88 years. Then the land was taxed to his youngest son, David, 21 years old.

David Downen married Elizabeth Oliver in 1808 in Christian Co., KY. Their second daughter, Jane, was born in Indiana in 1810. She married John Dixon in 1831. John died in 1873 and Jane in 1888. David Downen died around 1831 and Elizabeth (Betsy) in 1870. The Olivers and Downens had been neighbors all through the years of migration.

John and Jane Dixon had a daughter Missouri Jane, born in 1843, who married William David Crunk in 1863, when he was home on leave from the Civil War. They lived in Crunk Settlement, Marrs Township, near the Ohio River.

Their daughter, Carrie Evelyn Crunk, married James Arthur Wolfinger, a Marrs township farmer, Jan. 4, 1906. They had two daughters, Vivian Lucile and Miskel Virginia.

Miskel Wolfinger is a Home Economist and lives in Mt. Vernon, IN.

Vivian, a teacher, married Kenneth Jack Blackburn, a Black township farmer and dairyman, in 1932. Kenneth died in 1963 and Vivian maintains their home in Bufkin, near Mt. Vernon. Their children are James William who died in an accident at age three; Peggy Anne, a Dietician, married to James Edward Gross, a musician, of Lafayette, IN. They live in Highland Park, IL; Bonnie Jill, a teacher, married William Edward Koehler, an airline pilot, of Birmingham, MI. They live in Apple Valley, MN.

The Gross children are Tamara Kay and Candace Lee, who married Kevin Weber, of Chicago.

The Koehler children are Julia Ann, William Edward III, and Robert Kenneth.

The name Blackburn is English and found in the early history of Blackburn, a city near the industrial center of England. The family in America began with John Blackburn - 1752-1833 - who reared his family in Rockingham Co., NC.

GLENDA SUE (ANGERMEIER) ELPERS

Glenda Sue (Angermeier) Elpers, of Gibson County, born Aug. 11, 1951, parents Virgil and Margie Jean (Espenlaub) Angermeir of Black Township. Attended eight years of school at St. Matthews, graduated from Mt. Vernon High School in 1969.

Back Row: Glenn V. Angermeier, Paul L. Angermeier Front Row: Emma O.M. Espenlaub, Glenda Sue (Angermeier) Elpers

Graduated from L.P.N. School in 1970. Married to Jerome (Jerry) T. Elpers Aug. 26, 1972 of Gibson County, parents Virgil and Mildred (Kraft) Elpers of Vanderburgh County. To this union have been born Christy Anne, born Nov. 23, 1974. Her hobby is fishing. Sherry Lynne, born Dec. 24, 1975. She likes music like her great grandmother, Emma

O.M. Espenlaub, and plays the piano. Both attend Haubstadt School. Jerome (Jerry) is self employed and is a contractor.

ENDECOTTS

One early spring morning in 1763, Thomas Endecott and Joseph Endecott, 5th Generation in the colonies, descendants of Gov. John Endecott of Massachusetts Bay Coloney, assembled their families and headed south west from the Mt. Holly, NJ area.

Twelve years later Thomas Endecott and his family settled down in Lowgap, NC. Joseph took his family into South Carolina.

Daniel Boone, born across the Delaware River from the Mt. Holly area, lived a short distance away from Lowgap at Boones Crossing of the Yadkin River.

By 1796, Thomas was on the move again, taking Boone's wilderness trail into Bourbon County, WV-(KY), where he and his sons bought land along the Indian Creek. Within the year, Joseph aged 21, son of Joseph and his two sisters, Sara and Eunice, appeared on their Uncle Thomas' doorstep from South Carolina.

In 1811, Thomas Endecott Sr., Thomas Endicott Jr., Aaron Endicott, Wm. Davis, Jonathan Jaquess, and Wm. Casey tracked from their Cynthiana, KY homes up into the lower reaches of the Indiana Territory, scouting the lay of the land around the future Cynthiana, IN.

On Sept. 1, 1815, seven Endicott's of the 7th and 8th generation, set out for the Indiana Territory along with the Jaquess-Fraizer-Casey families and settled in what became Smith Township, Posey County.

In 1817, Wm. Davis brought his family to Smith Township and soon laid out Cynthiana, IN. He was accompanied by his brother John and family, the James Nesbit family, the Reuben Garten and widow Margaret McGhee Journey (mother of most of the companys wives).

Before 1819 old Thomas Endecott brought his young wife, Susan Turner Young Endecott, and their infant son, Absolum Turner Endicott, to settle near his descendants. (Note: Thomas Endecott and wife, Susan, lie buried in the southeast corner of Mt. Pleasant Cemetery five miles east of Poseyville. Writer Note: Tombstones were still in place and legible in mid-20s. Susans Lada Lamb couchant.)

Among the Posey County Endecotts that left their imprint on the county and state includes Dr. Samuel Endicott; Moses Endicott, Township Trustee and County Commissioner, and my great grandfather, James Casey Endicott who was serving in the state legislature, when he contracted Cholera and came home to die.

By 1850, every settler in the area was kin to the other settlers through marriage. For example, three Endicotts had married Nesbits. Four Endicotts had married into the Calvert family. The Kinships has increased until in the 1980's three out of four people living in Northwestern Vanderburg, S.E. Gibson County, and in Posey County Robb-Smith Townships have one or more common ancestors.

Sixty-nine Endecotts (Endicotts) are listed in the indexes of Coy's Posey County Cemeteries 1814-1976. In the Posey County telephone directory 1987, there is only one Endicott listed (Herbert E. of Rural, New Harmony).

In view of the information in the preceeding paragraph, one can conclude that the male Endicotts either ran to girl babies or ran for the Posey County border!

FRED D. AND CAROLYN SUE (CROWE) ESSARY

Mt. Vernon natives, Fred. D. and Carolyn Sue Crowe Essary, started their lives together in Shawneetown, IL on Apr. 22, 1954. They are the parents of three daughters: Cheryl Ann, born Mar. 30, 1955, Cathy Jo, born June 25, 1957 and Chawn Renae, born Feb. 3, 1964. Cathy married Dwight Howe of Vincennes on May 14, 1977. Their children are Jeremy David, born Feb. 6, 1981, and Amanda Dawn, bo,n Sept. 24, 1983. Chawn was married to Billy Gibbs from 1983 to 1987. Their children are Cayce Ann, born Apr. 2, 1985 and Courtny Jo. born July 13, 1986.

Fred, born on May 4, 1933 to John and Blanch Cooper Essary, is the brother of Geneva, James, Beulah, Guild (who died in infancy), Gene, John Robert and Virgil.

At age 17, his maternal great-grandfather, Ebeneezer John Cooper, worked his way to America from Hampshire Greenhut, England as a cabin boy. Traveling down the Ohio River to Mt. Vernon, and from there, riding an ox-cart to Poseyville, in 1854 he married Mary Barter, who died in 1897 shortly after giving birth to their daughter, Elizabeth. In 1860 he married Hester Ann Willis. They were the parents of James Elbert, Thomas, Nancy Ann and Cassandra. A circuit-riding Primative Baptist Preacher, he served a wide area, including Hamilton Co., IL where he and his family eventually settled. Fred's paternal great-grandparents Nathan, born in North Carolina, and Jane Vaughn Hudson Essary, of White Co., IL were early settlers of Hamilton Co., IL and many descendants still live there.

Fred and Sue Essary

Fred has been an employee of Indiana Farm Bureau Refinery since February, 1957 as a #1 Craftsman Pump-repairman.

Sue's parents were Owen C. and Bertha Ashworth Crowe. She arrived Dec. 10, 1935 to join her sisters, Harriett Louise (nicknamed Peggy at birth), and Wanda Lee.

Her father, a World War I veteran, was the son of Charles C. and Ida Mae Gray Crowe. Her grandfather, a master mechanic, owned his own garage in Mt. Vernon. Her great-great grandparents John Crowe and Samuel Wise Gray were Pioneers of Indiana in Washington County. Her maternal ancestors were early settlers of Posey County.

In 1810, the family of Moses, a circuit-riding Methodist preacher, and Eliza Davis Ashworth, came to Prairie Settlement. Their son, Christopher, married Elizabeth Jacquess Hirons, daughter of Jonathan Jacquess, Jr., who served in the Revolutionary War. Their son, William Feltcher married Barbara Ann Greathouse, daughter of Sampson and Sarah Welborn Greathouse. Sampson's grandfather was Herman Groetenhausen, who immigrated to America from Germany about 1709.

Sue's maternal great-grandparents were Samuel and Mary Jane Allen Hanshoe, who came to Indiana from Floyd Co., KY, prior to 1877. Her maternal grandparents were David F. and Ella Frances Hanshoe Ashworth. He was a farmer. His death in 1940 ended 59 years of marriage.

From 1970 to 1982, Sue owned Sue's Pet Palace at 114 W. Third Street. She now works for Posey County Council on Aging as the Senior Center Director.

FELDMANN—MAURER

My great, great, grandfather, Valentine Jacob Feldman, was born in Buhlertal, Germany. He married Barbara Gumbrecht, born in 1807 in Oberlustadt, Germany and died in Germany in 1858. A weaver by trade, in 1856 he and his 20 year old daughter Barbara and his 16 year old son George Anton Feldmann came to America and apparently went to St. Louis, MO. Family speculation handed down says he left to look for work, was ambushed, robbed and murdered at an unknown place and time. Two other children remained in Germany, one other came to St. Louis later and the other two settled later in New York area.

My great grandfather George Anton Feldmann, seated on the right in the photo, was born in Rheinish Bavaria (another source says Alsasce Lorraine) on July 11, 1840, reportedly obtained employment on a river boat from St. Louis plying the Mississippi and Ohio Rivers and learned the barber trade. At age 22 he married Regina Bünz (Benz) at St. Phillips in Posey County in 1862. She was born in 1842 in Baden, Baden, Germany. He became a U.S. Citizen in Posey County Oct. 7, 1867. The 1870 Mt. Vernon census lists his occupation as a barber which continued for his lifetime.

Felman-Maurer Family

The photograph pictures the six living children of the ten born to that marriage. A newspaper advertisement in 1882 lists his barber shop at three doors South of Third Street, West side of Main and "Shampooing, hairdressing and shaving done in the most satisfactory manner. Cigars and Tobacco always on hand." A newspaper article states that on Oct. 19, 1880 his barber shop, another barber shop and 12 other businesses were totally destroyed by fire which consumed the entire block. His shop contained six barber chairs. The family residence was 415 W Third Street, about four blocks West from the fire. His wife and newly born tenth child became exposed from the weather elements while watching the disaster and both died on October 27.

The child is buried in the mother's arm at St. Matthew Cemetery at Mt. Vernon. His second marriage was to Octavia Templeton in 1884 to which three children were born. He died Nov. 30, 1910 and is buried at St. Matthew Cemetery.

The fifth child was my grandmother, (pictured standing second from left), Anna Katherine Feldmann who was born Apr. 30, 1870 in Mt. Vernon. She was ten years old at her mother's death and went to Donaldsonville, LA to live with her mother's sister Sophia Bünz Wild for 16 years. Later she went to St. Louis living with relatives and gained employment in a wholesale milinery factory for three years, returning to Mt. Vernon and opened her millinery store in 1899. Newspaper advertisement and City Directory in 1899 recites: "Miss Katherine Feldmann, Fashionable Milliner, 119 W. Second Street, My Stock of Millinery Goods is the most Complete in the City. I have all the Latest Styles and Guarantee Satisfaction. Also Carry a Line of Stamped Goods and Fancy Novelties." She married my grandfather, George Maurer (born at Marine, IL, Jan. 25, 1871) on Oct. 13, 1901 at St. Matthews Church. Their children were Mary Odeline who married Clarence Bailey, now living in Vincennes, IN; Marjorie Celestine who married William Causey, now living in Richmond, VA; and my mother Pauline Louise (b. June 21, 1905), now living in Mt. Vernon, IN. My father was William Herbert Woods, born at Smith Mills, KY in 1905, died in Mt. Vernon in 1988.

My maternal grandmother, Anna Katherine Feldmann Maurer died Mar. 12, 1944 and my maternal grandfather George Maurer died Aug. 3, 1944. Both are buried at St. Matthews.

I am, Betty Ann Woods Kleinschmidt, the oldest of five living children, born in Mt. Vernon in 1924, my brothers and sisters are: Ellen Louise Hayden of Mt. Vernon; Willadee Ervin Goshorn of Port Townsend, WA; George Herbert Woods of Loogootee, IN; Robert Glenn Woods of Mt. Vernon, IN; and Harold Thomas Woods who died at age 2-1/2, is buried in Vincennes, IN.

I married my Stuckey School, Marrs Township and Mt. Vernon High School classmate, C. Eugene Kleinschmidt in 1944. His WW II military service was primarily at Fort Riley, KS, and living in Manhattan, KS, our oldest daughter Ruth Annette was born in 1945. We remained in Kansas after completing service in 1946, employed by Kansas Farm Bureau Insurance Company, residing in various cities, i.e., Manhattan, Garden City, Wichita, and Salina, KS. Our youngest daughter, Marilyn Kay was born in Wichita in 1950. We returned to our native Indiana in 1956, residing in Evansville. Ruth Annette graduated from Bosse High School, married Richard Hebeisen in December, 1964. Our grandson is Bryan Eugene Hebeisen born in 1974 and they reside in Jasper, IN. We moved to Fort Branch, IN in early 1965 and became owners of Rosemeyer Insurance and Real Estate Agency, where we now reside. Marilyn Kay completed high school in Fort Branch and Lockyear Business College in Evansville, and married Wayne L. Fischer in August 1980. Our granddaughter is Alison Leigh born in 1982 and they reside in Evansville, IN.
Submitted by Betty Ann Woods Kleinschmidt

ANN FARRIS (RANES) FISCHER

Ann Farris Ranes Fischer daughter of Francis W. Ranes and Mary Martha (Reeves) Ranes was born July 14, 1948 at the family farm north of Upton about 4-1/2 miles northwest of Mt. Vernon being delivered by her grandfather Dr. John R. Ranes. At age six she began her education at Grafton Elementary two-room school with Mrs. Loren (Nell) Walker teaching grades one-three. With the closing of Grafton she was transferred to Upton School for grade four with Mrs. Lena Addison as her teacher. The remainder of her schooling was in the Mt. Vernon City Schools where she graduated in 1966. In August of that same year she enrolled in the school of practical nursing in Evansville receiving her diploma in 1967. She was employed at Welborn Clinic and also at the Welborn Hospital and on Aug. 31, 1968 she was united in marriage to George Frederick Fischer son of George Joseph and Wilmetta (Reinitz) Fischer. Ann's employment was terminated with the birth of their first child a son George Tyler (Ty) on Dec. 31, 1971 who is presently a junior student at Mt. Vernon High School and is active in sports playing football and baseball. A second son Andrew (Andy) Ranes Fischer was born Jan. 13, 1974 and is currently a freshman at Mt. Vernon High School where he participates in football and is also an Explorer Scout Post #2412. On Dec. 14, 1978 a daughter Tiffany Meshal was born and is a 4th grade student at Farmersville Elementary School. She is a member of 'The Little Hoosiers' a Historical Society sponsored by Mrs. Norma Tiek, a 4th grade teacher at Farmersville.

Seated in front: L to R: Tiffany Fischer, Ann Fischer. Standing in back: Andy Fischer

Both George and Ann are very active in parent and support groups at school for their children. Ann is a member of D.A.R. and George is a 24-year employee of Mt. Vernon General Electric Co. The Fischer's reside on R.R. 4 Ranes Road in Rural Mt. Vernon.

FISHER

James Lewis Fisher came to New Harmony with his wife Effie (Harrison) and family in 1892. James, better known as Lewis, was born on June 17, 1857 to Mormon and Mary (Wade) Fisher in Huntingburg, IN. His father, Mormon, was also born in Huntingburg on Dec. 25, 1833 to William and Mary (Whitten) Fisher. Lewis' grandfather William was born near Cincinnati, OH on Aug. 9, 1791 and he was raised near Hardinsburg, KY. William served as a soldier in the War of 1812. He settled near Huntingburg as a farmer in 1817. Mormon served as a Captain during the Civil War in the Tenth Indiana Cavalry. He was a lawyer, State Legislator, postmaster and Mayor of Huntingburg.

Lewis was a farmer by trade. He and his family lived and worked the land across the Wabash River from New Harmony known as Cut-Off Island. He and his wife had ten children during their marriage: Ella, John, Hugar (Buck), Ross, Bertha, Frank, Sylvia, Alfred, Helen and Martin. Lewis died on Dec. 20, 1938 and Effie passed away on Nov. 21, 1924. Both were buried at the Maple Hill Cemetery, as are most of the descendants.

Genevieve, Geraldine, Edith, Myrtle, John Jr., Homer, Lewis, Donald

John Fisher was born in Huntingburg on Oct. 6, 1877. He married Myrtle Mae Stewart on May 23, 1901. They had nine children: Guy, Geraldine (Stanley Mitchell), Louis (Hazel Hyatt), Effie, Edith (Harry Linville), Edward Homer (Kate Bailey), Genevieve (Robert Wilson), Donald (Elizabeth Streamer) and John (Beatrice Brown). He and his family were members of the General Baptist Church in New Harmony. John died on May 21, 1930 and Myrtle died on Sept. 5, 1954. Both are buried in Maple Hill Cemetery.

Donald Fisher was born Dec. 17, 1919. He served in the U.S. Navy and fought in the Pacific during WWII. He married Elizabeth Streamer, daughter of Clarence and Cora Belle (Hunter) on Apr. 21, 1946. They had two sons, Dennis, born Dec. 15, 1949; David on Sept. 2, 1952, and six grandchildren. Donald died May 28, 1984.

The picture is the John Fisher family taken in April 1943. Top Row- Genevieve, Geraldine, Edith, wife (Myrtle). Bottom row - John, Jr., E. Homer, Lewis (Skeet) and Donald.

Edith Linville is the only one of John's children still living in Posey County. John Jr. and family live in Farmersville, LA. The rest are deceased. Several of Alfred, Hugar and Bertha's descendants still live in Posey County.

E. Homer and Kathlyn (Kate) Bailey were married July 9, 1937. He died May 13, 1969. However, she and their four daughters, - Dorita (Logan) born Nov. 2, 1938; Ginger (Little) born Sept. 21, 1940; Sharon (Saltzman) born Apr. 20, 1943; and Jane born Aug. 21, 1955 are living in Posey County. They have ten grandchildren and ten great-grandchildren. Cynthia Powell (Dorita's oldest daughter) died Oct. 12, 1988. Most of the rest are living in New Harmony or Mt. Vernon.

ORAL H. AND MELBA FLENER

Oral H. and Wallace Melba Trafford Flener are residents of Mt. Vernon. They were married Oct. 14, 1940 and had one daughter, Sharon Ann. She died Dec. 18, 1941. Both are members of the Mt. Vernon General Baptist Church.

Oral was born Sept. 20, 1919 in Ohio Co., KY to Elvis and Arrinda Ivy Smith Flener, the seventh of eight children. He served in World War II in Europe in Company K, 30th infantry, 119 Regiment, U.S. Army as a private from 1942 to 1944. Oral received a Purple Heart and Certificate of Merit for a patrol he was on in January 1945 that was deep in enemy territory for five hours in Belgium. Later he worked for Coastal Tank Lines for 34 years until he retired.

Oral's paternal great grandparents were Andrew Jackson (b. 1814-d. 1883) and Ester R. Romans Flener. Their eldest child was Vincent Flener born in 1846. He married Margaret Harmon. They had one son, Elvis, who married Arrinda Ivy Smith.

Oral's maternal great, great, great grandparents were Adam and ? Smith. They had one known son, Jacob, born in Pennsylvania and married Mary Barker in 1800. Her father was John Barker (Rev. War soldier). Jacob and Mary had one son, Daniel Morgan Smith born 1811 in Butler Co., KY. He was the first white child born in Morgantown, KY. Daniel married Polly Ann Flener Jan. 24, 1837. They had ten children. Columbus Barter Smith was the eldest known and in 1870 he married Arrinder Flener, the daughter of Andrew Jackson and Ester Romans Flener. Columbus and Arrinda had 12 children. Arrinda Ivy Smith was born Jan. 28, 1880.

Wallace Melba was born Aug. 27, 1911 in Posey County to Manford and Ethel Allyn Trafford. She married first, James Leonard Carter and had one daughter, Wanda Lee.

Oral and Melba Flener

Melba's paternal great, great, great grandparents were Edward or Edmund Trafford born in Maryland. He married Nancy Applegate in 1810. They had six children. John, the eldest, was born May 1, 1811 in Kentucky. He married Mary Phillips Sept. 28, 1834. They had six children. Elisha, the eldest son, was born Jan. 6, 1837 in Posey County and on Dec. 4, 1856, he married Mary Ann Erwin. She was the daughter of Jeff and Harriet Albright Erwin. They had three children, Marshall, Thomas, and Nora. Marshall was born in 1862 and married Arvilla Webb Nov. 5, 1882. Her parents were Jay and Sarah York Webb. Marshall and Arvilla had four sons, Enzla, Elisha, Manford, and Floyd. Manford married Ethel Allyn.

Melba's maternal great, great grandparents were Peleg and Mary Allyn. The second son, Francis, was born Sept. 15, 1803 in Cayuga, NY. He married Sarah Jane Jackson Oct. 17, 1824. Sarah was born in England and was the daughter of Henry and Jane Jackson. Francis and Sarah had seven children. The eldest son, Joseph, was born Mar. 3, 1836. On January 5, 1865 he married Rachel Ann Alldredge, the daughter of Anderson and Sarah Conover Alldredge. One of their daughters, Ethel, married Manford Trafford.

FLOYD FAMILY OF WALES

In the mountain region of Wales, a noble family of Floyd owned estates during medieval times. The estates were at the bottom of Dartmoor, which is one of the most beautiful parts of the English countryside.

John Floyd, born 1570, fought with the forces of Queen Elizabeth in the destruction of the Spanish Armada. He was knighted by the Queen, and married a lady of her court. He equipped his sons, Nathanial and Walter for their adventures in the new world. They landed in Jamestown in their own vessel, the "Bona Nova" in 1608. They traded with the mother country for years.

One descendant was Wlliam, signer of the Declaration of Independence.

Colonel John James Floyd, born 1751, friend of George Rodgers Clark and Daniel Boone helped to rescue Boone's daughter from the Indians. In 1780, he helped lay out and establish the town of Louisville. Shot by Indians, he died on Apr. 13, 1783. He was a descendant of Nicketti, daughter of Cleopatra, sister to Pocahuntas. High cheekbones, dark eyes and dark skin occurred in various members of the family for generations.

Henry Floyd Sr., my direct ancestor, came to Union County in 1805. His wife Nancy Ann Helm was the first white woman buried in Union County.

Henry, his sons Henry Helm and John Helm served in the Revolutionary War. He received 2,156 acres of land for serving with George Rodgers Clark as a Lieutenant. They are listed in the DAR index.

Ray E. Floyd Sr. and wife Virginia Floyd and son William Tony Floyd

Another son, Nathaniel Helm served in the War of 1812. His will of 1824, left a share of his estate to Leonard, son of Peter.

Nathaniel's son, Peter Wortham Floyd, married Emily Poole, Oct. 3, 1817. Their son, Leonard Hardin, born Aug. 2, 1819, come to Posey County in 1837. He and his mother are buried on the Floyd Homestead, owned by a McGinnes in 1989. Leonard owned much land, including where G.E. is located. His wives Indiana Daniels, and Mary Ann Daniels, sisters, are buried by the G.A.F. plant. He later married Matilda Moore.

William Lawrence Floyd, Leonard's son was Ray Floyd's grandfather. His son Leonard Hardin Floyd 4th had five children: William, Ray Edwin, George, Richard and Evelyn.

Ray Edwin Floyd Sr. born Oct. 2, 1910, married Virginia, born May 19, 1917, daughter of Fred and Frances Hess Baldwin. They married Nov. 18, 1933. Ray and "Virgie" had: Ray Jr., William, Helen Muth Quick, Tommy, and Carol S. Broomfield Rose.

William, his sons, William Wayne and Tony Edward, were living on Elm Street in 1989. Joseph Daniel lived in the country with Joseph Zachery and Katie Dawn. William Wayne's son William Ray lived on Jefferson Drive. William's daughter, Sheree, lived in Florida.

Tommy had two sons, Brian and Gordon.

Ray Jr. lived at Dyer, IN. He had no children.

Ray Edwin Floyd Sr. was a farmer, fisherman and hunter. He had lived on Mackey Ferry Road by the Wabash River until 1968. He drowned in the Wabash on Dec. 7, 1968, while checking his fish nets and beaver traps. He was never found.

EMERSON-FREEMAN

Elizabeth Mae Freeman was born in Gibson Co., IN on Nov. 22, 1888. Her father, Charles Freeman was born in England in 1857. He moved to Gibson County during his teen years. He married Emma Eliza Lumm. She was born in Bone Gap, IL in 1860. Charles was a farmer most of his life and died in 1936. Emma died in 1945.

Mae's husband was George Henry Robertson. He was born in Franklin Co., IL on May 15, 1890. Mae and Henry were married in Albion, IL on Apr. 7, 1910. Henry completed three years of school and Mae continued until the eighth grade. After attending Oakland City College and receiving a teaching certificate, she taught school for one year. They lived on a Gibson County farm, rearing three children; Herbert, Eva and Donald. In 1930 they moved to a Posey County farm where they lived until Henry's death on Oct. 4, 1963. Mae moved to Owensboro, KY soon after Henry's death. There she lived with her daughter, Eva, until 1980. Mae is now 100 years old and has lived in an Owensboro nursing home for almost nine years.

Herbert Robertson was born on Apr. 4, 1911 and died Jan. 23, 1984. He and his wife, Margaret, had three children. Two of them now reside in Vanderburgh Co., IN and the other one in Illinois.

Eva was born Friday, May 13, 1913. She and Clifford Emerson were married Sept. 2, 1935. Clifford was born Feb. 2, 1911 in Posey Co., IN. He graduated from Poseyville High School in 1929. Eva graduated from Cynthiana High School in 1931. Cifford managed A&P grocery stores in Indiana, Tennessee and Kentucky. He retired at age 60 because of a stroke and died Feb. 12, 1985. Eva died Dec. 31, 1988 in Owensboro KY. They had five children; Verna, David, Charles, Alan and Alice. Three of them live in Daviess Co., KY; one in Warren Co., KY; and one in Marietta, GA.

Donald, the youngest child of Mae and Henry Robertson, was born on Oct. 5, 1922. He and his wife, Marie, have four children. Donald and Marie now reside in Hot Springs, AR.

Clifford Emerson's father, Arthur Garfield Emerson, was born June 4, 1884. He was a farm hand most of his life, but for a while he was a railroader. He married Alberta Smith around 1910. Arthur died in 1964; Alberta died in 1918 during the Great Flu Epidemic.

DEMPSEY M. "BUD" FUNKHOUSER FAMILY

Dempsey "Bud" Funkhouser was born on Mar. 13, 1940, in Ziegler, IL. He graduated from Ziegler-Royalton High School and went to work in sales for the clothing retailer John Green Co. which had opened a store in Mt. Vernon, IL.

The company which was eventually purchased by P.N. Hirsch Co. opened a store in Posey County. Bud was given the task of opening and managing the local outlet and the Funkhouser family moved to Mt. Vernon, IN in the Spring of 1961. Bud is now self-employed in a retail business selling hardware and related lines. The store is known as Bud's True Value Hardware and is located at 413 Main Street here in Mt. Vernon. Bud is also a member of the Posey County Council.

Bud's parents are Velma (Lacey) Funkhouser and the late Dempsey Funkhouser. Velma's parents were Lee Lacey and Fanny May Aliff, both from Grand Chain, IL. Mrs. Funkhouser resides in Ziegler, IL.

Dempsey's (Bud's father's) parents were Carl and Edith (Brown) Funkhouser from Carrier Mills, IL. Bud also has a sister, Edith (Funkhouser) Lewis, who lives in Hopkinsville, KY.

The Funkhouser name is of German origin and although many Americans of the same name reside in the United States, most of the immediate relatives of this Funkhouser family settled in south-central Indiana and southern Illinois.

Grandsons of Bud and Carolyn. Left to right: Michael, Shane, and Nickolas

Bud's wife, Carolyn, is also a graduate of Ziegler-Royalton High School. Carolyn started the Fitness Factory exercise business which is currently doing business as The Cellar Gym located in the lower level of Bud's Hardware. The Funkhouser's are co-owners of that enterprise. Carolyn is currently employed as a real estate agent with Citizens' Realty in Evansville.

Carolyn is the daughter of Lela "Susie" (Carpenter) Miller and the late Melvin "Peck" Carpenter both from Christopher, IL. Mrs. Miller's maiden name was Doolin and she resides in Ziegler, IL.

Bud and Carolyn reside at 504 E. Fifth Street in Mt. Vernon. They have three children all of which graduated from Mt. Vernon Senior High School. Scott is attending Western Kentucky University in Bowling Green, KY and is a member of the swim team.

Teresa "Teri" (Funkhouser) Duckworth is the mother of Bud and Carolyn's middle grandson, Shane. They reside at 505 E. Grant Street in Mt. Vernon. Teri graduated as an L.P.N. from Deaconess School of Nursing in 1980 and is currently employed with Orthopedic Associates in Evansville.

Mark graduated from Indiana Vocational Technical College in 1980 and is currently enrolled at the University of Southern Indiana in Business Administration. Mark is employed for his father at Bud's Hardware.

Mark's wife, Kimberly (Batteiger) Funkhouser is the daughter of Gene Batteiger and Paula Etheridge. Kim graduated from Mt. Vernon Senior High School and is currently employed for her mother who is the Posey County Clerk.

Kim's grandparents are also part of Posey County's heritage. The late Carl and Ellen Batteiger lived on Ford Road in Marrs Township. Kim's mothers' parents are Martha Jean (Moye) Breeze and the late Marvin D. Breeze. Mrs. Breeze still resides in Mt. Vernon.

Mark and Kim, who are the parents of two other grandchildren of Bud and Carolyn's, reside with Nickolas and Michael at 703 Walnut Street in Mt. Vernon.

FAMILY OF JOHN GARNER AND ESTHER MEADOWS

The GARNER name was established as early as 1807 in Knox Co., IN, part of which later became Posey County. The family of John GARNER and Esther Meadows (married Dec. 20, 1811), was among settlers who traveled on a wagon train around 1837 from coastal Carteret Co., NC to Posey Co., IN. Others in the North Carolina Group were the families of Edward H. Bell, Jacob Benthall, brothers Joseph and Thomas Cully, James Breece, Thomas Quinn, and William Russell.

Early Carteret Co., NC records show a deed recorded on Dec. 20, 1824 for land sold by John and Esther Garner to Malachi Rigdon. As was the practice of the day, the court ordered private examination of Esther (by Moses Watson and Edward H. Bell) to ensure that she was not being coerced to sign away her dower rights against her will. Other Cateret County records list the appointment in 1826 of John GARNER as overseer of two roads in their Newport, NC community. Property owners and community leaders often shared the tasks for road maintenance before state and federal agencies assumed the responsibility.

GARNER families in North Carolina are aware of their Posey Co., IN connections through a set of letters written by Esther Garner to her sister, Sarah, back home in North Carolina. Sarah Meadows married Samuel Garner, John's brother, in 1811, remained in Carteret County, and are the progenitors of many North Carolina Garners. The letters have been passed down through five generations of Garners and are the subject of a book published recently by a Garner family member.

Esther's letters provided information to their "relations in Newport" from 1838 to 1845 about family events, church activities, local prices, and the life and death of relatives and friends in Indiana. Among Posey County events of interest are references to the Bethel Primitive Baptist Church near Mt. Vernon and the traveling "very able preacher of the Gospel" who provided "preaching almost every Sabbath" somewhere in the area.

John and Esther's children were all born in Carteret Co., NC. They are listed below with their offspring. All except Sidney raised their families in Posey Co., IN.

(1) Sidney Garner (a daughter 1815-1838), married Amos Bell in Carteret County in 1836 (Sidney died after only 18 months of marriage);

(2) Jabez Garner (a son b. 1820), married Mahala Mitchell (b. 1831) of Georgia in Posey County on Aug. 6, 1850;

(3) Casandra Garner (a daughter b. 1825) married John Hill, a Posey County school teacher from Pennsylvania, on Aug. 6, 1850 and had a son Homer S. Hill (b. 1846);

(4) Nancy Garner (a daughter b. 1829) married Jonathan Combs on Apr. 6, 1846 and had a son George Combs, b. 1848. Esther's husband, John is believed to have died between 1848 and 1850, as the 1850 census lists Esther as head of household.

Any Indiana researchers who discover these lines in their research are asked to contact the contributor of this article through the Posey County Historical Society.

(Sources are deeds, wills, censuses in NC Archives, and personal letters in the Garner family).

1838 Letter from Esther Garner in Posey County, Ind. to Sara Garner in Newport, NC

RICHARD E. AND KATHERINE (FISHER) GARRETT

Richard E. Garrett and Katherine A. Fisher were married July 5, 1974 in New Harmony, IN where they currently reside. Richard has three children from a previous marriage. They are Cheryl Garrett Deig born Oct. 3, 1963, Jeremy S. Garrett born Sept. 23, 1970 and Angela Garrett Wiltshire born May 14, 1965. Kathy has one child from a previous marriage. Her first husband, Allen R. Blaylock, died Apr. 10, 1972. Their son Jared Allen Blaylock was born Sept. 15, 1968 at St. Mary's Hospital in Evansville, IN. Richard and Kathy have one son, Lee Richard Garrett, born Oct. 19, 1983 at Deaconess Hospital in Evansville, IN.

Kathy was born Oct. 6, 1947 to Melvin O. and Evelyn Kramer Fisher. She graduated from New Harmony High School in 1965. Currently she is employed with Posey County National Bank, New Harmony, IN as Branch Manager. She has worked for the bank since 1972.

Richard was born Mar. 30, 1943 to James Marion Garrett and Edith Hanes Garrett. He currently is employed with PPG in Evansville, IN. He joined PPG in 1980 in the Maintenance Department.

Kathy's father, Melvin O. Fisher, was born June 14, 1912 on The Rebeyre Island. He managed the farming operations on the Rebeyre Island till his death on Sept. 16, 1975. As a young boy Melvin attended school on the cut-off Island in a one room school house. When not attending school he was kept busy helping with the family farming.

Kathy's mother, Evelyn A. Kramer Fisher was born Aug. 13, 1915 in Evansville, IN. She grew up in Evansville and graduated from Bosse High School at the age of 16. She came to New Harmony and took post graduate courses at the local high school before attending the University of Evansville. She passed away Nov. 2, 1979. Just a few months later Kathy's only brother, Stephen E. Fisher died. Steve was born Feb. 28, 1944 and died July 18, 1980. He graduated from New Harmony High School and Indiana State College at Terre

Haute. Steve left behind three children. They are Jarred, Barbara and Jason Fisher.

Kathy's maternal grandparents are Edward P. Kramer (b. May 12, 1882 in Evansville, IN d. Mar. 15, 1933 in New Harmony, IN) and Mayme Kemmerling Kramer (b. Jan. 12, 1884 New Harmony, IN d, Dec. 23, 1972 Framingham, MA). Mayme's father Jacob Kemmerling was born June 13, 1858, in Harmony Township. Jacob was the son of Charles and Elizabeth Kemmerling who came from Germany in 1852.

Kathy's paternal grandparents are Hugar (Buck) Fisher (b. July 2, 1888 Huntingburg, IN d. July 12, 1947 New Harmony, IN) and Nellie Stewart Fisher (b. Sept. 21, 1889 d. June 27, 1971 New Harmony, IN) Hugar and Nellie had seven children. They are Ralph Fisher, Melvin Fisher, Bill Fisher, Erna Mae Culiver, Jim Fisher, Wilbur Fisher and Betty Jo Hobbs. Kathy's great grandfather was James Louis Fisher (b. June 17, 1857 Dubois Co., IN d. Jan. 6, 1939 Posey County).

JAMES MARION AND EDITH HANES GARRETT

James Marion Garrett and Edith Hanes were married Aug. 17, 1929 at Carmi, White Co., IL. Their children are: Eva Lou, born Aug. 4, 1930, Harmony Township, attended Smith and Springfield Schools and New Harmony High School and received a G.E.D. certificate from White Co., IL; married Leo Gene Allen of White Co., IL. Their children are: David Marion and Gay Yvonne.

Alan Ray, born Nov. 2, 1931, Harmony Township, attended Springfield School, died Mar. 17, 1946, Vanderburgh County.

Connie Joyce, born May 2, 1934, Harmony Township, attended Springfield School and graduated 1952 from New Harmony High School; married George Dale Osborne. Their children are: Alan Dale, Ronald Keith, George Kevin, Jackie Lee, Ricky Elwood, Lisa Rene, Darla Kay, Joni Sue, Steven Eric. All nine children graduated from Mt. Vernon High School. Connie died Jan. 17, 1987, Vanderburgh County, and is buried at Pelham Cemetery.

Front row: James Marion Garrett, Edith Hanes Garrett; back row: Eva Lou Garrett Allen, Marilyn Garrett Rhodes, Richard Elwood Garrett, Connie Garrett Osborne.

Marilyn Ruth, born Sept. 25, 1937, Lynn Township, attended Springfield School and New Harmony High School; married Geraldee Biggs. Their children are: Gerald Lee, Mark Allen, James Lloyd and Harold Dee, who died at birth. Later, Marilyn was married to G.P. Rhodes and lives in Arkansas.

Richard Elwood, born Mar. 30, 1943, Vanderburgh County, attended Springfield School and graduated 1961 from Mt. Vernon High School, and served four years in the Air Force; married Wanda Kueber. Their children are: Cheryle Lynn, Angela Rae, Jeremy Scott. Later, Richard married Katherine Fisher Blaylock. Their children are: Jared Allen Blaylock and Lee Richard Garrett.

Marion was born June 10, 1907, Gibson County, to David and Flora Simpson Dedman Garrett. His brothers were Thomas Ellis, David "Bud" Elvis, and his twin brother, William Aaron; sisters, Clara Dedman Garrett and Eliza Dedman Axton. He attended Wiley School in Harmony Township, Bowman's Bend School in White Co., IL and graduated from the eighth grade at New Harmony. Marion and Edith moved to Lynn Township in 1936, where he farmed, raised livestock, did custom hay baling and logged in the winter months. They sold their farming interests in 1967 and moved into New Harmony. Marion went to work for the Posey County Highway Department, where his twin brother, Aaron, worked. After Aaron's death in 1969, he left the garage and did carpenter work and saw filing from his home shop. He died at his home on Mar. 16, 1987, the birthday of his granddaughter, Gay Allen Barbre. He had provided a good living for his family and had enjoyed nearly 80 years of a good life. He is buried at Maple Hill Cemetery beside his son, grandson and brother.

Marion's maternal lineage includes James and Elvira Davis Simpson, and John and Parthena Waters Simpson, early pioneers of Gibson County. His paternal line: Thomas and Elizabeth Johnson Garrett, Amos and Martha Neal Garrett and Presley and Elizabeth Baxter Garrett, also, early settlers of Gibson Co., IN.

Edith Hanes Garrett, born Feb. 11, 1910. Harmony Township, daughter of Nealy William and Stella Herring Hanes, lives in New Harmony. *Submitted by Marilyn Garrett Rhodes*

GILBERT-McFADIN

Ruth Anna McFadin was born July 2, 1917 in St. Louis, MO, the second child of George E. and Pauline (Gaiser) McFadin. In the spring of 1918 Ruth and her family returned to Posey County to live near the community of Upton.

Ruth attended Upton School and graduated from Mt. Vernon Senior High in 1935. She received her degree from Lockyear Secretarial School in 1936. She was a secretary for several companies in Evansville, IN.

Ruth and Gil Gilbert

On Oct. 27, 1945 Ruth married Hillard Gilbert in Morganfield, KY. Hillard or "Gil", as his friends knew him, was born Oct. 26, 1909, in Melber, KY. He was the son of David and Mada (Springer) Gilbert.

Gil was a navy veteran of WWII, a shipfitter, 2nd class (CB) USNR. He played the trombone in the CB band. After his tour of duty in the service, he worked as a sheet-metal welder until retiring in 1962 due to heart trouble. Upon retirement they took up residence on Upton Road, Mt. Vernon, IN in their house built by Ruth's brother-in-law, Fred Benthall.

Gil passed away on July 29, 1986 at his home and is buried at the Welborn Cemetery. The Gilberts were members of Trinity United Church of Christ. Gil was a member of the Evansville VFW #1114 and Ruth is a member of that auxiliary. Ruth was also a member of the Eagles auxiliary.

WILLIAM GONNERMAN

William Gonnerman, the son of Adam and Martha Ripple Gonnerman, born Jan. 5, 1856, in Solz, Province of Hessen-Nassau, Germany.

He came to America, alone, in 1873 at the age of 17. He located in Evansville, IN, and worked in a machine shop until 1884 when he came to Mt. Vernon. He had married Lena Alexander of Evansville, formerly of Germany, in 1876. They had three children.

He organized and launched the Keck-Gonnerman Company, with John Keck and Henry Kuebler in 1884. The foundry, as the machine shop was known, increased in size and was known as the largest foundry of its kind in the Mid-West. Makers of threshing outfits and steam engines. At the death of John Keck, in 1938, Mr. Gonnerman became President and held that office for many years.

He organized the Industrial Brick Company. He assisted in organizing People's Bank & Trust Company, and was Vice President. For years he was the head of Mt. Vernon electric utility.

Elected to the State (Indiana) Senate, in 1907 and served until 1909. He refused to be a candidate for renomination owing to business affairs.

Two other children had been born in 1884 and 1888. His wife died Apr. 5, 1891, age 35 years.

At the age of 68 he organized the Gonnerman Auto Company.

The foundry was his love and source of pleasure. He possessed a rare ability for machinery work and the foresight to plan ahead.

A devout member of Trinity Evangelical and Reformed Church, known now as Trinity United Church of Christ.

His home was always opened to friends and business associates. He was devoted to his family, all of whom lived in Mt. Vernon. His life was rich in service and achievement.

Mr. Gonnerman's death came Nov. 26, 1948, age 92. His five children have passed away and two grandchildren, leaving just two granddaughters as his descendants.

GOSS

William C. Goss was born Apr. 3, 1809 in New York. His wife, Permelia, was born Dec. 18, 1815 in Ohio. They came to settle in Point Township, Posey Co., IN in the 1840s. William was a farmer. He was a member of the Masonic Lodge. He died Feb. 11, 1861. Permelia died Mar. 25, 1877. Both buried in a country cemetery near their homeplace. William and Permelia had six children: James - born in 1839; Sarah - born in 1842; Mary - born in 1844; Martha - born in 1845; Robert B. - born in 1848; Henry D. - born in 1850. Robert B. Goss fifth child of William and Permelia, was a farmer and landowner in Point Township. He was Trustee of this township in 1880. He was noted for his skill in carpenter work. He built a home on his property which was located near a well known landmark in Point Township, Half-Moon Pond. He died Nov. 8, 1909 and was buried beside his parents.

William C. Goss

Henry D. Goss, sixth child of William and Permelia, was a farmer and landowner in Point and Black Township. Part of his farm bordered the Wabash River. He married Sarah Abigal Conlin, also of Point Township, on Sept. 30, 1880. She was born on Dec. 27, 1854. Her parents were Thomas and Mary Ann (Rowe) Conlin. They had three children: Cora Ann - born May 2, 1883; Frederick Conlin - born Apr. 4, 1885; and Thomas Robert - born Mar. 11, 1890. Henry D. Goss died Dec. 19, 1934. His wife, Sarah died Aug. 16, 1896. Both buried in Black Cemetery in Posey Co., IN. Cora Ann Goss, first child of Henry D. and Sarah (Conlin) Goss, married John Edward Schmidt. He was a farmer. They lived in Point Township in a home built by the Goss family on the original family farm. Cora and John had five children: Henry Edward, Robert Goss, Sarah Abigal, Pauline, and James William. Cora died Nov. 29, 1942.

Henry Edward Schmidt was born Nov. 2, 1908. Died Mar. 20, 1974. Married Mary Beste. Parents of four children: Lois Elaine, Kenneth Wayne, Everett Henry, and Mary Lucille.

Robert Goss Schmidt was born Mar. 10, 1913. Died Aug. 10, 1985. Married Regina Jarman. Parents of five children: Marjorie Ann, Carolyn Sue, Wanda Lou, Barbara Nell, and Robert Kent.

Sarah Abigal Schmidt was born Jan. 16, 1915. Married Herdis Bauer. Parents of two children: William Edward and Herdis Wayne.

Pauline Schmidt was born Feb. 7, 1917. Died Apr. 11, 1986. Married Elmer Schelhorn. Parents of three children: John Robert, Alan Lee, Jerry Elmer.

James William Schmidt was born Feb. 7, 1926. Married Juanita Goff. Parents of six children: Susan Diane, James Irvin, Patricia June, Rebecca Lynn, Timothy Leo and Debra Kay.

Frederick Conlin Goss, second child of Henry D. and Sarah (Conlin) Goss, married Elfrieda Schneider. No children. Frederick died in 1956.

Thomas Robert Goss, third child of Henry D. and Sarah (Conlin) Goss, married Anna Meir. Parents of two children: Charollotte Marie and Charles Robert.

Charlotte Marie Goss was born June 12, 1913. Died Sept. 30, 1964. Married Lovell Lanman. Parents of three children: Lois Ann, Joyce Marie, and Barbara Alice. *Submitted by Wanda Tichenor*

HORACE F. GREATHOUSE

Horace F. Greathouse and Emma Elizabeth (Betty) Greathouse reside on a farm in Lynn Township, Posey county, which was purchased in 1872 by Francis Marion Greathouse, after he returned from the Civil War. The Greathouses have cultivated this homestead for the past 117 years.

Horace F. Greathouse is the only son of Horace E. Greathouse, a German descendant, and Elizabeth Pritchard Greathouse, an English descendant. Horace E. was a 32nd Degree Mason, and Elizabeth was a 50 year member of the Order of the Eastern Star.

Horace F. Greathouse's sister, Emily, deceased, was wed to Carlton Carnahan. Mr. Greathouse has one half-sister, Margaret, who wed Daniel James.

On the 17th of December, 1948, Horace wed Emma Elizabeth (Betty) Mentzer, one of three daughters of Harry Mentzer and Gladys Smith Mentzer.

To Horace F. and Betty Greathouse were born four children, Roger Alan Greathouse, Christopher F. Greathouse, Julie Ann Greathouse, and Mark Andrew Greathouse. Their sons are loggers in the southwestern Indiana area, and Julie, a 1984 graduate of Indiana University of Bloomington, presently resides in Austin, TX. Horace and Betty have two grandchildren, Roger Alan Greathouse, Jr. and Brandi, the daughter of Christopher.

Mr. Greathouse was an active participant in implementing the consolidation of the township schools into the Mt. Vernon Metropolitan School District. He also was seated on the Corporation in 1958 to build Mt. Vernon Senior High School.

Additionally, he served many years as the Republican Precinct Committeeman of Lynn Township West. He and Betty are active members of the Harvestime Temple Church in Mt. Vernon. Mr. Greathouse is employed at General Electric.

JOHN AND PERMELIA GREATHOUSE

Permelia ("Millie") Milligan (c. 1802-1899) was half Indian and was adopted by the Milligan family in central Kentucky after she was found as an orphan at about age two. In 1816 she married John Greathouse (1792-1830), son of William R. and Rebecca Greathouse. John and Millie plus John's brother David and his wife, Sarah Kallender, came down the Ohio River on a flatboat about 1816. David and Sarah Greathouse settled about six miles south of McFaddin's Bluff in Posey County while John and Millie settled in Union Co., KY, at the mouth of Highland Creek (right across the river from David). John operated a mill and farmed corn and tobacco. John and Millie had one child, John Tecumseh Greathouse (c. 1819-c. 1880). John died from a fever in August, 1830. About 1835 Millie and her son sold the holdings in Kentucky and moved across to Posey County to be closer to family.

James Madison Greathouse ("Jim Matt")

In 1843 John T. married Louisa Jane Browning Greathouse (1820-1863), widow of John T.'s first cousin John Adams Greathouse, and became stepfather to Benjamin Franklin Greathouse. John T. and Louisa had four children: Aaron, James Madison, Sarah Ann, and William R.

David Greathouse was killed by river pirates on Jan. 23, 1827, on a trip to take produce to New Orleans. His widow Sarah married the hired man, Henry Stripe, in 1828. Following Sarah's death in 1853, Henry Stripe and Millie Milligan Greathouse were married in 1854. Henry died in 1877 and Millie in 1899. Sarah, Henry, and Millie are buried in the Greathouse Family Cemetery. John T. and Louisa Greathouse are buried in unmarked graves in the Greathouse Community Cemetery, located behind Greathouse School.

Aaron Greathouse (born 1845) served in Company K, Tenth Indiana Cavalry, during the Civil War and later married Fannie Mitchell

James Madison Greathouse (1847-1936) married Veronica Combs (1852-1921) on Mar. 29, 1871. James did not like the name Veronica, so he changed her name to Victoria. James farmed in Point Township and served as the township's trustee from 1909 to 1915. He and Victoria had six children: David A., Ida Belle, Eva, Flora May, James Clifford, and Bessie. (David, Ida, and James died in infancy.) Eva (1876-1949) married Edwin V. Spencer; Flora (1880-1935) married Edward Morlock; and Bessie (1888-1936) married Lee O. Bunner. James and Victoria Greathouse and Edward and Flora Morlock are buried in Bellefontaine Cemetery.

Sarah Ann Greathouse (born 1851) married James M. Dowell and had three children: Bertie, Alvin and Hattie.

William R. Greathouse (born 1853) married Rebecca Greathouse; their only child, Benjamin, died in infancy. *Submitted by Mrs. Vivian Morlock Taylor*

DAVID RAE AND KATHLEEN JANET (CURTIS) GREEN

David Rae and Kathleen Janet Curtis Green reside in Black Township in Posey County.

David was born in Posey County Sept. 2, 1933. He is the eldest son of Robert Edwin and Dorothy Layer Green. He attended grade school at Central Grade School, now named Hedges Central, and graduated from Mt. Vernon High School in 1951. He graduated from Indiana University in 1955 with an A.B. degree in Government.

From 1956 to 1958, he was a Lieutenant in the Air Force where he trained as a pilot, navigator and bombardier. He attended Indiana University School of Law from 1958 to 1959. From 1959 to 1960, he worked for State Farm Insurance as an Insurance Adjuster in Lafayette, IN. In 1960, when General Electric constructed a new plant in Mt. Vernon, he was one of the first 12 people hired. He worked at General Electric until 1984.

Kathleen J. (Curtis) Green and David Rae Green

In 1984, he joined his brother, Richard, at Mt. Vernon Auto Parts, a business that his father had begun in 1946. He also has a sister, Jana Lee White, who resides in Utica, KY.

David's paternal grandparents were Guy Barter and Jane Amelia Colton Green. His maternal grandparents were Henry Harrison and Magdalena (Lena) Christina Miller Layer.

Kathleen (Kathy) was born in Black Township in Posey County Feb. 23, 1936. She is the daughter of Wilford Russell and Katherine Schieber Curtis. She attended grade school at Jeffries School, a two room country school house with outdoor toilets. She graduated from Mt. Vernon High School in 1954. She worked in the office at the Mt. Vernon Oil Refinery and the Farm Bureau Oil Co. for two years.

In 1956, she resigned her job at the Refinery and moved with her husband to McAllen, TX where he was stationed with the U.S. Air Force. She is the youngest of six children, which include Charles, Elnora Martinelli, Geraldine McFadin, Eugene (deceased) and Barbara Nell. David and Kathy are the fourth generation descendents living in Posey County. They are of German and English heritage.

They are the parents of two daughters, Stephanie Rae, born on Jan. 25, 1957 in Enid, OK and Allison Lee, born on Apr. 28, 1966 in Deaconess Hospital in Evansville, IN.

Stephanie is married to David Murphy Fuelling. They were married July 2, 1976. Allison is married to Shawn Dee Nix and they were married Apr. 23, 1988.

Stephanie is Director of Printing at the University of Southern Indiana. She graduated from the University of Southern Indiana in 1978 with a degree in Art. Her husband is employed at the Farm Bureau Oil Company as an Oil Gauger. Allison attended Indiana University for two years and also Roger's Academy of Hair Design. She is a hairdresser at Lazarus's Department Store in Evansville, IN. Her husband is employed as Grocery Manager at Schnuck's Grocery store in Evansville.

David and Kathy are members of Black's United Methodist Church. David is interested in church activities, reading World War II books, deer hunting, yard and fruit tree tending and travel. Kathy is interested in church activities, Domestic Doers Extension Homemaker's Club, antiques, cooking for her family and travel. They have traveled to Germany, England, Wales, Ireland, also, Iceland, Denmark, Norway and Sweden. In 1989, they traveled to Figi, New Zealand and Australia.

In 1966, they built a home on 23 wooded acres purchased from Charles Black, which had been owned in the 1800's by Harrison's, who were Kathy's ancestors.

After a five year courtship, David and Kathy were married Apr. 9, 1955 in Trinity Church with Rev. August Binder officiating.

ROBERT EDWIN AND DOROTHY LAYER GREEN

Robert Edwin and Dorothy Layer Green are residents of Mt. Vernon. They married Dec. 6, 1931. Their children are David born Sept. 2, 1934, Jana Lee born Jan. 19, 1936, and Richard born Feb. 8, 1943.

Robert was born in Mt. Vernon Oct. 22, 1910, the youngest son of Gery B. Green and Amelia Jane Colton Green. Robert attended and graduated 1926-929 from Mt. Vernon High School. Operated a suit store on Main Street five years, moved and built a neighborhood grocery on Locust Street until World War II. He worked in Defense at Evansville Ship Yard until end of war, where he built and operated Mt. Vernon Auto parts for 37 years at Kimballand Fourth Street. Upon retiring his sons David and Richard continue to operate and own the business.

Dorothy born Dec. 11, 1912 to Henry H. Layer and Lena C. Miller Layer of Marrs Township, Posey County. Attended Renschler School for eight years, then attended Mt. Vernon High School 1927-1930. After marriage resided at 812 Locust Street in Mt. Vernon.

Her father was born May 29, 1879, death Feb. 23, 1942 and farmed the same farm he was born on. Her mother was born Aug. 22, 1893 died July 13, 1985.

David born Sept. 2, 1934 graduated from Mt. Vernon High School 1951, and Indiana University, Bloomington, IN, 1955. Served four years in Air Force, three years an adjuster for State Farm Mutual Insurance, Lafayette, IN moved to Mt. Vernon and worked at General Electric. After fathers retirement now connected with Mt. Vernon Auto Parts.

Married Apr. 9, 1955 to Kathleen Curtis, Feb. 23, 1936 daughter of Wilford and Katherine Schieber Curtis of Black Township. Their children are Stephanie born Jan. 19, 1957, married to David Fuelling and Allison married to Shawn Nix.

Jana Lee born Jan. 19, 1936 graduated from Mt. Vernon High School 1954, and Indiana University, Bloomington, IN, 1958. Worked for Western Kentucky Gas at Owensboro, KY 1958-1961. Has worked at Owensboro Davis County Hospital as a director of Dietary Service 1961 to present. Married William L. White Apr. 3, 1960 of Owensboro. Their children are Robert E. born Mar. 1, 1967, and Susan C. born Mar. 29, 1971.

Richard H. born Feb. 8, 1943 graduated from Mt. Vernon High School 1961, and Indiana University, Bloomington, IN 1966. Married Jacqueline Peck daughter of John T. Peck and Leola Miller Peck. Worked in Civil Service at Warren, MI, Texarkanan, TX, and Lexington, KY four years. Located in Mt. Vernon and worked at General Electric Company five years. Now connected with Mt. Vernon Auto Parts since 1975. Their children are Guy H. born Dec. 31, 1971, Gordon C. born July 29, 1974, and Gretchen M. Jan. 17, 1978

SIMON C. AND WANDA LEE (CARTER) GRIESS

Simon C. and Wanda Lee Carter Griess were born and raised in Mt. Vernon. Simon attended St. Matthews Catholic School and graduated from Mt. Vernon High School in 1946. After graduation he worked for his father in the family grocery on West Second Street. In 1952 he accepted a position at the Mt. Vernon Post Office. He retired as Postmaster in 1983. He was a past president of the St. Matthews Parish Council and the Greater Mt. Vernon Assn. He was a member of St. Matthew Cemetery Assn., Elks, Mt. Vernon Conservation Club and a director of the Black Township Water Corp.

Simon's great grandparents, John and Elizabeth Griess were born in Bavaria. Their son, Adam, was born in Bavaria in 1832. In 1855 Adam married Catherina Mann. Her parents were Christopher and Margaret Mann. Catherina was one of four children. Adam and Catherina Griess had 15 children. The eldest, Karl Phillip, was born Feb. 20, 1855 at Parker Settlement in Posey County. On Nov. 4, 1883, Karl married Elizabeth Baumgartner. Her parents were Jacob and Anna Doen Baumgartner. Elizabeth was born in Hesse Darmstadt, Ger. Oct.

Wanda and Simon Griess

29, 1861. Karl and Elizabeth had seven children. One of these was John Christian was born Apr. 8, 1889. He married Anna Margaret Maurer. She was one of eight children of Simon Francis and Isabell Betz Maurer. John and Margaret had three children, John Christian, Jr. born July 13, 1922, Simon C. born Oct. 23, 1928 and Anna Margaret born July 14, 1930 and died Dec. 21, 1930. John C. Jr., married Margaret E. Slusser in 1947 and they have seven children. Simon C. married Wanda Lee Carter in 1954 and they have no children.

Wanda Lee was born Jan. 26, 1931 to James Leonard and Wallace Melba Trafford Carter. She attended the James W. Riley grade school and graduated from the Mt. Vernon High School in 1950. She started work at the People's Bank and Trust Company as a bookkeeper and left after serving as Auditor. She was a past president of the Mt. Vernon Business and Professional Women and the Posey County Historical Society She was a member of the Friends of the Library, Indiana Historical Society, the Tri-State Genealogical Society and the Society of Indiana Pioneers.

Wanda's paternal great grandparents were James Jasper and Nancy Hutchcraft Carter. They were married May 2, 1872 in White Co., IL. Their son, James Albert, married Velaria Shores Dec. 7, 1895 in Carmi, IL. They had two sons, Orman, born Aug. 27, 1901 and James Leonard born July 9, 1909. James Leonard married Melba Trafford Mar. 12, 1928. Melba was the daughter of Manford and Ethel Allyn Trafford.

Wanda's maternal great grandparents were Francis and Sarah Jane Jackson Allyn. Joseph was the eldest of their seven children. On Jan. 5, 1865 he married Rachel Alldredge. Rachel was the fourth child of Anderson and Sarah Conover Alldredge. Joseph and Rachel had 14 children of which Ethel was the 11th. She married Manford Trafford on Jan. 3, 1905 and had one girl, Wallace Melba.

SAMUEL GRIFFIN

Samuel Griffin was the first Postmaster for the town of Griffin, IN named for him after he and W.T. Price donated land in 1879 for the P.D.&E. Railroad. Soon a corporation interrupted wheat cutting to layout and build the P.D.&E. Railroad. The same field where the south half was first known as Prices' Station laid out by W.T. Price, Aug. 11, 1881.

Mr. Griffin was born Mar. 14, 1826, and died Aug. 23, 1914, at the age of 88 years and was buried in the Griffin Mt. Pleasant Cemetery. He was born in northern Indiana, the son of James and Nancy Hummel. When his father died in 1828, he and his mother moved to Gibson County. He received a common school education and was married to Manda Short in 1851 who died in 1854. In 1856 he was married to Rebecca Wilkin and she died in 1890. Then he married Eliza Mobley Fisher in

1890. To this union was born Goldie Mae Griffin who died in infancy, leaving three step-children, John W. Fisher, Jane Fisher Stallings and William Fisher.

The only survivors at this time are Mrs. Belva Stallings Cox, who is 98 years old and lives in Sarasota, FL, and Mrs. America Fisher Welch who is 87 years and still a resident in Griffin. Samuel Griffin very proudly gave her her name, then a very popular name. He was the only grandfather she ever knew and their deep love for each other left her many happy memories. She also has antiques that belonged to her grandparents.

Mr. Griffin was one of the oldest settlers in Posey County and became a very prominent farmer who soon owned 1,250 acres of very fine fertile land in Posey and Gibson Counties. He was a self-made man without any means. As a farmhand, he worked at $5.00 a month for William Wilkin in Gibson County in 1844. He was then 18 years old and worked by the month until 1857 when he bought 160 acres of land in Edwards Co., IL. When Mr. Griffin bought his first acres he traded a shot gun and a mule for land. He moved from six miles northwest of Albion, IL to Posey County where he bought 200 acres in Bethel Township. In 1870 he bought 160 acres more and in 1876 he bought 134 more, continuing on until he owned 1,250 acres. Mrs. America Welch is the present owner of 160 of those acres.

COUNTRY SINGER "RAY GUYCE"

Ray Guyce was born on a farm near Wadesville, IN. Guyce received his first music lesson from his mother at the age of seven. "That first lesson was on the mandolin," he says, "but when I was nine, I switched to fiddle and guitar. I handle all the lead guitar work in my unit, and I double over on the swing fiddle."

Guyce's group enjoyed the unique distinction of performing on the first live television show to originate from Evansville, in September, 1948, over WIKY. But his big break came in 1955 when he embarked on a 50,000 mile tour for McConkey Artists' Corporation of Chicago. He made personal appearances all over the East Coast, the Midwest, New England, and Canada, sharing billing with such country and western stars as Lola Dee, Billy Holmes and Phyllis Brown of WLW's Barn Dance in Cincinnati, OH, and the late Moon Mulligan of "Grand Ole Opry"

Guyce recently signed a lifetime writer's contract with Broadcast Music, Inc. (BMI) a famous music publishing house, which guarantees publication of any song he writes.

He has a daughter, Linda Brashears and a granddaughter Mellisa Brashears who both reside in Dayton, OH, along with his former wife Ruby (Little Jo) Markland who was also a 12 year member of The Lonesome Valley Boys. unit, pickin the big upright bass and vocal work with Ray on shows and recordings. During the 70s the unit toured another 6,000 miles west as a male-female country duet billed as "Ray & Bebe Guyce" the (Country Sweethearts) who were heard regular over WPCO radio in Mt. Vernon, IN and their current record features Bebe's own composition titled "Please Let Me B/W Nobody Cries" written by Pete Olsen of New York.

Ray's parents were Bertha (Rothlei) Geiss and Anton C. Geiss both of Wadesville, IN where they resided on their farm just out of Blairsville, IN until 1962 when ill health forced them to move to Bloomington where Ray was located at that time. They both died in Bloomington, Anton in 1963 and Bertha in 1969, and are buried in Evansville. Ray moved back to the homeplace in the fall of 1969.

His grandparents were Anna (Koch) and Danial Rothlei. Dan was an orphan in Pennsylvania and later grew up here in Posey County. He worked as a carpenter, and cleared the ground here and built the buildings. He is buried at Parker Settlement. He fought in both the Civil and the Spanish American Wars. His wife Anna came here from Germany on a sail ship. She is buried in Evansville.

On his father's side Ray's grandparents were Lena (Balsmeier) Geiss and John Geiss both of Posey County. John worked as a painter. They are both buried at the Engleheimer Cemetery near Blairsville.

Ray had one brother who died shortly after birth, Freeman Anthony Geiss. He is buried at St. Wendel, IN Cemetery.

PHILIP HAGEMANN

Although New York City is his principal residence, Philip Hagemann was born and raised in Mt. Vernon, has an interest in farmland in Black and Point Townships, makes frequent visits to Mt. Vernon and maintains an active role in the musical life of Posey County.

His great-grandfather was Frederick H. Hagemann, who was described in the "Illustrated Atlas of Posey County" published in 1900 as "one of the most prosperous farmers of Posey County." Frederick was the son of Henry and Mary Weidkaup Hagemann and was born in what was then Prussia (in Schnathorst near Minden on the Wesar River) on Oct. 3, 1839. He attended the schools of his native province until his fourteenth year when he hired to a man named Herman Meyer for three years. He then went to work in Bremerhaven where he remained for two years on the public works. In 1859 he embarked on the sailing ship Magdalena for America, arriving in New Orleans, November 1st after a nine-week voyage. He then came to Evansville, IN, by steamboat, the trip requiring three weeks more. His first job, for about a month, was chopping wood for a man named Brinkmayer at 60 cents per cord. He worked at general labor until his 26th year, when he married Augusta Deusner, daughter of Philip and Amelia Esskuchen (sp?) Deusner, who was born in Evansville Aug. 9, 1850. This event was solemnized Mar. 14, 1867. For the first three years of their marriage they lived in Union Township, Vanderburgh County. They then moved to Henderson Co., KY, where they lived for four years in Horseshoe Bend before moving to Walnut Bottom. Six years later, in 1880, they moved to Posey County, where he purchased the Oatman Farm near Mt. Vernon. After living in the old Oatman homestead for 15 years, they built the large brick home (still standing) at the end of W. Second St. The 1900 Atlas stated: "Mr. Hagemann has 280 acres of fine land in Indiana and 650 in Henderson County, and also some valuable city property. His son, Philip, who is married and has one child, owns 397 acres in Posey County. Frederick, Jr. is also married and lives on his father's farm in Kentucky. Mr. Hagemann's success in life is due to his sobriety, industry and economy. He is a true blue Republican in politics, a member of the A.O.U.W. Society and he and his wife are members of Trinity Evangelical Church in Mt. Vernon."

Frederick (who died in Mt. Vernon in 1919) and

Philip H. Hagemann

Augusta (who died in Mt. Vernon in 1914) had nine children: Katie A. (born June 6, 1868; died in childhood); Philip Henry (born June 26, 1869; died Oct. 18, 1941), who married Dorothea Schelhorn (born June 26, 1873; died July 8, 1952) and had two children: Dora Anna and Harry Philip; Mollie A. (born Oct. 14, 1871; died in childhood); Frederick O. (born Jan. 12, 1874; died in 1930), who married Katherine Lurch and had two children: Mary and Ralph; Sophia V. (born Dec. 29, 1876; died June 4, 1960), who married Frank Wittmer and had no children; Elizabeth K. (born Dec. 29, 1878 died June 1, 1955), who married August Blosfield and had one daughter: Augusta; William L. (born June 16, 1881; died 1925), who married Amelia Kreie and had five children: Lucille, Frederick, Florence, Philip and Jeanette; Charles E., William's twin brother (born June 16, 1881; died in 1955), who married Bertha Gronemeier and had three children: Willford, Charles and Helen; Bertha P. (born Sept. 23, 1886; died Dec. 15, 1969), who married John Moore (1883-1910) and had one daughter: Martha.

Philip and Dorothea were married Mar. 1, 1893, and set up housekeeping in a small frame house less than two miles west of Mt. Vernon on Rte. 69. It was torn down when the tract of land on which it stood was sold to General Electric. It was near the present Dan Fox Recreation Center. (Frederick's large brick house was occupied for many years by the three daughters—Sophia, Elizabeth and Bertha—when all three were widowed relatively early in life. After their deaths it passed to Bertha's daughter, Martha Culley, and her family.) In April, 1908, Philip purchased a large brick house on the southwest corner of Fourth and Locust in Mt. Vernon. It had been built between 1836 and 1838 by Alexander McCallister, who moved his family there from Evansville. The McCallister estate sold the property to the Hagemanns, who owned it until Harry and Lorene Hagemann sold it in 1964 to the builders of the Plantation Apartments. Philip's entire life was spent in farming but for a period of time (perhaps around 1905 to 1919) he also owned a livery stable on lower Main Street, site of the present armory. The stable was destroyed by fire Sept. 11, 1919.

Philip and Dorothea had a daughter, Dora Anna (born June 26, 1896; died Feb. 14, 1969; she and her parents shared the same birthday), who married John F. Bernd (born Feb. 1, 1895; died Oct. 27, 1976). Both lived in or just west of Mt. Vernon their entire lives. John was in the U.S. Army for a brief time around World War I and was in farming with his wife's family. They were members of Trinity Church and local fraternal organizations. They had no children.

Philip and Dorothea also had one son, Harry Philip, who was born June 19, 1908, just after the family moved to the home on E. Fourth St. In 1932

Harry married Merium Lorene Knight. They lived with his parents on E. Fourth St. and stayed there until they built a new home on Sauerkraut Lane, two miles west of Mt. Vernon, in 1964. After graduating from Mt. Vernon High School in 1926 Harry attended, the Lockyear Business College in Evansville for one year but basically spent his entire life continuing the family farming operations until the late 1950s, when ill health forced him into a more inactive role. For a few years in the 1950s in the early days of television he also had a small business selling RCA television sets. He and his wife were members of local Masonic lodges and the Evansville Shrine Club, where he enjoyed playing in the Drum and Bugle Corps (he had played cornet in his student days). They were members of Trinity Church, she having transferred her membership in recent years from Mt. Pleasant General Baptist Church in Bufkin. She is a member of the Mt. Vernon Garden Club and continues to live in the home west of Mt. Vernon.

Lorene Hagemann was born in Bufkin to Henry Brugger Knight (born Sept. 17, 1886; died July 15, 1968) and Florence Blackburn Knight (born Apr. 27, 1888; died May 6, 1967), both lifelong Posey County residents. They had 11 children: **Maurice Brugger** (born Mar. 3, 1906; died Apr. 19, 1978); **Ivan Henry** (born Aug. 2, 1909; died Aug. 23, 1918); **Merium Lorene** (born Feb. 17, 1911); **Ina Mae** (born Oct. 23, 1913); **Jack Richard** (born Dec. 29, 1915); **Garland Thompson** (born Sept. 28, 1917); **Anabel** (born July 30, 1920); **Harriett Elizabeth** (born Dec. 8, 1922); **Estella Flo** (born Dec. 7, 1925); **Edsel Eugene** (born Aug. 28, 1927); **Mary Frances** (born Mar. 16, 1930; died Apr. 5, 1930). Henry and Florence were able to celebrate their 62nd wedding anniversary on Apr. 5, 1967. Both were enthusiastic amateur singers (soprano and tenor) and frequently sang at church services, funerals and other gatherings. In addition to his farm in Bufkin, for several years in the late 1920s Henry owned a butcher shop in Mt. Vernon (at several locations), selling home-killed meat hand delivered to his customers. Active in the local Democratic Party, Henry served as Posey County Treasurer from 1947 to 1950.

Harry and Lorene had one child, Philip Henry, born Dec. 21, 1932, at the residence on E. 4th Street. During his years in the public schools of Mt. Vernon he was active in musical and dramatic groups and was president of his senior class (1950). While a second-grader he began piano lessons with Nan Wellborn and later studied with Sister M. Flavia and Florence Schenk (local) and Allene Herron (at what was then Evansville College during his last three years of high school). He also played alto saxophone in high school. He continued playing both instruments while earning a Bachelor of Music Education degree at Northwestern University, Evanston, IL (Class of 1954). For the next two years he served in the U.S. Army, playing alto saxophone in army bands in Austria and West Germany. After his military discharge in September 1956, he immediately enrolled at Teachers College, Columbia University, in New York City, receiving a Master of Music degree the following May. For six years he taught at Roy W. Brown Jr. High School, Bergenfield, NJ, (choral and general music) followed by 16 years at the senior high school in Spring Valley, NY (choruses, music appreciation, history and theory, and productions of Broadway musicals). From 1959 to 1967 he sang with The Collegiate Chorale, one of Manhattan's leading amateur choruses.

During those years the group made a number of appearances at Carnegie Hall and the newly-opened Lincoln Center with the New York Philharmonic under Leonard Bernstein, William Steinberg, Joseph Krips and Loren Maazel. In 1967 he was appointed conductor of the County Choral Society of Rockland Co., NY, a short distance northwest of Manhattan, a position he continues to hold today. Early in his teaching career he began arranging songs for his student choruses and this led to the writing of original compositions. His first published choral piece was "Christopher Columbus", a setting of a humorous poem by Ogden Nash (1961). At the time of this writing at least 60 of his choral works have been published by several major companies and he has written many other works of various sorts. His most popular piece is a Christmas novelty called "Fruitcake" which was written in collaboration with Penny Leka Knapp and has sold nearly 100,000 copies.

In 1975 the County Choral Society gave a special concert at St. Patricks' Cathedral in which he conducted his **Mass for Women's Voices.** At Mt. Vernon's observance of the American Bi-Centennial at a program at Sherburne Park on July 4, 1976, Mr. Hagemann conducted a local chorus and brass ensemble in "The River, Time and Music", written especially for the occasion. His compositions have been performed in Lincoln Center and the Kennedy Center, by choirs throughout this country, including the prestigious Chicago Symphony Chorus, and by the Hong Kong Childrens Choir and groups in Canada, England and France. In the last ten years much of his time has been spent composing six operas, which have been produced in Indiana, North Carolina, California, Illinois, Ohio and New York. One of them, **The Music Cure,** received its premiere production at the New Harmony Festival of Music (1984), with which he has been involved several years beginning in 1981. In March, 1986, in New Harmony, the University of Southern Indiana sponsored a program of musical settings by Mr. Hagemann of works by the famous poet, John Ciardi, who was in attendance. In March, 1987, also in New Harmony, USI sponsored the premiere of Hagemann's opera, **The Six of Calais,** along with his adaptation of Debussy's **The Prodigal Son.** In 1983 he created the Hagemann Award for Musical Performance, an annual competition for Posey County high school musicians. He is a member of the American Society of Composers, Authors and Publishers (from which he has received a Composers Award for each of the last five years), the American Choral Directors Association and other professional organizations.

WILLFORD AND MARGUERITA HAGEMANN

Willford and Marguerite Hagemann have lived in Black Township, Posey County all of their lives. They are members of Trinity United Church of Christ. They were married in 1936. A farm west of town on Upton Road has been home for 52 years. They lived in a three-story brick home built by Spencers in 1881. They built a new home in 1965.

They have one son, David, born in 1939. He is married to Lana Clevenger and works at General Electric; they now occupy the old home. The Hagemann's have two grandchildren; David, Jr., born 1964 and married to Jo Marie Hedges, Nancy Sue, born 1968 and married to John Crum. They have two great grandchildren, Christopher Johnson and John David Crum.

Willford attended Main Street Elementary School and graduated from high school in 1925. Marguerite attended Jeffries Elementary School and graduated from high school in 1934.

Willford and Marguerite Hagemann Former Home Place - Built in 1881

Willford helped in operating the ferry at the foot of Main Street, which his father bought in 1923. He worked at Rosenbaum's Department Store on Main Street; later going to Jackson, MI where he worked for McClellan Five and Ten Cent Store. He returned to Posey County to take up farming. He was a federal inspector of fruits and vegetables in Indiana 1927-1936.

They continued as grain and livestock farmers in Indiana, Illinois, and Kentucky. The farms and businesses continued as a family operation until his father's death in 1955.

In 1942 they began Hagemann Sand & Gravel Co. on their farm in the Upton vicinity and later from the Henry Lang Farm. They loaded and shipped sand and gravel in railroad cars from a ramp they built at Upton Switch. In 1947 they began a sand and gravel operation on the Ohio River at Newburgh. In 1949 they formed Hagemann Readymix Concrete Inc. located on Wolflin Street, which they operated until retirement in 1969.

Willford was appointed to the original Mt. Vernon Planning Commission and served 1953-1969.

Marguerite was secretary to John Keck of Keck Gonnerman Co. on West Fourth Street 1934-1936. She was secretary and bookkeeper for the family business until retiring 1969. She is an inactive member of Gamma Psi Chapter of Kappa Kappa Kappa. She is an active volunteer of The American Red Cross.

Since retirement they have been developing West Heights; a residential development west of town.

Willford is the son of Charles E. and Bertha Gronemeier Hagemann. Charles was a prominent grain and livestock farmer and property owner. He was a livestock dealer and shipped much of his livestock on the railroad. His grandfather was Frederick Hagemann who came from Germany in 1859; also a successful farmer and land owner in Indiana and Kentucky. An account of his life can be found in the Illustrated Atlas of Posey County 1900. His grandfather August Gronemeier had a blacksmith shop and was a wagon maker. Willford had a brother, Charles and a sister Helen; both died of scarlet fever and diphtheria in 1914.

Marguerite's parents were Herman and Nancy Works Riecken. They were farmers in the Upton Community. Herman worked with Carl Weilbrenner at the Weilbrenner Orchard and later retired from Keck-Gonnerman Co. Her grandfather Heinrich Riecken was a farmer. He came from Germany and owned a farm in the Upton area. She has one sister Elizabeth "Betty" Thompson.

HALL-McMURRAY

Timothy Morris Hall graduated from Mt. Vernon High School and attended Vincennes University. He is a sales representative for Metropolitan Life Ins. Company in Evansville.

His sister, Jacquelyn Hall Carney, graduated from Mt. Vernon High School and attended Indiana State University at Terre Haute for two years. She now lives in Indianapolis with her two sons, Sean and Kevin Carney.

Tim's brother, Stephen T. Hall, was also a Mt. Vernon High School graduate. Steve joined the U.S. Marine Corps in January, 1967 and was killed in Vietnam Apr. 30, 1969 at age 21. He had served in Vietnam five months before he was hit by mortar fire while standing perimeter guard watch the night of April 29th. Before going to Vietnam Steve was stationed in Washington, D.C. for 18 months where he served in the Special Ceremonial Guard Company of the U.S. Marine Corps. While there he met and married Deborah Ellen Seel of Mt. Rainier, MD. They were the parents of a daughter, Mary Alsa Hall, born while Steve was in Vietnam. Mary lives in Hyattsville, MD with her mother and stepfather, Deborah and Ronald Lawhorne, and two brothers, Ronnie and Rick Lawhorne. She is currently in her second year at the University of Maryland.

Dr. Thomas J. Hall and wife, Magdalena Kuhn Hall

Tim's step-father and mother are Jim D. McMurray and Mary Catherine McMurray. Jim is the only child of the late Conway and Ruby Divine McMurray of Morganfield, KY. Conway was a distributor for Gulf Oil Company and served 16 years as sheriff of Union Co., KY. Ruby McMurray was a school teacher. Jim and Mary McMurray live in Mt. Vernon, IN.

Tim's mother, Mary C. Cox Hall McMurray, has two sisters: Wilma Lengelsen, widow of Edgar Lengelsen; and Laura Bullard, widow of Robert L. Bullard. Their parents were Lester and Lela Ludlow Cox. Lester had a brother, Arvin, and a sister, Clara. Their parents were William James Cox and Malinda Zerkiebal Cox. William Cox was a farmer and school teacher in Posey County. Lela had a brother, Elijah Ludlow, and two sisters, Mary Ludlow Curtis, and Aletha Ludlow. Their parents were Abe and Laura Rhodes Ludlow. Laura Ludlow grew up in Harrison Co., IN and Abe Ludlow was a farmer in Black Township.

Tim Hall's father, Thomas F. Hall, died by drowning as the result of a boating accident in the Ohio River in 1959 at age 38. He died six weeks before Tim was born. He was owner-operator of Hall Service Company at the time of his death. His parents were Morris F. Hall and Celia Ritzert Hall, who lived in the Caborn, IN area. Celia had a sister, Mary Ritzert Lilley, California; and two brothers Sylvester and Leroy Ritzert.

Morris Hall's parents were Thomas J. Hall (1862-1930) and Magdalena Kuhn Hall (1871-1930). Her brothers were Joseph and Aloyois Kuhn; her sisters were Anna Kuhn Moll, Olivia Kuhn Robinson, and Cecelia Kuhn Ofer.

Thomas J. Hall was a native of Lexington, KY and was a medical doctor in the Caborn, Grafton and Mt. Vernon area at the time of his death.

HANCOCK-HERRING

Amanda Elizabeth Hancock and Squire Mitchell Wilson Herring married in Posey County, May 22, 1875. Seven children, all born Harmony Township were: Infant, born and died Aug. 18, 1876; Stella Maud Aug. 13, 1877-Feb. 1, 1965, married Nealy Hanes. Children: Madeline, Edith and Nedra.

Mildred, Oct. 2, 1879-Nov. 25, 1969, married Frank Leslie Schnee. Children: Gellert Stancil, Marjorie Merikbed, Kathleen Maud, Helen Gertrude, Ruth Elizabeth, Earl Wilson, Edna Louise, Mildred Evelyn, and Amy Irene. Mr. and Mrs. Schnee, buried Bellefontaine Cemetery.

Front Row: Squire Mitchell Wilson Herring, Gilbert Herring, Amanda Hancock Herring; Back Row: George Antwine Herring, Stella Maud Herring Mildred Herring.

Alexander, June 14, 1882-July 17, 1966 Vanderburgh County, married Nathalie Mable Anderson. Children: Harold Vistol, Elma Grace, Issac Wilson, Fanny, Mary Louise, Alexander Junior. Mr. and Mrs. Herring, buried Hancock Cemetery.

George Antwine, May 19, 1886- Apr. 13, 1916, served U.S. Army 1912-1914, stationed in the Philippine Islands.

John Thruman, Sept. 2,-Sept. 8, 1888.

Gilbert M., Mar. 15, 1894-1908 LaCenter, KY.

Wilson, Oct. 27, 1848, Tupelo, MS-Mar. 8, 1905 Posey County, son of Alexander Flemnon and Lucinda Jane White Herring. He was a carpenter; he built several buildings in Harmony Township, among them were a barn for U. Williams, houses for himself, William Viets, E. Stallings, Baptist Church, possibly the Catholic Church. His father, Alexander F., Feb. 21, 1827, Georgia - Mar. 19, 1879, Harmony Township, married Jan. 16, 1848 to Lucinda Jane White, Feb. 1, 1828, Alabama—Feb. 4, 1868 Centralia, IL. Alexander F., enlisted, Rocky Ford, MS, March 1862 in the Confederate Army, listed as a deserter, August of 1864; he was found, a prisoner of war in Memphis, TN; signed the Oath of Allegence to the United States, Nov. 15, 1864. After the Civil War ended he started north with Lucinda and five children; daughters, Missouri Evaline Meredin died, Arkansas; Elvira died, Tennessee. At Centralia, IL, son Alexander Marion was born, July 16, 1867-July 11, 1868. February 4, 1868, Lucinda died. He arrived, Posey County by 1870 with son Wilson and daughters, Nancy Frances Emmaline, who married Elijah Anderson, and Sarah Margaret Rhoda, who married Benjamin Franklin Hancock, Amanda's brother.

Amanda, May 28, 1858, Posey County-Aug. 3, 1928, married Jan. 1, 1910 to David P. Aldrich, 1857-May 13, 1918. Amanda, her husbands five children and Alexander F. Herring are buried at Hancock Cemetery. Her parents were Jourdan, Sept. 2, 1832-Apr. 4, 1906, married Sept. 1, 1852, Posey County, to Elmiria Jane Dunivan, July 13, 1827-Feb. 17, 1881, Posey County. Their children: Mahala Angeline; Benjamin Franklin, Harriet Adeline, Amanda E., George Washington, William Henry, Willis, Stephen, Willa Mina, May Isabelle, Lemuel.

Jourdan's parents, Benjamin and Mary Butler Hancock, married Mar. 24, 1826, Grainger Co., TN, came to Posey County 1829-32, with sons Enoch, Oct. 15, 1828, Tennessee-Mar. 31, 1908 married Mary Stallings; John, Apr. 13, 1829, Tennessee-Aug. 15, 1857, married Catherine Taunt; Jourdan; Louisa, 1834-Sept. 26, 1859, married George Ira Williams; Susannah, 1839-ca 1877, married George H. Morgan. Their great, great granddaughter, Jane Morgan, a lawyer, died Dec. 21, 1988 in the plane crash at Lockerbie, Scotland. Urbin, Sept. 4, 1846-Aug. 31, 1869, married Dica Hayes; Martha J., 1849-May 26, 1918, married Jacob Merchanthouse. Benjamin, Oct. 27, 1801, Virginia Oct. 7, 1875, and Mary, Oct. 18, 1803 North Carolina-Dec. 18, 1876. His father, John Hancock, ca 1769, Virginia-ca 1850-51, Posey County. It is believed John married Mar. 30, 1797, Shenandoah Co., VA to Mary Featheringill. He came to Posey County, alone, by 1850 and lived with Benjamin and Mary until he died. His grave is marked with a sandstone rock at Hancock Cemetery. Others buried at Hancock Cemetery include, Benjamin, Mary, Jourdan, Enoch, Urbin, and numerous members of the Hancock/Herring families. *Submitted by: Eva Lou Allen*

HANES FAMILY

A man named Hanes came to America from England with four (4) sons and settled around Concord, MA, a section called New England. One son became the first Governor of one of the New England states after the Revolutionary war and the colonies became states.

Two brothers traveled south to Virginia. One crossed the mountains at the Cumberland Gap into Kentucky.

Summer 1954

James Watson Hanes was born Oct. 8, 1816, and married Elizabeth Martin Hanes. They crossed the Ohio River and settled in Southern Indiana, Robinson Township, in Posey County. At this time there were four children: Matilda E., six years old; William M., four; Sara, two; Mary J., one.

Three more children were born to this union; John, James and Robert. James W. was a Posey County farmer who lived to an old age.

William Marion was born Nov. 3, 1845 in St. Wendel, Robinson Township. His educational advantages were very limited but by contact with business life he acquired a good practical education. At the age of 21 he began farming for himself on a rented place, continuing seven years when he purchased 81 acres. Later he increased his acreage to 133 acres. On Oct. 16, 1867 he was married to Elizabeth Williams.

Mr. William Hanes became a prominent farmer in Smith Township and owned 165 acres of fine land on which he erected a fine farm house and good barns. He was a Democrat and cast his first vote for Seymour. He and his wife were members of the Regular Baptist Church and the parents of four children; George W., Anna Alice, Robert Andrew and William Casey. William Marion Hanes passed away Mar. 21, 1937 at the age of 91, one of Posey County's oldest citizens.

The son, William Casey, married Evelyn Pirtle Dyer in Sonara, KY on Jan. 24, 1912. They moved to the New Harmony area in 1913 making farming his profession until he retired and moved to New Harmony in 1962. To this union six children were born; Alice Marie Happel who resides in New Harmony, Laura Elizabeth Nilsen resides in Philadelphia, PA, Marguerite Tramelli of Black Eagle, MT passed away in 1987, Evelyn Frances Miesel resides in Terre Haute, IN, William Casey, Jr. resides in Boonville, IN, George Edwin passed away in 1931 at the age of three. William Casey Sr. passed away Dec. 8, 1976.

MR. AND MRS. ELBERT M. HANES

Elbert M. Hanes, son of Mathias and Martha (Stallings) Hanes, was born Aug. 28, 1895 in Center Township, Posey County. Mollie Mae Shelton, daughter of Charlie and Virginia Shelton, was born Apr. 13, 1908, in Union Co., KY.

Bert and Mollie were married on Oct. 6, 1929. Bert was a head salesman for Grand Union Coffee and Tea Company. After their marriage, Bert and Mollie, in quick succession, lived in Paducah, KY: Cleveland, OH; St. Louis, MO, Quincy, IL and back to St. Louis. In 1931 the couple decided that they had enough of that life and they returned to Center Township to farm. This was during the great depression when everything was so cheap. They sold corn for 15¢ per hundred weight, and eggs were 5 and 10¢ per dozen. Mollie and Bert (sometimes known as Chick) worked very hard on rented farms.

Elbert and Mollie Hanes

Mollie, having been raised in Kentucky, decided to put out an acre of tobacco. No one else in Center Township was raising tobacco. They thought perhaps it might help pay taxes at least. People came from all around to see the crop grow. It was lots of work. Bert said he never saw a crop that took 12 months to harvest. Bert borrowed a truck from his brother-in-law, Lemuel Causey, to haul it to Henderson, KY, to sell. They didn't get much more than expenses out of the crop, but it was a GREAT experience.

Bert soon bought a wheat thresher and did contract threshing. His father, Mathias (Pie) Hanes died Feb. 12, 1934. They then bought the tavern in Wadesville from Mr. and Mrs. Ed Ricketts. They sold the TAVERN in 1937 to Buck Owens. The owner of that same tavern now is Jim Thornburg.

On Apr. 13, 1938, Bert and Mollie, bought the Corner General Merchandise Store Building from George W. Norton and his wife. The Hanes stocked the old store in 1938 and ran it as a general store for nine years.

Many things happened in those years-World War II, gas rationing, and also many groceries were rationed. Bert worked at Republic Aviation during the War. At the store they bought and tested cream, sold Wolverine shoes, dry goods—you name it, and they had it.

One great entertainment was the women sitting around the old stove in the center of the store on Saturday nights waiting for their husbands to come from Wade's Tavern where they played cards. Free movies on the street were great attractions on Thursday night. The merchants supported the shows. This made good business for all the merchants after the show.

On Nov. 6, 1947, Bert and Mollie sold the store to John M. Tenbarge. Mollie kept on working for Johnny for some time. For about a year, Bert and Mollie rented Martin Stegmaier's little house. Next they bought a farm in Robb Township from Dave Hasting in 1947. They remodeled the house and moved to the farm in 1948. A short time later, Johnny was called back to the Naval Reserve. Then Bert and Mollie moved back in the store and ran it while Johnny was away. Bert farmed until his health failed, and the doctor ordered him to give up farming. In 1955 they bought the house Mollie now lives in from Clifford Nash. The farm was rented out and finally in 1960 was sold to Alfred Kiltz.

In 1956 Mollie was elected Posey County Republican Vice Chair "lady". She and Chick became very active in Republican politics. In 1958, the clerk of Posey County Circuit Court, Lawrence Lumm, was killed in a auto accident. Harold Handley, Republican Governor of Indiana appointed Mr. Hanes to fill out Lumm's term of office. Bert ran for the office in 1960 but was defeated. He served as an Auto License Examiner for four years. His health kept failing. The Hanes went to Florida for the cold weather months for seven years. They had to fly home in April 1975, when Bert's condition worsened. He was in and out of the hospital until his death July 7, 1975. He was a member of the First Christian Church in Wadesville, Masonic Lodge No. 632 in Poseyville and Scottish Rite and Hadi Shrine in Evansville, IN.

Mollie resigned as Posey County Republican Vice Chairman in 1974 after serving 18 years. She served for 16 years as Eight District Vice Chairman. She was elected to the Electoral College in 1976 and voted on December 13th in the House of Representatives in the Indiana State House in Indianapolis, IN.

Indiana went for Gerald Ford in the general election. She was happy to cast her vote along with the other 12 electors for Gerald Ford, who was defeated on Nov. 2, 1976.

Mollie has been very active as a volunteer in Cancer drives, and was on the Cancer board for ten years. She was also active in Heart fund drives, mental health gold lady for ten years, Posey County council on aging for ten years and on the Swirka Board for two years. She is a devout worker and charter member of the First Christian Church in Wadesville for 40 years. She is a member of the Eastern Star Poseyville Chapter No. 394 for 45 years and a member of the Daughter of the Nile ISIS Temple No. 41 in Evansville.

She is an avid traveler, domestic and foreign. She has traveled to Alaska, Australia, Hawaii and most of all the other states.

She celebrated her 80th birthday on Apr. 9, 1988 with a dinner and dance at the V.F. W. in Wadesville. There was about 400 family and friends in attendance. *Submitted by Mollie M. Hanes*

NEALY WILLIAM AND STELLA HERRING HANES

Nealy and Stella Herring Hanes were life long residents of Posey County. Nealy, born May 20, 1880, Robinson Township, at St. Wendel, was a farmer, married Jan. 10, 1906, Posey County, to Stella Maud Herring, born Aug. 13, 1877, Harmony Township, daughter of Squire Mitchell Wilson and Amanda Hancock Herring, She started school at "Bugtown", but soon moved to New Harmony where she finished the eighth grade. Nealy attended the Kansas City School near St. Wendel, through the eighth grade. Nealy and Stella had three daughters, all born Harmony Township. Madeline, born Oct. 16, 1908, attended Stewartsville and New Harmony Schools, married Princeton, IN to Ellis Garrett son of David and Flora Simpson Garrett. Ellis died at his home in New Harmony, July 3, 1960.

Edith, born Feb. 11, 1910, attended Stewartsville and New Harmony Schools, married Carmi, IL, to James Marion Garrett, a brother to Ellis Garrett. Their children are: Eva Lou, born Aug. 4, 1930; Alan Ray, born Nov. 2, 1931 died Mar. 17, 1946; Connie Joyce, born May 2, 1934 died Jan. 17, 1987; Marilyn Ruth, born Sept. 25, 1937; Richard Elwood, born Mar. 30, 1943.

Nealy William and Stella Herring Hanes

Nedra Nieta, born May 31, 1911, attended Stewartsville School, graduated 1929 New Harmony High School, and a 1941 graduate of Lockyear's Business College, then worked at Crown Pottery in Evansville. She married, McLeansboro, IL to George Daniel Nemetz of Hopewell, VA. She worked 14 years at the Fort Lee Army base near Hopewell before she and George returned to live in Mt. Vernon. George died Apr. 22, 1981.

Nealy was the son of James Thomas and Malinda Yeager Hanes of St. Wendel. He died at his home at

"Bugtown", Feb. 11, 1952, on his daughter, Edith's birthday. He and Stella are buried at Maple Hill.

James Thomas and Malinda Yeager Hanes raised their family in the St. Wendel area where Mr. Hanes owned and farmed several acres of land. Their children were: Jessie C., who died aged two; Martha Frances; Ephriam M.; Welzie Thomas; Ora Madison; Emory Eldon; Florence Effie; Grace; Arcie; Nealy William; and twin sons, who died as babies. James T., born Mar. 29, 1852 died at Nealy's home, June 30, 1931. His parents were James Watson and Elizabeth Martin Hanes. He and Malinda, who died May 19, 1928, Poseyville, are buried at Liberty Cemetery at Cynthiana. Malinda's parents were George M. and Martha Williams Yeager. George M., born Sept. 1, 1817, Campbell Co., KY died Dec. 20, 1895, Gibson County, is buried at Liberty. Martha Ann, born 1820 to George and Audra Journey Williams, burial site unknown. The Yeagers, of German descent, can be traced to Nicholas Yager, a member of the 1717 Germanna Colony of Virginia.

James Watson Hanes, born Oct. 8, 1815 near Lexington, KY, married Oct. 27, 1842, Vanderburgh County to Elizabeth Martin daughter of Thomas and Fanny Marcus Martin. The Martin lineage descends from John Martin, born 1596, died 1673, a member of the Virginia House of Burgesses.

James W. and Elizabeth settled about 1840, on the Hanes Homestead near St. Wendel. He died July 15, 1897. He and Elizabeth are buried at Mt. Pleasant Cemetery near Poseyville. James W.'s parents were James, born 1788, Virginia, died ca 1851-52, Posey County and Katherine, born 1791, Virginia, died October 1849, Posey County. The Hanes Cemetery in the St. Wendel area, where James and Katherine were buried has been destroyed by PROGRESS. *Submitted by Nedra N. Nemetz*

TROY STEVEN HANES AND DONNA (KUBIK) HANES

Troy Steven Hanes and Donna Marie "Kubik" Hanes reside in Westmont, IL. They both graduated from Hinsdale South High School in 1972. They married on Sept. 22, 1973 in Clarendon Hills, IL. Troy "Steve" to friends and relatvies was born on Jan. 29, 1954 in Williamson Co., Herrin, IL. He was the fifth of six Hanes children with four other half brothers and sisters.

Although Troy was never a resident of Posey County his ancestral heritage has a deep background there.

The Hanes family came to America from England. A man named Hanes with four sons settled around Concord, MA, in the section called New England. One son became the first governor of one of the New England States after the Revolutionary War and the colonies became states. Two brothers traveled south to Virginia, one crossed the mountains at the Cumberland Gap into Kentucky. (ref. The Hanes Family Tree, by Marie Happel, October 1975.)

One of the two brothers is said to have the name Peter. Peter and wife Mary Hanes (gggg grandparents) had five sons. David 1786, Rache, Eli, William, and James 1788. All five were supposed to have been born near Richmond, VA. Prior to Oct. 8, 1815 James Hanes left Virginia to Lexington, KY. His wife Katherine, (ggg grandparents) maiden name, birth date, place or date of marriage unknown. They had six children. James Watson, Oct. 8, 1815, William R. June 3, 1820, Charles C. Oct.

Troy Steven, Donna, Kim and Kristin

17, 1887, Sally Retta 1821, Georg T., Lucinda July 15, 1811. The children were believed to have been born in Lexington, KY.

By 1832 James and Katherine Hanes resettled in Indiana. On July 7, 1832 James Hanes (Farmer) purchased what is believed to be his first land in Robinson Township, Posey County.

James W. Oct. 8, 1815 - July 14, 1897 married Elizabeth Martin Feb. 8, 1824 - Jan. 17, 1912 on Oct. 27, 1842 in Vanderburgh Co., IN (gg grandparents). Seven children were born; Matilda E. 1844, William Marion Nov. 3, 1845 - Mar. 21, 1937, Sarah F. 1848, Mary J. 1849, James Thomas Mar. 29, 1852 - June 30, 1931, John G. 1854 - 1929, Robert A. 1855 - Sept. 4, 1941.

James Thomas Hanes was a farmer, just as his father and grandfather were. Some of the land he owned and farmed was owned and farmed by his father and grandfather before him.

James T. and Malinda Yeager Hanes July 12, 1852 - Mar. 19, 1928: (g grandparents) daughter of George and Malinda Yeager (gg grandparents) married Mar. 1, 1875 had 12 children all born in Posey County. Jessie C., Martha Frances, Ephriam M., Nealy William, infant twin sons B&D, Welzie Thomas, Ora Madison, Emory Eldon, Florence Effie, Grace, Arcie.

Emory Eldon Hanes Apr. 22, 1889 - Feb. 10, 1953 married Eathel Sue Barton Apr. 17, 1889 - Apr. 30, 1926 on Jan. 11, 1918, (grandparents) (her parents Anson and Sophia A. "Blackburn" Barton (g grandparents).

They had four children; female Nov. 26, 1918 B&D, Kenneth Barton, Jessie Melvin, Harley Elbert. The three boys were born in Wadesville on the Anson Barton Farm by Dr. Auburn. Emory was a World War I Veteran. A plaque in the Mt. Vernon Coliseum (1917 Honor Roll 1918, To Those of Posey County Who Served In The World War) has his name on it.

Kenneth Barton Hanes July 24, 1920 married Nora Jean Husar (Oct. 16, 1928) on Mar. 4, 1950, Posey Co., IN. Their children; Ronald Wayne, Roger Allen, Jacqueline Sue, Kenneth Ray. All born Davis County Hospital, Owensboro, KY.

Jessie Melvin "Jeep" Hanes June 30, 1922 married Anna Bell Scott Apr. 20, 1920, Evansville, IN, no children.

Harley Elbert Hanes July 12, 1925 - Feb. 23, 1986 married Roberta Vee Fricker Robertson June 24, 1921 on Jan. 10, 1945 in Marion, KY. Roberta was widowed with four children - they are Bonita, Johnny, Vera, and Brenda Robertson. Together they had six children Eathel Sue, Kenneth Douglas, Judith Delores, Phyllis Jean, Troy Steven and Gregory Eldon Hanes.

Bonita Ruth Robertson Sept. 28, 1938 married George Anthony Peska Mar. 12, 1937 on May 7, 1966. Their child Michael George.

Johnny Howard Robertson Nov. 16, 1939 married Estelle May Barry May 31, 1942 on Nov. 15, 1958. Their children Sara Lynn, Lisha Ruth, Barry Steven, Paul David, Amanda, Holly Teresa.

Vera Hollie Robertson Feb. 4, 1942 married Roger Lee Oxford Aug. 21, 1941 on Aug. 20, 1959. Their children; Tammie Vee, Natalie Gay, and Bernard Todd.

Brenda Kathleen Robertson Apr. 1, 1944 married Norman Richard Thompson July 15, 1929 children; Norman R. Jr., Mary Ann, Harold Thomas July 16, 1962 - Oct. 1, 1980, Mavine Kathleen, M. Lynn.

Eathel Sue Hanes Oct. 11, 1845 married Richard Arthur Wiegel Jan. 8, 1943 on Nov. 18, 1967. Children; Richard Harley, Ginger Ann.

Kenneth Douglas Hanes Sept. 3, 1946 married Diana Sue Robison Dec. 6, 1946 on Sept. 18, 1965. Children; Scottie Douglas, Adam Wade.

Judith Delores Hanes Biggerstaff Aug. 1, 1947 married Samuel Thomas Rubenacker Sept. 25, 1942 on Mar. 5, 1970. Child Johnny Elbert Biggerstaff.

Phyllis Jean Hanes July 8, 1948 married Edward Francis Bradley III Nov. 2, 1944 on Feb. 4, 1966. Children; Roberta Ann, Edward Harley.

Troy Steven Hanes Jan. 29, 1954 married Donna Marie Kubik Sept. 16, 1954 on Sept. 22, 1973. Children; Kimberly Diane, Kristin Marie.

Gregory Eldon Hanes Aug. 1, 1956 married Rebecca June Randolph Dec. 4, 1958 on Aug. 27, 1977. Children; Ryan Gregory, Cody Jared, Evan Michael Wayland, Jordan James.

In 1955 Harley left Indiana and came to Illinois to find work. After finding employment at Electromotive in LaGrange he brought his family to live in Lemont. In 1961 he moved them to Clarendon Hills, IL where he lived until his death in 1986. His wife still lives in that home.

RAYMOND C. HAPPE

Raymond C. Happe is a resident of Mt. Vernon, IN. He was born on Bluff Road Dec. 20, 1920. After the death of his father, the family moved to Evansville, IN where Ray attended St. Boniface Grade School. He graduated from Reitz High School in 1939.

Raymond C. Happe died Sept. 7, 1989, and was buried at St. Joseph Cemetery in Evansville, IN.

Raymond C. Happe

After high school, Ray worked for a few years as a factory worker. Ever since Ray was a young man, he had hoped that someday he would be able to return to Posey County and engage in farming as his father had done for so many years. In 1946 his dream came true when he purchased what was known as the John Derrington farm.

Ray is the son of Edward and Theresa (Strobel) Happe who are both deceased.

Ray has a sister, Clara McCrarey of Evansville, IN and a brother Walter Happe who is deceased.

LARRY W. HARMS FAMILY

Larry W. Harms Sr. was born on Oct. 30, 1946 in Evansville, IN. He graduated from the old Evansville Central High School and served in the Navy in Vietnam and in the Arab-Israel war of June, 1967.

In December 1967 he went to work for Mead Johnson & Co. He graduated from I.T.T. in 1970 with a degree in Electronic Engineering, and studied Management at I.S.U.E., now the University of Southern Indiana.

Mead Johnson and Co. was merged into the Bristol Myers Corporation in 1968. Larry was transferred to Posey County in 1972, as one of the first employees of the Bristol Myer's Mt. Vernon Plant.

Larry's parents were Esther (Whipking) Harms and Floyd G. Harms. The Whipking family came from Prussia, Germany in 1850 and settled in Huntingburg, IN. Esther Whipking's mother was from the Ball family of Poole, KY. Her grandfather, Madison Ball, was in the Civil War and his brother fought on the other side.

From Left to Right - Beth, Diana, Mary, Larry, Jr., Larry W. Harms Sr. 1988

Floyd Harms' grandfather, Jacob Harms (1838-1916), (son of Lewis and Ellen Harms) came from Braddorg, Germany in 1857 by way of ship from Bremerhaven to New Orleans. He came to avoid the civil war that was developing in Germany, and settled in Bone Gap, IL.

Jacob married Sophronia Brown (1835-1872), a direct descendent of John Alden and Priscilla (Mullins) Alden, who came from England to America on the Mayflower in 1620.*

Jacob's oldest son, John L. Harms, moved to Posey County in August of 1888 and married Eliza J. Barnett. They are buried in the Bone Gap cemetery.

After the death of his first wife, Sophronia, Jacob married her cousin, Sarah Lambert (1842-1933), daughter of David and Cyrena (Michels) Lambert. David Lambert came from Haxey, Lincolnshire England at age 14 with his parents, John and Mary Ann (West) Lambert, in 1829.

The Michels came to Illinois from Maine in 1818. They have been traced back to James Michels and Rebecca Pendor, married on Dec. 11, 1746 in Boston, MA. Jacob and Sarah were the great grandparents of Larry Harms.

Larry's wife, Mary, is a graduate of Reitz High School and is the daughter of Dotson Nolan (from Georgia) and Lucille (Evrard) Nolan from St. Marks, IN.

Mary's paternal grandmother, Fanny (Quinn) Nolan, still resides in Millidgeville, GA.

The Evrard family has been traced to Andre Pierre and Mary Elizabeth (Gravet) Pierre of Les Bulles, Belgium, born in 1808 and 1805 respectively. They were the parents of Elizabeth (1838-1920) who married John J. Evrard (1831-1892). John and Elizabeth were the parents of John Baptist Evrard (1860-1910) who was Mary Harms' great grandfather.

Larry and Mary reside on Seibert Lane, near the Uebelhack Turkey farm, with their son, Larry Harms Jr. Larry's daughters, Diana and Beth graduated from Mt. Vernon High School and attended U.S.I. He has two children who reside in Evansville, IN, Cheryl and Daniel. Cheryl and Ronald Mullen are the parents of Larry's three grandchildren, Heather, Eric, and Tabatha.

The Harmses are members of St. Matthew Catholic Church and were active for several years in the Boy Scout Troop 475 in Mt. Vernon.

*

1. John and Priscella (Mullins) Alden came from England to America on the Mayflower in 1620.
2. Their son Joseph Alden married Mary Simmons.
3. Their son Joseph Alden Jr. married Hannah Dunham.
4. Their son David Alden married Abigal Shaw.
5. Their son Barnabus Alden married Elizabeth Patterson.
6. Their daughter Esther Elizabeth Alden married Nathen Gould on May 7, 1801.
7. Their daughter Lydia Gould, born in Massachusetts in 1814, married John Brown.
8. Their daughter Sophronia Brown married Jacob Harms.
9. Their son was John L. Harms.

DAVID AND OLIVE HASTING MICHAEL AND NANCY HASTING

David Erin Hasting, born Dec. 17, 1906, was the oldest child of William Edward and Anna Bell Hasting. His mother died in childbirth when he was almost four. As a young boy, Dave worked on his father's farm in Point Township. In the summer, he also worked for Fuhrer-Ford Scale House in Point Twp. weighing grain, and for Jeff Callahan's threshing rig, starting out as the water boy and firing the engine the last four years he worked.

In 1924, while a junior in High School, Dave experimented with radios and built the first broadcasting station in Mt. Vernon for Pearson Furniture Co. (they sold radios). Their call letters were 9CJZ. They played records, and broadcast Crunk's Orchestra playing live. He attended Purdue University in Agriculture from 1925-1928. With the advent of the Depression, he returned home to help on the family farm and took over completely when his Dad moved to California in 1939.

He married Olive Blanche Ayers, daughter of Thomas and Sina Ayers Jan. 27, 1940 in Paducah, KY. She was born in Brown Co., IN May 30, 1914. Olive attended Indiana University from 1932-1934 in music. She is an accomplished piano player, and in her teenage years played for the silent movies in Nashville, IN. She met Dave while living with her sister and brother-in-law in Evansville. She worked at Evansville Titles Corp. and Ideal Pure Milk before her marriage to Dave.

Dave bought Eilert Equipment, the International Harvester Dealership, in 1941. He expanded the franchise to include Oldsmobile and Hudson automobiles. The automobile franchise was sold in 1956. The IH dealership was discontinued in 1985.

During WWII Dave was a pilot with the Army Air Corp, and was stationed in Texas, Mississippi, Kansas, and Indiana. While he was gone Olive managed Hasting Equipment Co.

After the War Dave purchased planes and became a flight instructor in Mt. Vernon for several years.

Other business interests Dave was involved with over the years include: Mt. Vernon Appliance Store; E.B. Schenk Hardware; starting a fertilizer service that later became Custom Farm Service; and as Sec.-Treas. of Mt. Vernon Realty Co., he built and sold houses.

Dave and Olive had two children: Judith Ann born Sept. 27, 1945; and Michael Erin born Feb. 18, 1953.

Michael Erin graduated from Purdue University with a B.S. in Mechanical Engineering in 1975 and received his M.S. in Mechanical Engineering in 1977.

Mike worked at Arkla Industries in Evansville and then at the family International Harvestor Dealership first as Parts Manager, then as General Manager until the dealership closed in 1985. He now farms in Point Township.

Mike married Nancy Vanada Nov. 10, 1979. She was born Nov. 9, 1954 the daughter of Chester and Betty Vanada in Warrick Co., IN. They met at Purdue where she received her B.S. in Agriculture in 1975 and added a teaching certificate in 1976. She started Hasting Plants and Produce in 1982 - a greenhouse and U-Pick Garden operation on the family farm in Point Twp.

Mike and Nancy have one child, Daniel Erin, born July 30, 1987.

Mike enjoys working with and has a collection of antique International Tractors including the F-30 on steel he used as a boy helping clear ground on the farm, and an award winning WD-40, the first diesel farm tractor ever made. He also has in his collection Model A & Model T Ford Automobiles, Ford & K.R. Wilson Tools and a Keck Gonnerman Steam Engine, Separator & Tractors.

THE HASTING FAMILY & DR. WILLIAM EDWARD HASTING

The Hasting family first came to Posey County, from Delaware, in the 1830's. Goodspeed's History lists a Nehemiah Hasting voting in the 1835 election in Point Township. He was of English descent. Nehemiah died at a young age leaving his son William Thomas Hasting, born Dec. 21, 1829 (in Delaware City, DE) as a ward of Eli Aldredge of Black Township until he was 17.

William married Sarah Jane Booth Oct. 8, 1857. The daughter of John Booth, she was born Feb. 21, 1838 in Point Township. Of their seven children, only four lived to adulthood: Thomas Jefferson, David Henry, William Edward, and Ida May. William Thomas purchased his first property in Point Township in 1860. William died Jan. 31, 1885, Sarah died Nov. 7, 1907.

William Edward, their fourth child was born Aug. 10, 1867. He became a Dr. of Medicine, taking his pre-med at DePauw University and his Medical Degree at Washington University in St. Louis. After his graduation in 1897, he spent three years first as superintendent of the Merchants Hospital of St. Louis, then as superintendent of the Employee's Hospital of East St. Louis, and returned to Mt. Vernon in 1900. One of the first Doctors in the state to use X-Ray machines, he lost a hand to overexposure. He married Anna Bell, who had emi-

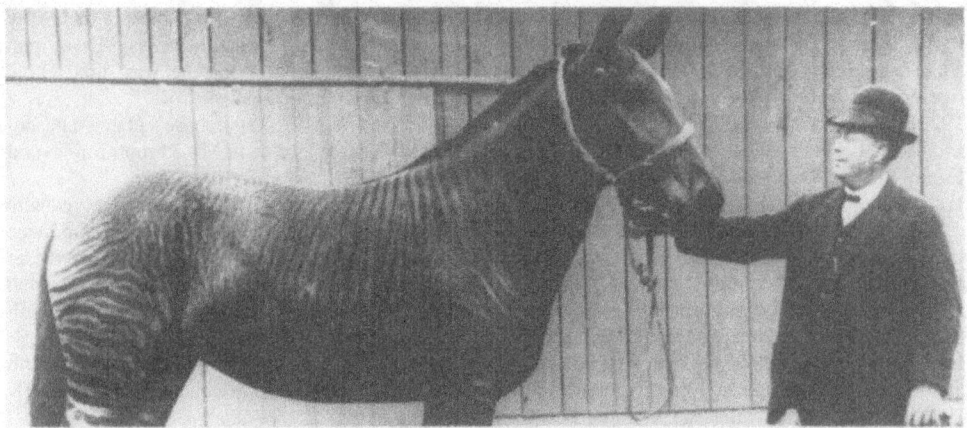
Dr. William Edward Hasting ca. 1918 with one of his Zebroids

grated to Kentucky from Newtownbutler, Ireland, on Dec. 16, 1905. She was the daughter of John Bell and Sarah Bryans Bell, and was born June 18, 1872. William Edward and Anna had two children, David Erin born Dec. 17, 1906, and Anna Bell born Apr. 28, 1908. Mrs. Anna Hasting died Nov. 6, 1910 following a caesarean operation at her home. The infant preceeded her in death by two days.

Dr. Hasting left the Medical profession and devoted his time to his extensive farming operation (close to 1,000 acres) in Point Township. A large livestock breeder, "Doc" built the state's largest barn which covered two acres of ground (320' x 280'). He experimented and developed "zebroids", a cross between zebras and white arabian mares. These were intended as hybrid draft animals, and proved very strong, but continued to have a wild streak. The zebras were purchased from the Hagebock and Wallace Circus headquartered in Hamburg, Germany. As an interesting note, the USDA had experimented with zebroids in Beltsville, MD, but had no success as the zebroids were too small. "Doc" had befriended Hagebock, from the Circus of that name, who encouraged him to try again using the Grevy's zebra, a larger zebra. The results were successful. Many Posey County residents still remember visiting the Hasting farm in Point Township to see the zebras and zebroids. The advent of the farm tractor led to the discontinuance of the zebroid experiment.

"Doc" Hasting weathered the depression with his farm, but decided enough was enough after the 1937 flood, and moved to Redlands, CA in 1939. He died there Sept. 13, 1957.

CHARLES AND STELLA HAYNES

Charles and Stella Haynes, 1633 Hawthorne Drive, Mt. Vernon, IN have resided in Posey County for the last 22 years. Charles was with Babcock & Wilcox until 1980 when the plant closed. He is now employed at General Electric Company. Stella is a Vice President, People's Bank & Trust Co. They have one son, Charles William (Bill). Bill graduated from Mt. Vernon High School in 1981 and graduated from Purdue University, School of Engineering in 1985 and is employed by Pritsker, Indianapolis, IN.

Charles is the son of Walker W. and Virgie Mae Haynes, Owensboro, KY and both are deceased. Charles has one sister, Margaret Mills, Albuquerque, NM.

Stella is the daughter of Raymond and Lula Spencer Legg, Owensboro, KY. Her mother died in 1983. She has two sisters, Ruth Rhodes, Evansville, IN and Anna Raye Montgomery, Leitchfield, KY.

HEIN-PAPENMEIR

Everett Hein and Velma (Papenmeier) Hein are residents of rural New Harmony, living on a farm purchased by Everett's grandfather, Sidney Johnson in 1890. Everett was born here and attended New Harmony Schools, graduating in 1942. He is farming and has worked as a machinist at Whirlpool Corporation in Evansville, IN.

The Johnson family came to New Harmony, IN from North Carolina; Sidney (1858-1919) was the sixth child of Camma Johnson (1815-1899) and Rachel (Staley) Johnson (1820-1884). He was married to Jane (Wade) Johnson (1864-1943), they had two children; Winston Johnson (1893-1969) and Lena Johnson, while living on the farm at New Harmony, IN. Lena Johnson (1899-1975) married Edward Hein (1895-1952) in October, 1921, after Edward returned from the Army serving in World War I. Everett, born Aug. 20, 1923 was the oldest of two children.

Everett M. Hein and Velma Hein

Everett's paternal great grandfather, Dierdrich Hain (1794-1873) and wife Barbara, along with five children came to America from Permson, Germany in 1839. Arrived at Baltimore, MD, to Philadelphia and Pittsburgh, traveling the Ohio River to Evansville and Darmstadt, their families then moving on to Stewartsville, IN.

Deirdrich's fifth son was named Henry Hein (1848-1932), was married to Caroline Kohler, died after the birth of two children; his second wife, Magdalena (Zohonsinger) Hein (1857-1902). They had six children, and Edward was the youngest.

The name Hein is adopted in America, from German spellings of Hayn, Hain and Hyne.

Velma, born Mar. 4, 1928, the oldest of two daughters, born to William (1897-1986) and Sadie (Daub) Papenmeir (1900-1964). She attended Waterman School, graduating from Wadesville High School in 1946.

Her father, William, the second child from a family of nine, was born to Gustav Papenmeier (1867-1938) and Mary (Dickaut) Papenmeier (1876-1963). Her great grandparents, Friedrich William Philipp Papenmeier (1823-1900), left the German Army with the rank of Colonel, and married Wilhelmine (Webel) Papenmeier (1831-1890) in Hummerson, Germany and brought their family of four children to America, circa 1865. Their fifth child, Gustav was born in America.

Velma's maternal great great great grandparents, Casper Daub (1808-1891) and Elizabeth (Stenernagel) Daub (1810-1873) made their way to America from Hesse Darmstadt, Germany in 1857, locating in Robinson Township, Posey Co., IN, where the father engaged in farming. They raised six children, the fourth child, Henry Daub (1848-1917) was married to Catherine (Oeth) Daub (1848-1917). Their oldest child, Henry A. Daub, (1871-1926) was from a family of seven children, married Anna (Winternheimer) Daub (1878-1973). There were five children born to this marriage, of which Sadie (Velma's mother) was the oldest.

Everett and Velma Hein were married June 18, 1950, they have three children, JoBerta Hein (Home Economist), born May 22, 1951, Marwin Lee Hein (G.E. Color Technician), born Mar. 27, 1956, and Kristy Lou Hein (Executive Secretary), born Dec. 31, 1962. The family are members of Johnson United Methodist Church and active in many community organizations.

HENGSTENBERG-GULICHER FAMILY HISTORY

According to a report written by Anna-Marie Stock (Neisen) when she was in grade school, from information supplied by her mother, Emma Winiger Stock, the Hengstenberg Family came up the Mississippi River from New Orleans on a cattle boat in 1857 after boarding ship at Bremen in 1856 from Westfalen (Westphalia), Germany, to spare their sons from military conscription. (Of course, Germany as a country did not exist until Bismarck united it in 1881. Up to that time it was a conglomerate of small principalities and kingdoms, such as Bavaria, Baden, Württemberg, Hessen, and Preuszen (Prussia), which was the home of the Hengstenbergs and Gülichers, wife Anna Wilhelmines'.) They had been friends of the Lengelsens*, which had come from the same area nine years earlier, and were probably influenced by correspondence during that time; when they arrived at West Franklin, the women and children waited there with their possessions until the men could go over the hills to Lengelsens and come back for them.

Anna Wilhelmine Gulicher Hengstenberg, Mine Luise Hengstinberg, Peter Casper Wilhelm Hengstenberg

October 26 was the date that their purchase of approximately one-half a section of land was recorded, on whose highest point above sea level they built a log house with overview of most of the acreage, which stood until the late 1960's (a couple of these logs of oak and poplar were purchased and made into benches, being preserved by descendants).

Hengstenberg Hill was the highest point directly east of Mt. Vernon about 12 miles and about one mile from the Ohio River. The Old Salem Church building now stands on the exact site, where the south entrance will use the brick floor of the old cellar, the property having been sold to Dr. Welborn about 1919 and the homesite reclaimed 1973 by purchase from his daughter by Hengstenberg descendants 117 years to the day after it was originally purchased. Until the electric power plant was built across the road, partly on Hengstenberg property, one could see all the way to Mt. Vernon and even see the river when the water was up. Now most of that is blocked by a high wall of earth. It is reported that the land agent took Peter Casper Wilhelm to the hilltop and told him he could have all the land he could see that he could clear. Wm. Waller, Welborn's son-in-law, who farmed the land for a time, related a story that it took six teams of oxen to pull just one large log out of the valley just west of the homesite. It seems appropriate that **Hengstenberg** means **"Hengst am Berg"** "stallion on the hill/mountain".

A history of the Anglo-Saxon Invasion of Great Britain names the first seafaring Saxons who led it—brothers **Hengest** and **Horsa.** Could they have been related? Correspondence with a Ruth Hengstenberg in New York informs us that the history dates back to 1237 and that the line includes mostly ministers and teachers. One such was associated with Martin Luther; one was a pastor of the Gülichers, church in Wiblingwerde (highest hill in the Sauerland), and his wife's tombstone is there. Some were located in Fröndenberg and Werdohl. Peter Gülicher of Holland, also a Lengelsen descendant, visited family haunts here in 1979 and has compiled several books on the history of the two families. Most know the family name because of business concerns in Düsseldorf and Esslingen, which produce vinegar, salad dressings, and various canned vegetables. This author visited there in 1974 and met the owner, Kurt Hengstenberg.

The amount of property obtained enabled the Hengstenbergs to furnish a homesite for son Wilhelm and wife, Elisabeth Schimmel, around the bend to the south; to daughter Emma and husband, Adam Winiger from Switzerland, across the road (where P.C. Wilh. died); to son Karl and wife, Annie Nölle, down in the valley to the west beside a stream; and another homesite there to son Friedrich, who married Dora Schnack. The oldest daughter, Hulda, married Jacob Orth and lived along the highway to Mt. Vernon; their log house has been moved to the USI campus and is known as the Grimes House. She had her children in the same house where she was born and died there at 21, (daughter Ida survived). The youngest daughter, Mina, only child born in this country, lived at home with husband Eduard Lengelsen. Daughter Ida, a midwife for whom many babies were named, married Adolph Nölle and lived mostly in two houses in West Franklin, where she cooked mussels gathered from the river, and sometimes found pearls. (She died in Evansville at 2609 W. Virginia—formerly known as Law Ave—in 1929, where niece Emma Winiger Stock and husband, Will, lived approximately 50 years.) It was Ida who carried on correspondence with relatives back in Westfalen until her death, therefore enabling a descendant in the early 70's, through old letters and pictures, to re-establish contact with the Gülichers and then visit them and old homesites in 1974. A good picture of Ida was obtained through a sad event of those times: Ida and her sister-in-law were required to have their pictures taken when the First World War came along, as the two old ladies were foreign-born aliens: "Ich und die Anna—mir könnten noch Spion sein!" ("I and Anna—we could be spies yet!")

As already noted, there was a long-standing closeness with the Lengelsens, involving intermarriage with them on at least four occasions: with Ed Lengelsen; Adolf and Anna Noelle, whose mother was a Lengelsen; and then in old age Hermann Diedrich Lengelsen married the widow (a Schnepper) of Hermann Diedrich Hengstenberg. Both families had brought not only their children but their parents and thus quite literally their entire extended family.

The Gülicher family tree is in possession of descendants, in a direct line from 1660; there has always been a Karl Gülicher on the **Claumberg,** the hill next to the church, which is approximately 1000 years old.

JOHN AND MARGARET HERRMANN

Johann Hermann, Jr., was born on Aug. 10, 1827, in Bavaria, Germany; he was the son of Johann Herrmann, Sr., and Magdalena Wagoner. On Aug. 20, 1851, he married Margaretha Hempfling, born in Bavaria on Aug. 21, 1833. John and Margaret lived in Mt. Vernon and had seven children: Barbara, Simon, Elizabeth ("Ella"), Christina (Feb. 3, 1859-Dec. 25, 1902), Carolina, John G. (born 1866), and Sophia (1869-1905). John Jr., was a farmer and acquired extensive land holdings in Posey County. John, Margaret, Sophia, and Christina are buried in adjoining plots in Bellefontaine Cemetery.

John Herrmann, Jr.

Elizabeth married Lawrence Leopold and had one daughter, Ferne.

John G. married Tilley H. Stephens and became a judge.

Christina married Nicholas Weyer on June 17, 1877. Their children were Charles Edward (1878-1915) and Anna Sophia (1880-1881). Nicholas died several months before the birth of Anna. Christina returned to her parents' home with Edward, and Anna was born there. On Feb. 7, 1889, Christina married a widower, John A. Drake. Christina died on Christmas Day, 1902, and John moved to Florida to live with a married daughter.

Margaret Herrmann died on Oct. 15, 1905, and John Herrmann, Jr., died on Nov. 4, 1915.

Edward Weyer, their grandson, married Ida May Laslie (1883-1943) on Sept. 28, 1903. They lived in Wadesville on a farm rented from John Herrmann. Edward farmed and also worked in a men's clothing store. Edward and Ida had three children: Irene Isabel (1904-1983), Alice Christine (born 1906); and Albert Edward (1915-1966). Edward died on Sept. 2, 1915, about two months before his grandfather. *Submitted by Mrs. Vivian Morlock Taylor*

JOHN AND ROSE HIRSCH

It was melon time in Posey County, in 1916, when John L. Hirsch came to Poseyville, from Haubstadt in Gibson Co., IN, to open a retail grocery store. His first store, handling groceries and shoes, was located at the corner of Main and Locust streets. The store, known as the old Opera House Building, was situated where Effinger Appliance Company is presently located. Upon entry into the U.S. Army in August of 1918, John L. Hirsch sold the store to T.J. Williams, who continued the operation of the grocery for a number of years. After World War I, occupancy of the present location of the J.L. Hirsch Company, at the corner of Main and Cale streets was made. The property and building was owned by Joseph Ziliak, the Father of Rose Ziliak Hirsch.

John L. Hirsch & Rose Ziliak Hirsch

The make-up of the store was "general", selling dry goods, shoes, piece goods, linoleum, furniture, groceries, hardware, and 'what-have-you'. These were the years of the "cracker barrel era". Practically all food-stuffs had to be packaged and measured. For example, bread was all unwrapped and unsliced, coffee had to be ground; pickles and sauerkraut, crackers and flour - all had to be measured and weighed. Self-service was unheard of in those days!...Deliveries were made by horse and buggy, supplanted in due time by the Model T. Ford. Store hours were from 6 a.m. to 6 p.m., and on Saturdays until mid-night or later.

As the years slipped by, employees had come and gone but John L. Hirsch stayed right on the job. ....In 1938 Charles Hirsch began his association with the Company, showing special interest and talent for dry goods merchandising. Robert ("Bob") came on the scene with full-time employment in 1948, and from the start showed interest and aptitude in the grocery and meat department. Both Charles and Bob became partners in the business in 1958 and are now the owners and managers of the Dry Goods and Grocery Departments, respectively, of the J.L. Hirsch Company.

On June 5, 1917 John Lawrence Hirsch and Rose Anna Ziliak were married at St. James Catholic Church, R.R. 1 Haubstadt, IN. Rose was a native of Vanderburgh Co., IN. ...Subsequent to his return in 1918 from World War I, John and Rose took up residence in Poseyville, remaining in Posey County throughout their lives.

Seven children were born to John and Rose. Clinton, was ordained a Priest in 1945 and received the papal honor of Monsignor in 1967. ... Linus, died in 1936, at the age of 16, while still a student at Poseyville High School. ...Charles, married Erma Nix in 1947, and the couple has resided in Poseyville to the present time. Erma was associated with the Farmers Bank and Trust Co., for 47 years. Charles continues his artistic Water Color Paintings at the current time, having his studio in their residence on N. Cale Street, Poseyville. ...Herman, the fourth son, graduated from St. Louis University Medical School in 1952 and served the people of Mt. Vernon, IN, for more than 25 years, before becoming Medical Director at the General Electric Company in Mt. Vernon, where Dr. Herman is presently employed. He married Mary Jane Higgins of Kansas City, MO, in 1953 they have four children. ... Mary Ann married Thelman Reising at St. Francis Xavier Church in Poseyville in 1947, and of their marriage, three children were born. Thelman, has been, and still is, associated with the family-owned Poseyville Grain and Feed Company. ... Rita Clair married Harry Kuhlman of Cleveland, OH, in 1953 and subsequently took up residence first in Indianapolis, and for the past 30 years, have lived in Kokomo, IN. They have five children. Harry is deceased. ... Robert married Kathryn Bayer at St. Anthony Catholic Church, Evansville, IN, in 1953. They have five daughters. Since their marriage, Robert and Kathryn have resided in Poseyville on N. Cale Street.

The paternal ancestors (Hirsch Family) settled in Gibson Co., IN, in 1848, coming from the village of Heilingenstein, Rheinbagern (on the Rhine) in Germany. ...The Ziliak Family came from the town of Mulhousen, in Alsace, near the borders of Germany, France and Switzerland. The Ziliak Family settled in Vanderburgh Co., IN, also in 1848. ..."Respect the past, to live better in the present, with a view to the future."!

ALBERT MORRIS AND GLOANNA DIXON HODGES

Morris, born Sept. 28, 1928, moved to Posey County, Point Township, at the age of two, from Providence, KY with his parents, Albert Jennings Hodges and Virgia Lorene Harkins and sister, Laura Elizabeth. His grandparents, were Albert Hayes and Elizabeth Jennings Hodges; maternal grandparents, Thomas and Laura Price Harkins. His ancestors came west from the Carolinas through Cumberland Gap.

Gloanna, born Jan. 5, 1931, daughter of Douglas Dixon and Lola Deuischer, is eldest granddaughter of John Oscar Dixon, Point Township, listed in 1913 Posey County History, of early John Welborn - John Dixon families.

Children of Morris and Gloanna Hedges 1963, Marcie, four years, Douglas three years, David, two years, Gayle one year.

Mother, Lola, was daughter of William Thomas Deuischer, whose father came from Germany. Lola's mother, Lela Thomas, was daughter of Enoch Thomas and Esther Moore-early Thomas and Noel families. Lola's brother, Lloyd Edward Deuischer, was killed, Dec. 1, 1944, in World War II in France.

July 27, 1952 Gloanna and Morris were married. 1950-51 Morris was in Army in Korean conflict. After army discharge, he worked at Servel Inc., later Indiana Farm Bureau Oil and Refinery. For ten years after school, Gloanna worked in Evansville as oil accountant. May 7, 1958 daughter, Marcia Ann born. June 20, 1959 son, Douglas Morris. December 20, 1960 son, David Albert. February 17, 1962 daughter, Gayle Sue.

1963 Morris helped people with their automatic clothes washers after regular work hours. 1967 Hodges Repair Shop began after Homer Tomlinson died, the dealer for RCA-Whirlpool appliances. Hodges became the dealer for Whirlpool white goods appliances and Maytag.

Gloanna is receptionist-bookkeeper while Morris sells, repairs and delivers appliances. The children helped in business as they were growing up and attended Indiana State University Evansville now University of Southern Indiana.

Marcia graduated 1979 and became Certified Public Accountant. She worked in Indianapolis; then returned to Posey County and worked for Haynie Travel Service, Evansville.

Douglas received ISUE Business Associate degree and now employed by Evansville Appliance Parts. June 25, 1983 Douglas married Debra Ferguson and lives in Evansville. Debra, a graduate of ISUE, is personnel director for Gertha's Nursing Center.

David graduated ISUE, engineer in Technology degree and is employed by Southern Indiana Gas & Electric Co. as engineering service representative.

Gayle graduated 1983, passed certified public accountant exam and employed by Bristol-Myers USNPG (Mead Johnson) in Accounting Dept. July 23, 1988 Gayle married James Howard Priest III, who she met in Business classes at ISUE. He is certified Public accountant at Gaither, Koewler, Rohlfer & Luckett Co., Evansville. His parents live in Vanderburgh County.

July 27, 1985 Marcia married Robert Wayne Schneider, son of John Doerr Schneider and Coquella Daphane Ogles Schneider. Robert's paternal grandmother was Mary Jane Redman (Point Township) - early Redman - John Welborn families. Robert is 1980 Purdue graduate in landscape management.

September 21, 1988 Marcia and Robert had a son, John Albert Schneider.

CECILIA AND HERMAN C. HOEHN

Cecilia Maurer and Herman C. Hoehn were married at Saint Matthew Catholic Church in Mt. Vernon on Feb. 10, 1914 and moved to their home at Grafton in Black Township, Posey County. Herman was the only son of Charles Hoehn and Mary Ann Black. He was born in the family home in Lynn Township in 1894. His father came from Germany with his parents in 1853 as a six week old infant. The son of Blaze and Josephine Pfister Hoehn was a farmer all his life. Mary Ann Black was a native of Posey County.

Cecilia Maurer born in 1890, was a daughter of Simon Maurer and Isabelle Betz. Isabelle was born

Cecilia and Herman C. Hoehn

in St. Wendell and Simon was born in Armstrong, IN. He was born and raised in a grocery store.

Herman and Cecilia had 11 children, Mary Louise, Herman C. Jr., Joseph Edward, Simon Blaze, Pauline, Dorothy J., Teresa, Clarissa D., Paul James, Agnes Ann and Pat.

Mary Louise was born Jan. 14, 1915 and married Floyd French in 1970. He was a Lynn Township farmer.

Herman C. Jr. was born Oct. 4, 1916 and died 1978. He married Geraldine F. Thomson in 1953. He served in the U.S. Army, 1942 to 1945, and was discharged as a Sergeant. They had 13 children: Charles Wm. married to Tamara Anderson with children - Seth and Aaron, Andrew Francis married Nancy Herron, children- Andrew Jr., Lindsay, Keren, and Jeffrey, John Anthony married Anita Kizee, children - Joseph and Benjamin, Martha Jean married Paul Breeze, children - Sarah and Lauren, Mary Jane married Bill Rhoades, children - Carly, Dennis Michael married to Denise Kay Wagner, Pauline Cecilia married Scott Gerard, children - Cecelia Jane and Alexander, Joan Elizabeth married Mahammed Khajo, children - Janon, Daniel Martin, Christin Ann, Carl Louis, Matthew Herman and Janet Marie, all single.

Joseph Edward was born Sept. 2, 1918 and died May 17, 1986. He married Hazel M. Reeves in 1945 after serving in the U.S. Army from 1942 to 1945. They had six children: Rita M. married Charles Mansfield, Sharon Irene married David Miller, children - Susan Diane and Adam Anthony, Paul James married Janet Lynn Perry, children - Ryan Patrick, Nicholas Scott and Traci Lynn, Mary Ann married Michael Shrode, Teresa Louise married Dale Spivey, children - Damon Dale and Christopher Joseph, James Herman married, first, Sherri Lynn Toelle, children - Shannon, second, Sherry Lynn Carey, children - Joseph James and Justin Ashley, third, Tammy Gayle Barnes, children - Bret Andrew and Kelley Nichole, fourth Kim Maybee. Hazel died May 26, 1986.

Simon Blaze, born in 1920, married Patti Lou Henn in 1950. They had three children: Timothy George - single, Thomas Blaze married Deana Lou Head, children - Susan Deane and Simon Blaze, Toni Lou married Bryan Keith Lyke, children - Jason Andrew and Joshua Lee.

Pauline, born in 1922, entered the Benedictine Convent on Sept. 8, 1943 and became Sister Irene. She is now a retired teacher.

Dorothy J., born in 1924, married Charles A. Weinzapfel in 1952. They had six children: Mary Jo married Donald Musgrave, children - Jeremy, Tyler and Ryan, Steven married Vandra Rialdo, children - Sarah and Stephanie, Michael and Barbara are single, Martha married Tom Dick and had one daughter - Julia, and Rosemary married David Del Toro.

Teresa, born in 1926, entered the Benedictine Convent on Sept. 8, 1945, and became Sister Mary Sharon. She was a teacher for 30 years and is now in Chicago.

Clarissa D., born in 1927, married Frank M. Parrish in 1957. Their four children are: Kathy Ann married David R. Nelson, Carolyn Marie married Jonathan D. Mason, children - Nicholas James and Christopher Dane, Martin Joseph is single and Nancy Louise married Michael D. Marshall.

Paul James was born and died in 1929.

Agnes Ann was born in 1932 and is a retired nurse.

Pat was born in 1933 and married Loretta Goebel Feb. 15, 1958. They have five children: Benny married Kathleen Elpers, children - Kayla Nicole, Kurt Owen, and Kelsey Jo; Mark married Edith Meinert. Linda married Donald Martin, children - Brooke Amanda, Matthew Henderson and Daniel Coty; Donna married Gerald Goebel; Julia is single. Pat served in the U.S. Army as a Sergeant. He and his sons are farming the old home place.

DON AND LEE ANN HOENERT

Don and Lee Ann Hoenert reside in an early 1900s two-story remodeled farmhouse in Robinson Township. They were married Feb. 24, 1963 at St. Paul's United Methodist Church in Poseyville. Their children are Tim, born July 22, 1964; Greg, born June 20, 1967; Shelly, born Oct. 28, 1968; and Beth, born Aug. 27, 1971.

Tim married Johlene Boring Aug. 6, 1988 at Carrollton United Methodist Church in Carrollton, IN. Tim earned a B.S. in Agricultural Engineering from Purdue University. Tim farms with his father. Johlene, also a graduate of Purdue, is an accountant at SIGECO. Greg and Shelly both attend Purdue University and Beth attends North Posey High School.

Donald William, born May 8, 1939, is the son of Harold and Ethelene (Brandt) Hoenert. He attended grades 1-4 at Hartman School and grades 5-8 at Martin School. He graduated from Mt. Vernon High School in 1957 and Purdue University's Short Course in 1961. Following in his father's and many of his ancestors' footsteps, Don is a swine and grain farmer.

Front Row: Beth Hoenert; Middle: Left: Johlene Hoenert, Right: Shelly Hoenert; Back Row: Left to Right: Tim, Lee Ann, Don, and Greg Hoenert

Harold and Ethelene were married Nov. 24, 1937 in the home of Ethelene's parents on Peters Road in rural Wadesville. Ethelene, born May 9, 1913, was the only child of William and Katherine (Damm) Brandt. Ethelene's grandfather, Simon Brandt, came to America from Minden, Germany when he was eight years old. Simon married Lousia Schroeder May 8, 1881. Louisa's mother, Anna (Berger), was born in West Phalia, Germany and her father, Frederick, was from Exter, Germany.

Harold, the fourth son of Frederick and Magdalena (Roedel) Hoenert, was born on May 12, 1915. Harold died Oct. 21, 1963 in a farming accident. Harold's grandfather, Conrad Hoenert came from Detmold, Germany when he was ten. Conrad possessed another skill in addition to farming. He wrote a poem in memory of his mother's death, a copy of which is still in the family.

Lee Ann Caroline was born Apr. 18, 1940, the daughter of Clarence and Meta (Espenlaub) Mahrenholz. She graduated from Poseyville High School in 1958. She earned a B.S. in Home Economics from Indiana State University in 1962 and a M.Ed. in 1985. Lee Ann is a home economics teacher at New Harmony School.

Clarence and Meta were married Dec. 20, 1928. Meta, the fifth child of eight of Herman and Sophia (Donner) Espenlaub, was born May 12, 1906. She died Dec. 15, 1987. Meta's great-grandparents, Henry and Barbara (Baumann) Donner, immigrated from Wurtenburg, Germany in 1839. Henry, who was a mechanic, purchased a farm in Robinson Township.

Clarence, born Nov. 22, 1904, is a retired farmer. Clarence's father, Fred Adolph, married Caroline Tiemann Apr. 25, 1893. Fred's brother owned the ground that the University of Southern Indiana is built on. A lane to the apartments is called Mahrenholz Lane.

Clarence's grandparents, Frederick Ludwig and Sophia (Nagel) Mahrenholz, came to the United States in 1850 from Ohlendorf, Germany to escape religious oppression. A little town with the name of Mahrenholz is located in northern Germany. Fredericks' father, Henry was a linen weaver in Germany.

All of Don and Lee Ann's ancestors came from Germany and have settled in southern Indiana where they have remained over the years.

HORACEK-ALLBRITTON

David E. and Maryhelen Horacek Allbritton are residents of Clearwater, FL. Maryhelen is a native of Mount Vernon, IN, a graduate of MVHS (1972) and the youngest daughter of Thomas E. and Ilse Horacek, who are mentioned elsewhere in this book. Maryhelen married David in 1976, graduated with a B.A. degree from Eckerd College in St. Petersburg, FL, in 1983 and is employed as a guidance counselor and occupational specialist at Tarpon Springs High School, in Tarpon Springs, FL. Through her grandmother, Cecil Thomas Horacek (1892-1967), Maryhelen is a descendant of the Thomas, Eblin and York families who pioneered Posey County around 1813. These early settlers came from Pennsylvania, North Carolina and Tennessee. Her maternal roots are German; her grandfather still lived in Germany at the time of this writing.

David, son of Attorney Owen and Peggy Allbritton, is a native of Clearwater and a fourth generation Floridian. His father is judge of Pinellas County Circuit Court. His mother is a descendant of the Estes family who spent many years in Puerto Rico, and Columbia, South America. Her father was regional V.P. for the Singer Sewing Machine Company.

David graduated from Clearwater High School (1969) and attended North Carolina Wesleyan College in Rocky Mount, NC. He is a building contractor and operates Designwise Building Contractors Inc.

Maryhelen and David are the parents of twins, John Daniel and Jennifer Elyse, born in 1987. David Justin, a son of David's previous marriage, born in 1972, also lives with them. The Allbrittons are members of the First Methodist Church in Clearwater. *Submitted by Ilse Horacek*

HORACEK-ANGEL

Dennis E. Angel and Constance J. Horacek were married in August 1971, at Black's Chapel Methodist Church in Posey County.

Dennis, born in 1950, is the oldest son of Jack and Wanda Angel; their biography appears elsewhere in this book. He is a descendant of the Row(e) family who settled in McFadden's Bluff in 1809. One of the early Rowes is credited with changing the town's name to Mount Vernon. Dennis graduated from MVHS in 1968, and served with the U.S. Army for three years, serving time in Korea. For 15 years he was associated with his grandfather, Everett Ashworth, in farming the Ashworth farm on Ashford Road in Posey County. Since his grandfather's death, Dennis is owner of the farm. He and his three sons work 900 acres of land and raise a herd of beef cattle. He has two brothers, Stephan Angel, of Chicago, IL, and Jeff Angel of Posey County.

Connie, born in 1951, is the oldest daughter of Thomas E. and Ilse Horacek. Their family history is recorded in this book also. She has spent her entire life in Posey County. A graduate of MVHS, class of 1970, she also graduated from Lockyear's School of Business in 1972. She is associated with her husband in farming, drives a school bus, and is employed at the Posey County Recorder's office. Through her paternal ancestors she is a descendant of the Thomas, Eblin and York pioneer families who settled in Posey County around 1813. Connie's maternal ancestors were residents of Germany. Her 89-year-old grandfather is still living in Munich, Germany, at the time of this writing. Connie has one brother, Roger T. Horacek of Posey County, and one sister, Maryhelen Allbritton of Clearwater, FL.

Dennis and Connie Angel are parents of twins, Christopher Scott and Bryan Neal, born in 1973, and Brock Edward, born in 1974. The three teenagers farm with their father and attend Mount Vernon High School. *Submitted by Ilse Horacek*

HORACEK-JACKSON

Roger Thomas Horacek and Peggy Lee Jackson were married October 1969 at Olive Chapel Methodist Church in Posey County.

Roger, born in 1948, is the oldest son of Thomas E. and Ilse Horacek. Their biography appears elsewhere in this book. He is named after his great-grandfather, Roger Robinson Thomas, who was a grandson of Posey County pioneers James Thomas and Mary Eblin. (They were of Welsh origin. Mary's father fought in the Revolutionary War. The Thomases were Quakers. They settled in Posey County in 1813.) Roger's great-grandfather Horacek was a native of Prague, Czechoslavakia. He and his family emigrated to Chicago, IL, around 1880.

Roger graduated from MVHS in 1966, and from Vincennes University School of Printing in 1967. He fought with the 25th Infantry Division in Vietnam and was awarded the Purple Heart. Following his discharge from the Army, Roger graduated from Lockyear's College in Evansville and has been employed by the Mount Vernon post office for 14 years.

He has two sisters, Connie Angel, of Mount

Vernon, and Maryhelen Allbritton, of Clearwater, FL.

Peggy, born in 1949, is the oldest daughter of Roy Lee and Lillie Mae Bishop Jackson of Posey County. Her father's family came to this county from Tennessee. Peggy's mother is a native of Birmingham, AL; she spent most of her childhood in North Carolina. Peggy graduated from MVHS in 1967. For five years she was employed as a teller by People's Bank and Trust Company in Mount Vernon. Since 1986 she is an employee of General Electric. She has two sisters, Patricia Ann Adkins, of Crestview, FL, and Juanita Lynn Jackson, of Mount Vernon.

There are three sons in the Horacek family. Roger Thomas II, born in 1973, attends MVHS at the time of this writing. Robert Shane was born in 1978, and Rodney Lee in 1979. The Roger Horacek family's home is on a ten acre tract of land on the Springfield Road in Posey County. *Submitted by Ilse Horacek*

THOMAS E. AND ILSE HORACEK

Thomas Eugene (Gene) Horacek and Ilse Dorsch met in Munich, Germany in 1945 while Gene was with the U.S. Army. They were married in 1947 in Morganfield, KY, and have since then resided in Mount Vernon.

Gene was born 1920 in Mount Vernon. His mother, Cecil Thomas Horacek was the daughter of Carrie York and Roger Robinson Thomas and a descendant of the Thomas-Eblin pioneer families who came to Posey County from Pennsylvania and Tennessee in 1813. Among this family were early Posey County legislators, mayors and sheriffs. They were of Welsh descent and Quakers. The York family settled in this county in 1812, coming from Randolph Co., PA. They originated in Yorkshire, England. Cecil Thomas (1892-1967) married Peter Thomas Horacek (1890-1969) in 1919. The Horaceks emigrated from Prague, Czechoslavakia, to the U.S. around 1880 and settled in Chicago.

Ilse Horacek

Gene grew up in Mount Vernon, graduated from MVHS in 1938 and from Lockyear's Business College in Evansville in 1941. He served with the U.S. Army during World War II. Following his discharge he was employed at the Mount Vernon post office as a rural mail carrier until he retired in 1978.

Ilse, born in 1930 in Munich, Germany, to Konrad and Thea Dorsch, came to Mount Vernon in 1947 as a war bride. She became a U.S. citizen in 1953. Her mother died in Munich in 1985; her ashes were buried at Beech Grove Cemetery in Posey County. Ilse's father still lives in Munich and is a frequent visitor in Mount Vernon. Ilse is active as a genealogist and historian and writes for the Mount Vernon Democrat.

Gene and Ilse have three married children: Roger Thomas Horacek, Constance Jean Angel, and Maryhelen Allbritton; they and their families are mentioned elsewhere in this book. There are also eight grandsons and one granddaughter in this family. The Horacek's second son, John Daniel Horacek, died in 1953 at the age of three years. *Submitted by Ilse Horacek*

CATHARINE LOUISE HOWARD

Catharine L. Howard, the daughter of Silas Greene and Catharine Mann Howard was born in Mount Vernon, at 711 Mill Street on Aug 16, 1903. Her father's family came to Mount Vernon about 1872 from Obion Co, TN. The Mann family emigrated from Gaugrehweiler, Rheinpfalz, Germany, in 1858 and settled in Mount Vernon in the early 1860's.

Catharine has lived her entire life in this city. She graduated from Mount Vernon High School in 1921 and graduated from Indiana University in 1925. In 1936 she received her Master's degree in education from I.U. At I.U. she was a member of Delta Zeta social sorority, I.U. Memorial Committee and a member of International Student Club. As a Latin major she was also active in the Classical Club. For two years she was appointed to the council of the YWCA and in her senior year was YWCA president. As a junior she was elected to Mortar Board, an honorary organization based on campus activities and scholarship.

Catharine L. Howard

Following her graduation from I.U. she taught Latin, English and speech at MVHS from 1925 though 1968. In 1928-29 she organized the first dramatic club, called the Footlight Performers. She instituted a chapter of National Thespian and served as the society's southern Indiana representative.

As head of the English department she developed a curriculum that received recognition from Indiana colleges. She was invited to serve on the Indiana English Curriculum Committee and the Executive Board of Indiana Council of Teachers of English.

She has been a member of Sunbeam Chapter No. 1 of the Order of the Eastern star since 1921 and is a past matron. She was elected to the first board of the Greater Mount Vernon Association. As a member of Kappa Kappa Kappa she held offices in both active and associated chapters. She served as Province One officer for southwestern Indiana. For five years she served on the Tri Kappa State Constitution Committee and scholarship committees.

Catharine is a life-long member of Trinity United Church of Christ and has held active positions in Sunday School, council and women's work.

She is a member of two honorary professional groups: Delta Kappa Gamma, and Pi Lamba Theta.

Locally she served on the Alexandrian Library Board and is a member of Tuesday Club. She has also been actively involved in the University of Evansville Theatre League and the Good Samaritan Home auxiliary.

During the last 15 years of her retirement she has been moderately active in her former organizations. She also has written the stories of her Mann and Howard ancestors. She spends her time reading, visiting with friends and maintains an active correspondence with hundreds of her former students.

STOY AND MARY ELLIOTT HUGHES

Stoy and Mary Elliott Hughes, Rt. 5, Mt. Vernon, IN, lifelong residents of Point Township in Posey County. Parents of four children; Dewey Hughes, Sandra Hughes Winiger, Karen Hughes Bauer and Robin Hughes. Fourteen grandchildren; Tracey Hughes Carson Dewey, Douglas Dustin and Devlin Hughes of Hudson, FL. Stoy, Kelly and Sabrina Winiger Schelhorn, Ka Lee, Debroa, Denyse Bauer, Matthew and Mary Bauer deceased, Jay Goodman, GGC, Shay Hughes, Criston Carson, Joshua and Justin Winiger, Zachary, Matthew and Kayce Winiger.

Stoy, 2nd son of Ed and Pearl Yeida Hughes; 1st son, Kelly Hughes, daughter Medea Louise, deceased.

Mary, 3rd daughter of Willard and Mae Drew Elliott; 1st and 2nd daughters deceased also 1st and 2nd sons deceased.

Stoy and Mary celebrated their 50th wedding anniversary in 1988.

Sandra Hughes married Arthur Winiger, Jr. Karen Hughes married D.L. Bauer (deceased). Dewey Hughes married Sharon Burks, Robin Hughes married J.C. Goodman (divorced).

JAMES

Samuel L. and Francis Randolph James lived in Bardstown, KY, in the late 1790s. They were the parents of two sons: Enoch R., born 1800, and Thomas R., born 1802, both in Bardstown. These two young men married sisters, Esther S. Lowry in 1822 and Anna Lowry in 1823 respectively.

Enoch R. and Esther moved to Louisiana, then returned to Mt. Vernon in the early years of the town's history. They had five children: Lawrence, Dewitt, Juliet, Mary, and Cornelia, some of whom were believed born in Mt. Vernon. Several years later, Mary married the Honorable Alvin P. Hovey, a prominent lawyer of Mt. Vernon. Mr. Hovey was elected to one term as Governor of Indiana but was killed as a result of injuries in a train wreck. In addition to a steamboat operation, Enoch R. was involved in real estate in Mt. Vernon. He had a hand in many subdivisions, and many deeds and abstracts, as well as a street in Mt. Vernon, carry his name. He was granted a bank charter and he and his sons, Lawrence and Dewitt, operated a bank for a period of years. He was a member of the board of directors that built 15 miles of plank road between Mt. Vernon and New Harmony. He also carried the rank of Colonel during the Civil War and was in charge of a few hundred troops with headquarters in Mt. Vernon. They saw no real action, but did a lot of guard and patrol duty along the Ohio River, fearing the Southern Army would raid across the river. He served as City Councilman, and performed other civic duties, as well as serving one term as State Senator.

Back Row - Luther James; Middle Row - Mary (James) Boyer, Anna James (McCoy), James James, Nellie (James) Terrell; Front Row - Betty James - Later (Searcy and Seiler) and Maurice James.

Thomas R. and Anna also moved to Louisiana where they had two children: a daughter whose name is possibly Margaret Jane born in 1826 and a son, Thomas R. Jr. born 1827. Thomas Sr. died in 1827 leaving two small children. Anna died in 1867. There is no other record of Margaret. Thomas Jr. came to Mt. Vernon to live with his uncle, Enoch R. He was educated at Depauw University of Central Indiana, the first college west of the Allegheney Mountains. He was given a job as shipping clerk on one of the six combination freight and passenger steamers operated by Enoch R. on the Ohio and Mississippi Rivers between Cincinnati, OH, and New Orleans, LA. He then set out on his own and in 1859 married Olive M. Beckley and returned to Mt. Vernon. They purchased three acres of land which is still held by his grandson. They built a log home and had six children: Alvin H. born 1863, James born 1864, John born 1867, Annie born 1869, Lawrence born 1873, and Maggie born 1878. During his lifetime, Thomas Jr. taught school in the area and served as Justice of the Peace. Thomas Jr. died in 1895 and Olive died in 1918. Their son Alvin H. James married Annie Smith and had four children. Lawrence married but had no children. John never married. Annie married Sherman York and had seven children. Maggie died at age 15.

James James married Anna McCoy in 1889 and they had five children: Luther born 1891, Mary born 1893, Nellie born 1898, Betty born 1905, and Maurice born 1909. James died in 1946 followed by Anna in 1950. Their son Luther married Pauline Williams and had a son Albert Luther born 1914. Albert Luther married Edith Haughey and they had four children: James, William, Mary Beth, and Ellen. His son James had two sons who are the only ones to carry on the James surname. Albert Luther later remarried to Edith's sister, Esther Haughey. Luther died in 1946. Mary married James Boyer and had four children: Malcom, James (who was a POW in WWII), Dorothy born 1924 who later married an Overton, and Frederick born 1926. Mary died in 1931. Nellie married Arthur Terrell and had nine children: Kenneth Leroy, Edgar, Juanita, Anna Ruth, Glen, Robert Eugene, Frances Sue, Billie, and Donny. Nellie died in 1953. Betty married Roy Searcy in 1923 and they had five children Evelyn Marjorie born 1924, Everett Ray born 1926, Alvin Luther born 1928, Paul Edwin born 1930, and Emil Eugene 1934. Roy Searcy died in 1952 and Betty remarried in 1958 to John W. Sailer. Betty continues to live in Posey County. Maurice married Mildred Garner in 1929 and they presently live on James Street in Mt. Vernon.

Most of Betty's five children, 12 grandchildren, ten great-grandchildren, and two great-great-grandsons continue to reside in Posey County.

Evelyn married Royvan McKinnies in 1941 and they had three children: Betty Ann born 1942, Van Lee "Chip" born 1946, and Danny Ray who died in infancy in 1947. Betty Ann married Arthur Stierley, Jr. in 1961 and they have three children. Terri Lynn born 1962 married David Koch in 1983 and they have one son, Christopher David born 1986. Vicki Lee born 1965 married Orvel Schroeder in 1986 and they have one son, Patrick Benjamin born 1989. Randy Ray born 1966 married Anita Murphy in 1985. Van Lee married Bonnie Tomlinson in 1983 and she has one son, Ken Wayne born 1966.

Everett married Alice Summers in 1946 and they had three children: Donna Faye born 1951, Linda Ruth born 1955, and Everett Ray Jr. born 1960. Donna married James Delancy in 1974 and they have two children: Gregory James born 1976, and Crystal Faye born 1982. Linda married Casey Jay Almond in 1974, and they have two children: Tiffany Lynn born 1978, and Jarod Casey born in 1988.

Alvin married Dorothy Brandt in 1951 and they have two children: Deborah Susan born 1954, and Cynthia Lynn born 1961.

Paul married Sadie Chaplin in 1952 and they have four children: Kathy Louise born in 1953, Stephen Paul born in 1955, Roy Eugene born in 1957, and Dennis James born in 1964. Stephen married Jayne Usher in 1977 and they have one son, Nathan Stephen born 1986. Roy married Ruth Johnson in 1979 and they have two children, Timothy Robert born in 1981, and Jackie Lynn born in 1984. Dennis married Stephanie Cohoon in 1988.

Emil married Anna Marie Benthall in 1955 and they had two children: Brian Daryl born 1960 who died as a child in 1967, and Nelda Fay born in 1964.

EVELYN FITZGERRELL JENKINS

Evelyn Fitzgerrell Jenkins was born Dec. 20, 1907. She is the youngest of four children born to Daniel Graham Fitzgerrell and Mary Almira Turpen. Her sisters were Dalpha Fitzgerrell Gale and Fay Fitzgerrell Wiley. A brother James Daniel died at the age 11. Dalpha married Virgil Edgar Gale Sept. 29, 1923 and their one child, George Graham Gale married Dorothy Inglis of Evansville. They live in Whitter, CA. Fay married Fred D. Wiley in 1916, and were the parents of three children. Their one surviving child, James D. is married to Patricia Garrett and lives near New Harmony. Evelyn went to Oakland City College and Indiana State College at Terre Haute, then began her teaching career in Stewartsville. She taught there three years and was transferred to Poseyville where she continued teaching for 42 years until her retirement in 1972. She married Carl Jenkins July 26, 1945. Carl was born Dec. 13, 1902, died May 10, 1966. He was the son of George Jenkins and Anna Carroll Jenkins of Gibson County. Carl, also a teacher, taught 33 of his 37 years at New Harmony. Evelyn resides north of Poseyville in the house built for her grandfather, Daniel Fitzgerrell, in 1879.

Evelyn's great-grandfather, James Fitzgerrell was born in 1777, married Elizabeth Ray May 10, 1810. They came to Indiana in 1814, first to Gibson County, then to Robb Township where they purchased their first land in 1831. James and Elizabeth were the parents of 14 children, nine boys and five girls. Evelyn's grandfather, Daniel was their tenth child. He married Harriet Lisbia Graham Aug. 13, 1826. They were the parents of eight children, Evelyn's father, Daniel Graham, the youngest child was born Mar. 8, 1867. He married Mary Almira Turpen Jan. 7, 1892. The daughter of James and Mariah Durham Turpen, she was born Jan. 9, 1866. James Turpen was the son of Solomon and Susannah Turpen of Warrick County. Mariah Durham was kidnapped as a young child and nothing is known of her ancestry. The Daniel Grahams Fitzgerrells began their married life in a log cabin near the present house, and their first child, Dalpha, was born there.

Evelyn's great grandmother, Elizabeth Ray is a descendant of the Lewis Family of Langlesly, England. William Lewis was Justice of the Peace and High Sheriff of Langlesly, 1549, 1557, and 1572. He was also a member of Parliament.

THE WILLIAM F. JOEST FAMILY - WADESVILLE

Josephine A. Seibert Joest was born on Feb. 19, 1906, on a farm in the Mt. Pleasant area near Poseyville. Josephine was one of nine children born to John Seibert and Elizabeth Gries Seibert. John Seibert emigrated from Germany to the St. Wendel area in 1889. Elizabeth Gries was born in 1872 near St. Wendel. John and Elizabeth were married in 1893.

William F. Joest was born May 3, 1899, on a farm east of Wadesville. William was one of eight children born to Leonard John Joest and Margaret Koch Joest. Leonard John, the son of Leonard and Elizabeth Effinger Joest, was born in a log house in Wadesville. In 1869 the family moved to a farm east of Wadesville purchased from William Watson. Leonard and Margaret were married in 1892 and purchased the family farm in 1894.

William graduated in 1917 from Wadesville High School. After serving in the US Army in World War I, Bill left the family farm to attend Lockyear College in Evansville. After graduation, he was employed at Servel. Although he enjoyed his job, he longed to return to farming. William used the money he had saved to buy the William Forcum farm in 1923.

William and Josephine were married May 10, 1927. They became the parents of four children, LaVerne, Bill, Mary Ann and Jerome.

William and Josephine were among the first Posey County farmers to use lime and fertilizer to improve their crops. During the Great Depression, while Josephine kept the farm running with the help of their children and hired hands, Lawrence and Pete Koch, William worked in Soil Conservation in the county agent's office in Mt. Vernon. He helped introduce such concepts as crop management and terracing to Posey County farmers.

William was also instrumental along with Jim Wiggins, Floyd Moye, Floyd LaDuke, Aloys and Joe Denning, among others, in forming the Posey County Farm Bureau. Josephine was a member of the Wadesville Ladies Farm Bureau Chorus which traveled to the Indiana State Fair and on Sept. 10, 1939, these 21 women sang their way to first prize.

In 1951, Bill and Josephine purchased the original Joest family farm from the heirs. Then in 1953 they bought the William Strauss farm to complete the Joest family farm.

William was appointed a Posey County councilman in the early 1950s and served until the mid-1960s. In a Mt. Vernon newspaper editorial, Bill was lauded for his efforts on behalf of his constituents.

William and Josephine retired from active farming in 1961. Today only the infirmities of old age have restricted their activities. As the oldest of 22 grandchildren and 25-great grandchildren, I am proud to call them "Grandma and Grandpa." *Written by Judith Holder O'Leary*

JOHNSON-GRABERT

Charles Thomas Johnson III and Mary Blanche Grabert were married Sept. 21, 1935, in St. Louis, MO. They have two children, Sara Ann and David Michael.

Mary Blanche was born in Mount Vernon, Oct. 21, 1914, to Andrew J. Grabert (1878-1940) and Minnie Stahl Grabert (1879-1919). She attended local schools, graduating from MVHS in 1932. Her father, Andrew J. Grabert (1878-1940), was the eldest of ten sons born to George Michael Grabert (1841-1919) and Louisa Susick Grabert (1857-1947). Louisa came to this country from Germany with her mother and two brothers, Charles and Frederich, when she was about six years of age. George Michael Grabert, a native of Wuerttemberg, Germany, was a large land owner in Black Township at the turn of the century and one of the early founders of Trinity Church. Mary B.'s mother, Minnie Stahl Grabert (1879-1919), was the daughter of Daniel E. and Mary Blanche Moore Stahl. Daniel Stahl came to Posey County from Boonesboro, MD; his ancestry going back to Daniel Boone. Mary Blanche Moore was the daughter of Solomon Moore (1828-1875) and his first wife, nee Mary Keelin (1826-1868), of Black Township.

Charles T. Johnson III (1914-1973) was the son of Charles T. Johnson, Jr. (1890-1958), a captain in the U.S. Army during both World Wars, and Inez L. Williams Johnson (1890-1975). His maternal grandparents were John S. and Lizzie May Smith Williams. His paternal grandparents were Charles T. Johnson, Sr. (1866-1933) and Deirdre Duff Johnson (1878-1956). Charles T. Johnson, Sr., was a prominent Mount Vernon business man and civic leader. The Johnsons entertained Franklin D. and Eleanor Roosevelt in their home in Mount Vernon during the Roosevelt's campaign trip in 1920.

Charles T. Johnson III graduated from Mount Vernon High School in 1931. After graduating from Stinson School of Aviation, in Long Island, he enlisted in the U.S. Marine Corps and saw action in the South Pacific during World War II. Following his discharge, he graduated from Purdue University in 1949 with a ME degree. He was a member of the Masonic Lodge in Bradford, PA. Mr. and Mrs. Johnson have lived also in New Jersey and Illinois. While they lived in Akron, OH, in 1973, Mr. Johnson passed away. After living for several years in Lake Zurich, IL, Mary Blanche Johnson returned to her native Mount Vernon in 1988.

JOHNSON-McFADIN

Georgia Irene Johnson was born in Black Township, Posey County on Jan. 23, 1920, the third daughter of George E. and Pauline (Gaiser) McFadin. Irene attended Upton School and graduated from Mt. Vernon Senior High in 1937. She obtained a degree from Lockyear Secretarial School in 1938. She was a medical secretary in Evansville, IN for 20 years. During the WWII years she was a civilian cadette with the USO. She enjoys playing the piano and listening to big band music. Irene helped her parents by working at their family owned furniture store in Mt. Vernon from June of 1947 to March of 1960.

On Feb. 26, 1956 Irene married Leo Curtis Johnson at Mt. Vernon, IN. Leo, known to his friends as "John" was born on July 25, 1917 at

"Leo" John and Irene Johnson

Waverly, OH to Joseph and Alice (Steiner) Johnson.

John served in the United States Navy eight years and went around the world twice by ship. He was one of only a few survivors of his ship at the invasion of Pearl Harbor. He was then in the United States Coast Guard for four years and was on the "Voice of America" ship. After his marriage he worked in the construction field, drove a Greyhound bus and before his retirement in 1979 worked for Babcock and Wilcox for 16 years.

On June 1, 1980 John died of cancer in Evansville, IN. He is buried in the Welborn Cemetery. Irene continues to reside at her family's homeplace on Upton Road, Mt. Vernon.

The Johnsons were members of Trinity United Church of Christ in Mt. Vernon. John was a member of the Evansville VFW #1114 and Irene is a member of that auxiliary.

ROBERT A. AND PATRICIA M. JOHNSON

Robert A. and Patricia M. Johnson are residents of Harmony Township. Robert was born in the house in which they live. Sixty acres of this farm have been in the Johnson family for six generations, since before the 1811 earthquake in this area. The home presently occupied was built in the early 1900s.

Robert was born in 1921. He is the son of Dr. Arthur L. and Lula (Barrett) Johnson. He attended school and graduated from New Harmony High School in 1939. Robert, like his father and other Johnson ancestors, has raised beef cattle as well as feed crops until recent years. His father, Arthur L., a veterinarian, was born in 1885. His wife, Lula, was born in 1884 at the Barrett Homestead near Stewartsville, IN. They were married in 1908. Robert's sister, Lela (Johnson) Grey and her husband, Harold Mel Grey also live in Harmony Township. Lela, a retired teacher, taught in New Harmony, NY and at Eastern Illinois University at Charleston, IL. Lela and Robert's brother, George William Johnson (deceased) was married to Juanita (Doss) Johnson. Their son Barrett George Johnson and his wife Merry Ann (McCullum) Johnson reside in Tallahassee, FL. Their two children are George Jett and Jennifer.

Robert's ancestors who have resided in Harmony Township are his grandfather, William Jett Johnson whose wife was Cassandra (Randolph) Johnson, great grandfather Elias Johnson, Jr., great great grandfather Elias Johnson, Sr. and great great great grandfather Moses Johnson, who came to Harmony Township from Virginia by way of Kentucky.

Robert's maternal grandparents were George M. Barrett and his wife Mary Louise (Schneck) Barrett of Stewartsville, IN. George M. Barrett was a Civil War cavalryman whose faithful horse named Fly was his steed in all the battles and skirmishes in which George M. Barrett took part. The horse lived to the amazing age of 37 years. Old Fly's skeleton is part of a museum display at the New Harmony Workingmen's Institute.

The Barrett Homestead property near Stewartsville is presently owned by Barrett George Johnson. This land was part of land purchased from the United States government in the presidency of Andrew Jackson.

Patricia M. (Hallinan) Johnson was born in Evansville and attended school there, graduating from the University of Evansville. She has been a teacher and volleyball and track coach in the Evansville Vanderburgh School System. She stopped teaching in 1983 after teaching 37 years at Reitz High School.

Her parents were James Michael Hallinan and Agnes C. (Hoing) Hallinan. Her father was born in Evansville and her mother in Darmstadt, IN. She has one sister, Joan (Hallinan) Croce, a teacher in West Germany at the Ramstein Air Base. Joan has two daughters and two sons. Patricia's deceased brother James Edward Hallinan and his wife Betty Jo (Logel) Hallinan have two sons and twin daughters.

Patricia's paternal grandfather, Peter Hallinan, came to the United States from Ireland as a 13 year old stowaway, during the Irish potato famine. Her paternal grandmother was Margaret (Davis) Hallinan.

Patricia's maternal grandparents were Anton Hoing and his wife Johanna (Tepool) Hoing who lived at Darmstadt, IN where they had a dairy farm and apple orchards.

Robert and Patricia were married in 1953 in Evansville, IN.

JAMES E. AND EVELYN L. JOHNSTON

James E. and Evelyn L. Johnston reside in Mt. Carmel, IL. Evelyn graduated Mt. Vernon High School class of 1968. James graduated Reitz Memorial High School, Evansville, IN. They are both graduates of The University of Evansville. James and Evelyn were married in 1973. To this union have been born Sarah Elizabeth, Aug. 21, 1979, and Emily and Julie, Sept. 18, 1982.

James E., Evelyn L., Sarah E., Emily A., and Julie K. Johnston

James was born in 1948 at Parris Island, SC, the son of William C. and Josephine (Strange) Johnston. William C. Johnston was born in Hoboken, GA, September 1917. He served 20 years in U.S. Marine Corps. Josephine Johnston was born Feb. 29, 1920, in Loogootee, IN. James served three years in the U.S. Navy aboard the U.S. Tripoli. He received the Vietnam Service Medal and the Vietnam Campaign Medal. He is a financial services representative of John Hancock Insurance.

Evelyn was born in 1950 to Charles F. and Ruth (Curtis) Scherer, natives of Posey County. She is a staff nurse at St. Mary's Medical Center, Evansville, IN. Her father was born Sept. 4, 1922. He retired from farming in 1987. Her mother was born in 1926. They were married in 1946. They are also the parents of Charles F. Scherer, Jr. of Anchorage, AK.

Evelyn's paternal grandparents were Fred and Dora (Thienes) Scherer. Fred was the son of Charles and Emma (Lurker) Scherer. Like his parents and many of his antecedents, Fred was a farmer. Charles was the son of Charles and Christina (Grabert) Scherer. Charles born in Baden, Germany, 1821, immigrated to the U.S. in 1854.

Evelyn's maternal grandparents were Mack and Mary Ina (Ludlow) Curtis. Mack a farmer and real estate broker, was the son of George B. and Mattie (Row) Curtis. George Curtis was a farmer.

George Rowe, the great grandfather of Mattie Row Curtis was born in 1750, as his parents were coming to this country. He served in the Revolutionary Army. The family migrated west to Ohio, and after a few years, they moved to Kentucky. In the early 1800s, the Rowe family came to Posey County with several other families by wagon train.

KECK

Louis Henry Keck was one of 12 children of Andrew Keck, who immigrated from Germany in 1835 to settle in Marrs Township. Louis was a farmer in Marrs Township until he relocated to Mt. Vernon. He became an industrialist and was Secretary-Treasurer of Keck-Gonnerman Corp. Louis H. Keck married Nannie Foshee of Mt. Vernon. Four children were born of this union, Louis D. Keck, Emily Keck Shrode, Robert Andrew Keck and Helen Keck Yow.

Robert Andrew was born in 1898 in Mt. Vernon, where he resided until his death on Dec. 2, 1973. He married Louise Hopkins in 1920, daughter of Edgar W. and Hattie Tente Hopkins of Chicago. Louise was the granddaughter of Christian F. Tente, a merchant in Mt. Vernon. She was born in 1898 in Mt. Vernon.

Robert Andrew and Louise have three sons. Robert Andrew Keck, Jr., James Hopkins Keck and David Michael Keck. Robert, Jr. was born in 1922 in Mt. Vernon. He served in the South Pacific with the U.S. Navy during the Second World War. In 1948 he graduated from Indiana University with a degree in business. He married Phyllis Jean Deig of Mt. Vernon in 1953. They have one daughter, Krista Jean, born in 1957. Krista married Rex Townsend of Chicago, IL, in 1988. They reside in Newport News, VA. Krista is office manager for Gust Newberg Co. She received her degree in business from Indiana University. Rex is a construction superintendent with Gust Newberg Co., a graduate of Southern Illinois University. Robert, Jr. retired from Whirlpool after 29 years as supervisor of Product Planning.

James Hopkins Keck was born in 1924. He served with the U.S. Navy in the South Pacific in the Second World War. He married Edith Jensen of Racine, WI in 1952. They have two children, Donald Hopkins, born in 1960, and Eileen Ruth, born in 1962. James is an engineering graduate of Tri-State College. He was a product engineer at Jacobsen Corp., a division of Textron Corp., until

Robert Andrew Keck

his retirement. They resided in Racine, WI. Donald graduated from the University of Wisconsin. He is engaged in the electronics industry in Wisconsin. Eileen is a bookkeeper in a dental office in La Quinta, CA.

David M. married Joan Carol Hitchcock of Indianapolis in 1956. David and Joan attended Indiana University where he received a degree in law and practices in Evansville, IN. Joan's degree is in home economics and she is a tax preparer for George S. Olive Co. in Evansville, IN. They have three sons, Jonathan David, born Oct. 9, 1959. He married Angela Thompson on Aug. 24, 1985. They have one son, Logan Michael, born Dec. 16, 1988 at Murphreesboro, TN, where they now reside. Jonathan graduated from the University of Evansville and is a sales representative for Bristol Myers Company. Angela is an electronics technician for IBM. Andrew Gareth, born on Dec. 26, 1961, resides in Salt Lake City, UT, where he is engaged in graduate studies in mathematics at the University of Utah. James Michael, born in Evansville on Apr. 14, 1965, resides in Knoxville, TN. He is a manager in a Spinnakers restaurant. He graduated from Purdue University with a degree in restaurant and hotel management.

In 1924 Louise and Robert purchased a Federal-style home built by Mr. Mann in 1853, where Louise still lives. She maintains an artist studio and has exhibited her works widely throughout the Tri-State area. She has worked in oils, water colors, and prisma colors. Also, she has sculpted figures which are cast in bronze by the lost wax process. Her early education was in music, specifically, the violin.

Robert graduated from the University of Michigan in 1920 with a degree in business. He then joined the family business of Keck-Gonnerman Company which manufactured threshing machines, steam engines, pea and bean hullers, saw mills and other farm implements. He continued his career with the company until retiring as president. In retirement he continued his lifelong interest in farming by managing several farms and selling farm real estate. He also served for many years as a director of Peoples Bank and Trust Company. He was president of the Indiana Implement Dealers Association.

WILLIAM H. KECK

William H. Keck was born Aug. 15, 1919. He graduated from Indiana University. He was commissioned a 2nd Lieutenant in the U.S. Army, served 19 months in Europe during World War II, awarded the Bronze Star and discharged with the rank of Major.

He worked for Indiana Tractor Sales, Ford Tractor Distributor, two years, returning to Mt. Vernon upon the death of his father in December, 1947. He and his brother, John R. Keck, then took over Keck Motor Company.

William married Ellen Emison of Vincennes Apr. 3, 1948. Their children are Katherine L., born June 26, 1955; Kenneth E., born July 6, 1956 and died July 7, 1956; Richard A., born June 1, 1958, is Vice-President of Keck Motor Company; and Sarah R., born Feb. 24, 1961. Richard, a graduate of Indiana University, is married to Mary Ann Schmith of Tipton (see Richard Keck biography). They have three children: Elizabeth, born 1981; Joseph, born 1984 and Ross, born 1987.

After the death of Ellen Keck in January, 1980, William married Patricia Barefield October, 1982. She lived in Mt. Carmel, IL, the widow of James Barefield, and mother of two children—James Barefield and Jennifer Barefield Stewart.

William H. Keck

William Keck has been active in community affairs. He is past president of Kiwanis, Chamber of Commerce, United Way and Western Hills Country Club. He was very instrumental in developing Southwind Maritime Centre. He has served on the Indiana Port Commission since 1970 and is its chairman. He currently serves as trustee of Deaconess Hospital, is a director of Peoples' Bank & Trust Company; Old National Bank; Old National Bancorp, a holding company; and Southern Indiana Gas & Electric Company.

He has been active in the automobile industry, serving on Ford National Dealer Council in 1964. In 1960 he was winner of Indiana Auto Dealer Council in 1964. In 1960 he was winner of Indiana Auto Dealers Herman Goodin Civic Service award and received Honorable Mention in Time Magazine's recognition for community service. He is a Mason and has been active in the Methodist Church.

Parents of William are Grover C., born Aug. 31, 1884, and Lena Highman Keck, born Aug. 4, 1886. They were married Oct. 12, 1916 and were parents of John R. Keck, born July 24, 1917, and William. Grover attended Purdue University. Lena was the daughter of Robert Wilson Highman and Sarah French Highman. Lena attended DePauw University. Robert Highman was a respected farmer in Lynn Township, served as Township Trustee and later County Commissioner.

Grover started the automobile agency as a division of Keck Gonnerman Company (see Keck Motor Company history). In 1924 he formed Keck Motor Company. The Ford line was added in 1912 and Mercury in 1939. Ford tractors were also sold. Keck Motor Company is the oldest Ford agency in Indiana and the 23rd oldest nationally.

Parents of Grover Keck were John and Addie Franck Keck. John, born Aug. 7, 1851, was reared on his father's farm in Marrs Township. In 1877 he initiated a foundry named Woody & Keck (refer to Keck-Gonnerman history). John married Addie Franck on Mar. 20, 1877. She was the daughter of

Valentine Franck, a market gardner of Louisville, KY. Another son, Franck L., was born June 16, 1882.

John's parents were Andreas and Rosanna Grossman Keck. Both were born in Waldrennach, Germany. Andreas arrived in the United States in 1830, locating on a Marrs Township farm. Andreas died in 1876. Rosanna died in a fire at the family home in 1862. Andreas was a farmer, an untiring worker, possessing the frugality of the German race and known as a man of strict honesty.

RICHARD A. KECK

Richard A. Keck, Vice-President of Keck Motor Company, is the son of Ellen Emison Keck (deceased) and William H. Keck (see William Keck history for ancestry). Richard is a graduate of Mt. Vernon High School and Indiana University in 1980.

He is married to Mary Ann Schmith of Tipton, IN, who is also a graduate of I.U. They are parents of three children: Elizabeth Ellen, born in 1981; Joseph William, born in 1984 and Ross Edwards, born in 1987.

His mother, Ellen Emison Keck, grew up in Vincennes, IN and was a graduate of DePauw. Her parents were Ewing and Tuley Shepard Emison.

Richard is Vice-President of Kiwanis Club, has served on the Board of Western Hills Country Club as treasurer, is a member of the Board of Directors of the Chamber of Commerce and the United Way.

ALVIN HENRY AND MARTHA FRANCIS KEITEL

Philip Keitel, the grandfather of Alvin Keitel came to America from Baden, Germany. (Prussia). Philip and his wife, Margaret Hostadt Keitel and their sons Frederick, William, and a daughter Frederica Keitel along with a brother of Philip, Andrew Keitel, boarded the good ship Donau in Bremen Germany in August 1880 and sailed for America, arriving in New York Sept. 1, 1880. From there they traveled to Indiana, finally settling in Posey County. Along the way another daughter Sophia Keitel was born in Kentucky. Philip and Margaret had three more daughters, Barbara, Margarite, and Lena Keitel. All born in Indiana. The family settled in Posey County in Black Township. When Philip died, he was a caretaker of Bellefontaine Cemetary in Posey County. Frederick Keitel, the first child of Philip Keitel was five years old when the family sailed to America and 22 years old when he married Karolina Furst. Karolina Furst had also come from Germany. Frederick and Karolina had nine children, Louise, Magdelina, William, Fred, Alvin, Margaret, Carl, Paul, and John Keitel. Alvin Henry Keitel, the fifth child of Frederick and Karolina Keitel was born in Posey County and lived his entire life in Posey County. Alvin was born Mar. 2, 1909.

Alvin later married Martha Frances Alldredge the fourth child of Benoni Stinson Alldrededge and Maud Della Curry. Alvin and Martha tended a farm in Point Township near Hovey's Lake in the early years. Later the family moved into Mount Vernon where Alvin began working for the Stephan Implement Company. Out of this union, there were three children born. Norma Jean, John Alvin, and Bonnie Rae Keitel. Norma Jean Keitel married Paul Healy and the couple had three children, Jerry Alan Healy, Coretta Ann Healy, and Gregory Duane Healy. Norma then moved to Kentucky where she married Billy Royce Barclay. This couple had one child, Bonnie Rose Barclay. Bonnie Rose Barclay was only 15 years old when she died in a tragic automobile accident. John Alvin Keitel married Ruth Cleo Kincade and the couple had three children. Rhonda Jean, Dale Lee, and Mickey Allen Keitel.

Bonnie Keitel married Gilbert Lengelsen and had three children. Ramona Kae, Robin Renee, and Rachele Fay Lengelsen. The Lengelsen family also immigrated to Posey County in 1848 from Germany. Of all the children of Alvin and Martha Keitel, only John Alvin and Ruth Keitel still reside in Posey County with their son Mickey Allen Keitel. One grandson, Jerry Alan Healy still lives in Posey County with his daughter Lacey. Norma Jean now lives in Kentucky and Bonnie Rae lives in Florida. There are many Keitels living in Posey County now who are descendants of Philip and Margaret Keitel. Some are descendants of Andrew Keitel, the brother of Philip. There are many Keitels in Germany and some of them immigrated to other parts of America.

BEN W. KERCHER FAMILY

Ben's ancestors stemmed from Germany. The Kerchers came from Biblis (Hessen-Darmstadt) in the 1840s, and settled in Vanderburgh County. Ben was born in German Twp. on Mar. 3, 1895, the third son of Fred (1869-1954) and Elizabeth Nurrenbern (1869-1898) Kercher. The Kerchers moved to Point Twp. in 1912 and farmed until 1923 when they moved back to Evansville.

The Dennings also came from Germany. They arrived from Furstenau (Hanover) in the 1830s and bought land in Spencer County. Minnie was born Dec. 8, 1896 at St. Meinrad. She was the oldest daughter of Henry (1864-1951) and Theresia Fischer (1871-1950) Denning. The Dennings moved to Point Twp. in 1910.

It was in Point that Ben and Minnie met and courted. Ben was drafted in May, 1918, but missed having to go overseas because he caught the dangerous Spanish flu. By the time he was well again and had trained with a different Company, the Armistice was signed. He was discharged in May, 1919 and married Minnie September 23 at St. Matthew Church.

They first farmed land owned by Minnie's father on Bonebank Road. From there they moved to Schlachter corner, where Ben bought an 80 acre farm. Henry (1926-) and Lavita (1929-) were born there. Several years of poor crops forced the sale of the farm. After living in the Wabash bottoms for about a year, they rented a farm (Jones Place) just off Ditch Road in Point. Dennis (1934-) was born there.

The end of their farming came with the wrath of the '37 flood. Having to leave their home from an upstairs window onto a boat, they were taken to Mt. Vernon. When they returned after the flood, most of their possessions were either destroyed or stolen. The attempt at farming after the flood failed. They moved to Mt. Vernon permanently in late '37. Leroy (1938-) was born in Mt. Vernon.

The next four years found the family struggling to exist. Ben had various jobs getting a job on the WPA. The family thought the $12 a week from the WPA was a lot of money.

In 1940 Ben was hired at the IFB refinery, and in 1943 they bought their West Third St. home. Ben worked at the refinery in various capacities until he retired in 1956. He died of cancer later that year. Minnie lived almost 26 more years, doing the things she liked best: gardening, growing flowers, quilting, and watching TV.

Their children all married. 'Cookie' married Bob Freimiller in 1946. Bob worked for SIGECO and has been a Mt. Vernon city councilman for many years. They have four children. Henry married Patricia Murray in 1947. He worked for Sohio in Cleveland until retirement in 1983. Henry and Pat had six children. Dennis married Joan Fuller in 1963. He works for Emerson Electric in St. Louis, and has three children. Leroy married Helga Abt in 1965 while in the Air Force. He works for Westinghouse in Pittsburgh, and has three children.

KLEINSCHMIDT

Seated center in the picture is CLEMENS CONRAD KLEINSCHMIDT and his wife BEATRICE MABEL WOODS KLEINSCHMIDT. The remainder of the picture are the children who wish to present the known KLEINSCHMIDT family history.

Our paternal great grandfather was CONRAD KLEINSCHMIDT, born in LIPPE, Detmold, Germany in 1830 (d. 1902) immigrated to the United States in 1860 and became a naturalized citizen the same year. Later that year he and his brother Charles H. (also known as Karl) purchased 116 acres of land in Section 21 in Marrs Township, about 2-1/2 miles West of West Franklin and near the Ohio River. In February 1861 he married Henrietta Amalia Reineke (b. 1842; d. 1908), the daughter of August and Wilhelmina Tieman Reineke who also immigrated from LIPPE, Detmold, Germany and were farmers in western Perry Township in Vanderburgh County.

Norma Jean Keitel Barclay, John A. Keitel, Bonnie Keitel Lengelsen, Alvin Keitel, Martha Keitel

Ben and Minnie Kercher, holding grandchildren, Michael Kercher, Gary Freimiller, with Wayne Freimiller standing between.

Kleinschmidt Family

To this marriage came our paternal grandfather HENRY AUGUST CONRAD KLEINSCHMIDT in May 1862 (d. 1943); Wilhelmina Maria Kleinschmidt in 1869 (d. 1948); Conrad F. Kleinschmidt in 1872 (d. 1965) and Frederick Kleinschmidt in 1880 (d. 1972). A double wedding took place at Immanuel Church on Oct. 25, 1886 when HENRY A. C. KLEINSCHMIDT married Maria Elizabeth Dembersmier and his sister Wilhelmina Maria Kleinschmidt married August Dembersmier, a brother to Maria Elizabeth Dembersmier.

Our paternal grandfather, HENRY AUGUST CONRAD KLEINSCHMIDT and grandmothers children were: Wilhelm August Kleinschmidt (b. 1892), was mortally wounded in France in 1918 during World War I; CLEMENS CONRAD KLEINSCHMIDT, our paternal father, born in 1894 (d. 1970), married Beatrice Mabel Woods (b. 1906; d. 1968); Flora Maria Klein-Kleinschmidt (b. 1897; d. 1983) married Elmer Hahn; Henry B. Kleinschmidt (b. 1902; d. 1980) married Mary Elizabeth Duckworth; and Clarence Frederick Kleinschmidt, born in 1909 and died seven months later.

Seated on the right in the picture is: Anna Marie (b. 1923) married to Edgar K. Oschman, now living in Evansville, IN, whose children are Sandra Elaine McCormick of Rural Wadesville, IN; Steven Eugene Oschman of Mooresville, IN: and Sherri Ann Green of Mooresville, IN. Standing far right is: Clement Eugene (b. 1924) married to Betty Ann Woods, now living in Fort Branch, IN, whose children are Ruth Annette Hebeisen of Jasper, IN; and Marilyn Kaye Fischer of Evansville, IN. Standing third from left is: Flora Geraldine (b. 1926) married to Harold Cotner (d. 1981) whose child is Jerry Wayne Cotner. She later married Billy J. Morris and live in Mt. Vernon, IN. Standing second from left is Charles Henry (b. 1928) married to Jean Davis, now living in Mt. Vernon, IN; whose children are Charles Alan Kleinschmidt of Bloomington, IL; Brian Leonard Kleinschmidt of Indianapolis, IN and Carol Jean Kleinschmidt of Greeley, CO. Standing first from left is: Harold Lloyd Kleinschmidt (b. 1930; d. 1988) married Martha Shoemake of Mt. Vernon, IN, whose children are Patricia Lynn Garrett of Newburgh, IN; Linda Sue Roby of Lockport, LA, and Connie Jean Fuelling of Mt. Vernon, IN. Seated first on left: Helen Joyce (b. 1936) married to Russell Garrett of Lockport, LA whose children are Lisa DeAnn Zerinque, Jr. of Raceland, LA; Terri Sue Gautreauz of Lockport, LA; and Melea Joyce Garrett, a student at McNeese University of Lake Charles, LA. Jackie Clyde Kleinschmidt, another son of Clemens Conrad Kleinschmidt and Beatrice Mabel Woods Kleinschmidt who was born Dec. 16, 1932 and died Dec. 26, 1932.

A majority of the deceased are buried at Immanuel Church Cemetery on Ford Road in Marrs Township. *Submitted by Clement Eugene Kleinschmidt*

KREUTZINGER FAMILY

James Knight Kreutzinger was born to Henry Philip and Esther Knight Kreutzinger on Jan. 17, 1859, in Point Township, Posey County. His father, Henry Philip Kreutzinger, who was born Aug. 1, 1831, in Menden (Prussia), Germany, came to the United States with Henry Philip's grandparents in 1839. They settled near St. Philips in eastern Posey County.

Later, Henry Philip's parents, Herman and Ernestina Kreutzinger came to this country bringing the other children of the family. His parents, who died in 1847 and 1853, left Henry to look after his siblings. For a time, Henry was an overseer of slave labor in Union Co., KY.

When his brothers and sisters were grown, he returned to Posey County where he married Esther Knight. She was born Apr. 28, 1838, in London, England. Esther Knight Kreutzinger died Nov. 3, 1880. After her death, Henry Philip served as Trustee of Point Township three terms. He was then elected County Commissioner and served two terms. He died Mar. 5, 1915.

James Knight Kreutzinger, an only child, married Anna Margaretha Schmidt on Mar. 29, 1882. Anna was the daughter of John Philip Schmidt and Anna Margaretha Zimmerman. John Philip Schmidt (1824-1913) was brought from Germany to this country by his parents in 1857. Anna Margaretha Zimmerman (1823-1889) was born in Germany.

From the marriage of James Knight (1859-1921) and Anna Margaretha Schmidt Kreutzinger (1864-1944) there were two sons and six daughters: Edmund Philip (1883-1942) married Edith Hall of Ridgway, IL; Esther (1885-1981) married George W. Denham of Kentucky; Lydia (1886-1905); Beatrice (1888-1973) married Benton O. Blake of Wadesville; Henry James (1891-1968) married Rose Whitaker of Rensselaer, IN: Marguerite (Rita) (1893-1975) married C.H. Mendenhall, of Evansville; Dorothy (1895-1987) married Glenn Henderson of Bloomington; and Ruth Elizabeth (1906-19_) married Nathan Hall of Bloomington.

James Knight Kreutzinger was a carpenter who later became a traveling salesman of advertising. Of his children, Edmund, Beatrice, Dorothy and Ruth each taught for several years. His son, Henry, retired from the Allison Division of General Motors in Indianapolis. Rita was employed by Indiana Bell Telephone before her marriage. Of this family's descendants, only one granddaughter, Mildred Beatrice Blake, still resides in Posey County.

For other survivors, see the Benton O. Blake family history.

CHARLEY AND VERA LAWRENCE

Charley and Vera Lawrence are residents of Mt. Vernon, IN. Both are graduates of Mt. Vernon High School. Charley graduated in 1946 and Vera graduated in 1947. Charley and Vera were married on Mar. 25, 1949 in Mt. Vernon. They have three sons, Tony, David and Jon. Tony Michael was born on Sept. 25, 1951, David Duane was born on Mar. 25, 1954 and Jon Thomas was born on Mar. 21, 1959. Charley was born on Mar. 17, 1928 to Charles E. Lawrence, Sr. and Mildred Bailey Lawrence. Charley Jr. was active in sports in High School, namely, football and basketball. Charley took a pre-engineering course in High School in preparation for going to Evansville College in the fall of 1946 in which he studied mechanical engineering, drafting and surveying. After leaving college, Charley was engaged in the engineering department at Swift & Co. and worked for a short time with an architect at Whirlpool. A few years later, he started his own business of remodeling and building houses. Charley actually started seriously building homes about 1958 and has been doing that ever since. Charley is president of Charles Lawrence Homes, Inc. His primary occupation now is developing land into subdivisions and building houses. To date, Charley has built approximately 700 homes in and around Mt. Vernon, primarily in his two subdivisions the Lawrence Addition on the Northside of town and the Park Ridge Subdivision and Country Club Estates in the northwest part of town in the Western Hills Country Club area. When Vera graduated from High School she went directly to the county Auditors office and worked there approximately three years. After that she went to the Indiana Farm Bureau Refinery and worked there for approximately two years prior to starting a family. Presently she is Vice-President of Charles Lawrence Homes, Inc. and works in that capacity.

Charley and Vera Lawrence

Tony married Yvonne Vaal of Mt. Vernon and they have three children, Angela - age 14, Duane - age seven, and Michael - age three months. Tony works with his father and is Secretary of Charles Lawrence Homes, Inc. He graduated from Indiana State University at Terre Haute, IN with a degree in Industrial Management. David lives in Los Angeles, CA and works as an attorney for a large law firm Cotkin, Collins, and Franscell. He married Patricia Lafferty formerly of East Orange, NJ. They have no children. He graduated from Indiana University with a degree in Business and he graduated from the University of Arizona Law School. Jon lives in Bloomington, IN and is in the computer business. He is not married. He graduated from Indiana University in Bloomington with a degree in Business.

Charles E. Lawrence, Sr. was born on Jan. 30, 1903 in Mt. Vernon, and has lived in Mt. Vernon his entire life. Most of his early years were devoted to working in grocery stores for his father and owning and operating grocery stores in Mt. Vernon until approximately 1948. At that time he went to work for the Mt. Vernon Lumber Co. and stayed there for several years. Then in approximately 1960 he went to work for his son Charles Jr., in the home building business and to this date he is still working for the firm. He and Mildred live at 358 Audubon Drive, Mt. Vernon and are active in the First United Methodist Church. Charles Sr. has a brother Leonard who lives in Princeton, IN. They are the sons of Charles L. Lawrence who came from Owensville, IN and was born Feb. 16, 1878 and died July 1, 1941. Charles L. Lawrence married Mathilda Springer who was born Sept. 14, 1878 and died July 3, 1964. They both moved from Mt. Vernon and lived in Princeton in their latter years. Mildred was born to John A. Bailey and Mattie Henson Bailey on Sept. 2, 1901. She attended Mt. Vernon High School. John A. Bailey was born 1869 and died 1959. Mattie Henson was born 1868 and died 1945. John A. Bailey was engaged in farming his entire life. Charley's sister Joan was born May 20, 1934. She graduated from Mt. Vernon High School and Indiana University. She married Lloyd Novak and they have twins Nancy and David who both attend Depauw University. The Novak's presently live in Evansville, IN.

Vera was the last of nine children born to Lester F. Redman and Margaret Schierbaum Redman. Vera was born on July 8, 1929. Lester F. Redman was born Sept. 17, 1884 and died Dec. 6, 1970. Margaret Schierbaum Redman was born Dec. 29, 1885 and died Aug. 25, 1979. Lester F. Redman was engaged in farming his entire life. The Schierbaums' came from Germany.

JOHN H. AND ESTHER C. LEFFEL

John Herbert and Esther C. (Rode) Leffel, 702 Mulberry Street, Mount Vernon, IN were married Dec. 1, 1943 by Reverand Charles Maier at Fort Leonard Wood, MO while Mr. Leffel was in Service of World War II.

John Herbert was born Feb. 28, 1910, attended St. Matthew's Parochial School and Mt. Vernon High School and graduated from Purdue University with a degree in Civil Engineering in June 1935. He was appointed to the Office of Posey County Surveyor, September 1937 and elected to said Office on the Democratic Ticket on the first Tuesday of November 1938 and each succeeding election day until retirement on Jan. 1, 1989. He is the fourth generation of the Leffel family to reside in Posey Co., IN.

Esther C. (Rode) Leffel, Dec. 24, 1910 educated at the Assumption Parochial School, Central High School and Lockyear's Business College of Evansville and employed by Hulman Wholesale Grocery until marriage. She is the daughter of Adam B. Rode (1875-1922) and Frances (Kraft) Rode (1881-1969) of Vanderburgh Co., IN.

To this union were born four children: Mary Beth, Aug. 16, 1945 educated at St. Matthew's Parochial and Mt. Vernon High School and graduated from St. Louis University with a degree in Special Education. She married Raymond P. Linder of Widner, AR Sept. 2, 1967 at St. Matthew's Catholic Church by Rev. Raymond Smith. To this union were born three sons: Jonathan Hilary, born Apr. 17, 1970; Benjamin Charles born June 7, 1971 and Nathaniel Paul born Apr. 23, 1974. The Linders reside in Helena, MT.

Standing left to right John H. II, John H. I, Esther Geoffrey. Sitting left to right Mary Beth - Holly Ann

John Herbert Leffel, II, Nov. 1, 1947, educated at St. Matthew's Parochial and Mt. Vernon High School, attended Indiana University and Indiana State University and received his Masters in Business Administration. He married Karen Sue Bell daughter of Kenneth and Sue Bell of Chicago, IL on Sept. 17, 1977 and to this union three sons were born: John Herbert III, June 30, 1978; Kenneth Edward, June 9, 1981 and Geoffrey Dean on Dec. 29, 1983. John is employed as Stock Broker w/ Shearson Lehman and Hutton in Indianapolis.

Holly Ann Leffel, Dec. 10, 1953, educated at St. Matthew's Parochial, Mt. Vernon High School and graduated from Indiana State University in 1975 with a degree in Therapeutic Recreation. She has been employed with Southwestern Indiana Mental Health Center, Evansville, IN since 1976.

Geoffrey Adam Leffel, Sept. 26, 1955, educated at St. Matthew's Parochial, Mt. Vernon High and graduated from Indiana State University with a degree in Business Administration. He married Stacy Lynn Wiley, daughter of Gordon and Glenda Wiley of Beaumont, TX on Apr. 19, 1986 at Neu Chapel at the University of Evanville and resides in Warrick Co., IN and has a son, Kyle Geoffrey, born Sept. 6, 1987. Geoffrey is a Stock Broker with Merrill Lynch Pierce Fenner and Smith, Inc., Evansville, IN.

Herbert and Agnes Mary (Pfeffer) Leffel, natives of Posey Co., IN were the parents of three children, all born in Mt. Vernon, IN. Louise Douglas (1901-1956), Martha Mary (Feb. 22, 1906-Mar. 21, 1906) and John Herbert Leffel.

Louise was educated in Mount Vernon Schools and graduated from High School in May 1919. On Sept. 3, 1926 was married to Carl Kissick in Tulsa, OK. To this union were born two children: Mary Carol (Mar. 8, 1931) and James Herbert, (Jan. 25, 1937) at Tulsa, OK.

HERBERT LEFFEL, second oldest son of John C. and Minnie (Brinkman) Leffel born Apr. 24, 1877, attended the public schools of Mount Vernon, IN and learned the Newspaper business in the "Western Star" Office which was owned by his father, John C. Leffel. He became a partner with his father in publishing the Western Star Newspaper. After the death of John C. Leffel, he continued the publishing of the Newspaper until his death in Mar. 24, 1945. Herbert Leffel married Agnes Pfeffer (Sept. 3, 1878 - Aug. 7, 1969) daughter of John and Minnie (Gerke) Pfeffer, Jan. 18, 1900 at St. Matthew's Catholic Church by Rev. T.B. Luebberman.

DANIEL and BARBARA (Reinchenbacher) LEFFEL, both born in Karlsruhe Baden, Germany, where they were also married. In 1832 they immigrated to the United States and for several years resided in New York City. They changed locations several times, and the latter part of the 1840s located in Center Township, Posey Co., IN where Daniel Leffel purchased large tracts of land, the town sites of Blairsville and Wadesville being a part of his original purchase. In 1854 he moved to Mount Vernon and engaged in merchandising. His death occurred Mar. 24, 1873 at the age of 66 years and that of his wife, who was related to Eddie Reichenbacher, the World War I Ace, occurred Feb. 3, 1894. They were parents of six daughters and two sons.

JOHN C. LEFFEL the oldest son of Daniel and Barbara Leffel, (May 8, 1850 - June 7, 1935) and at the age of 15 became an apprentice in a harness shop at St. Louis, MO. In 1867 he returned to Mount Vernon and assisted Tom Collins, the editor and proprietor of the "Democrat" in getting out the newspapers. October 1875, Mr. Leffel established the Mount Vernon "WOCHENBLAT" the first and only German paper to be published in Posey County. In 1877 the first issue of the "Western Star" appeared as a Democratic Paper. In 1885 the publishing of the "WOCHENBLAT" was discontinued. John C. Leffel married Minnie (Brinkman) daughter of Henry and Margaret (Hahn) Brinkman on July 2, 1871 at the Salem Church, Marrs Township by Rev. J.J. Fox. To this union was born four sons and three daughters. John C. Leffel died June 7, 1935 at the age of 85. Mrs. John C. Liffel was born July 8, 1853 and died Feb. 28, 1907 at the age of 54.

MARTHA AND LELAND LEIGH

Martha and Leland Leigh are residents of 2916 Springfield - Oliver Road of Mt. Vernon, IN. Martha and Leland were married in 1961 in White Co., IL. Martha was born in 1925 Posey County and Leland was born 1923 in Sallisaw, OK and have one daughter, Leann. Martha was married to Larkin Overton in 1945 and to this marriage two sons were born, Keith and Steven Overton.

Martha's parents were Otis Oral and Daisy M. Pritchard Carroll. Martha graduated in 1943 from Mt. Vernon High School, was employed by Vanderburgh County T.B. Assn.

Leland attended Harrison School in Sallisaw and was a WWII Veteran. Leland retired in 1988 from A.D.M. Milling Company after 29 years.

Leland's parents were Arthur and Vivian Morris Leigh of Sallisaw, OK. Leland's father was a member of the Cherokee Indian Tribe in Sequoyah County and had a roll number with the Cherokee Indians.

Otis and Daisy Carroll

Otis Oral Carroll born 1880 and married in 1913 in Evansville, IN to Daisy M. Pritchard, who was born 1888. Otis was the son of John R. and Virginia Adsett Carroll. His wife was the daughter of Florian and Elizabeth Heck Pritchard.

They were the parents of five children: Margaret, William, Erma, Mary K. and Martha. Margaret and Mary K died early in life.

Otis and Daisy resided on a farm north of Farmersville during his years of successful farming and livestock raising. Was an active Republican and a member of Posey County Alcholic Beverage Board, Black Township Advisory Board, Masonic Lodge and Modern Woodman Lodge.

Otis and his brother-in-law, Walter T. Allen were owners of a steam engine and wheat thresher and did custom work for farmers in the Farmersville area.

My grandfather, John R. Carroll born 1843 in McNairy Co., TN and died in Posey County 1919. He married Virginia Adsett born in 1845 in Posey County. John R's parents were Stephen and Nancy Glenn Carroll. Virginia's parents were Ann Hithman and Jarman Adsett.

To this marriage nine children were born: Nora, Logan, Samuel, Ollie, Victoria, Albert, Otis, Bertha and Walter.

John R. was in WWI in the 46th Ohio Reg. Vol. Inf. 1862 to 1864. He was wounded in 1862 at Pittsburgh Landing, Shiloh Tennessee. He often talked about the roar of the cannon's of the Civil War Shiloh Battle which they could hear from their home in Purdy, Tennessee.

John R. and Virginia are buried in French Cemetery in West Lynn Township of Posey County.

Stephen Carroll and Nancy Glenn, both of Orange County, married in Hillsborough, NC on Thursday, Sept. 25, 1828. Their first three children were born in North Carolina before they migrated to McNairy Co., TN. Their children were: Wesley, Susan, James, William Henry, Benjamin, Elizabeth Ann, Martha Jane, John R. Charles, Franklin and George Washington; all of whom migrated to Posey County in 1864.

LENGELSEN FAMILY HISTORY

Though the name **Lengelsen** is presently carried only by a widow of Edgar, and a Ruth (former librarian) living in Mt. Carmel, IL, and by one Gilbert Lengelsen and family, now living in Florida, Lengelsen descendants are prominent in this area's life and scattered throughout the country.

Fritz Lengelsen born 1825-died 1914

The spelling of **Sen** probably does not have a connection with **son** or Scandinavia, but was thought by Pastor Helmut Lengelsen of Iserlohn, Germany, to be abbreviated from Lengelhausen (houses of Lengel). The first Lengelsen in this country, Hermann Diedrich, was born 1798 in Werdohl (e), Westfalen (Westphalia), his son Fritz in 1825 in Wintersohle a cluster of buildings recently saved from destruction and declared a national historic site. Nearby, also on the Lenne River, stands the community of Lengelsen, and this author visited the town **Pungelscheid,** with part of its medievel wall still standing, where the family is said to have originated. Also the church records in Werdohl were perused by four Lengelsens in 1978 — Luise and Pauline Burgdorf (also in 1974), Charlotte Lengelsen Burnett, and Peter Gülicher of Holland, who visited relatives and sites here in 1979. **Lüdenscheid** was the district and the largest nearby town, part of the province **(Regierungsbezirk)** Arnsberg, a part of Prussia **(Preuszen).** They spoke **Plattdeutsch,** or Low German.

This descendant had the pleasure of meeting in Germany counterparts Hermann (who had been a prisoner of war in Louisiana during World War II"), Lengelsen, Peter Friedrich ("Fritz), and whose father died of starvation as an American prisoner in Germany). Peter Friedrich Wilhelm ("Friedehlm") a jeweler, and Helmut, local pastor, one author of **"Evangelische Westfalen",** and overseer of the Women's Guild in the Evangelical Church of Westfalen/Lippe. His one son, Thomas, is a minister; the other, Burkhardt, an employee of Union Carbide, who visited Evansville briefly in December, 1983, and attended the Gemania Männer - and Damenchor Christmas concert, where he could sing the German national anthem as well as at home!

The two sons, Peter Friedrich and Casper Diedrich Wilhelm, were of the age to be conscripted for military service; 1848 was also the time of revolution in Germany, so the entire family, including son-in-law Peter Wilhelm Nölle, migrated, sailing on the ship Diana to New York. Hermann Diedrich purchased 87 acres in Marrs Township about one-half mile from the present Salem Evangelical Church on what was once State Highway #10 (the Old State Road), now known as the Old Lower Mt. Vernon Road, in some sort of partnership with Heinrich Assenberg. They became founding members of the church, where many Lengelsens remain active. One descendant, with help from others, saved their second sanctuary from destruction in 1973 by moving it—and one of the most faithful volunteers in this effort was one man—first, second, and third cousin!—related through Becker, Hengstenberg, and Lengelson.

The most original building on the Lengelsen Place, the log barn, fell in recent years, having failed to find anyone who would repair it. (One of the siding boards (poplar) on the front was approximately two feet wide and 20 feet long—an indication of the trees used for the lumber.) This author believes, due to its structure including one floored room, that they stayed first in the barn. The original house burned (perhaps due to a hired hand's careless smoking) about 1900, probably destroying family records and pictures—the straw pillows the main thing being saved! A second structure included logs from the old Schwartz Place down the road east, and six generations have been in it, seven on the place, which remains in the family, farmed by a descendant. Unfortunately the Indiana-Michigan Utility Company, and SIGECO ran a railroad through a corner in the 1970's.

*The oldest picture of the congregation, 1892, shows Fritz and Ida Lengelsen and Ferdinand Grebe, among others identifiable. The Lengelsens had long arms and tended to bring them together with folded hands in front of them, perhaps not knowing what else to do with them!

The accordian was the musical instrument of the Lengelsens, played by Eduard Albert, and Clem Lengelsen, Freada Herign, and Clara Boerner Stephan. Hermann Diedrich and Christine Elisabeth had at least four children in Germany: Anna Maria Dorothea, who married Peter Wilhem Nölle; Casper Diedrich Wilhelm, who married Caroline Grebe from Minden, Westfalen, sister of Ferdinand, and lived in a log house on land adjacent to Fritz near the intersection of the Old Lower Mt. Vernon and West Franklin Roads, the latter later branching into Grebe and Welborn Roads, continuing to West Franklin. Caroline, who married Ferdinand Grebe; and Peter Friedrich, who married Wilhelmine Ohose of Hanover.

PETER FRIEDRICH (FRITZ) LENGELSEN

Peter Freidrich (Fritz) Lengelsen was born in Prussia in 1825. During this period in time, Prussia was expanding under the rule of Friedrich Wilhelm III, and Lutherans were suffering persecution for their religious beliefs. Also during this period, the young men were forced to serve in the military. When King Wilhelm III used the military to enforce his edicts, it put the young men in the position of enforcing unpopular laws against their own families. Immigration seemed to provide the only viable solution, and from 1830 to the early 1850s, an estimated 6000 fled to the freedom of America. In late 1847, Hermann Diedrich Wilhelm Lengelsen, the father of Peter Friedrich Lengelsen, made the decision to immigrate to America. The family, which included Peter Friedrich, Casper Diedrich Wilhelm, Peter August, Caroline, and Louise Lengelsen traveled to Bremen, where they boarded the good ship "Diane" and sailed to America.

Peter Friedrich Lengelsen

The family landed in New York on Jan. 22, 1848. From there they traveled to Posey County where they settled near St. Phillips in a small community known then as Heusler, because the post office was located in Dr. Heusler's house next to the cemetery. On Oct. 15, 1848, Hermann Diedrich Wilhelm Lengelsen in partnership with Heinrich Assenberg bought some land and began farming. About a dozen families organized a congregation and named it Salem. Hermann Diedrich and his family were members of this congregation. The congregation was being served by a missionary from Germany named Heinrich Toelke. By 1880, Salem Church had a constitution and Peter Friedrich (Fritz) Lengelsen was the president of this organization. The Salem United Church of Christ is still in existence today. By this time Peter Friedrich had married Wilhelmina Ohose, who also immigrated to America with her family, and the couple had seven children.

Of all the descendants of Peter Friedrich Lengelsen and his brothers, there are no male Lengelsens living in Posey County on this the 175th Anniversary. However, many Posey County families are related to the Lengelsens through marriage, for instance the Burgdorfs, Beckers, Noelles, Hengstenbergs, Uebelhacks, Struehs, Barenbergs, Grebes, and Wilma Lengelsen, to mention a few. Most of the Lengelsens and some of their descendants are buried in the Salem United Church of Christ cemetary near St. Phillips. *Submitted by Gilbert I. Lengelsen*

GERALD R. LEWIS

Gerald R. Lewis, son of John Ellis and Beulah Fay (Stiff) Lewis of Warrick Co., IN, was born in Posey Co., IN on Aug. 4, 1940. He was educated in the Warrick Couny school system and attended Evansville College. Gerald married Gloria Smith, daughter of Robert and Paula (Harris) Smith. They have three children, Paula, born in 1960, Troy, born in 1963, and Tricia, born in 1974. Gerald has owned and operated his own company, Quality Coatings, Inc., for the past 15 years. Gerald's g-g-g-g grandfather was Alexander Lewis who made the journey from Virginia to Mercer Co, KY in 1788 settling on the Dicks River. In 1798 he came to Christian Co., KY and settled on a farm of 600 acres on the W. Fork of Pond River. Alexander was born circa 1755 in Virginia and was married circa 1775 to Elizabeth. The names of their children (believed to be listed in order of birth) were: Robert, Margaret (Peggy), Nancy, and John.

Gerald, Troy, Gloria, Tricia and Paula

These children were all married in Christian Co., KY. Robert, born circa 1780, married Hannah Grace, daughter of Henry Grace on Apr. 26, 1813. They had six children: John Alexander, Patsy, Nancy, Margarette, Mahala, and Susan. Alexander's daughter, Margaret (Peggy), married William Cargill on Jan. 24, 1804 and moved to Posey Co., IN. Alexander's other daughter, Nancy, married John Cargill on Nov 27, 1803. John Lewis, son of Alexander and Elizabeth, was born circa 1790 in Mercer Co., KY but was educated in Christian Co., KY. He married Susannah Oliver, daughter of John Oliver, on Oct. 15, 1811. Shortly after their marriage, they also moved to Posey Co., IN settling in Marrs Township near the Ohio River on several hundred acres. They became two of the earliest settlers in this area. "Col." John Lewis was a very successful farmer, building a 5,000 acre estate before his death on Feb. 3, 1856. "Col." John and his wife Susan had eight children: Robert Alexander, Patsy, Jane, John, James, Elizabeth, Nancy, and Martha. Robert Alexander was born Mar. 26, 1814. He married Martha (Price) Martin on Mar. 30, 1835. He was a farmer in Marrs Township of Posey Co., IN until his death on Aug. 10, 1848. Robert and his wife Martha had five children: James Alexander, John, Thompson Price, Nathaniel, and Aurilla Jane. Thompson Price Lewis was born June 8, 1840. He married Elizabeth J. Green, daughter of Thomas S. Green and his wife Mary, on Nov. 3, 1858. He was a very successful farmer until his death Sept. 4, 1922. Thompson Price and his wife Elizabeth had 12 children: Mary Jane, James Robert, Udora, Nathaniel, Patsey, William David, Orila, Price, Ellsworth, Edward, Thompson, and Oscar. Price Lewis was born Aug. 18, 1874. He married Viola Hartley, daughter of Henry Hartley, and Abigale (Horton) Hartley, in 1897. Price Lewis farmed until his death on Dec. 9, 1938. He and his wife Viola had nine children: Raymond Price, Mildred, Fanny, Hartley J., John Ellis, Edward, Myron, Mary Katherine, and Martha. John Ellis Lewis was born on Jan. 19, 1910. He married Beulah Faye Stiff, daughter of Arthur Stiff and Bruce (Johnston) Stiff, on Dec. 23, 1929. He was a farmer until starting his own construction company. John Ellis died July 31, 1962. He and his wife Beulah had six children: Robert Gene, Deloris Dean, Carolyn Sue, Gerald Ray, Ronald Lee, and Donald Roy.

BARNETT AND CAROLYN LOEHR

Barnett Herbert Loehr born Dec. 16, 1904, son of John Herbert Loehr and Eva Whipple. He was one of five children.

Carolyn Evelyn Bell Loehr born Apr. 3, 1908, the daughter of George Wesley Bell and Attie May Pruitt. She was one of nine children.

Barnett and Carolyn were married Dec. 23, 1924. In December of 1988 they celebrated their 64th wedding anniversary. They had five children, 11 grandchildren and ten great grandchildren.

Their children: Lois Lawanda Loerh died of scarlet fever February 1932 at the age of six. Barnett Edmund Loehr (Jack) drowned in backwater January 1943 at 15.

Herbert Earl Loehr married Marrie Mann 1947. The father of Mickie Jay Loehr, Nancy Wallace Spencer (Dan), Barnett Ray Loehr and Mickie Wayne Loehr.

Barnett and Carolyn Loehr

Joyce Marenda Loehr married Glen Briesacher 1949. Children Glen Arnold Jr., Timothy Bruce (wife Gloria Danford), Daniel Brian (wife Brenda Brewer) David Allan, Gigi Joyce (husband Mark Kozinski).

Marion Samuel Loehr married Sue Lewis, children are: Sam Ray, Stacey Keith (wife Cindy).

Great grandchildren: Eric Len Wallace, Whitney Danielle Spencer, Clint Alexandra Loehr Sellers, Phalen Marshal Loehr, Heather Melissa Briesacher, Tiffany Deseree Briesacher, Daniel Brian Briesacher, Jr., Carrie Lyn Briesacher, Dustin Keith Loehr, and Emily Jane Kozinski, born May 1, 1989.

Barnett and Carolyn were born just on the other side of the Wabash River in Illinois. Barnett was six and Carolyn was 15 when they first moved to Point Township. Carolyn says that once you've tasted the Point Township soil and it gets in your blood, you will never want to leave. They both lived close to Half Moon Pond when they first came to Mt. Vernon.

After working all week the neighbors would all get together at each others home and have a dance. It was at one of these dances that Carolyn and Barnett met. Barnett says that night they danced until daybreak. Barnett remembers he had to walk Carolyn home with the soles off his shoes because he had worn them off dancing. Carolyn says walking home after a dance and traveling by Half Moon Pond could bring a chill down ones spine. It was so dark sometimes there wasn't a moon or a star in the sky. The wind would be rushing through the trees, the old owl would give a few hoots and the cricket would play a symphony.

Barnett was a farmer, his father was a farmer. He remembers working for 25¢ a day and later when he got a dollar a day he felt like a rich man. A lot of rabbits, quails and squirrels found their way into the frying pan. One year Barnett killed 199 squirrels and not a one went to waste. Trapping and selling the pets helped to buy Christmas for the children and provide the extra's needed for the cold winter. But every jar was full of canned vegetables, fruit and jellies, when one of the kids would need a new pair of shoes the chickens would hide for a week, because they knew Carolyn was taking them to market to buy new shoes. She would pick wild blackberries and sell to the town people. Once she had the back seat of the Old Model A full of berries and the car caught on fire. Before she worried about the fire she got her berries out of the car.

Barnett and Carolyn remembered the days of moonshine and homebrew. Barnett says that he would be plowing in the field and look up to see Carolyn and the kids coming across the field bringing him a cold bottle of homebrew that she had cooled in the well. The bottle would have cold drops of water on the outside. He said a man felt like he was a millionaire with just the simple things in life.

The depression was a terrible thing to a lot of people, but to Barnett and Carolyn they were so poor they really didn't notice much difference. The 1937 flood caused havoc. Barnett and Carolyn had to take refuge at the coliseum in Mt. Vernon with all the other people who was forced out of their homes by the flood. Then when the water went down, they found their home had floated down in the field. But they lived in it right where it was at with no kitchen floor, until they could build another house. Later they found their kitchen table high in a tree with the pecan crackers still in the drawer where the flood had taken it.

Carolyn and eight other people founded the Point Township Nazarene Church. They raised the money to build a church. Through the effects of Carolyn and the other eight a lot of people came to know the Lord. In fact Dallas Robinson the minister at the Point Township Church now, went to the old church as a little boy.

Barnett and Carolyn live on Graddy Road close to Hovey Lake. At 84 Barnett still farms his plot of ground and at 81 Carolyn still fills her jars and prepares for the cold winter. She rides around on her mobile cart and takes care of her nine cats and looks over the land she loves so much. Barnett finds enjoyment in his dog Scottie, when Carolyn isn't looking he loves to watch Scottie send a few of Carolyn's cats running up the nearest tree.

Sometimes you feel like you can hear the voices of the past residents of Point Township in the Wind. I'ts like they want to tell us to protect this special place in the world. If you will just stop to listen you can hear the echo of their voices. Those voices will comfort you in time of sorrow and rejoice with you when you are happy.

The spirits of the past that made Mt. Vernon what it is today. That spirit still lives in Mammy and Pappy Loehr.

MARION SAMUEL LOEHR MINALYN SUE LOEHR

Sam and Sue (Lewis) live in Mesa, AZ. Both graduated from Mt. Vernon High School, Sam class of 1954, Sue class of 1956. They married Aug. 31, 1957. They have two sons, Samuel Ray born Mar. 21, 1959 and Stacey Keith born Feb. 23, 1962. Sam Ray is single and lives in Prescott, AZ. Stace married Cindy Valenzuela, of Mesa. They have a son Dustin Keith born May 16, 1988, they live in Gilbert, AZ. The Loehr's lived in Mt. Vernon, as did their ancestors, until July 1969.

Sam born Aug. 18, 1936 in Point Township, the baby of five children of Barnett and Carolyn (Bell) Loehr. He attended Black School in Point, a two room school house. He is a Staff Engineer for Motorola.

Sam's father born Dec. 16, 1904 in White Co., IL, is still working his farm in Point. His mother, born Apr. 3, 1908 in Gallatin, IL, is still keeping their home. They were married Dec. 23, 1924 and just celebrated their 64th Anniversary.

Sam's paternal grandparents were John and Eva (Whipple) Loehr, both born in Posey County, John Nov. 22, 1870 and Eva Aug. 1, 1872. John was the son of John and Margret (Cost) Loehr. Eva the daughter of Marion and Liza Whipple.

Sam's maternal grandparents were George and Attie May (Pruiett) Bell. George son of George and Fina (Perdue) Bell, born Oct. 3, 1875 in Tennessee. Attie May daughter of Ezra and Evalyn (Butler) Pruiett, born Nov. 8, 1880 in Gallatin Co., IL.

Sue was born Dec. 30, 1937 in Poseyville, IN, the eldest daughter of four, to Wm. Harold and Laura E. (Thompson) Lewis. She has worked for the Mesa School District for the past 19 years.

Sue's father was born May 6, 1912 in Poseyville, IN. He retired after 32 years with Bucyrus Erie Company in Evansville and still lives in Mt. Vernon with his second wife Evelyn (Broadhead). Sue's mother born Sept. 6, 1916 in Mt. Vernon, died Oct. 11, 1959. Harold and Laura were married May 6, 1936. Margo Ann (Lewis) Ramsey, their second daughter, born Oct. 17, 1939. Maria Elean (Lewis) Nelson, their third daughter, born Dec. 14, 1943. Monica Clair, their fourth daughter, born May 24, 1953 died in infancy Aug. 3, 1953.

Sue's paternal grandparents were George and Minnie (Osborn) Lewis of Poseyville. George born Dec. 12, 1871, son of James and Keyia (Cox) Lewis. James born June 22, 1825 from North Carolina. Minnie born Oct. 2, 1874 to Potiphar and Hannah (Scales) Osborn. Potiphar born Dec. 13, 1829 and Hannah born Feb. 4, 1839.

Sue's maternal grandparents William and Minnie (Watkins) Thompson of Mt. Vernon. William born Jan. 22, 1885 to John and Elizabeth Mary (Brune) Thompson. John born Apr. 22, 1853 to Louis T. and Nancy (Underwood) Thompson. Louis T. fought in the Civil War in Sherman's Army. He was the son of Stephen and Bridgette Ann (Lampkins) Thompson. Stephen was born in North Carolina around 1806. Bridgette was from Virginia. Louis T. immigrated from Kentucky to Perry Co., IN with his parents in August 1840. He married Nancy Oct. 13, 1850. In 1871 they moved their 12 children to Posey County east of Mt. Vernon. In 1886 they bought the Taylor Redmen farm. (This information was found in the 1900 Atlas of Posey County with pictures of Louis and Nancy). Nancy daughter of John and Jane (Bridges) Underwood formerly of South Carolina. Elizabeth Mary (Brune) Thompson born Dec. 8, 1858 to Frederick and Sophia (Damm) Brune. They came to America from Prussia (Germany) around 1850 with Sophia's parents William and Elizabeth Damm. Frederick born Apr. 21, 1831 and Sophia born May 10, 1830.

Minnie (Watkins) Thompson born Feb. 15, 1888 to Clinton and Laura (Barter) Watkins. Clinton was the son of Robert and Nancy (Crunk) Watkins who were married May 16, 1846 in Posey County. Laura (Barter) Watkins was the daughter of Job and Sarah (Bell) Barter, married May 1, 1862. Job was the son of William and Elizabeth (Downen) Barter. William came from Houl England in 1812. Elizabeth daughter of Job and Mary (Robinson) Downen of South Carolina. Job son of Josiah and Mary Downen. Josiah born in the 1740s served in the American Revolution. (See Photo Page 177)

CLIFFORD LOUIS MAAS

Clifford Louis Maas was born Aug. 29, 1905. The son of Michael and Estella (Alldridge) Maas. He was a native and lifelong resident of Mt. Vernon.

Clifford's paternal great grandparents were Moses Maas, born 1817-died 1870 and Henriette Siesal, born 1823-died 1847. Their son, Jacob Maas was born 1847 in Dalgesheim, Germany. He came to the United States from Germany when he was 13. He first went to Georgia and later to Mt. Vernon. His cousins, Abe and Isaac Maas were the founders of Maas Brothers department store in Tampa, FL. His cousin, Charles Klein, a noted dramatist and playwright, was drowned when the Lusitania was sunk by the Germans in World War I. Phillip Klein, his son, was a pioneer movie playwright and producer. Jacob married Eva Jarodzki in 1874. She was born in 1856 in Bromberg, Germany and died in 1919. They had five children, Moses, born 1878 and died 1931; Michael, born 1879 and died 1940; Reuben G., born 1881 and died 1920; Louis, born 1883 and died 1918, and Henrietta, born 1885 and died 1971.

Jacob Maas built the first movie theatre in Mt. Vernon at 128 Main Street. It was the "Colonial".

Michael Maas, Jacob's son, operated and managed the early movies in Mt. Vernon. First the "Dreamland", then the "Empress" and last the "Vernon".

Clifford's maternal great grandparents were Louis M. Jarodzki, born 1822 in Nakel, Germany and died 1883 and Sarah Somen, born 1833 in Norwich, England and died in 1887. They were married in 1848.

Louis M. Jarodzki purchased real estate at the corner of Main and Second streets Aug. 9, 1879 for £800. He established a mercantile business which he operated until his death. He left his estate to his wife, Sarah and children - Esther, Eva, Minnie, Max, Adolph and Otto. Eva Maas bought the business and operated it with her husband, Jacob Maas.

TIM AND JOANNE MALONEY

Tim Maloney was born near Ridgway, IL the son of Edward D. and Sallie (Mecum) Maloney. On Aug. 7, 1952, he was married to Joanne Poole the daughter of James and Lena (Hardesty) Poole of Eldorado, IL. Tim and Joanne lived near Ridgway, IL until 1960 when they moved to Mt. Vernon, IN. Tim is employed by General Electric and Joanne by K-Mart Corp. They have three children; James, Bridget, and Elizabeth.

James is an accountant in Evansville. Bridget is an accountant in Mt. Vernon and is married to Greg Wehr, they have one daughter, Whitney. Elizabeth is a dietician and is married to Bruce White. They live in Crown Point, IN.

JOHN DOSS AND PAMALLA KAY (McGREW) MANN

John Doss and Pamalla Kay (McGrew) Mann are long time residents of New Harmony. Posey County has always been home for John D., his parents, grandparents and great grandparents.

John D. born Oct. 12, 1946, is the fourth son of six children born to John Henry and Jancie Louise (Cartwright) Mann. Their other children are as follows: Billy Joe, Joan, Michael, Donald Wayne and Marilyn Sue. He attended grade school in Wadesville and graduated in 1964 from North Posey High School. After spending two years in the Armed Services, which included a tour of duty in Vietnam, he was employed by General Electric in Mt. Vernon. He is still employed there in Research and Development.

John D. is a member of Holy Angel Catholic Church. He is also an active member of the local Kiwanis Club. John D. had been known to work diligently to help those in need.

His parents have always lived in Wadesville where his maternal grandparents, Josephus Cartwright and Mamie (Allison), ran a grocery store.

Pamalla was born Mar. 31, 1947, in Muskogee, OK to the union of Holland James and Avon Elizabeth (Corder) McGrew. Her family, who had lived their entire lives in Oklahoma, came to Indiana in 1949 to look for a job in the oilfields.

She attended New Harmony Public School and graduated in 1965. Her graduating class of 33 was the largest to graduate to that date. Her first-grade class held 66 children. Pamalla is an active member of the local First Baptist Church. She also has taught at the Christian Harmony Preschool for the past eight years. Geneology has always been a love of Pamalla's and she is working hard at preserving the history of her family for future generations.

Pam and John are also the parents of one daughter, Peggy Ann, born Jan. 15, 1975.

This year Pamalla has undertaken the task of homeschooling her daughter to insure her a Christian education.

Holland, born Aug. 6, 1923, in Webber Falls, OK, was a well respected citizen of New Harmony. He was a deacon of the First Baptist Church, a hard worker, and a family man. He was employed by the Ashland Oil Company. His untimely death on Feb. 22, 1973, at age 49 was mourned by many.

Avon E. born Mar. 7, 1947, in Webber Falls, OK. She is an active member of the First Baptist Church. She is employed by Charles Ford Memorial Home in New Harmony.

Holland and Avon are also the parents of another daughter, Vickie Darcell (McGrew) Vallejos. Vickie, born Sept. 18, 1956, now resides with her husband Ralph and two children, Sarah age nine and Joshua age five in Jeffersonville, IN. Vickie is a registered nurse and is employed by the local "Visiting Nurses Association."

DON S. AND PAULA F. MATHEW

Don S. and Paula F. Mathew reside in Lynn Township on land that has been in the Mathew family since 1816. Paula was born Apr. 16, 1944 in Mt. Vernon, the second daughter born to Paul E. and Vivian G. (Slygh) Keitel. Paul's father came to America from Germany as a young boy. Paula has worked at General Electric since 1963 after graduating from Mt. Vernon High School in 1962.

Middle of Chair Don, Back of Chair Paula, Left Arm of Chair Denise, Right Arm of Chair Steven

Don was born Mar. 12, 1946, in Vanderburgh County, the third of four children born to Elbert Elwood Sr. and V. Berneice (Wolfe) Mathew. Don and Paula were married Aug. 31, 1968 and have two children: Denise D. born Mar. 13, 1971 and Steven D. born Mar. 14, 1975. Don has also worked at General Electric since graduating from Mt. Vernon High School in 1964.

Don's paternal grandparents were Jesse Alvis and Ethel (Johnson) Mathew. Ethel's parents were Rigdon and Emma (Aldrich) Johnson. Jesse Alvis was the son of Lytle and Grace B. (Gregory) Mathew. Jesse Alvis being named after both grandfathers: Jesse who married Sarah Wiley and Alvis Gregory who married Charlotte Wilson.

Alvis Gregory owned a livery stable in Mt. Vernon located on the East side of Main Street between 4th and 5th Street.

Jesse's parents were Caleb and Mary (Nash) Mathew who were married in Posey County on Sept. 23, 1816. Caleb for a short time served in the War of 1812 in Pennsylvania.

The Mathew, Nash, Wilson, Saltzman families all moved from Butler Co., PA to Posey County, all settling on land near each other and inter-marrying. Reports say the Mathew, Wilson and Saltzman's came down the Ohio River on a flat boat.

IVA NEWMAN MAUCK

Iva Newman Mauck, who is now retired and living at Westminster Village Kentuckiana, (a retirement center) Clarksville, IN, grew up in Cynthiana, IN. She is very busy in her retirement enjoying all the activities at W.V.K. such as trivial pursuit, bridge, bingo, sing-a-longs, coffee hours, vesper services, etc. Her hobby for many years has been feeding the birds and she has four bird feeders on her balcony of her second floor apartment. She buys bird seed ten and 15 pounds at a time. She also still loves to play the piano, including duets with a neighbor. Her love is classical music and still plays from memory Rachmaninoff's Prelude in C# Minor and Braham's Hungarian Dance #7. A Bach Prelude, Chopin Prelude in C#, Beethoven's Moonlight Sonata and her own arrangements of favorite hymns are among her favorites as well as an old piano arrangement of the Indian Love Song, "By the Waters of Minheuouka". She also loves to read!

Before 1982 Iva lived in Owensville, IN for 38 years, where her husband, Robert G. Mauck, owned and operated a Tractor and Farm Implement Service and Repair Shop and carried a line of International Harvestor parts for many years.

Iva Newman Mauck

She was very active in clubs, church work, and gave many book reviews. She is written up in 'Indiana Lives' by the Historical Record Association in 1967 and is a great, great granddaughter of Joseph Endicott, who was one of the early settlers of Posey County in 1815. She is also a descendant of John Endicott, first Governor (appointed by the King of England) of Massachusetts Bay Colony and on the first Board of Overseers of Harvard University.

Iva is also a member of Eastern Star, Daughters of the Nile (Shriner's Wives) of Evansville, D.A.R. and served on the Owensville Carnegie-Library Board for 20 years.

Before her marriage she taught school 20 years - 17 of which were in Greeley, CO - auditorium teacher in a platoon system. While there she was president of the Greeley Classroom Teachers, twice delegate to Colorado Teachers Association Business Meetings and head of the Nature Section one year at Colorado State Teacher's Convention in Denver.

She also served several years on a local advisory board for the House of Neighborly Service, a Presbyterian National Missions Service for Spanish speaking people. Before that she attended Indiana University one year, then transferred to James Millinkin University and Conservatory of Music for two years. There she received a Certificate in Piano playing. After teaching primary two years at Atkinson, IL, she moved with her family to Colorado where she received her A.B. degree in Education at Colorado State College of Education - now Northern Colorado University.

She graduated from the Cynthiana High School in 1918 and while in her late teens gave piano lessons to a large number of children in the Cynthiana and Poseyville area. She also clerked in her father's store and was active in the Presbyterian Church.

Iva was the daughter of Schuyler C. and Ada Rebecca Newman, born in Vangerburg County (Armstrong Township) Mar. 6, 1900. Her family moved to Cynthiana in 1903 and in 1905 her father opened up the Lumber and Building Material business, which included a Planing Mill. Later this included a grain business. About 1922, after selling the business he bought a general merchandise store (back when coffee was two pounds for 25¢ and had to be ground when sold and men's overcoats were $11.95.) He was active in the Presbyterian Church and Civic Affairs and was written up in the 1913 Posey County History. Her brother, Maurice T. Newman, was a bookkeeper in a Greeley, CO bank and died in 1938.

Iva Newman Mauck believes that to be happy one must keep busy.

McCONNELL

Eldon Eddie and Darlene McConnell are residents of Mt. Vernon, both are graduates of Mount Vernon High School class of 1964. They married Jan. 18, 1969. Their children are: Christina, born Apr. 18, 1973 and Angela, born Jan. 3, 1984.

Eddie was born Nov. 28, 1946 in Hardin Co., IL, the oldest son of Eldon Leroy and Pauline (Davis) McConnell. The family moved from Cave-in-Rock to Manteno, IL, there Eddie attended Manteno High School from 1960-1963. Eddie served with the US Army in Germany. He is now an electrician at General Electric where he has been employed since March 1968. His antecedents include the Bryants, Griffith and Stark families of Spencer Co., IN.

Darlene was born Oct. 4, 1946 to Willard H. and Martha (Walker) Gerth natives of Posey. She worked at the Credit Bureau of Posey County, Inc. until 1972. She has written and published three books of local historical interest.

Her father was born Apr. 6, 1918. He retired from ADM Mill after 23 years in 1983. He died May 19, 1988. Her mother was born Feb. 21, 1923. She

Eddie, Darlene, Chrissy, and Angela

worked for Otis Allyn Abstractor and the Credit Bureau of Posey County, Inc. They are also the parents of Beverly and W. Scott Gerth.

Darlene's paternal grandparents were Albert and Nellie (Reed) Gerth. Albert was the son of William and Margaret (Martin) Gerth. William immigrated from Buhl, Baden, Germany with his parents in 1847. He apprenticed under his father and, after serving in the Union Army, became an accomplished local barn and bridge builder. Margaret, his wife, had located near Caborn in 1867, with her parents Michael and Rosina (Gabel) Martin. Her family was of German descent. Albert married Nellie the daughter of Willard and Amy (Bell) Reed. Willard, a Bufkin farmer, was a native of Warrick Co., IN. His grandfather served in the Rev. War. Amy was born at Bufkin to James and Elizabeth (Lamb) Bell. The Bells are from Carteret Co., NC.

Darlene's maternal grandparents are Loren Donaldson Walker, deceased, and his wife Nell Lee York. Loren, a farmer and school bus driver, was the son of Cornelius and Cora (Donaldson) Walker. Nell a retired teacher, is the daughter of Sherman and Anna (James) York. While a child her family homesteaded lottery land near Fort Cobb, OK. She is now Mrs. Robert Guffey. The Yorks arrived from Randolph Co., NC about 1812. Nell's grandparents were Thomas Jr. and Olivia Mariah (Beckley) James. The grandmother was French. Her grandfather was the son of Thomas and Anna (Lowry) James, who were married in Mount Vernon on Christmas Day 1823. Their son was born in 1827 in Baton Rouge, LA. Thomas Sr., a man of great promise, died young. His widow and small son made their home with her brother-in-law and her sister Enoch and Esther (Lowry) James in the Old James homestead overlooking Robin Hill, the home their brother William J. Lowry built in 1836. The James were from Virginia. The Lowrys are Irish.

THE McDURMONS

Mary Eliza McDurmon - her family and ancestors

Mary Eliza McDurmon was born Sept. 14, 1897 at Mount Vernon, IN, the daughter of John McDurmon, Morganfield, KY and his wife Sally Emma Fuhrer McDurmon, Mount Vernon, IN. The children born to this family were:

1. Arthur Leo McDurmon (1893-1901). 2. Alex Fuhrer McDurmon (1885-1972); Married Rose Hoehn; 12 children. 3. Anna Ruby McDurmon married Frank Hellenberg-4 children (1888-1963), 4. Leonard Howard McDurmon (1890-); Married Anna Watson Thielman; two children. 5. Zeb Sullivan McDurmon (1892-1986); Married Lucille Martell; one daughter: Emma M. Lackey. 6. Mary Eliza McDurmon (McFadden) (1897-1974); six children, 12 grandchildren.

John McDurmon (1856-1943) and Sally Emma Fuhrer McDurmon (1860-1924) were married in April of 1881 in Mount Vernon, IN, where their six children were born.

The parents of John McDurmon were Michael McDurmon of Sulphur Springs, KY and Mary Ann Berry (1842-1870); they were married in 1855. After the death of Michael, who was killed in action while serving with the Confederate Army during the Civil War, Mary Ann married for the second time to Thomas Jackson in 1863, in Morganfield, KY.

The only brother of John McDurmon who could be traced was William who was said to have died at the Klatz home in Point Township, IN, around 1880. He was 20 years old and was buried in the Greathouse Cemetery north of the church.

Sally Emma Fuhrer McDurmon, John McDurmon

Sally Emma Fuhrer (1860-1924) and John McDurmon (1856-1943) were married Apr. 24, 1881. John was 25 years old and Sally Emma was 20 years old.

Sally Emma Fuhrer was the daughter of Leopold Fuhrer (? - 1876)and Eliza Westerman (1816-1873) were married in May, 1846 in Steubenville, OH. Children of this union were:

1. Mary Frances Fuhrer (1848-1943) b. Mount Vernon, d. Houston, TX. 2. Morris Alexander Fuhrer (1849-?) b. Mount Vernon. 3. Ernestine D. Fuhrer (1851-1852) 4. George Robert Fuhrer (1853-?) b. Mount Vernon 5. James Leo Fuhrer (1855-1858) b. Mount Vernon. 6. Caroline Ernestine and Kate Amelia (twins) (1858-?) b. Mount Vernon. 7. Sally Emma Fuhrer (1860-1924) b. Mount Vernon. 8. Richard Leonard Fuhrer (1867-1876) b. Henderson Co., KY (opposite Mount Vernon)

Eliza Westerman Fuhrer was the daughter of James Alexander Westerman, Wakefield, England (b. 1790, Yorkshire England, d. 1868, Sharon, PA) and Sara Scholaise (Sara Schofield, 1795-1836), who married in Paris. There were nine children born to this marriage: 1. James (1819-1884), 2. Eliza Westerman Fuhrer (1821-1873) b. Cateau, France, d. Mount Vernon. 3. Joseph (1824-1830). 4. Thomas (? -1843). 5. David (? -1850). 6. Robert (? - 1862) Killed in the Civil War. 7. Carolina (dates unknown). 8. Ernestine (1831-1847). 9. George (1836-1918).

James A. Westerman went with his father, Robert Westerman of Wakefield, England, to Paris in 1816, where they were in the cotton spinning business. From Paris, they went to Cateau, France; most of the children of James and Sara were born near Paris in Cateau or Pontrois. James A. came to America in 1829 and subsequently purchased a farm near Cleveland, OH in 1832. His son James was with him, but the rest of the family stayed in France until 1836 when some members joined them in America. There are many interesting letters from those remaining in France to the family members in the "new" world. James A. and son James first came to Pittsburgh, PA where they originally set up a cotton spinning factory that was later destroyed by fire. From Pennsylvania and Ohio the Westerman family branched out, one going as far as the Dakota Territory.

THE McFADDENS

The McFaddens of Posey Co., IN (West Lynn Township) were farmers from the time of the marriage of great grandfather Noah Sr., to Sarah Albright (1821) and a resulting dowry of land now owned by Douglas McFadden of Washington, D.C.

Noah Sr., had three sons who lived to marriage age and left descendants. (1) Noah Jr., the son of James and America McFadden, had children by his first wife Maggie (Noel), and four sons by the second. The last grandson Kenneth died in Oregon in 1988. Another son, Oral, lived and died in Savannah, IL. The youngest, Philocus Polk McFadden married Malinda Bundy (the name as written in the 1850 census was Bonda).

Malinda, was the daughter of James Bundy, Sr. (1800-1837) and sister of "Uncle" Benoni Bundy and "Aunt" Caroline Huston, who moved to Kansas. James Sr., Benoni, Uncle Billy and his son James are buried in the Alexander Cemetery on Bundy Road, Lynn Township.

Polk McFadden (1844-1895) had an older brother; Enoch who married Emily (Aldredge), they had a daughter Ida who married Charles Weir. A son Enoch did police work in Evansville, then joined the sheriff staff in Los Angeles, CA. Enoch McFadden (and some eight or nine brothers and a sister, Catherine) are buried in McFadden Cemetery on Lower New Harmony Road.

The Noah and Florence (Gano) Family; John Hanig, Charles, Hazel, Merle G.

Children of Polk and Malinda were James, Enoch, Benoni, Noah, Idella (who married Julius Alexander) and Hanie, who was accidentally killed in a hunting accident on Hovey Lake.

James and Isabell (Aldrich) had sons Ivan who had sons Ivan Jr. of Florida and Robert of Maryland.

Benoni and wife Ora (Hunt) had three sons; Fieldon of Wyoming, Goebel in the New Harmony Nursing Home, and Basil who had Jim and Ora Dell Butler.

Idella and her husband Julius Alexander had daughters Mable and first born Lena, who married Paul Addison, also sons Carson and Morris. There were no grandchildren.

Noah McFadden married Florence Amanda Gano of French Hugenot descent, on the Gano (Ganeau) side, and a Dutch ancestor on the grandmother side (nee Amanda). Thus three ancestors can be traced back to participation in the Revolution. Mrs. McFadden's grandfather, Henry Beavers Gano is buried in the Civil War Cemetery at Knoxville, TN. He is listed as dying of pneumonia, as did many soldiers; her father John Gano and wife Sarah (Aldrich) are buried in Black Cemetery.

Noah McFadden and Florence (Gano) had five children. The youngest died as an infant. The family lived next to the old McFadden school at the junction of Raben and Lower New Harmony Roads.

John Hanie was an ex-sheriff (as were Uncle James and Enoch); John Hanie and wife Agnes (Notter) have a daughter Evonnee and a son Daniel. Daniel has two children. Vonnie and husband Wm. Grabert have one daughter and, to date, one grandson - Joshua Smith.

Charles and wife Lee of Mattoon, IL, had Noah Edward McFadden, then twins Martha Thompson and Paul McFadden. Paul is buried in the Noah and Florence McFadden Plot of Bellefountain Cemetery, as is Gilbert Cox, Hazel's husband. Hazel is the only girl in the Noah & Florence McFadden family Wm. Cox, present sheriff of Posey County, is her son. He and Lillian, two daughters and two sons, Dwaine and Darrin, also three grandsons to date.

Merle G. McFadden (1903) started teaching at age 18 at Old McFadden School. He also served in the Bureau of Ships, Washington, DC and later decommissioned the Naval Supply Base 717, of New Guinea, in 1946. He was principal in Stewartsville School, taught in Evansville and in Cleveland Heights, OH until retirement in 1969.

He and his wife Ethel (Reynolds), also a teacher, and an artist, moved to Grand Chain Road in West Lynn Township. Ethel died Dec. 24, 1981 and is buried in Stewartsville. Joan McDurmon and husband Alex (Butch) McDurmon provided the first grandchild James. James is sheriff of Spencer County (Rockport) sons Jason and Joe are great-grandsons. Both are good Jr. and Senior High School students. Joel aspires to be another Audubon, or an artist like his grandmother.

Merle has spent his winter months with son Thomas S. on Lake Sanier in Georgia, but prefers Summers near the Wabash in Posey County.

Tom and wife Janet (Humphrey) became grandparents on Dec. 9, 1988, when little Nicholas George Pugh was born to Diana (McFadden) and her husband Darrell of Signal Mt., TN. Michael and John T. are college age and as yet unmarried. Tom is expecting to build a home this spring in Jacksonville, FL where he will continue with a national computerized building company.

Much information about the early McFaddin-McFadden settlement at the "Rocks" (1905) and at McFadin Bluff (1909) is found in Posey County libraries. A painting of the Bluff is at the Workingmen's Institute in New Harmony.

The McFaddens are descended from John McFadin's oldest son William who died at his "hotel" on the N.E. corner of 2nd and Main Streets. The related McFadins of Posey County retained the old North Carolina spelling, and are descended by way of Andrew's son Roly, a full brother of (Slim) Andy Jr. Slim Andy's two sons A. Hogan and Squire migrated westward as did William's son John. John was killed by Civil War partisans in Missouri.

More McFadin-McFaddens have left Posey County than remain. Seven cemeteries account for most who remained. William's relatives were buried on Givens Road Cemetery without markers. Andrew Sr. was buried across the street from the

Mt. Vernon water works but others were largely buried at old Bradley Cemetery, now completely destroyed. Roly McFadin's family members are buried near by at Gill Cemetery. McFadden Cemetery holds early Noah McFadden Sr. members except later ones buried at Beech Grove, or Belfountain. Later McFadins are buried at Welborn Church Cemetery.

A nephew of Wm. and Andrew, son of Elias McFadin who was killed by Indians came with his uncles to Indiana Territory. He became known as Tiddle-de-dum for his musical talents. He had three daughters who married Monroe, Hackett, and Peel. He left Posey County in the 1850s, to live with the Peel family in their new home in Springfield, IL. There were three Peel grandsons John, Andrew, and Thomas and four daughters. Monroes and Hacketts are known as teachers and writers.

Andrew Sr. and second wife had three sons. Son (Slim) Jim and Samuel had one son each; both died early. Daughters are known to have married into the following families; Templeton, Erwin, White, Young. Others need further tracing.

There is a marker on Barren River, KY, opposite the mouth of Drake Creek, to the McFadin settlement, (a crude fort giving protection against Indian raids). Bowling Green became a nearby city.

The D.A.R. provided a marker for captain James McFadin and the John McFadden (17-1776) home fort, where his parents, eight sons and one daughter lived. The county is now Rutherford and the nearest city (about three miles East) is Rutherfordton, NC. Wm. took part in the Revolution at Cowpens and was later paid for oats furnished for horses of the South Carolina militia.

FIELDON BENONI McFADDEN FAMILY

Fieldon Benoni McFadden (1893-1953) married Mary Eliza McDurmon (1897-1974) (the McDurmons are another early Mount Vernon family) in Mount Vernon in January, 1922. They had four sons and two daughters.

Fieldon was educated at Indiana State, Terre Haute. His first venture west was into North Dakota where he taught school briefly, returning to Mount Vernon. He enlisted in the U.S. Army Corps on Sept. 21, 1917, during World War I. He rose to the rank of Sergeant on Oct. 10, 1918, during his service in France. On July 26, 1919, he received his discharge. After his marriage to Mary E. McDurmon, he again traveled west, in the spring of 1926. Leaving Savah, IN, where he had operated a small grocery store, he traveled by automobile and first visited the Wyoming towns of Lander and Casper. He chose to settle in the little town of Pinedale, WY, where he became the manager of the Pinedale Cash Store, a general merchandise business.

In the spring of 1928, Fieldons' wife Mary Eliza and his two sons, John Stinson and Elbert Howard (both born in Mount Vernon) followed him to Wyoming. They traveled by train as far as the coal-mining town of Rock Springs, WY. Upon their arrival there, the then very bleak, desert-like countryside caused Mary to have many misgivings about the move to Wyoming. She admitted to crying most of the 100 miles north to Pinedale; she also said that the taxi driver was less than sympathetic. She was pleasantly relieved when they reached their destination; Pinedale was a very small town nestled among the beautiful peaks of the Wind River Mountain Range. The log home they lived in still stands today, and is being lived in by Pinedale residents. Their son, Pat, and their daughter Mary Yvonne were both born there. Although Mary adjusted to the rugged life in Wyoming, she never got over her love for Indiana and especially Mount Vernon. She visited as often as possible, returning yearly to see her family. Her last visit was in September of 1973, just a few months before her death on Jan. 4, 1974.

Fieldon Benoni McFadden, Mary Eliza McDurmon McFadden

In the summer of 1933, the family moved to the larger town of Rock Springs, where Fieldon had accepted a position as Manager of the W.W. Scott Wholesale Company. In 1935, Fieldon, along with E.C. Hobson, a Purina Mills representative, purchased the W.W. Scott Wholesale business. In 1936, Fieldon bought Hobson's interest and from that time it became known as the F.B. McFadden Wholesale Company. On Fieldon's death in 1953, the three sons, Elbert H., Pat, and Michael, continued to operate the business with John Stinson joining them in 1964. Elbert H. is President of McFadden Wholesale, Pat is Vice-President, Michael is Treasurer, with John Stinson as Sales Manager.

Children Alice, Jeann and Michael were born in Rock Springs following the move from Pinedale. The children of Fieldon Benoni and Mary McDurmon McFadden are:

1. John Stinson McFadden (b. Dec. 22, 1922). Wife: Wilmot Curnow McFadden

Children: Maureen Mary (m. Dan Pedry) (b. 1946), Susan Genevieve (m. Dennis Duncan) (b. 1955), Wilmot Christi (m. Charles Bice) (b. 1947).

Grandchildren: Scott John Pedry, Sarah Genevieve Pedry, (Stacey Jeannette 1966-1980), Jessica Stacey Duncan, Katherine Wilmot Bice, Christopher Charles Bice.

2. Elbert Howard McFadden (b. 1926) Wife: Lucille Taucher McFadden (Rock Springs).

Children: Gene H. McFadden, Mary Anne Katana McFadden, Dale McFadden, Terry Brennan McFadden.

Grandchildren: Jeanie McFadden, Julie McFadden, Kelly McFadden, Eileen McFadden, Christopher McFadden.

3. Pat McFadden (b. 1928) Wife: Reka Santini McFadden (Rock Springs).

Children: Pat McFadden, Jr. Linda McFadden (Attorney-at-Law, California).

4. Yvonne Mary McFadden (b. 1931) Husband: Alex Unguren (Rohnert Park, CA).

Children: Dr. John Fieldon Unguren (m. Suzanne Berger).

Grandchildren: Michelle Unguren, Ross Unguren, Allison Unguren.

5. Alice Jean McFadden (b. 1933) Husband: Rudy Cristanelli (Rock Springs).

Children: Wayne A. Cristanelli, Jayne B. (Adams), June M. (Hansen).

Grandchildren: Rudy Cristanelli, Matthew Cristanelli, Jason Cristanelli, Amber Adams, Kimberly Hansen.

6. Michael Fieldon McFadden (b. 1939), Wife: Marlene Noble (Rock Springs).

Children: David M. McFadden, Paul A. McFadden.

ANCESTORS AND FAMILY OF FIELDON BENONI MCFADDEN

Fieldon Benoni McFadden was born on Sept. 6, 1893, Posey Co., IN, in Savah, the original site of the family home (and Post Office). His brother Goebel and wife, Georgia, still reside there. Goebel has the abstract of title to his present home and surrounding area that shows that President Andrew Jackson signed the deed of the land to James McFadden. Goebel has abstracts of legal dealings of the past one hundred years and the law books of his great grandfather. "Polk", Benoni, Fieldon, and Goebel's son, Don were born in this house. Fieldon Benoni McFadden was the son of Benoni Stinson McFadden and Ora Dell Hust. They were married on Dec. 23, 1892. Other sons of this marriage are Goebel McFadden (1901-) and Basil McFadden (1903-1938). Ora Dell Hust McFadden was the daughter of John Hust and Ellebeth Messmore of Springfield, IN. John Hust was a soldier in the Civil War. Ora Dell's great grandfather, Ruben Altizer, born in 1776 is buried in Springfield.

Benoni Stinson McFadden (1869-1949) was born in Posey County, the son of Philocles **Polk** McFadden and Malinda Bundy McFadden. Philocles **Polk** (1844-1894) was the son of Noah Webster McFadden (1802-1879) and Sarah Albright McFadden (1804-1868). Noah W., in turn, was the son of William McFadden who married twice, his second marriage was to Rachael Hendricks Hogan (widow). William and Rachael were married Oct. 18, 1789. William died in 1811. William was the son of John Stephens McFadin and Hannah. Other sons of John Stephens and Hannah were:

1. Captain James McFaddin, an officer of the Virginia Militia. 2. John Jr. who served in the South Carolina Militia. 3. Samuel McFadin - buried in Christian City, KY. 4. Elias McFadin - killed by the Indians in Tennessee - his son Andrew II (Tiddle-de-dum-a musician) is credited as being the first to settle McFadden's Bluff in 1805. On a hunting trip in 1795, Andrew, a native of North Carolina crossed Kentucky to the Ohio River, in Indiana, and to the bluff overlooking the Ohio River. Later in 1804 he brought his family there, making them the first settlers there. After he had built his house, Andrew (Slim) and William McFadden (cousins) followed him there and gave the settlement the name of McFadden's Bluff, later to become Mount Vernon.

5. Andrew "Slim" McFadden of the Virginia Militia was an Indian fighter under General William Henry Harrison (later to become the President of the United States). "Slim" was credited with firing the first shot in the Battle of Tippecanoe on Nov. 18, 1811. "Slim" Andrew subsequently traveled to Texas. 6. Andrew McFadin (Sr.) - Virginia Militia - Mount Vernon 1805. 7. Stephen McFadden - (1760-1836) - North Carolina. 8. Alexander McFadden was a Minute Man at the age of 16 years in the American Revolution.

William, himself, was a member of the South Carolina Militia during the Revolutionary war.

John Stephens McFadden (1700-1776) was born in Garagh, Northern Ireland and married Hannah (no last name was found). He came to America in

1718. At the same time his father, Andrew (McFadden (1675-) and his mother, Mercy Mallory, also came, settling near Rutherford (present name), NC.

Andrew McFadden (1675-) was born in Inverness, Scotland and emigrated to America from Northern Ireland. Andrew and his family came to America for religious freedom. In Northern Ireland at that time, citizens were expected to embrace the beliefs and rituals of the Church of England, the McFaddens were Scottish Presbyterians and did not feel that they could abide by the English Law. After settling in North Carolina members of the McFaddens, McFaddin, McFadin family members were to branch out into Tennessee, Kentucky, Ohio, Indiana. Some went even further afield to Texas and other Western States, yet others settled in a few New England States.

GOEBEL AND GEORGIA McFADDEN

Geobel and Georgia McFadden reside in Lynn Township on the farm homesteaded by Goebel's Great-grandfather, Noah McFadden in 1821. They were married in 1921.

Goebel was born Nov. 10, 1901 to Ben and Ora Dell McFadden in Posey County. He has been a farmer all his life. He attended Mt. Vernon High School and graduated from the Chicago School of Auctioneering. He was an auctioneer for a number of years. He also was an independent school bus operator for 42 years without an accident. He was also active in the Democratic Party and a delegate to the Democratic State Convention.

Goebel is a direct descendant of Andrew McFadden, who was born in Inverness, Scotland in 1675. Andrew McFadden came to America in 1718 from Northern Ireland after petitioning the Governor of the New England Colony for rights to colonize. Andrew McFadden settled with his wife and six children in Maine only to be burned out by Indians in 1723. Andrew's son John Stephen McFadden, later migrated to Rutherfordton, NC where he built a plantation and erected Fort McFadden. The Fort was destroyed in 1777 by British loyalists. John Stephen McFadden and his sons, James, William, and Andrew McFadden served the American cause during the American Revolution.

Goebel and Georgia McFadden

William and Andrew left Fort McFadden at Rutherfordton, NC after serving in the American Revolution, for which they received land bounties in Kentucky. They first settled near Bowling Green, KY later moving to Indiana when that part of the Northwest Territory, north of the Ohio River, was opened for settlement. William and Andrew settled McFadden's Bluff in 1805, which later became known as Mt. Vernon. William's son Noah McFadden, who was Goebel's great-grandfather, was one of the first settlers in Lynn Township in 1821 and served as a justice for the township.

Goebel's grandfather, Polk McFadden who was Noah McFadden's son and a prominent Posey County farmer, was a Southern sympathizer during the Civil War. Typical of the time, Goebel's maternal grandfather, John Hust, served in the Union Army's 144th Indiana Regiment during the Civil War.

Goebel's maternal great-great-grandfather, Elias Altizer, was the first overseer of the poor in Lynn Township and furnished material for the first county courthouse at Springfield in 1817. Elias Altizer sold land in Harmony township to the Rappities in 1815; land he had recorded in 1811.

Georgia was born Feb. 10, 1905, in Clinton Co., KY to Martin Alexander and Addeline Guffey. She moved with her family as a little girl to Posey County. Georgia was a registered practical nurse and an active civic leader. She has been a 4-H leader, active in the Posey County Cancer Society, and in the Savah General Baptist Church. She has also been active in the Posey County Women's Democratic Club. Georgia's Grandfather, George Carr was sheriff of Clinton Co., KY. Her great-uncle, Preston Leslie served as attorney general and governor of Kentucky and later governor of Montana Territory.

Goebel and Georgia have three children Donald, who resides in Lynn Township and farmed with Goebel, a daughter, Malinda Walls, who is a former teacher and resides in Seattle, WA, and Douglas, an attorney who resides in Washington, D.C. They have three grandchildren, Kirby and Cindy Walls and Anne McFadden. Georgia's brother, Robert Guffey, resides in Mt. Vernon.

McFADIN-GAISER

George Ellis McFadin was born in Black Township on June 3, 1886, the son of Enoch and Belle (Castiller) McFadin. He farmed with his father until 1912 when he went to St. Louis, MO. In St. Louis George was employed as a conductor by the United Railways Company of St. Louis.

George and Pauline McFadin

There on July 16, 1914 at the Wagoner Memorial Church, George married Pauline Rosina Gaiser, the daughter of Martin and Christina (Walz) Gaiser. Pauline was born on July 17, 1893 in Centralia, IL. Just prior to her marriage, Pauline attended a Secretarial College in St. Louis. The McFadins, in time, had a family of eight children.

Two of their children, Elvera then Ruth were born in St. Louis. In 1918 George and Pauline brought their family to Posey County to live in Black Township near the Upton community and there they resided the remainder of their lives. Six more children were born to them in Posey County: Irene, Woodrow, Paul, Lola, Doris, and Shirley. All eight children are surviving and all except Elvera and Shirley currently reside in Posey County.

Elvera lives in Evansville, IN. Shirley lives in Brentwood, CA.

George farmed for many years. He also owned a tavern in Mt. Vernon in the 1940s. McFadin's Orchard, the family's business, occupied a lot of their time while their children were growing up. From June, 1947 till their deaths, they owned and ran McFadin's Furniture Store on Main Street, Mt. Vernon. For several years after George's death, Pauline found consolation in managing the furniture store.

The McFadin home was always busy on Sundays as it served as a neighborhood gathering place after church. Pauline prepared delicious German meals for the whole family to enjoy, even in her later years.

George died July 9, 1952 in Evansville, IN. Pauline past away on Dec. 26, 1960. They are both buried at Welborn Cemetery. Pauline was a member of Trinity United Church of Christ in Mt. Vernon.

McFADIN-PHILLIPS

Wilfred LaRue Phillips was born June 27, 1926, in Mt. Vernon, IN, the son of Wilfred, and Mary E. (Benthall) Phillips. LaRue attended Central School. He graduated from Mt. Vernon Senior High in 1944 and earned his Bachelor-of-Arts Degree in Education from Evansville College in 1959 and his Masters-of-Science Degree in Education from Indiana State University at Terre Haute in 1964. LaRue taught and coached three and one half years in Illinois. Then upon moving to Mt. Vernon, he was an employee of People's Bank and Trust Company for several years after which he went back to teaching and coaching for the Mt. Vernon School District. He taught at the Mt. Vernon Junior High for 23 years and retired from the teaching occupation there in 1988.

LaRue and Doris Phillips

LaRue was a technical Sargeant in the U.S. Army during WWII. He was awarded the Purple Heart after being wounded in fighting on Cebu in the Philippines in May, 1945.

On Dec. 29, 1951, at Lynnville, Warrick Co., IN, LaRue married Doris Jean McFadin, born Feb. 9, 1929, in Black Township. Doris is the daughter of George E. and Pauline (Gaiser) McFadin.

Doris attended Upton School and graduated from Mt. Vernon Senior High School in 1946. She received her Bachelor-of-Arts teaching degree from Evansville College in 1950 and later earned her Master-of-Science degree at Indiana State University in Terre Haute. She then taught at the Mt. Vernon Senior High and several years in Illinois. After moving back to Posey County, Doris taught at Hedges Elementary. She has taught the past 24 years at the Mt. Vernon Junior High where she serves as chairperson of the Language Arts Department.

Doris and LaRue are members of Trinity United Church of Christ in Mt. Vernon where they taught Sunday School for many years. LaRue is a member of the Masonic Lodge at Mt. Vernon. He is a member of the Evansville VFW #1114 and Doris is a member of that auxiliary. Doris belongs to the National Council of Teachers of English and the Indiana Council of Teachers of English.

The Phillipses have two daughters, Delene Schmitz and Deena Cortus. They also have two grandchildren, Hans and Carly Schmitz. They reside at 5621 Upton Road, Mt. Vernon, IN.

OSCAR McGENNIS FAMILY

Oscar McGennis and Inez Redman were married, St. Louis, MO in 1928. His parents were William S. and Eliza White McGennis. The McGennis came to America from Ireland, the Whites from Wales. Both had soldiers in the Revolutionary and Civil Wars and the two world wars. Oscar had two brothers and six sisters. Oscar was employed at the Chevrolet Assembly Plant in St. Louis for 15 years. They came to Indiana (Point Twp.) in 1937 and engaged in farming and eventually owned farms in Point Twp. The family was active in Farmers Chapel Church until it disbanded, they then became members of Zoar Methodist Church. Oscar was an active member of the Odd Fellows Lodge, Methodist Men, P.T.A., 4-H, Farm Bureau, and the Republican Party. He served as a party delegate to the state convention and circuit and federal juries numerous times. He also helped consolidate the schools in the Mt. Vernon Metropolitan School District. He was a member of the committee to pick sites for the schools. In 1965, he and Inez re-opened the Hovey Store and operated it successfully until July 1969. After moving to their newly built home, he went to work at the Wabash Toll Bridge. He worked there until 1976 when he retired, August 29, he died from heart failure 9:30 P.M. the same day. He is buried beside son Thomas in Bellefontaine Cemetery.

Ann, Inez, Oscar, Allen McGennis

Six children were born to them. They attended Blacks Grade School and Mt. Vernon High School. Eugene was born Sept. 2, 1929, St. Louis, was in Navy during the Korean conflict, lived in California and there married Barbara Yeager. Two sons, Mark and Rick. They divorced and he married Patricia Gough, came to Posey County and worked at Alcoa in Warrick County. Patricia died Oct. 17, 1980, he died Oct. 31, 1981, buried in Bellefontaine Cemetery.

Mary Jane was born Feb. 13, 1936, a graduate of Deaconess Nursing School and is married to Russell Halco. They have a daughter and a son, and live in Ohio.

Allen was born Nov. 30, 1938, is married to Loyce (Erwin). They have two daughters, and two sons. He and sons own and farm in Point Twp.

Ann (Thompson) was born Jan. 10, 1941. She married Paul Thompson and they live in Mt. Vernon, IN. They have two daughters and one son.

Thomas was born Mar. 3, 1946. He was a member of the U.S. Army, 1965-1969 when he became ill, his father gave a kidney for transplant at Cleveland Clinic in 1968. Tom died Sept. 9, 1969. He is buried in Bellefontaine Cemetery.

William was born Feb. 19, 1950. He served in the U.S. Army from 1969 to 1971. He married Mary Ann (Nurrenbern) and they have one son and one daughter. They live in Mt. Vernon, IN.

McKINNIES

James McKinnies was born in 1807 in Tennessee. He married Jane Elkins and they had seven children. One son, Daniel, was born in 1844 in Indiana. Daniel married Sarah Catherine Wilson in 1866 and had three children, two of whom died in infancy. The surviving child was Leroy, born in 1888. In 1909, Leroy McKinnies married Stella Causey and they had three children: Zona Marie born 1912, Okal Mae born 1916, Royvan born 1919.

Zona married James Earl Travers in 1928 and they have four children: Eugene Earl born 1929, Marilyn Jean born 1934, Connie Earlene born 1947, and Teresa Rendell born 1952. Zona's family currently resides in Kentucky and Tennessee. Eugene is presently married to Jeannine Buckle and has three sons, Steven Earl born 1949, Kim Eugene born 1954, and Eugene Earl "Bubby" born 1968; three grandchildren, and one great-grandchild. Marilyn married Roy K. Pindell and has three children: Deborah Lynn born 1954, Duane Keith born 1956, and Russell Kevin born 1957. Deborah is presently married to Robert Davidson and has three sons: Ryan Thompson born 1976, Jeffrey Thompson born 1980, and Robert Davidson III born 1985. Duane married Theresa Banz and has one daughter Brittany born 1986. Russell married Donna Sullins and has two sons, Michael Sullins Pindell born 1980 and Dustin born 1983. Connie is presently married to Larry Barker and has two children, Kristi LaDonna born 1968 who married Rick Pompell in 1988, and Larry Heath born 1974. Teresa "Rendy" married William Donald Hopper and has two children, Jamie Bree born 1978 and William Nathan born 1982.

Earl and Zona Travers, Okal and Archie Blackburn, Evelyn and Royvan McKinnies

Okal married Archie Blackburn in 1933 who died in 1985. They had three children: Donald Lee born 1933, Dorothy Mae born 1935 and Dolores Marie born 1938. Donald is presently married to Jan Lindsey (1971). He has two children, Jennifer Anne born 1958 and Donald Lee Jr. "Buddy" born 1960. Jennifer has three children, Carrie Ann Mominee born 1979, Jamie Lynn Mominee born 1981, and Andrew Lawrence Lindenschmidt born 1988. "Buddy" married Danette Lumpkin in 1987. Dorothy Mae is presently married to Edward Hall. She has two sons Eugene Doyle Minton born 1956 who married Debra Morgan in 1985, and Wesley Brewer born 1968. Dolores "Tootsie" married Marion Thomas "Mac" McKnight in 1958 and they have three children: Thomas Bruce born 1961, Timothy Brian born 1964, and Tamra Beth born 1966. Thomas married Kimberly Zier and has a son Joshua Thomas born 1988. Although Okal's children have moved to Texas and Florida, Okal resides in Posey County.

Royvan married Evelyn Marjorie Searcy in 1941 and they had three children: Betty Ann born 1942, Van Lee "Chip" born 1946, and Danny Ray who died in infancy in 1947. Royvan served three and one-half years in World War II as a charter member of the 82nd Airborne 325th Glider Infantry and has six combat stars. Royvan served the Wadesville U.S. Post Office for 17 years, nine of which he served as Postmaster. Their daughter Betty Ann married Arthur Stierley, Jr. in 1961 and they have three children: Terri Lynn born 1962, Vicki Lee born 1965, and Randy Ray born 1966. Terri married David Koch in 1983 and they have one son, Christopher David born 1986. Vickie married Orvel Schroeder in 1986 and they have one son, Patrick Benjamin born 1989. Randy married Anita Murphy in 1985. Van Lee served three years in the U.S. Army including one year in Vietnam and is presently married to Bonnie Tomlinson (1983) who has one son, Ken Wayne Tomlinson born 1966. Royvan's family continues to reside in Posey County, where Royvan, Chip, Randy and now Christopher, as the fourth generation, enjoy farming.

TREVA ALLDREDGE MILES

Treva Alldredge Miles, second child of Eileen Butler Alldredge and Myron Lee Alldredge of the Upton Community met and married her husband in Evansville, IN. After graduating from the University of Evansville with a degree in Elementary Education, she taught first grade at Highland School on the north side of Evansville. It was during her teaching days that she met Alan Page Miles, a native of Logan Co., KY. A graduate of the University of Kentucky, he was working as a Mechanical Engineer for Alcoa, Warrick Operations, Newburgh.

He had just finished a 13 month tour of duty as First Lieutenant, Ordnance Corps, 635th Military Intelligence Detachment (October 1968 - October 1969) in The Republic of Vietnam. His parents are Martha Louise Page Miles and Robert Parnell Miles, both natives of Logan Co., Russellville, KY. His father died in the Spring of 1986. He has two sisters: Mary Nell Miles Robertson and Carol Ann Miles Watkins.

Alan and Treva were married at Neu Chapel on the campus of University of Evansville, June 19, 1971. They restored the Bob Coleman (Manager of the Evansville Braves) home on South Alvord Blvd. and began their family. A son, Lee Alldredge Miles, was born Oct. 4, 1973; and their daughter, Jenny Lou Miles, was born Nov. 15, 1975. They moved across the street to a larger home (the Dr. Haggins homestead) and remained on the Blvd. for eight years. In 1979 the family built a colonial home on the far eastside of the city in Brookshire Estates. The children have spent their entire school years in this area.

Alan, Lee, Jenny and Treva Miles, Summer 1985

Alan continues to work at Alcoa and Treva has never worked outside the home since the children were born. Alan's present position at Alcoa is Implementation Manager of the Computer Integrated Manufacturing System. The family attends Aldersgate United Methodist Church and volunteers time to church and community service. Alan is Scouting Coordinator for Boy Scout Troop 383 and serves on the Troop Committee. He also works with the Methodist Youth Fellowship program.

Treva is Fund Raising chairman for the Scouts and has been a children's choir director for many years. She and Alan have taught elementary Sunday School for ten years. She works weekly with a youth mission project, preparing and serving lunch and providing recreation for Harrison High School students. This project is named "Tuesdays." She also is a 4-H leader for her daughter's club.

The children are in Youth Choir and M.Y.F. members at their church. Lee is active in scouting, and Jenny is in 4-H and soccer. Both are musicians: Lee plays alto saxophone in Harrison High School Marching Band, Pep Band, and All-City honors Band. Jenny plays cello in the Plaza Park Middle School Orchestra. She, also, is in the All-City Honors Orchestra.

The family cherishes family gatherings, holidays and getting back to their roots in Russellville, KY and also Posey County.

MILLS

My first Mills ancestor in Posey County was David Alexander Mills. His father, Alexander Mills, died in South Carolina in 1777.

David, his 14th child, was born Jan. 26, 1776, in Georgia, died Dec. 19, 1838. His wife, Mary (Polly) Summers, born Dec. 3, 1782, in Virginia, died Aug. 29, 1860. Both buried in Mills Graveyard near Farmersville. Tradition that Mary was part Indian.

Their daughter, Mary, also called Polly, born Feb. 10, 1817, married John Lewis Benner, born July 11, 1807. He, and his parents John Frederick Benner and unknown wife, were born in Hesse, Germany. They came to this country in 1819 and joined Mr. Rapp's colony in New Harmony. They left the colony and John F. Benner operated a mill in Marrs Township. Among the men who came to the mill was David Alexander Mills who invited John Lewis to visit and meet his daughters. He accepted and at first sight, chose Mary. John Lewis Benner died May 29, 1861 in Posey County and Mary died Jan. 17, 1904 in Omaha, IL at the home of her son Felix. They are buried in Old Union Cemetery in Posey County.

Nancy Benner, their 11th child (of 12 children), born Dec. 9, 1850, married Frederick Wolfinger, born June 24, 1840 Frederick's parents, John and Elizabeth Grossman Wolfinger, were born in Germany. After their marriage, they came to this country, settling near Allentown, PA, where their first child George was born. Other children born after they came to Posey County were Louis, Frederick, Elizabeth, Charles Dixon and Ann.

Frederick farmed about 500 acres in Marrs township; served in the Civil War in major battles and had his horse shot out from under him, was injured but recovered. After the war, returned to farming and operated a threshing machine. Their children were Mary Elizabeth, called Molly, Joseph Welborn, Otis Alvin, James Arthur, Fred and Eleanor. Frederick died Nov. 11, 1907 and Nancy Jan. 3, 1929. They are buried in Bellefontaine cemetery.

James Arthur, born Nov. 24, 1880, married Carrie Evelyn Crunk, born Feb. 15, 1884, daughter of William David and Missouri Jane Dixon Crunk of Marrs Township. Arthur was a graduate of Lockyears Business College in Evansville, played cornet in a band, was ordained a Deacon in the General Baptist Church Sept. 20, 1925, served many years as Superintendent and teacher of Sunday School, was a 50 year member of the Masonic Fraternity and his wife was a 50 year member of the Eastern Star. He farmed in Marrs township, then worked with Sears Roebuck Company in Roofing Sales, then during World War II with Chrysler Corporation in Evansville and Chicago.

After the war, remained in Chicago working for a clothing manufacturer. Retired, lived a year in Phoenix, AZ and returned to Mt. Vernon in 1951.

Mr. Wolfinger died June 28, 1965 and Mrs. Wolfinger June 12, 1984. They are buried in Bellefontaine cemetery.

Their daughter Vivian attended Oakland City College, taught in elementary school, then home bound children, married Kenneth Jack Blackburn in 1932. Members of Mt. Pleasant General Baptist Church.

Their daughter Miskel Wolfinger graduated from Oakland City College and Indiana University, taught school briefly, then worked for public utility in Public Relations and Consumer Services.

See sketch of Josiah Downen for descendants of Vivian Wolfinger Blackburn. *Submitted by Miskel Wolfinger*

PAUL AND ERMA MITCHELL

Paul Eugene and Erma Joyce (Montgomery) Mitchell were married on Aug. 28, 1954 at the Evangelical United Brethren Church, now Faith United Methodist Church in Mt. Vernon and presently reside at 1213 Jefferson Drive, Mt. Vernon. They are the parents of four children: Steven Lee, Scott Alan, David Eugene and Julie Ann - all graduates of Mt. Vernon High School. Steve, a Mt. Vernon Junior High math teacher, reserve baseball and freshman basketball coach is a graduate of ISUE. He married Betsy (Hall) and they have a daughter Abbey. Scott, a Murray State graduate, works at G.E. He is married to Terri (Allen). They have two children, Nikki and Tim. Dave and Julie, both USI graduates, live in Evansville. Dave is an Investment Officer for Old National Bank. Julie is a Dental Hygieniest for Jay Bigham, Newburgh and Kevin Dillman, Mt. Vernon.

Paul was born May 1, 1929 in Mt. Vernon to Lee and Martha Josephine (Ingle) Mitchell who were the parents of seven children: Lela, Harold, Roscoe, Elwood, Elizabeth, Paul and Ronald. Paul attended school the first three grades at James Whitcomb Riley School which now serves as the Administrative offices of the Mt. Vernon School System. He attended grades four through seven at the Central Elementary School which later burned and was replaced by the present Hedges Central Elementary School. Paul graduated from Mt. Vernon High School in 1948 and started working for Farm Bureau Oil Company where he has been continuously employed for 41 years. Two years of this employment was interrupted by services in the United States Army during the Korean Conflict.

Paul and Erma Mitchell

Paul's paternal grandparents were T.C. Mitchell and Sallie (Oakley) Mitchell. His maternal grandparents were William and Julia (Ausley) Ingle.

Erma, the eldest of five children, was born Sept. 20, 1929 in Posey County to Mabel (Rutledge) Montgomery and Malcolm Montgomery, who were also the parents of Frieda (Hundley), Malcolm, Jr., Marilyn (Newman), and Mary Jane (Embrey). Mabel, born May 19, 1910, lives in New Harmony, but Malcolm, born July 9, 1903, who was a farmer in Posey County, passed away Mar. 14, 1973.

Erma attended Caborn, Jeffries, Stewartsville and Springfield grade schools, graduating from New Harmony High School in 1947, after which she attended Evansville College. For the past 19 years she has worked as an aide and reading assistant for the Mt. Vernon School System.

Erma's maternal grandparents were George and Mary (Rickens) Rutledge, the parents of nine children. Her maternal great grandparents were John and Sarah (Dunlap) Rutledge and Charles and Louise (Kemmerling) Rickens. Charles came to America from Germany as a young man, settling in Vanderburgh County. He later moved to Posey County where he married and spent his remaining years. Charles' parents (Erma's great-great grandparents), Deidrick and Rebecca Rickens, remained in Germany.

Erma's paternal gandparents were George and Emma (Young) Montgomery, the parents of seven children. George was a farmer and horse trader of Irish descent.

MONROE-McFADDEN

Edwin Monroe, born in New York, came to Mt. Vernon with a nine year old brother after their parents, Joshuwa and ___ Fairchild were massacred by Indians. They arrived on a flatboat with the McFadden family.

During his younger years Edwin flatboated to New Orleans. On July 16, 1840 he married Miranda Jane McFadden (Record book 2, page 422, Posey Co., IN). After their marriage they bought a farm near Farmersville, north of Mt. Vernon and lived there the rest of their lives. They had ten sons (I have a photograph of them) and four daughters. Their son William was my Great Grandfather. He married Luona Wilson. (See Monroe-Wilson for their history). Miranda's father, John McFadden was said to

139

Sons of Edwin and Miranda Monroe— Front Row - Ed Monroe, Unknown, Nat, William and Unknown. Back Row - One and two unknown, Center - Charles and Hack, Last unknown.

have been an Indian Scout and a friend of Daniel Boone. He took up a section of land where Mt. Vernon now is located. McFadden's Bluff is said to be the location of his business. *Submitted by William R. Martin, Evansville, IN and Helen L. Robertson, Woodland Hills, CA.*

MONROE-WILSON

William Monroe, born in 1858 to Edwin and Miranda (McFadden) Monroe and Luona Wilson, born in 1865 to Adam Franklin Wilson and Milissa (Bigelow) Wilson were married in Posey Co., IN in 1883. Their children were Edmund Franklin, Wilson P., Glenna Marie, Irene, (my grandmother) Luona, James Henry, Paul, Ira Hackett and Elsie. Williams' brother James Monroe married Mary Wilson, Luona's sister resulting in a number of double cousins.

Back Row: Wilson, Glenna, and Edmund; Front Row: Irene, William with James Henry, Luona with Paul and Ona. Insert: Ira and Elsie taken at a later date.

In the early 1900s William and Luona moved to a farm in Southern Illinois in the community of Gibsonia in Gallatin County building a large two story home on a hilltop overlooking a beautiful fertile valley to the south and across another to the Ohio River near Shawneetown, IL. Both William and Luona died on this farm but were buried with their ancestors in the Bellefontaine Cemetery north of Mt. Vernon, IN.

The Adam Franklin Wilson farm, south of Mt. Vernon was still owned by a member of the Wilson family as late as the early 50's (and may still as of this writing) when I visited there with my Grandmother, Irene. *Submitted by Great Grandchildren: William R. Martin, Evansville, IN Helen Robertson, Woodland Hills, CA*

MORLOCK

Eugene Earl and Ima Lee (Nelson) Morlock were residents of Posey County before retiring and moving to Florida. Eugene and "Shorty" were married in Norman, OK in February of 1943, where he was stationed with the Marine Corps. After a stint in the service during W.W. II, Eugene returned to Posey County to join his wife and young daughter and to farm with his father. Jeanne was soon joined by two younger brothers, David and Jeffrey. The three Morlock children were raised on the Morlock farm near Oliver and all three graduated from North Posey High School. Jeffrey is a G.E. employee living in Vanderburgh County with his wife JoLee and daughters Samantha and Alison. Jeanne is an X-ray tech and lives in Mt. Vernon with her husband Dennis Carr and their two children Laura and Kevin. David lives on the Old Causey farm near Springfield with his wife Candace and three children David W., Robert E. and Kimberly R., he is a G.E. Employee and farmer.

Eugene Earl and Ima Lee (Nelson) Morlock

Eugene is the son of Fred E. and Macil Gladys (Greene) Morlock, he was born in Point Twp. Posey County on Feb. 3, 1921. Ima Lee is the daughter of Sherman O. Nelson and Mary Catherine Mobley, she was born in Illinois.

Eugene's father Fred E. Morlock was born on Mar. 8, 1898 in Point Twp. to George and Elizabeth A. (Bayer) Morlock. He was one of six children, Evalyn (Silber), George, Emma (Hutchinson), Frieda (Roos), and Ralph. Macil is the daughter of Thomas and Rosetta (Nelson) Greene who lived in the Springfield area. Fred and Macil were united in marriage on Jan. 7, 1920. Of this union there were three children.

Eugene's grandfather George Morlock was the second of six children born to Christian II and Maria Christina (Willman) Morlock, who were married in Posey County on Jan. 27, 1868. His siblings were Fred A., Mary A. (Reinitz), John H., Edward, and Emma C. (Cullman). Christian II died at an early age and the children were raised by their mother, living in Mt. Vernon proper and Point twp. Great-grandmother Christina immigrated to America with her parents Johann A. II and Ann (Zimmerman) Willman from Altheim, Germany in 1854. Christian Morlock II was born in Ohio to Christian I and Louisa ( ) Morlock who were of German descent coming from Baden, Germany via Ohio to Marrs Twp. around 1837 with their four children, Louisa M. (Zehner), Christian II, Andrew and George. Christian I was a farmer and operated the Brick Yard at Morlock pond on Tile Factory Road. Christian I and Louisa are buried in Belfountaine cemetery, leaving many branches on the Morlock family tree to reach out in all directions in the Posey County area and beyond. Research into the past continues......

CHRISTIAN MORLOCK, SR.

Christian Morlock, Sr., (1808-1870) was born near Heidelberg in Baden, Germany. He and his wife Louisa (1809-1869) came to America about 1830 and lived for a few years in Cincinnati, OH. Their son Christian, Jr., was born in Cincinnati in 1834. In 1837 or 1838 they moved to Posey County and bought land to farm in Marrs Township. They had three other children: Louisa, George, and Andrew. In the 1850s the family moved into Mt. Vernon, and Christian established a brickyard on East Fourth Street. He made many of the bricks used in Mt. Vernon for sidewalks, chimneys, and foundations. After Louisa's death in 1869, Christian married Clara, who is listed as his wife in the 1870 census. Christian and Louisa are buried in Bellefontaine Cemetery.

Christian Morlock, Jr., (1834-1880) married Catharine Lang (1842-1861), and they had one child, Christian Morlock III (1861-1880). Catharine died on May 3, 1861, as a result of the complications of childbirth and was the first person buried in "German Cemetery," later renamed Bellefontaine Cemetery. In 1868 Christian, Jr., married Maria Christina Willmann (1845-1924), and they had six children: Frederick (1868-1907), George (1870-1943), Mary (1872-1919), John (1873-1956), Edward (1876-1949), and Emma (1879-1973). Christian had a farm about three miles east of Mt. Vernon.

On Feb. 29, 1880, Christian III died at age 18. His father caught a cold at the funeral, developed pneumonia, and died on March 4. Christian, Jr., and Christian III are buried next to Christian, Sr., and Louisa in Bellefontaine Cemetery.

Christian Morlock, Jr.

In the next generation, Frederick married Mary Roos and had seven children: Lillie; Frederick, Jr.; Irving; Louis; Arthur; Mary; and Rose. Frederick, Sr., was treasurer of Posey County and a trustee of Point Township. He later moved to Cincinnati.

George Morlock married Elizabeth Bayer and had six children: Emma; Evalyn; Frederick; Freida; George, Jr.; and Ralph.

Mary Morlock married George Reinitz, and they had 13 children: George, Jr.; Addie; Katie; Lillian; Edward; William; Frederick; Pauline; Walter; Emily; Victory; Harry; and Margaret.

John Morlock married Louise ("Lulu") Lang, and they had two children, Margaret and Emma.

Edward Morlock married Flora May Greathouse, and they had three children: Hazel May, James Edward, and Dorothy Vernon.

Emma Morlock married William Cullman and they had six children: Anna; Emma; William, Jr.; Florence; Louis; and Paul. *Submitted by Mrs. Vivian Morlock Taylor*

DAVID E. AND CANDACE R. MORLOCK

David E. and Candace R. Morlock were married July 22, 1967 in Mt. Vernon and now reside on a small rural farm just north of Springfield. They have three children, David William born Oct. 2, 1971, Robert Earl born Sept. 23, 1972 and Kimberly Ruth born Dec. 20, 1977.

David was born Sept. 9, 1948 in Evansville, the middle child of Eugene E. and Ima Lee (Nelson) Morlock. David has one sister Ima Jean Carr born Oct. 24, 1943, and one brother Jeffrey Lynn born Dec. 22, 1954. David served in the Marine Corps after his graduation from North Posey High School. Dave is an electrical instrument technician at General Electric where he has worked for the past 20 years. Someday Dave plans to farm.

Candace is a Lawrence County native who came to Posey County in 1953 to live with her step parents, Willie and Ruth (Schelhorn) Nowling. Candace is the ninth child of Willis and Ethel M. (Nowling) Wilkerson. Candace has five brothers, Hershal, Cecil, William, Dale and Frank, she also has four sisters, Mary E., Blanch (Huffman), Rosie (Wilson) and Mary K. (Jenkins), which all reside in the Jackson and Lawrence County area. Candace graduated from Mt. Vernon in 1966 and went on to become a Licensed Practical Nurse and worked several years in a nursing home in Evansville before quitting to start her family.

Front Row - Kimberly Ruth, Candace Ruth, David Earl; Back Row- Robert Earl, David William

David's father Eugene E. Morlock was born on Feb. 3, 1921 in Point Twp. to Fred E. and Macil (Greene) Morlock. He was one of three children. Ima Lee was born on Aug. 9, 1924 in Illinois, and is the daughter of Sherman O. Nelson and Mary Catherine Mobley. Ima Lee is one of three children also, Doris Nelson and Harry Kries live at Salt Lake City, UT. Eugene and Ima Lee resided in the Springfield area before retiring and moving to North Port, FL.

The Morlocks are descendants of Christian II and Christina (Willman) Morlock. Christian I and Louisa Morlock immigrated to America from Germany. The Morlocks migrated to Posey County from Ohio sometime in the 1830s, settling in Marrs Township. Christian II married Christina Willman Jan. 27, 1868 in Posey County. Of their children George Morlock married Elizabeth Bayer July 31, 1892 in Posey County. Of their children Fred E. married Macil Greene Jan. 7, 1920 in Posey County and of their children Eugene E. married Ima Lee Nelson Feb. 6, 1943 in Norman, OK. And of course of their children David E. married Candace R. Wilkerson July 22, 1967 in Posey County and of course it is now left in the hands of their children to continue to see that the Morlock name is carried for many more generation to come.

JAMES EDWARD MORLOCK

James Edward Morlock, son of Edward and Flora May Greathoues Morlock, was born on Aug. 11, 1901, in Point Township, Posey County. He married Alice Christine Weyer, also a native of Posey County, on June 27, 1937. They have one child, Vivian Alice Morlock Taylor, born in 1942 (now Mrs. Charles E. Taylor), and one grandchild, Scott Charles Taylor, born in 1974.

James Morlock was graduated from Mount Vernon High School in 1919. He earned his bachelor's degree from Evansville College in 1927, his master's from Indiana University in 1931, and his doctorate from Ohio State University in 1947.

He wrote **The Evansville Story** (1956) and published a revised edition in 1981. He wrote **The Greathouse Family in Indiana** (1977) and edited **Was It Yesterday?** (1980).

James E. Morlock

He began his teaching career at age 18 at Renschler School in Posey County later taught at Greathouse and Lawrence Schools. He taught at Wadesville High School from 1926 to 1931 and was principal from 1929 to 1931. He began teaching at Evansville College in 1931 and stayed there until his retirement 43 years later. He taught sociology (and, in the early years, economics and American history), was head of the Sociology Department (1946-1972), and was Dean of Men (1936-1968). He retired in 1974.

He was president of the Southwestern Indiana Teacher's Association (1931), member of the Evansville Museum Board (1936-1956), president of the Southwestern Indiana Council of Social Work (1942), president of the Indiana Academy of Social Sciences (1954), president of the Evansville Park Board (1956), president of the Evansville-Vanderburgh School Board (1956-1960), program chairman of the Southwestern Indiana Historical Society (1954 to present), and president of the Evansville-Vanderburgh Public Library Board (1981-1982) with service on that board from 1973 to 1987.

He was a lay leader of the Methodist Church and is a member of the Methodist Temple in Evansville. He was the first sponsor of the Methodist Student Movement there and taught Sunday School. He was elected to Phi Kappa Phi (academic honorary) and Pi Gamma Mu (social science honorary). He was named Evansville College's Favorite Professor in 1961, and he was the Kiwanis Layman of the Year in 1977. He has been a member of the Downtown Kiwanis Club of Evansville since 1941. He organized and conducted tours to the eastern and western United States, Mexico, Europe, and the Holy Land between and 1938 and 1970. *Submitted byVivian Morlock Taylor*

RALPH MORLOCK FAMILY

Ralph and Rose Morlock are residents of Point Township. They were married May 5, 1934. Their family consists of one daughter Shirley, who is married to Sam Blankenship and they live in Point Township, also. The Blankenships have one daughter Susan, a graduate of Murray State and the University of Kentucky. She is married to Lucas Stone and they reside in Bloomington, IN, and one son James, a graduate of Purdue University and he resides at home. The Morlocks have a son Larry who is married to the former Lois Lanman.

Ralph and Rose Morlock

They have a son Christian who attended Wabash College and a daughter Abigail attended Ball State at Muncie, IN and they reside in Columbus, IN.

Ralph was born Jan. 13, 1909 in Point Township, the youngest son of George Morlock and Elizabeth Bayer Morlock. George was the oldest son of Christian and Louisa Morlock who lived east of Mt. Vernon where George was born. After the death of his father his mother moved her family to western Black Township. Ralph's mother was the daughter of Mr. Bayer and Margaret Bayer. They came from Germany and lived in Union Township in Vanderburg County. After the death of Elizabeth's father, her mother re-married and they also moved to western Black Township. When George and Elizabeth were married they moved on the Morlock farm in Point Township where Ralph now resides. The George Morlocks had three sons, Fred, George and Ralph and three daughters, Emma, Evelyn and Frieda.

Rose was born June 22, 1915 in Point Township. She is the youngest daughter of Robert Hargrove and Lawra Eaton Hargrove. Robert and Lawra Hargrove moved to Point Township from Union Co., KY in January 1910. They had four girls, Mattie, Pearl, Juanita and Rose, and four sons, Roy, Jesse, Charles and George Franklin. George Franklin died at the age of two years and nine months of pneumonia. Robert was a farmer in Point Township. Their son Jesse enlisted in World War I and was the first Posey County soldier to be listed as missing in action in Posey County. He was a prisoner in the German camp of Rastatt until the end of the war and returned home the next April.

Ralph was a farmer until his retirement. They still live on the farm that has been in the family over 100 years.

DENNIS EUGENE MOUNTS

Dennis E. Mounts was born on May 8, 1944 in Evansville, IN. He graduated from the old New Harmony High School. He attended Southern Illinois University, University of Evansville and University of Southern Indiana. In 1976, he graduated from Indiana College of Mortuary Science in Indianapolis, IN with a degree in Mortuary Science and, in 1987, from Lockyear College with a degree in Professional Accounting-Computer Systems Analyst.

Dennis is a letter carrier for the United States

Postal Service and is working at helping his father with his tax accounting business, Mounts Tax Service, in Posey Co., IN. Earlier, he was the funeral director at several funeral homes and even owned and operated his own funeral home, Mounts Memorial Chapel, Inc. in Poseyville, IN for awhile. He has been a notary public in Posey Co., IN for over 20 years.

Dennis E. Mounts

Being an impaired hearing person has not slowed Dennis at all. He has been and is involved in so many activities that there are too many to list individually. Among them is a long and colorful Scouting career. He has been with the Scouts for over 20 years, earlier achieving the rank of Eagle, and later being a Scoutmaster and winning various awards for his endeavors. Also he is involved in many historical societies, including genealogy organizations. He was a water safety instructor for the Red Cross swimming and lifesaving programs for the handicapped. He is a charter member of General Thomas Posey Chapter of the Sons of the American Revolution.

Dennis' parents are Manford E. and G. Roberta (Holder) Mounts. The Mounts family came from the Swiss Palatinate, Germany to William Penn's colony of Pennsylvania in 1682 and settled in Indiana Territory in 1811.

An avid genealogist, Dennis discovered that he is descended from 42 pioneers who arrived in Indiana prior 1830; that one of his ancestors served with Abraham Lincoln in the Black Hawk War; and the Mounts family tree is populated by seven Revolutionary War Veterans.

His ancestor, Lt. Thomas Montgomery (1745-1818), from whom he is eigthth degree in descent, served in assisting in the establishment of American Independence during the War of the Revolution under the command of Brigadier General George Rogers Clark in the Northwest Territory campaigns. His wife, Martha (1740-1803), was the daughter of Captain Joseph (1676-1767) and Jeanne (de Vigne) (1703-1792) Crockett. Joseph was in Colonial Militia, having been commissioned Captain of Foot in Augusta County Militia, 1752, in the colony of Virginia. Jeanne was the first European child born on Manhattan Island in the colony of New York.

Samuel Utley (-1662), another ancestor of Dennis of 12th generation, immigrated from Yorkshire, England to the colony of New Plymouth in New England about 1647. It makes Dennis eligible for membership in the Order of Founders.

Dennis also is a member of National Society of the Sons and Daughters of the Pilgrims due to the fact that his ancestor, Robert Montgomery, of the 10th generation, came from Ireland and landed at Jamestown on the James River in the colony of Virginia in 1666.

Dennis is the author of **Thomas Posey: The Making of the Soldier and the Statesman.** He also has written numerous genealogical and historical books. He edits a genealogical journal called the **The Posey Patriot.**

MANFORD E. MOUNTS FAMILY

Manford E. Mounts, a life-long resident of Posey Co., IN, was born on Dec. 13, 1920 in Bethel Township near Griffin. He graduated valedictorian from the old New Harmony High School and served three years in the U.S. Air Force in World War II. He was stationed as cryptographer on the Island of Tinian in the South Pacific where the first atomic bomb was stored. He was on the duty the night the bomb was dropped on Hiroshima, Japan.

He was a civil service employee of the United States Government as a rural mail carrier; a position he held for 25 years at New Harmony and Mt. Vernon Post Offices in Posey Co., IN. He was employed by George Koch & Sons in Evansville, IN as cost accountant, payroll clerk and timekeeper for three years. At present he owns and operates Mounts Tax Service as a tax consultant and accountant. He has been in the tax-bookkeeping business for 31 years. In 1982 he was elected Auditor of Posey Co., IN and in 1986 he resigned and moved to Columbia, TN where he started a business in connection with General Motor's new Saturn plant. In 1988 he moved back to Posey Co., IN. He is presently employed by Cleve Corporation as an accounting clerk in Poseyville, IN.

Roberta and Manford Mounts

Manford served as first chairman on the Posey County Civil Defense Board which he helped organize. He is a member of Johnson United Methodist Church; Veterans of Foreign Wars Post 3851 for 33 years, past commander, adjutant and member of American Legion Post for 41 years; Troop Committee of the Boys Scout of America for 22 years; Posey County Farm Bureau; and Kiwanis Club.

Manford's parents were William Edgar Mounts and Mary Elizabeth Stallings. The Stallings family came from England to James City Co., VA in 1635 and settled in Indiana Territory in 1811.

William E. Mounts' great-great grandfather, Mathias Mounts (1752-1818), was the first person to deliver mail on foot in what was then the Indiana Territory. He carried the mail along the old Buffalo Trace early in the 18th century. His wife, Mary Molly (1754-1854), daughter of Lt. Thomas (1745-1818) and Martha (1740-1803) (Crockett) Montgomery, was a direct cousin of Davey Crockett. Manford's wife, Roberta, is a graduate of the old New Harmony High School and is the daughter of Frank Cox Holder and Annie Viola Moore, all born in Posey Co., IN. Her ancestor, "General" Joseph Cox (1791-1865) was the veteran of the War of 1812, and another, Jesse Moore (1802-1889), the Black Hawk War veteran.

Manford, known by many as "Mutt", and Roberta reside in Wadesville, IN. They are the parents of three children: Dennis, a college graduate with two degrees, is a letter carrier with U.S. Postal Service; Carol Lynn Julian, a secretary for law firm, Bamberger Foreman Oswald & Hahn of Evansville, IN; and Ricki Dean, a law student at University of Southern Indiana. Dennis and Ricki graduated from the old New Harmony High School and Carol from North Posey High School. The couple also have a granddaughter, Amy, a junior at North Posey High School.

MOYE-YEWELL

George Moye was born and has lived in Posey County, except thru war years of World War II and the Korean War. George's parents George W. Moye and Delia M. (Hogan) Moye were from Gallatin Co., IL. George married Avis Yewell in the year of 51 at Vellejo, CA. Avis's parents Frank L. Yewell and Gladie Voyne (Flener) Yewell are from Kentucky. *Submitted by Avis Moye*

MUMFORD FAMILY

Thomas Mumford, Sr. came to New Harmony in the year 1818. He was a native of Hertfordshire England and came to New Harmony to teach in the Maclure-Fretageot School. In 1842 he married Louisa Maental, daughter of the now well-known folk painter, Jacob Maental. A fine collection of Maental's paintings are in the Workingmen's Institute, New Harmony, and other galleries across the country.

The children of Thomas and Louisa were Mary, Frances Amelia, and Thomas Mumford, Jr. At this time the Mumfords lived in New Harmony and were merchants. Thomas Mumford, Jr. acquired land in Bethel Township near Griffin, and would drive his buggy to and from New Harmony to manage the farms. Mary married Eugene Thrall, founder of Thrall's Opera House, in 1867. Thomas, Jr. married Emma Bishop in 1870. The Bishop family came from Connecticut to reside in New Harmony. Amelia married Sam Hill and moved to New Jersey. He made his fortune manufacturing "Poslum," a popular cure-all salve. They had one daughter, Louise, who never married.

Thomas Mumford, Sr.

Thomas Mumford, Jr. and Emma had four children. Bessie married Harry Pitcher from Albion, IL, and lived many years on Alma Plantation in Louisiana. William married Hazel McCurdy of Evansville, the daughter of Col. McCurdy who built the McCurdy Hotel. Eloise married Ruffin Claiborn, and they both died at an early age in Louisiana.

Eugene Bishop married Elsa Frenzel of Indianapolis. She had one son, Thomas Frenzel Mumford before she died in the flu epidemic of 1914. Dr.

Mumford then married Aliene Booker of Louisville, KY. Dr. Mumford was a prominent orthopedic surgeon in Indianapolis.

Thomas F. Mumford married Letitia Sinclair of Indianapolis. She is the granddaughter of Thomas Taggert of French Lick, IN. They moved to the Mumford Family farm after Tom served in World War II, and raised six children.

Thomas F. Mumford, Jr. married Nancy Smith; they have two daughters, Anna Letitia and Eloise. Richardson Sinclair Mumford married Janine Shiveley of Carmel, CA; they have one son, Richardson S. Mumford, Jr. Elizabeth Bishop Mumford married Stephen Wilson from Connecticut; they have one son, Samual Bishop Mumford. Christopher Mumford married Margaret Crane from New Hampshire, presently soon to be a doctor. Michael Mumford married Nancy Jane Smith from Barnstable, MA; they have one daughter Anne. Bishop Mumford married Elizabeth Reynolds of New Harmony.

Thomas Frenzel Mumford died July 17, 1975.

At this writing, January 1989, Letitia still lives at the family home on the farm. Her sons, Christopher and Bishop, also reside on the hill and operate Mumford Farms.

MURPHY-WILSON

George Washington Murphy, son of Noah and Elizabeth (Vandaveer) Murphy, was born July 30, 1855 and died May 7, 1928. George, was the youngest of nine children. November 23, 1878, he married Cornelia Ellen Wilson who was born Dec. 23, 1856 and died Dec. 20, 1898. She was the second child of eight born to John and Sarah Boyle Wilson.

They were the parents of two daughters, Ina May, who died at age ten from scarlet fever and Ora Wilson, born Mar. 30, 18875 and died Apr. 5, 1931.

On Feb. 7, 1906, Ora married Robert Alexander Lamar, who was born Sept. 3, 1881 in Spencer Co., IN, on the Lamar homestead, one mile south of Lamar, the town having been named after his grandfather John S. Lamar. His parents were Trusten W. and Sarah Kennedy Lamar. His mother Sarah immigrated from County Down, Ireland with her parents in 1848 when she was six years old. Robert died Dec. 23, 1959.

They were the parents of five children, Hazel Ina, Malcolm Murphy, Sarah Mae (died in infancy), Marcella Ruth (died in infancy), and Carol Renee. Hazel Ina, died on Aug. 22, 1972 at the age of 65.

Malcolm Murphy married Wyiona Gardner on Oct. 2, 1930. They are the parents of two children, Betty Frances Espenlaub and Alan Lamar. Betty married Don Espenlaub on Sept. 14, 1952. They are the parents of three children, Donna Kaye Drew of Monroe City and twin sons, David of Evansville and Dennis of Poseyville. Alan married Jo Ann Etherton on Oct. 29, 1960. They are the parents of three children, Scott Alan, Kathi Bryant and Christopher Aaron, all of Poseyville.

One hundred acres of original land grant land that was settled by Thomas Murphy who came in covered wagon from North Carolina to settle in 1812, remains in the Murphy family and is owned by Malcolm Murphy and Wyiona Lamar and Carol Renee Lamar.

ANTON NIEMEIER

Anton (Antony) Niemeier (1847-1897), the son of Meinolph and Bernardina (Munstermann) Niggemeyer (German spelling), was born in Anrochte, Germany. Anton sailed as a stowaway from Hamburg, Germany in April 1865, at the age of 18 to escape compulsary military training. Anton married Mary (Goebel) on July 27, 1872, and had one child Henry Niemeier (1874-1946.)

Anton Niemeier, Anna Katherine (Wolf) Niemeier

Henry Niemeier married Caroline G. (Hartmann) and they had one child Clara C. Niemeier (1906-1988). Mary (Goebel) Niemeier died and Anton Niemeier married Anna Katherine (Wolf) (1851-1915), daughter of Peter and Helena (Oehn) Wolf on July 2, 1878. Their children were Peter John (1880-1880), Anton Peter (1881-1948), married Walburga Rickert (see Anton Peter Niemeier), Bernard Frank (1882-1955), married Margaret Bushkill, Anna Katherine (1884-1959), married Edward Lewis, John Henry (1886-1964), married Louetta Benner and Margaret Deig, Margaret (1888-1965), married Clement Kueber, Helena Mary (1890-1975), married Roscoe E. Ruminer, Philip Jacob (1893-1953), married Elizabeth Konrad and Mary Anna (1894-1975), married Herman G. Muehlenbein. Anton was engaged in farming in Marrs Township and is buried in St. Phillip's Catholic Cemetery.

ANTON PETER NIEMEIER

Anton Peter Niemeier (1881-1948) the son of Anton Niemeier and Anna Katherine (Wolf), (see Anton Niemeier), married Walburga (Rickert) Niemeier (1881-1976), on Sept. 18, 1900.

Anton Peter Niemeier, Walburga (Rickert) Niemeier

Their children were John Anthony (1900-1900), Lula Teresa (1901-1974), married Thomas Hunt and Clem Munsterman, Elnora Catherine (1905-1977), married Timothy Henry Kaffenberger, Olivia Barbara (1907-1975), married Anselm J. Kaffenberger, Raymond Clem (1910-1981), married Dorothy P. (Munsterman) and Rose (Betz) Munsterman, Lillian Mary (1912), married Charles Knowles and resides in Evansville, Rosetta Catherine (1915-1957), married Erwin Brown Willis, Rapheal George (1917), married Erma Elsie (Carroll) and Helen Vivian (Zenthoefer) and resides in Evansville and Louetta Marie (1920), married Joseph M. Etienne and resides in Evansville.

Anton was a farmer and he also owned a Keck-Gonnerman Steam Engine and separator. He thrashed wheat every year throughout the Marrs Township Area. During the winter months he used his steam engine on a large sawmill. Many barn patterns were sawed at different locations east of Mt. Vernon.

Anton and Walburga are buried in St. Matthews Catholic Cemetery.

FRANZ (FRANK) NIEMEIER

Franz (Frank) Niemeier born Oct. 13, 1840 and his sister Maria Christina born Apr. 30, 1838 in Anrochte, Germany (parents were Meinolph and Bernardina (Munstermann) Niggemeyer (German spelling of Niemeier), left on May 12, 1861 for America. A friend drove them to Lippstadt, Germany, and Rheda, Germany, from there by train to Bremen, Germany.

Maria Brugger Niemeier; Franz (Frank) Niemeier

On May 17, 1861, they went on a small boat out into the harbor and waited for a steam boat to pull them several miles out into the sea. Due to bad weather and lots of wind, they had to lay still until May 23, 1861. Some days they gained some distance, and lost time quite often. Many sad things happened, a baby born - died, put into ocean, on June 13, 1861, a seven year old boy died. June 18, 1861, five more people died. A sailer went on deck to get some dry clothes, deck was wet, he slipped and fell, and was lost, all that died went down in the ocean. Finally on July 18, 1861 they saw land and they had to wait for permission to come in. A steam ship had to come bring them in. On July 21, 1861, they landed in Baltimore, MD on the Ship Ferdinand. Their intention was going to Evansville because they had friends living there. When they went to the train station, the train to Evansville, IN was down for repairs, so they went to Cincinnati, OH, then to Evansville, and then to Posey County St. Phillip's area. There Frank lived with friends and worked for farmers, bought land and built a small house, later added to the house and married Maria (Brugger) on May 12, 1868 in St. Wendel Catholic Church. Maria was born on Feb. 24, 1849. Maria was the daughter of Franz Heinrick Brugger and Maria Theresia (Daub). Frank and Maria had the following children: Heinrick (Henry) (1869-1869), Anton F. (1870-1926) married Theresia Inkenhaus, Maria (1872-1873), Frank H. (1874-1958) married Margaret Koressel, Clemens P. (1878-1963) married Wilhelmina Waterman and Mathilda Stratman, Henry F. (1881-1963) married Josephine Kercher, Catherine (1882-1962) married Barthol Kercher, George S. (1885-1972) married Magdalena Rexing and Lena Litzelmann, Anna (1888-1973) married

George Kruse, Elizabeth (1892-1977) married Theodore Rexing.

There were 42 grandchildren. Maria died on June 23, 1909 at age 60 and Frank died on Oct. 18, 1919 at age 79. They are buried in St. Phillip's Catholic Cemetery.

Mildred Kruse has the diary that Franz (Frank) Niemeier wrote while traveling on the Ship Ferdinand to America.

RAYMOND A. NIEMEIER FAMILY

Raymond A. Niemeier was born on Dec. 10, 1935 in Mt. Vernon, IN. He graduated from Mt. Vernon High School in 1954. Raymond's parents were the late Dorothy P. (Munsterman) Niemeier (1913-1956), and Raymond C. Niemeier (1910-1981). They were married on June 16, 1934 in St. Matthews Catholic Church. They are buried in St. Matthews Catholic Cemetery.

Raymond's grandparents were Anton Peter Niemeier (1881-1948) (See Anton Peter Niemeier), and Walburga (Rickert) Niemeier (1881-1976), and Henry Munsterman (1872-1950), and Amelia Barbara (Dietz) Munsterman (1878-1950). Raymond's great grandparents were Anton Niemeier and Anna Katherine (Wolf) Niemeier (see Anton Niemeier), and Frank Munsterman (1846-1909), and Eva (Lautenschläger) Munsterman (1846-1909), and Henry Dietz and Mary (Kohl) Dietz.

Raymond A. and Linda Niemeier

Raymond's wife, Linda, is a graduate of Reitz High School and Lockyear's Business College. Linda was born on Oct. 11, 1940 in Evansville, IN. Raymond and Linda were married on Nov. 12, 1960 at Sacred Heart Rectory in Evansville, IN. Linda is the daughter of the late Victor S. Hesson and her Mother, Imogene (Wright) Hesson resides in Evansville, IN. Linda's grandparents were Allen Adam Hesson and Ada Mae (Totten) Hesson and Wayne E. Wright and Etta (Wallace) Wright. Linda's great grandparents were George Burton Hesson and Laura Ann (Bryant) Hesson and Homer E. Totten and Mary (Trafford) Totten of Posey County.

Raymond and Linda reside on Darnell School Road in Marrs Township with their son, Ryan Raymond Niemeier, born on Mar. 14, 1971, graduated from Mt. Vernon High School and is attending Ball State University and Troy Victor Niemeier, born on June 21, 1973 is a student at Mt. Vernon High School.

Raymond is engaged in farming and Linda works in Evansville for a Trucking Company.

RAYMOND C. NIEMEIER FAMILY

Raymond C. Niemeier was born on June 27, 1910 in Marrs Township. He attended the Crunk School and St. Matthew's where he graduated. His parents were Anton Peter Niemeier and Walburga (Rickert) Niemeier (see Anton Peter Niemeier Family).

Sitting - Raymond C. and Dorothy Philipine (Munsterman) Niemeier; Standing: Rosetta Catherine (Niemeier) Willis and Clem Munsterman

Raymond married Dorothy P. (Munsterman) on June 16, 1934 in St. Matthews Catholic Church. Dorothy was born on Jan. 3, 1913 in Texas City, IL. Dorothy's parents were Henry Munsterman and Amelia Barbara (Dietz) Munsterman.

Raymond's sister Rosetta Catherine (Niemeier) Willis and Dorothy's brother Clem Munsterman were the ones in the wedding picture with them.

Raymond and Dorothy had one son, Raymond Anthony Niemeier born on Dec. 10, 1935 in Mt. Vernon, IN (see Raymond A. Niemeier Family).

Dorothy died on July 31, 1956 (age 43) and is buried in St. Matthews Catholic Cemetery.

Raymond then married Rose (Betz) Munsterman on Apr. 22, 1961 at Corpus Christi Church in Evansville.

Raymond died on July 14, 1981 (age 71) and is buried in St. Matthews Catholic Cemetery.

Rose (Betz) Munsterman Niemeier resides on Davis Road (used to be called Rickert Road).

Raymond was a farmer in Marrs Township until his death.

ALBERT T. AND LOUISE R. NOELLE

Albert T. and Louise Noelle are residents of Mt. Vernon, having been born and reared in Marrs Township, Posey County. They were married in July, 1943. They have two sons Albert T., II (Toby) and Richard A. who lives on the 100 year old Noelle farm near West Franklin. Toby is married to Janice Wing Liendecker.

Albert was born in 1918 to Carl and Selma (Hausmann) Noelle. He has two sisters Ellen and Arline. Albert served in the U.S. Army for five years during WWII in the Pacific theater receiving a battlefield commission. He is retired from 27 years with Farm Bureau Insurance. He continues to be active in community affairs.

Carl was born April, 1896 to Frederick and Anna (Berger) Noelle, the youngest of nine children, all deceased. Selma was born September, 1896 to Tobias and Louisa (Schisler) Hausmann, the oldest of seven children. Selma and a brother Edward Hausmann are living. The Noelle and Berger families and the Hausmann and Schisler families are of German origin and were farmers.

Louise was born March, 1921 to Roscoe and Helena (Niemeier) Ruminer. Other children are Venita, Arlene, Anthony and Angela. Louise worked for USDA and as deputy clerk of Posey Circuit Court. She has been an active member of the Daughters of the American Revolution.

Roscoe was born June, 1890 to Edward and Louisa (Feldbush) Ruminer. He was a farmer and schoolbus driver. Helena was born November 1890 to Anton and Catherine (Wolf) Niemeier.

Edward Ruminer was born to Michael and Jane (Marrs) Ruminer. He was a farmer, operated a saw mill, wheat threshing and corn husking and shredding equipment, a cloverseed huller, powered by Keck Gonnerman steam engine. He also raised sheep and a few horses. His son Roscoe worked for him.

Jane was the daughter of Urban and Susanna (Martin) Marrs. Urban was the son of James and Anna (Shannon) Marrs.

James served in the Revolutionary War coming from Virginia through Tennessee and Kentucky to the present site of Evansville. He acquired property in that area, died there and is buried at the site of the Old Court House. Marrs Township was named for Samuel Marrs, brother to Urban Marrs.

Edward and Louisa Ruminer, Michael and Jane Ruminer and Urban and Susanna Marrs are buried in the Old Union Cemetery on Wildeman Road, Marrs Township.

For further information on the Ruminer and Marrs families see History of Posey Co., IN, Goodspeed, 1886 and Illustrated Atlas of Posey Co., IN, 1990.

STEPHEN M. AND HEIDEMARIE W. NOON

Stephen M. and Heidiemarie W. Noon reside in Oberwildenau, Federal Republic of Germany, one hour north of Munich and 20 miles west of Czechoslovakia. Posey County is their official residence in the United States while performing official duties for the Department of Defense in Germany. Stephen (Steve) graduated from Mt. Vernon High School with the class of 1959. Heidiemarie (Heidi) graduated from the Kindergarten Teachers College of Mainz, Germany in 1959. Steve and Heidi were married on Oct. 4, 1978 in Terre Haute, IN, after several months as penpals.

Steve was born July 24, 1941 at Farmersville, just north of Mt. Vernon in Posey County, the eldest son of Samuel Topper and Mary Ruth (Allen) Noon. He attended Hedges Central Grade School, Mt. Vernon High School and Indiana State University. Steve is a career Department of the Army Civilian working on the V Corps staff, G3 Training, in Frankfurt, FRG.

Stephen M. and Heidemarie W. Noon

Heidemarie Waltraud Dost was born Nov. 27, 1941 at Prague, Czechoslovokia, the youngest daughter of Otto Woldemar and Emma Rosa Ann (Bossceker) Dost. The Dost family was caught in Prague during the hostilities at the end of WWII in

1945 while Mr. Dost was a prisoner of war in a British POW camp in Egypt. Escape to West Germany took Mrs. Dost and her three children more than three months and over coming unbelievable threats, hardships, illnesses, and dangers. The family was finally reunited in Coburg in May 1948 upon the release of Mr. Dost from the POW camp. Heidi's sister Rosemarie Elizabeth Peter, born Apr. 24, 1936 at Ejram, Zagreb, Yugoslavia, and her husband Helmut Peter, reside in New Jersey. Heidi's brother Wolfgang Alfred Dost, born Sept. 13, 1938 at Altenburg, Thuering, East Germany, and his wife, Ingrid (Geffckin), reside in Munich, FRG.

Steve has two brothers and one sister, Stanley Richard of Posey County, Dennis Allen of Henderson, KY, and Anna Vivian of Aberystwyth, Wales. Steve's parents, Samuel and Ruth (Allen) Noon, were married Aug. 29, 1940 in Mt. Vernon. Samuel Topper Noon, born Apr. 28, 1918 in Posey County, was the youngest son of Stanley S. and Anna Margaret (Topper) Noon, who married Nov. 10, 1895 in Mt. Vernon. Stanley S. Noon, born Jan. 30, 1867 in Harrison Co., IN, moved to Mt. Vernon, married Anna Margaret Topper, and farmed in Point Township. Anna Margaret Topper, born Aug. 5, 1877 in Posey County, was the daughter of Samuel and Katherine (Klotz) Topper, who married Dec. 13, 1876 in Mt. Vernon.

Steve's great grandparents, Jasper John (Jack) and Catherine Susan (Jenkins) Noon, married Sept. 7, 1865 at Mauckport, IN, and were successful farmers in Harrison County. Jasper Noon was an enlisted soldier in the Civil War.

Samuel Topper, born Aug. 18, 1853, was the son of Richard and Julia (Jarrett) Topper, married Feb. 27, 1850 at Evansville, IN. Richard Topper was born at Cherry Hill Estate, 35 miles south of Liverpool, England, Apr. 23, 1823, and emigrated through New Orleans to Posey County where he became a very successful farmer.

Steve's great grandmother, Katherine (Klotz) Topper, born Mar. 11, 1856 at Tiefenbach, Hessen, Germany, emigrated at the age of three with her parents, Johann Heinrich Klotz, born Dec. 11, 1821 at Tiefenbach, Germany, and married Anna Margretha (Friedrich) Klotz, born Feb. 29, 1824 at Tiefenbach, Germany, and married Oct. 4, 1840 in Tiefenbach, to Harrisburg, IL, then moved to Posey County. Steve has researched this branch of the family and traced seven complete generations beyond Katherine, all in the Tiefenbach area just west of Giessen and north of Frankfurt. Church records in the castle at Braunfels were destroyed during the Thirty-Year War preventing further research.

Steve's great-grandparents, George Washington Akers, born Feb. 22, 1861 in Posey County, and Nancy Matilda (Peerman) Akers, born Feb. 23, 1870 in Posey County were married in Mt. Vernon, IN on Oct 18, 1889. George's father, John Akers, born in 1826, and Elizabeth (Van Zandt) Akers, born Nov. 30, 1841, were married in Mt. Vernon on May 21, 1859.

Steve and Heidi plan to reside in Posey County upon retirement from civil service.

WILLIE AND RUTH S. NOWLING

Willie and Ruth S. Nowling were married Apr. 8, 1943 in Bedford, IN. Willie had been a life long resident of Lawrence County and Ruth a life long resident of Posey County. Willie had worked at Charleston, IN where he met and befriended the Schelhorn brothers, after their jobs were over up there they all returned to Posey County where he met Ruth.

In September 1942 Willie and three of the Schelhorn boys, Dale, Harvey, and Walter enlisted for a stint in the service during WWII. Willie enlisted in the Navy and was placed aboard a submarine chaser. In 1943 while on leave Ruth and Willie were married and Ruth made her residence in Lawrence Co.

Willie and Ruth Nowling

Willie is the son of Cartha and Besse (Beavers) Nowling, he was born in Lawrence County on Mar. 4, 1915. He was one of four children, Kathleen (Goen), Eula (Hackney), and Ethel (Wilkerson). His only living sister, Kathleen still resides in Lawrence Co., IN.

Ruth is the daughter of George and Ida (Brandt) Schelhorn, and she was one of five children, Elmer, Harvey, Dale and Walter. Walter is the only living brother and resides in Mt. Vernon. Ruth was born Jan. 24, 1923 and was raised in Posey County.

In 1945 Willie was discharged from the Navy and they lived in the Lawrence County area for a couple of years before returning to Posey County. Willie worked all over the states as a boilermaker, working with Ruth's brother Dale. In their work they traveled from Minnesota to Florida.

In 1953 they decided to take and raise a niece, Candace R. Wilkerson, who was the daughter of Willie's sister Ethel. Candace continues to live in Posey County, after graduation from Mt. Vernon High School she went on to become a Licensed Practical Nurse. She married David E. Morlock July 22, 1967. Willie and Ruth have three grandchildren from this union, David William born Oct. 2, 1971, Robert Earl born Sept. 23, 1972 and Kimberly Ruth born Dec. 20, 1977.

Willie retired in 1978 and in the winter months he and Ruth like to take their camper and go to Florida. Willie enjoys fishing in the Okeechobee lake. Ruth enjoys painting and doing crafts.

Ruth is a descendant of Jacob Schelhorn who immigrated to Posey Co., IN from Saxony, Germany before 1849. Jacob was a cooper in the Mt. Vernon area in 1860. He married Margaret (Engle) in June 1849. They had nine children, John F., William, Mary, Caroline, Henry, Charles, Edward, Hannah and another daughter, name unknown.
Submitted by Ruth S. Nowling

MR. AND MRS. ELMER NURRENBERN

Elmer Nurrenbern and Carolyn Riner met at the Crystal Heights dance hall in 1944, and were married in 1946 at St. Agnes Church in Evansville. They now are members of St. Matthew's Church in Mt. Vernon. They moved to Mt. Vernon to begin married life together on the farm on the Tile Factory Road, where they are still living today, only in a different home.

Elmer received his education in St. Agnes School in Evansville. He also completed the Dale Carnegie Course.

Sitting: Elmer and Carolyn Nurrenbern; Standing: Linda Nurrenbern Gray, Glen Nurrenbern Joyce Nurrenbern Fellows, Janet Nurrenbern Dunigan

Carolyn graduated from Mt. Vernon High School in 1946. They started out in grain farming and milk production. Elmer is the third child of six children, born to Julia Rollett and Robert Nurrenbern, of Vanderburgh County. He had brothers, Walter, and Edward, and three sisters, Helen, Margaret and Clara. Carolyn Riner was the second child of Elva Oeth Riner, of Vanderburgh County, and formerly of Mt. Vernon, and George Riner, of Atlanta, GA. She had a brother George Riner, Jr.

Elmer and Carolyn had four children. Linda Gray, of Newburgh, Joyce Fellows, of Lansing, MI, Glenn, of Evansville, and Janet Dunigan, of Muncie, IN. All four children are graduates of Mt. Vernon High School. They also have seven grandchildren. Stephanie and Andrea Gray, Derek, Aaron, and Tonya Fellows and Tiffany and Shawn Nurrenbern. With the arrival in Mt. Vernon of G.E. and B&W, there became a need for new homes, so in 1965-66, Elmer and Carolyn decided to develop their farm into a subdivision and build homes. They called their new addition Country Terrace, and named the streets for popular area birds. At the time they were in the country, but a few years later the area was annexed into the city of Mt. Vernon. Son, Glenn joined the family homebuilding business after graduation from high school.

In 1970 there became a need for apartments in Mt. Vernon, so Elmer built the first building of what is now known as Brookside Apartments, behind their home on Tile Factory Rd. In 1975 the second building was built. In 1986 Elmer retired from the homebuilding business, and now he and Carolyn are actively engaged in managing and maintaining the Brookside Apts.

Elmer and Carolyn are active members of the Evansville, State, and National Homebuilders Association, and have served as their director, and also Presidents of the local Association of Homebuilders, and Homebuilders Auxiliary.

BILLY A. AND ANN M. NUSSEL

Billy A. Nussel and Ann M. (Jerger) were married July 22, 1961. They reside in Marrs Township. Their children are: Catherine A., born/died Oct. 10, 1962; Dale A., June 1, 1964; Elaine R., July 8, 1966; and Fay A., June 15, 1968.

Dale is majoring in Engineering at Purdue University; Elaine graduated from Marian College Indianapolis in May of 1988 with a B.S. in Account-

145

ing; and Fay is majoring in Pre-law at the University of Evansville.

Elaine, Fay, Billy, Ann, and Dale Nussel

The Billy A. Nussel family is the fourth generation of Nussel's to reside in Posey County. Mr. Nussel's great grandfather, John Conrad Nussel, at nine months of age along with his mother, Anna Barbara (Fleischman), left from port of Bremen, Germany and after a voyage of 42 days on the ship Luise arrived Oct. 2, 1843, at Baltimore, MD.

Jon G. Nussel and Anna Barbara resided in Posey Township, Clay Co., IN. John Conrad, the eldest of eight children grew up in Clay County and volunteered on Oct. 15, 1863, for the Union Forces in the Civil War. He served with Company E, 124 Regiment Indiana Infantry until his discharge on Aug. 31, 1865.

John married Sara (Crumbel) in Clay County on Nov. 23, 1870. They had two children: Henry, Oct. 3, 1871 and Mary Ann, Nov. 11, 1873. Sara, died Jan. 4, 1875.

John C. Nussel and Eunice (Osborn) were married, on Aug. 30, 1876. They moved to Mt. Vernon, IN, in 1877. John was a building contractor and carpenter, constructing many of the large elevated grain storage barns in the local bottom lands of Indiana and Kentucky. John C. Nussel died on Feb. 17, 1930 and was the Local Commander of Harrow Post, Grand Army of the Republic at the time of his passing. Children of John and Eunice were Edward and his fraternal sister Sophia born on Nov. 10, 1877. Sophia died at the age of 12 and was buried in the North Cemetery. A third child Bertha was born on Nov. 18, 1880 and died at age of one. Edward Nussel remained a resident of Mt. Vernon and followed his father's trade as a carpenter. Edward married Nellie (Stull). He passed away on Apr. 14, 1956. They had one child, Arthur A. Nussel, born Sept. 13, 1915. On Feb. 2, 1935; Arthur married Mary Elizabeth (Hutchinson), born Feb. 6, 1919, daughter of Thomas and Carrie (Rhein) Hutchinson. Arthur worked for Keck Gonnerman Company as a Sheet Metal Draftsman until 1954, and Mt. Vernon Milling Company until his death Dec. 6, 1980. Their children are: Billy A., Nov. 17, 1935; Barbara A. (Higgins), June 14, 1938; Tommy E., born June 28, 1941, died Mar. 1, 1946; Judy C. (West), Jan. 28, 1946; John A., Nov. 16, 1948.

Billy A. Nussel attended Riley and Central Grade schools and graduated from Mt. Vernon High School in 1954. He attended Evansville College before being drafted into the military service for two years 1958-1960. (US52469585). He is presently employed at General Electric Co., in Electrical Engineering. He was a charter member of Mt. Vernon Civitan Club. He served as a precinct committeeman for Black Eight and Marrs Center for many years and served as the Posey County Democratic County Chairman from 1979 to 1984.

Ann M. (Jerger) Nussel was born Aug. 10, 1936, in Washington, IN, and graduated in 1954 from Washington Catholic High School. She met Billy at Evansville College where she graduated in 1958 with a B.S. degree. She was employed at hospitals in Vigo, Green and Vanderburgh counties until her marriage in 1961. She is a member of the St. Matthews Church; American Medical Pathology Association; and Mt. Vernon Business and Professional Women's Club.

Billy and Ann purchased radio station WPCO in 1983 and presently manage the station.

FRIEDA NEBE OETH

Frieda Nebe Oeth will be 100 years old June 2, 1989. She is the youngest daughter of Charles Nebe 1853-1899 and Elizabeth Dietz Nebe 1857-1897, both natives of Germany. The Nebe family arrived in New York City from Dusseldorf, Germany. The Dietz family came from Gaugrehweiler, Germany, arriving in New Orleans, coming North by the Mississippi River. Friedaricka had two older sisters, Emma Caroline 1882-1945, who never married, and Charlotte 1887-1971, who was the wife of Edward G. Schneider 1887-1958.

Frieda graduated from Mt. Vernon Public Schools, High School Department 1907 (27 members) and the Mary Jane Gilbert Memorial, Private Sanitarium (school of nursing), in Evansville, IN in 1914. This building is now owned and occupied by Hadi Shrine. She did most of her nursing as a private duty nurse and especially enjoyed caring for children. Her work took her into homes of humble circumstances as well as the affluent and traveled to out of State Clinics and Hospitals with some of her patients. She had compassion for all her patients and made lasting friendships with many of the families.

On Dec. 14, 1935 she married Ferdinand Oeth 1879-1956. He was a machinest and operated his own thrashing machine during grain harvest. He had two children by a former marriage to Edith Uhde 1884-1934, Raymond L. Oath Mar. 12, 1908 and Ruth Emily Jan. 24, 1920, Raymond resides in Speedway, IN and Ruth Beery lives in Tucson, AZ. They continue to keep in close contact with their "Mother". She has one niece, Sarah E. Carr of Mt. Vernon.

JOHN AND ORA PACE

John and Ora Pace arrived in Posey County in February of 1937. They came from Southeast Missouri with their four sons, Irvin, Stephen, Edward and John, Jr. They settled on a farm known as the "Stallings" place, located about five miles East of New Harmony on the Poseyville Road. John was born in Murray, KY on Nov. 18, 1885. He grew up in Kentucky and was, at various times, a potter, tobacco grader, and grocer. He arrived in Mississippi Co., MO about 1913 where he met Ora Kathryne Reeves. With the assistance of her brother, they eloped and were married in Cairo, IL on Aug. 2, 1915. All four of their sons were born in Mississippi County. While in Missouri, John operated a restaurant, a grocery, and was a farmer. After living through several river floods in Southeast Missouri, the flood of the Mississippi River in the winter of 1936/1937 was, as he said: "the last one for me." He declared: "I'm going to find a farm on a high hill and live where I'll never see another flood." He found just such a place in Posey County.

It was during the Great Depression that he purchased the farm which did not appear to have been farmed for several years. Trees and underbrush had grown out 20 to 30 feet from the fence-rows and all the low lying areas had overgrown with ash trees and underbrush. It was a cold, harsh winter and not long until planting time. John and his four sons went to work clearing the trees and brush from the fence-rows and low areas. By spring the farm was readied and planted.

John and Ora Pace Farm

John Pace was a man of sterling character, and a hard worker. It was these traits that earned him the respect of all his neighbors. He worked the farm alone after all four of his sons entered the military services during World War II. Irvin, the eldest, was in the Navy and served in the Pacific; Stephen, as an Army Sergeant serving in Europe, was a part of the D-Day invasions of France; Edward served in the Army Air Force and John Jr., the youngest son, was in the Army and served in the Panama Canal Zone.

None of the sons returned to the farm after the war was over so John worked the farm alone until he retired in 1950. On retiring, he entrusted the farm to a very competent renter. He and Ora moved to Evansville where they spent the remainder of their lives. Ora died on July 17, 1979 and John died on Oct. 16, 1981. The farm remains in the possession of the four sons and is still being farmed by the same renter chosen by John Pace. The four sons, having never returned to the farm, are living in various parts of the country. Irvin and John, Jr. are living in Evansville; Stephen is living New York City and Edward is living in Corpus Christi, TX.

PAUL-BANKS

Joseph William Paul and Ella Banks were married during World War I at St. Patrick's Church, Pond Settlement, IL in 1917. Joe, born in 1890, was the oldest son of Peter and Magdaline Paul who came to Gallatin County from St. Wendel, IN in Posey County in 1884. After Joe and Ella were married, they moved to Enfield, IL and in 1918 their first son, Philip Frances, was born. They moved back to a farm south of Ridgway, next to his father's farm and a second son, Clarence, was born in 1920. In 1921, a daughter, Mary M. was born and two

Eula and Joseph Paul

years later, a third son, Leo Clyde, made four children in the Paul family. Two more girls were added when Laura Rita was born in 1926 and Patricia in 1930.

Joe and Ella decided that a move to St. Wendel in Posey County promised better opportunities, so they moved to a farm southeast of St. Wendel, IN. This was near where Joe's grandfather, Francis Paul, lived after arriving from Mombach Hesse Darmstadt, Germany in 1845.

Ella died in 1965 and is buried at St. Wendel. Joe was married again in 1971 to Emma Maser of Evansville, IN. They moved to Evansville where he lived until his death in 1981, age 91. He was buried beside Ella in St. Wendel Cemetary.

EDWARD A. AND DOROTHEA D. PENCE

Dorothea Dietz Pence, a life-long resident of Mt. Vernon, was born Dec. 16, 1903. She was married June 2, 1930, to Edward A. Pence, who came to Mt. Vernon in 1926 as a teacher of biology and U.S. history and as the coach of basketball and football. He was deceased Nov. 12, 1976.

During World War II Pence was principal of Central School; he then continued teaching biology and finished his career at the high school as guidance counselor. Following retirement he was academic counselor at Deaconess Hospital School of Nursing in Evansville. His father was a United Brethren minister; his family roots were in Whitley County, IN. He earned his bachelor's degree at Indiana Central College and his master's degree at Indiana University.

Dorothea and Edward Pence.

Mrs. Pence's father William P. Dietz, born Oct. 6, 1874, and deceased June 6, 1959, was a proprietor of a barber shop in the 200 block on Main Street and was a participating member of the Mt. Vernon Dramatic Club and active in other civic affairs. He was the youngest of 13 children born to Phillip Dietz, a cabinetmaker, and Charlotte Dexheimer Dietz both of whom were born in Gaugrehweiler, Germany, and came to the United States in 1867. Phillip Dietz, 1820-95, was the son of John Friedrich and Louise Petri Dietz; Charlotte Dietz, 1828-1905, was the daughter of Christian and Charlotte Dexheimer, all of Gaugrehweiler.

Mrs. Pence's mother, Ida Maus Dietz, was born Mar. 1, 1874, and deceased July 16, 1968. Ida Maus's mother came to the United States from Germany as a widow with a young son, John Graf, following the death of her husband and her parents within a six-month period, and later married Conrad Maus.

Dorothea Pence graduated from Mt. Vernon High School in 1922, and attended Evansville College. She worked in the Alexandrian Free Public Library and the high school library prior to her marriage. She is remembered for her children's story hours at the library and in area schools. Later she was well known for her scores of book reviews in the Mt. Vernon and Tri-State area.

The Pences have been active members of Trinity United Church of Christ, where members of Mrs. Pence's family have been members since the time of their migration. Mrs. Pence was president of the Synodical Women's Guild, participated in the merger of the Evangelical and Reformed and Congregational Christian Churches to form the United Church of Christ, and was the first woman to serve as moderator of the Indiana-Kentucky Conference. At Trinity her active participation included teaching Sunday School classes for many years.

She also was a charter member of Gammi Psi Chapter of Kappa Kappa Kappa and a long-time member of Tuesday Literary Club.

The Pences had no children but scores of students were close to them and frequently visited their home at 521 Mulberry St.

GEORGE L. PFISTER JR. AND GLORIA J. PFISTER FAMILY HISTORY

George L. and Gloria J. Pfister are life long residents of Mt. Veron, IN. They both graduated from Mt. Vernon High School. George was in class of 1941 and Gloria in class of 1948.

George served in the U.S. Navy from November 1941 until December, 1946. He was stationed on the Destroyer USS *Morris* the entire length of World War II serving in the South Pacific. Following his discharge, he worked at several different jobs until he was employed by Texaco Inc. in 1951. He worked at the river terminal in Mt. Vernon until his retirement in December 1984.

Following graduation, Gloria worked in the legal department of Indiana Farm Bureau Refinery for three years. She returned to a full time job in January, 1968 and has been working at Bayer Insurance Agency for 21 years.

George L. and Gloria J. Pfister

George and Gloria were married May 27, 1950, and they have two sons. Michael Louis was born Jan. 24, 1952 and resides in Mt. Vernon. He graduated from MVHS in 1970 and is married to Troy Redman, also a lifetime resident of Mt. Vernon. They have three children - Tara Loy, born Apr. 16, 1982; Michael Keith, born Jan. 10, 1984, and Julia Chrystine, born June 7, 1987. Mike is a maintenance mechanic at GAF Corp and also has his real estate license.

Thomas Eugene was born Mar. 16, 1955 and resides in Lakeland, FL. He is married to Karen Miller, who was reared in Lake Hamilton, FL. Tom graduated from MVHS in 1973 and from USI in 1977 with a degree in communication. He is presently an insurance adjuster and a scuba diving instructor. They are expecting their first child in May, 1989.

George is the son of George L. Pfister, Sr. and Florence Scheller Pfister. George Sr. worked at Fuhrer Ford Mill over 40 years and from 1944 until his death in 1975 lived in the Pfister home at 623 Walnut St., Mt. Vernon, IN. George, Sr.'s parents were Louis and Lina Gerwig Pfister. Louis's family came to America from Alsace Lorraine in the early 1800s and settled in Posey County. Louis was a business man in Mt. Vernon, being active in banking and real estate. He was one of the founders of Mt. Vernon Building & Loan Assoc. which later became Mt. Vernon Savings & Loan Assoc., and later merged with Mid West Federal Savings & Loan. Louis born Jan. 11, 1862, and Lina, born Dec. 17, 1861, were married Apr. 18, 1885. Lina's father was Joseph Gerwig, who came from France and became a naturalized citizen in October, 1858. He served three years in the Civil War with the 25th Regiment of Indiana Vet Infantry Volunteers.

Florence's parents were Adam Scheller and Barbara Effinger Scheller. Adam also served in the Army during the Civil War.

Gloria's parents are Will K. and Lillian Dietz Thomas. Will, born Aug. 13, 1905, and Lillian, born Sept. 25, 1910, were married in February 1930. Will worked for a number of years as a butcher. In 1945 he began working at Indiana Farm Bureau Refinery and was there until his retirement. He passed away in January, 1978.

Will's parents were Matthew Thomas and Zella Allyn Thomas. His grandparents were William B. and Mathilda Jones Thomas. Matthew was employed at the Hominy Mill and later became a rural mail carrier serving Point Township and R.R. #1 Mt. Vernon for over 40 years. He often told stories of carrying mail on horseback.

Zella was the daughter of Francisco Allyn and Harriet Bradley. Harriet Bradley's great grandfather was Cornelius Bradley who was a private in Capt. Henry Dobson's Co in New York and fought in the Revolutionary War. He came to Posey County in the early 1800s. He was born in 1755 in Ireland and died Aug. 26, 1840 in Posey County. Matthew and Zella were members of the Bethel Primitive Baptist Church at Farmersville.

Lillian's parents were William J. Dietz and Sophia E. Boerner Dietz. Their home was in Huessler Dome area near Salem Church. William's father was John J. Dietz, born May 12, 1833, and came to the U.S. from Wurtemburg, Germany in 1854. His mother was Elizabeth Strueh, born May 12, 1833. John and his brother came to Mt. Vernon and opened a blacksmith shop.

In 1859, he bought land in Marrs Township and farmed. The land is still owned by his heirs. John was considered to be one of pioneers of Posey County and a highly respected citizen. According to his obituary taken from the Western Star, his funeral cartage was the largest ever seen in the County.

Sophia's parents were Adam Boerner and Wilhelmenia Burgdorf. They also lived in Marrs Township and all attended Salem Church. Adam came to the U.S. from Hessen Waussau, Germany and Wilhelmenia came from Braunschweig Germany. Adam signed his naturalization papers Mar. 27, 1917. Witnesses to his moral character included Louis Pfister.

George and Gloria presently reside at 81 Park Ridge, Mt. Vernon, IN, moving there in August,

1980, after residing 30 years at 220 W. 9th, Mt. Vernon, IN, which was George's parents home while he was growing up. They are members of Trinity United Church of Christ.

PHILLIPS-BENTHALL

Wilfred Phillips was born in Black Township on Dec. 12, 1895, the son of Charles and Victoria (Carroll) Phillips. He attended Farmersville Elementary School and graduated from Mt. Vernon Senior High in 1915. He received his certificate from Indiana State College to become a teacher in 1917. He taught at College Point School in Point Township. He then served in the United States Army in WWI as a Sergeant. His tour of duty included 13 months spent in France. Upon completion of his Army duty he resumed teaching at Prairie School in West Black Township.

Wilfred and Mary Phillips

Soon after his return home from the service, Wilfred married Mary Edna Benthall on Oct. 18, 1919 at Evansville, IN. Mary was born Oct. 28, 1900 in Black township, the daughter of John D. and Honora (Blackburn) Benthall.

Wilfred obtained his teacher's license in 1920. Later that same year he began working at People's Bank and Trust Company in Mt. Vernon where he remained 45 years until his retirement in 1965. Many knew Wilfred as "Bud" or "Uncle Bud".

Wilfred and Mary were the parents of six children: Mary Elinor, born Mar. 3, 1922 and died Mar. 9, 1922. Naomi Jean was born Aug. 21, 1923 and resides in Poseyville, IN. Wilfred LaRue was born June 27, 1926 and resides on Upton Road. Gerald was born Dec. 4, 1933 and resides in the town of Mt. Vernon. Gerald's twin sister, Geraldine resides at Comstock Park, MI. The sixth child, Phyllis Sue lives outside of Carmi, IL and was born Feb. 18, 1938.

The Phillips family resided for 37 years at 705 East Fifth Street. Mary and Wilfred were members of the Bethel Primitive Baptist Church, the first church in Posey County, as they had been since they were children. Mary was a past worthy matron of Sunbeam Chapter, No. 1, Order of the Eastern Star, serving in that office at the same time her husband, Wilfred, was worthy patron of the Mt. Vernon Masonic Lodge. Mary was a member of the Victoria Camp, Royal Neighbors of America, and a charter member of the Black Township Community Club.

Mary said her last farewell to Wilfred, her husband of 45 years, on Sept. 24, 1964. Wilfred found his life to be "empty" without his Mary and so on Nov. 4, 1967 he took for his second wife, Nell York Walker. Wilfred died on Nov. 23, 1969. *Submitted by Delene Schmitz*

CHARLES AND VICTORIA (CARROLL) PHILLIPS

Charles and Victoria Carroll Phillips married in Posey County June 5, 1892. They reared their family north of Farmersville on land homesteaded by his grandfather, Elisha Phillips upon his arrival from New York. Charles (July 7, 1860-Oct. 2, 1941) was a carpenter and farmer; a quiet, hard working person. He was caretaker of Moore Cemetery near his home for many years. He carried a stone jug of drinking water and a scythe and mowed by hand. His grandfather, Elisha, his father, Moses, himself and his young son, Anson (May 13, 1893-Oct. 18, 1895) makes four generations of his family buried there. Their other children were Wilfred (Dec. 31, 1895-Nov. 23, 1969), Angie (Anna) (July 22, 1897-Aug. 22, 1973) Bertha (Aug. 24, 1899-Aug. 30, 1974) and Vera (May 7, 1905-Feb. 23, 1985).

Moses Phillips' home was a two story house, facing west on the older section of road. The road was rerouted and ran through the Phillips land. Charles therefore built his home facing east on the new part of what is now S.R. 69. Vera and husband, Leo Parker later built their home on the north side of his. Anna built across the highway on the southside of Phillips Road.

Charles and Victoria (Carroll) Phillips

Victoria, (Sept. 8, 1874-May 8, 1956) was the daughter of John R. Carroll, who was born in McNairy Co., TN. He married Virginia Adsit in Posey County. She assisted the doctors at childbirths and nursed the sick. She, her sister, Bertha Carroll, her brother, Samuel and his first wife, Abbie West Carroll were members of Bethel Primitive Baptist Church in Farmersville. Meeting time was the third Sunday each month as part of a circuit. Many years of family dinners were enjoyed at her home on church day with all four children and their families. Anna and husband, Joel Cox, while living on the Greathouse Farm on Springfield Road, took their four children to church by horse and buggy. Lorene and Charles Joseph sat in the seat between their parents, Lela sat at her mother's feet on a stool made by her father, and Walter on his mother's lap. They crossed Big Creek on the W.T. Washer covered bridge at Solitude.

Charles and Victoria had 19 grandchildren; many of whom still live in Posey County.

CLIFFORD PRITCHARD

Clifford Pritchard, son of John Fowler and Emma Heck Pritchard, grandson of William Fowler and Florence McDonagh Pritchard, was born Oct. 13, 1888 in Phillips Township, White Co., IL. He was a farmer all of his working life, and spent a greater part of that time in the area of Crossville and Phillips Township, until he moved his family to Ellendale, ND in 1929, possibly looking for new challenges to conquer. At this time there was a great depression and also a drought and the family suffered many reverses and decided to return five years later, to more familiar country, trying to get their fortunes reversed.

Clifford and Sarah had a family of seven children:

Victor Clifford was born Nov. 11, 1919. He married Bernadine Tolley in 1942, and they had six children; Kenneth Wayne, who lived four days, Victor Clifford, Jr., David Lester, Larry Eugene, Harold Robert and Helen Denise.

William Leonard was born Oct. 28, 1920. He married Nina Wolf in 1943, and they had four children: Wayne William, Pamela, Nita Jo and Mariann.

John Franklin Pritchard was born Apr. 5, 1922. He married Edith Toth, and they had eight children; John F. Jr., James Clifford, Gail Elaine, Joan Ellen (Joni), Judith Ann, Jean Frances, Robert Dale, and Paul Edward.

Edwin Eugene (Doc), who was born July 24, 1923. He married Olive Dennison in 1946 and they had a family of three; Monty Edwin, Rebecca Pearl and Steven Roy.

Lewis Ed (Sed) who was born Jan. 19, 1925. He married Mary Alice Timms and they had a family of seven children; Jacqueline Kay, who was killed in an auto accident June 30, 1966, Gayle Lewis (male), Danny, Rick, Debby Sheila and Tony.

Edna Frances, who was born Feb. 22, 1926, and died June 22, 1933 at Ellendale, ND.

Norma Jean who was born Sept. 24, 1928. She married Ralph Simmons and they had three children: Lonnie Ray, Judy Lavon and Brenda Joyce.

Clifford's first marriage to Julia Knight took place July 26, 1909 in Phillips Township, and they had two girls by that union; Velma who was born Mar. 29, 1910 and Zola Grace, whose birthdate was Sept. 29, 1912.

About the time World War II began, Cliff moved his family to Indiana, at one time living around Oaktown, and then moving to Flat Rock, IL and farming there until his retirement. He purchased a farm in Flat Rock and was in partnership with his son William. He was a good farmer, introducing innovations which improved farming in the areas where he lived.

He had introduced yellow soybeans to southern Indiana and Illinois around 1934 and before World War II and had better than average yield. He also pioneered fall plowing in order for the ground to be better broken up for spring planting. He used much large equipment, plows, combines and tractors, all of which made for doing a bigger than average job of farming.

He died Feb. 4, 1957. Buried in Price Cemetery, Russelville, IL.

FLO AND ELIZABETH PRITCHARD

Florian Percival Pritchard born May 27, 1853 in Posey Co., IN who married Elizabeth Heck Jan. 2, 1878 in Posey County. Elizabeth was born Mar. 14, 1858 in Posey County, whose parents were Joseph and Elizabeth Schaffer Heck.

Florian was the eighth son of William F. and Florence Macdonagh. Florian had a twin brother Volney, and Florian was born 2-1/2 minutes after Volney.

Flo and Elizabeth Pritchard

Florian and Elizabeth had a son, Julian and five daughters, Fannie, Daisy, Elizabeth, Grace and Jessie.

Julian died at an early age. Fannie was married to Mark Kahn and her second husband was George N. Wall. Daisy married Otis Carroll; Elizabeth married Horace E. Greathouse; Grace married Simon Hempfling and Jessie married Edward Robins and her second husband was Robert S. Adams.

Florian was a farmer and land owner in Posey County. He sold his farm in 1917 and bought a home in Mt. Vernon and retired.

Florian died Feb. 6, 1935 in Posey County and Elizabeth died Nov. 11, 1943 in Indianapolis, IN at the home of Jessie Robins Adams. Both are buried at Maple Hill Cemetery in New Harmony, IN.
Submitted by Martha Carroll Leigh

JOHN F. PRITCHARD

The following information was taken from obituary in Carmi, IL paper May 3, 1931 (The Carmi Democrat-Tribune).

John F. Pritchard, son of William Fowler and Florence McDonagh Pritchard was born in New Harmony, IN, Oct. 20, 1859; died May 2, 1931 at his home in Crossville, IL at the age of 80 years, six months and 12 days.

He had eight brothers: Henry Turner Pritchard, Thomas McDonagh Pritchard, William Austin Pritchard, William Shakespeare Pritchard, Norman Lockley Pritchard, Voleny Walter Pritchard, Julian Peter Pritchard, Florian Percival Pritchard. At that time Florian was the only one surviving, and lived in Mt. Vernon, IN.

The Pritchard family came from England about the year 1842, the two older brothers being born in Ellesmere, Shropshire, England.

John Pritchard carved his name as a deep and lasting influence on his generation and upon this community. He was a neighborly man and a splendid man to serve as a friend. He was a farmer, blacksmith, carpenter, was a member of the Episcopalian Church in New Harmony until he moved to White Co, IL in 1887.

John Pritchard was united in marriage to Emma Heck on Dec. 22, 1878. To this union were born five children: Louis Pritchard of Crossville, IL, Vol Pritchard of Indianapolis, IN, Kate Pritchard Spencer of Carmi, IL, Clifford Pritchard of Ellendale, ND, and Dorothy Pritchard Sawyer also of Ellendale, ND.

He was preceeded in death by his loving companion on July 6, 1922. He was again united in marriage to Emma Owen on July 12, 1924, who with the above named children, one brother and 18 grandchildren are left to mourn their loss.

He has been fast failing in health especially within the past three years, during which time he has received every care and attention from his faithful companion.

Funeral services were held at the Baptist Church in Crossville at two o'clock Sunday afternoon, May 3rd, conducted by Elder W.D. Arnold. Interment was made in the New Harmony Cemetery. Boultinghouse & Archer were the funeral directors.

JOHN FRANKLIN PRITCHARD

John Franklin Pritchard, born in Crossville, IL on Apr. 5, 1922 to Clifford and Sarah Hon Pritchard, married Edith Elizabeth Toth on Feb. 13, 1943 at Cleveland, OH. John served in the U.S. Navy from September 1942 until January 1946 and settled in Cleveland, where his family was raised. John and Edith were parents of eight children: John F. Jr., born Jan. 26, 1944: James Clifford, born Feb. 26, 1945: Gail Elaine, born Nov. 28, 1946; Joan Ellen, born Mar. 29, 1948; Judith Ann, born Oct. 18, 1949; Jean Frances, born Feb. 8, 1956; Robert Dale, born Feb. 1, 1959; and Paul Edward, born Dec. 1, 1960.

John spent his growing up years mainly in the area around Crossville, IL and a five year period in Ellendale, ND. He was quite active in sports in high school — in track, softball and was captain of his basketball team three years at Crossville Community High School. Was 12 letter man.

While in the Navy, he taught electrical theory and electrical mathematics in The Navy Electrical School in Detroit, and also served in the South Pacific about 13 months, on the USS Collingsworth, APA 146. Received the Purple Heart and four battle stars.

The children presented us with 14 grandchildren: John Jr., married Sandra Lee Beck, and has two sons, John III and Rob: James Clifford married Anita Park and has two children, Alece Michelle and Christopher Lynn; Gail Elaine married Joseph Bohanon and has three boys, Michael Joseph, Joel Christopher, and David Alan; Joan (Joni) married Lyle Stusek, and they have one son, Charles Michael; Judith Ann is married to Donald E. Winchell and they have four daughters, Darlene Marie, Sarah Anne, Julia Elizabeth and Laura Elaine; Jean married Michael J. Bowen and has two children, Jarrod Mathew, and Hallie Juliana. These children all reside in Lake Co., OH at the present time.

John has been employed in several capacities during his working career in production and maintenance in manufacturing plants, engineering and machine designing and robotics, as a certified manufacturing engineer, for many years until retiring in 1982.

THOMAS McDONAGH PRITCHARD AND WIFE RUTH ROBINSON

William Fowler Pritchard and his wife, Florence McDonagh Pritchard, along with their two sons born in England, Henry Turner Pritchard and Thomas McDonagh Pritchard, emigrated to America from Derbyshire, England in the early 1840s.

The oldest son, Henry Turner, passed away shortly after their arrival to New Orleans, where they first settled.

Thomas McDonagh Pritchard, the second son, came down the Ohio River by boat with his parents, probably to Evansville and then by wagon to New Harmony, IN, on the banks of the Wabash in 1847 where he grew up. He was one of nine sons born to William Fowler and Florence McDonagh Pritchard.

Thomas McDonagh Pritchard

He served in the Indiana Regiment Volunteers for three years during the war, 1862 through 1865. Shortly after his discharge from service, he married Ruth Robinson in Posey County. Ruth Robinson was the daughter of Wilhemenia Evans and Henry Robinson. Wilhemenia Evans was the daughter of Oliver Evans, son of the inventor of steam engines and mill machinery.

Thomas and Ruth Louise Pritchard were members of the "Workingmens Institute", "Thespian Society" and they performed in the New Harmony Opera House. They were also active members of the Episcopal church in New Harmony.

There were four children born to Thomas McDonagh and Ruth Louise Pritchard. One girl, Annie, and three sons, Harry, Neef and Leonard.

Annie was the oldest and was a pretty woman with warm brown eyes and her mother's amiable disposition. She grew up in New Harmony and married Richard Richards of New Harmony and three children were born to them.

Harry Pritchard was the oldest son. He married Marietta Reno. Harry and Marietta had six children. Many of their descendants are settled in California and Washington.

Neef Pritchard, the second son was named for his great, great, grandfather. Neef also married and settled in California.

Leonard Pritchard was the last child born to Thomas and Ruth, as Ruth passed away shortly after Leonard's birth. His grandparents, Henry and Wilhemenia Robinson raised him for a while. Wilhemenia and her daughter, Nell Robinson ran a millinary shop in New Harmony, so Leonard was farmed out to different members of the family and had a rather difficult childhood. He grew up and married Lizzie Russell also of Posey County. One son, Vern Osborn Pritchard, was born to them.

Vern Osborn Pritchard married Pearl Edwards in the State of Illinois, Gallatin County. Vern was a member of the Operating Engineers Local #181. He worked at the Shipyards in Evansville, IN, during WWII. Other projects were the Atomic Plant in Central City, KY; the Kentucky Dam; Bernheim Forest Toll Road, in Kentucky and the bridge in Shawneetown, IL. He also was a farmer.

Vern and Pearl Pritchard settled in Shawneetown, IL and had seven children. Vernon Leon, Norman Edward, David Osborn, Mary Agnes, Leonard Delano and William Gene Pritchard. Six of their children are still living as of this writing. Vern and Pearl are both deceased and are buried in Hogans Cemetery in Shawneetwon, IL.

Thomas McDonagh Pritchard and Ruth Louise Robinson Pritchard have many living descendants in the United States in this year of 1989.

After Ruth's death, Thomas married again to Mary Metcalf and they had four children. The first three died at birth or shortly after. Arthur, a son grew up and became a pharmacist in California. He is deceased with no descendants. *Written by Mary Pritchard Zampino.*

WILLIAM FOWLER PRITCHARD AND FLORENCE MACDONAGH PRITCHARD

William Fowler Pritchard was born on June 13, 1818 in the small rural market town of Ellesmere, Shropshire, England near the Welsh border. His father was Thomas Pritchard (1795-?), a maltster born in Ellesmere as had been a considerable number of previous generations of Pritchards, and his mother was Juliana Fowler (1793-1822), christened (and presumably born) in Newcastle-under-Lyme, Stafford, England. William had a younger sister, Juliana Mary Pritchard (1821-?), who did not come to America.

William Fowler Pritchard; Florence MacDonagh Pritchard

Florence MacDonagh, William Fowler Pritchard's wife, was born in Chesterfield, Derbyshire, England on May 5, 1819. Her father was Thomas Austin MacDonagh, a wine merchant rumored to have been born in Portugal, and her mother was Dorothy Needham (1787-?), born in Chesterfield. She had an older sister, Celia (1821-?) and a younger brother, Thomas Austin MacDonagh Jr., christened on Feb. 24, 1824. Nothing further is known of Florence's sister, but her brother also emigrated to New Harmony where he died on July 21, 1869. He is buried in Maple Hill Cemetery south of New Harmony.

Little is known of William and Florence's life in England except that they moved (probably with his father) to Liverpool by Nov. 12, 1838 when their first child, the first of nine sons, Henry Turner, was born. There is a record of their marriage on Sept. 23, 1840 in Liverpool where William's occupation is listed as "cabinet maker." A second son, Thomas MacDonagh, was born in 1841 in Liverpool.

The family emigrated to the United States between 1841 and 1844, landing in New Orleans where a third son, William Austin was born on Nov. 19, 1843. The family lived for a time in New Orleans where William Austin died in 1844 and Henry Turner died on May 12, 1845. The family subsequently traveled up the Mississippi river, living for a period in Waterloo, IL near St. Louis. They then moved up the Ohio river, reaching Covington, KY opposite Cincinnati where the fourth son, William Shakespeare, was born in 1845.

In 1847 William and Florence moved to New Harmony in Posey County and helped establish the New Harmony Dramatic Association. William Fowler acted in these productions as well as built sets for them, and Florence acted in them. William was for a period after he first arrived in New Harmony in the silk business. A fifth son, Julian Peter, was born in 1848.

William took part in the Gold Rush while Florence and the three surviving boys remained behind in New Harmony (Florence was pregnant with the sixth son, John Fowler, who was born in 1850 while William was in California). William left New Harmony on Apr. 1, 1850 and arrived in Sacramento on Sept. 24, 1850, continued his theatrical career and returned to New Harmony by ship via Nicaragua in 1852. He kept a journal of this trip which is being prepared for publication.

After returning to New Harmony, William Fowler Pritchard settled down to his main profession which was cabinet making. He had quite a reputation in this craft but was reported to be a questionable farmer even though he did some farming around New Harmony at some period during his life. He also got into the undertaking business, building both coffins and, in 1859, a hearse. He also resumed his work in the theater with a group called the New Harmony Thespians between 1855 and 1860.

The twins Volney Walter and Florian Percival were born on May 27, 1853 and Norman Lockley in 1857. Volney died on Mar. 22, 1881 without issue.

During the Civil War William Fowler Pritchard served with his son William Shakespeare as a musician with the Regimental Band of the 25th Regiment, Indiana Volunteers.

William and Florence are known to have owned at least two lots in New Harmony. The first was bounded by North, Granary, Main and Brewery Streets where they presumably lived in the Harmonist house on the property. The second was bounded by Church, Steam Mill, Short and First Streets where it is believed the two Williams built a substantial two story house with a workshop behind.

William Fowler Pritchard died on Aug. 12, 1875, probably in Albion, Edwards Co., IL on the farm of his son William Shakespeare and is buried in Maple Hill Cemetery. Florence lived on in an addition to the workshop which William Shakespeare built for her and was active with St. Stephen's Episcopal Church where she has a memorial window. She died on Aug. 9, 1896 and is also buried in Maple Hill Cemetery. Up to the end of 1988, there have been 421 descendants of this couple, a number of whom still live in Posey County and the surrounding counties of Indiana, Illinois and Kentucky.

WILLIAM SHAKESPEARE PRITCHARD AND CHARLOTTE EMILY METCALF PRITCHARD

William Shakespeare Prichard was the fourth son of William Fowler (1818-75) and Florence (MacDonagh) Pritchard (1819-96) and was born in Covington, Kenton Co., KY on Dec. 1, 1845. He moved with his family to New Harmony in 1847.

Charlotte Emily Metcalf, William Shakespeare Pritchard's wife, was born on July 24, 1853 in Albion, Edwards Co., IL to Arthur Edward Metcalf (1822-90) and Charlotte Conyngton (1819-68).

They were married on Dec. 28, 1876 near Albion, Edwards Co., IL at the home of her father.

During the Civil War William served with his father with the Regimental Band of the 25th Regiment, Indiana Volunteers. He later served as a soldier with Company D, 74th Indiana Regiment where he participated in Sherman's march to the sea.

William Shakespeare Pritchard, Charlotte Emily Metcalf Pritchard

William alternated between carpentry and farming. He helped his father build at least one house in New Harmony. He also did plumbing, stonemasonry, and electrical work.

They moved to a farm near Albion in 1876 where two children were born: Thomas MacDonagh Pritchard (Jan. 10, 1878-May 5, 1962) and Julia Mary Prichard (Jan. 30, 1880-Oct. 3, 1967).

In 1881 they moved back into Posey County, to a farm near Stewartsville and later rented the Col. Jule Owen farm outside of New Harmony. The family began a series of moves outside of Posey County in 1884 (mainly between California and Albion, IL), eventually ending up in Pullman, Whitman, Co., WA in 1904. Two further children were born during this period: Florence Conyngton Pritchard (Nov. 4, 1885-Nov. 3, 1918) and Walter Howard Pritchard (Aug. 24, 1887-Nov. 24, 1834). In Pullman he stopped farming and is known to have built at least five houses and to have invested in real estate, including helping his sons buy their first farm acreage.

William is known to have visited New Harmony in 1916, a few years before his death on Oct. 22, 1920 in Orange, Orange Co., CA. Charlotte died on Jan. 10, 1930 in Whittier, Los Angeles Co., CA.

This branch of the prolific family of William Fowler and Florence Pritchard has thus far generated 28 descendants, but only Tom and Julia ever resided in Posey County (and only as children):

Thomas MacDonagh Pritchard had Earl Hampton Pritchard (1907-) and Anna Lucille Pritchard (McGlade) (1909-). Earl had Philip Norman Pritchard (1948-) who is the author of this article and Pamela Lynn Pritchard (1950-); all three have been back to New Harmony, Posey County for one or more Pritchard family reunions. Anna had Jo Ann McGlade (Morgan) (1935-) and Charles Jerry McGlade (1938-). Jo Ann had John Steven Morgan (1957-), Anne Michelle Morgan (1959-60), Christopher William Morgan (1961-) and Meredith Ellen Morgan (1966-). Jerry had Brenda Jo McGlade (1961-), Michael Sean McGlade (1962-), Patrick Erin McGlade (1970-) and Kelly Sue McGlade (1971-). John had Grant Evan McGlade (1984-).

Julia Mary Pritchard had no children.

Florence Conyngton Pritchard (Lawrence) had Jesse Conyngton Lawrence (1913-) and Margaret Pritchard Lawrence (1914-), neither of whom have any children.

Walter Howard Pritchard had Charlotte Pauline Pritchard (1913), John Robert Pritchard (1917-1969), and William Christian Pritchard (1923-). Bill had Christopher James Pritchard (1951-), Mary Kay Pritchard (1953-) and Nancy Lynn Pritchard

(1954-). Chris had Jessica Michelle Pritchard (1985).

JOHN ROBERT AND SADIE (ARNOLD) RANES

John Robert and Sadie (Arnold) Ranes were a part of the Mt. Vernon community for 40 years. Dr. Ranes practiced medicine in Mt. Vernon from 1911 until the last few years of his life, most of those years from his office at 117 East Second Street. He also owned and operated Ranebo Fruit Farm located northwest of the city near Upton, IN.

John R. Ranes was born Apr. 30, 1881, in White Co., IL, reportedly in a covered wagon. He was the fifth child of Henry Ranes, a carpenter and laborer, and Eliza Ellen Redman Ranes. John was reared in Gibson County, near Owensville, IN. He attended Richland School and Princeton High School and then Oakland City College. It was while he was a student at the college that he met and married Sadie Arnold of Warrick County, also a student at the College. She was the daughter of John Granville Arnold and Barbara Ellen Hall (Barnett) Arnold. (Sadie was born Dec. 2, 1880, and died Feb. 26, 1956.) They were married on Dec. 25, 1904.

Seated in front: L to R. John R. and Sadie A. Ranes, Standing in Back: L to R Harold W., J. Kenneth, and Francis W. Ranes

After three years at Oakland City College, John and Sadie moved to Indianapolis, IN, where he enrolled in medical school. He was graduated in 1908 from the Indiana School of Medicine. He practiced in Indianapolis for a short time, and then moved to Union in Pike County before removing to Mt. Vernon in 1911.

During all the years they were in Mt. Vernon, the Raneses were active members of the Mt. Vernon General Baptist Church.

He was the quintessential country doctor, making house calls in all kinds of weather, delivering as many as eight or ten babies a week in the homes of his patients, and dispensing medications sometimes from his own stock. He had to be a specialist in all areas and often received meat or produce in return for his services.

His death, as his life had been, was given to the betterment of mankind, as he allowed researchers to use his terminal condition to come nearer a cure for cancer. He died Oct. 23, 1951, in Billings Hospital in Chicago, IL.

Three sons were born to Dr. and Mrs. Ranes.

Harold Wilbur was born Apr. 12, 1907; he died Mar. 1, 1988. He was married to Eleanor von Stetton Jan. 16, 1932. They had three children: Jacqueline (Mrs. Howard Young), Juanita (Mrs. Gene Bertolet), and Ronald. Following Eleanor's death, Harold married Betty Hartzell (Aug. 31, 1941), and they had one son, Paul Timothy.

John Kenneth was born Sept. 16, 1910. He was married to Ruby Vines, the daughter of Percy and Amy (Ashworth) Vines, Dec. 2, 1932. (Ruby passed away Oct. 20, 1988.) They had no children.

Francis Willard was born Aug. 10, 1917, and he died Nov. 9, 1957, of injuries sustained in an accident at the Mt. Vernon Milling Company. Francis was married Mar. 22, 1940, to Mary Martha Reeves, the daughter of Charles, Sr. and Ollie (Farris) Reeves. To them were born three daughters: Barbara Judith (Mrs. David Whitten), Nancy (Mrs. Cecil Sexton), and Ann (Mrs. George F. Fischer).

REDMAN HISTORY

Mary Jane (Redman) Schneider was the daughter of George Taylor and Mary Elizabeth (Clarkston) Redman. George Taylor was born Mar. 17, 1868. He married Mary Elizabeth on Sept. 2, 1891. They had eight children. George Taylor died in 1938, the same year as his daughter, Mary Jane. Mary Elizabeth died in 1947. Both are buried in Blacks Cemetery.

George Taylor was the son of Edward and Margaret (Greathouse) Redman. They had four children. Edward was in Civil War. Margaret died 1874. Buried in Greathouse Cemetery. Edward died 1913. Buried Blacks Cemetery.

Edward Redman was the son of Joseph and Elizabeth Ann (Davis). Joseph was born 1803, and married Elizabeth Feb. 17, 1830. They shortened the name from Readman to Redman.

Joseph Redman was the son of Edward Readman, Sr. and Mary (Moran), from England. They came to Posey County in 1820. Edward, Sr. died in 1837.

The Schneider-Redman History can be cross-referenced with the Redman-McGennis History.

READMAN (REDMAN) FAMILY

History known goes back to Edward Readman Sr. who came to England from Ireland in 1780. He married Mary Moran, an English girl. Edward Jr. was born 1789, Joseph 1803, Mary 1807, David 1810. They came to North Carolina 1815 and to Posey County 1820. Were not listed in 1820 Census. Edward Sr. died in 1837. Burial place of he and wife not known. Edward Jr. married Anna Pickles Sept. 9, 1826 in Mt. Vernon. Joseph and Elizabeth Ann Davis of Tennessee married Feb. 17, 1830. Mary to Zenori Mills Apr. 3, 1826. David to Maria Givens in April 1830. Second marriage to Elizabeth Knight. Joseph and Elizabeth homesteaded farm land west of Mt. Vernon. They shortened the name to Redman.

Children were Eliza, born 1834 married S.G. Curtis, Susan C., 1836, married James G. Smith. John in Civil War lived in Northern Posey, no record, buried in Soldiers Plot at Bellefontaine Cemetery. Edward 1841 was in Civil War, married Margaret Greathouse. William, 1843, married Ruth D. Kitchel. George, 1846, married Anne Row, Taylor. 1850, married Martha Greathouse, she died in 1875, buried in Greathouse Cemetery.

Margaret Greathouse was daughter of Sarah Welborn and Sampson Greathouse. His father was William and Mary Owen. Father of William was Herman Graethousen who came from Germany in early 1700s. William was in Revolutionary War, Washington Company Militia. Children were John and David. William died in Pennsylvania. The sons came to Indiana, settled near Hovey Lake and in Kentucky.

David married Sarah Callander in 1806. Children were Sampson December 1806, George March 1811, John 1818 and Alonzo Dow 1820. David died 1827. Children educated at Greathouse school and church went on to higher education.

Front Row Schneider children and Ralph Fuller, 2nd Row: Ruth Kitchel Redman, Mary J. Schneider, June Curtis Rowe, Mary Clarkson Redman, Margaret Redman. Back Row - Phillip Schneider, Walter Rowe, Loren Redman, George Redman, Esee Redman

Children of Sampson and Sarah Welborn Greathouse were Barbara (Ashworth), Margaret (Redman), Sarah (Klotz), Elizabeth (Harris), George (Martha Hirshman), John A. (Elizabeth Browning), Alonzo (Esther White) died 1842. He married Philomena Stinson.

Children of Margaret and Edward Redman were Alice born 1866, died 1866, George Taylor Mar. 17, 1868, Nora (Martin) 1870, Sampson 1873 (Eliza Huff). Margaret died in 1874, buried in Greathouse Cemetery. Edward's mother lived with them until she died 1879. Edward then married a widow Angeline York. Charles, a son died 1915. Angeline died 1912 and Edward 1913, buried in Blacks Cemetery.

George Taylor married Mary Elizabeth, daughter of John S. and Mary Chamberlain Clarkson Sept. 2, 1891. John was born in Lincoln, England 1849. He left wife and four daughters to go back to England. Never heard of again. His wife later married Ben Gibson, he died 1918 and she 1922, buried in Concord, IL.

Children of George and Mary Redman were Cora (Fordice) 1892. Esco Redman Feb. 3, 1895 (Lena West), Iva (Fuller) Nov. 17, 1897, Mary Jane 1898 (Phillip Schneider), Nora 1900 (John Abbrederes), Loren Redman 1903 (Zola Moit), Inez 1908 (Oscar McGennis) and Margaret 1910 (George Bottomley). They attended Prairie School and Prairie Church. Prairie School burned in 1926 and the flood of 1937 destroyed the church. George T. Redman died in 1938 and wife Mary in 1947. Buried in Black's Cemetery.

HERBERT WALTER AND ETHEL MAE REDMAN

The marriage of Herbert Walter Redman and Ethel Mae Alldredge Sept. 20, 1908 united two pioneer Posey County families. The wedding took place at the Alldredge home in Upton.

Ethel Mae, born May 23, 1890, was the daughter of John Sam and Mary Louisa (Redman) Alldredge. John Sam was a direct descendant of John Alldredge who, with his six sons, arrived in Posey County with the second boatload of people from North Carolina coming to the new McFadin settlement. This was probably in 1810 although the records aren't clear on this point. John Sam was the son of Samuel who was the son of John. Mary Louisa was the second wife of John Sam. They were married Sept. 18, 1887. Three daughters were born to this union: Elsie, Ethel and Edith.

Herbert Walter, born Nov. 20, 1887, was the son of James Walter and Martha (Bray) Redman. They were married in 1886. James Walter was the son of Henry C. and Lisa (Bottomley) Redman. This branch of the Redman family came from England, however they settled for a while in Maryland before coming to Posey County.

Herbert and Ethel Redman

Herb and Ethel lived in Mt. Vernon after their marriage, Herb was a barber at the Dietz barber shop but later set up his own shop on Main Street. In the late 1920's when women started cutting and curling their hair, Herb branched out into the beauty business and became the owner of the first beauty shop in Mt. Vernon. Two daughters were born to Herb and Ethel: Hallie Lucile and Janice Fern.

Hallie Lucile was born May 17, 1910, the day before the earth went through the tail of Halley's Comet, an event that some thought would kill all life on earth. That did not happen, but to commemorate the historic event, John Sam insisted that the new baby be named Hallie.

Hallie Lucile graduated from Mt. Vernon High School in 1928. She received her B.A. degree from Evansville College and her M.A. from Bread Loaf School of English, Middlebury College, Middlebury, VT. She also did graduate work at Northwestern University School of Speech. She began teaching in Mt. Vernon in 1936 and, with the exception of five years, she continued to teach there until her retirement in 1975. During World War II she was an American Red Cross Hospital Recreation Worker. The school year of 1956-1957 she taught at Mid-Pacific Institute in Honolulu, HI. She still lives in Mt. Vernon.

Janice Fern graduated from Mt. Vernon High School in 1930. In 1929 she won the first beauty contest in Posey County. She was judged the most beautiful girl in Posey County. After graduating from Washington University School of Nursing in 1934, she married Dr. Harold Lees Joslyn from Malden, MO. Dr. Joslyn became an associate of Dr. Horace W. Soper of the Soper Mills Clinic in St. Louis. When Dr. Soper retired, Harold took over the clinic and remained there until 1978 when he suffered a stroke that partially paralyzed him. In 1983 he and Janice moved to Mt. Vernon where they still live. They have one son, James Richard Joslyn, who lives in St. Louis.

CHARLES REEVES

Charles Reeves born Oct. 10, 1882 at Upton, IN the son of James N. Reeves (1822-1897) and Martha Street Lashbrook Reeves (1839-1888). Around 1893 James N. Reeves and his children left Upton in two covered wagons for Wolf City, TX their journey took about 13 months as the sojourners stopped along the way to work and refill their food supplies. Their stay in Texas was short lived and the family started their trek back to Upton in their covered wagons where on Nov. 11, 1897 James died suddenly (it is believed from pneumonia) and was buried in Poplar Bluff, MO. The children continued their journey home. The entire return trip took about nine months. Upon their return to Upton, Charles did farm work; and on Sept. 24, 1900 was united in marriage to Ollie Farris daughter of Willis Farris (1853-1889) and Mary Skipworth Farris (1854-1937). On Mar. 21, 1903 a son Virgil was born and on June 9, 1924 he married Grace Culley daughter of Fred Culley. Virgil passed away Dec. 9, 1979, is buried in Bellefontaine Cemetery. In 1911 Charles and family moved to Mt. Vernon and Charles worked for the L&N Railroad during which time their son James William was born Dec. 11, 1911 and in August 1932 James was united in marriage to Florence Hageman daughter of William and Amelia (Kreie) Hageman.

L to R: Ollie and Charles Reeves

James passed away Nov. 14, 1947 and is buried in Bellefontaine Cemetery. Some time later Charles began his employment at the Home Mill Grain Company located on North Main Street and thence on to the Fuhrer Ford Grain Company where he was employed about 35 years. During this time a daughter Marjorie was born on Mar. 31, 1915 and on Jan. 9, 1935 was married to Milford Blackburn son of Walter and Martha (Knight) Blackburn; Marjorie passed away May 30, 1968 and is buried in Bellefontaine Cemetery. Another daughter Mary Martha, born July 29, 1921 and on Mar. 22, 1940 married Francis W. Ranes son of Dr. John R. and Sadie (Arnold) Ranes; Another son Charles LaVern was born Jan. 9, 1924 and was united in marriage on Oct. 10, 1946 to Bonnie Stokes daughter of Henry and Gertie Stokes.

In his later years Charles worked at Servel where he retired in 1947.

Charles' great grandparents were James Reeves born Jan. 5, 1795 in Georgia and Ann McAndrew Reeves born Oct. 5, 1799 in Virginia. They were married Dec. 29, 1816 in Jefferson Co., TN by Justice of the Peace William Hill. They are listed in the Jefferson County Census of 1830. About 1830 they moved to Posey Co., IN and settled in Black Township near the "Plank Road". Both James and Ann McAndrew Reeves are buried at Moore Cemetery on State Road 69 near Solitude, IN.

Charles was a member of the Independent Order of Odd Fellows Lodge #49 and his wife was a member of Helen Rebekah Lodge #245. They were both members of the Mt. Vernon General Baptist Church. Charles passed away Mar. 31, 1959 and he and his wife are buried at Welborn Cemetery at Upton.

REINEKE-MEIER

Henry August Reineke was born in Robinson Township, Posey County on Mar. 14, 1886. Henry was the son of August and Anna (Brandt) Reineke. He attended Schroeder School. He was a lifelong farmer in Robinson Township.

Henry and Carrie Reineke

On Nov. 26, 1914 Henry married Caroline Meier at Zion United Church of Christ, Lippe. "Carrie", as her friends knew her, was born Jan. 3, 1895 and was the daughter of George and Sarah (Lang) Meier of Posey County. Carrie also went to Schroeder School. Her grandfather, John Lang, built the house in which the Reineke family lived.

Henry and Carrie had a family of four children. The first, a boy, was stillborn. Both Marie and Esther, their daughters, presently live in Robinson Township. Henry, their other son died in 1987.

The Reinekes were also members of Zion United Church of Christ. They were active Farm Bureau members.

Henry died Sept. 18, 1967 and Carrie followed on Jan. 27, 1979. Both are buried at Zion United Church of Christ Cemetery.

ELIJAH DUGAN RENO

Elijah Dugan Reno (son of George b. 1751, VA, grandson of John b. 1720 Virginia, and great grandson of Louis b. 1676 in Paris France) of Virginia Huguenot heritage, was born in 1780 in Westomoreland Co., OH. He and his father George, earned their living taking flatboats down the Ohio and Mississippi Rivers to New Orleans. Every boatman from Cincinnati to New Orleans knew him and addressed him as "Hard on the Twine" which meant to pull hard on the ropes when the flatboat was caught on a sandbar or some hidden snag. After delivering their cargo of produce from the "upper country" they would dismantle the flatboat, sell the lumber and "hot foot" it back to Ohio. They would then build another flatboat for the next trip to New Orleans.

Harry Pritchard; Mary Etta Reno

In 1818 he married Mary Noggles in Dearborn Co., IN. Nine children were born in Dearborn County; Jessie Noggle, Elijah D., Robert Hart, Mary J., Catherine, Eliza, Daniel Lynn, and Eleacta

Ann. The family moved to the Solitude area of Posey County in 1832 and their tenth child, Lavina, was born in 1834. Elijah died in 1844 and is interred at Goad's Cemetery. Mary died in 1875 and is interred at the Black Cemetery on Highway 69 near Solitude.

Robert Hart Reno, second son of Elijah Dugan Reno was born in Dearborn Co., IN in 1820. At the age of 27 he enlisted in the Army at Lawrenceburg, IN. His war service as a volunteer commenced at the mouth of the river Rio Grande to Vera Cruz, Mexico. Robert Hart was married four times: to Mary Hobby, Elizabeth Swenerton, Mrs. Mary Hurst, and Malinda Allison. (Allison's antecedents are the Bacon, Cummins and Pennypacker Posey County pioneer families). The first four children of the Reno/Allison marriage are: John Ed, Charles, Cordelia Belle, Julius, were born in Solitude. Marietta Reno, the fifth child was born in St. Joseph, MO in 1872.

A Posey County newspaper clipping tells of his honesty,

"While returning from Mt. Vernon last Tuesday, Mr. Samuel Arthur lost his pocket book containing between three and four hundred dollars. It was found by Mr. Hart Reno and returned to the owner, who, as may be imagined was glad to recover his property. Such instance of honesty in these dishonest times are worthy of record."

Hart's obituary states that he was one of the original Posey County Republicans and was noted as one of the shrewdest farmers in the county. Hart died at Solitude in 1892 and is interred at the Black Cemetery on Highway 69 near Solitude.

Marietta Reno, while young, returned with her family to Posey County. She married Harry Pritchard (son of Thomas MacDonagh Pritchard and Ruth Robinson) at Posey County in 1894. They raised and raced Standardbred Horses. Their children are Thomas Neef, Leland Paul, Julius Holbert, twins Elva and Alice Elma and Aline. Marietta died 1963 in California.

Alice Pritchard was born in 1905 at the Streater, IL racetrack where her father was racing Standardbred horses. She visited Posey County many times. She married Thomas Williams, a furniture retailer, in California. They had one child, Patricia. Alice is now 84 years old and currently resides in Balboa, CA.

Patricia Jannetta Williams was born in 1933 in Glendale, CA. She married Leland Edward Finley in 1956 at Orange Co., CA and currently resides in New Castle, CA. She has three children: Thomas, Susan, and James and 11 grandchildren. *Submitted by Patricia Williams Finley, fourth great-granddaughter*

MAURICE J. AND LAJUAN REISING

Maurice J. "Lefty" and Lajuan Reising were married Sept. 21, 1948, and since January, 1949 have resided at their home on the corner of Cale and Dean Streets, Poseyville. To this union were born Gwendolyn "Gwen" Marie, Sept. 10, 1949; Gregory "Greg" Neal, July 3, 1951; Gabriel "Gabe" Eugene, Feb. 17, 1958; and Gayle Angela, May 27, 1960. All four children were baptized at St. Francis Xavier Catholic Church, attended St. Francis Elementary School, North Posey High School, and obtained various college degrees. Gwendolyn married John R. Scott, Ph.D., of Ft. Collins, CO, Aug. 9, 1974. Their son, Eric Tyler, was born Sept. 5, 1983. Gwendolyn is employed as data analyst for the National Atmospheric Deposition Program at the Natural Resource Ecology Laboratory, Colorado State University, Ft. Collins. Gregory Reising, Ph.D., is a Counseling Psychologist and Coordinator of Clinical Services at Towson State University, Towson, MD, and also maintains a private practice. Gabriel Reising, M.D., specializes in Anesthesiology and practices at Ball Memorial Hospital, Muncie, IN. He married Susanne (Stemler) May 15, 1982. Their son, Nicholas Christian, was born Sept. 10, 1986. Gayle Reising is a production Geologist with Exxon Oil Corporation in Corpus Christi, TX.

Maurice, the son of Nicholas and Katherine (Emge) Reising, was born Sept. 17, 1919, the fourth of five children. Upon graduation from St. Francis Xavier Elementary School and Poseyville High School, he was employed by Davis Downen Motor Company of Poseyville. After serving in the Army Air Force during WWII, he became a partner in his father's business, the Poseyville Grain and Feed Company. A lifelong member of St. Francis Xavier Church, Maurice is a past Commander of the American Legion and has been its Finance Officer for over 40 years. Maurice's grandparents were Philip and Kathryn (VerWayne) Reising, and Emil and Christina (Knapp) Emge.

Lajuan, the second child of Otto J. and Veta (Strickfaden) Forler, was born Dec. 27, 1924. Reared on the family farm west of Chrisney, IN, she graduated from Midway Elementary, Chrisney High School and Lockyears Business College. After marriage, she resigned employment with Indiana Bell Telephone Company, Evansville, IN to rear her children. In 1987, with help and guidance from her then grown children, she authored and compiled the centennial **History of St. Francis Xavier Church.** Lajuan's grandparents were Ernest V. and Adelaide (Kromel) Forler, and John W. and Louisa (Arensman) Strickfaden.

John W. Strickfaden moved his family to Poseyville from Chrisney in 1907. He and his son, Clayton, operated a general Blacksmith Shop on Church Street just south of Main. They also made brooms. Veta, the youngest of their four children, was employed by the Poseyville News and was a member of the drama cast directed by Matt Weatherly which put on many excellent plays in the area. Misfortune befell the family in 1916; Blanche, the oldest daughter, and Catherine, Clayton's wife, both died, leaving infant, Louveta Logsdon, and toddlers, Leota and Leora. Veta assisted her mother and family in rearing these three nieces. The family moved to a farm east of Chrisney December, 1918.

NICHOLAS AND KATHERINE REISING

Nicholas and Katherine (Emge) Reising were married Sept. 17, 1907. They built a residence on St. Francis Avenue, Poseyville, where they spent their entire married lives. Children born to this union were: Warner, 1909 (who married Lorena Joest) Flavian, 1912 (married Mary Elizabeth "Betty" Schafer); Elinor, 1917; Maurice, 1919 (married Lajuan Forler); and Thelman, 1925 (married Mary Ann Hirsch).

Nicholas, the son of Philip and Kathryn "Katherine" (VerWayne) Reising, was born Oct. 4, 1883 in Smith Township, east of Poseyville. He was educated at St. Wendel Catholic and Buttermilk Schools. A respected pillar of the Poseyville community, he spent his life in the family Poseyville Grain and Feed Company business.

Philip Reising was born Feb. 13, 1857 near Armstrong in Vanderburgh County. He farmed for several years east of Poseyville near Mt. Pleasant before moving to town. He purchased interest in a grain business and built a residence on the corner of St. Francis Avenue and South Street. Children born to Philip and Kathryn in addition to Nicholas were Peter, Rose, Elizabeth Schenk, Theresa, Anthony "Tony", John, Mary Gillis, and Juliana Hirsch. Kathryn was born in 1861.

Philip Reising's parents, Peter and Eva Katherine (Streit) Reising, were both born in Hörstein, Germany. They were married Feb. 22, 1852. Since their first child was born in America in 1854, it is assumed that early after their marriage they immigrated to the United States. The Peter Reising homestead is in Vanderburgh Co., IN, approximately 12 miles northwest of Evansville and southwest of the Armstrong Community. The property still remains in the Reising family. Philip's siblings were John, Theresa Fehrenbacher, and Frank. Eva Katherine's parents were Peter and Katherine (Saepel) Streit, also of Germany.

Peter Reising was born Dec. 4, 1818 at 11 o'clock in the morning at Hörstein, Germany. He was the third child of George Paul Reising, the Burgemeister, and Anna Maria (Sittinger) Reising.

Katherine (Emge) Reising was the tenth of 11 children born to Emil and Christina (Knapp) Emge. Her siblings were George, Peter, John, Emil, Frank, Mary Anslinger, Lona, Anna, Elizabeth Walters, and Christina. Katherine was born Jan. 30, 1883 on the family's farm east of Poseyville (presently owned by Elbert Allen). The family moved from this farm to one a mile north of Poseyville (present Raymond Seibert farm), and later resided on the corner of Locust and Pine Streets, Poseyville (present Allison Nursing Home). After Emil's death, his widow and two daughters, Anna and Lona, having no method of transportation, moved "close to church" to the residence north of Main Street at St. Francis Avenue (the present Odilo Jochim home).

Emil Emge, who was born in Germany Jan. 9, 1840, learned to walk on the boat while his family was immigrating to America. His wife, Christina, whose parents were John and Elizabeth (Schmidt) Knapp, was born Sept. 29, 1841. Emil and Christina are buried in St. Francis Xavier Catholic Cemetery, Poseyville. Emil's father, George Emge was buried at St. Wendel, IN.

THELMAN E. REISING

On June 25, 1947, St. Francis Xavier Church in Poseyville, IN was the setting for a summer wedding uniting Mary Ann Hirsch and Thelman Emil Reising. From this union three children were born, Lawrence (Larry) Joseph, Apr. 30, 1950, Ellen Ruth, Oct. 26, 1951, Brian Ray, Oct. 24, 1961.

Larry graduated from Magister Noster Latin School, Evansville, IN, attended St. Meinrad College, St. Meinrad, IN, graduated with a Bachelor of Arts degree in English from St. Louis University, St. Louis, MO. After earning a Bachelor of Arts degree in Art from University of Evansville, Evansville, IN, he went to University of Iowa, Iowa City, IA, was a teaching assistant, won a scholarship to Skowhegan, ME. Graduated from University of Iowa with a Masters of Art degree and a Masters of Fine Arts degree. Received a commission for a sculpture called "Sky Dance" from Mrs. Jane Owen, which is located at New Harmony Inn. He now resides in Denver, CO and has a business called City Visuals.

Ellen graduated from North Posey High School,

then went to St. Mary-of-the-Woods College, Terre Haute, IN, she earned a Bachelor of Arts degree in Business. She worked at the Fashion Shop, Evansville, IN, as an assistant manager, moved to Springfield, IL, as accounts receivable manager at a ladies apparel store. Met her husband, David R. Rice from Elmhurst, IL, and was married Dec. 6, 1975. Later moving to Washington, D.C. area where both are employed by Unisys Corp., Ellen is a financial analyst and David is a computer scientist, they reside in Burke, VA.

Brian graduated from North Posey High School, and entered the School of Engineering, Purdue University, West Lafayette, IN, co-oping with Ashland Oil Co., Ashland, KY. Completing the five year program. He graduated with a Bachelor of Science degree in Chemical Engineering. Presently attending Lewis University, Romeoville, IL, working towards completing a Masters Degree in Business Administration. He married Tracy Cain, Indianapolis, IN, Sept. 29, 1984, moved to the Chicago, IL area. He is plant supervisor for Ashland Chemical Co., Calumet City, IL, and Tracy is manager of financial accounting for Insurance Company of Illinois, Chicago, IL, they are presently residing in Orland Park, IL.

Mary Ann was born Nov. 29, 1925 to John and Rose Hirsch. After graduating from Poseyville High School she worked for seven years at J.L. Hirsch Co., store owned by her parents John and Rose Hirsch. The family being raised she returned to work for three more years, then retiring.

Thelman was born Feb. 13, 1925 to Nicholas and Katherine Reising. He graduated from Poseyville High School, worked at Poseyville Grain and Feed Co. (a family owned business) for a year, before entering the United States Army, was assigned to the 45th Infantry Division, in the European Theater of Operations for two years. After being discharged from the Army he returned to the family business for 43 more years, served as President of the company from 1984 until retirement.

DAVID A. RITZERT FAMILY

David, the son of Leroy J. and Veronica (Folz) Ritzert was born Mar. 8, 1941. On June 25, 1966 he married the former Ruth J. Gries. She is the daughter of John and Luella (Schauss) Gries, and was born Mar. 14, 1943.

Melissa, Rachel, Michael, Rodney, Bryan, Kristine, Ruth, and David

David graduated from Mt. Vernon Senior High School in 1959. Ruth was a graduate of the 1961 Class of Mater Dei High School (Evansville).

They moved to a home on Caborn Road, Marrs Township, when they married in 1966, and still reside there today.

They are the parents of three daughters and three sons. Kristine, born Aug. 10, 1967 will be married on Mar. 17, 1989 to Roger Deig. Michael, born July 28, 1968. Rodney, born Dec. 31, 1969. Melissa, born Sept. 13, 1972. Rachel, born Feb. 7, 1976. Bryan, born June 26, 1977.

All six children attended St. Matthew Parochial School, and three oldest have already graduated from Mt. Vernon Senior High School. Kristine will graduate from The University of Southern Indiana (Evansville) in 1989.

The family has made their living operating a Dairy and Grain farm since David and Ruth were married. They bought David's parents' Dairy and Farming operation in 1970, and operate it as a family farm today.

The family attends St. Matthew Catholic Church in Mt. Vernon, and are all very active members in the parish.

WILLIAM HOWARD ROBERTS

William Howard Roberts, known to his family and friends as Howard, was born July 11, 1938 in Evansville, IN. He was the only child of William Harlan Roberts and Alice Maud (Harris) Roberts. Howard attended school in Evansville, graduating from Central High School in 1956. He also attended Evansville College where he studied business. Howard enjoyed all kinds of sports, but baseball was his favorite. He played the position of catcher. While in high school he played varsity baseball and lettered in that sport.

Although Howard was born in Indiana he spent much of his life traveling between Indiana and Sarnia Ontario Canada. Alice Harris moved to Evansville, IN in the mid 1930s to work and live with her father's older sister Alice Harris Pickett. Mrs. Pickett and her husband Jack owned the Home-a-fect Photography Studio in Evansville. Young Alice, as Howard's mother was called by her family, met Harlan Roberts at the Walnut Street Baptist Church, which she attended with her Aunt Alice Pickett. Harlan and Alice were married in 1936 in her home town of Sarnia, Ontario Canada. Before their marriage, Harlan agreed that Alice could spend at least six weeks of every year with her family in Canada. Since Howards' maternal Grandfather was a railroader and worked for the Canadian National Railroad, the family was allowed to travel to and from Canada on his railroad pass.

Wm. Howard Roberts

Howard's paternal grandparents were Nathaniel Roberts born Jan. 12, 1877 in Scottsville, KY, died Mar. 16, 1927 also in Scottsville, KY. He married Mary Isabelle Spears on Apr. 20, 1897. Mary was born Oct. 13, 1873 in Allen Co., KY and died Jan. 1, 1947 in Evansville, IN. Nathaniel's parents were James Herd Roberts born in 1853 in Putman Co., TN and Mary Frances Haynes born 1856 also in Putnam Co., TN. Mary Isabelle Spears' parents were Daniel W. Spears born May 9, 1837, died Jan. 16, 1894 in Scottsville, KY. Between 1859 and 1860 he married Melviney Mitchell born Jan. 15, 1840 and died June 22, 1911. Melviney was one of the daughters of the Reverand George Mitchell born ca 1809 died ca 1885 who married Nancy Ann Wolfe Feb. 18, 1828 in Scottsville, KY. All of the above families were involved in local politics and the Rough Creek Baptist Church. Thompson Spears, the father of Daniel Spears, was born in Virginia ca 1805 and was a farmer and a land speculator. The father of James Herd Roberts was Henry Roberts born in Craven County, NC ca 1821 and his wife Elizabeth was born Nov. 11, 1826 in North Carolina and died Dec. 31, 1885 in Scottsville, KY.

The maternal grandparents for Howard were Joseph Howard Harris born Feb. 21, 1891 in Sarnia, Ontario Canada died Oct. 12, 1957 in Sarnia married Dec. 5, 1913 to Matilda Potter born Feb. 21, 1891 (same day and year as her future husband) in Belfast, Northern Ireland. She was the daughter of Hugh Potter and his wife Sara Wilson. Joseph Howard Harris's parents were William Samuel Harris and Jeanette Pilkey (Pelshae the French spelling) born ca 1864, died Jan. 27, 1909 in Sarnia, Ontario. Marilda Potter was always called "John" by her husband. She came to Canada in 1912. She was supposed to have originally come to the United States on the Titanic but because the ship's steerage class was too full she was made to wait for the next ship. The next ship was destined for Canada so her voyage ended there. She always considered that change a true blessing. She was a typical "Irish Coleen" with red hair, blue eyes and rosey cheeks.

In November of 1958 Howard married Sharon Elizabeth Farmer. Sharon was born and raised in Evansville, IN. She is the youngest child of Robert E. Farmer Sr. and his second wife Viola Marie Mabry. Robert Farmer, Sr. was born June 21, 1893 died Aug. 10, 1980 married Nov. 10, 1936 to Viola Marie Mabry born Feb. 3, 1913. Sharon graduated from Central High School in 1955. She graduated from Evansville College in 1958 with a degree in Education. She received her Master's Degree in 1967 from the University of Evansville. Sharon taught school in the Evansville-Vanderburgh School Corporation for 27 years before retiring in January 1986.

Sharon's paternal great grandparents were Robert H. Brainard born July 22, 1850 in Hancock Co., KY died Aug. 8, 1921 in Evansville, IN. He married Lucinda Chissenhall born ca 1852 in Eastern Posey County the daughter of Allen McClain Chissenhall and Mary Elizabeth Uzary. Robert Brainard was the son of Alonzo H. Brainard born Nov. 4, 1823 in Holley, NY died June 2, 1873 in Evansville, IN. He married Katherine Linxweiler Apr. 7, 1847 in Hancock Co., KY. Alonzo's father was Otis Brainard born Jan. 12, 1801 in Haddam, CT died Apr. 5, 1847 in Swanton, VT. Otis was the son of Ezra Brainard Junior born May 11, 1769 in Haddam, CT died Nov. 15, 1833 married Mabel Porter Mar. 9, 1786. Ezra Junior was the son of Ezra Brainard Senior. The Brainard family of Haddam, CT was a very influential group. They married in to many well known East Coast families such as the Stanley's, Porter's, Hobart's, Pitkin's, Egglestons, Spencer's, Gaylords', Goodwin's, Cowles' and St. John's. The progenitor of the Brainard family in America was Daniel who arrived from England in 1642.

Sharon's maternal great grandparents were Robert Elmbridge Mabry born Apr. 11, 1848 in

Mississippi, died Feb. 22, 1916 in Fairfield, IL. Robert was a Republican politician who served in the Illinois Legislature a number of terms before his death. He was also a realtor and the clerk of the Wayne Co., IL Court for a number of years. His first wife was Mary Ellen Davis born Apr. 11, 1847 in Gibson Co., IN. Robert's father was Seth W. Mabry born Feb. 9, 1816 died Feb. 5, 1901 in Fairfield, IL. Seth's first wfe was Martha Ann Bell born Jan. 16, 1819 in Tennessee died Feb. 24, 1861 in Wayne County Illinois Court for a number of years. Seth's father Benjamin Mabry was a Methodist-Episcopal Preacher born Feb. 21, 1794 in Franklin Co., NC married Aug. 30, 1813 Delilah Zorah Murphy. Benjamin's father was Seth Mabry born ca 1752 who married Elizabeth Seawell June 16, 1771 in Brunswick Co., VA. The Mabry progenitor in the United States was Francis Mayberry, who arrived in Henrico, Charles City, and Surry Co., VA between 1672 abd 1679 from England. He married Elizabeth Gilliam in 1685. Francis Mayberry was thought to have been involved in "Bacon's Rebellion" which foreshadowed the American Revolution. Elizabeth Gilliam's family was among the Mecklenburg Signers.

In 1972 Howard purchased the local Mt. Vernon, IGA store at 1320 North Main Street. In 1982 he purchased U-Save IGA on Fourth Street. Howard was well beloved by his employees. To show his appreciation for his employees, Howard took most of his employees to the World's Fair held in Knoxville, TN in 1982. He paid for the entire overnight trip. He had been nominated for outstanding IGA Retailer of the Year several times and was a past president of the Retail Merchants Association of Mt. Vernon. At the time of his death on Mar. 28, 1987 he was serving a 5th term as a Senator for Wetterau Foods Incorporated, the parent company for IGA. He was a member of Lessing lodge, Scottish Rite and the Hadi Temple of Evansville. He served as President of the Mt. Vernon Optimists Chapter and was a member of Grace Baptist Church in Evansville, IN. He was survived by his wife Sharon, one daughter Makaila Jean Blackburn, his son-in-law Wayne Blackburn, one granddaughter Whitney Lynn Blackburn and his mother-in-law Viola Marie Mabry Farmer and three cousins he helped to raise Marc, Jacklyn and Edyn Roberts of Sarnia, Ontario Canada. Also a number of Aunts and Uncles both in Canada and Evansville, IN.

DALLAS LEE ROBINSON

Dallas Lee Robinson, born Mar. 12, 1941 in Point Township to Harry L. Robinson and Marie (Yeida) Robinson. Both lifelong residents of Point Township. Harry was the son of George and Lottie Robinson. Marie was the daughter of William H. and Pearl (Burlinson) Yeida. Dallas was one of ten children: Charlotte Pearl (deceased), Delores Ray (Benner), George William, Dallas Lee, Rose Marie (Moore), Rita June (Sherrety), Dennis Wayne, Linda Gayle (Garrett), Harry Lee, Jr., and Helen Diane (Hollis).

Dallas attended Black Elementary School for eight years. Attended Mt. Vernon Sr. High graduating in 1959. Entered the U.S. Navy in March 1960, spent six months in service, returned to Mt. Vernon employed by A&P Tea Company.

He married Barbara Ann Mercer of New Harmony, Sept. 17, 1960. Barbara is the daughter of Damon J. and Wilma (Goff) Mercer. Dallas and Barbara moved to Huntingburg in 1961, where they spent seven years active in politics there served on the city council. Dallas felt a definite call from God to minister in 1968 and begin the course of study for ordination that year. The family returned to Point Township in March 1969 to open the Point Township Church of the Nazarene which had been inactive since 1956.

Dallas Lee Robinson and Family

Four children all born in Huntingburg are: Troy Lynn, Roger Lee, Vicky Ann, Dawn Marie.

Roger married Louise Sage a Navajo Indian, while the Robinson's worked among the North American Indians in 1982-83. Roger and Louise have two children Donita Marie and Nathaneal Lee. Vicky is married to Steve Schmittler from Grayville, IL, they have a son Steven Lee. Dawn has a son Brandon Joseph.

The Church in Point has experienced unusual growth which has helped to bring about a change in the image and character of Point Township and its residents.

Dallas is involved in Nursing Home Ministry, Senior Citizens, Mt. Vernon Ministerial Association, Posey County Thrift Shop, and has worked several years on the Point Election Board.

HAROLD AND HELEN ROEHR FAMILY

Helen Barbara Louise Seifert was born June 15, 1914 in Caborn, IN. She attended Caborn Grade School and graduated from Mt. Vernon High School.

Helen was one of three children of Edward and Amelia (Herchelman) Seifert. Edward's parents were William and Louisa (Rosner) Seifert who had ten children. William's parents were John and Anna Margaret (Lehman) Seifert who had eight children. John's parents were Nicholas and Eva (Wagner) Seifert who had six children Nichols arrived from Gerstenfeld, Germany in 1839. In 1840 he purchased land in Posey County. Nicholas and Eva's descendants have resided in Posey County since 1840.

Harold Henry Roehr was born Jan. 20, 1912 in Posey County. He attended Neu School. through eighth grade.

Harold and Helen Roehr 1987

Harold was one of six children of Henry Simon and Lula (Menikheim) Roehr. Henry's parents were Friedrich Simon Wilhelm and Anna (Schroeder) Roehr who had four children. Friedrich's parents' were Simon August Conrad and Catherine Amelia (Frevert) Roehr who had six children. Simon and Catherine arrived from Lippe Depmold, Germany in 1867 and settled in Posey County near Zion Lippe United Church of Christ.

Helen and Harold were married on July 27, 1935 at St. John's Methodist Church in Caborn. They bought their first home in Caborn where they resided until 1957 when they purchased Helen's parent's home and farm just northwest of St. John's United Methodist Church in Caborn. They lived on the farm until October 1986 when they built a new home in Mt. Vernon where they currently reside. Their home on the farm was sold to their grandson and his wife Brett and Trudy (Williams) Stock.

Helen and Harold have one daughter, Barbara Jean, who married William Gilmore Stock in November 1957. Barbara and Gil have three children, Brett Alan, Jeffrey Lynn, and Jennifer Ann.

Harold and Helen farmed for several years and eventually entered into the chicken business. They supplied several grocery stores in Mt. Vernon with their eggs. After leaving the chicken business, Harold was a self-employed painter and wallpaper hanger.

Helen and Harold are members of St. John's United Methodist Church.

DR. ROPP AND WIFE GLADYS

Dr. Ropp and his wife Gladys came to New Harmony July 1931. They made many friends and he established a large practice in the surrounding communities. He served as Mayor for the town, President of Ford Memorial Home, President of Posey County Medical Society, a member of the Workingmens Institute, served as Major in Flight Service in World War II and a member of the Masonic Lodge. He loved plants and flowers and spent most of his leisure time in gardening and on a farm near Petersburg. Dr. Ropp was honored in 1981 for his 50 years of service to his community. The same year the couple celebrated their Golden Wedding.

Dr. Ropp and wife Gladys

Gladys an elementary school teacher from Gibson County was a wonderful homemaker and worked in his office the first year. She also substituted at the public school for many years when she was needed. She worked and held office in the Methodist Church and later worked in the Episcopal Church on Altar Guild, she was an honorary member of Tri Kappa Sorority, a past matron of Eastern Star and a Grand Representative to the state of Kentucky.

The Community was saddened when Dr. Ropp

passed away Feb. 25, 1987. He was a kind and generous man to the poor and needy and everybody's friend.

ROWE FAMILY

These are the historical facts of the beginnings of the Rowe family, many of whom are still living in this area.

George Row was born on the Atlantic Ocean in 1750, as his parents were coming to this country from either Germany or Holland. The father, Martin Row, settled his family near York, PA, from where he, and later his son, George, enlisted in the state militia. Martin Row was killed by Indians in 1766, during the absence of his wife, young George, and some other children. They had gone to the mill to have grain ground. Two children, left at home, shared the fate of their father.

Martin Row was a private in Captain Weaver's company at the time of his death. He had served five of the six years of his enlistment term. His son, George, then about 16 years old, served out his father's term and enlisted for another six years in the Revolutionary Army for himself, totaling some seven years.

George Row married Margaret Weaver in 1770 while serving as a first lieutenant in Captain Dapper's company.

After a few years, George decided to go West, and moved his family to Ohio, where they lived long enough for their two oldest children to marry. These two new families stayed in Ohio, and George with the rest of his family, moved on to Kentucky, where the two youngest children were born.

From there, sometime in the early 1800s, George, with the families of Milton Black, Absalam Duckworth, William Alexander, Thomas Servier, and the Todds, came to Posey County by wagons. These families all settled in various parts of the county. George and his wife and family settled with 14 of their 16 children in Black Township near Upton, where he farmed until his death in 1818. George and his wife, with three of their children, are buried in a tiny family graveyard behind the site of the big brick house where they lived on Upton Road. The burial site is unmarked and unknown.

Of the 16 children of George and Margaret Row the following named are all whose history is known: namely, John, George, Martin, Michael, Andrew, Samuel, Jacob, Mary Eve, Elizabeth, and Julia. Samuel was the father of Mary Ann Rowe Conlin, and is also credited with suggesting the name of Mount Vernon. for the early community at a town meeting, as his father, George, was an ardent admirer of George Washington, whose home in Virginia was called Mount Vernon. John Row is credited with changing the spelling of the name from Row to Rowe in 1854.

George Row, the pioneer, was one of the few Revolutionary War soldiers buried in Posey County, whose military service was proven.

EARL E. ROWE AND RUTH (NOLAN) ROWE

Earl E. Rowe and Ruth (Nolan) Rowe are residents of Mt. Vernon, IN. Living in Posey County, Black Township, all of their lives, they were married in Henderson, KY, Sept. 21, 1940.

Earl, the fourth born child of Ben Rowe and Elsie (Jeffries) Rowe, was born on Feb. 16, 1919. Ruth, the daughter of Arthur Nolan and Henrietta (Fellemende) Nolan, was born on May 18, 1919.

Earl was a farmer in Black Township, farming with his father. In 1956 his father retired and moved to Mt. Vernon, IN. Earl then continued to farm on his own until 1980, when he retired due to heart trouble. Earl and Ruth then moved to town in 1981 where they live now.

Earl has one brother and three sisters. Norman, the oldest, married Florence Beste. Mary, living in Indianapolis, IN, married Melvin Granneman. Juanita, married Elmo Adams and lives in Lebanon, IN. Marjorie, living in Evansville, IN, married Cecil Holtzmeier, now deceased.

Ruth has one sister, Pauline, living in Evansville, IN, married Robert Crider, now deceased.

Earl and Ruth have two children. Dennis Earl, born Aug. 26, 1944 and Carolyn Sue, born May 3, 1949. Dennis is married to Kathy DeKemper. They have two sons, Dennis Matthew and Todd Christian. Dennis is self employed in the advertising business in Evansville, IN. Kathy is a school teacher at Castle High School in Warrick County. Carolyn Sue married Leroy Lindenberg. They have three children, Julia Ann, David Scott and Amy Sue. Leroy is an employee of General Electric Mt. Veron. Sue is an employee of The Metropolitan School District as a bookkeeper at the Mt. Vernon High School.

Earl's paternal grandparents were Walter Rowe, a rural mail carrier in the 1920's, and Jane (Curtis) Rowe. Maternal grandparents were Robert Jeffries and Louise (Whipple) Jeffries. They were farmers in the Upton area.

Ruth's paternal grandparents were Charles Nolan, a farmer in Point Township and Sarah E. (Sherretz) Nolan. Maternal grandparents were George Fellemende and Henrietta (Weiss) Fellemende.

NORMAN AND FLORENCE ROWE FAMILY

Norman and Florence are natives of Posey County, each children of long time farming families in Black and Point Township.

Norman, born in 1912, was the oldest child of Benjamin and Elsie (Jeffries) Rowe. Benjamin was the son of Walter and Jane (Curtis) Rowe. Elsie's parents were Robert and Louisa (Whipple) Jeffries. They were all early settlers in western Black Township. Norman has a brother, Earl, and three sisters, Mary, Juanita, and Marjorie.

Norman Wayne, Rita Rowe French, Florence, Norman, Sharon Rowe, Barbarette and Steve Rowe.

Florence was born to Fred and Emma (Roos) Beste in 1914 and was the youngest of their surviving children—two having died in infancy. Fred was the son of Mr. and Mrs. Frederick Beste..Mrs. Beste's maiden name was Folz. The elder Mr. and Mrs. Beste were natives of Prussia, Germany, and embarked from Bremen, Germany, arriving in the United States in 1858 at the port of New Orleans. Emma was the daughter of Michael and Barbara (Grottentahler) Roos, who emigrated to America from Wurtemberg, Germany, landing in New York City, in 1866. Florence has three brothers, Alfred (deceased), Edward and Fred, and two sisters, Clara (deceased), and Mary.

Norman's and Florence's education began in two-room schoolhouses in rural southwestern Posey County. Norman started high school in 1927 at which time the school was located on College Avenue and Fifth Street. In 1928 the school site was changed to the corner of Sixth and Canal Streets. A new school was built and it was there that Norman and Florence first met. Florence graduated from high school in 1932. They were married in 1935 and lived on the Rowe farm until the record breaking 1937 flood washed away nearly all their possessions and severely damaged their home. It was then they moved to Mt. Vernon where Norman worked as a carpenter and building contractor, and drove a school bus until 1939 when he went to work for the initial building of the Indiana Farm Bureau Oil Refinery located west of Mt. Vernon. He continued his employment there for 37 years, and retired as a supervisor in operations in January 1977.

They built their home on the corner of Sixth and Harriet Streets in 1941 and reside there yet today. They had five children: Steve, Dolores, Norman Wayne, Sharon and Rita. Dolores, who was born in 1944, died at the age of two. The others attended Hedges Central Elementary, Mount Vernon Junior High and graduated from Mount Vernon High School.

Steve was born in 1942. He married Sandra Barfield, a Mount Vernon High School graduate, now deceased. They had two children, Mark and Sarah. Steve received the Doctor of Veterinary Medicine degree from Purdue University and served two years as captain in the Army Veterinary Corps. He continued his education at the University of Michigan where he received training in laboratory animal medicine and a MS degree in Pathology. During the past 15 years, Steve has worked in medical research at Battelle Laboratories in Richland, WA.

Norman Wayne was born in 1948. He served two years as a radioman in the U.S. Navy during the Vietnam war. He graduated from Purdue University with a B.S. degree in Industrial Management and Chemistry and a MS in Environmental Engineering. He married Judith Ohaver, of Birmingham, MI. They have two sons, Jeffrey and Daniel. Norman is now vice president of technical operations with Wm. Leman Inc., a mint oil refinery in Bremen, IN. Judy teaches elementary school in Bremen.

Sharon was born in 1949. She attended Indiana State University where she studied journalism. She completed her studies as an apprentice at the Fort Lauderdale News in Fort Lauderdale, FL. She is currently a Realtor Associate with Merrill Lynch Realty in Coral Springs, FL. She resides there with her husband, Jerry Barbarette, a native of Hazelton, PA, their son Troy, and her daughters, Lori and Tami Newcomb.

Rita was born in 1951. She received a degree in business from Indiana University. She studied accounting at Purdue and is a licensed CPA. She married Tracy French of Indianapolis and they have two children, Trevor and Hannah. They reside in Ithaca, NY where Tracy teaches at Cornell University and Rita works for an accounting firm.

RALPH CURTIS ROWE

Born in 1892, died in 1966. His parents were George Walter Rowe, (a farmer and rural mail carrier) born in 1859 and E. Jane Curtis Rowe born in 1852. Ralph married Jessie K. Schierbaum, daughter of Henry Clay Schierbaum and Magdelena Schwartz, in 1917. To this union three children were born, M. Eugene, Leland E., and Mrs. Peggy Cullman and six grandchildren, Judith and Stephan Rowe, Michael and Ronald Rowe, Jeffrey and Gary Cullman.

Ralph was Chief of Police of Mt. Vernon in the late 1930's and Sheriff for six years in the early 1940's. His family can be traced in Posey County from about 1806. The first was George Row born in 1750 on a ship on the Atlantic Ocean as his parents (Martin Row) emigrated from Europe. To him was born Jacob in 1793, and to Jacob a son named George W. in 1832. The name changed from Row to Rowe in 1854. To George W. a son was born in 1859 and named G. Walter and to G. Walter was born Ralph, Benjamin and Mrs. Mary Hines.

WILTON RUEGER

Wilton V. Rueger born Jan. 18, 1918, the year of the big snow "22 inches" in Posey County to Edward Rueger 1891-1963 and Odelia (Miller) 1892-1987. Wilton's family includes Malcom 1915-1979, Warren, Darwin, and Ruth Naab.

Paternal grandparents, Gottlieb Rueger 1861-1934, and Lena (Niehaus) 1868-1961. Great Grandparents Andrew Rueger 1826-1882 and Margaret (Brehm) 1838-1910. Maternal grandparents, Lorenz Miller 1851-1911 and Margaret (Wimpelborg) 1859-1925. Great grandparents, Heinrich Niehaus 1827-1900 and Angeline (Brockmole) 1829-1923.

Wilton farmed before going to the Army in WWII serving 1941-1945 in Central and Western Pacific, Tec 5 Radio Operator, H Q Co 2nd BN, 165th Infantry. After returning home Wilton worked for Farm Bureau Corporation 1946-1983. Avid sportsman, he played baseball in Tri-County League for Al's Aces Team, Bowled 27 years in same league, Golf with Farm Bureau Refinery Men's Club. Wilton life-long member of Immanuel Church, Immanuel's Brotherhood, American Legion, Elks, belongs to Salem's Clabber Club, Senior Bowling League.

Wilton and Betty Rueger

Wilton diagnosed at Mayo Clinic in 1988 having dementing disease "Ricks" which is indistinguishable from Alzheimers.

Wilton married Betty (Bess) Grebe in Salem Church 1954, Betty born in 1929 to Albert Grebe 1902-1975 and Marie (Graff) 1907-1969. They had Al's Standard Service Station on Hwy 62 from 1929-1975. Betty's family includes Joan Niehaus, Albert, F. J., Judy, and Bonnie Frost. Betty graduated from Reitz High School 1947 and Lockyears Business College 1949 and worked at Anchor Supply as Secretary/Stenographer and at Mt. Vernon License Branch. A leader in Girl Scouts and Cadet Outpost Primitive Camping was chose "Hidden Heroine" in 1976 by scouts. Sunday School teacher Salem and Immanuel Churches, also Bible School Crafts Instructor, Red Cross Water Safety Instructor of Memorial Coliseum Pool, Certified Jr. Bowling Instructor. Belongs to Immanuel's Women's Group, Legion Auxiliary, Farm Bureau Ladies Golf Club, Mt. Vernon Women's Softball League and Bowling teams. Helfrich Ladies Golf Club winning Club Championship three years and Evansville Courier City Tournament nine-hole champion 1984 and 1985. In River City Senior games received gold medals in golf and bowling.

Maternal grandparents, John Graff 1880-1955 and Elizabeth (Mahrenholz) 1881-1946. Paternal grandparents Ferdinand C. Grebe 1878-1945 and Caroline A. (Boerner) 1881-1970. Great grandparents Ferdinand Grebe 1835-1918 and Caroline (Boerner). 1834-1922. Great grandfather, Louis Graff 1839-1913 volunteered in the Union Army in 1862 serving 32nd Regiment Indiana Voluntary Army Infantry, fought and was wounded in Army of the Cumberland, promoted to Sergeant, the color bearer in 1865. Returning home to farm after the war he married Henrietta 1845-1929 and planted a fruit orchard. Betty's mother told how they took apples and pears to town by wagon and team. Six pear trees were still bearing fruit in fall 1988. Wilton and Betty have resided on Tile Factory Road since building home in 1954. Their daughters are Terri A. McCormick and Debbie K. Wells, grandchildren are Jennifer and Matthew McCormick and Audrey Wells.

Wilton and Betty have lived in Posey County all their life and ancestors have come from Germany, Bavaria, Switzerland and Holland.

DON C. RUSSELL

Don C. Russell has been a lifelong resident of Posey Co., IN. His grandparents Isaac and Alice Russell came to Posey County from Tennessee and they moved back and forth. Their union produced 11 children and five of their offsprings settled eventually in Posey County. Isaac and Alice Russell are buried at Beach Grove Cemetery in Posey County. One of their sons, Bodie Russell, is Don's father. He met Ora Copas in Red Boiling Springs, TN. They married and came to settle in Posey County. Their five children were all born in Posey County, they are Etheleen, Don C., Elenora, Louise and Beverly. Don C. was born in 1926 in Lynn Township. He went to school in the country and later attended Mt. Vernon High School, graduating in 1945. Two days after graduation he left for the Army. It was still wartime in Europe and US Armed Forces were being shipped overseas. Don C. went to Germany. There he met and married Linda (Sieglinde) Ronge, a German. She was born in Breslau which was the capitol of Selisia (Schlesien). That particular part of Germany now belongs to Poland. Linda and her parents Theodor and Martha Ronge, were forced out of their home since they were German citizens. Linda ended up living in Furth (near Nurnberg). There she worked for the U.S. Armed Forces as an interpreter for the Judge Advocate Section. Don was stationed in Nurenberg with the Military Police. They were in charge of the security in and around Furth/Nurnberg and also were in charge of Security during the War Crime Trials at the Palace of Justice in Nurenberg.

Don and Linda were married in 1948 and came to Mt. Vernon in the Fall of that year. They are the parents of three children Robert Gene Russell who lives in Indianapolis, IN; Christine Russell DeKemper (wife of Robert DeKemper); and Carolyn Sue Russell Reineke (wife of Dennis W. Reineke). Both Christine and Carolyn live in Orlando, FL with their families.

Don and Linda's grandchildren are Cinda M. Russell (daughter of Bob); Amber Nikole DeKemper (Christine's daughter); Brandon and Dustin Reineke (Carolyn's sons).

WILLIAM RUSSELL

William Russell born 1755, North Carolina. No proof he served in Revolution. Like many other North Carolinians he migrated westward. The name of first wife is unknown. She may have been Lucretia born 1770-1780; died before 1840. William married (2) Sarah and divorced 1846.

After stops in Tennessee and Kentucky William's family arrived in Posey County before 1815. Their children were: (1) Lucretia, born 1793, married Nov. 8, 1815 John Ridenour who had Henry, 1815-20, married Aug. 3, 1835 Jane Downen; son, 1815-20; William, 1818/9 married July 23, 1841 Belinda Bradley; Mary, 1820-25, married July 10, 1841 Jeremiah Holbert; John, 1829, married 1849 Anny; Elizabeth, 1837.

William Alexander Hunt; Sarah A. Russell Hunt

2. John Russell, 1801, married Apr. 24, 1822 Margaret Butler. Both died before 1850. According to census John and Margaret had eight children. Only four are identified as minors in Probate Book E, page 225: Nancy Jane born before 1830, married Sept. 14, 1843 William Thompson; Martha Ann; John born 1833, (in home of William Thompson, 1850) age 17; Thomas, 1836, married Feb. 14, 1856 Sarah C. Shryock, 1841- , (daughter of Valentine Shryock and Mary George) who had Sarah A. Russell Oct. 19, 1858, died Jan. 10, 1924 Hamilton Co., IL, married Aug. 22, 1879 Jackson Co., AR, William Alexander Hunt; Edward Russell, died young, daughter probably Jane.

3. Hester, 1801, married Jan. 4, 1820 Israel Chamberlin (See Chamberlin section).

4. Thomas, 1800-1810, died before 1840, married June 9, 1826 Celia Cook. Celia with her crippled son Francis were living in poor house 1860. Francis died May 28, 1863, Celia died after September 1879. In 1830 census they had a daughter born 1827-30. She may be Emily who married Joel Chamberlin.

5. William 1804, died before May 1858, Arkansas, married Dec. 13, 1822 Charlotty Culley Posey County. She died before 1847. (daughter of Thomas Culley) William went to Lawrence Co., AR where,

on behalf of his eight children made claim for one-ninth of estate of Thomas Culley Sept. 21, 1847. William Jr.'s children: Elizabeth, 1827; Jane 1828 died January 1871, married Sept. 30, 1847 Calvin Ragsdale; William, 1831, married Mar. 19, 1855 Drucilla Garett; Henry, 1833; Lucinda, 1836, married 1854 Champion Hunt; Cynthia Ann, 1837, married June 27, 1856 Wilson Guthrie; Galena, 1840, married June 18, 1860 John Franklin Newton; Lucretia.

6. James 1804. Tennessee; died before March 1858, married Apr. 23, 1825 Margaret Thomas. Children: Clarissa, 1826, married William Breeze; need proof that George, Jane and John F. were children of James: Nancy, 1834, married Wesley Dunn; Lucretia, 1835; William 1838; Hester, 1840, married Mr. Dunn.

7. Samuel, 1806, Kentucky; died before Sept. 15, 1886, married Lucinda Breeze. Children: William 1832/4, married Ann; James, 1839, married Ann E.; David, 1840, married Martha; George, 1842; Harriett, 1846; Richard, 1847; Jay W., 1852, married Cassa J. Culley; Martha, 1859.

8. Elizabeth, 1810, Kentucky; died before Oct. 29, 1843, married May 23, 1833, Covington Breeze. Children: William; John; Elitia.

9. Russell daughter, married John Nott, who received a full share of William Russell Sr'.s estate June 1858.

THE EDMOND RUTLEDGE FAMILY

Edmond E. Rutledge was born Nov. 2, 1907, the son of George and Mary (Rikens) Rutledge of Stewartsville, IN. On Oct. 11, 1930, he married Elsie Elizabeth Eakins born Oct. 4, 1907, daughter of Richard and Bertha (Fisher) Eakins of New Harmony, IN.

The couple lived four years in New Harmony where Ed worked for Cook's Construction Co. and later on the construction of the Bridge over the Wabash River and on the construction of Highway 66.

In 1934 the family moved to Stewartsville where Ed engaged in farming. In August of 1939 he bought a farm in Wadesville. For a time he also worked at Bucyrus-Erie Co. in Evansville.

In 1942 as a member of the Republican Party, Ed embarked upon a political career in the county which involved three offices and 24 years. He was elected trustee of Center Township in 1942 and was re-elected in 1946. In 1954 he was elected sheriff of Posey County and the family moved to Mt. Vernon. He was re-elected to that office in 1958. In 1962 he sought election to the office of Posey County Assessor and won. He was re-elected to that post in 1966. A man does not serve in elective office 24 years without having had the trust and respect of his fellow citizens. In 1970 he retired from public office, and the family returned to Wadesville. Ed died Aug. 3, 1988. Ed and Elsie have four children:

Virginia Sue born Apr. 1, 1932, graduated from Wadesville High School in 1950. On Sept. 29, 1950, she married Donald Eugene Wenderoth son of Homer and Eugenia (Becker) Wenderoth. For several years she operated The Golden Hairpin Beauty Salon, The Golden Opportunity Shop and The Body Shop in Wadesville. Donald and Virginia have three sons Robert Eugene born May 17, 1953, Kent Wayne, born Aug. 18, 1955 and Bart Alan, born Apr. 18, 1959. (See Wenderoth-Cavett).

A. Jane born June 24, 1935, graduated from Wadesville High School in 1953. In 1958 she was appointed Postmaster at Griffin, IN and still holds that position. Jane married Kenneth Earl Rodgers born Aug. 6, 1933, son of Edgar Rodgers and Georgia (Jobe) Rodgers. Jane and Kenneth have one son Jeffrey Alan born Apr. 9, 1954. Jeffrey graduated from Owensville High School in 1972. On Nov. 22, 1975, he married Carol Ann Hipp born June 15, 1954. A son Ryan Scott was born Apr. 10, 1977. He is in the sixth grade at North Elementary. A daughter Jennifer Sue was born Apr. 9, 1980. She is in the third grade at North Elementary. Jeff is engaged in farming with his father in Griffin and resides in R.R. 2 Poseyville.

Stephen Earl born June 2, 1942, graduated from Mt. Vernon High School in 1960. He married Judy Patricia Wells born June 4, 1943, daughter of Harry Wells and Mildred (Wade) Wells. Steve and Judy have one son Keith Alan born July 15, 1961. Keith resides in Fort Lauderdale, FL. Steve resides in Griffin, IN and is employed at B&M Plastics in Mt. Vernon, IN.

Sara Ann born Nov. 30, 1945, attended Mt. Vernon High School. On Jan. 22, 1965 she married David Keith Houchins, son of Earl and Helen (Yarbor) Houchins of Griffin, IN. A son Jon David was born Oct. 27, 1965. He graduated from North Posey High School in 1983, and attended Kentucky Wesleyan College and the University of Southern Indiana. On Jan. 28, 1989, he married Malicia Shea McCune born Jan. 4, 1964. Jon works at GAF in Mt. Vernon and resides in Poseyville, IN. Malicia and Jon are expecting a child later this year. A daughter Melissa Dawn was born June 3, 1967. She graduated from North Posey High School in 1985. On June 4, 1988, she married William Ambrose Hopf Jr. born Feb. 17, 1956. They have one son Sean Michael born Apr. 1, 1989 She resides in Poseyville. Sara and David were divorced in 1983. Sara resides in Wadesville.

SANDERS

Elvis Sanders was born in Wadesville, IN on Sept. 15, 1893. He was the fourth child born to Henry and Elizabeth Ann (Williams) Sanders. Other children were Orvil and Gilbert Sanders. Elvis joined the Army in WWI at Jefferson Barracks in St. Louis, MO. He was discharged at Fort McArthur in San Pedro, CA on Jan. 30, 1922. It was in Redondo Beach, CA at a dance that he met his wife, Esther Payne. They were married in 1920 and were the parents of four children.

Earl (decased), Dorothy, Patrick (deceased), and James (deceased).

Henry Sanders the father of Elvis, was the son of William and Mary J. (Organ) Sanders. Henry was born June 20, 1859 at Oliver, IN. He married Elizabeth Ellen Williams in Posey County on June 20, 1885. Henry died in Indiana, and is buried at Mt. Zion Baptist Cemetery.

Elvis Sanders

Elizabeth Ellen Sanders the mother of Elvis, was born in Posey Co., IN, on Sept. 26, 1871 and was the daughter of Richard Wyman and Elizabeth Ann (Cox) Williams. Other children were, John, Joseph, Permelia.

Zephorriah, William, Azzarah, Lucretia. The parents of Richard Wyman were Joseph and Sarah (Carney), other children were Bryant, Robert, and Joseph. Elizabeth died Sept. 7, 1932 at Los Angeles General Hospital in L.A., CA.

William Sanders the paternal grandfather of Elvis, was born in Kentucky and was first married to Lucretia Dunbar on Sept. 12, 1840 at Posey Co., IN. They were the parents of five children, John T., Robert, Martha J. (Cox), William Harrison, and Hugh. After the death of Lucretia he married, Mary J. Organ and they became the parents of seven children, Charles, James W., Henry, George Washington, Mary E. (Reich), Susan (Cobb), and Lattica (Cobb).

Elizabeth Ann Cox the maternal grandmother of Elvis, was the daughter of John "Duck" and Polly (Cox) Cox. They were the parents of three other children, William Eli, and Mary (Williams) Cox. The parent's of John "Duck" were Joseph and Elizabeth (Hunsaker) Cox. Joseph was from Kentucky. He fought in the conflicts of Tippecanoe and the War of 1812.

Elvis and his mother, Elizabeth Ellen (Williams) Sanders, and his sons Earl and Pat are buried at Pacific Crest Cemetery in Redondo Beach, CA. James Sanders was lost at Sea.

Richard Wyman, Elizabeth Ann (Cox) Williams. Joseph Williams, Sarh (Carney) Williams, John "Duck" Cox, Polly Cox, Joseph Cox are all buried at the Fillingim Cemetery, Center Twp. Posey Co., IN. *Submitted by Dorothy M. Kerr (daughter of Elvis Sanders).*

SCHELHORN-QUINZER

George Nicholas and Anna Maria (Bauersachs) Schelhorn emigrated to Posey County in 1838. He was born in Coburg, Germany, Nov. 9, 1809 and she in Lieban, Germany, Feb. 25, 1809. The three year old daughter Ernestine, born Oct. 21, 1835 in Coburg, Germany accompanied her parents to Posey County. They were farmers and purchased 160 acres of land under the Treaty of Vincennes Land Grant. The Schelhorn farm was located 1/4 mile west of St. Peters United Methodist Church in St. Phillips. In 1847 a son Theodore was born. They were original members of St. Peters United Methodist Church in St. Phillips founded in 1844. Peter Schmicker was the first church minister. George Nicholas Schelhorn served during the Civil War. He passed away Aug. 21, 1871 and his wife Anna Maria, Apr. 22, 1884. Their son Theodore who never married passed away in 1921. They are buried in St. Peters United Methodist Church Cemetery in St. Phillips.

The Schelhorn's daughter, Ernestine was married to Adam Quinzer in Mt. Vernon on Jan. 5, 1855. He was born in Baden, Germany in 1831 and was a cabinetmaker. Their home was located at 1137 Main Street and his woodworking shop was behind his home. The Quinzers had eight children. Caroline born in 1856 passed away at age four. Henry the second child was born July 1859. He married Annie Brink in Mt. Vernon on July 19, 1885. The Henry Quinzers lived at 1133 Main Street and he was a farmhand. The marriage produced three daughters. Two died at birth and were unnamed. The third child Florence was born Jan. 9,

1887. On July 30, 1905 Florence Quinzer married Edward Gaines. Shortly thereafter they along with Henry Quinzer moved to the south and were employed in a lumber company.

Left; Bettye (Muir) Quinzer, Right; Elizabeth Quinzer, dated 1895

Charles Quinzer was born in Mt. Vernon on Aug. 15, 1861. On Feb. 8, 1899 he married Emma Schuler. He was a farmer in "Sand Hills." Emma Quinzer died Aug. 12, 1909. He passed away Feb. 22, 1949 and is buried in Bellfontaine Cemetery. The only child Audrey was born Apr. 29, 1899. She married John Loehr in Carmi, IL on Feb. 13, 1915. They had two children Francis Earl and Charles. Francis Earl died as an infant and is buried in Blacks Cemetery. Charles was born July 15, 1915 and is a farmer married to Golda Baldwin. Audrey Loehr passed away Mar. 1, 1984 and is buried at Black Cemetery.

John Quinzer was born in Mt. Vernon, Jan. 5, 1863. He was a woodworker for Keck Gonnerman Foundry which manufactured steam driven wheat threshers. On Mar. 26, 1885 he married Bettye Muir. She was the daughter of Henretta and James Muir. The marriage was performed by Rev. J.W. Ashbury. The John Quinzers had four children. Lena was born May 10, 1886 and died Aug. 11, 1886. The other children were Dorothy Louise, born Aug. 12, 1887, Ethel Ray Mar. 18, 1890 and Johnnie Grace Mar. 8, 1896. John Quinzer spoke fluent German and he and his family were members of the Trinity Evangelical Church. Bettye Quinzer passed away in 1898 and John Quinzer, Nov. 6, 1937. Both are buried in Bellfontaine Cemetery. John Quinzer's eldest daughter, Dorothy Louise married Charles Guy Morehead of West Franklin, IN on June 21, 1906. The marriage was performed by Rev. Frank Duerking of Mt. Vernon. Charles Guy Morehead the son of Joseph and Mary (Hudson) Morehead was born in West Franklin on June 10, 1885. His parents came to Indiana from North Carolina through the Cumberland Gap. His occupation was molder, and his father was co-owner of Sailor/Morehead Hardware Store in Mt. Vernon. There were three children, Charles Guy II, born June 8, 1907, Mary Elizabeth, June 7, 1911 and Ethel Lucille, June 27, 1917. Both Charles Guy II and his sister Ethel Lucille were killed in an automobile accident near Springfield, TN on Nov. 6, 1968. Charles Guy Morehead passed away Feb. 14, 1920 and wife Dorothy Louise on June 23, 1974. Both are buried in Bellfontaine Cemetery in Mt. Vernon.

Ethel Ray Quinzer, John and Bettye Quinzer's next daughter was married to George Harvey Martin on Oct. 25, 1908 in Mt. Vernon. He was the son of George and Ida Belle (Gaines) Martin and was born in Gentryville, IN, Mar. 23, 1884. The marriage was performed by Rev. Charles E. Servinghaus. His occupation was motorman on Evansville and Ohio Valley Railroad which operated between Mt. Vernon and Grandview, IN. The Martins had three children, Agnes Madeline born Oct. 28, 1910, George Harold, Feb. 17, 1913 and Pearl Louise, Oct. 22, 1915.

Agnes Madeline Martin attended Mt. Vernon High School and was a telephone operator in Evansville. She married Guerdon Earl Cobb, the son of Thomas and Corilla (Bassett) Cobb on Jan. 11, 1930. The marriage was performed by Rev. Rake, Pastor of First Baptist Church in Evansville. Guerdon Cobb was born in Rumsey, KY, May 25, 1910. His occupation was Maintenance Supervisor for National Furniture Company. They have two daughters, both born in Evansville, Bettye Jean, Nov. 4, 1930 and Patricia Joan, Nov. 2, 1938. The Cobbs moved to California in 1967. Agnes Madelin (Martin) Cobb passed away June 4, 1986 and is buried at Rose Hill Cemetery in Whitier, CA.

George Harold Martin, only son of Ethel and George Martin graduated from Central High School in Evansville, Lockyears Business College and the Air Force Institute of Technology, Dayton, OH. He was a civilian employee for the Department of Defense at Wright-Patterson Air Force Base, OH. He married Jean Hagan, a Registered Nurse from Grandview, IN on May 30, 1942 in St. Louis, MO. During WWII he served overseas with the 25th Air Depot Group. The function of the Air Depot Group was to move aircraft into the European theatre of operations. At the end of WWII he was reassigned Wright-Patterson AFB, OH. In 1946 he attended a dinner at the Engineers Club in Dayton, OH honoring Orville Wright. Orville Wright was described as slight in build and very shy. During President Dwight Eisenhower's administration he was Project Manager for the V.I.P. Aircraft fleet and had the opportunity to fly in the Presidential aircraft the "Columbino." At the time of his retirement in 1977 he was Deptuy Director for logistics in the F-15 Project Office.

Pearl Louise Martin, the third child attended Central High School in Evansville and was married to Charles Owen on Oct. 12, 1947. They had no children.

Johnnie Grace Quinzer, youngest daughter of John and Bettye Quinzer married Thomas Raymond Bradford in Carmi, IL on Aug. 21, 1919. He was a molder and she worked at Scholey's Laundry in Mt. Vernon. There were three children. Leo Frank born Aug. 30, 1921 and died Mar. 10, 1922. He is buried at Bellfontaine Cemetery in Mt. Vernon. Raymond, Jr. was born Jan. 11, 1923. He graduated from University of Evansville and earned a Masters Degree from University of Southern Illinois. His occupation was high school history teacher at Crystal Lake, IL. He served in the Armed Services during WWII. He married Beaulah Foster Hale, a Registered Nurse from Narrows, VA on Apr. 28, 1951. There was one daughter, Lisa, born Oct. 9, 1960 in Mt. Vernon, IL. Jack Darrell Bradford, the youngest son was born Feb. 4, 1924 in Mt. Vernon. He graduated from Central High School in Evansville where he was a cheerleader. He served in the Armed Forces during WWII. His occupation was co-owner of an Engineering Drawing business in Evansville. Jack Bradford married Doris Marie Bost of Hillsboro, IL on Sept. 4, 1948. There were three children, Karen Sue, Brent Allen and Scott.

Elizabeth Quinzer was born in Mt. Vernon on Mar. 4, 1865. She was engaged to be married to a handsome young man who was killed in an accident. Her heart was broken and she remained unmarried. She moved to Cincinnati, OH to live with her sister Ollie and brother-in-law, Ottis Miller, where she remained until her death. The sisters came to Mt. Vernon frequently by train to visit relatives and always gave silver coins to their young grand nieces and nephews. She died in Cincinnati, OH May 22, 1948 and is buried at Memorial Park Rest Haven Cemetery in Cincinnati.

Lilly Quinzer was born Sept. 13, 1866 in Mt. Vernon. She married George W. Miller, Apr. 13, 1890 in a double wedding ceremony with her sister Molly Quinzer and Fredrick Seppich. The ceremony was performed by Rev. B.F. Rawlins of First M.E. Church in the home of parents Ernestine and Adam Quinzer at 1137 Main Street. George W. Miller was born in Posey County in 1857. His father was John Miller and his mother Eliza (Douvoan). His occupation was cigar maker. Shortly after marriage, the George W. Millers moved to New Richmond, OH. There were three children, sons Mark, Gilbert and daughter Sonoma. George W. Miller passed away in Ohio and his wife Lilly on July 9, 1946. Both are buried in Grandview Cemetery, New Richmond, OH.

Molly Quinzer was born in Mt. Vernon, Oct. 11, 1871. She married Fredrick Seppich on Apr. 13, 1890 in a double wedding ceremony with sister Lilly. He was born in Evansville, June 6, 1870, the son of Johan Adam Seppich and Lucetta (Rappey) Seppich. His occupation was barber. There were five children Claude Arthur, Henry Edward, Charles Mike, Esther and Elizabeth. They all were born in Mt. Vernon. In 1909 the Seppichs moved to Evaston, WY where son Charles Mike died and was buried. While living in Evanston, a neighbor asked the Seppichs if they would be interested in starting a small dry goods store. Since they had planned to move on to Ogden, UT, they told the neighbor no. He was J.C. Penny. After moving to Ogden, the Seppichs joined the Mormon Church. Fredrich Seppich died Apr. 1, 1949 and Molly (Quinzer) Seppich, Oct. 12, 1950. Both are buried at Aultorest Memorial Park Cemetery, Ogden, UT.

Ollie Quinzer was born in Mt. Vernon, Nov. 14, 1874. She married Ottis Miller of Mt. Vernon on Oct. 15, 1893. His parents were Ottis P. and Ann (Lindsey) Miller. Shortly after marriage they moved to Cincinnati, OH. They owned and operated a successful furniture store business in Cincinnati. Their only child was son Clyde. He served in the Navy during WWI and became an Attorney. Ottis Miller died 1937, son Clyde, Jan. 1, 1964 and wife Ollie, Aug. 31, 1964. The Millers are buried at Rest Haven Cemetery, Cincinnati, OH.

Adam Quinzer, the Patriarch of the Quinzer family, died in 1896 and wife Ernestine (Schelhorn) Quinzer, Apr. 5, 1913. She was living with daughter Ollie in Cincinnati at time of her death and was brought to Mt. Vernon by river boat for burial. Both are buried in Bellfontaine Cemetery.

George Nicholas Schelhorn had two nephews, Jacob and Peter Schelhorn who also emigrated to Posey County from Germany. Many of their descendants still live in Posey and Vanderburgh Counties.

JACOB E. SCHELHORN FAMILY

Marriage records and the 1880 census suggest that a group of three or four Schelhorns came to Posey County, from Germany. According to the census records, Jacob Schelhorn was born in Saxony, while Peter and Leanom, who quite probably were brothers, were born in neighbouring Hanover.

Although Jacob and all of his known descendants have spelled their name Schelhorn, some records of them use the form Shelhorn.

Jacob E. Schelhorn came to Posey Co., IN, from Saxony, Germany, before 1849 and he was a cooper in Mt. Vernon, IN, in 1860. Jacob married Margaret Engle also from Saxony, Germany. They had nine children, John F., William, Mary, Caroline, Henry, Charles, Edward, Hannah and a daughter name not known.

John F. Schelhorn married Mary Kramer in 1872. They had eight children, Katherine, John, Carrie, Mary, Emma, William, Edward and George W. who was my grandfather. John F. Schelhorn was a preacher and preached in a church at Parker Settlement.

George Schelhorn; Ida (Brandt) Schelhorn 1910

George W. Schelhorn married Ida Julia Brandt in 1910. They had five children, Harvey, Elmer, Dale, Walter and a daughter Ruth. George for many years owned and operated a blacksmith shop in his native Robinson Township, in 1935 the blacksmith shop burned down and George was burned very bad, after recovering from his injuries he later farmed in Point and West Black Townships.

Harvey Schelhorn was a skilled mechanic and a specialist in diesel motors, he served in World War II and during his time in the Army he served as an interpreter, which came easy for him because German was the language that was spoken in his home. Harvey never married and died at age 42.

Dale was a boilermaker by trade and a veteran of World War II. He died in 1976 at the age of 62. He had two sons and two stepdaughters, one son was killed in a gun accident at the age of 13, the other son William resides in Texas, both stepdaughters live in the Mt. Vernon area.

Elmer was a retired farmer and county highway employee. He lived in the Bufkin area at the time of his death. His nickname was "Speed" and he married Cora Pauline Schmidt in 1937 and had three sons, John, Alan and Jerry, all living in the Posey County area.

Walter who is the only son still living is married to Verna McCarty, and they have two daughters, Terri and Connie. Terri lives in Mt. Vernon and Connie in Evansville. Walter worked many years as a skilled truck driver for Marathon Oil and later worked at the B&W Plant. He now is employed at the courthouse in Mt. Vernon.

Ruth is the only girl and she resides in Lynn Township along with her husband Willie Nowling, who is a retired Boilermaker and they have one stepdaughter, Candace (Wilkerson) Morlock. Ruth worked at the plastic factory for many years. Ruth has three grandchildren, David, Robert and Kimberly Morlock.

We really never listen when our ancestors talk of the olden days and of their native lands, we should as they could share many memories and tell many stories that we will never have the opportunity to hear again when they are gone. *by Candace R. Morlock*

CHRISTIAN EDWARD SCHMIDT FAMILY

Christian Edward Schmidt, the third child of John Phillip and Margareth Zimmerman Schmidt, was born on July 18, 1860. On Jan. 7, 1886 he married Henrietta Fellemende. The entry in "Die Bibel oder die ganze Heilige Schrift des Alten und Neuen Testaments", published in 1886 reads "was married at the home of the bride Shartta Daudistle". Edward, as he was more commonly known, and Henrietta "Yetta" had six children. Only three, John Raymond, born Oct. 6, 1886, Minnie Augusta, born Oct. 15, 1891 and Charles Walter, lived to reach maturity. Edward and Yetta lived across the road from the original family home on Holler Road in south west Posey County.

Charles Walter Schmidt was born on May 27, 1896. On Aug. 31, 1920 he maried the daughter of Jacob John and Anna Louisa Bockstahler, a neighboring farmer. Edna Louise Bockstahler was born on Jan. 21, 1900 and was the third of four children. Edna frequently tells of how her parents moved from Dale, IN to Posey County with all their possessions packed in two large trunks in the back of a horse drawn wagon. They also brought with them a few chickens and a milk cow was tied to the back of the wagon. The journey took over two days and two nights. Charlie both farmed with his father Edward and served as a rural mail carrier for nearly 30 years. Charles and Edna had three children who lived to maturity.

Melvin Charles Schmidt was born on Sept. 23, 1921 at the home of his Grandmother Bockstahler in south west Posey County. He was married on Aug. 8, 1942 to Dorothy Louise Muelbauer of Evansville, IN. Melvin and Dorothy had two daughters, Carol Ann, born Oct. 8, 1946 and Nancy Louise, born Apr. 30, 1948. Dorothy passed away on May 26, 1988. Melvin currently resides in Sidney, OH along with his oldest daughter, Carol Ann.

Dalton Morris Schmidt was born on Feb. 22, 1924 at the home of his parents. He was married on June 19, 1965 to Susan Mildred Harbin in Westminster, SC. Susan and Morrie currently reside in Huntsville, AL with their two sons, Charles Harbin Schmidt, born Mar. 2, 1968 and William Arthur Schmidt, born July 14, 1970. Morrie works for the National Aeronautical Space Administration as an engineer and Susan teaches school.

Annetta Faye Schmidt, the youngest of Edna and Charles' children was born on Mar. 21, 1941. She is married to Donald Ray Parke and they currently reside in Newburgh, IN. Annetta works for Koch Originals of Evansville and Don is a school teacher at Heritage Hills in Dale, IN. The couple have no children; however Donald has four sons from a previous marriage. The youngest, John, resides with Annetta and Donald.

Charles Schmidt died on Nov. 23, 1960 at the family farm. Edna no longer resides at the family farm; however, she still owns the property. Currently the house is rented out and the farm lands are being farmed by Edna's cousins the Rieses of south west Posey County. Edna lives in Mt. Vernon with Melvin's younger daughter, Nancy Louise. She still enjoys good health and is active in Senior Citizens, the Posey County Farm Bureau extension group she helped found in the 1930s. Edna still attends Zoar United Methodist Church, where her family has gone for over 100 years. Nancy is a bookkeeper for the Second Chance Halfway House in Evansville, IN. She serves as the secretary/treasurer of the Black Township chapter of the Posey County Farm Bureau.

JOHN PHILLIP SCHMIDT

John Phillip Schmidt and his wife Ana Margareth Zimmerman Schmidt, were the first generation of the Schmidt ancestors to live in America, they came from a village called Ueberau in Germany.

They bought 80 acres in western Black township in 1875 and upon their deaths it was willed to their youngest son Philip Schmidt who was never married.

John Heinrich their eldest son, a farmer in western Black township married Pauline Schieber, they had two daughters and seven sons.

Hugo the fourth, son of John and Pauline Schmidt married Malinda Jones on May 3, 1908. She was the daughter of David and Sara Miller Jones, who also were farmers in western Black Township.

Hugo and Malinda farmed until 1937, then they bought Zimmerman blacksmith shop in Grafton, in later years he was a cemetery custodian.

They had two children, Rosa Lena and John Philip Schmidt. John moved to California and married Grase Thoresen from New York. They have three children, Judi, Stephen, and Carol who all live in California. Carol Pulice has a daughter Jessie the only great grandchild of Hugo and Malinda.

Rosa married Otto Richard Rowe the eldest son of Harry and Mattie Bradford Rowe, who were farmers in western Black township.

They had no children and he passed away in 1962.

In 1931 Philip Schmidt deeded the Schmidt home place to Otto and Rosa and he made his home with them until his death.

Rosa still has the Schmidt place which has been in the Schmidt name for over 115 years.

The House is still being lived in that was built by Philipp and Margareth. Rosa is a member of Black Chapel Church, The United Methodist Women, Busy Homemakers Extension Homemakers Club, Black Township Farm Bureau, Posey County Farm Bureau Auxiliary, and the A.A.A.R.P. Group.

ROBERT GOSS SCHMIDT

Robert Goss Schmidt was born Mar. 10, 1913 in Point Township, Posey Co., IN about five miles south of Mt. Vernon. He was the son of John Edward and Cora Ann (Goss) Schmidt. Robert was named for his Great Uncle Robert B. Goss. He received his schooling at the Spencer Grade School and Mt. Vernon High School. The Schmidt family farmed and raised livestock. Robert worked on the farm as a boy and continued to do so as a young man. He was married to Regina Ann Jarman. She was born on Oct. 4, 1938, a native of Clarksville, TN. Robert and his family lived in the Wabash bottoms near Half-Moon Pond in a home built by his Great Uncle Robert Goss. In 1950, they moved to a farm and home in Gibson Co., IN located in Montgomery Township. He lived on this farm where he raised grain and livestock until he retired in 1982

He was a member of the United Methodist Church, Order of Eastern Star, and Masonic Lodge He died Aug. 10, 1985 and was buried at Antioch Cemetery about four miles south of Owensville, IN

Robert's great-grandparents were Philipp and Anna Margaretha (Zimmerman) Schmidt who came from Ueberau, Germany to settle in Black Township, Posey County in 1855. Philipp was also a farmer. Robert's grandparents were John H. and Paulina (Schieber) Schmidt who lived on a farm near Philipp. This Philipp's farm is still in the Schmidt family today. It was heired by Rosa Rowe, a great-granddaughter of Philipp, from Mt. Vernon. She lives near this farm today. Robert's great-great-great grandfather was James Conlin who came to Point Township in 1818 to settle and build a log cabin. He owned several hundred acres of farmland at that time in Point. These ancestors are buried in the Conlin Cemetery in Point Township near Bone Bank. His Goss relatives were also early immigrants to Posey County coming in the 1840s. His great grandfather Frederick Schieber and great grandmother Barbara (Storg) Schieber, German Immigrants settled in Posey County, Point Township in the 1840s. Frederick and Barbara owned a farm also. Frederick was a Union soldier in the Civil War.

Robert Goss Schmidt 1913-1985

Robert and Regina are the parents of five children: 1. Marjorie Ann born Nov. 29, 1938. Married Donald Peugh. One child: Kelly Sue; 2. Carolyn Sue born Jan. 15, 1941. Married Phillip McKinnon. Children: Michael, Robert Frederick, David Lane; 3. Wanda Lou - born Sept. 6, 1944. Married Terry Tichenor. Children Todd Eric, Tadd Evan; 4. Barbara Nell - born Dec. 21, 1946. Married (1st) Wayne Gwaltney. Child: Keith Wayne. Married (2) Aaron Riggs. Children: Tara Leigh, Aaron Leon II; Great grandchildren of Robert and Regina are: Robert Goss Gwaltney, son of Mr. and Mrs. Keith Gwaltney, and Brandon Michael son of Mr. and Mrs. Robert Frederick McKinnon.

RAYMOND H. AND LUCY SCHMITT

Raymond and Lucy (Weinzapfel) Schmitt's farm is in northeastern Posey County where Smith and Robinson Townships meet. Original acreage was purchased by John Watson in 1832 from the US Government. Albert Schmitt (Ray's grandfather) purchased it in 1871, Bernard (Ray's father) 1917, Ray and Lucy in 1956. This original acreage has been in the Schmitt family for 118 years.

Ray and Lucy were married Aug. 30, 1952 at St. Phillips Catholic Church. Their children are: Patrick, Leonard, Theresa (Windhaus), Ralph, Carl, and Agnes (Reidford).

Ray's grandfather, Albert Schmitt came to the US from Alsace-Lorraine with his parents. His three year old sister died enroute and was buried at sea. Albert served in the Indiana Infantry during the Civil War from 1862-1865. He married Margaret (Tieken); they had eight children, including two sets of twins; Bernard and Martin, Mary (Dietsch) and Mary (Knapp). Other children were; Gerhardt, Elizabeth (Martin), Ann (Seib) and Theresa (Gries).

Front: Raymond and Lucy Schmitt; Back: Lt to Rt. Leonard, Carl, Ralph, Patrick, Theresa, Agnes.

Ray's parents Bernard and Gertrude (Gries) purchased adjoining acreage from Henry Baehl in 1927. Their children were: Joseph (deceased), Margaret (Halbig), Leo, Edwin, Helen (Simon), Wilfred, Raymond, Anthony, Albinus, Urban, Jerome, and Bernard.

Ray's maternal great grandparents were Johann and Mary, Ann (Staab) from Bavaria, Germany. Conrad Gries (Ray's grandfather) married Gertrude (Oppel) and their children were; Margaret, Mary Kunigunda, Elizabeth (Seibert), Joseph, and Mary Ann (Elpers). After his wife died he marred Elizabeth (Knapp) Ray's grandmother and their children were: Conrad, John, Peter, Gertrude (Ray's mother), Lena (Will) and Catherine (Scheller-Gumbel).

Lucy's ancestors came from Alsace-Lorraine in 1838. Fr. Roman Weinzapfel, a young seminarian came to Vincennes, IN. Lucy's great grandfather Michael (brother of Roman) came in 1847. He settled in St. Philip and married Katherine Helfrick in 1847. They had 11 children and one son Henry moved to Windhurst, TX and ran a general store. Another brother Franz came to America and there are two versions; one that he came and didn't like it and returned, second his clothes arrived but he didn't.

August (Lucy's grandfather) frequently traveled with Fr. Weinzapfel visiting his mission parishes in southern Indiana. August spoke French, German, and English, and was a look-alike of Abe Lincoln. He married Rose (Weber) an orphan, in 1855. They had eight children; Katherine, Josephine, and Michael moved to Arizona, where Michael was a railroad engineer for the Southern Pacific Railroad. Frank ran a country store in St. Philips.

Joseph Weinzapfel (Lucy's father) married Berndena Mueller in 1919 at St. Matthew's Church Mt. Vernon. Their children are: Charles, Mary Margaret (Mesker), Mildred (Blankenberger), Rose (Nellis), Lucy (Schmitt) Louis, Martha Ann (Schmitt).

Farm ownership in Marrs Township: Ernest Willman from US Government 1845, Andrew Deig 1863, Michael Weinzapfel 1880, August 1884, Joseph-1933, Louis 1972. Weinzapfel ownership 109 years.

Lucy's maternal ancestors were: great grandparents Louis and Joanna Mueller from Germany, grandparents Lawrence and Margaret (Kirchoff) Mueller who lived in Black Twp. Other relatives who live in the Posey County Area include: Gerths, Deigs, Stratmans, Steinkamps, Fischers, and Hartmanns.

REINEKE-SCHMITZ

Earl Henry Schmitz was born on Oct. 28, 1926, in Robinson Township, son of Moses and Lorena (Hoell) Schmitz. Earl attended Waterman School in Robinson Township. In 1940 Earl began farming and raising livestock full-time with his mother and father on their farm. Earl and Moses went throughout the county making and selling molasses through the fall months. Moses and Lorena were both born in Robinson Township. They had nine children-five of whom yet survive. They are Earl, Charles and Charlotte (twins), and Paul and David (twins).

Earl and Esther Schmitz

On July 31, 1948 Earl took for his bride Esther Louisa Reineke. Esther was born on Sept. 10, 1926, the daughter of Henry August and Caroline (Meier) Reineke. Henry and Caroline were the parents of three children: Marie, Esther, and Henry. Esther went to Schroeder School in Robinson Township and in 1940 she began farming with her father and mother. After their marriage, Esther and Earl began crop and dairy farming together with Esther's parents.

Esther and Earl are the parents of three children, Carl, Albert, and Nancy, all of whom reside in Posey County. They also have six grandchildren.

Earl is a member of the Robinson Township Conservation Club and Posey County Farm Bureau. He spent 16 years as a Marrs Township volunteer firefighter and is now on its board-of-directors. Esther and Earl are members of Zion United Church of Christ on Ford Road. They reside at 925 Dutchman Rd., Wadesville, IN.

ALBERT FRED SCHREIBER

Albert Fred Schreiber was born in Mt. Vernon, IL on Apr. 8, 1912. His parents were Wm. Fred Schreiber and Carrie A. Renner. Carrie Renner's parents were William Renner and Mary Juncker. Fred Schreiber's parents were Henry Schreiber and Bertha Dietz. Henry Schrieber's parents were Michael Schrieber and a woman named Elizabeth. Michael Schreiber was born in Germany and came to America sometime before 1850. Michael's first wife died on board ship and was buried at sea. When in America Michael lived in Southern Indiana. Michael married second wife and had about eight children.

Some of the Schreiber's had large families. Michael's third wife had a son whose name was Henry. Henry was Albert Fred Schreiber's grandfather. All three of Michael Schreiber's wives were named Elizabeth. Michael was born in 1800 and died in 1881.

Albert Schreiber's father worked in a railroad car

shop while in Illinois. Later Fred and his wife Carrie moved to Southern Indiana and started farming. Fred and Carrie's two daughters Esther and Dorothy were born. Esther married Raymond Hoenert and Dorothy married John Maurer. Fred Schreiber had three brothers, William, Phillip, Arthur and one sister, Elizabeth. William died when very young. Albert Schreiber married Lillian Roedel and farmed with Fred Schreiber. Albert was also a substitute mail carrier. Albert's chief interest in sports was baseball.

Albert's first wife died of cancer. Albert's second wife was Helen Burgdorf Clark and they lived in Evansville, IN.

After retirement Albert and his wife like to travel. They traveled by bus, trailer and motorhome.

CARL A. AND DELENE I. SCHMITZ

Carl A. and Delene I. Schmitz reside in Robinson Township. Posey County has always been home to them as it was to their parents and grandparents. The Schmitzes reside in Carl's maternal family's homestead as have the past five generations since John Lang built the house in 1859 at 929 Dutchman Road, Wadesville.

Carl, born Mar. 12, 1951, is the son of Earl and Esther (Reineke) Schmitz. He attended first grade at Waterman School, the last year the one-room school was in session. He graduated from North Posey High in 1969. Like his parents and many of his antecedents, Carl has been a dairy (registered holsteins) and crop farmer since 1967 and is co-owner of Dutchman Farms, Inc.

Carl has a Posey County brother, Albert, and sister, Nancy Dougan. Esther's parents, Henry and Caroline (Meier) Reineke, married in 1914. Henry's grandmother, Florentine (Osterhausen) Reineke, immigrated from Holzhausen, Lippe, Germany to Robinson Township. As a teenager, Caroline's grandfather, Fred Meier, came from Germany and made Robinson Township his home also.

Delene, Carl, Hans, Carly Schmitz

Carl's grandfather, Moses Schmitz, married Lorena Hoell in 1921. Moses' grandfather, Joshua, came from Waltheim, Germany to Posey County.

Delene was born Nov. 26, 1953, the daughter of Wilfred LaRue and Doris (McFadin) Phillips. She graduated from Mt. Vernon Senior High in 1972. She earned a B.S. Degree in Business from Indiana University, Bloomington, in 1975. Delene is a Posey County real estate broker and appraiser. Delene's sister is Deena Cortus.

Carl and Delene were married on July 21, 1979 at Zion United Church of Christ where they are members. To this union have been born Hans, July 30, 1984, and Carolina, "Carly", on Sept. 24, 1985.

Carl is a member of the Robinson Township Conservation Club, and the National and Indiana Holstein Associations. He and Delene are chairpersons of the Posey County Farm Bureau Dairy Committee and are members of the Evansville Young Dairymen Assoc., and the Southwestern Indiana Holstein Assoc. of which Carl is treasurer. Delene is a member of the American Assoc. of University Women, Indiana University Alumni Assoc., Posey County Historical Society, and National, State, and Evansville Associations of Realtors, and Zion's Women's Guild.

Delene's grandfather, George E. McFadin, married Pauline Gaiser. The town, McFadin's Bluff, later to become Mt. Vernon, was named for Andrew McFadin, Sr., George's great-grandfather. Andrew fought in the Revolutionary War and settled in Posey County in 1805 coming from North Carolina.

Elisha Phillips traveled with his family down the Ohio River in a flatboat in 1818, stopping at Farmersville. Elisha married Electa Annable, whose ancestors came to America on the **Anne**, the second ship to arrive after the **Mayflower**. Wilfred Phillips, Elisha's great-grandson and Delene's grandfather, served in WWI. He married Mary Benthall and worked for 45 years at People's Bank and Trust Co. in Mt. Vernon.

Mary's great-great grandparents, Jacob and Catharine (Canady) Benthall, migrated to Posey County from North Carolina around 1828, along with the Bells, Canadays, and Culleys. Many of these families' descendents live and prosper in Posey County today.

SCHMITZ-HOELL

Moses Schmitz was born on Jan. 17, 1896 in Robb Township, Posey County. Moses was the son of Charles and Mina (Roesner) Schmitz. Moses farmed in Robinson Township after attending Waterman School.

Moses Schmitz and Lorena Hoell marriage

On Mar. 10, 1921 at St. Peter's United Church of Christ at Parker Settlement Moses married Lorena Elizabeth Hoell. Lorena was born on Feb. 18, 1899 in Robinson Township, Posey County. She was the daughter of George E. and Gertrude (Metz) Hoell. Lorena attended Waterman School also.

Moses and Lorena made their home at Downen Road, Robinson Township. They had a family of nine children. Those surviving to this day are Earl Henry, Paul and David (twins), and Charles and Charlotte (twins). Norman died of scarlet fever at age 13. Alberta passed on in 1930 of summer complaint. John and Stephan were both stillborn.

Moses was a Legionaire. His father, Joshua, was a charter member of the Memorial Baptist Church on Marx Road.

Moses died Sept. 25, 1967 and Lorena followed him on May 10, 1976. Both are buried at Memorial Baptist Cemetery.

SCHNEIDER HISTORY

According to Elfrieda Lang's History of Trinity, 1953 based on Original Returns of the 8th U.S. Census, 1860, the first Schneider to come to Posey County was John Schneider. He was born Sept. 16, 1831 in Hessen-Cassel, Germany. He married Louise Mahrenholz.

Louise, daughter of John and Louise Mahrenholz, born Mar. 17, 1831, in Hanover, Germany. John Schneider was a carpenter. With Henry Brinkman, John built the first Trinity Church in Mt. Vernon in 1857. After moving to Mt. Vernon, John and Louise had eight children:

Right to Left: Paul P. Schneider Nov. 25, 1916, Charles A. Schneider, Jan. 9, 1920, Ervin M. Schneider Oct. 13, 1921, Earl O. Schneider Sept. 1, 1923, Mary R. Reich June 10, 1925, Wm. C. Schneider Sept. 3, 1927, John D. Schneider Apr. 9, 1929

1. John (married Anna B. Zergiebel) born 1856-died 1930. He farmed at Mt. Vernon, then operated implement, feed, and seed store.

2. Elisabeth L. (Thomas J. Willis) born Sept. 30, 1858.

3. Conrad (Katherine Peter), born Jan. 16, 1860-died Apr. 3, 1929.

4. Louisa born 1869-died 1873 age four.

5. Augusta born Jan. 29, 1871-died June 28, 1872. Both Louisa and Augusta died of cholera.

6. Charles (Mary Downen), birthdate unknown.

7. Minnie, birthdate unknown.

8. Mary (George Downen), birthdate unknown. Died Sept. 25, 1925.

John Schneider died Sept. 20, 1872. Louise (Mahrenholz) Schneider died May 12, 1900. Both buried in Bellefontaine Cemetery, Mt. Vernon, IN.

Their third child, Conrad, nicknamed "Coon", married Katherine Peter Nov. 9, 1884. Katherine, born Nov. 26, 1868, daughter of Phillip and Sarah (Smith) Peter.

Conrad and Katherine also had eight children:

1. Elfrieda (Fred C. Goss), born Nov. 13, 1885-died Oct. 30, 1966.

2. Edward George (Charlotte Hammer nee Nebe) born July 15, 1887-died July 13, 1958.

3. Phillip Charles (Mary Jane Redman), born Aug. 22, 1889-died Apr. 23, 1968.

4. Clarence Otis (Hazel Cora Walls), born Aug. 10, 1891-died Aug. 26, 1973.

5. Alvin Conrad (Minnie Katherine Renschler), born Oct. 5, 1893-died Mar. 2, 1971.

6. Ruth K. (unmarried), born Apr. 8, 1896 - died July 23, 1914 (during appendicitis operation).

7. Raymond A. (Sue), born Dec. 14, 1898-died Mar. 30, 1952. Raymond served in WWI - then was drafted WWII.

8. Doris (Winston Richard Brown), born Nov. 23, 1911 - still living.

Conrad Schneider died Apr. 3, 1929. Katherine (Peter) Schneider died Nov. 26, 1942. Both are buried Bellefontaine Cemetery, Mt. Vernon, IN.

Their third child, Phillip Charles, was born in Posey County on Aug. 22, 1889. He married Mary Jane Redman in 1914. He was a lifelong farmer. Farming first with his father in Point Township, and later farming with his sons. In later years he also farmed in Illinois, near Omaha and Eldorado. He was a member of Trinity United Church of Christ. After the death of his first wife, Mary Jane, he was married three more times. Second wife, Myrtle, third-Zenia, fourth-Hazel.

Mary Jane (Redman) Schneider was born Oct. 20, 1898, to George Taylor and Mary Elizabeth (Clarkston) Redman. She attended Prairie School and Prairie Church.

Phillip and Mary Jane Schneider had seven children:

1. Paul Phillip (1st Dorothy Ousley - 2nd Mary Yates) both deceased. Born Nov. 25, 1916.

2. Charles Arthur (Evelyn Reich), born Jan. 9, 1920.

3. Ervin Malcolm (Mettis Irene Johnson Weatherford), born Oct. 13, 1921.

4. Earl Otto (Betty L. Woods), born Sept. 1, 1923.

5. Mary Ruth (Earl Phillip Reich) born June 10, 1925.

6. William Conrad (unmarried), born Sept. 3, 1927.

7. John Doerr (Coquella Daphane Ogles), born Apr. 9, 1929.

All seven children of Phillip and Mary Jane Schneider were born in Posey County. All seven children are still living.

Phillip Charles Schneider died Apr 23, 1968 in Eldorado, IL at age 79 of natural causes. Mary Jane (Redman) Schneider died May 8, 1938 at age 39 from complications from gallbladder. Both are buried Bellefontaine Cemetery, Mt. Vernon, IN.

Their last child, John Doerr, was born in Point Township, Apr. 9, 1929. He married Coquella Daphane Ogles on Sept. 23, 1950 (now divorced). He attended Lawrence Elementary School in Point Township for eight years and graduated May 1948 from Mt. Vernon High School. He owned and operated Schneider Excavating for 28 years as well as farming in Point Township. He has traveled widely, including most of South America, Mexico, Canada, and several countries in Europe and Africa.

Coquella Daphane (Ogles) Schneider was born in Kentucky, May 26, 1933, daughter of Clarissa Ogles.

John Doerr and Daphane Schneider had six children:

1. John Conrad (Janice Marie Porter - now divorced), born Nov. 22, 1951. Professor at Mississippi University, Starkville, MS one son-Adam.

2. Robert Wayne (Marcia Ann Hodges), born Oct. 3, 1953. Attended Purdue University. Grounds Supervisor-Red Geranium Enterprises - New Harmony, IN. one son - John Albert.

3. Ronald Dale, born Sept. 4, 1955, died Apr. 14, 1981-self-inflicted gunshot wound.

4. Cheryl Lynn (Peter Macconi), born Apr. 1, 1960. Two daughters - Michelle and Melissa.

5. David Glen (unmarried), born Apr. 1, 1960. Cheryl and David are twins.

6. Donna Gwen, died at birth Sept. 20, 1961.

The most recent addition to the Schneider line is John Albert, born Sept. 21, 1988, to Robert and Marcia Schneider. His paternal grandfather is John Doerr Schneider. His great-grandmother was Mary Jane (Redman) Schneider.

SCHROEDER

David Edward Schroeder was born at home May 24, 1940 in Posey County in a farm house on what is now called Shroeder Lane.

David was born the youngest son to Albert Simon Schroeder and Matilda nee Jung. Both are now deceased. They were life-long farmers on 90 acres now owned by their eldest son, Raymond. David has a sister, Gertrude Lewis of St. Louis and an elder brother, Harold on Copperline Rd., who builds homes and develops real estate.

David's grandparents, Henry Carl, born Feb. 27, 1859 and Bertha nee Espenlaub were large farm owners on Downen Road in Posey County. Henry's father, Frederick Wilhelm Schroeder was born Oct. 30, 1827 in Exter, Germany. He came to Indiana purchasing a farm on Boberg Road, Posey County. His farm is presenlty owned by Edgar Boberg.

David married Lennita Ann Bumb at St. Paul's U.C.C. in Evansville Oct. 22, 1961. They lived in Evansville for a few years having a son Allen David Aug. 14, 1962. They purchased, in the meanwhile, 7-1/2 acres in Posey County, planning and building their "dream home" and anxious to move in before their daughter, Shannon Elaine arrived June 14, 1968. The home is located in Parker Settlement. They have planted many fruit and nut trees and have flowers and flowering shrubs with nostalgic memories, such as "Albert's Fire Bush" (David's father's contribution), an "Aunt Huldy Bush", a beautiful shrub with purple berries in fall, and King Alfred daffodils given to them from Lennita's mother, Martha and deceased father, Edgar Bumb's home place.

They enjoy raising a large family vegetable garden each year, sharing their fruits, nuts and vegetables with family and friends. Their best yield is Lima Beans.

One change David and Lennita would like to make in their home is the dining room. They'd like to enlarge it to make more room for family and friends to gather for meals on special occasions and for the grandchildren they hope to have someday.

Their son, Allen lives at home, but owns two acres in Posey County next to James Paul's Saw Mill in Blairsville. Mr. Paul's son, Andrew, and Allen are best friends. Allen built a garage/bachelor pad there and intends to build his home on the property. His interests are Taekwondo, restoring old cars, collecting coins and rare comics. He is employed at Sermersheim's Corvette Corner, Evansville.

Their daughter, Shannon works for Sermershiems. She is living at home and attended Beau Madame Modeling School. Shannon hopes to move to Florida within a few years.

David works for Sermersheim's Corvette Corner. He belongs to the Masonic Lodge in Poseyville and the Scottish Rite in Evansville. He loves hunting and collecting old guns.

Lennita works for Whitmore's Custom Woodworking, Evansville. She enjoys art work, and collecting Depression Glass.

David and Lennita hope to take a Caribbean Cruise for their 30th Anniversary.

All are members of St. Peter's U.C.C. at Parker Settlement.

SEIFERTS OF POSEY COUNTY

The name Seifert was derived from the German Word Sigifrith which means "Victory" or "Peace". It has several spellings and is a common name in the province of Saxony where it was spelled Siefert, Seiferth, Seyfert, Seyferth, Seifart, and Seyfarth.

Nicholas Seifert, his wife Eva and their five children Johannes, Margaretha, Andrew, Martha and Jasper left the farm near Gersfeld, Germany by way of the port of Bremen on the square-rigged ship "Julia" and sailed to the United States. They landed at the port of New Orleans on Nov. 23, 1839. On Jan. 23, 1840 Nicholas bought land in Marrs Township about one mile northeast of the present St. John's United Methodist Church. The land has been owned by succeeding sons and is now owned by Paula A., Norma Jean and Timothy Jon Seifert. A sixth child of Elizabeth was born in 1841. Later Eva died and Nicholas married the widow Frances Winemiller, a neighbor. She had eight children: Jacob, William, Catherine, Sara, Roswell, Julia, Nancy, and Jane. Later Martha and Jasper Seifert married Jacob and Jane Winemiller. Andrew married Rebecca Underwood.

St. Johns United Methodist Church at Caborn - 100 years old 1987

In 1853, Nicholas, his wife and three of their children moved to Franklin Co., IL. Nicholas bought land there on July 12, 1853 near the town of Whittington. The name was spelled Cipher, Sipher, and Cypher. Nicholas lived here until his death on Nov. 17, 1870. He had established a cemetery on his farm and is buried there south of Whittington.

The other three children continued to live here in Posey County. Johannes married Margaretha Lehman, Margaretha married Freiderich Kramer, and Elizabeth married John Zimmerman.

St. John's United Methodist Church was built in 1887 and celebrated the 100th Anniversary on Sept. 13, 1987. Many of Nicholas Seifert's descendents were prominent members in the erection of the church, and many descendents still attend the church. All of the Seiferts who lived in Posey County are direct descendents of Nicholas and Eva Seifert. *by Laverne Seifert*

NANCY VIVIAN RANES SEXTON

Nancy Vivian Ranes Sexton daughter of Francis W. Ranes and Mary Martha (Reeves) Ranes was born Sept. 7, 1943 at Oliphant Nursing Home in Mt. Vernon being delivered by her grandfather Dr. John R. Ranes. She grew up at the family farm north of Upton about 4-1/2 miles northwest of Mt. Vernon. Her first years of education began at Grafton Elementary School, a 2-room school with Mrs. Loren (Nell) Walker her teacher for grades 1-4; her 5th and 6th grade teacher was Mr. Carl Curtis and her 7th and 8th grade teacher was Mr. Emmet Knowles. Nancy graduated from Mt. Vernon High School in 1961 and in June of that same year began employment with Mead Johnson Company International Office in Evansville.

163

Seated in Front L to R. Nancy Ranes Sexton, Louann Woodford. Standing in back: L to R Cecil Sexton, Jeff Woodford.

On June 20, 1964 she was married and on Dec. 23, 1965 a son Jeffrey Ranes Woodford was born and is presently a Sargent in the United States Air Force stationed at Homestead Air Force Base in Florida. On Apr. 17, 1987 he was united in marriage to Miss Sybil LouAnn Miller daughter of Larry J. and Martha (Doss) Miller of Greenville, KY.

Nancy has pursued employment in the secretarial field and is presently a medical office manager in a surgeon's office in Pittsburgh, PA. where she resides with her husband Cecil Sexton, Jr. son of Cecil Sr. and Mary Elizabeth (Snodgrass) Sexton of Owensboro, KY. Nancy is a volunteer member of the American Cancer Society; a member of Pittsburgh Symphony Guild; a member of Pittsburgh Association for the Blind; is a Medical Researcher and Counselor with cancer patients and their families. Cecil is vice president of marketing and sales for Genix Enterprises—a computer information service company in Pittsburgh, PA.

JOHN KITCHELL AND EVELYN MARIE SHERRETZ

John and Marie have been residents of Poseyville, IN for the last 22 years. John is presently Posey County Auditor and Marie is a Registered Nurse. John attended Mt. Vernon High, Class of 1956, University of Evansville, Class of 1961, and College Advanced Transportation, Class of 1971. Marie attended Elnora High School, Class of 1959 and Deaconess School of Nursing, Class of 1962. They have three children: Adam Trent born Aug. 19, 1964, married Deanna Fenwick on Oct. 4, 1985 and have a daughter Lyndsay Ann born Mar. 2, 1987. Ardith Ann born Mar. 2, 1967, married Robert Craig Jordan Nov. 12, 1988, reside in Evansville, IN. One other son, Aaron Joshua born Aug. 22, 1978 at home.

Marie was born in Daviess Co., IN on Feb. 2, 1941, the oldest child of George and Helen Dickie (Stringer) Wildridge. Her antecedents include the Stringer, Wildridge, and Hunter families of Daviess Co., IN.

John was born June 2, 1938 in Point Township, Posey Co., IN. John is the oldest son of William H. born Dec. 21, 1911 and Marguerite C. (Johnson) born Aug. 14, 1917 in Union Co., KY. William and Marguerite were married May 25, 1936. They also have another son Richard J. born June 27, 1950 that resides in Madisonville, KY and a daughter Marjorie E. Franklin born Dec. 21, 1941 who resided in Mt. Vernon, IN.

William D. Sherretz born July 12, 1873 father of William H. came to Point Township in 1886 from Hamilton Co., IL on a farm three miles from McLeansboro. His father Wallace Livingston was born in Tennessee and married Martha Davis of Kentucky. Wallace's grandfather was from Germany and married a Bell from Kentucky whose grandparents were also born in Kentucky.

John, Marie Sherretz, Josh and Ardith (children)

William D. married Clara May Kitchell Aug. 31, 1895. Clara's father was John Welborn Kitchell a farmer who married Caroline M. Greathouse on Mar. 4, 1874. Her father was Lorenzo Dow that married Parthenia Stinson, youngest daughter of Benoni who was a well known preacher and one of the founders of the General Baptist Denomination. Lorenzo was the youngest son of David. He was born Sept. 5, 1818 in Point Township. David Greathouse a farmer born 1790 in Brown County, OH near Aberdeen settled in Point Township in 1816 about six miles south of McFaddins Bluff close to the Old Greathouse School presently standing that was built in 1911 and the Greathouse Cemetery. The Greathouses' spelled "Grotehausen" in Germany settled in Philadelphia in 1709 when they came from Heidelburg, Germany.

John Kitchell's father was Jake who came from Pennsylvania and married Margaret Welborn. He too was a farmer.

EDMOND RAY SMYTH

Edmond "Ray" Smyth (Nov. 24, 1925) and his wife, Nancye "Ruth" Oliver Smyth (Sept. 25, 1918), moved to New Harmony, February 1959, from Washington, PA with their two children, Edmond Oliver Smyth (May 25, 1946) and Rebecca Ann Smyth (Aug. 30, 1947). They had lived in Pennsylvania only a short time and were all originally from Lee County in eastern Kentucky.

Ray Smyth was an oilfield electrician for Continental Oil Company in Griffin, an electrician for Industrial Contractors in Evansville, a maintenance man for the Executive Inn, and manger of the Black Cat Tavern in Evansville for many years. He died in the Veterans Hospital in Lexington, KY Aug. 18, 1986 from complications following surgery.

Ruth Smyth is retired and still living in New Harmony. She worked for Alfred Owen in Owen's Variety Store for 21 years. Edmond Smyth graduated from New Harmony High School in 1962 and attended the University of Evansville. He is a U.S. Air Force veteran and worked at B&W in Mt. Vernon, Western Electric in Evansville, and Tri-State Communications. He now resides in Evansville and is self-employed as Comm-Tech Services, Electronic-Communications.

Rebecca Smyth graduated from NHHS in 1963, worked at the Main Cafe and Owen's Market in New Harmony, and attended Eastern Kentucky University in Richmond, KY. She began teaching at New Harmony in the fall of 1971, still lives in New Harmony, and teaches first grade at New Harmony School.

ANTHONY SPAHN AND DORETHA (WASSMER) SPAHN

Anthony John Spahn and Doretha Faye Wassmer are residents of Posey County, Marrs Township, near St. Phillips. Anthony and Doretha married on Nov. 3, 1962, at St. Benedicts Catholic Church in Evansville. They attend St. Philips Church where Anthony is a Eucharistic Minister. Their two adopted children are David Anthony born on Aug. 28, 1971 and Laura Marie born on Dec. 5, 1974.

Anthony was born on Oct. 29, 1934 in Vanderburgh County, the oldest son of John Martin and Rosa Sophia (Goedde) Spahn. The family moved from Evansville to St. Wendel where they farmed, Mr. Spahn also worked in a factory. Anthony attended St. Wendel Catholic School through 8th grade. He served in the U.S. Army from October 1954 to 1956, 13 mo. of this time in Germany. Anthony graduated from Lain Technical Institute in 1960 as a Tool Designer. He worked for 13 years as a Design Draftsman at Babcock Wilcox in Mt. Vernon. He is now employed as a Rural Mail Carrier for the Mt. Vernon Post Office.

John Martin Spahn was born on Sept. 2, 1908, Rosa (Rose) was born on Mar. 13, 1908. They were married Aug. 30, 1933 at St. Wendel. John Martin's parents were John A. & Lena (Koch) Spahn, their home was in Robinson Twp., Posey County. Rose's parents were Frank A. and Mary C. (Laugel) Goedde. John and Rose are the parents of seven children. They are Anthony, Francis, Edgar, Frederick, Eugene, Marylene Spahn Hunt, and Virginia Spahn Miles.

Three interesting books are in Willard Library in Evansville. Doretha helped author "Spahn History, St. Wendel, IN, 1838-1988." Tri-State Southwestern Indiana, Southern Illinois and Western Kentucky Connections at Evansville, IN (November 1984) contains both the Spahn and Wassmer five generation ancestor charts. This book also contains the charts from Doretha's cousins, William Wassmer and Mary Ann Wolf Baehl. William Wassmer wrote a Wassmer Family History Book in March, 1978.

Anthony, Doretha, David, Laura

Doretha Wassmer Spahn was born on Sept. 22, 1938 in Posey County, Robb Township, her parents are Sylvester (deceased, June 25, 1958) and Wilfrieda Sauer Wassmer. Doretha went to St. Francis Xavier Grade School and Robb Township High School (Poseyville), graduating in 1956. She graduated in 1959 from St. Mary's Hospital School of Nursing, Evansville. Doretha is presently employed at the Evansville-Vanderburgh County Department of Health in the Tuberculosis Clinic. Doretha has an avid interest in Geneology.

In June of 1988, Anthony, Doretha and their daughter Laura spent two weeks in Germany,

Switzerland, Austria and Liechtenstein. Laura is 14 years old and in the 8th grade at St. Philips School. Her interests are piano and sports. Her brother, David, is 17 and a Senior at Mater Dei High School in Evansville. He recently joined the Marine Reserves.

The Sylvester Wassmer farm home is located about two miles North of Poseyville off Highway 165 near the Black River twin bridges. Doretha's brother, Robert J. (Bob) Wassmer and his wife Sue Reynolds Wassmer live about a half-mile further north on the Posey-Gibson County Line. They are the parents of five children, Steve, Pam Wassmer Spahn, David, Kevin, and Mike, all living in the Poseyville—Wadesville area.

Doretha's paternal grandparents were Andrew Wassmer and Matilda Hillenbrand Wassmer. Doretha's great-great grandparents were Wendelin Wassmer and Katharine Mueller Wassmer. St. Wendel, IN is named in his memory and in honor of his patron, St. Wendelin. Wilfrieda Sauer's parents were John Sauer and Mary Martin Sauer.

Both the Spahn and Wassmer families are of German descent.

AUSBURN T. STEPHENS FAMILY

Ausburn T. Stephens, son of Ezra and Dollie H. Stephens, was born in New Harmony. After his marriage to Mary Alexander in 1938 he has lived in Mt. Vernon, but his ties to New Harmony have been maintained. He worked for a few years as deputy Treasurer of Posey County before joinng the staff of Peoples Bank and Trust Company where he worked for 40 years.

Ausburn and Mary Stephen's daughter, Jane E. Norris and her husband, R. Scott Norris, are residents of Mt. Vernon. They have two children, Julia Ann, 11, and Amy Lynn, three. Jane was born Nov. 24, 1950, and graduated from Mt. Vernon High School in 1969. Scott was born May 28, 1948 and graduated from high school in Ethopia, where his father was stationed as a Lieutenant-Colonel in the United States Army. Jane and Scott both graduated from Depauw University Jane in 1973 with a B.A. Degree in English, and Scott in 1970 with a B.S. Degree. He also earned his Master's Degree at Depauw in 1972, and from there entered the Indiana School of Dentistry, getting his D.D.S Degree in 1976. He is practicing dentistry in Mt. Vernon.

R. Scott, Amy Lyn, Jane and Julia Ann Norris

Jane is a descendant of several early pioneers Posey County families. In this family her great, great grandfather, James Stephens, was born in 1780 in Virginia, and his wife, Sarah Trail Stephens, was born in Maryland in 1796. They came west to Covington, KY, where a son, Ausburn Trail Stephens was born in 1819. He married Elizabeth Hume in Kentucky in 1842. They had five children, one of whom was Ezra Stephens, the father of Ausburn T. Stephens (named for his grandfather) who resides with his wife, Mary in Mt. Vernon.

Ezra Stephen's parents moved to Indiana from Kentucky in 1855 when he was two years old, and bought land in Lynn Township where they prospered.

Later Ezra married Dollie Louise Heckman. Her parents were both from Germany. They were Rosina Bach and Peter Heckman. They were both born in the same town in Germany, but came to this country separately.

Ezra Stephens, besides his interest in farming, was involved in several businesses in New Harmony. He was the founder of the First New Harmony National Bank in 1903. In 1911 he purchased a flour mill and operated it for several years before selling it to the Couch family. He also owned and operated a grain elevator, buying and selling grain. During these years he maintained an active interest in Posey County politics and affairs.

Parthena Stephens, a daughter of Ausburn T. Stephens, and a sister of Ezra Stephens, married Christopher Wilson. They were the parents of Ezra Wilson. He and his wife, Zulah, were parents of Arleta Wilson Manning and Kenneth Wilson, residents of Mt. Vernon, today, making them and their children direct descendants of James Stephens, who was the first of this family to come to this part of the country. Arleta's son, Charles Milton Manning and his wife, nee Doris Schwartz, have two daughters, Robin and Miriam. Arleta's other son, Shannon, does not live here. Kenneth Wilson and his wife Hazel have a son, Kenneth Don Wilson, although he and his family do not live here.

STIFF-LEWIS

Beulah Faye Stiff, daughter of Arthur Stiff and Bruce (Johnson) Stiff, was born on Apr. 28, 1914. She was born on a small farm located between Mt. Vernon and New Harmony on Rush Creek. By the time she was of school age she was living in Mt. Vernon where she obtained her education. Beulah married John Ellis Lewis, son of Price Lewis and Viola (Hartley) Lewis. They had six children: Robert Gene, Deloris Dean, Carolyn Sue, Gerald Ray, Ronald Lee, and Donald Roy.

Beulah's great grandfather was Milton Stiff of Saline Co., IL who was born in Kentucky circa 1803 and moved to Gallatin Co., IL before 1840. Milton's parents were both born in Virginia. Elbert (Milton) Stiff married Minerva Donahoo whose father was born in Kentucky and whose mother was born in Tennessee. The names of their children were: Rebecca A., Angeline, Lewis, Eliza, Thomas J., Henry, Sarah J., Solomon, and Lorinda. Rebecca A. Stiff was born circa 1834 married Charles L. Ashby on Jan. 13, 1853. Angeline Stiff was born circa 1837 married John Hamilton on Dec. 9, 1855. Lewis Stiff was born circa 1844 and married Nancy E. Johnson on Mar. 23, 1872. Eliza Stiff was born circa 1844 and married Robert M. Carlisle on Aug. 29, 1878. Thomas J. Stiff was born circa 1845 and married Louisa J. Conley on Oct. 25, 1877. Henry Stiff was born circa 1848 but died young. Sarah J. Stiff was born circa 1848 and married Jerome Tolbert on Jan. 26, 1871. Solomon Stiff was born circa 1854. Lorinda Stiff was born circa 1856 and married Jefferson Duncan on Mar. 18, 1877.

Beulah's grandfather was Thomas Jefferson Stiff of Saline Co., IL. On Oct. 24, 1877 he married Louisa J. Conley, daughter of John J. Conley and Susan Ward. John Conley was born in Ohio as was his wife Susan. Louisa Jane Conley was born Nov. 12, 1859. Susan Ward's father was born in New York, her mother in Ohio. By 1880, Thomas J. Stiff and his wife Louisa were living in Independence Township, Saline Co., IL. By 1900, the family had moved to Golconda Precinct of Golconda Village, Pope Co., IL. Thomas J. Stiff died Oct. 12, 1902 in Brownfield, Pope Co., IL. Louisa Jane (Conley) Stiff died July 12, 1906 in Pope Co., IL.

John and Beulah (Stiff) Lewis

They had the following children; Dora, Cora, Arthur, Della, Eva, Oliver, Rosa, and Virgil. Dora Stiff was born Sept. 25, 1878 and married first Ruben R. Givens on Jan. 14, 1899 then second marriage to Ross Threlkeld on Aug. 22, 1913. Cora Stiff was born Nov. 9, 1880 and died July, 1881. Arthur Stiff was born Feb. 9, 1880 and married Bruce Johnson on July 4, 1907. Della Stiff was born on July 15, 1888 and died Aug. 27, 1888. Eva Stiff was born on Dec. 8, 1889 and died the same day. Oliver Stiff was born on Dec. 8, 1889 and married Boneta McEntire on May 11, 1913. Rosa Stiff was born July 19, 1892 and married Clarence Simmons on Oct. 16, 1911. Virgil Stiff was born Nov. 7, 1896 and died Nov. 11, 1977. He had a military burial at Old Beech Cemetery in Posey Co., IN.

Beulah's father was Arthur Stiff who was born in Saline Co., IL. Arthur married Bruce Johnson, daughter of John T. Johnson and Mary Alice Jennings of Simpson Township, Johnson Co., IL. John T. was born in Illinois but his father and mother born in Tennessee. Mary Alice Jennings was born in Illinois as were her mother and father. Arthur Stiff lived in Brownfield, Pope Co., IL until moving to Posey Co., IN around 1909. The family then moved to Mt. Vernon, IN (Barter Street), whre they resided nearly 50 years. Arthur was employed by the railroad as a section-hand and also farmed some land near his Mt. Vernon home with a team of mules until around 1950. Arthur died Dec. 7, 1964 and is buried at Old Beech Cemetery. Bruce (Johnson) Stiff is also buried there having passed away on July 27, 1976. They had the following children: Rosa Lee, Earl, Lily May, Beulah Faye, Cora, Merle, Mary Lucile, Verlin, Doris Ellen, and others who died young. Rosa Lee was born Feb. 26, 1908 and married Robert Hutchinson on July 9, 1923. Earl Stiff was born July 22, 1909 and married Esther Mallory on July 1, 1939. Lily May was born Feb. 2, 1910 and died Feb. 26, 1913. Beulah Faye was born Apr. 28, 1914 and married John Ellis Lewis on Dec. 23, 1929. Cora was born Jan. 9, 1916 and died Mar. 12, 1919. Merle was born Mar. 9, 1919 and died Mar. 12, 1920. Mary Lucile was born Jan. 9, 1921 and married Norton Rowe on Nov. 1, 1939. Velin was born Feb. 26, 1926 and married Lois Claxton on Nov. 22, 1945. Doris Ellen was born Nov. 3, 1929 and married first Bob Johnson then married second Donald Clevenger on Feb. 25, 1948.

BRETT AND TRUDY STOCK FAMILY

Trudy Jean Williams was born on Feb. 17, 1964. She is the daughter of Ned Owen and Mary Elizabeth (Dixon) Williams. She grew up in rural Poseyville. Trudy is the second of four children. She graduated from North Posey High School in 1982 as Salutatorian. She graduated magna cum laude from the University of Southern Indiana in 1986 with a bachelor of science degree in accounting. While attending the university, Trudy worked part-time in the University's Business Affairs office as a clerk/typist. During the winter of 1986, Trudy began working at Harding, Shymanski & Company in Evansville as a staff accountant and is currently there as a Certified Public Accountant.

Brett and Trudy Stock 1978

Brett Alan Stock was born on Feb. 24, 1961. He is the son of William Gilmore and Barbara Jean (Roehr) Stock. He lived in Caborn until 1970 when the family built a home in Parker Settlement. Brett is the oldest of three children. He graduated from North Posey High School in 1979. Brett joined Core Laboratories in the summer of 1980 and continues to work as a Supervising Chemist with the company. Brett is a member of Poseyville Masonic Lodge #632 and the Ancient Accepted Scottish Rite N.M.J. Valley of Evansville, IN.

Brett and Trudy were married on May 12, 1984 at St. Paul's United Church of Christ in Evansville. During their first two years of marriage they resided in rural Wadesville. During the fall of 1986 they purchased Brett's grandparents' (Harold and Helen Roehr) home in Caborn. This property has been in the family since approximately 1846.

Brett and Trudy are members of St. Paul's United Methodist Church in Poseyville.

WILLIAM GILMORE STOCK & BARBARA JEAN (ROEHR) STOCK

Gilmore Stock, oldest son of four born to Emil & Vellora Stock who lived in Marrs Township, attended Stuckey School, graduated from Mt. Vernon High in 1955 and attended University of Evansville.

Barbara Jean (Roehr) Stock, daughter of Harold and Helen Roehr of Caborn in Marrs Township, attended Caborn School and graduated from Mt. Vernon High in 1956.

Married in November 1957 at St. John's Methodist Church in Caborn. Resided in Caborn for 13 years, then moved to present home in Robinson Township near Parker Settlement.

Gilmore was employed by Citizens Bank in Evansville, Farm Bureau Refinery and presently is employed by Moorman Mfg. Co. He was hired by Moorman's as a salesman in the northern Posey County area, promoted to District Sales Manager covering all of Posey County and part of Vanderburgh. For the past four years he has been State Sales Manager covering the southeastern part of Indiana and part of Kentucky.

Stock Family; Front Row L-R Barbara, Gilmore, Trudy (William Stock) Back Row L-R Jeff, Jennifer, Brett

Barbara was employed by the Posey County Extension Service for six years after that becoming a full time homemaker and mother. For the past 11 years has been employed by the newspapers in Evansville. Worked in the Press Business Office for seven years and for the past four years secretary to the Advertising Director.

We have three children: Brett, Jeff and Jennifer.

Brett was born February 1961, attended grade school at Marrs and South Terrace Elementary and graduated from North Posey High and attended USI. He is married to the former Trudy Williams of Poseyville and resides in Caborn. Brett is employed in Evansville by Core Laboratories, Inc. Jeff was born July 1964, attended grade school at Marrs and South Terrace Elementary and graduated from Noth Posey High. He attended Purdue University and graduated with a degree in Genetic Biology. Jeff presently resides in Cincinnati, OH and is employed in the research department at the Childrens Hospital Medical Center doing genetic research. Jennifer, born in October 1971 attended South Terrace Elementary and will graduate from North Posey High in 1990. She is president of her senior class and plans on attending college after graduation.

HAROLD NORRIS SUITS

Harold Norris Suits, the first child of Miles Harold and Elsie (Belt) Suits was born Apr. 21, 1943 in Livingston Co., KY. He graduated from Mount Vernon High School in 1961, and served active duty in the U.S. Navy from 1961-1963. He is now a mechanic at General Electric, where he has been employed since May 1977. Harold Norris married Beverly Ellen Gerth, born Oct. 17, 1950, and a 1968 gradute of Mount Vernon High School, in 1970. She is the daughter of Willard and Martha (Walker) Gerth. They are the parents of Brent Norris born Jan. 13, 1971 and Shane Evan born Feb. 7, 1975. They reside in Mount Vernon. His brothers are Ronald Eugene born Mar. 20, 1945 and Gary Dale born June 24, 1946.

His father's parents were Livingston Co., KY residents James Denfer Suits (1868-1948) and his wife Flora McDaniel (1891-1967), his father the last of eight children born to this couple, at Lola, KY Feb. 20, 1923. His mother's parents were Charles Harley Belt (1891-1967) and his wife Lula Kimsey (1901-1974), their child Elsie Marie was born July 27, 1923, at Tolu, Crittenden Co., KY. Harold Norris's great-grandparents were William and Ellen (Curnel) Suits, William and Alice (Watson) McDaniel, James O. and Lizzie (Thorp) Belt and Samuel and Henrietta (Johnson) Kimsey.

Beverly's mother's family decends from Alexander and Alias Mills of Wilkes Co., GA. Their youngest child David Alexander Mills (1775-1838) and his wife Mary Summers (1782-1860) settled in Posey before 1807. They were the parents of 12 children: Felix J. (1799-1873); Zimri (ca 1800-bef. 1860); Bethania Robb (1802-1885); Sarah Duckworth (1803-); James Seaborn (1804-bef. 1869); Fielden Nicholas (1805-1885); Susanna McFadin (1808-1884); David A. (1812-1854); William (1814-1861); Mary (Polly) Benner (1817-1904); Thomas (1819-) and Nancy Welborn (1821-1896).

Their son Zimri married Mary Redman a native of England in 1826.

Their children were: Alexander Mills (1829-1904); Jane Cully (1837-bef. 1870) and Susanna Donaldson (1833-1888). Beverly's ancestors Susanna married George Gale in 1849. He died in 1857, leaving her with their children to raise, Marindia Gale (1850-), Mary Jane Utley (1852-1874?), Zimri Gale (1854-1937), Augusta Wier (1856-1933), and George W. Gale (1857-bef. 1870). She became the third wife of William B. Donaldson (1817-1874) in 1866. Their children were Lanora Moore (1868-1931) and Cora J. Walker (1871-1938) the wife of Cornelius Walker.

(See Walker-York sketch).

JOHN M. AND WILLA J. TENBARGE

John M. and Willa (Billie) J. TenBarge are residents of Wadesville. John graduated from Poseyville High School in 1941 and attended two years of college at Brown University in Providence, RI. Willa J. graduated from Cynthiana High School in 1943 and attended Vincennes Business College. They were married Feb. 4, 1948. They have five children: Janet Lee, born Oct. 26, 1949; John Stephen, Dec. 11, 1950; James Michael, Mar. 18, 1956; Jean Ann, July 23, 1958; and Thomas Benjamin, Apr. 29, 1964.

John was born June 17, 1922 in Poseyville, the youngest son of John B. and Mary Reuter TenBarge. Willa J. was born in Otwell, IN on Oct. 29, 1925, the youngest daughter of William and Portia Traylor Mulkey. She moved to Posey County in 1930. After graduation from Vincennes Business College, Willa worked as a secretary until she married John. After graduation from Poseyville High School, John worked as a welder on LST ships at the Evansville Ship Yard until he joined the Navy in November 1942. Upon completion of the Navy V-12 program, he was commissioned an Ensign at Notre Dame University. He then served as a line officer on a Navy Destroyer until being placed on inactive duty in June 1946.

John M. TenBarge and Willa J. TenBarge

In September 1947 he purchased a grocery store in Wadesville from Elbert and Mollie Hanes. In February 1948 he and Willa were married and they moved to Wadesville. In March 1951 John was recalled to active Navy duty during the Korean War. He served 16 months as a Lieutenant on a Destroyer. During this period Willa, with their two children, moved to Poseyville, and Mollie Hanes operated the store until his return.

John and Willa operated the store (Johnny's Market) for 35 years, selling it to the Wendroths in 1983. In 1964 John and Willa built the Snak Shak restaurant in Wadesville and operated it for ten years. In 1973 they became part owners in T's restaurant in Poseyville. In 1984 they became part owners in T-Mart, a convenience store in Poseyville. In 1988 they sold their interest in both businesses and retired.

John was President and General Manager of The Wadesville Telephone Company, Inc. for 35 years, from 1950 until 1985. He was President and Resident Manager of Wadesville Homes, Inc., a low income housing project located in Wadesville for 23 years, from 1965 to 1988. He was one of the organizers and first President of the Wadesville Center Township Volunteer Fire Department. He served as President of the Wadesville Athletic Club for 20 years. He was an organizer and board member of the German Township Water District that brought a community water system to the Wadesville area.

John served as the first President of the Posey County Area Plan Commission. He also served as the first President of the Posey County Park Board.

JOSEPH C. TEN BARGE FAMILY

Joseph C. Ten Barge Sr. was born on Feb. 24, 1920 in Poseyville, IN. He graduated from the old Poseyville High School in 1938. He was a basketball player and was a captain of his team. In 1941 he was called to serve in the United States Army. While stationed in Hawaii he was recalled to the States for Army Air Corps training. He obtained his commission and was a B26 Bomber pilot until the end of the World War II. During High School Joe had worked for the local Texaco Agent and after the war he worked for Ray Bloom the Texaco Agent in Poseyville, IN. Joe attended Evansville College.

Joe's parents were Mary (Reuter) Ten Barge and John B. Ten Barge, local jeweller. Joe's grandfather, Bernard "Uncle Ben" Ten Barge ran a restaurant in Poseyville, IN. Joe has two brothers, John M. Ten Barge of Wadesville, IN and Maurice Ten Barge of New Haven, IN.

Seated: Joseph C. Ten Barge Sr. Carol Ann Ten Barge Standing (Left to Right) Joseph C. Ten Barge Jr. Carol Jo (Ten Barge) Droege Donald Cotrell Ten Barge

On Aug. 6, 1949 Joe married Carol Ann Cottrell, daughter of George B. Cottrell and Mildred (Antle) Cottrell. George B. Cottrell's parents were George N. Cottrell and Dolly (Cook) Cottrell, both from Warrick Co., IN. After graduating from Poseyville High School George B. Cottrell attended Butler University and Mildred Antle attended Lindenwood College in Missouri. Mildred Antle's parents were Peter "Pete" Antle and Delia (Carroll) Antle.

Joe's wife, Carol, after graduating from Poseyville High School attended the University of Chicago. Carol has four sisters, Betty Ruth Wade, Mary Lois Finn, Nancy Baker and Priscilla Rutledge and two brothers, George Antle Cottrell and Rodger Anthony Cottrell.

Joe and Carol have three children, Carol Jo, born in 1950, Joseph C. Ten Barge Jr., born in 1952 and Donald Cottrell Ten Barge, born in 1957. They have seven grandchildren. Samuel W. Lawrence III, Christine Carol Droege and Michael Edmund Droege are the children of Carol Jo and James Droege. Ryan Joseph Ten Barge, Andrea Marie Ten Barge and Jason Christopher Ten Barge are the children of Donald and Olivia "Lee" (Thornburg) Ten Barge. Dorian is the son of Joseph Jr. and Christine (Horn) Ten Barge.

Joe and Carol have always resided in Poseyville, IN. Since 1951 they have been in business for themselves, first operating Ten Barge Texaco Service and at present operating Ten Barge Oil Co, Inc., T-Mart Inc. and T's Restaurant, all in Poseyville, IN.

WILLIAM CLINTON THOMPSON ANNA MARJORIE THOMPSON

Bill and Ann, lifelong residents of the Mt. Vernon area have one daughter, Pamelia Jeanne, born July 15, 1945, who is married to Fausto Agostinelli of Milano-Vaprio D'Adda, Italy.

Bill was born July 14, 1923, at 821 Canal Street. He was the youngest child of William Lewis and Minnie Blanche (Watkins) Thompson. His oldest brother Frederick Gerald was born Aug. 5, 1912, died July 30, 1972, was married to Lenora Cobb, May 5, 1934. Two sons of this union were Gerald Harlan, born July 27, 1935, died Mar. 6, 1982; and Frederick Charles born Aug. 24, 1944.

He had a sister Laura Elizabeth, born Sept. 6, 1916, died Oct. 11, 1959, who was married to William Harold Lewis.

Bill attended Central Elementary and graduated from Mt. Vernon High in 1941, and Kansas City Watch-repair School in 1948. Ann attended Dunn, Upton, Black, and Central Elementary School, and later graduated from Mt. Vernon High in 1940. Ann earned a Medical Technology Registry and an Associate of Science from the University of Evansville, and a B.S. in Health Services at the University of Southern Indiana.

Bill and Ann met in high school and married July 12, 1942, at Cupid's Corner in Yuma, AZ by Rev. J.G. Anderson with Robert Lee McCain and June McKenzie as attendants. Mr. Thompson was stationed at Camp Mahan Naval Base in San Diego.

When Bill was two and a half years old, his father died on Dec. 18, 1925, and at five years old, his mother died on Oct. 1, 1928. From age two he lived in the home of Charles, Edith, and Charles Robert Hutson, whom he regarded as his younger brother.

Bill's military experience began in Company "F" Fifth Infantry Indiana State Guard with his friends Harold "Bud" Cox and James Goss. He was discharged on Mar. 1, 1942, with the rank of Sergeant to enlist in the United States Navy. He was accepted on Apr. 17, 1942, and traveled from Evansville to Indianapolis to the Naval Training Station in San Diego. He entered Quarter-master Training School and completed the course on Oct. 23, 1942, with high scores.

Bill was transferred to the Little Creek (Norfolk, VA) amphibious unit and served on the U.S.S. L.C.I. (L) #20 in North Africa (Oran, Algiers, Casablanca), Sicily (Gela, Palermo), and Italy (Salerno, Anzio) where his ship was bombed. In spring of 1944, he returned on the U.S.S. Buchner to Norfolk, VA. In the Spring of 1945, he left on L.S.T. #984 for Japan. Crossing the international date line on June 23, 1945, he was initiated into the Order of the Golden Dragon.

Mr. Thompson arrived at wars end in Yokahama, Japan, where he boarded the U.S.S. General Sturgis leaving Yokahama on Sept. 26, 1945. On board the Sturgis were two friends that were also from Mt. Vernon; they were Marshall Overfield and Marvin Pharr. Marshall kept him filled with steaks. Bill was discharged in Saint Louis on Oct. 17, 1945, as Quartermaster 1C. Bill died Mar. 13, 1983, at his home, 418 East Third.

Bill's paternal family consisted of his father William, Charles H., John Joseph, Minnie Agnes (Shaw), Julia Ann, and Rose Elizabeth (Ashworth). The family of John Henry, Bill's grandfather, is listed in the Posey County Atlas 1900, under Lewis T. and Nancy Underwood. Lewis T's brothers and sisters were William, born 1826; Henry Reason, born 1832; Lucinda, born 1835, married Elias Underwood and later Henry James; Julia Ann, born 1837, married Stephen Claycomb; George Rowan, born 1839; and Joseph, born 1841 (died in infancy). Stephen, father of Lewis T. was born between 1804 and 1806, died Oct. 19, 1867. He married Bridgette Lampkins, who died Aug. 8, 1841, and later Catherine Murphy, daughter of Abraham and Mary, died Nov. 16, 1910. Catherine married Stephen on Jan. 15, 1843. Their children were Henry Abraham, Mary E., Stephen D., and Lydia.

Stephen came from North Carolina to Perry County traveling part of the journey by flatboat. His destination was Louisiana or Texas. He planned to stay at Rome's Landing through the winter, but remained there for a lifetime near Leopold. He gave 40 acres of land to the Saint Augustine Church. He was god parent to many of the community. Due to financial reverses resulting from the Civil War and the developing of marital problems, he committed suicide. This act caused a rift in the family with the Catholic Church as burial was not allowed on sacred soil.

Bill's maternal family consisted of his mother Minnie Blanche, who had eight brothers and sisters: Anna Barter (Wolfinger), French, Edith (Hutson), Robert C., Paul, Clara "Doll" (Dausman), William Gilbert, and Martha Elfrieda (Teeter).

Minnie's father Clinton Watkins had three sisters and one brother: Americus Mandela, Martha (Hutchinson), James Milton, and Laura (Allison).

Clinton's father was Robert and his mother was Nancy Crunk.

Nancy's father was William Duncan Crunk and her mother was Nancy Hunter.

William's father was John. Nancy had two brothers and one sister: William, James, and Fanny.

Ann's father was Richard Harvey Head and her mother was Flora Tongate. Ann had two brothers: Ernest Coleman, died at 21 months old, born Nov. 11, 1916, and James Dorsey, born Mar. 22, 1919, died Nov. 10, 1971.

167

HERMAN J.W. AND CHRISTINE (ROCKER) UHDE

Herman Uhde was a lifelong resident of Posey County. Born Dec. 13, 1879, to Ludwig (Louis) Uhde (1842-1918) and Dorothea (Stallman) Uhde (1845-1914), Herman was one of nine children.

Ludwig (Louis) was born in Germany and came to Posey County in 1866 via New York and Huntingburg, IN. Dorothea (an orphan) also came to Posey County from Germany. Following their marriage, they settled on 80 acres in what is now Black Township near Upton, four miles northwest of Mt. Vernon.

Here they built a four-room log home. As their family grew, so did the home—to 11 rooms. The house was torn down in 1970.

Louis Uhde was a successful lifelong farmer. With the help of his wife, three sons and six daughters he accumulated several acres of Posey County farmland.

Herman and Chrstine Uhde

Herman Uhde married Kunigunde Gebbhard (1884-1912) in 1905. Four children were born to this union: Clara (one year), Otto H. (Ellen Bottomley), Ralph F. (Ethel Rhodes), and Oscar H. (Lucille Cotner). At their marriage, they moved onto the farm and lived there together with their family until her death in 1912.

Christine E. (Rocker) Uhde (1884-1954) was the daughter of William Rocker (1836-1910) and Katherine (Damm) Rocker.

William Rocker was born in Heffel, Darmstadt, Germany and came to New Orleans, LA in 1855. After a few years, he moved to Evansville, IN, where he met and married Katherine Damm on May 4, 1869. Four children were born to this couple, three girls and one boy.

In January, 1876, William moved his young family to Columbus, KY on the Mississippi River where he engaged in the manufacture of potteryware. He followed this business successfully until 1907.

Upon William's death and the death of his wife, the youngest daughter, Christine, came to Evansville, IN by steamer. Here she visited cousins in both Evansville and Robinson Township in Posey County, where she was introduced to the young widower, Herman Uhde, by a Robinson Township school teacher, William Riecken.

The couple married May 17, 1914, in the home of William and Kate (Damm) Brandt. Following the marriage, they traveled to Upton by horse and buggy to live in the homeplace.

To this union were born seven children: Albert (two weeks), Clifforded E. (Sudia Mercer), Harold L. (Ruby Walker), Gilbert L. (Margaret Madden), Adrene C. (Edward J. Lutterman), Katherine D. (Woodrow McFadin, Sr.), and Clarence E. (Dorothy Walters).

With the help of his wife and nine children, the farm prospered once more. A landmark barn was built on the property in 1921 from lumber cut from the farm. It still stands as sturdy as when it was built and where all the many descendants have played.

Christine Uhde passed away Nov. 15, 1954. Herman Uhde spent his entire 89 years in the house and on the farm where he was born. He died Apr. 27, 1969. His son Harold and wife moved from the city of Mt. Vernon into a new house on the farm in 1970 and lived there until Harold's death in 1976.

A fourth and fifth generation family, Woodrow McFadin, Jr. (Theresa Blakley) and their three children, now live on and farm the farm.

REV. HILARY F. VIECK

Rev. Hilary F. Vieck, son of Christopher and Cecelia (Kaiser) Vieck, of Rural Route 5, Vincennes, IN, was born Aug. 1, 1929. He attended St. Thomas Grade School, St. Meinrad High and College ('43-'51), St. Meinrad School of Theology ('51-'55). Vieck was ordained on June 4, 1955 by Bishop Henry J. Grimmelsman, of Evansville, at the Assumption Cathedral in Evansville.

Rev. Hilary F. Vieck

Father Vieck's first assignment was to St. John's Catholic Church, Loogootee, IN in August of 1955. Other assignments were St. Mary's, WA; St. Mary's Hospital, as Chaplain; St. Philip Neri, Bicknell; Corpus Christi, Evansville; and St. Matthew's, Mt. Vernon. The latter assignment began on Aug. 11, 1981.

As pastor of St. Matthew's, Rev. Vieck has been instrumental in initiating a strong religious education program in the school of St. Matthew's and the religious education program for young and adults. During this period there has been additonal properties purchased. In 1983 St. Matthew's parish purchased the Fogas property on the corner of 4th and Walnut. This has been used as a rental office space and a dwelling-apartment. In 1988 the lot and Chalman building on the corner of 5th and Walnut was acquired from David Schroeder. The house was demolished and the entire space has been made into a parking lot.

As a leader in the community, Rev. Vieck has served as president of Mt. Vernon Ministerial Association for two different one-year terms. He has also been active in the Posey County Soil and Water Conservation Development. In 1983 and 1986 he was awarded as conservation Minister of the Year. Father Vieck is a member of the Elks Lodge and Western Hills Country Club of Mt. Vernon. Father Vieck has been a priest for 34 years.

DR. L. JOHN AND MARGARET K. VOGEL

Lawrence John and Margaret Kennedy Vogel grew up near Lamar in Spencer Co., IN, and came to Mt. Vernon in 1944.

Dr. Vogel was born at Mandan, ND, where his father homesteaded and lived there and in Kansas until he was five years old. His parents were Robert Frederick and Louise Wohlleb Vogel and his grandparents were Lawrence and Katherine Held Vogel and John and Caroline Beren Wohlleb. Dr. Vogel graduated from Grandview High School, attended Evansville College and received his MD degree from Indiana University School of Medicine.

Margaret's parents were Kenneth K. and Anna Menninger Kennedy and her grandparents were David F. and Anna Schreifer Kennedy and August V. and Caroline Obrecht Menninger. Margaret graduated from Dale High School and Indiana State Teachers College, Terre Haute.

Dr. L. John and Margaret K. Vogel

Dr. Vogel began his Family Practice in Mt. Vernon Feb. 7, 1944, at 422 1/2 Main St. From July 1952 to July 1954 he served as a Medical Officer in the Army at Fort Sam Houston, Camp Breckinridge, Camp Atterbury and Fort Knox. He resumed his practice in 1954 at 131 West Third St., built a new office at 722 Main Street in 1968, and moved to the Mt. Vernon Medical Center at 1900 West Fourth St. in 1977. In 1978 he was joined in practice by his son Dr. Gordon Vogel who had specialized in Internal Medicine. He retired in January 1987.

The Vogels raised four children who all attended Hedges Elementary School and graduated from Mt. Vernon High School.

Stanley John Vogel was born Nov. 14, 1944, graduated from Wabash College and Washington University School of Medicine, St. Louis. He served a residency in Internal Medicine at the University of Michigan, was a Medical Officer in the Army at Heidelburg, Germany, 1974-76, returned to Washington University for additional training and in 1978 began his practice of Hematology and Oncology in Topeka, KS. He married Sandra Kay Williams, daughter of Bill and Essie Williams, June 14, 1969, and they have two sons: David born 1971 and Byron born 1974. Sandy is Director of Development for Washburn University School of Law.

Anne Louise Vogel was born Sept. 13, 1946, graduated from Earlham College and received an MAT degree from Washington University. She married Ronald L. Rossi of St. Louis June 28, 1970; they live in St. Louis and have three children: Susan born 1977, John born 1979 and Adam born 1984. Anne teaches mathematics in the Burroughs School.

Gordon Allen Vogel was born Feb. 8, 1950, attended Wabash College, graduated from Washington University School of Medicine, and served a residency in Internal Medicine at Ohio State University. He married Gayle Stubbs of Birmingham,

AL, Mar. 10, 1979, and they have two sons: Todd born in 1981 and Mark born in 1985. Gayle is Chief Microbiologist at Deaconess Hospital.

Ellen Vogel was born Aug. 18, 1956, graduated from DePauw University and received an MBA degree at Washington University. She married William Seeman of Connecticut June 22, 1980; they live in Gales Ferry, CT, and have a daughter Stephanie born in 1986. Ellen is an accountant for United Nuclear Corporation.

John and Margaret are members of Trinity United Church of Christ; both have been School Board members and have been active on various boards and in community organizations.

WALKER-YORK

James W. Walker (1833-1926), the son of John and Sarah Walker, was born in Posey County. He was a landowner at Savah, IN and a Union Soldier. He married Martha D. (Patsey) York (1835-1919) on Sept. 16, 1857. Patsey's father, William York (1806-1881) the son of Samuel York, migrated from Randolph, NC and married Sarah (Sallie) French (1807-d. bef. 1878), the daughter of James French. Their ancestors were large landowners at Savah and through this family's philanthropy land was given for Walker School and Bethesda General Baptist Church.

To this union were born: Margaret (Meg) Carrell (1858-1935), Thomas (1860-1936), Sarah (Sallie) Aldrich Veron (1862-1935), James Lowrey (1864-1946), Cornelius Augustus (1867-1946), Lemuel E. (1869-?), Delmar Didimus (1871-1953), Emma E. Hironimus (1875-1952).

Cornelius Augustus married Cora J. Donaldson (1871-1938) in 1892. Born to this union were Loren Donaldson (1893-1961), Fred Augustus (1899-1966), Cornelius, a Savah farmer and Cora are buried at Beech Grove.

James W. and Martha (York) Walker

Loren Donaldson Walker, their oldest son was a farmer near Savah and what is now Harmonie Park and drove a school bus to Smith School. He married Nell Lee York (1900-) Nov. 6, 1920. She is a native of this county the daughter of Sherman O. York and Annie L. (James) York. Nell was working as a teacher in South Metropolitan School District when she retired in 1966, having first taught in one and two room schools over the county. Three children blessed this marriage, all living at this time, Ruby Lee (1921-) graduated 1939 from Mount Vernon High School and worked at the A&P Food Store, Garment Factory, and retired from the Farm Bureau Refinery in 1983 after over 32 years. In 1946 she married Harold Lester Uhde (1919-1976) the son of Herman J. (1879-1969) and Christine E. (Rocker) Uhde (1884-1954). After Harold's death Ruby married in 1978 to Alvis Meeks (1923-). There are no children to either union.

Second child: Martha Ellen (1923-) a lifelong resident of Posey graduated in 1940 from Mt. Vernon High School, she was employed by Kilroy and Espenscheid Lawyers, Draft Board, Otis Allyn Abstractor, and the Credit Bureau of Posey County. She was married in 1946 to Willard H. Gerth (1918-1988) the son of Albert Charles (1890-1956) and Nellie S. Reed (1889-1953). Three children blessed this union; Darlene Ann McConnell (1946-), Beverly Ellen Suits (1950-) and Willard Scott (1958-). See Eldon & Darlene McConnell and Harold and Beverly Suits sketches for family continuation.

Third child: Gerald Fred Walker (1934 -) was born in Posey County. He graduated in 1953 from Indiana State School for the Deaf, Indianapolis, IN. Gerald served his apprenticeship in linotyping with local newspapers then worked at United Color Press, Dayton, OH. Gerald is now custodian with Mt. Vernon Metropolitan School district working at the high school.

WALLACE

Zenas and Anna Wallace were both born in Gibson County, but moved to Posey County and went to school 12 years together, graduating in the class of 1915 from Cynthiana High School. They were married July 26, 1919, and moved to Gibson County where they raised their six children, who all graduated from Haubstadt High School. All those years, however, they lived not very far removed from Posey County, living on Highway 68 just beyond the county line, then west of 65, back on 65 north of Cynthiana, then east of New Liberty Church in 1927, and then in 1935 to the then Julia Lowe property almost adjacent to the county line. In 1960 they bought the small farm that had belonged to the Newman girls just east of Cynthiana, and they spent the rest of their time back in Posey County.

In 1969, they celebrated their 50th Wedding Anniversary with a family celebration and reception at New Liberty Church.

Zenas farmed, and in 1966 became a rural sub mail carrier out of Cynthiana, which he kept until shortly after his 80th birthday. He died suddenly Dec. 16, 1977.

Zenas and Anna Wallace

Zenas was born Mar. 24, 1897, the son of Emanuel Fritz and Kissiah Elizabeth Blythe Wallace. His brothers were Elzie, Floyd, Neal, Arch and his sister Margaret Rice.

His antecedents include the Mangrum, Gwaltney, Boren, Murphy and Douglas families. The Wallaces came from Ireland to Maryland, Virginia, Kentucky and then to Gibson Co., IN. The Boren's came from Ireland to Pennsylvania, Maryland, to Kentucky, Tennessee and then to Gibson Co., IN.

Anna was born June 25, 1897, to Alpha Erwin and Melva Ethel Knowles Gee. Anna died Feb. 18, 1986. She had brothers John and Melvin and sisters Iona Williams and Helen Wilhite.

The Gees had lived in Warrick County, but originally came from Massachusetts by way of Geauga Co., OH. The Knowles family came from Delaware to Georgia, Tennessee, Kentucky then to Indiana.

Antecedents were Carter, Boren, Chastain, Pomeroy.

Zenas and Anna had six children, Melvin Wayne, who married Ruth Heiser. Their daughters are Linda and Becky.

Rachael married Al Burklow, then Dave Lefton, and mothered his two children. Ruth Anna married C.F. Funkhouser and had children, Coral Ann, Martha, Richard, Darrell, John and Bradley.

Mary Jane married Forrest Brown and her children are Jack and Judy. After Forrest's death, Mary married Henry Lippert.

Kenneth Wesley married Marilyn Dearing and their children are Sandra, Terry, Donna and Lori.

Nancy Lee married Glenn Ramsey and had children David, Susan, and Mark. *Submitted by Ruth Funkhouser*

GEORGE WALLING

George Walling, born in Posey County Nov. 29, 1916, is the seventh of eight children born to Hugh Lawson and Charlotte (Ward) Walling. His parents named him Ulysses for Dr. Ulysses Whiting, the attending physician. Knowing he was uncomfortable with the name Ulysses, a high school teacher nicknamed him "Chick". In 1945, when he obtained a copy of his birth certificate, he discovered Dr. Whiting had named him George. All legal documents bearing his name had to be corrected.

His father was born in White Co., IL and his mother in Posey County as were his siblings Mabel Margaret, Homer Alonzo, Edith, twins Norton Hugh and Norman Ward, John Felix and an unnamed boy who died at birth.

George graduated from Mt. Vernon High School and recieved bachelor and master degrees from Indiana State University.

For the 1941-42 school year, he taught in Lawrence Co., IN.

During World War II, George served in the Air Force from July 1942 to December 1945. He trained at the Air Force Armament Training School at Lowry Field, Denver and the Air Force Base in Waycross, GA.

Assigned to the 311th Fighter Group Headquarters, George left to serve overseas with the 10th Air Force in the China-Burma-India Theater. His squadron was located at Dinjon in Assam, a Province in northern India. The 311th defended the Brahmaputra Valley, protected the northern air route to China and offensive operations against Japanese troop and supply concentrations in northern Burma in preparation for a drive to the south by General Stilwell's Chinese-American forces.

George's duty at Headquaters was to transpose information received from Intelligence onto maps the pilots used on missions.

After one year in India, the Group Headquarters were moved to Tingkawk Sakan, Burma, to further co-operation between ground and air units in the C-B-I Theater.

Following three months in Burma, the entire group moved over the Hump to China where the group was assigned to General Chennault's 14th Air Force - known as the "Flying Tigers". Group

169

Headquarters were based at Pungchacheng. Here the primary mission assigned the group was protection of B-29s and their bases.

Before T/Sgt. Walling was discharged from service in December 1945, he was awarded a Bronze Star Medal for Meritorious Achievement. During his 41 months in service, he encircled the world.

George returned to Mt. Vernon and became an Industrial Arts teacher for the Evansville-Vanderburgh School Corporation.

On Dec. 22, 1947, George married Jean Alice Stinson in the Salem Methodist Church at Evansville. Rev. Robert E. Green officiated. Jean, born in Vanderburgh County Feb. 25, 1923, is the daughter of Walter Addison and Martha (Niehaus) Stinson - both natives of Vanderburgh County.

George and Jean have three children - Donald Edwin, Alice Jean and James Alan. The family attended the First Methodist Church during the 14 years they lived near Bufkin in Black Township. In 1962 they moved to Perry Township, Vanderburgh County.

George taught at Culver and Perry Heights Schools for a total of 39 years before retiring in 1982.

WILLIAM L. WASSMER FAMILY

William Wassmer was born Oct. 21, 1935, one mile north of Poseyville on Highway 165.

His great, great grandfather Wendel Wassmer, along with his brother Marcus, came from the Black Forest area (Schwarzwald) of the State of Baden approximately 1830. They were barrelmakers by trade and worked in Toronto, Canada for six years before deciding to walk south to America, due to the extreme cold winter in Canada. They walked to Southern Indiana to what is now the St. Wendel area and decided to stay due to the good white oak timber in that area. Less than a year later, they decided to walk back to Toronto and back to their old jobs, but when they arrived there, Canada was having very difficult times and again the two boys walked, for the third time, the trip from Toronto to southern Indiana, this time to stay for good.

The year was 1836 or 1837, Wendel purchased 40 acres. June 18, 1838, partly where the church and cemetery is today. He donated seven acres for a church and cemetery and the first log church was built in 1842 and numbered 20 families. It was built in five days and the first priest was Father Roman Weinzapfel.

St. Wendel was named in honor of Wendel Wassmer and his patron Saint Wendelin, the patron saint of Rural Folk (554-617). Wendel's brother, Marcus, never married and lived with Wendel and his family until his death in 1846, at the age of 36.

William L. Wassmer Family

The present church was built in 1853, directly over Marcus's grave. They lived across the road close to where the St. Wendel Bank sits today.

Wendel (1801-1894) married Katharina Mueller (1820-1899), daughter of Nicholas and Catherine (Betz) Mueller, on May 4, 1841, at the home of Martin Kohl. Mass was held in the peoples homes before the church was built.

They had ten children of which my great grandfather Marcus (named after Wendel's brother) was the oldest son. Wendel and Kate lived all their lives close to the church.

My great grandfather Marcus (1843-1918) married Magdalena Miller (1850-1939) in 1869 and they had 17 children of which grandfather Andrew Wassmer was the oldest son. They also lived all their lives close to St. Wendel.

My grandfather Andrew (1872-1941) married Matilda Hillenbrand (1873-1959) on Nov. 14, 1899 and they had eight children of which my father Clem Wassmer (1900-1972) married Mary L. Sauer (1912-) in 1932 and they had seven children. They lived all their married lives north of Poseyville, my mother and brother still live there.

William married Eileen Elpers, daughter of Alois and Marie (Halbig) Elpers, on Aug. 30, 1948. They have two daughters, Rhonda (b-1960) and married to Greg Davis, and Gayla (b. 1962) married to David Straw. William and Eileen have one grandchild, Leah, daughter of David and Gayla Straw. Rhonda and Greg live in Colorado Springs, CO, and David, Gayla and Leah live in Wadesville, TN.

William and Eileen lived all their married life at their present address, two miles north of Poseyville on Hwy. 165. *Submitted by William L. Wassmer*

CHARLES THOMAS WEILBRENNER

Charles Thomas Weilbrenner and Myra (Volz) Weilbrenner are residents of Western Black Township. Thomas graduated from St. Matthew's Catholic School in 1956, Mt. Vernon High School in 1960 and Purdue University with a B.S. in Agriculture Economics in 1964. Tom's high school graduating class of 1960 was the last class to graduate from the old high school at 6th and Canal Street (site of the present junior high school). Myra graduated from St. Theresa Catholic School in 1962, Rex Mundi High School in 1966, and Devry's Beauty School in 1967, all of them in Evansville, IN. Thomas and Myra were married on Nov. 29, 1969 at St. Joseph Catholic Church in Evansville. They have two children; Julie Ann and Alex Jay.

Myra (Volz) Weilbrenner was the oldest of four children of Leo and Ann Volz of Evansville. Her brothers are Rex Volz and Phillip Volz of Evansville and Nicholas Volz of Mt. Vernon. Leo was the eighth of 12 children of Nicholas (1885-Sept. 30, 1952) and Katherine (1882-July 13, 1950) Volz of Siberia, IN, located near St. Meinrad, IN. Leo (born Apr. 5, 1920) grew up on the family farm. At the age of 20 he moved to Evansville. In February 1942, he joined the Air Force and served with distinction, serving mainly in the South Pacific. At his discharge during May of 1945 he had attained the rank of Staff Sergeant. On Sept. 28, 1946 he married Angela Ruxer of St. Meinrad, IN. Angela (born Jan. 3, 1926) was the fourth of five children born to Frank and Aurelia (Feb. 26, 1908-Apr. 4, 1985) (Becher) Ruxer at St. Meinrad. Both Leo and Ann's families are of German descent.

Thomas was the oldest child of Charles Manford (July 31, 1907-Feb. 10, 1984) and Dorothy (Lynch) (born July 23, 1904) Weilbrenner. Tom has one sister, Ann Tepool of Wadesville, and one brother, George Andrew Wielbrenner of Mt. Vernon. Tom farms in Western Black Township in partnership with his brother Andy. Manford worked at People's Bank and Trust Company and before that at First National Bank for several years in addition to operating Hillcrest Orchard west of Mt. Vernon - the same farm on which Tom now lives. Manford was the oldest of three children of Carl A. (Mar. 4, 1880 - Mar. 28, 1950) and Anna (Mann) (Mar. 14, 1881-July 27, 1964) Weilbrenner. Their other children were Louise married to Robert J. Moll and Helen deceased. Carl and Anna were married on Oct. 25, 1906 and lived at the family home at 518 College Avenue (site of the present library). Carl operated a grocery store in Mt. Vernon along with operating a fruit orchard and nursery (started in 1911) in Western Black Township. Carl was regarded as one of the outstanding horticulturist in the nation as well as a pioneer in the grafting of fruit and nut trees. In 1939 Carl produced the largest peach ever grown in the world (26 1/2 oz.), as far as the official record of the USDA is concerned. On Carl's farm was a log house used as a fruit packing house-that was one of the oldest buildings in Posey County having been constructed by the father of George D. Rowe in 1818. An English Walnut tree, on the family farm, planted by Carl was the first of its kind grown east of the Mississippi River.

Carl Weilbrenner was the third of five children of George Andrew Weilbrenner and Henrietta (Gronemeier) Weilbrenner. George was born on Dec. 15, 1849 in Germany and came to America when he was two years old. For three years his family lived in New York City and moved to Mt. Vernon in 1854. He went to public schools here and helped his father in the grocery business. Later he became part-owner and, after his father's death, took over the store. The grocery store, located at 415 Main Street, was later the site of Gronemeier Hardware Store and Bud's Hardware. He and his wife were married in 1875. Henrietta was born Aug. 11, 1854 and died Dec. 14, 1917. George died on Aug. 31, 1914 after a ten month siege of sickness caused by a fall in an elevator shaft at his grocery store.

George's parents had five children and were born and raised in Oberschiff Oim Boxbergym Baden, Germany and came to America in 1851. George Michael Weilbrenner was born June 17, 1824 and died on Oct. 1, 1898. His wife Caroline (Ries) Weilbrenner was born Sept. 7, 1821 and died on July 18, 1873.

Dorothy (Lynch) Weilbrenner was the only child of Thomas Lynch (Mar. 12, 1980-Mar. 11, 1943), born in Winston-Salem, NC, and Della (McGee) Lynch (1884-February 1962), born in Terre Haute, IN. Mr. Lynch was a coal mine superintendent in Linton, IN at his death. Dorothy, born in Terre Haute, IN graduated from DePaul University at Greencastle, IN with a Bachelor of Arts degree in 1927. She taught in a high school near Bogalosa, LA for a time, worked in the 4-H Department at the University of Illinois, worked as a Home Agent in Ottawa, IL, worked at Purdue University as State Leader of Rural Housing, and worked as 4-H agent in Green Co., IN (Bloomfield). On Feb. 5, 1935, Dorothy came to Mt. Vernon as the first Home Demonstration Agent for Posey County during her tenure here, she organized the first 4-H Clubs in the county. During the 1937 flood, Dorothy was in charge of preparing meals at the Coliseum for all people in the county made homeless by the rising Ohio and Wabash Rivers. She and Manford were married on July 12, 1940 at St. Matthews Church in Mt. Vernon. Dorothy's family is of English descent.

LAWRENCE NICHOLAS WEINTRAUT AND ANNA A. WEINTRAUT

Lawrence Nicholas Weintraut was born in Shelby County on Nov 5, 1898. He was the son of Peter Weintraut, a farmer, and Elizabeth Bachmann Weintraut. While Lawrence was attending Jasper College he became acquainted with Anna A. Maurer. She was visiting a brother, Joseph, a student at the same school.

Anna was the daughter of Simon F. Maurer and Isabelle Betz Maurer. Both her parents were of German descent. They had six children all born and raised in Posey County. Simon Maurer owned and operated a grocery store all his life. The store was located on West Second Street in Mt. Vernon, IN.

Lawrence and Anna were married at St. Matthew Catholic Church in Mt. Vernon on July 13, 1920. After their marriage they resided in Shelbyville, IN for the first two years and then moved to Posey County for their entire married life. Their children are Elizabeth Ann, Lawrence Nicholas, Jr., Rosemary, Jane Irene, Joan, Joseph E. and Martha Isabelle. Lawrence was an identical twin and he and Anna had two sets of twins.

Elizabeth Ann married Donald Murphy Fuelling. Their children: Donna Marie, Stephen Craig, Ann, Mary Jane, David Murphy, Martha, John Nicholas, Nancy Elizabeth, Anthony James, and Sally Rose.

Lawrence Nicholas Weintraut, Jr. married Pauline Woods and their children are Lawrence Nicholas Weintraut III, this name has been carried on for three generations, Marie, Jeffrey, and Andrew G.

Rosemary the third child born to Lawrence and Anna Weintraut died in 1956.

Jane Irene is retired from Indiana Bell Telephone Company. She resides at the family home for 51 years with her sister Martha Isabell. Martha graduated from St. Mary's School of Nursing and is employed at General Electric Company.

Joan married Arthur Ashworth and they reside at RR #1, Mt. Vernon, IN. Their children are: Arthur Jr., Susan Ann, Kathleen, and Amy Louise.

Joseph E. is a twin brother of Joan. Joseph married Jenny Sue Fuelling and their children are: Jody Ann, Matthew Lee, Mark G., John Joseph, and Betsy.

JOE T. AND MARY ANN WEINZAPFEL

Joe T. and Mary Ann Weinzapfel are residents of Marrs Township, Posey County. They reside at their family farm on 6712 Old Lower Mt. Vernon Road, where they've lived for the last 17 years.

Joe and Mary Ann married Oct. 3, 1953 when he returned from the armed forces, resided in Vanderburgh County until 1955 when they moved to Posey County, and rented farmland until they moved to their present address. They are the parents of four sons and one daughter. Rick J. born Apr. 12, 1955, Steve B., born Apr. 17, 1956, Ronnie W. born Sept. 26, 1958, Bart A. born Sept. 10, 1961 and Holly A. born Dec. 31, 1966. All are graduates of Mt. Vernon High School.

Rick graduated from Purdue in 1977 with a Bachelor's Degree in Agronomy, married Katherine D. Maier of Wadesville Feb. 25, 1978. They have two daughters Jennifer L. born Mar. 13, 1982 and Megan L. born Oct. 26, 1985.

Joe T. and Mary Ann Weinzapfel

After graduation from MVSHS in 1975 Steven went into farming with his dad. He married Debra L. Brown of Mt. Vernon Mar. 18, 1978. They have two children Amy M. born Apr. 21, 1979 and Brent A. born Dec. 22, 1981.

Ronnie graduated from Purdue in 1978 with an Associate Degree in Animal Science. He married Maria C. Moers from Evansville June 14, 1980 and are the parents of three children Ashley M. born Dec. 4, 1982, Krista D. born May 22, 1985, and Ryan M. born Dec. 30, 1988.

Bart graduated from MVSHS in 1979 and works at Bristol Myers in Evansville where he resides.

Holly will graduate in May of 1989 from the University of Southern Indiana with Bachelor's degrees in both Business Administration and Marketing. She currently resides at home.

Joe was born in Vanderburgh County, on Jan. 27, 1931 and went to school at St. Phillip's in Posey County and Reitz Memorial in Evansville. He was born the son of Alois and Mary A. (Humpert), Weinzapfel born Sept. 23, 1891 and Mar. 27, 1894 respectively, and the youngest of seven, five brothers, Anthony, Clarence, Bernard, Linus, Paul (Pete) and one sister Mary Rose Naab. He served 21 months in the army during the Korean Conflict from 1950-1953, 14 of which were served in Korea. He has been a self-employed farmer since then. He also served 12 years (1970-1982) on the Posey County Council and has been a director of People's Bank and Trust Co. in Mt. Vernon since 1972. He is owner and manager of Weinzapfel Farms along with the three oldest sons Rick, Steve, and Ron.

Joe's paternal grandparents were Frank and Elizabeth (Soellner) Weinzapfel. Maternal grandparents were Anton and Anna (Schutte) Humpert. His great grandparents were Michael born 1820 and Catherine (Helfrich) Weinzapfel. Michael immigrated to the United States in 1847 from Ungersheim-Canton Scultz on the Upper Rhine. This is the Alsace area of France which at that time belonged to the Germans and is now the property of France.

Mary Ann was born in Nov. 9, 1930, the daughter of Alfred J. and Margaret (Ritzert) Mohr. She attended St. Matthew's School and is a graduate of MVHS. She has one sister Rosalie C. Spindler and three brothers Alfred A., Henry J. and Gerald Mohr. Her father Alfred J. was born in 1904 in Louisville, KY. Her mother, Margaret B. Ritzert was born in 1900 to Henry J. (born 1864) and Mary A. (Dobes) (born 1870) Ritzert, has one sister Olivia Wargel. Her grandfather was a prominent farmer in the Caborn area. Her paternal great grandfather, Michael Ritzert born 1801 in Biblis came to America in 1847 with his children, one of whom was Henrich Ritzert—Margaret's paternal grandfather. He was born Nov. 17, 1828 in Biblis-Darmstadt Hesse. He came to America in 1847. Barbara Krach born June 24, 1834 in Diedesheim came to America in 1856. The two married Jan. 6, 1857.

THE WENDEROTH-CAVETT FAMILIES

The Wenderoth family came to the United States from Germany. Henry Wenderoth, Senior and Fredrika Bender were married aboard ship by the captain in 1856. They settled in the area near Memphis, TN, where it is believed he found work in the mills. This couple were the parents of six children. One of these children was Ralph Henry Wenderoth who was born Jan. 5, 1864. About 1874 a yellow fever epidemic hit the Memphis area and Henry, Sr. and Fredrika both died. The other children remained in the South, but Ralph Henry came to Indiana as a young boy. As a young man, he lived at the home of Chris Schlosser on a farm northeast of Wadesville. While living there, he married Laura Cavett. She died two years later. A few years after that, he married Laura's sister, Ida Bell Cavett.

The Cavett family came to Indiana from Pennsylvania. Andrew Cavett, Sr. and his wife, Sarah, were the parents of Andrew, Jr., who came to Indiana in 1815. He married Nancy Lowe of Maryland. Andrew, Jr., was prominent in the settlement of Posey County. He was an Associate Judge for 14 years and a Justice of the Peace for many years. This couple was the parents of several children including William Cavett. William was born on the farm northeast of Wadesville in 1820 and lived there until his death in 1841. In 1841 he married Jemima Dorsett and they became the parents of seven children. In 1857 Jemima Dorsett Cavett died, and William later married Elizabeth Wade. Elizabeth bore William three children including Laura Alice Cavett Wenderoth and Ida Bell Cavett Wenderoth. William was a township trustee and an active Republican.

Henry and Ida Bell Wenderoth continued to live at the Cavett farm where they raised their family. The farm was considered one of the best in Posey County. They were active in the work of the Farm Bureau, the Primitive Baptist Church, and many community projects. Ida Bell Wenderoth was a charter member of the Wadesville Community Club. This couple were the parents of Bessie Lee Cox, Catherine Hidbrader, William Henry Wendertoh, and Homer Cavett Wenderoth.

Bessie Lee Wenderoth was born May 28, 1889. She attended Terre Haute Normal School (now Indiana State University), and she taught school for several years. She married Lemuel Potter Cox and was very active in community projects. Her special interests were the Red Cross, Farm Bureau dramatics, Farm Women's Chorus, and food service in the public schools. She died in 1972.

Catherine Alliene Wenderoth was born Aug. 11, 1891. She attended school at Terre Haute and at Mrs. Blaker's school in Indianapolis. She taught several years in the primary grades at Wadesville. She married Herman Hidbrader, and they lived on a farm west of Wadesville until her death in 1930.

William Henry Wenderoth was born June 1,

1895. He attended the Cavett School and the Wadesville Public School. For many years he was associated in farming the Wenderoth farm, specializing in raising grain and pork. He served in the U.S. Army during World War I. After retirement from farming, he moved to Wadesville where he died Dec. 22, 1977.

Homer Wenderoth was born July 12, 1899. He attended Indiana University and served in the Army during World War I.

After a short term of teaching school, he joined the staff of Farmers Bank & Trust Company. He worked his way up to President of the bank. He was influential in the fine growth of the bank. He was married to Eugenia Myrtle Becker. They were the parents of three sons: Robert Lee, who was killed during World War II; Jack Bernard; and Donald Eugene. Both Jack and Donald are members of the Board of Directors of the Farmers Bank & Trust Company, and they both live in Wadesville. Homer died on May 3, 1970. Eugenia died Nov. 16, 1987.

Jack Bernard Wenderoth was born June 17, 1927. He attended the Wadesville Pubic School and served in the U.S. Army during the Korean War. He retired from National City Bank in June 1988, after 40 years. He married Betty Louise Letterman on Sept. 12, 1950. A daughter, Bobbie Christine, was born Apr. 18, 1953. A son, David, was born Jan. 19, 1957. On July 21, 1968 Betty Wenderoth died. Jack married Diana Kay Ellerbrook on Aug. 9, 1969, and a son, Shane Alan, was born to them on Dec. 6, 1970. Bobbie, Jack's daughter, lives in Louisville, KY and works at the University of Louisville. David married Suetta Powers June 6, 1981. They have one daughter Tiffany Nicole born Dec. 25, 1981. They live in Murray, KY. Shane is a senior at North Posey High School and after graduation will attend Purdue University in the fall.

Donald Eugene Wenderoth was born Apr. 10, 1931. He also attended Wadesville Public School and served in the U.S. Army during the Korean Conflict. Don is Merchandising Manager at Indiana Farm Bureau Cooperative Association in Mt. Vernon, IN, where he has been employed for 40 years. He married Virginia Sue Rutledge (see Rutledge Family history) in 1950. They became the parents of three sons and a daughter. Robert Eugene Wenderoth born May 17, 1953, graduated in 1971 from North Posey High School. On Apr. 26, 1975 he married Donna Jean (Lizotte) Backus born Mar. 24, 1948. Donna is the mother of Tammy Marie born Aug. 15, 1965 and Scot Michael born June 3, 1971. Robert and Donna are the parents of one son Brad Eugene born June 23, 1977. He is in the sixth grade at North Elementary. Scot is a senior at North Posey High School and Tammy married Scott Oxley, Feb. 21, 1987. They have one son Zachary Scott born Aug. 14, 1987. Robert is employed at General Electric in Mt. Vernon, IN. He resides in Wadesville where he is very active in the Wadesville Fire Department & Rescue Team. He is a member of the Wadesville Christian Church.

Kent Wayne born Aug. 18, 1955, graduated from North Posey in 1973 and Vincennes University in 1975. On Dec. 21, 1974 he married Karen Ann Ross born Sept. 9, 1957. A daughter Kayce Ann was born Nov. 16, 1977. She is in the fifth grade at North Elementary. A son Kory Wayne was born Aug. 29, 1980. He is in the second grade at North Elementary. On Apr. 2, 1986 Kent and Karen were divorced. On July 11, 1987 he married Sandra Darlene (Davis) Sturges born May 14, 1962. Her daughter Megan Marie Sturges born Feb. 23, 1982 is in the first grade at North Elementary. Kent and Sandra have one child.

Kent is employed at General Electric in Mt. Vernon, IN. He resides in Wadesville where he is a member of the Wadesville Fire Department. He is a member of the Wadesville Christian Church.

Bart Alan born Apr. 18, 1959, graduated from North Posey High School in 1977. He attended Indiana University for one year before transferring to Indiana State University of Evansville. He graduated from there in 1982 with an Associate Degree in Computer Science. In the fall of 1982 he enrolled in Indiana State University, Terre Haute and graduated in 1985 with a BS in Electronic Technology. On Aug. 25, 1984 he married Mona Kay Rone born Feb. 21, 1963. They have one son Brock Alan born Nov. 11, 1987. Bart is employed at Electronics Research Inc., in Newburgh, IN. He resides in Wadesville where he is a member of the Wadesville Fire Department. He is a member of the Wadesville Christian Church.

A daughter Jane Ann born Sept. 8, 1963 died at birth.

WERRY FAMILY

Philip Charles Werry (age 55) and his wife Eleanor (age 40) with their son Chester Leslie (age 19) came to Posey County from Warrick County in the year of the Great Depression, 1929. For the Werrys it was a new beginning. Courage, endurance, and hard work were the tools they brought with them to build their new life in Poseyville. By 1930, the Werrys had purchased the property at the corner of Cale and Fletchall Ave. and thus began one of Posey County's most prominent businesses, the P.C. Werry and Son Funeral Home.

Philip C. Werry was born (Mar. 26, 1874) and raised on a farm in Spencer County near the small town of Tennyson, IN. He was the son of Frank (born Aug. 24, 1850) and Mary Gemlich (born Dec. 17, 1855) both of whom were born in Warrick County. Philip had four sisters (Catharine Margaret, Laura Maria, Rosa Anna and Mattilde Jeliua) and one brother (Leslie Edward). As a small boy, Philip helped his father on the farm and attended school in a small one room school house near Tennyson. He also attended Ebinezer Methodist Church where he became the church organist. Philip's first real job was working for the U.S. Postal Service as a mail carrier. Later in 1880, at the age of 14, he added a second job and worked part-time for the mortician in Tennyson, Mr. John Alfred Billups.

Philip C. Werry (left), Chester L. Werry (Center), Eleanor Werry (Right)

John A. Billups and his wife Sarah Campbell started the funeral business in the small town of Tennyson in the year 1880. Their furniture store near downtown Tennyson served as a funeral parlor as well. By 1895, Philip Werry became a full partner and the "Billups and Werry Funeral Home" was formed.

John and Sarah raised four lovely daughters in their large white frame house in Tennyson. Girtha was the oldest, then Eleanor, Lucy and Lunetta.

By 1904 the young Eleanor, age 15, (born June 3, 1889) and Philip C. Werry were married. Philip took his bride to live on the Werry farm where they lived until after their only child Chester Leslie Werry was born May 7, 1910, during a severe electrical storm.

In 1912, the Billups and Werry Funeral Home opened in Booneville, in an excellent location, only two blocks from the center of town. Chester Werry attended high school in Boonville and was one of the "bruisers" who played football during THE GOLDEN ERA of 1928. Although active in the athletic department in high school and college, Chester also advanced in the field of music.

When the Werrys moved to Poseyville, in late 1929, Chester very quickly became the dominant figure in the business of P.C. Werry and Son. Philip's health was failing and Chester was needed to direct the business. Soon the home at the corner of Sharp and Fletchall Ave. became a funeral home. The family not only offered funeral services, but also the only ambulance service for the northeastern and central sections of Posey County.

Although busy with the family business, Chester still had time to relax and enjoy his violin. While preparing for a concert at the Methodist Church, he met a young pianist named Ruth Elizabeth Jaquess, and, after two years of courtship, they were married at the home of the bride on Cale Street. Ruth was the daughter of James Smith Jaquess, who's great great grandfather was Jonathan Jaquess Jr., one of Posey County's founding fathers. Ruth's mother was Emma Sands, who's father fought in the battle of Mobile during the Civil War.

Together Ruth and Chester were a winning team. They worked hard and the funeral business prospered. Ruth took care of the flowers and the music, and also worked on the books. Chester carried on with the funerals and the ambulance work. During the Second World War, Chester was the Air Raid Warden for Poseyville. He held classes in first aid and was responsible for blackening out the town during "Blackouts". The ambulance business was, however, a business all it's own! It was dangerous, back breaking and very often, thankless.

Ruth and Chester had two children. James Philip was born Aug. 31, 1934. Judith Ann was born Nov. 22, 1936. The two children grew up during the happy days of the 40's and 50's. They both graduated from Poseyville High School. Jim completed his studies at the Indiana School of Mortuary Science in 1953. He attended the University of Evansville (Evansville College) for two years and then served in the U.S. Army in the Quartermaster Corps at Fort Riley, KS.

On Sept. 14, 1955, Jim married Phyllis Anne Wilkinson (born July 16, 1935) of Stewartville, IN. Phyllis is the daughter of Ermal and Lydia Doll Wilkinson. Jim and Phyllis have three sons Philip Alan (born July 6, 1958), John Adam (born Dec. 3, 1960), and Paul Richard (born June 15, 1964).

Judith Ann graduated from Indiana State Teachers College (Indiana State University) in June of 1959. She was married to Robert H. Lindell of Shenandoah, IA. Bob and Judy have four children; James Robert (born Mar. 21, 1960), Jeffrey Alan (born July 23, 1962), Kathleen Suzanne (born Sept. 1, 1966), and Carl David (born Feb. 18, 1972).

By 1946 P.C. Werry and Son had expanded to include the Bixler-Werry Funeral Home in Cynthiana, IN, and in 1950 to include the Shoultz-Werry Funeral Home in New Harmony, IN. By the early 1960's Werry Funeral Homes were incorporated.

Jim and Phyllis moved to the new brick funeral home in New Harmony in December 1957. Together they expanded the funeral business to the central and southern parts of the county. Being interested in New Harmony, they became active in the town's affairs. Jim served on the town board (1961-1965). He was Posey County Commissioner (1967-1970) and served on the White County Bridge Commission for two terms (1972-1978 and 1985-1991). Phyllis is an active member in the Methodist Church, Tri-Kappa Sorority, Posey County Cancer Society, and Friends of the Library.

Philip C. Werry died in 1951 at the old Shoultz-Werry Funeral Home. Eleanor did not follow Philip until 1988. Ruth Werry died at the age of 64, in 1974, and Chester died of cancer in 1983. Today, 1989, Jim and Phyllis's three sons have joined the family business. Each attended the School of Mortuary Science at Vincennes University. Philip married Janet L. Anderson of Carmi, IL. They have a daughter Heather Diane (born Jan. 25, 1985) and a son Chad Alan (born Mar. 23, 1987). John attended the University of Southern Indiana and University of Evansville. He married Gayla Uhde of Mt. Vernon, IN. They have a daughter, Amanda Sue (born Dec. 2, 1987). Paul, also continued his education at Purdue University.

As of today, 1989, the Werry Funeral Home business has spread from the 19th Century (1895) through most of the 20th Century (1989) and will surely continue well into the 21st Century. The business started through the efforts of John Billups and Philip Werry and grew and expanded through the hard work and self sacrificing of Ruth and Chester. Jim and Phyllis sustained their efforts and turned the business into a solid and most promising future for their sons and their sons to be. It's a heritage of which to be proud. It has spanned more than five generations.

HENRY AND MARGARET WEYER

Heinrich Weyer, son of Georg P. Weyer, was born Apr. 14, 1823, in Germany and migrated to Posey County, probably in the 1840s. On Sept. 24, 1851, he married Margaretha Hart, born along the Lower Rhine in Hesse-Darmstadt, Germany, on Oct. 17, 1828. Margaretha moved with her family to Posey County; her brother operated a blacksmith shop at Parker Settlement.

Henry and Margaret Weyer lived on a farm of 34 acres at the northeast edge of Blairsville. They had eight children: Nicholas (1856?-1880); Henry, Jr. (died 1893?); Louis William (1863-1930); Anna (1865-1884); George; John W. (1869-1909); Bertha (1871-1951); and another daughter, possibly Barbara, who died in infancy. Henry, Sr., died Feb. 29, 1896 and was buried in the family cemetery at Blairsville. Margaret later lived with her daughter Bertha Schweitzer in Evansville and died Aug. 27, 1920; she was buried in Locust Hill Cemetery in Evansville.

Nicholas was born about 1856 and confirmed in 1868. In 1877 he married Christina Herrmann (1859-1902), and they lived at Blairsville. Their son, Charles Edward ("Ed") Weyer, was born Jan. 1, 1878; and a daughter, Anna, was born on Sept. 25, 1880, shortly after her father's death. (Anna died on Apr. 17, 1881.) Christina and Edward went to live with her parents, John and Margaret Herrmann. Nicholas was buried in the family cemetery at Blairsville.

Margaret Hart, Wife of Henry Weyer

On Sept. 28, 1903, Edward Weyer married Ida May Laslie (1883-1943), daughter of the Rev. Theophilus Alexander Hall Laslie and Sarah Isabell Davis Laslie. Edward and Ida lived at Wadesville on a farm rented from Ed's grandfather Herrmann. They had three children: Irene Isabel (Aug. 29, 1904-Aug. 20, 1983); Alice Christine (born Sept. 18, 1906); and Albert Edward (Mar. 31, 1915-Apr. 10, 1966). Irene was a teacher and artist; she did not marry. Alice taught music, English, and Latin for 14 years. She married James E. Morlock on June 27, 1937, and has one daughter, Vivian Alice. Albert worked in the field of public health in Costa Rica, Liberia and the Bahamas. On Jan. 27, 1939, he married Dora Dean Halliday, and they had one daughter, Dora Diane.

Edward and Ida Weyer are buried at Bellefontaine Cemetery, and their daughter Irene is beside them. Albert is buried in Gates Mills, OH. Dora and Diane live in Belize, Central America. Alice and James Morlock live in Evansville, IN.

Henry Weyer, Jr., second son of Henry and Margaret, and William A. and Anna by his first wife and Edward by his second wife, Minnie. William had three wives and ten children; Anna and her husband had five children; Edward died in childhood.

Louis married Elizabeth Schuessler on May 29, 1890, and had four children.

Anna died at age 19.

George married Katharine Schweitzer and had four children. His second wife was named Lillian.

John married Ida Houser and had three children.

Bertha married Jacob Schweitzer, Jr., on May 19, 1892, and had five children. *Submitted by Mrs. Vivian Morlock Taylor*

DAVID AND BARBARA JUDITH WHITTEN

David and Barbara Judith Whitten are residents of Oakland City, IN. They were married June 22, 1962, at the Mt. Vernon General Baptist Church. This union has been blessed with a son, Michael Vern, born Oct. 19, 1964, and a daughter, Melanie Francene, born Dec. 17, 1966.

Judy was born Jan. 26, 1941, into the home of Francis Willard and Mary Martha (Reeves) Ranes. She was born at the Ranes home at Ranebo Fruit Farm, northwest of Mt. Vernon, near Upton, IN. Her grandfather, Dr. John R. Ranes, delivered her. She attended Grafton School, where she received an excellent educational background under the tutelage of such fine teachers as Lorene Kishline, Nell Walker, and Carl Curtis. In 1959 Judy was graduated from Mt. Vernon High School; she received a bachelor of arts degree from Oakland City College in 1962 and began teaching English and German at Francisco High School that year. Her professional career was interrupted for a time when their children were born. She returned to teaching in 1969, teaching English at Oakland City College on a part-time basis. In 1976, she added to those duties that of being Director of Alumni Affairs. When responsibilities of the alumni work increased, she retired from the classroom to take on the full-time responsibilities of the Alumni Office, a position that she has at this writing.

Seated: David and Judy Whitten. Standing (l to r) Melanie holding Mallory Wood, Steve Wood, Michael Whitten, Karen holding Brittney Whitten.

Judy was accepted to membership in the National Society Daughters of the American Revolution in 1979, having been approved for membership through her Revolutionary ancestor Aaron Redman, the great-grandfather of John R. Ranes.

David was born Aug. 21, 1940, in Vanderburgh Co., IN. His parents are Vern Prentice and Bertha (Atkinson) Whitten. He was graduated from F.J. Reitz High School in 1958, attended Oakland City College from 1958 to 1960, and was graduated from Indiana State University in 1962. He earned his master of science degree from Indiana State University in 1968. He is employed by the Visiting Nurse Association of Southwestern Indiana as a speech language pathologist. David is a member of the Descendants of the Mayflower through his lineage from Isaac Allerton.

David and Judy are active members of the Francisco General Baptist Church, where David is a deacon, music director, and Sunday School teacher.

Their son, Michael, is a math teacher and coach at Pike Central High School. He was graduated from Wood Memorial High School in 1982 and from Oakland City College in 1986, becoming the fourth generation of his family to have attended or been graduated from OCC. He was married to Karen Dillon July 19, 1986. On May 2, 1988, they were blessed with a daughter, Brittney Rachelle Whitten.

Melanie, their daughter, was married to Steve Wood on Dec. 22, 1984. They live in Flint, MI, where Steve is Youth Pastor at the First General Baptist Church. Melanie teaches at a day care center. They were blessed with a daughter, Mallory Kristene Wood, May 7, 1988.

JAMES D. WILEY

James D. Wiley of New Harmony and Patricia K. Garrett of Griffin, were married Feb. 9, 1958. They now reside in Harmony Township, Posey County. Jim was born May 12, 1932, graduated from New

Harmony High School in 1951. He and his sons, Timothy, born Dec. 16, 1961, and Todd, born Feb. 28, 1967 farm around 1200 acres in Posey County. Pat, born Oct. 30, 1936, graduated from Griffin High School in 1954 and is presently employed at Allyn Abstract Co. in Mt. Vernon. The first child, Tracy Ann, born Oct. 30, 1960, married, married Richard N. Burks Apr. 4, 1981 and have one child, Jennifer Ann, born Sept. 17, 1986. The Burks family reside on the home place and Jennifer is the seventh generation of the family to live there. Jim's father, Fred D. Wiley, born Mar. 9, 1982, died in 1980, was the third child of James D. and Hannah Penfold Wiley.

Back Row L-R: Todd Wiley, James Wiley, Tim Wiley, Rick Burks, Front L-R: Tracy A. Burks, Jennifer A. Burks, Patricia Wiley

Hannah's grandfather, Abraham Penfold, immigrated from Surrey County, England. Fred's grandfather, Sam, son of the James Wiley that purchased the land in 1840, was born in a log cabin where the family lived until a frame house was built during the civil war. In 1859 Sam married Elizabeth Jackson, the daughter of Jonathan Jackson and Mary Norbury of Chester, England. Jonathan manufactured silk in his factory in New Harmony. Jim's mother Fay Fitzgerrell, born Dec. 1, 1893, died in 1970, was a native of Robb Township. She was the daughter of Daniel Graham Fitzgerrell and Mary Almirah Turpen. Fay's great-grandfather, James Fitzgerrell, was the son of Lawrence Fitzgerrell and Esther Ellis Fitzgerrell. Lawrence immigrated from Ireland and settled in Virginia. Fay's maternal grandmother, Mariah Durham was kidnapped as a child and nothing is known of her ancestors. Jim's sister Virginia, was a member of the Community of the Transfiguration in Cincinnati, OH until her death in 1978.

Pat is the second of five children born to Virgie Haggard, Garrett, Racine. Virgie was born July 19, 1912, died 1977. Pat's brother, Gordon Garrett, was born May 9, 1934 and died Oct. 8, 1982. She has a half brother, Alan Racine of rural Evansville, two half sisters, Joan Racine Hunckler of Vincennes, and Virginia Racine York of Griffin. Virgie was the oldest of seven children born to Louis "Doctor" Haggard and Emma Pearl Lumm Haggard. Mr. Haggard came from Illinois, married Emma June 7, 1911 and settled first in Gibson County. They were living in Griffin at the time of the 1925 tornado, but moved to a farm west of Griffin in the early 1930s. Pat's father, Harrison B. Garrett, born June 14, 1889, was the son of Elebe Garrett and Mary Ireland. His great-great-great grandfather was Presley Garrett. After Harrisons death Aug. 9, 1938, Virgie married Delmar.

A. Racine, also a great-great-great grandson of Presley Garrett.

MARVIN AND NAOMI WILLIAMS FAMILY

Sherri Beth and Larry M. are the daughter and son of Marvin and Naomi Williams of Cynthiana, IN.

Sherri graduated from North Posey High School and attended Ball State and has an associate degree in Science from U.S.I. An honor graduate of Deaconess Hospital School of Radiologic Technology, she is a licensed Radiologic Technologist.

Larry graduated from Hallsville High School, Hallsville, MO and Missouri University at Columbia and served four years in the Air Force. Larry and Patricia Hauser, daughter of Bernard and Rachel Hauser of Kansas City, MO, were married Dec. 10, 1977. They have one son, Mark.

Sherrie and Ken Seibert, a graduate of North Posey and Purdue University and the son of Raymond and Martha Seibert of Poseyville, IN, were married Oct. 9, 1976. They reside near Poseyville and have three sons, Kevin John, Scott, and Kyle.

Larry M. Williams and wife Patricia, son Mark, Sherri and Ken Seibert and sons Kevin John and Scott, 1984.

Naomi, a Gibson County native is a descendant of early Posey County residents. A maternal grandmother Emily Sharp born Sept. 15, 1830 was the daughter of George and Rebecca (Garrett) Sharp. George's parents were Thomas and Rachel (Elliott) Sharp. Rebecca's parents were Pressley and Elizabeth (Baxter) Garrett, who, along with the Simpson's and Water's were early settlers of Gibson County. The Sharps came from Carrol Co., MD.

Emily and William Holloman were married in Posey County, Dec. 11, 1855 and settled in Paris, now Stewartsville. Emily is a devout Methodist, and their children Rebecca, Nancy and Alfred were quite active in the Sunday School there where William owned a flour mill until his death in 1877.

In 1901 Emily and a granddaughter, Ava, went to Lake Co., FL where they homesteaded 125 acres on the Sauet Johns River near Paisley. Emily died there in 1916 and Ava in 1933.

Nancy born in 1858 married Wm. A. Sharp in 1877. Wm. the son of Harrison and Eliza C. (Sharp) Sharp born in 1854, was a farmer and master carpenter. He helped build "The Old Red Bridge" at The Upper Hills. Their children were Effie, Myrtle May, Florence, Oscar and Albert. The girls attended school in the Stewartsville area after Nancy's death in 1895.

Myrtle married George Williams in 1901. George's father Charles was a White Co., IL Civil War Soldier. His maternal grandfather, Daniel Bidwell was a Revolutionary War Veteran.

Myrtle and George were parents of seven children. Their second daughter, Sadie married John Straw. They were parents of five children; Naomi, Earl, Edward, George and John.

Naomi a graduate of Griffin High School attended Lockyears Business College and graduated from Kidwell's School of Hairdressing.

She and Marvin Williams were married Dec. 15, 1945. Marvin attended Knox Co., IN schools and in 1937 came to Posey County with his parents the late Everett and Edith (Thompson) Williams. He is a descendant of the pioneer Joseph Wood, Revolutionary War soldier and an Irishman by birth who settled on the River Du Shee in Knox Co., IN in 1807. His maternal grandfather, Eli Butler, served in the Civil War, as did a paternal grandfather, John R. Williams.

Marvin's paternal grandmother Mary Lincoln was a third cousin of Abraham Lincoln.

Marvin is a retired farmer and construction worker and a veteran of World War II. *Submitted by Naomi Williams*

NED O. WILLIAMS FAMILY

Ned and Mary Beth (Dixon) Williams live in Robb Township. Posey County has always been their home. They were married Sept. 26, 1959.

Mary Beth the youngest child of Otto and Thelma (Blakley) Dixon was born Dec. 15, 1937. Her paternal grandparents were William Thomas and Gertrude Mary (O'Nan) Dixon and her maternal grandparents were Richard King and Lizzie (Wallace) Blakley. She graduated from Reitz High School in 1956. She works in the Insurance Business.

Ned Owen, second son of Elwood and Ella Fern (Stallings) Williams was born Nov. 26, 1938. He has a brother Jack who lives in Washington, IN and a sister Penny Wade. He was graduated from Poseyville High School in 1956. He attended short course at Purdue University. He was raised on the farm on which his Mother still resides.

Ned O. Williams Family

His father Elwood Williams was born Dec. 16, 1905 and his mother Ella Fern was born June 1, 1906. They were married Aug. 8, 1925.

Ned's paternal grandparents were Thomas Owen Williams, born 1876 and Hettie (Grant) Williams born 1876. They were married Nov. 17, 1897 in Posey County. They had four children.

Ned's paternal great grandparents were William Hume born 1850 and Serelda (Westfall) Williams born in 1851. They were married in 1875 in Posey County. The Williams family imigrated from England in 1637 to Massachusetts, then on to Kentucky and Posey County, Williams Hume Williams' great grandfather, William Williams, born in 1731 was a signer of the Declaration of Independence.

Ned's paternal grandmother Hettie was born in 1876 to Andrew Jackson Grant and Wilemina (Shelton) Grant. He was a school teacher and was a cousin of Alonzo K. Grant, who was a former sheriff of Posey County.

Ned's maternal grandparents, Harry Stallings born 1875 and Lucy (Wells) Stallings born 1878 were married in 1898. Harry's parents Leander Stallings born 1849 and Lodema (Elsperman) Stallings born 1854, lived in Center and Robb townships in Posey County. The Stallings family imigrated from Scotland to North Carolina and then to Posey County. The Elsperman family came from Germany. Lucy Wells Stallings was the daughter of Lycurgus and Diana (Jones) Wells. Diana Jones Wells was the daughter of Peter Jones, who served under William Henry Harrison. He made Captain and as a Secretary of Harrison signed a treaty with the Indians.

Ned and Mary Beth now live on the former Lawrence Doll farm which his father owned and which he tends today. During the first 11 years of marriage, they lived on the former Greenberry Young Farm located southeast of Poseyville.

They are the parents of four children, Julie born 1961, Trudy (Stock) born 1964, Matthew born 1970 and Heidi born 1972.

JOHANN ADAM WILLMANN, JR.

Johann Adam Willmann Jr., (1817-1882) and his wife, Anna Maria Zimmermann Willmann (born 1819), with five children left Altheim in Hesse-Darmstadt, Germany, and landed in New Orleans on Oct. 20, 1854. They settled in Posey County, and Johann became a farmer. Their children were Maria Christina (1845-1924), Elizabeth, Katharine, Mary, and Frederick (1852-1929). Johann and Anna are buried without a marker in the Zion-Lippe Church Cemetery.

Maria Christina (called Christina) married Christian Morlock, Jr., and they had six children: Frederick, George, Mary, John, Edward, and Emma. Christina and Christian were married on Jan. 27, 1868, and Christian died on Mar. 4, 1880, when Emma was barely five months old. Christina sold the land east of Mt. Vernon about 1883 and bought 120 acres in Black Township on the boundary with Point Township. This land had belonged to Andrew Morlock, Christian's brother, and was purchased from Andrew's widow. Christina eventually bought more land and later divided it among her children, whose descendants still own most of it.

Maria Christina (Willmann) Morlock

Elizabeth Willmann married Chris Dolgner.

Katharine ("Kate") Willmann married Henry Meyer, and they had five children: Molly; William; Carrie, Henry, Jr.; and Kate.

Mary Willmann married Conrad Meier (Maier?) in 1863, and they had seven children: Conrad, Jr.; Mary; John; Frederick; William; Margaret; and Lulu.

Frederick Adolph Willmann married Wilhelmina Johanna Korte in 1872, and they had seven children: George, Sylvia, Lillian and Millie (twins), Lydia, Arthur, and Flora. Frederick was a minister.

The church record in Altheim provided the following information. Anna Maria Zimmermann's parents were Peter Zimmermann (1791-1866) and Anna Catharina Sauerwein. Johann Adam Willmann, Jr., was the son of Johann Adam Willmann, Sr., (1784-1863) and Anna Maria Crämerin. Johann, Sr., was the son of Philipp Ernst Willmann (1747-1819) and Catharina Willand (1746-1823). Philipp's parents were Georg Heinrich Willmann (1711-1753) and Margarethe Roth (1716-1782). Georg's parents were Johann Nickol Wüllman (1687-1749) and Anna Margaretha Sauerwein (1681-1765). Johann's parents were Wolf Georg Wüllmann (1648-1741) and Elizabeth Willand. Wolf was the son of Matern Wüllmann (1608-1685) and his wife, Catharina (died, 1674). *Submitted by Mrs. Vivian Morlock Taylor*

JAMES B. (JACK) YAGGI & ALICE P. YAGGI

We have lived in Mt. Vernon, Posey Col., IN all our lives; both graduated from Mt. Vernon High School, James in 1936 and Alice in 1938. We married in August 1942, and are the parents of two sons, James Bernard II born in August 1946, and Roger David born in April 1948.

James was born Jan. 20, 1917 in Mt. Vernon, and Alice was born Jan. 29, 1921 just outside of Mt. Vernon on one of the Philip Hageman farms. (The house has since been torn down.)

James and Alice Yaggi

James joined the Indiana National Guard, Battery B, a Mt. Vernon group in September 1940. The Guard was activated in January 1941 where he served until November 1945 after active duty during World War II in the South Pacific.

James is the son of Ivan B. Yaggi and Inez Harriett (Ashworth) Yaggi. Ivan's mother was Mary Augustus (Edwards) Yaggi who came to Mt. Vernon from Perry Co., IN after the death of her husband, John. She and her five children lived here until the children were grown when they moved to Indianapolis. Ivan remained here and later married Inez Harriett Ashworth, a daughter of David F. and Ella Hanshoe Ashworth.

Alice's parents were George L. Pfister, Sr. and Florence C. Scheller Pfister. He was a son of Louis and Lina Gerwig Pfister. She was a daughter of Adam Scheller and Barbara Effinger Scheller. Adam Scheller served in the Civil War. George L. Pfistger worked for over 40 years at Fuhrer-Ford Milling Co. (now A.D.M.)

Ivan had opened a plumbing and heating business in 1939 at 125 Main St., Mt. Vernon, IN, after operating from his home since 1935. After World War II, James joined his father in the business, and he and his brother own and operate the business in the same location today. James' two sons, James II and Roger have joined them in the business. It is the oldest in the area.

GEORGE ELBERT AND GRACE YORK

George Elbert (born in Posey County Nov. 6, 1914), and Grace (born Apr. 6 1921 in Gibson County) York were married June 17, 1939 and have four children, Larry, David, William and Nancy. They also have seven great-grandchildren.

Elbert is the son of William Elisha and Bertha Henrietta (Brandenstein) York. His father, a carpenter, died in 1958. His mother died in 1984.

Elbert's third great-grandfather, Henry York, married Katherine Links June 16, 1825 and resided on a farm in Point Township with their five children. Henry is believed to be descended from the Yorks of Randolph Co., NC. Their oldest son, (William) Elisha, born about 1827, married Mary Angeline Donovan Feb. 11, 1851. They had one child, John Marshall, Aug. 1, 1857. Elisha died about 1859 and Angeline married James Reeder. She died Nov. 30, 1865. Her son, raised by the Stallings family, married Sydney Taylor, daughter of William and Elizabeth (Britton) Taylor, on Oct. 12, 1880. They had four children, William Elisha (Elbert's father), George, Arthur and Mary Nettie. Mary Nettie, who married Kenneth Whitmore, is still living.

Elizabeth Britton York was descended from the Britton and Stuart (Stewart) families who moved from the Carolinas to Christian Co., KY, then to Posey County in the early 1800s.

Bertha York was the daughter of August and Caroline "Lena" (Oschman) Brandenstein. August's parents were Peter and Wilhelmina (Gephardt) Brandenstein. Peter, a brickmaker, was born in Germany in 1820 and filed his oath of allegiance on Oct. 9, 1854 in Vanderburgh County. He died Sept. 27, 1882. Wilhelmina, daughter of Phillip Gephardt and his wife, a Schenk, was born in Germany Nov. 3, 1829 and died Apr. 10, 1909. Lena was born in Germany May 30, 1863. Only she and her father, Louis John Oschmann, survived the journey to America, arriving in New York in July 1869. They came to "Lippe" in Marrs Township where other Oschmanns resided.

Grace is the daughter of Earl Malcus and Maude Mable (Hudson) Matsel. Her mother, born Dec. 13, 1897 in Pike County, died in 1974. Her mother's family were from eastern Kentucky. Her father, born Feb. 17, 1899 in Gibson County to John Wesley and Manecia (Smith) Matsel, died June 23, 1980.

John Wesley was the son of John Jerry and Mary E. (Austin) Matsel. His father died when he was young and all the remainder of his family, except one sister, died in an epidemic in 1877. His maternal grandfather, Benjamin Austin, was born to Elisha and Martha (Fox) Austin Dec. 6, 1816 in Warren Co., TN. Benjamin married Lucinda Emmerson, the daughter of William Emmerson of White Co., IL, Feb. 23, 1937.

Henry Matsel, father of John Jerry, was born in New York Dec. 6, 1796 and died July 12, 1879. His wife, Sarah, born Apr. 7, 1804, died Oct. 26, 1869. They are buried in a small graveyard on the farm where they lived west of Carmi, IL.

Manecia (Smith) Matsel's grandmother was Sally Davis, daughter of Robert Clark and Elizabeth (Redwine) Davis, whose families came to

Indiana from Rowen and Montgomery Counties, NC. These families settled in Gibson County and northern Posey County.

LARRY KEITH AND VIRGINIA ALICE YORK

Larry born Feb. 26, 1941, and Virginia, born Aug. 23, 1948, were married Apr. 15, 1966 and reside in Griffin. They have two children, Angela, born July 1, 1967, and Stephen, born Dec. 24, 1969. Angela has two children, Ashley and Megan Cawthon, born Mar. 15, 1985 and Feb. 7, 1987, respectively. Angela is married to James Counts, a Floridian.

Larry is the son of George Elbert and Grace (Matsel) York. He graduated from New Harmony in 1959, served six years in the Army and joined the Posey County Sheriff's Department in 1970, where he is a detective. See his parents' biographies for his family history.

Virginia is the daughter of Delmar "Jack" and Virgie (Haggard) Racine. She graduated from North Posey in 1966 and began working for Allyn Abstract Company in 1970, where she is now manager.

Her father, Jack, was born Aug. 25, 1910 and died Feb. 8, 1972. He worked for Texaco for over 30 years and hand-made fishing nets, which he sold or used in the river himself.

Larry and Virginia York

Her mother, Virgie, was born July 19, 1912 and died Sept. 18, 1979. She married Harrison Garrett and had two children, Charles Gordon, now deceased, and Patricia. After Mr. Garrett's death, she married Jack and had three children, Joan, Virginia and Alan. Her many talents included painting, woodworking and refinishing antiques.

Virginia's paternal grandfather, William "Ozzie" Racine, married Lillie Lucas, the daughter of McFarland and Julia (Robinson) Lucas. Ozzie and their young daughter, Bessie, died in the 1918 flu epidemic, leaving Lillie to raise her four sons alone.

McFarland and Julia are both descended from many Gibson County pioneers. Julia's great-grandfather, Over River Jordan, died in Gibson County in 1826.

Ozzie was descended from Rene and Marie (Loysel) Racine, natives of Fumichon, Normandy, France, whose son, Etienne, immigrated to Canada and married Marguerite Martin May 22, 1638. Etienne and Marguerite's great-grandson, Jean Baptiste Racine (dit Ste. Marie), came to Vincennes, IN, and married Anne-Jeanne Dudevoir Nov. 23, 1756. Jean, a Commandante at Fort Vincennes, and his son, Francois, born Nov. 20, 1758, served in the Revolutionary War. Francois married Marie-Therese Compagnot Nov. 15, 1787. A son, Henri Orra, was born to them about 1800, probably after they moved to Lawrence Co., IL, around St. Francisville. Most of the French, at this time, were farmers, fishermen and trappers. The Racines, along with the Tougas families, were among the first settlers in that part of Illinois. The Tougas men, all very tall, were famous for their bravery in dealing with the Indians.

Henri married Eleanore Tougas, daughter of Francois and Genevieve (Valle) Tougas (dit Laviolette), Aug. 15, 1828. Eleanor's grandfather, Joseph Tougas, also served in the Revolution. Henri and Eleanor were the great-grandparents of Ozzie Racine.

Ozzie's father, Alfred Henry, married Sarah Garrett on Jan. 12, 1884. Sarah was descended from Presley and Elizabeth (Baxter) Garrett of Gibson County.

Virginia's maternal grandparents were Louis Doctor and Emma Pearl (Lumm) Haggard. The Haggard family came to southern Illinois from Tennessee around 1850. The Lumm family to southern Illinois via Virginia and Ohio.

ROBERT AND SHIRLEY YORK

Robert and Shirley York are residents of Mt. Vernon, IN. Robert was born in Mt. Vernon and is a life long resident. Shirley was born in Monet, MO. She spent most of her pre-teen years in Kansas and Oklahoma prior to moving to Mt. Vernon.

Robert was born Dec. 4, 1941, to Robert and Harriet (Patrick) York. Robert was born the fourth of ten children. Shirley was born June 30, 1942 to Allen and Dorothy (Beal) Hendrix. She was an only child.

Robert and Shirley are the parents of one child, Dwayne Eddie. Dwayne resides in Wilmington, NC with his wife, Wendy, and their daughter, Felicia.

Robert was employed by the Mt. Vernon Fire Department. He started his employment with the department, Jan. 1, 1965, and retired Jan. 31, 1989. During the time of his service, he served as Assistant Fire Chief from 1972 through 1985.

Shirley currently is employed at the Mt. Vernon Democrat, where she has worked since 1979.

LAWRENCE JOSEPH ZELLER

A silver and bronze star holder, Larry Zeller, the oldest son of Clarence and Mary (Paul) Zeller, was an inspiration to all who knew him. He was born to Clarence and Mary (Paul) Zeller, on Jan. 8, 1948 in Evansville, IN. Larry attended St. Wendel School and one year of high school at Mater Die, Evansville. He then enrolled at North Posey High School in Posey County and graduated in May, 1966. His father was in construction of homes in Indiana, Kentucky, and Illinois, so Larry was engaged in carpentry with the family business, when he was drafted into the United States Army on Nov. 8, 1967. He had made application to attend electronics school in Indianapolis, but felt a deep sense of duty and patriotism. After serving for several months in the War Zone, Larry was awarded the National Defense Service Medal, Combat Infantry Badge and the Sharpshooter Badge with automatic rifle and rifle bars.

Larry Zeller was killed in Vietnam on New Year's Day 1969, only moments after the Christmas Holiday cease fire period ended. While on ambush patrol with Company D, 1st Battalion, 27th Infantry, they were attacked by a large Communist force. Specialist Zeller received a fatal wound in Binh Boung Province from a rocket grenade while directing the men after the platoon leader was wounded. Zeller had been in Vietnam since Apr. 25, 1968.

Larry Zeller

The Silver Star was awarded for gallantry and the Bronze Star awarded for meritorious service in connection with military operations against a hostile force. The medals and citations were presented posthumously to the parents, Clarence and Mary Zeller. Services were held at St. Wendel's Catholic Church on January 10, with burial in the church cemetery, St. Wendel, IN.

Larry has a brother, Dennis and two sisters, Ruth Ann Champlain and Rita Janet. His grandparents were Joe and Ella Paul of St. Wendel, IN.

ZELLER-PAUL

Mary M. Paul grew up on a farm south of Ridgway, IL. She was the oldest daughter of Joseph and Ella (Banks) Paul. After attending Bradley School and St. Joseph Parochial School in Ridgway, she moved with her parents to St. Wendel, IN after the Flood of 1937. Mary was born Dec. 26, 1921.

Mary found employment in a defense plant in Evansville as World War II was raging. She dated Clarence W. Zeller, then he went into the service. After a tour of duty in Europe, Clarence returned to the United States the day following the Fourth of July in 1945. They made plans for marriage only a few weeks later on July 23, 1945 in Holy Trinity Catholic Church, Evansville, IN. Clarence then went to Camp Cooke, CA, while Mary went to Los Angeles, CA, where she stayed until Clarence was out of service.

Clarence and Mary Zeller

Clarence and Mary returned home to Posey County where they received a warm welcome after the trying times of war. They returned to California in 1946 but this step showed no promise, so the couple came to St. Wendel in Posey County, to farm and raise cattle. Their home has been blessed with two sons and two daughters. Lawrence Joseph was born on Jan. 8, 1948 and Dennis William on Jan. 7,

1953. Lawrence (Larry) was killed in the Vietnam War on Jan. 1, 1969 whie on ambush patrol. He received the Silver Star and Bronze Star for heroic action.

On Dec. 6, 1954, a daughter, Rita Janet was born and four years later their youngest child, Ruth Ann was born on Oct. 25, 1958.

Meanwhile, Clarence was a self-employed carpenter and built houses in Indiana, Kentucky, and Illinois. The two sons helped in the carpentry with Dennis continuing the family business but Larry's time was cut short when he entered the service and was killed in Vietnam.

Clarence has now retired but they continue to live on the family farm, southwest of St. Wendel, which is now known for its three-acre vineyard and fine grapes. Clarence and Mary attended classes put on by Purdue University to learn the crafts of grape growers.

Mary has kept busy helping others, especially after the loss of their son, Larry. She found that helping the mentally ill patients at the Evansville State Hospital was what she could do best in memory of her son. She is a Gold Star Mother and was the recipient of the Luise Whiting Award for the volunteer hours in 1979, when she had put in 1500 hours of work. The nine years since that date sees Mary still having volunteer hours every month. Hours as a seamstress, as well as assisting with luncheon for hospital patients who are war veterans are a part of Mary Zeller's life.

Clarence and Mary are active members in St. Wendel Catholic Church. They also keep in close touch with their son, Dennis and family, also their daughters, Rita and Ruth and their families.

RITA JANET ZELLER

Rita Janet Zeller was born Dec. 6, 1954 in Evansville, IN. She was the first daughter of Clarence and Mary M. (Paul) Zeller. Her mother is the daughter of Joseph W. Paul and Ella (Banks) Paul of St. Wendel. She attended St. Wendel Grade School and graduated in 1969 from eighth grade.

Left to right, Tamera Lee, Rita, Lisa Weiss

Rita graduated from North Posey High School in 1973. She married Dennis Weiss in 1975 and they had two daughters. Tamera Lee born Sept. 14, 1975 and Lisa Ann born Apr. 20, 1979. She is now divorced and lives near St. Wendel in Posey County.

ZELLER-SHAW

Dennis William Zeller is the second son of Mary M. (Paul) and Clarence W. Zeller. He is the grandson of Joseph and Ella Paul from Posey County. Dennis was born Jan. 7, 1953 at Welborn Baptist Hospital in Evansville, IN. He grew up on the family farm that is located near St. Wendel, IN. He helped his grandfather, Paul, take care of the cattle and the farm. Dennis also helped his father in the family construction business. Dennis attended St. Wendel Grade School and graduated from the eighth grade in 1967. He then attended North Posey High School and graduated in 1971.

Zeller Family; Back Row: - L&R Alex, Katherine, April, Dennis, First Row - Amy, Andrew, Amanda

Dennis married Katherine S. Shaw in June of 1975. Katherine is the oldest daughter of Robert E. Shaw and Suzanne (Schlosser) Shaw of Crawfordsville, IN. She was born on Nov. 2, 1953 in Wabash, IN. Katherine graduated from Crawfordsville High School in 1972 and from the University of Evansville in 1976. She is currently a homemaker. Dennis is a self-employed carpenter, having taken over his father's business in 1981. They have five children: Andrew Robert Sept. 13, 1977, Amy Denise born Oct. 5, 1980, Amanda Sue born Aug. 9, 1982, April Marie born Apr. 25, 1986, and Alex William born Nov. 28, 1987. They live near St. Wendel, IN on the family farm.

Left to right: Stace, Sam, Sam Ray and Sue Loehr

Early 1920's Automobile Department of Keck Gonnerman Company.

CLUB ORGANIZATION BUSINESS, HISTORY

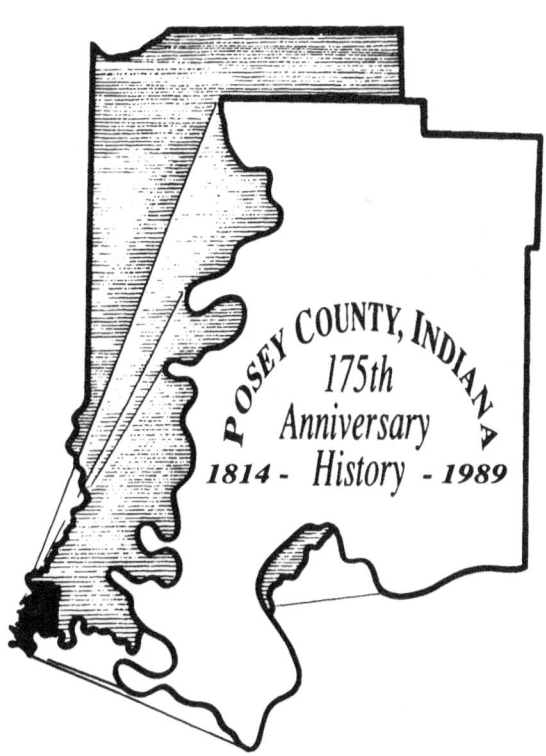

THE AMERICAN LEGION, OWEN DUNN POST 5

The American Legion, largest organization of war veterans in history, was born at a caucus of the first Expeditionary Force in Paris, France, March 15 to 17, 1919. In St. Louis, Mo. May 8, 1919, a general caucus produced the blueprint of the American Legion. Stimulated by Ambrose W. Harbert, the first meeting to affect a local Legion organization was held in the Mt. Vernon city hall on June 12, 1919. Thirty-four men signed a charter application. The application was held open for a grand homecoming sponsored by the War Mothers in September. An additional 123 names were added. Total 155.

For several years, the new Legion met at different places, among them, the city hall, Modern Woodmen Hall and the library club room. In 1926, the World War Memorial Coliseum was erected and it became the meeting place until 1947.

Ambrose Harbert, who was instrumental in forming the local Legion, preferred not to be commander, and this resulted in the election of Merle Weisinger as the first post commander. An early function was to name the post Owen Dunn Post 5 in honor of the first Posey County boy to die in battle. Owen Dunn was killed at Chateau Thierry, July 14, 1918. Another early function was a request to civil authorities that Nov. 11, 1919 be declared a holiday. The request was granted.

In 1947, the Legion purchased the residence of Dr. Raanes at 203 Walnut St. With some remodeling, this became the Post home until 1965. In that year, this building was razed and the present home was constructed. This new home is not only put to good use by the members, but is also frequently rented to public for reunions, wedding receptions and meetings of all kinds.

At one time, the Post sponsored a Boy Scout troop and a baseball team, an oratorical project, a child welfare program, and Christmas baskets for the needy. Each year, we send four boys to Boys State, an outstanding educational force developed by the Legion. The Auxiliary also sends three girls to Girls State. Another activity, which the public is probably more aware of, is the participation of the Legion Firing Squad and Color Guard at military funerals.

At this time, the total membership, comprised of the Legion, the Womens Auxiliary, and The Sons of the Legion, is 1040.

THE MOUNT VERNON COTERIE

Mount Vernon's first literary club was organized on November 23, 1896, by Myra Ruminer (Mrs. Walter) French. Eight local ladies met at Mrs. French's home and instituted a group which had the aim of stimulating intellectual development and general culture of its members. The club was named the Mount Vernon Bay View Reading Circle after the Bay View course of study which the club followed for the first year. Later the name of the growing circle was changed to Mount Vernon Coterie. The club's motto "More Light" was chosen and the carnation became its flower with the colors of green and white.

Ninety-three years after its founding, members of Coterie meet once each month to enjoy book reviews, lectures and other cultural programs. Their civic activities include sponsoring literary programs for the public, placing books in the local library and, each year, giving a cash award to a high school senior who plans to continue study in the field of English.

Present members are Lou Bayer; Leona Becker; Erma Boatman; Mary Breeze, chaplain; Lucy Brown; Marjorie Burkhart; Elizabeth Carpenter, vice-president; Sarah Carr; Rachel Conlin; Irma Cox, Edna Dietz; Elka Lee Forthoffer; Esther Grabert; Ilse Horacek, president; Mary Lloyd Hurley; Wilma Jacobs; Mary B. Johnson; Janice Joslyn; Mary A. Kleeschuilte, secretary; Gladys Krug; Lydia Lurker; Twila Paul; Lucile Redman; Donna Reineke; Lillian Rowe; Phyllis Stevens; Elizabeth Uebelhack; Olie Williams, treasurer; and Lucille Ziegler.

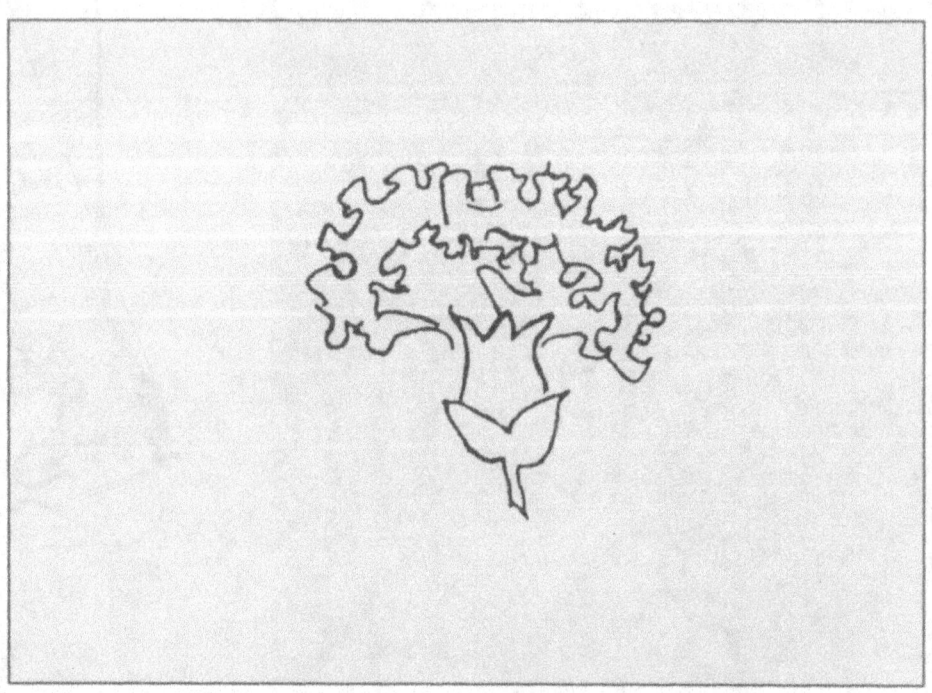

Second and Store Street building in Mt. Vernon built by Slim Andy McFadin before his death in 1845. Masonic Hall is on the top floor.

Maas Building, South East corner of Second and Main, parking lot now

Farmers Bank & Trust Company

During the late 1800's, banking for Wadesville residents was as an informal transaction.

In addition to running a general store and handling other ventures, James Cross also served as the community's banker. However, when Mr. Cross loaned money, he often was not re-paid for the debt. Therefore, when his store burned in 1905, it was never re-built.

A need for local banking service prompted the people of the area to open a bank for Wadesville. On October 7, 1907, the Farmers National Bank was organized. The first directors of the bank were Warren Wade, Dan Williams, Cornelius E. Miler, John Heckman, John M. Hunter, Conrad Kolb, James A. Cox, G.B. Causey, and Joseph M. Nash. B.O. Warren was the first cashier. The Articles of Association which were filed September 28, 1907, also carried the names of Charles W. Ratcliff, William H. Roesner, Joel Bailey, Z.P. Watson and I.E. Record as shareholders. Capital stock was $25,000.00 to be divided into shares of $100.00 each.

Early minutes of board meetings are missing, but statements to the Treasury Department show immediate and consistent growth. The first report is dated December 3, 1907 — less than two months after the bank's organization. According to this report Farmers National Bank already had $15,390.00 in capital stock and $9,756.06 in checking deposits. Loans of $562.75 had been made, and lawful money reserve in the bank included $260.00 in gold coin and $383.00 in silver dollars.

By February 14, 1908, capital stock had increased to $21,180.00. In addition, checking deposits totalled $23,515.64 while loans had grown to $25,622.98.

Few changes were made in bank personnel for several years until Dan Williams resigned as cashier in December, 1920. L.P. Cox, who had been assistant cashier, was then elected cashier.

In 1925, the bank's name hit the newspaper headlines. On May 11, seven armed bandits kidnapped Mr. Cox and his wife, Bessie, and forced them, at gun point, to go to the bank and open the vault. When the bandits were captured, the story and pictures of the robbers were carried in the May 30, Evansville Courier and Journal.

The next event of historical significance came after the Wall Street "crash" of 1929. During the early 30's many banks were having trouble and were forced to close their doors. In some cases, they were never to open again. Every time another bank closed, frantic people rushed to their own banks to demand immediate withdrawal of the money in their accounts. However, nothing like this happened at the Farmers National Bank. Patrons had enough trust in the institution that they took the events in stride. Miss Elizabeth Schroeder, a retired 49-year employee and officer of the bank, told this story:

The Wadesville bank took a one day "holiday", increased the capital stock from $25,000.00 to $50,000.00 and reopened on March 30, 1933 for "business as usual." During the uneasy times, bank employees did not even draw their salaries.

She recalled another incident which demonstrated the level of trust people had for the bank personnel. W.W. (Happy) Anderson had an account at the bank, but he also had some money "stashed" away at home. When he heard of the shortage, he loaned Miss Schroeder money to eat on for the week.

In 1933, Martin Stegmaier was elected a director to replace Henry Wenderoth who resigned due to poor health and old age. In 1934, L.P. Cox resigned after being elected Treasurer of the Fourth District, A.C.A. in Louisville, Kentucky. At the same time, Homer C. Wenderoth was elected to the Board of Directors and became cashier while Edward J. Mann was named assistant cashier. In 1936, the name J.B. McKinnies also appears on listings for board members.

A major re-organization of the bank occurred in 1940. During that year all assets were transferred from Farmers National Bank to Farmers Bank & Trust Company. On June 20, 1940, an application was made for the opening of a branch bank. Poseyville had been without its own banking facility since the banks there closed following the 1929 Stock Market crash. The branch in Poseyville opened October 7, 1940 with Edward J. Mann as manager and Paul C. Fletchall as assistant manager.

On March 1, 1949, the capital stock was increased from $50,000.00 to $100,000.00. Later that year, A second bank robbery occurred. On September 24, the thieves gained access by cutting a hole in the roof of the bank. Contents of eight safe deposit boxes were taken as well as $472.00 in cash. The robbers were later caught.

Mr. L.P. Cox died October 31, 1949, and Edward Mann became a director of the bank. Homer Wenderoth was promoted to vice president at the same time.

On January 30, 1950, plans were made to enlarge the original Wadesville building and put in a new vault and vault door.

On October 6, 1953, Mr. Wenderoth became president of the bank and Z. Earl Cox, became vice president. Virgil Williams was appointed as a director to fill the vacancy made by the death of Mr. Stegmaier. On October 26, 1959, Director Louis Wasem resigned, and Ralph Schuler, an attorney in Poseyville, was elected to the board.

On February 6, 1962, a resolution was approved to raise the capital stock of the Farmers Bank & Trust Company to $200,000.00 to consist of 20,000 shares.

In 1965, the Wadesville office underwent a second physical alteration with a change of the exterior to a contemporary design which included a drive-up window. The interior was also completely remodeled to allow for the much needed increase in space. The grand opening for the remodeled structure was held in the summer of 1966.

Total assets of the bank had swelled to $23,723,996 by 1972. Capital stock was again doubled to $400,000 from $200,000.

Another two-for-one stock split occurred just two years later, in 1974, as capital stock was increased to $800,000. The bank had grown to over $35 million in assets, which represented a 50 percent increase in two years.

In 1976, to satisfy a need for added banking convenience for Poseyville customers, a free-standing walk-up and drive-thru banking facility was erected behind the main building, at the corner of Locust and Fletchall Streets.

Another remodeling of the Wadesville office took place in 1977 and included the consolidation of the bookkeeping department. The installment loan department was also consolidated and moved to the Poseyville Office.

As a result of the bank's customer base expanding eastward toward Evansville, construction of a new branch at St. Philips began in 1978. Total assets exceeded 50 million, and capital stock

1914 Board of Directors for Farmers Bank & Trust Company

was increased to $1,600,000, another two-for-one split. In March, 1979, an open house was held to celebrate the opening of the new facility in St. Philips.

In 1980, the Poseyville lobby was redesigned with the teller line being moved to the other side of the room. This provided more space for needed offices.

Capital stock was increased 50 percent to $2,400,000 in 1981.

In December of 1983, the Board of Directors made a decision to form a one bank holding company, Posey Bancorporation, effective January 1, 1984, with Farmers Bank & Trust Company as its wholly-owned subsidiary.

By the end of 1984, assets of the bank had grown to over $85 million. With this growth, the bookkeeping department had out grown its space at the Main Office in Wadesville. A new Data Processing Center was built at the intersection of Highway 66 and 165. This strategic location was chosen to house the bookkeeping and data processing functions and also featured drive-thru banking. The installment loan department was then moved from Poseyville to the vacated bookkeeping area at the Main Office.

Farmers Bank also took one more step into the world of modern banking that year by going "on line" with a computer banking system offered by Mellon Bank of Pittsburgh.

In the summer of 1985, the new Processing Center underwent a facelift. Expanded parking facilities, improved drainage and a wider lane around the building for delivery trucks and drive-thru traffic were included in the improvements. Approaching the end of 1985 assets had topped $92,000,000 with Farmers Bank remaining the largest bank in Posey County.

In 1986, the bank announced its plans to merge with First National Bank in Owensville. This location would become the bank's third branch.

On December 31, 1986, President Paul C. Fletchall retired from the bank. He had accumulated 45 years of service.

Automated teller machines were installed in Wadesville, Poseyville, and St. Philips during the first quarter of 1987. Later that year, a machine was also installed in Owensville. The machines were part of the MoneyMover and PLUS System networks. Since the machines were available seven days a week and 24-hours a day, customers could choose when they wanted to do their banking.

The merger with the Owensville bank was completed in April, 1987.

The loan administration department moved from the back of the Main Office to the Processing Center basement in 1987. Remodeling began at the Main Office that fall. The drive-in was removed, three offices were added, and the interior was completely redecorated. The improvements were finished by the early part of 1988.

In December of 1987, the bank announced plans to merge with CNB Bancshares, the holding company for Citizens Bank in Evansville and four other affiliate banks. The merger transaction was completed on June 30, 1988.

At the end of 1988, the bank's records indicated over $114 million in assets. Deposits totalled about $102 million while loan figures were $71 million.

MEMBERS OF THE BOARD OF DIRECTORS INCLUDED:

Rex E. Blase, Director Emeriti
Herbert A. Cox, Director
Kenneth Eisterhold, Director
Paul C. Fletchall, Director
James D. Higginbotham, Director
Virgil B. Williams, Director
Dale S. Martin, Director
Philip Mowrer, Director

Dwight L. Nestrick, Director
Verner Partenheimer, Director Emeriti
Paul G. Wade, Chairman of the Board
Don E. Wenderoth, Director
Jack B. Wenderoth, Director
Marvin Huff, Jr., Director Emeriti
Darwin Zehner, Director Emeriti

BRISTOL-MYERS

EVANSVILLE, IN, April, 1989 — Bristol-Myers U.S. Pharmaceutical and Nutritional Group, which today operates plant, laboratory and office facilities at both its Evansville and Mt. Vernon, Indiana locations, had its roots in the Tri-State area for the greater part of the Twentieth Century.

Founder Edward Mead Johnson broke away from the Johnson & Johnson family business and formed the American Ferment Company in 1900. The firm name changed and was incorporated as Mead Johnson & Company in Jersey City, New Jersey in 1905.

In 1915, the founder came West seeking a better location. On Evansville's Westside he found an 11.34 acre property with buildings which once housed The Evansville Cotton Manufacturing Company. He liked what he saw. The old cotton mill had its own power plant and rail spur, a good water supply, and it was located near an inexhaustible source of corn to provide the basic corn starch raw material in the company's first major product called Dextri-Maltose® — a revolutionary new carbohydrate milk modifier for feeding infants. Following purchase of the property, plant conversion went rapidly, and Mead Johnson production began in Evansville on April 1, 1916.

The Evansville firm continued to grow and expand it's line of nutritional products. Biochemistry research begun by Mead Johnson scientists in 1923 produced many of the first products providing standardized vitamin supplement potencies. Pablum®, introduced by Mead Johnson in 1933 as the world's first pre-cooked fortified cereal, would become the first solid food fed to an entire generation of more than 30 million American babies.

This began a period of accelerated company growth from the 1930s through the 1950s. Mead Johnson began pharmaceutical research in 1952, and soon after started developing pharmaceutical specialties in several therapeutic areas. Soon the company saw the need to acquire more land for future growth and expansion. In 1957 Mead Johnson bought 600 acres of Posey County property divided by the then new Highway 62 just east of Mt. Vernon, IN. for expected later development.

In 1967, Mead Johnson & Company was acquired by Bristol-Myers Company, a diversified international marketer of pharmaceuticals, nutritionals, home care and beauty items which is headquartered in New York City. Since its acquisition by Bristol-Myers, the Evansville firm has seen several expansions and more than $200 million in capital improvements.

The old Evansville Cotton Manufacturing Company complex on Evansville's Westside which Mead Johnson & Company converted and began production of its first major product, Dextri-Maltose® on April 1, 1916.

In late summer of 1970, site preparation got under way for the initial construction at Mead Johnson Park on half of the property near Mt. Vernon south of Hwy. 62. Completed in August, 1972, the first phase development included buildings for Nutritional Sciences and Biochemistry, plus a Vivarium and power house all covering approximately 130,000 Sq. Ft. at a cost of $10 million.

On January 12, 1977, Bristol-Myers Company's Board of Directors announced a $17.7 million expansion of manufacturing and warehousing at Mead Johnson Park. In June, 1979 Mead Johnson conducted dedication ceremonies of its new facilities near Mt. Vernon. Completed and in operation were a 150,000 Sq. Ft. Warehouse, a 150,000 Sq. Ft. Pharmaceutical Packaging Plant, a Sterile Drug Production Building, plus a complex housing an employee cafeteria, offices, and training facilities. In 1981 the company completed two expansions to its Mead Johnson Park facilities on the south side of Hwy. 62 — a 65,000 Sq. Ft. warehouse addition to support future production growth, and an 18,000 Sq. Ft. addition to its Drug Safety Evaluation facilities.

In 1983 Mead Johnson announced plans to build a modern 181,500 Sq. Ft. finished goods warehouse at Mead Johnson Park which became its first construction north of Highway 62. Completed in 1984 at a cost of $6.4 million, incorporated into the new warehouse were many novel features, including driverless Automatic Guided Vehicles to transport stock and advanced security detection equipment. Also, completed in July, 1988 was a new Distribution Services Center built adjacent to existing pharmaceutical packaging and warehouse buildings south of Hwy. 62.

With these latest additions, the company now has nearly 850,000 Sq. Ft. of buildings under roof at its Mead Johnson Park site in Posey County. Major projects completed at the Firm's Evansville plant site have included a new $14 million Nutritional Production Building put into operation in 1982, and a 28 million, 190,000 Sq. Ft. new office building, Administration Center East, completed and occupied in 1987.

In September, 1985 it was announced that the business units of Bristol Laboratories Pharmaceutical Division, Bristol-Myers Oncology Division, Mead Johnson Pharmaceutical Division and Mead Johnson Laboratories would become part of the newly created Bristol-Myers U.S. Pharmaceutical Group.

Today, the restructured Bristol-Myers U.S. Pharmaceutical and Nutritional Group (USPNG) operates six divisions headquartered in Evansville, IN, and markets an extensive array of infant and adult nutritionals, vitamin supplements, hormone replacements, analgesics, antibiotics, cardiovascular agents, cold/cough remedies and chemotherapeutic anti-cancer products.

Farm Bureau Insurance in Posey County

The first office in Posey County of the Farm Bureau Insurance was located in Poseyville in the old elevator at the North edge of town by Omar Wiggins, Agent and Mgr. In 1940 the office was moved to the Farm Bureau Co-Op Store on Main St. in Poseyville. The office stayed at this location until 1964 when it moved to the "old Post Office building" on the corner of Main and Locust, which was purchased from Mr. Edward Meinerding by the Posey County Farm Bureau, Inc.

1988 brought with it new beginnings for the Farm Bureau as they moved into a modern building erected in the same location as the "old Post Office," which had been torn down. After having the temporary location of the office in the Keck Building while the new one was under construction, the office moved into the new building in July, 1988 and an Open House was held on Aug. 28, 1988.

The Agency has a second office located in Mt. Vernon which was opened in 1950 and moved into a new building at 1701 N. Main St. on April 21, 1969.

The Poseyville Office has two secretaries and two agents. The Mt. Vernon Office his three secretaries and three agents.

Jim Luse of Princeton, In. is Agency Manager for Gibson-Posey agency. Richie Moore is County Manager for Poseyville and Mt. Vernon Offices.

Overall the Farm Bureau has played a major role in the development of Indiana and Posey County, beginning in 1919 when Indiana Farm Bureau, Inc. was organized. In 1925 the Indiana Farm Bureau became the state agent for the State Farm Mutual Insurance Company of Bloomington, IL. In 1935 the Farm Bureau Mutual Insurance Company of Indiana was organized at termination of the contract with State Farm Mutual.

In 1937 Hoosier Farm Bureau Life Insurance Company issued its first life policies on June 11. In 1945 the Farm Bureau Fire and Tornado Insurance Company was incorporated and in 1948 the Farm Bureau Fire and Tornado Insurance Company merged with the Farm Bureau Mutual Insurance Company.

In 1964 on July 1, "Life" company changed from a mutual to a stock company and name changed to United Farm Bureau Family Life Insurance Company. then in 1966 on January 1, the name of the "Mutual" company changed to United Farm Bureau Mutual Insurance Company.

News Publishing Company

For 122 years the pages of the MOUNT VERNON DEMOCRAT have supplied the latest news to its readers in Posey County and subscribers in nearly every state in the Union.

Founded in 1867 by Thomas Collins with the motto "Democratic at all times and under all circumstances," the MOUNT VERNON DEMOCRAT has seen many changes in style, type, ownership, publishers and editors. From its earliest years as a four page weekly, it grew to a daily newspaper in 1891, and then reverted to a weekly during the days of World War I.

The MOUNT VERNON DEMOCRAT grew to great popularity under the ownership of Edward Alles who bought the paper in 1918. He published a daily edition with the help of editor Orvan Hall, who became a legend of accuracy, correctness and in-depth reporting. In his later years Hall owned and edited the paper. In 1966 he sold Mount Vernon's only newspaper to Garth Whipple. Changes in policy, style and printing techniques took place and in 1979 the former privately owned paper was sold to Landmark Community Newspapers, Inc.

Since then several general managers and editors have continued with the same goal set by its founder 12 decades ago—to supply the reading public with the best possible news coverage.

A century ago hot metal linotype machines were used; today modern offset equipment produces newsprint with electronic speed. Computers have replaced typewriters and pictures accompany most stories. From one small upstairs newsroom on the two hundred block of Main Street, Mount Vernon's popular newspaper moved into its own brick building on the corner of Fifth and Main Streets over sixty years ago. A fire burned much of the office and records in 1946, but the "Democrat" came back bigger and better.

Under the present management of Tim Rutherford and 25 employees, the bi-weekly issues of the MOUNT VERNON DEMOCRAT are mailed to nearly 4000 subscribers.

Keck Motor Company

One of southwest Indiana's oldest auto agencies, and Indiana's oldest Ford dealer, was established in 1907. Grover C. Keck started the dealership as a division of Keck-Gonnerman Company. Keck-Gonnerman Company manufactured threshing machines and steam engines and was organized by John Keck, father of Grover.

The first garage was located on West Fourth Street. Many cars were sold including Oakland, General, Packard, Studebaker, E M F, Thirty and Cadillac. The Ford franchise was added in October of 1912. In 1916 the agency became an exclusive Ford dealership.

As the business expanded, the firm in 1917 built a new two-story garage building at Sixth and Main Streets. In 1924 Grover C. Keck purchased the auto division and formed Keck Motor Company. The Mercury franchise was added in 1939 and the business continued without change until the death of Grover Keck in December, 1947.

In January 1948 John R. Keck and William H. Keck, sons of Grover, took over the automobile agency. They continued to operate the dealership together for 33 years. In September of 1980 Richard A. Keck, son of William, joined the firm upon the retirement of John R. Keck.

In July of 1982 a fire destroyed the garage building at Sixth and Main Streets. The firm relocated at its present address on Highway 62 at the west edge of Mt. Vernon.

Today, Keck Motor Company is the oldest Ford dealership in the State of Indiana operated by the same family. It is the twenty-third oldest Ford dealership in the United States.

Rosenbaum Jewelry, Inc.

303 Main Street

Founded 1890 by Isaac Rosenbaum, O.D. an Optometrist and Jeweler. Upon his death, ownership passed to Charlot R. Carr, his younger daughter. Now owned by the third generation, Jim N. Bohn, grandson of the founder. We continue to offer the same tradition of value and service in this century as in the last.

PEOPLES BANK & TRUST COMPANY

People's Bank & Trust Company was organized August 9, 1907 and opened for business at the corner of Fourth and Main Streets with capital of $50,000. Joseph Kelley was Chief Executive Officer.

In March 1933, President Roosevelt closed all banks (called Bank Moratorium). People's was given the highest rating available and was able to reopen at the end of the Moratorium.

During the late 30's and all of the 40's "People's" grew slowly and they remained the only bank in Mount Vernon! In 1954, the assets were approximately $7,000,000.

That same year a group of Old National Bank directors headed by Walter A. Schlechte and Bill Carson purchased over 70% of the stock and assumed control of the bank. They selected K.W. Goss to replace Joseph Kelley as a director and Chief Executive Officer.

Joseph Kelley deserves a tremendous amount of credit for guiding the bank through two depressions and two wars. He formed a very sound capital base on which the new owners could build.

PEOPLE'S BANK & TRUST COMPANY

Since that year a large portion of stock purchased by the Old National Bank group was sold to local investors.

In the late 50's the area was classified as one of the six "most depressed areas" in the U.S. Out of concern several key people such as Verne McClellan, J. Dee Crabtree, Bill and John Keck, and K.W. Goss embarked on selling a self-improvement program for the area. With this plan they were able to attract a new industry, General Electric. It was the first new industry in years for the tri-state.

Other industry following were Babcock and Wilcox (which later closed), Bristol Myers (Mead Johnson), G.A.F. and numerous satellite industries.

In 1985 the bank building was placed on the National Historic Register.

On June 30, 1986 People's Bank merged with Old National Bank Corp. At that time total assets were $100,000,000.

Then to continue their endeavor to better meet the needs of their customers, People's Bank opened a new branch on August 8, 1988 at 1320 Main in the Mt. Vernon IGA. The branch is opened seven days a week, being the first of its' kind in Posey County.

On Feb. 7, 1989 G. Roger McCormick was named President and Chief Executive Officer of the bank when K.W. Goss retired.

Covered Bridge over Big Creek at Solitude on the Plank Road

FAMILY TREE

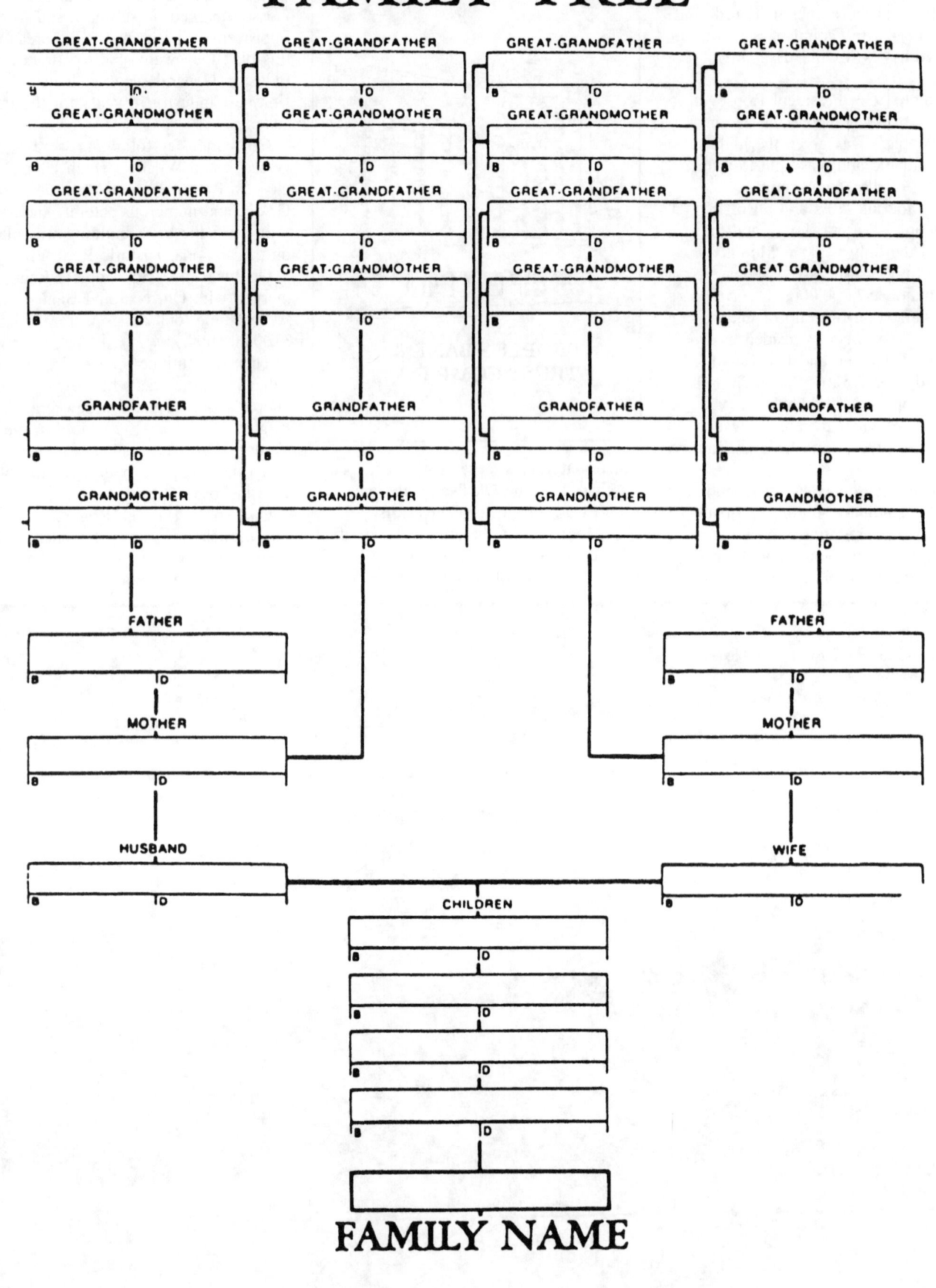

FAMILY NAME

INDEX

Agostinelli, Pamelia (Thompson) Agostinelli Fausto, 86
Alexander, William A., 86
Alldredge, Bruce R. and Christi, 86
Alldredg, Myron Lee and Eileen D., 87
Allyn, Otis Barton, 87
Almon, Don and Sandra, 87
Angel, Jack E. and Wanda D., 88
Angermeier, Virgil G. and Margie Jean (Espenlaub), 88
Ashworth, 88
Ashworth, Zola, 89
Austin, Eugene Jr. and Margie, 89
Axton-Hancock, 89
Bach, Judge and Mrs. Steve, 90
Baker, Bruce, 90
Barrett, Calvin and Lela Cox, 90
Becker, Family History, 91
Becker, Allyn A., 91
Bennett, James M., 91
Bergstrom, Gerald Elmer, 92
Binder, Rev. August E. and Amanda D., 92
Blake, Benton Ola and Beatrice (Kreutzinger), 93
Blake, James Isaac and Delia Ann (Wade), 93
Blackford, Garland and Hoyt and Geraldine Sue, 94
Brandt, F. William, 94
Briesacher, Glen and Joyce, 94
Broadhead, 95
Broadhead, Walter Jr., 95
Bundy, Paul Howard and Dorothea I., 95
Burks, George Cassius Sr., 96
Burks-Whitman, 96
Byrd-Bayer, 96
Canale, Thomas J. and Rhonda L., 96
Carl, Charles Allen and Veatrice Jo, 96
Carr, Cullen W. and Sara E., 97
Carr, Dennis J. and Ima Jean, 97
Challman, William Bower M.D. and Dorothy Brubaker, 98
Chamerlin, James, 99
Cleveland, Guy E. and Amelia, 99
Champlain-Zeller, 99
Collier, 99
Conlin, Charles, 100
Conlin, James, 100
Copeland, French, 100
Cortus-Phillips, 100
Cox Family, 101
Cox, Harold L., 101
Creek, Darrell and Donna, 101
Culley, A. Lloyd and Martha M., 102
Culley, Thomas Jr., 102
Cullman, Louis and Dorothy, 102
Cullman, Emma and William, 103
Cummins, James Clinton, 103
Curtis, Glenn and Dolores A., 103
David, 104
Deig, 104
DeKemper, 104
Denning, Henry J., 104
Dieterle, William F. and Dorothy F., 105
Doane, 105
Droege, Arvin and Anna, 106
Downen, Josiah, 106
Elpers, Glenda Sue (Angermeier), 106
Endecotts, 107
Essary, Fred D. and Carolyn Sue (Crowe), 107
Feldmann-Maurer, 107
Fischer, Ann Farris (Ranes), 108
Fisher, 108
Flener, Oral H. and Melba, 108
Floyd Family of Wales, 109
Emerson-Freeman, 109
Funkhoser, Dempsey M. "Bud", 109
Garner, John and Esther Meadows, 110
Garrett, Richard E. and Katherine (Fisher), 110
Garrett, James Marion and Edith Hanes, 111
Gilbert-McFadin, 111
Gonnerman, William, 111
Goss, 111
Greathouse, Horace F., 112
Greathouse, John and Permelia, 112
Green, David Rae and Kathleen Janet (Curtis), 112
Green, Robert Edwin and Dorothy Layer, 113
Griess, Simon C. and Wanda Lee Carter, 113
Griffin, Samuel, 113
"Guyce, Ray" Country Singer, 114
Hageman, Philip, 114
Hageman, Willford and Marguerita, 115
Hall-McMurray, 116
Hancock-Herring, 116
Hanes Family, 116
Hanes, Mr. and Mrs. Elbert M., 117
Hanes, Nealy William and Stella Herring, 117
Hanes, Troy Steven and Donna (Kubik), 118
Happe, Raymond C., 118
Harms, Larry W. Family, 119
Haynes, Charles and Stella, 120
Hein-PaPenmeir, 120
Hengstenberg-Gulicher, 120
Herrman, John and Margaret, 121
Hirsch, John and Rose, 121
Hodges, Albert Morris and Gloanna Dixon, 122
Hoehn, Cecilia and Herman C., 122
Hoenert, Don and Lee Ann, 123
Horacek-Allbritton, 123
Horacek-Angel, 123
Horacek-Jackson, 123
Horacek, Thomase E. and Ilse, 124
Howard, Catherine Louise, 124
Hughes, Stoy and Mary Elliott, 124
James, 124
Jenkins, Evelyn Fitzgerald, 125
Joest, William F., 125
Johnson-Grabert, 126
Johnson, Robert A. and Patricia M., 126
Johnston, James E. and Evelyn L., 126
Keck, 127
Keck, William H. 127
Keck, Richard A., 128
Kercher, Ben W., 128
Kleinschmidt, 128
Kreutzinger, 129
Lawernce, Charley and Vera, 129
Leffel, John H. and Esther, 130
Leigh, Martha and Leland, 130
Lengelsen Family, 131
Lengelsen, Peter Friedrich (Fritz), 131
Lewis, Gerald R., 131
Loehr, Barnett and Carolyn, 132
Loehr, Marion Samuel and Minalyn Sue, 132
Maas, Clifford Louis, 133
Mann, John Doss and Pamelia Kay (McGrew), 133
Mathew, Don S. and Paula F., 133
Mauck, Iva Newman, 134
McConnell, 134
McDurmons, The, 134
McFaddens, The, 135
McFadden, Feldon Benoni, 136
McFadden, Fieldon Benoni Ancestors, 136
McFadden, Goebel and Georgia, 137
McFadden-Gaiser, 137
McFadden-Phillips, 137
McGinnis, Oscar, 138
McKinnies, 138
Miles, Treva Alldredge, 138
Mills, 139
Mitchell, Paul and Erma, 139
Monroe-McFadden, 139
Monroe-Wilson, 140
Morlock, 140
Morlock, Christian Sr., 140
Morlock, David E. and Candace R., 140
Morlock, James Edward, 141
Morlock, Ralph, 141
Mounts, Dennis Eugene, 141
Mounts, Manford, 142
Moye-Yewell, 142
Mumford Family, 142
Murphy-Wilson, 143
Niemeier, Anton, 143
Niemeier, Anton Peter, 143
Niemeier, Franz (Frank), 143
Niemeier, Raymond A. Family, 144
Niemeier, Raymond C. Family, 144
Noelle, Albert T. and Louise R., 144
Noon, Stephen M. and Heidemarie W., 144
Nowling, Willie and Ruth S., 145
Nurrenbern, Mr. and Mrs. Elmer, 145
Nussel, Billy A. and Ann M., 145
Oeth, Frieda Nebe, 146
Pace, John and Ora, 146
Paul-Banks, 146
Pence, Edward A. and Dorothea D., 147
Pfister, George L. and Gloria J., 147
Phillips-Benthall, 148
Phillips, Charles and Victoria (Carroll), 148
Pritchard, Clifford, 148
Pritchard, Flo and Elizabeth, 148
Pritchard, John F., 149
Pritchard, John Franklin, 149
Pritchard, Thomas McDonagh and Ruth Robinson, 149
Pritchard, William Fowler and Florence Macdonagh, 150
Pritchard, William Shakespeare and Emily Metcalf, 150
Ranes, John Robert and Sadie (Arnold), 151
Redman, 151
Readman (Redman), 151
Redman, Herbert Walter and Ethel Mae, 151
Reeves, Charles, 152
Reineke-Meier, 152
Reno, Elijah Dugan, 152
Reising, Maurice J. and Lajuan, 153
Reising, Nicholas and Katherine, 153
Reising, Thelman E., 153
Ritzert, David A. Family, 154
Roberts, William Howard, 154
Robinson, Dallas Lee, 155
Roehr, Harold and Helen Family, 155
Ropp, Dr. and Gladys, 155
Rowe Family, 156
Rowe, Earl E. and Ruth (Nolan), 156
Rowe, Norman and Florence Family, 156
Rowe, Ralph Curtis, 157
Rueger, Wilton, 157
Russell, Don C., 157
Russell, William 157
Rutledge, Edmond Family, 158
Sanders, 158
Schelhorn-Quinzer, 158
Schelhorn, Jacob E. Family, 159
Schmidt, Christian Edward Family, 160
Schmidt, John Phillip, 160
Schmidt, Robert Goss, 160
Schmitt, Raymond H. and Lucy, 161
Reineke-Schmitz, 161
Schreiber, Albert Fred, 161
Schmitz, Carl A. and Delene I., 162
Schmitz-Hoell, 162
Schneider, 162
Schroeder, 163
Seiferts, 163
Sexton, Nancy Vivian Ranes, 163
Sherretz, John Kitchell and Evelyn Marie, 164
Smyth, Edmond Ray, 164
Spahn, Anthony and Doretha (Wassmer), 164
Stephens, Ausburn T. Family, 165
Stiff-Lewis, 165
Stock, Brett and Trudy Family, 166
Stock, William Gilmore and Barbara Jean (Roehr), 166
Suits, Harold Norris, 166
Tenbarge, John M. and Willa J., 166
Ten Barge, Joseph C. Family, 167
Thompson, William Clinton and Anna Marjorie, 167
Uhde, Herman J.W. and Christine (Rocker), 168
Vieck, Rev. Hilary F., 168
Vogel, Dr. L. John and Margaret K., 168
Walker-York, 169
Wallace, 169
Walling, George, 169
Wassmer, William L. Family, 170
Weilbrenner, Charles Thomas, 170
Weintraut, Lawrence Nicholas and Anna A., 171
Weinzapfel, Joe T. and Mary Ann, 171
Wenderoth-Cavett Families, 171
Werry Family, 172
Weyer, Henry and Margaret, 173
Whitten, David and Barbara Judith, 173
Wiley, James D., 173
Williams, Marvin and Naomi Family, 174
Williams, Ned O. Family, 174
Willmann, Johann Adam, Jr., 175
Yaggi, James B. (Jack) & Alice P., 175
York, George Elbert and Grace, 175
York, Larry Keith and Virginia Alice, 176
York, Robert and Shirley, 176
Zeller, Lawrence Joseph, 176
Zeller-Paul, 176
Zeller, Rita Janet, 177
Zeller-Shaw, 177

Notes

NOTES

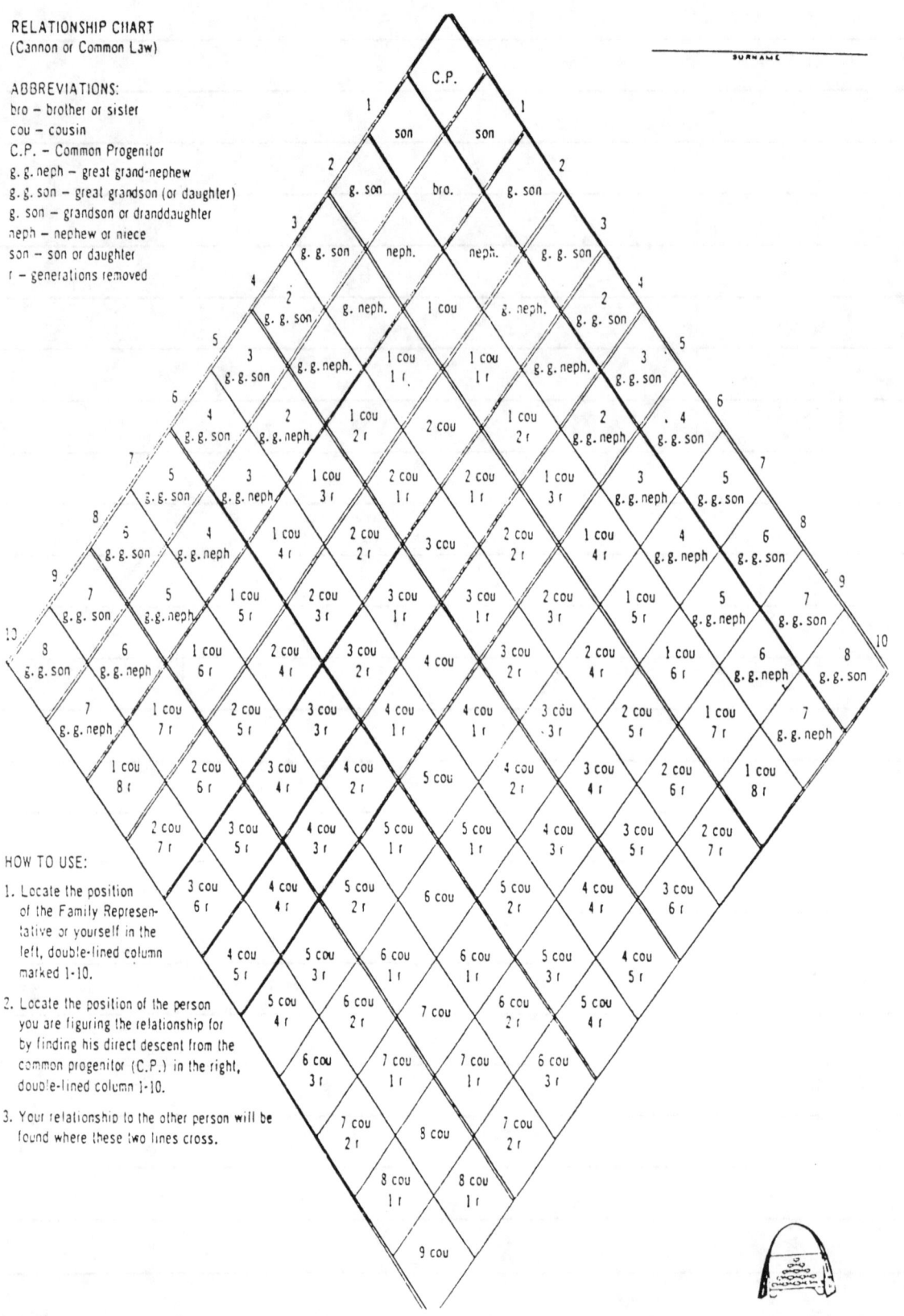

Upton Train Wreck; 5 men, 230 sheep & 9 mules died in the the July 15, 1905 wreck, 5 miles S.E. of Upton.

www.ingramcontent.com/pod-product-compliance
Lightning Source LLC
Chambersburg PA
CBHW082100230426
43670CB00017B/2904